SARTRE

Also by Ronald Hayman available from Carroll & Graf

Proust

SARTRE

A BIOGRAPHY

RONALD HAYMAN

Carroll & Graf Publishers, Inc.
New York

Copyright © 1987 by Ronald Hayman

All rights reserved

Published by arrangement with the author.

First published by Simon and Schuster.

First Carroll & Graf edition 1992

Carroll & Graf Publishers, Inc.
260 Fifth Avenue
New York, NY 10001

Library of Congress Cataloging-in-Publication Data

Hayman, Ronald, 1932–
    Sartre / Ronald Hayman.
      p.   cm.
    Includes bibliographical references and index.
    ISBN 0-88184-875-1 $15.95
    1. Sartre, Jean Paul, 1905- —Biography. 2. Philosophers—
France—Biography. 3. Authors, French—20th century—
Biography.
B2430.S34H386   1992
194—dc20
[B]   92-35246
                                    CIP

Manufactured in the United States of America

Acknowledgments

In the four years I have been working on this biography I have become greatly indebted to many people who have helped in different ways. The first words of thanks must go to George Weidenfeld, who suggested I write it, to Simone de Beauvoir, who was generous with both time and encouragement, and to the Arts Council of Great Britain, which gave me welcome financial support.

I am grateful to all the friends, colleagues, acquaintances, and critics of Sartre who talked to me in Paris, including Colette Audry, Simone de Beauvoir, Roland Castro, Jean Cau, Michel Contat, Anne-Marie Cazalis, Robert Gallimard, Roger Grenier, Geneviève Idt, Serge July, Robert Misrahi, Albert Palle, Marcel Péju, J.-B. Pontalis, Jean Pouillon, David Rousset, Nathalie Sarraute, Olivier Todd, and Michelle Vian. I also learned a good deal about Sartre and the history of the period from conversations with Ronald Aronson, Catharine Carver, Howard Davies, Val Doulton, Maurice Druon, Shusha Guppy, Quintin Hoare, Douglas Johnson, Leo Labedz, Richard Mayne, David Pryce-Jones, George Steiner, and Paul Webster.

I am especially grateful to Lisa Appignanesi, Ronald Aronson, and Catharine Carver, who at various stages read all or part of the book in typescript and gave me their comments. I would like to thank Alice Mayhew, my editor at Simon and Schuster, for all her help and encouragement throughout the period of working on the book; and to Henry Ferris and the copy editor, Louise Lindemann, for their help in preparing the American edition. Juliet Gardiner, my editor at Weidenfeld, has been extremely helpful throughout with constructive criticism. I'd also like to thank Linden Lawson for help on both text and pictures and Elspeth Henderson for help on pictures.

I am grateful to Gilles Chouraqui, the French cultural counselor, who gave me letters which gained me entry to the Bibliothèque Nationale and to various archives in Paris. I must thank Mme. Boulez and Mme. Dauphragne, who helped me to find archive material at the Ecole Normale Supérieure, and all those who helped me at the Lycée Louis-le-Grand.

I would not have been able to read the unpublished second part of Sartre's *Critique de la raison dialectique* but for Robert Gallimard's kindness in consenting and that of Patrick Camiller (Verso Books) in lending me a typescript. I am grateful to Howard Davies for letting me read his unpublished doctoral thesis on *Les Temps Modernes* and to Quintin Hoare for lending me Jean Pierre's unpublished memoir of experiences with Sartre in the army. For giving me books and reprints of articles I am indebted to Howard Davies, Geneviève Idt, and Paul Webster; for putting me in touch with people who could be helpful I would like to thank Ronald Aronson, Simone de Beauvoir, Judith Bumpus, Annie Cohen-Solal, Michel Contat, Rémy Dreyfus, Maurice Farhi, Shusha Guppy, Gabriel Josipovici, Olivier Todd, Paul Webster, and Martin Woollacott.

The translations from the French are my own.

Contents

PREFACE   9
LIFE BEGINS TOMORROW   15

PART I.
FOR A PRIVATE FUTURE (1905–31)

1. Poulou   31
2. Nitre and Sarzan   40
3. School for Superiors   54
4. The Beaver   73

PART II.
FRIENDLY TEACHER (1931–39)

5. Provincial Schoolmaster   87
6. A German Credo   97
7. Back to Bouville   111
8. Intimacy   121
9. Breakthrough   129

PART III.
WAR (1939–45)

10. The War Profiteer   149
11. Stalag   172
12. In Occupied Paris   179
13. The Future Reappears   204

PART IV.
SEARCHING FOR A THIRD WAY (1945–57)

14. Making a New Start   225
15. Chief Existentialist   232
16. Democratic Revolutionist   254
17. Communist Values   270
18. Under Oath to Hate   288

PART V.
TOWARD REVOLUTION (1957–68)

19. Back to Philosophy   331
20. Freudian Interlude   351
21. Unofficial Ambassador   369
22. "Kill Sartre"   381
23. Writing Is Neurosis   393
24. Halfway to Revolution   406

PART VI.
BEYOND COMMUNISM (1968–80)

25. With the Maoists   437
26. Fading Vision   454
    Not a Conclusion: Sartre's Continuing Life   477

CHRONOLOGY   485
ABBREVIATIONS   513
NOTES   515
BIBLIOGRAPHY   535
PHOTO CREDITS   541
INDEX   543

Preface

If one man towered above the postwar intellectual ferment and made his personal feelings impinge on political history, it was Jean-Paul Sartre. No intellectual has ever exerted greater influence on politics or let politics exert more influence on the development of his thinking. Sartre's life during the period 1945 to 1980 intertwined at a surprising number of points with major historical events. Before the war he was just a French provincial schoolmaster struggling to establish himself as a writer, and it looked as though he stood little chance, even if he succeeded, of making himself heard outside that segment of the reading public interested in philosophical fiction. He was highly articulate but physically unimposing, lively but ugly, with spectacles and a squint, friendly but diminutive, strong enough to make himself the dominant figure in a small group of friends but unlikely, it would have seemed, to make himself into a world historical figure. So how did it happen?

It would have been impossible in any other country, and even in France it could have happened only at this phase in cultural history. With the memory of the German army's quick and crushing defeat of their country and the ensuing occupation for four years still fresh in the minds of the people, morale in France was extremely low when Sartre suddenly found himself the chief spokesman for a fashionable new philosophy. Existentialism appealed mainly to young people who could not model themselves on their demoralized seniors and who discovered only after the war how much pleasure was to be had from jiving to the music the Nazis had banned as deriving from the culture of an inferior race. In reality Sartre's philosophy had nothing to do with jazz or with the life-style adopted by disaffected young people who gladly called themselves Existentialists, a label popularized by newspapers, magazines, and radio programs. But Sartre featured the word "freedom" prominently in his pronouncements, and freedom seemed especially desirable after the years of conformity and restraint.

Sartre was not just a philosopher. His first novel, *La Nausée,* came out in 1938. He established himself as a playwright during the occupation, and his next two novels were published soon after the liberation. Already he was finding, as he would throughout his career, that the philosophical ideas would pollinate the plays and novels; the plays and novels would help to popularize the philosophy. His reputation developed rapidly. In newspapers and magazines, his face became as familiar—not only in France but throughout the world—as that of any actor or jazz musician. Though he had wanted fame and had daydreamed about it since childhood, he soon found it less enjoyable than he had expected but discovered it was something he could use. It constituted another area of activity, and he could cultivate fruitful connections between it and the others.

To remain internationally influential, as Sartre did for thirty-five years, you have to make sure that you do not get bored with your own image: Sartre never lost faith in the importance of the contribution he had to make. One of his first steps to consolidate his power was to establish himself as editor in chief of a monthly magazine, *Les Temps Modernes.* In 1945 he was hoping that two other leading French writers, Albert Camus and André Malraux, would join the editorial board. And although neither would work under his leadership, the magazine's continuing importance would help his fame eclipse theirs. Camus was an editor before Sartre was. After editing the clandestine paper *Combat* during the occupation, he remained editor when it came out into the open and commissioned Sartre to write for him—first on the siege of Paris and then on the United States, when a party of French journalists was invited there. After a time Camus's literary ambitions no longer allowed him to continue working as an editor. But Sartre, whose ambitions did not remain primarily literary, gave little of his working day to editorial work while nominally remaining the editor of *Les Temps Modernes* until the end of his life. While Camus became more solitary, more isolated, Sartre continued to be surrounded by a coterie.

As De Gaulle's minister for cultural affairs (1959–69), Malraux became more involved in party politics than Sartre ever did, but unlike Sartre, Malraux did not manage to keep the pipelines open between one area of activity and another. Neither writer was politically consistent. Though he was never a Marxist, Malraux was a revolutionary activist in China during the twenties and later fought in both the Spanish Civil War and the Resistance before moving to the right. Sartre's sympathies were always with the left, but after making his philosophical debut as an impassioned advocate of individual freedom, denouncing Marxism as deterministic and the Communist party as undemocratic, he aligned himself with Marxism and relegated Existentialism to being a mere "ideology." Marxism, he declared, was the only valid philosophy for our time. But in the seventies he announced that he was no longer a Marxist.

Instead of reducing his importance, these inconsistencies enhance it. Better than any of his contemporaries, he incarnates the dilemma of the intellectual torn between creativity and commitment, unable to concentrate on literature or philosophy when to campaign against oppression and injustice might possibly alleviate suffering. Appalled by the apathy of powerful politicians, he was determined to use whatever political power he could muster. During the Cold War his knowledge of social injustice in the United States combined with his ignorance of social injustice in the Soviet Union (a country he had not yet visited) to make him more anti-American than most of his non-Communist contemporaries. He believed that nothing was more important than stopping Europe from aligning itself with the United States against the Communist bloc, and he fought as hard as any private individual could for European neutrality.

Only when this battle was lost did he move decisively to the left, never joining the Communist party but making himself more useful to it than anyone else. His fame had become a political weapon, an intercontinental ballistic missile. His face was irresistibly attractive to press photographers; his eminently quotable pronouncements were translated into dozens of languages and relayed all over the world. When he was invited to the Soviet Union, to Cuba, to China, to Brazil, it was partly for the publicity that his presence guaranteed. He was a charismatic ambassador representing no country and was bound by no conventions. Yet he was not an unbiased observer. The declared enemy of colonialism and of the bourgeoisie, he would not tell the whole truth about what he saw. But his reactions made an impact on the nonaligned and especially on the young.

Throughout his life he had a special relationship with students. Though he had less influence on them than certain other Marxist intellectuals, such as Louis Althusser and Henri Lefebvre, who as university lecturers were in daily contact with them, Sartre's books were one of the main theoretical sources through which French students absorbed Marxist ideas. In the latter part of his career, Sartre had no audience clearly in mind when he wrote, but he was nothing if not a moralist and believed that only the young could preserve their moral integrity because their seniors were hopelessly entangled in materialistic compromises. Even among the French working classes, there seemed to be no real concern about the sufferings of the oppressed in the Third World, whereas students were less uncaring. Addressing himself to them and encouraging other radical writers, both in *Les Temps Modernes* and in books, to stir up dissidence among them, Sartre played an important role in building up the pressure that would explode in the students' rebellion of 1968, though, like most of the students, he was himself ambivalent on the question of whether he wanted a revolution.

His first major philosophical work, *L'Etre et le Néant,* had promised that he would follow with a book on moral philosophy. If he failed to fulfill that promise, it was not because he had not devoted enough time to the task. He concluded that social conditions were inimical to ethical behavior, and *Saint Genet* is not so much a biography of Genet as a countermorality which centers on the equation of criminal and saint. Salvation can be achieved only through opposing the values hallowed by convention. The criminal must act out the aggression projected on him by the law-abiding citizen who conceals his own viciousness.

Here, already, Sartre's standpoint is potentially revolutionary, but his attitude to revolution was complicated by his attitude toward the Communist party. In *Les Communistes et la paix* he directly equated the working class and the party. Without the party the workers have no sense of their own collective identity; without the party there can be no revolution. But in 1968, when the students brought the French people closer to revolution than they had been since the turn of the century, the party sided with the forces of reaction. In July 1968 Sartre accused the party of betraying the revolution, and in August, when Warsaw Pact troops marched into Czechoslovakia, he condemned the Soviet Union. Twelve years earlier, he had condemned the Red Army's intervention in Hungary but in 1962 began accepting invitations to Moscow. After the invasion of Czechoslovakia he never went there again.

During the last twelve years of his life, his two major ambitions were to effect a reconciliation between Marxism and psychoanalysis, so that Freudian insights could be combined with dialectical thinking, and to coordinate the clashing leftist groups which had emerged out of the student rebellion. Without ever calling himself a Maoist, even when he finally said he was no longer a Marxist, Sartre gave the French Maoists the benefit of his fame. If his name was a weapon, he added it to their arsenal. It appeared on the cover of Maoist publications which, nominally, he was editing. But he did not pretend to agree with the contents. He was working simultaneously on his massive biography of Flaubert, probably the most Freudian biography ever written.

The question of how Sartre made himself into a world historical figure cannot be answered briefly. The whole of this book is an answer. But if I had to sum it up in one sentence, I would say that more courageously, more stubbornly, more cleverly, and more passionately than anyone else in this century he used his life to test ways of facing up to the evils of contemporary history. If he was not always honest, it was partly because honesty was a luxury he could not afford.

Life Begins Tomorrow

WHEN Jean-Paul Sartre was buried on April 19, 1980, a crowd of over fifty thousand converged on the procession and on the Montparnasse cemetery, while even more people watched on television. No philosopher has ever had a bigger audience for his funeral, though it was not his philosophy that had made him famous. In France, a country where intellectuals are still honored, he had for thirty-five years been the most celebrated intellectual. His face was familiar to people who had never seen him; his sayings were quoted by people who had never read his books. Witold Gombrowicz called him the Eiffel Tower of French culture. As a philosopher he was less original and less influential than Wittgenstein or Heidegger, but Sartre's importance does not rest on any single area of activity: we can say of him what he said of Proust— that his genius lies in the totality of his work considered as "the totality of the manifestation of the person."

As a playwright Sartre was highly successful but less innovative and less significant than Beckett or Ionesco. As a novelist Sartre completed only one work, *La Nausée* (*Nausea*), his other three novels being parts of an unfinished tetralogy. The bulk of his writing time was devoted to political journalism and biography, but he can hardly be called a journalist, while his biographies of Baudelaire, Genet, and Flaubert are not biographies in the usual sense of the term. "Writer" might look like the best one-word description of Sartre, but it is inadequate. Quantitatively his output was prodigious—his bibliographers have calculated that he averaged twenty pages a day throughout his long life[1]—but it was only when he was briefly in the army that he wholeheartedly pitched most of his time into writing. Before the war he would have liked to be a professional writer, but he had to earn his living as a schoolteacher until 1944, when he was almost forty. After the war his working life had two centers. He never enjoyed himself more than when he was philosophizing in his study, but his conscience was easier when he was functioning as a partyless politician, agitating, using his influence to champion the international underdog, fighting capitalism and imperialism, making speeches, editing a review, demonstrating, attending meetings, helping to organize political movements, traveling around the world, writing articles and books calculated to influence communism from outside.

This part of his life was governed by his fame and his eagerness to be useful. Because he attracted so much attention from the media, his presence was constantly in demand, and he was generous with it, but this caused increasing discontinuity between his public life and his writing. The young Sartre cared enormously about his relationship with his readers. He revised, reshaped, rewrote energetically, often following Simone de Beauvoir's canny advice, and in 1946 he maintained that the author's work is incomplete until the reader has collaborated by letting the book slowly disclose itself until it is "a unified object."[2] But once Sartre had become a public man his needs changed. Some energy went into maintaining his image. Should he visit the United States during the Vietnam War? Should he reject the Nobel Prize? Should he declare himself in favor of Israel's survival as an independent state? These decisions were not made without careful calculation about how his supporters would react. No longer depending on books to give him a relationship with the public, he no longer worried about whether readers would—or could—collaborate with him. Writing had become a private activity. He even took to working in his room instead of writing in cafés. He had always been careless about losing manuscripts; he became less interested in whether his books were published, of if published, read, or if read, understood. Few people can have read the million and a quarter words that make up his Flaubert biography and still fewer can have digested them. There was no question, latterly, of cutting, revising, reshaping to make a book more accessible; what mattered to Sartre was the relationship he had with his own intellect while sitting at his desk.

Though the best of his work is important, his importance depends no less on his central position in European intellectual history since the vogue for existentialism, which started in 1945. He could not have remained in this position thirty-five years if he had been averse to either inconsistency or opportunism. His uneven trajectory illustrates the problem of the intellectual caught between the impossibility of having and the impossibility of not having a relationship with the Communist party. Even his philosophical pronouncements were liable to be adulterated by *Realpolitik*. In 1957, when he decreed that existentialism could hand itself over to Marxism if only Marxism would "take on the human dimension [i.e., the existentialist project] as the basis for anthropological knowledge,"[3] he was behaving like the leader of a small country offering to make a deal with an irresistibly aggressive neighbor—he was an ideological Dollfuss trying to negotiate with a Communist Hitler. Wanting to change Marxism, Sartre believed that his best chance lay in offering a conciliatory package; had he succeeded, his main importance would have been as a political philosopher, but he failed.

Even if he solved none of the problems he tackled, he plunged into them more deeply than anyone of comparable intellectual acuity, and it will go on being impossible to ignore him as a model. He confronted not only the difficulties created by the divergence of Soviet practice from Marxian theory but also the problems produced by the disintegration of the great colonial empires, while he experimented in different ways of making both his literary activity and his physical presence into political weapons. Like Brecht but unlike Flaubert or D. H. Lawrence, he cared too much about public issues to immerse himself in fiction about personal relationships. Though he theorized authoritatively about commitment in literature, he became—no less than other committed writers—a rope in a tug-of-war between the compulsion to develop his artistic potential and the obligation to exert influence through didactic writing and political action.

He was not ineffectual. In France he had more influence than anyone else over intellectual opinion. He raised the temperature of anti-American feeling, made it harder for anti-Semitism to surface, and improved the intellectual standing of the Communist party. He played a major role in politicizing a whole generation of French students, and the leaders of the 1968 rebellion had mostly absorbed Marxism through a Sartrian filter; during the same year his influence contributed—Czech witnesses tell us—to the slackening of oppression during the Prague Spring.

Though he managed to complete nine original plays, seven short stories, and several screenplays, nearly all his other major projects in literature and philosophy were abandoned. How could the subject be closed? Why should it be? If his energy had not been diverted into political action, he might have tried harder to complete literary and philosophical projects, but this is by no means certain. He deeply disliked bringing anything to a conclusion. In 1938, as soon as *La Nausée* appeared in the bookshops, he started planning to revive the central character, Antoine Roquentin, in a sequel. At the end of both his major philosophical books, *L'Etre et le Néant* and *Critique de la raison dialectique*, he indicates that the work is not to be regarded as complete. The gesture appears to be made more for his sake than the reader's, though there are those who applaud his failure to finish projects: He is shattering "the myth of the coherently finished text, the myth that the contradictions that gave rise to the work have been resolved by an apparently cohesive textual narrative."[4] But he tried hard not to leave his pledges unredeemed. After ending *L'Etre et le Néant* (1943) with a promise to follow it with a book on ethics, he went on until 1949 struggling with the problem of goodness: the notebooks contain even more words than the book, but he finally gave up. After finishing the first volume of the *Critique* in 1959, he wrote 782 pages (about 200,000 words) of the second. All this unpublished work was not entirely wasted. Some of the material from the abandoned book on ethics went into *Saint Genet;* some of the ideas from the unfinished second volume of the *Critique* went into the Flaubert biography. The ideal way to read Sartre's work is not as a series of separate books but as a discontinuous and open-ended whole.

In the tetralogy *Les Chemins de la liberté* (misleadingly translated as *The Roads to Freedom*) he had relatively little difficulty in completing the first three volumes: nothing needed to be concluded. He wrote 223 pages of the last volume, *La Dernière Chance,* and he did not give up hope of finishing it until nine years after publishing the third volume, *La Mort dans l'âme* (mistranslated as *Iron in the Soul*). Other uncompleted projects include the autobiography, the enormous biography of Flaubert, *La Psyché* (a phenomenological psychology), a book on Mallarmé, one on Tintoretto, *Les Communistes et la paix* (an apologia for the party, abandoned in 1956 after Soviet tanks invaded Hungary), and *Pouvoir et liberté,* a collaborative book based on conversations with Benny Lévy (Pierre Victor).

Toward the end of his life interviewers often questioned Sartre about the mass of unfinished work, but less is to be learned from his answers than from the sequence in *La Nausée* when with an exquisite mixture of pleasure and pain Roquentin decides to give up his work on a historical biography. "The true nature of the present stood revealed. It was what exists, and everything that was not present did not exist. The past did not exist. . . . For me the past was only a retreat: it was another way of living, a holiday, passivity." But Roquentin can now picture the subject of his abandoned book, the Marquis de Rollebon, more vividly than ever before. "I sighed, let myself lean back against my chair with a feeling of unbearable deprivation." His immediate future will contain no holiday in the past.

Two of the crucial questions about Sartre are "Why did he keep changing tack?" and "Why did he go on committing himself to labors that even he—and no one has been more of an intellectual Hercules—couldn't possibly have accomplished?" I cannot believe anybody has ever written more greedily and sensually than Sartre did. Even when he was in his twenties his satisfaction when a woman yielded him her virginity was almost eclipsed by the satisfaction of plucking words out of the air to describe the seduction, moment by moment, in a long letter to Simone de Beauvoir. He was never more impatient than just before starting to write. According to Jean Cau, who worked as his secretary from 1946 to 1957, he would come into the flat, when he had slept elsewhere, and immediately sit down on the hard chair at his desk, never stopping to take off his jacket and tie.[5] He never typed, and the fountain pens he used—his friend Michelle Vian has kept several of them—feel as strongly impregnated with his physical presence as the stems of the pipes he smoked.

When he was writing letters, diaries, and short articles, his pleasure was unalloyed; when he worked at long-term projects, it was tarnished by ambivalence. Other work would be clamoring for his time, and simultaneously he would feel guilty about enjoying words instead of taking action. Something survived from his passionate boyhood identification with the heroes of adventure stories, from his fantasies of himself as the dashing rescuer of beautiful victims, and this helped to color his abortive adult forays into the Resistance and political activity. His constant restlessness derived partly from a mixture of romantic optimism and jaded guilt feelings. Even when he was writing about politics he felt that he should be fighting more actively against injustice; he also believed that he was wasting his talent as a writer. In 1969 he complained that almost everything he had written was "exactly the opposite of what I wanted to write."[6] He felt as though he had spent the major part of his life working, like a hack, on commission, or like a journalist, in response to current events. This feeling is relevant to all those moments of conflict which had been prefigured by Roquentin's triumphant surrender—moments of reluctantly fending off a seductive alternative to keep faith with the project at hand, or moments of deliciously treacherous capitulation.

The betrayal was fourfold—a betrayal of his readers and his intentions, combined with a more conscious betrayal of literature and his talent for it. If anyone in France was qualified to succeed Gide, Claudel, and Valéry it was Sartre, who instead took a principled pleasure in refusing to support literature as an establishment or as a way of life, treating it rather as a myth in need of demolition. According to Roland Barthes, Sartre's importance lies partly in his being the man "situated at the precise historical point of literature's disintegration."[7] If the reason Leonardo da Vinci failed to complete any of his works is that he had such a high regard for the greatness of art, Sartre failed for the opposite reason.

Not that he could possibly have succeeded. His Flaubert biography was intended to swallow the ocean of available data. "We have at the outset no assurance that such a summary is possible and that the truth is not multiple." His object in the second part of the *Critique* was nothing less than to prove that history added up to a single truth, a single meaning which could be explained without postulating a divine, extraterrestrial observer. The Marxist viewpoint was valid, Sartre believed, only if dialectical materialism could be made to reveal the unity of history. Could its "diverse multiplicities" be viewed as "connected and merged in their very oppositions and diversities by an intelligible totalization from which there is no appeal"?

No doubt Sartre would have achieved less if he had not set himself impossible tasks; he poised himself in a highly unusual way between the past and the future. He pictures consciousness as a blank, aimed like an arrow at the task ahead. This idea derives from Husserl, but we need to look at Sartre's temperament to see why Husserl's intentionality appealed to him so strongly. It is no accident that one of his favorite words was *dépasser* (go beyond, subsume, transcend): like a runner, waiting for the starting pistol with his weight poised forward, or like a child trying to fall asleep on Christmas Eve, Sartre found it almost unbearable that the future hadn't already begun. *La vie commence demain.* Simone de Beauvoir has written shrewdly about his indifference to the present and the past. "Sartre refuses to admit that he has any identity connecting him with his past . . . He rarely reminisces." He could talk with critical detachment about what he had said, written, or done: "The truth is that he has already stopped recognizing himself in the old Sartre he is talking about. What he really is, he believes, exists in the future, and in consequence he never feels any vanity about what he has done in the past. . . . On the other hand he displays immense pride when he talks about what he's expecting to do. This is the metaphysical and unpersonal pride of a liberty which tries to be absolute, which refuses to be constrained by circumstances."

He was afraid of possessions, afraid they would possess him or anchor him to one place, one situation, one identity. Had he been inclined to keep the money he earned, he could have become extremely rich; instead he not only spent, gave, and tipped with compulsive generosity, but supported a small retinue of dependents. The busier he became, the easier he found it to give money rather than time, attention, or sympathy. Nor did he ever want to own space. For much of his life he made his home in hotels or in his mother's little flat, where his room was so small that he could not have kept many books in it, even if he had not been in the habit of discarding them as soon as he had read them. (His formidable memory had been strengthened by a lycée education, which involved learning long passages by heart.) The narrow couch became his bed at night, and in the morning, when Jean Cau arrived, "a fearsome smell of tobacco and nocturnal breathing, spread into an atmosphere you could cut with a knife, jumped at my face and into my throat."[8] Cau then worked at a table which had to be cleared for lunch if Sartre was going to eat with his mother.

But with space on paper Sartre was lavish. He never squeezed additions or alterations into a margin, and whenever he had to cross words out he started a new sheet. He was in Italy with Michelle Vian when he wrote the preface to André Gorz's *Le Traître*. Arriving at the post office to mail the manuscript to the Paris publisher, she found that the cost of postage would have left them without enough cash to pay their hotel bill. With a pair of scissors she snipped off the unused paper from each page.[9]

Sartre felt most at home in cafés and restaurants where he could annex space by dominating the conversation and exhaling smoke. He noticed that pipe-smoking made him feel like settling wherever he was, watching people and talking through reassuring clouds of smoke. But, like Kafka, he never felt more free than when he was writing, creating an imaginary space. Paper as magic carpet; pen as wand. But if he felt uncomfortable with the literary conquest of imaginary space, his discomfort had one of its roots in the awkward relationship his mind had with his body. After a paradisal infancy centered on the belief that he was beautiful, he systematically tried to reject his body. To reassure his mind that it had nothing to fear from sibling rivalry with his maltreated body he consistently ignored all the messages it sent out. He resisted fatigue, treated pain as if it were a challenge. To step up his productivity he made reckless use of drugs and stimulants, taking sedatives when he needed to relax. He resented the time he had to spend on washing, shaving, cleaning his teeth, taking a bath, excreting, and he would economize by carrying on conversations with Cau through the bathroom door. He had no personal vanity, took no pleasure in buying clothes. His shoes were bought for him by his mother—his small feet were the same size as hers. When his smoke-stained teeth began to decay, he refused to waste time on seeing a dentist, but even when his face was swollen with an abscessed gum, he would stubbornly settle down to work at his desk. He took immeasurable pride in his intellect—"I've got a golden brain"[10]—but the punitive attitude to his body was based on the feeling that it could be written off. Occasionally he took exercise to keep fit, but the interest flickered only briefly. Nor did he want to have his squint corrected surgically. If his constitution had not been exceptionally strong, he could not have treated it so ruthlessly. Throughout his life he smoked excessively, overworked exorbitantly, ate and drank carelessly. He had no hankering for the kind of balance W. B. Yeats craved:

> Labour is blossoming or dancing where
> The body is not bruised to pleasure soul . . .

Sartre went on bruising the body to pleasure mind, trying incessantly to outpace himself. When he defines man as the creature who is not identical with himself, he has Heidegger's philosophy as one of his models and his own habits as the other.

Nietzsche observed that all philosophy is "the confession of its author and a kind of involuntary unconscious memoir." With his pronouncements the philosopher is pointing to the "relative positioning of the innermost drives in his nature."[11] Sartre's declaration of war against the idea of the self points to his hostility against the self as represented by the body. Even his insistence on free will and his resistance to determinism hinge on his refusal to see his own existence as conditioned by uncontrollable physical characteristics. The body, which he had not chosen, could be disregarded: his contempt for it encouraged him to believe that the individual self had no existence. Throughout his career he would find various ways of escaping from the first person singular—into a partnership, into fictional characters, into groups, into political movements, into theories about the collective, into the self-oblivion induced by drink or drugs or extreme fatigue. In 1956–57 he made his most extremist pronouncements against the individual ego, praising Soviet man for subordinating his identity to the group and questioning whether anyone can ever accurately say "I did it." Sartre's fanatical faith in the powers of the conscious intellect and his resistance to Freudian ideas about the unconscious are equally rooted in the same inner drive. Needing to believe that the human mind was capable of anything and everything, he was irked by the notion that it might be incapable of coming fully to grips with itself.

Privately he was more interested in dominating a group than in subordinating himself. Almost invariably friendly, he liked the effect he could have on other people more than he liked other people, and in conversation he took pleasure in pleasing. With his musical voice and his quick mind he had a genius for small talk ranging from fantasy to gossip to practical advice. As a companion he was charming, droll, endlessly entertaining. He talked rapidly, trying to catch up with his racing thoughts. With new acquaintances he seldom failed to make a favorable impression, but in a foreign city he was reluctant to ask a stranger the way, wanting neither to be seen as a middle-class tourist nor to "inflict a disagreeable presence" on anyone in the street.[12]

Though the drug-taking habit had its origins in a campaign to increase output, he began to take pleasure in the violence he was doing himself. For about twenty years he "abused drugs a great deal" (as he put it) but never so much as when writing the *Critique*. He was taking corydrane and orthodrine. The unpublished Part 2, which was more ambitious, could hardly have failed, had he completed it, to be his most important philosophical work, but, not content with sabotaging his chances of writing in a lucid and organized way, he was deliberately putting his life at risk: "As soon as one passed a certain point, one began to be destroyed, and the risk was a reality. One liked having blurred ideas which were vaguely interrogative and which then disintegrated. It also meant one could drop dead, but there was no knowing when."

Like Nietzsche, Sartre took an almost religious pleasure in the sense of battling against himself. There could be no complete dichotomy, of course, between mortifying the flesh and fighting the brain. In the same way that he resisted fatigue, he resisted his own ideas, challenged them, questioned whether it wouldn't be better to turn them upside down. Philosophically the habit of dialectical reversal was picked up from Hegel. Karl Marx, who had also picked it up, found, like Sartre, that it encouraged him to leave books unfinished. Both Marx and Sartre tended to define their position by making someone else's untenable and later to make their own untenable. They were both liable to start a book on the basis of convictions that would be repudiated before it was finished.

Without setting out to provide a rationale for this habit of leaving projects uncompleted, Sartre does this in the *Critique,* arguing that human action always tends to become something different from what was intended. When a man looks back at his work, simultaneously recognizing and failing to recognize himself in it, acknowledging that it isn't what he wanted to do but that he couldn't have done it any better, he is being forced "by an immediate dialectical movement to acknowledge necessity as freedom's destiny in exteriority."[13] This is a form of alienation, which invariably begins as soon as the individual objectifies himself in action. Other people can immediately rob him of his intention. Sartre was basing his ideas about human activity on his own activity as a writer, and there may be a connection between his misgivings about stolen or deflected intentions and his pleasure in abandoning positions he had formerly maintained. Inevitably this involved him in betraying friends, admirers, and supporters who had rallied around the idea as soon as they saw it flying from his flagstaff, but since their support had helped to rob him of his intention, they deserved to be punished.

Even when he was young, his attitude to fans and supporters was highly ambivalent. Following the loss of his infantile omnipotence, the loss of his mother when she remarried left him with an uncomfortable awareness of a dichotomy between the impression he had of himself and the impression other people had of him. His strongest need was to be in command of their reactions to him. Lusting for fame, which could bring this power, he was aware of his brain as an aggressive weapon. Part of his need to keep shifting positions was the need to bring the weapon constantly into play. The boxer can never afford to think about what he did in the last round: what matters is what he is doing now. If other people got stuck with yesterday's ideas, that was because they were the audience. He was the champion.

But that's not all there is to it. Working and living were not separate in this man whose main activity was writing. Long before he took to using the ugly word "totalization" he was practicing an instinctive dialectic in which each part of his life must relate to the whole and the whole to each part, while the living subject makes his peace with the image he tries to form of himself from outside. Sartre's passion for biography starts out on an impulse, already strong in childhood, to visualize his own experience from the viewpoint of posterity. He tries to live biographically. He can never surrender himself to the experience of the moment without remembering that it is already sliding into the past. As he says in *Les Mots,* "Try as I might to throw myself into whatever I took on, into work, anger, friendship, I'm always about to deny the self in me that wants it. I'm betraying myself in the middle of passion by the jubilant anticipation of my future treachery." With one eye on the biography that remains obstinately in the future, he can never enjoy the present. The book he's writing, the woman he's kissing, the words he's saying can never engage his full attention. The part belongs to the whole, and the alternative futures never stop trying to push each other out of the way. Like Roquentin he comes closest to being himself at the moment of changing his mind. The insistence on betrayal and self-betrayal leads to a certain passivity, but it is closely intertwined with activity in liberating himself from attachments in day-to-day living. Nauseated or not, Roquentin's self-critical consciousness is the part of him that functions best; Sartre similarly observes himself observing, while the revulsion from emotional commitment is encouraged by identification of the self with consciousness as he portrays it—something which has no ballast and no substance. Nothing in his life must be allowed to obstruct transparency. Austerely puritanical and ruthlessly ambitious, he sacrifices himself, his projects, his lovers again and again, while the destruction fuels his self-aggrandizement. His political passions are generous, and the generosity is genuine but compromised. He condemns givers of gifts as aggressors seeking power over those who accept, but he gives relentlessly while remaining endlessly on guard to protect himself against the generosity of others. When given presents, he gives them away; borrowing ideas he conceals his indebtedness, even from himself, knowing anyway that he will soon discard what he has taken.

His capacity for change was heightened by his awareness that we must never expect to recognize ourselves in our completed work, that books and actions deviate like children from parental intentions. Sartre had an extraordinary capacity for change. Disliking the idea of the static self and refusing to be tethered philosophically, politically, or personally to any commitment, he believed he could transform his life like a snake sloughing off dead skin.[14] Even physically he changed more than most people do, the slight, narrow-shouldered boy growing into the wide, squat man who was dubbed by his American friends "Mr. Five-by-Five." When he was twenty-four, his ambition, he told Simone de Beauvoir, was to become both Stendhal and Spinoza; later, applying philosophy to politics and *Realpolitik* to philosophy, he tried to negotiate a peace treaty between Marx and Freud. When this diplomacy failed, he fell back on a gigantic biography of Flaubert founded on a combination of Marxist and Freudian insights. By then the young Sartre who never voted had turned into the radical knight-errant who rode on international airlines. The mature Sartre never tired of demonstrating, agitating, signing manifestos, making political speeches, attending rallies, though, to seasoned politicians, he still seemed politically immature, incurably naïve. Despite his formidable intellect, he never quite arrived at what he called "the age of reason," at adult stability, though the young writer who made up his mind that success would never induce him to spend less time enjoying cafés, movies, or girls had grown into the compulsive worker who always wore moccasins to avoid wasting time on tying shoelaces.[15] But the young man who declared that all anti-Communists were swine had turned into an old man

who declared that the Communist party was the worst enemy of freedom, and the champion of individual freedom had denied freedom to
the individual.

But while he took an almost perverse pleasure in asserting his own
freedom through protean self-transformation, he could neither learn
from his mistakes nor keep hold of his most valuable insights. He had so
much faith in his ability to form new theories that he forgot the old
ones: rather than build higher on an old foundation he would start all
over again with a new one.

HE had two styles of writing because he had two methods of writing.
When he wanted to achieve a polished prose, as in *Les Mots*, he would
fill only the first three lines on each page, leaving space for multiple revisions of each sentence. Nor would he ever take drugs while writing
what he considered to be "literary" works. But for him the distinction
between "literary" and "philosophical" books was less meaningful than
the distinction between work which demanded painstaking writing and
work which did not. If while talking, teaching, or lecturing, he approximated thinking out loud, in most of his writing he approximated talking, teaching, or lecturing. His predominant feeling was that style
should take care of itself and that a writer should not waste time on
painstaking revision of each sentence. He still enjoyed the process of
finding the right words and arrranging them in the right order but forbade himself to believe that the task of writing was any more than the
task of extricating sentences from himself, as if the book already existed
inside his consciousness. Drugs not only had the effect of encouraging
this illusion but seemed to speed the process of extrication, and, as he
went on working in this hurried way, Sartre came to depend less and
less on either observation or research: he wrote as if everything he
needed was already present inside his brain.

This was something he increasingly needed to believe as he grew
older. The future was shrinking as demands on his time were increasing.
Always unrealistically optimistic about completing at least some of the
projects that were in abeyance, he had more and more reason to hurry.
The quality of his writing deteriorates as he relies less on new observation, information, research, more on knowledge he has accumulated,
and more on drugs that seemed to make him go faster. In chasing after
his ideas, he was also chasing after the creativity that had deserted him.

Much of his better, earlier, writing had depended on his ability to
chronicle the play of consciousness, dovetailing the drama into accurate
description of external circumstances. Some of his best prose is to be

found in *La Nausée*, which is written in the form of a diary, and in his army diaries, *Carnets de la drôle de guerre*. In these fictional and factual journals the pulse of the sentences excitingly follows the rhythm of Sartre's thinking, whereas the latter part of the Flaubert biography is written in amorphous sentences with flaccid rhythms. Judging by the number of words he was producing each day, the army diaries were not written any more carefully, but the life Sartre was living then was more conducive to good writing, though he never shut himself off entirely from new experiences and new social contacts, on which observations could have been based. While he was teaching he was alert to the people around him; *Les Chemins de la liberté* rests on his prewar friendships in Paris and on his experiences in the army and the stalag; his later writing is not nourished to any comparable extent by the life that was going on all around him. He was allowing himself to be seduced by his own powers of analytical improvisation, rather like a composer who refuses to compose except by improvising.

Sartre's fluency was prodigious, but even in his earliest fictions the narrative impulse was liable to be overtaken by impulses toward description, analysis, and satire. As he chronicled the movements of a consciousness, he was at the same time not only philosophizing about the nature of consciousness and the nature of reality but also competitively measuring himself against other chroniclers. The crude feeling "Anything you can do I can do better" was elaborated into a sophisticated game of pastiche. But once he had proved that he was capable of becoming the greatest French novelist since Proust, he lost interest in both artistry and art. "Artistic activity," he wrote in *L'Idiot de la famille*, "consists of devaluing the real by realizing the imaginary."[16] Though he had been moving toward this position since his early work on the image, it does not seem that his sabotage of his own artistry was entirely deliberate, even if destructive and self-destructive tendencies were at work. Is he rationalizing these tendencies in himself or justifiably exposing them in Flaubert when he condemns the great novelist for making the world unreal by making himself into an artist?

For Sartre, the activity of philosophizing had never been entirely separate from forming theories based on generalizations. Traveling when he was young to new countries, he would start to formulate theories about them before he had given himself time to observe what was going on around him; later on, at editorial meetings of *Les Temps Modernes*, he would talk authoritatively and at length about books he had not read or films he had not seen, constructing elaborate theories on the basis of what he had been told by a friend.[17] This tendency is paralleled in his later books by the pronounced drift toward abstraction. On a minimum of observation and research he erects a vast superstructure of theory. At the same time his growing distaste for literary artistry accompanied a growing aversion to subjectivity, interiority, and individuality. Temperament and political conviction both pushed him toward the collective. A glance at the essays collected in the ten volumes of *Situations* shows how as time passed he concerned himself less and less with literature, art, and the private self, more and more with politics and public issues. His mind was such that almost any experience or observation would prompt theoretical generalization, but he is at his best as a writer when he is drawing more on recent memories of experience and observation than on his reflective abstractions. In *L'Etre et le Néant* the brilliant analysis of interpersonal relationships seems no further removed from Sartre's private experience than the examples based on observation of café life. But implicit in his later, much more grandiose idea of totalizing history is the dismissal of private experience as irrelevant. This is requisite anyway if the intellectual is to do what Sartre said he must do—put himself entirely in the service of the masses.

IN this introduction I have approximated the method Sartre uses in his biographies. I have tried to give a synchronic impression of the whole man, summarizing tendencies and generalizing about traits which remained more or less constant while providing only the sketchiest indications of development from one phase of his life to the next. He stuck more rigidly than most men do to the strategies he evolved for dealing with everyday life. He worked, for instance, between fixed hours and regularly went abroad at the same time each year. But one of his reasons for needing rigid patterns was that he cultivated discontinuity so assiduously. He loved changing his mind, rejecting principles that had been vital, making a fresh start. He was consistent in nothing—not even in his love for freedom. But the full story of his divagations needs to be told chronologically.

PART I

FOR A PRIVATE
FUTURE

(1905=31)

①

Poulou

SARTRE was only fifteen months old when his father died. "The death of Jean-Baptiste was my greatest piece of good fortune. I didn't even have to forget him."[1]

If Jean-Paul Sartre was an intellectual adventurer, his disposition was partly inherited from Jean-Baptiste, whose restlessness was exacerbated by the need to escape from France and a joyless family in which the parents scarcely spoke to each other. Eymard Sartre, Jean-Baptiste's father, was a country doctor in the Dordogne, a bright man who had written a medical book while still in his twenties. He married a pharmacist's daughter under the misapprehension that her family was rich, and he never forgave her when he found it was not. Their son broke free by passing the highly competitive examination to study at the Ecole Polytechnique and then joining the navy.

While Jean-Paul Sartre, who was five foot two, owed his diminutive stature to his father, who was half an inch shorter, his disposition to literary intellectuality could have derived from either side of his family or from both sides. His mother was a cousin of Albert Schweitzer, whose father, Louis, a pastor, was the youngest of three brothers. The oldest of the three, Karl (or Charles, as he later called himself), came to France after it surrendered Alsace-Lorraine to Prussia in 1871. A passionate anti-Prussian, he was working in Mâcon as a German teacher when he married Louise Guillemin, daughter of a Catholic lawyer. After publishing essays about Hans Sachs and Guillaume d'Aquitaine, Karl Schweitzer collaborated with another teacher, Emile Simonnot, on a series of textbooks for teaching English, German, and French. The first of the four children Louise bore Karl was a girl, who died in infancy; the other three, two boys and a girl, were brought up as Catholics, their Protestant father having little to do with their education. Anne-Marie

was the youngest, and she was twenty-one when her brother Georges
introduced her to Jean-Baptiste Sartre.

The boys had met at the Ecole Polytechnique. After Jean-Baptiste
left in 1897 to join the navy, he was sent on the frigate *Melpomène* to
Senegal and then to China,[2] where he contracted enterocolitis, though
he seemed to have recovered his health by 1903, when he met Anne-
Marie in Cherbourg. Within a few weeks they were engaged, and they
were married in Paris on May 5, 1904, when he was twenty-nine and
she was nearly twenty-two.

Granted six months of unpaid leave, he stayed with his wife throughout most of her pregnancy, but failing in his efforts to extricate himself
from the navy, he had to leave home in the middle of May 1905. On
June 21 the baby made his entrance into the world, nearly a month
late. He was given the names Jean-Paul Charles Aymard. It was not
until November that he met his father, who was delighted with him:
"He laughs at everything, moves incessantly, wriggles, yells at the top of
his voice, laughs at noises but never cries. His look is curious, intelligent
and very gentle . . . He's very advanced for his age."[3] But the happiness
of the trio gave way to fear when the enterocolitis returned, compounded by bronchitis. The baby was nine months old when it became
obvious that his father was dying. The family went to a small farm near
Thiviers, Jean-Baptiste's birthplace, where he died on September 17,
1906, at the age of thirty-two.

To qualify for a widow's pension Anne-Marie had to convince the
navy that her husband's death was due to his enterocolitis; this took her
nearly a year.[4] With no income, no career, no means of earning a living,
she retreated to her parents' home in Meudon, where she was treated as
if she was still an adolescent. Mother and son shared a room, known as
the children's room, and she could neither accept an invitation to dinner without permission from her father nor stay out later than ten. As
the child soon learned, his mother had no authority that could not be
overruled by Karl and Mamie—the names by which he knew his
grandparents.

At sixty-two Karl Schweitzer was still a handsome man. Though his
fine white beard was stained with tobacco, he looked so much like God
the Father that his fellow parishioners sometimes ran away from him in
church or flung themselves at his feet.[5] At meals he would gesture silently with a forefinger when he wanted one of the women to pass him
the salt.

The boy's life was dominated by the strong-willed old man, whose
wife no longer tried to resist him. She had withdrawn into her mi-
graines, her bedroom, her bed, resigned to the infidelities that rein-

forced the pride he took in his appearance. At sixty-five he started an affair with a former pupil, an unmarried teacher, which continued until she left to work in Algeria.[6] Nor did he approve of his daughter's sexual abstinence. He was annoyed when she resisted the advances of a bald German doctor who often came to lunch and tried to kiss her. When Anne-Marie complained, she was told that she was either making things up or making her father look inhospitable. Meeting few men and liking none of them, she concentrated her emotional energy on her small son, who had everything done for him: he was washed, dressed, undressed; his shoes were put on, his hair brushed. He seldom cried, was never noisy.[7] It was easy to win praise from his mother. He was fair, rosy-complexioned, with plump cheeks and curls. Endless photographs were taken; Anne-Marie retouched them with crayons. Never having had a sister, she tended to emphasize the female side of her son's nature. If Gustave Flaubert's mother was like a daughter to the husband who was nine years her senior, Sartre's mother was still a daughter to her parents while bringing up her son as if he were a girl. His curly hair was allowed to grow long; his clothes were girlish. He may even, like Lucien in his 1938 story "L'Enfance d'un chef," have felt scared that he would actually turn into a girl.

His cross-eyed look and his defective vision had their origin in a cold he caught while vacationing at the seaside resort of Arcachon. When he was three or four his right eye was left with only 10 percent vision.

AT the age of sixty-seven Charles Schweitzer was forced to retire from the school at Meudon, so he moved to Paris with his three dependents and founded an institute for teaching French to foreign students. The family settled into a sixth-floor flat at 1 Rue Le Goff, near the Gare du Luxembourg. When Lucien's family moves to Paris, it is "like a magnesium flash" for the boy. He "could no longer sleep because of the cinemas, cars and streets."

Like his mother and her brothers, Sartre was brought up Catholic; few religious memories were to stay with him apart from a vague feeling that God could see him when he set fire to the net curtains with a match.[8] Poulou, as he was called, was taken quite often to church, but mainly to hear the organ music.[9] If he came to associate the Mass with virtuous behavior, it was chiefly because his mother told him that a good boy could stay still as a statue in church. He tried hard not to move his feet and to keep his chair from creaking.

Less effort was involved in winning admiration from his grandfather, who used to take his childish pronouncements with a seriousness that encouraged a nonstop performance. Sometimes Poulou could even perform in costume. At a party held to celebrate the anniversary of the institute's opening, he was dressed as an angel in a blue muslin dress, with stars in his fair curly hair and on his wings; he moved seraphically among the guests offering them oranges from a basket. But stardom did not save him from feeling bitterly jealous of his grandfather's fifty-year-old collaborator, Emile Simonnot, an ugly man with a waxed mustache and a dyed forelock, who came to dinner every Thursday. On one such evening Charles said: "Someone's missing: it's Simonnot."[10] No one ever said: "Someone's missing: it's Poulou." The boy resolved to make himself indispensable, and later, as he admitted, he would let himself be drawn into love affairs partly to make sure that his presence was required and his absence felt.

Gradually the child realized that his grandfather was hostile to the girlishness his mother was cultivating in him, most particularly his long hair. After sustained arguments had failed to influence his daughter, Charles took the boy to a barbershop, saying "We'll give your mother a surprise." Most family surprises led to exclamations of delight, to hugging and kissing, but this one led to weeping from behind the closed door of the bedroom. Without his long blond curls Poulou was undeniably ugly.[11] According to a letter Sartre wrote in 1925, this incident occurred when he was five. (According to the autobiography of his early years, *Les Mots,* he was seven.) Finding it more difficult now to charm the adults, he tried harder, sometimes too hard. And unaccustomed to failure, he became vindictive when other children outshone him.

Les Mots is also misleading in suggesting that the boy taught himself to read by taking precocious advantage of the books on his grandfather's crowded shelves. The fact is that Sartre's early intellectual development was conditioned by coaching from his grandfather. Teaching and music were the two family traditions: seven generations of Schweitzers had taught in Alsatian schools.[12] Charles had felt frustrated when his own children had been put into the hands of Dominicans; this made it all the more gratifying to tutor the responsive little nine-year-old. "I've made myself the schoolmaster of my little man, to whom I teach history and geography while learning them myself. Really nothing is so delicious as cultivating and planting seeds in these little intelligences."[13]

The soil was fertile, and the boy already gave signs of being literary. Sartre's own chronology is unreliable, but probably he was not much more than seven when he began to exchange letters in verse with Charles, helped by Anne-Marie and a manual on versification. Here was another way of winning praise from the grown-ups. Presented with a copy of La Fontaine's *Fables choisies,* he began to rewrite them in alexandrines. He constructed adventure stories, writing in exercise books with violet ink. For "Pour un papillon" he borrowed the title, characters, and plot from an adventure story about a professor sailing up the Amazon with his daughter in quest of a rare butterfly. The boy was given a small typewriter by his uncle Emile,[14] and his next story, "Le Marchand de bananes," was lovingly copied out by his mother and handed around for admiration.

As a dedicated teacher, Charles naturally reveled in the achievements of his young pupil. "His kind of aptitude is characteristically verbal . . . he dreams of nothing but adventures and poetry. But these are pretty useless in the twentieth century. Aggressive and eloquent, he's got more of the wherewithal, alas, for becoming a lawyer or a Deputy. In the meantime he's healthy and has the happiest character in the world, he sings all day."[15] The diligent student modeled himself on the septuagenarian. Later on he would make strenuous efforts to be unlike his grandfather; he was possibly rebelling against the memory of Charles's impressive library when he made a virtue of owning few books.

But the first reaction against the old man's influence came from Anne-Marie. One day, taking her son to the Jardins du Luxembourg, she stopped at a kiosk that sold boys' comics, serial adventure stories such as *Cri-cri, L'Epatant, Les Vacances, Les Trois Boy-Scouts,* and *La Tour du monde en aéroplane.* Rabelais and De Vigny became matters of less urgent concern than the Eagle of the Andes and the iron-fisted boxer. Anne-Marie also found him books of adventure stories. Though the boy tried to hide the comics, Charles discovered that his efforts were being undercut.[16] But he was wise enough to impose no veto, and Sartre always remained a devotee of thrillers.

Movies were another weapon his mother could use against high culture. At the Panthéon, in the Rue Soufflot, violet light bulbs glowed against the wall while a badly tuned piano accompanied the latest installment of the silent thriller serial. Anne-Marie also took him to boulevard movie houses, where he could see such thrillers as *Fantômas* and *Les Mystères de New York.* He watched beautiful young girls rescued in the nick of time from deadly perils—handsome horsemen galloping across plains while a sweet-faced girl waited, bound and helpless, as a flame moved inexorably along a fuse leading to a barrel of gunpowder.

In the early evening, while Charles was teaching at the institute and his wife was reading novels in her room, Anne-Marie, at the piano, would unwittingly provide the background music for the adventure stories her son acted out in the old man's study, playing all the parts himself—heroes, villains, victims, lovers, girl friends.

A star in private, he was a pariah in public. In the Jardins du Luxembourg he would lean against a tree, hoping that some of the other children would ask him to join in a game. Was he being ignored because of his size? His mother shared his uncertainty. At home she could accept his smallness, but in the park she wanted to plead that he be allowed into the magic circle of game playing. Her anxieties were exacerbated by her mother's doleful predictions: "He'll have the build of a Sartre." Despair and self-disgust increased his tendency to believe he was performing for an invisible public that withheld its admiration only when he was guiltily comforting himself in bed.

He soon learned that performing could secure love. He was about eight when Anne-Marie bought him a set of glove puppets, and whenever he had a little money, Poulou treated himself to a new one. He had a Jew, a policeman, Punch, a character called Bu-Ba-Bo, and several others. In an old children's book, *Monsieur le Vent et Madame la Pluie* (*Mr. Wind and Mrs. Rain*), which had probably belonged to his mother, one of the characters had magic puppets that came to life if they were touched three times with a ring, and he liked the idea that they could enjoy independence. He began to write plays for them, which he performed in the bathroom. Later, taking the puppets to the Jardins du Luxembourg, he would make a seat into a little stage, crouching behind it and making the puppets appear on his raised hands. Speaking in a high-pitched voice as if performing only for himself, he hoped to attract the attention of other children, and in this way he managed at last to make friends with a freckled girl his own age, Nicole.[17]

WHEN Sartre was eight it was Charles who found a school for him. In 1913, taken to meet the headmaster of the Lycée Montaigne, the boy was recommended as advanced for his age and was put into the eighth class. But in his first dictation he made so many mistakes that Charles was told he ought to be in the tenth. Annoyed, the old man took him away from the school and engaged a tutor, who came almost every day until the family left for a long vacation at Arcachon, where the boy was sent to the *école communale*. The teacher, M. Barrault, had a small beard, pince-nez, and halitosis. Poulou had a special desk, next to the rostrum, and even during recess he had to stay with M. Barrault instead of playing with the rough working-class boys.

In the autumn, back in Paris, he was taken by Anne-Marie to the Poupon school, where the mothers sat behind the semicircle of children, watching the teacher. After a term here he was entrusted to another tutor, Mademoiselle Marie-Louise, who chattered depressively about her loneliness. She would give anything to have a husband, anyone at all. Subsequent tutors were less demoralizing but less memorable.

While Poulou went on writing stories, the idea of writing for posterity gradually began to insinuate itself. Reading *L'Enfance des hommes illustres,* he compared the childhood of Rousseau, Bach, Raphael, and Molière with his own. Each trivial childhood incident seemed to prefigure their adult greatness; his own future would redeem present events from insignificance.

IN August 1914, when Germany declared war, France was engulfed in a surge of patriotism, and the boy was swept along in the excitement while being deprived of his favorite weeklies, which had disappeared from the bookstalls. He had only recently discovered Buffalo Bill, Sitting Bull, and Texas Jack; where were they now? Charles explained that the publisher was German. Meanwhile other writers were remodeling their adventure stories along patriotic lines: intrepid schoolboys were replaced by more topical heroes; regimental mascots bulked large, together with orphans from Alsace and the children of soldiers. Occasionally a heroic schoolboy fired a few shots. At Arcachon in October the nine-year-old author tried to combine individual heroism with the collective predicament in a story about a private who captured the Kaiser, challenged him to single combat, and forced him to sign an ignominious treaty giving Alsace-Lorraine back to the French.

If the war years were the happiest in his childhood, one reason was that he experienced a new closeness with his mother, who now eclipsed Charles in importance and confided everything to her attendant knight, her little man, as he did to her. He could confide in her unreservedly; in the presence of other people they were sometimes allies, sometimes conspirators. "In a shop or café the assistant would strike us as funny and on the way out my mother would say: 'I didn't meet your eyes. I was afraid I'd burst out laughing in her face.' "[18] As her confidant he shared her fear of brash men in the street. He never forgot the pasty complexion and waxed mustache of a straw-hatted man who accosted them one day near a bookstall. Protecting her against predatory males, the boy forgot his own maleness.[19]

Of course he was often reminded of it. Vacationing at the age of ten with his grandparents at Vic-sur-Cère, he tried to impress a young woman with an invented story about a girl who had hurt him so badly that he wanted to take vengeance on the whole sex. "I'd like to see the

boy when he's twenty," said the young woman. "I'm sure all the girl
will be mad about him."

In October 1915 he was finally sent to school after the two years o
individual tutoring, with only the brief intervals at the school in Arca
chon and the Poupon school in Paris. He started at the Lycée Henri IV
as a day student in the sixth form. The teacher, M. Ollivier, had to di
vide his attention among the whole class, and it was hard for Sartre to
compete with boys accustomed to answering questions in class. He did
equally badly in written work: his first essay put him at the bottom of
the class. Charles threatened to take him away from the school, but his
mother arranged a meeting with M. Ollivier, who refused to give him
private lessons but agreed to keep an eye on him.

It was surprisingly easy to make friends. Unlike the children in the
Jardins du Luxembourg, his classmates accepted him as their equal
After trying so hard to be special, he wanted nothing more than to be
like the others. He joined in their laughter, repeated their jokes, echoed
their catchphrases, accepted their values and unwritten laws. Jeering
and insults were prohibited: offenders were encircled and coerced into
apologizing. After school each afternoon the boys ran about shouting in
the Place du Panthéon, and they played ball between the Hôtel des
Grands Hommes and the statue of Rousseau. Most of the mothers knew
each other, and although Anne-Marie was informed by one of these
that "Poulou puts on airs," the two sons remained friendly.[20]

At the end of the term M. Ollivier summed up Sartre as an "excellent
child, but not at all thoughtful. Hardly ever gives the right answer first
time. Must accustom himself to thinking more." He did. By the end of
the school year the verdict of his teachers was that he was "excellent in
all respects."[21] Learning about ancient Egypt, Greece, and Rome,
Sartre especially enjoyed Duruy's history of Rome, which was full of
good stories. He consumed books voraciously, even when he understood
only part of what he was reading.

The boy who came out top of the class was a plump day boarder,
Bénard, who "looked like a baby chick." The son of a dressmaker who
was not on social terms with the other mothers, he was sensitive to the
cold, always wore a long woolen scarf, and had to stay indoors while the
other boys played outside; he waved to them through the window. In
class he never raised his hand to answer a question but always knew the
answer when asked. When he died at the end of the winter, forty boys
sobbed behind his coffin.[22]

Soon after Sartre and his classmates had been moved up to the fifth
form the door opened in the middle of a Latin lesson and the porter
ushered in a boy who looked so much like Bénard that Sartre thought

he was a ghost. Asked his name and his father's profession, the new boy said that he was Paul-Yves Nizan, the son of an engineer. He had steel-rimmed spectacles and a rather aquiline nose. He and Sartre developed an immediate rapport when they spoke during recess; while Nizan's squint, which differentiated him from Bénard, gave him something else in common with Sartre. At first Nizan gave the impression of being virtuous and shy, but he was neither. "Overcome by violent, inner emotions, he did not shout out, but we saw him turn white with rage and stammer: what we took for mildness was nothing but a temporary paralysis."[23] More sophisticated than the other boys, Nizan cultivated a cynical attitude and spoke ironically of his parents, whom he secretly adored. Sartre spent a lot of time chatting with Nizan, who wanted to be a writer.

During these two years at the lycée Sartre scarcely had time to think of himself as a writer. Exercise books were for dictation, composition, logical analysis, and arithmetic. The French teacher, M. Noël, pronounced him to be "among the best in the class at French . . . already a store of literary knowledge and a very alert memory."[24] He had not escaped his literary vocation: "My mandate became my character."[25] Later on he would try to convince himself that he had no superego, but surreptitiously it had taken control of him: he was already committed.

(2)
Nitre and Sarzan

IN April 1917, when his mother remarried after letting the boy monopolize her for nearly twelve years, Sartre sustained a loss from which he never fully recovered. He had felt completely secure in his possession of her; as he had drawn closer to adolescence, the only rival male, his grandfather, had been growing weaker and less threatening. The young mother, who had briefly flowered into womanhood while Jean-Baptiste was alive, had gladly slipped back into childhood when suddenly, at the age of thirty, she was no longer one of the children and no longer Madame Sartre. She was Madame Mancy. Later, describing Baudelaire's reaction (at the age of seven) to his own mother's second marriage, Sartre wrote: "Just now he had still been fully immersed in the communal and religious life of the couple he formed with his mother. This life had ebbed like a tide, leaving him alone and dry. He has lost his justifications. He discovers shamefully that he is separate, that his existence has been given to him for nothing. His fury at having been evicted is mixed with a feeling of profound failure."[1] In this as in subsequent biographies Sartre is at his best when writing autobiographically.

Anne-Marie's motives for marrying may have been more complex than they seemed to her son. The paternal grandfather, Dr. Eymard Sartre, had been the boy's deputy guardian, but when he died at the age of seventy-seven in October 1913, his son Joseph succeeded to the position. Anne-Marie had never been on good terms with her brother-in-law, and she convened a family meeting in April to arrange for her new husband to take over the role. So Joseph Mancy displaced both Joseph Sartre and Charles—the two rival claimants to authority over the boy. Mancy also solved all her financial problems at a time when it was becoming increasingly awkward to remain dependent on her father. What she miscalculated was the extent to which her son would feel betrayed.

Sartre stayed on with his grandparents while his mother moved into a flat with her husband, who was a naval engineer. Like Sartre's own father, he had graduated from the Ecole Polytechnique, and though Mancy had met Anne-Marie before her first marriage and had paid court to her in Cherbourg, he would not, as the son of a railwayman, have been considered a suitable husband. Later, working in Paris as manager of the Delaunay-Belleville companies, he had stood a much better chance, as he knew when he had gotten in touch with her again. He was, according to Sartre, "a tall thin fellow with a black mustache, a rather furrowed face, a very big nose, rather beautiful eyes, black hair."[2]

When he was put in charge of the Delaunay-Belleville shipbuilding yards in La Rochelle, he settled there with his new wife, and in November the boy moved into their flat. In the Rue Le Goff flat Anne-Marie had made her son feel that they were living on money that was not theirs; in La Rochelle, where Mancy earned a high salary and gave the boy a daily allowance, he felt even more alienated than before from the source of income. Leaving Paris, leaving his school and losing his friends, he would have felt disoriented even if he had not had to confront the domineering stranger who had taken his mother away and, worse still, the new image that she presented as a subservient wife.

It was impossible for Mancy to win the affection of his stepson, though he tried hard, even taking time after dinner to tutor him in geometry.[3] One evening, when the boy was answering a question, his insolent tone made his mother storm out of the room. The lesson proceeded more peacefully, but Anne-Marie came back and slapped her son twice across the face. Mancy shouted at her angrily. Feeling unloved and unwanted, while everything in the world seemed unstable, the boy worried more than ever about being ugly. His mother's identity appeared to have changed as dramatically as her name. She listened respectfully when Mancy held forth at the dinner table about politics and the responsibilities of the employer; to the boy his stepfather seemed intolerant, prejudiced, and narrow-minded.

In this atmosphere the grand piano became a source of solace. Anne-Marie played a good deal, and so did Sartre, teaching himself from the scores of operettas and graduating to duets with his mother. Struggling alone with pieces by Schumann, Beethoven, and Bach, he did not worry about fingering but tried to get the tempo right, going patiently over the same passages again and again, attending more to the shape than the detail.[4]

At the local coeducational lycée he felt like an outsider. Diminutive, unattractive, and cross-eyed, he was a natural victim for the tough schoolboys: they "would hang around ships and sailors and so on—an atmosphere which instilled in them more than the ordinary amount of energy and violence."[5] They got into fights with pupils at the religious school, the Ecole des Bons Pères, and with local street urchins. Retail-store apprentices were the natural enemies of the more expensively dressed lycée boys.[6] One day Anne-Marie came out of a store to find her son rolling on the ground, fighting viciously with a strange boy.[7] He enjoyed fighting, though his size put him at a disadvantage. As in Paris, boys were visibly affected by the absence of their fathers in the army, but in La Rochelle the boys acted as if they too were fighting a war. Violence could break out on the slightest provocation. "One of my school friends chased his mother with a knife—she had given him pota-toes and he didn't like them."[8]

Though less aggressive, Sartre had to compete with classmates who felt challenged by the presence of a boy wearing smart Parisian knick-erbockers. When they tried to impress him by talking boastfully about girls and orgies, he made out that he was no less of a man than they were. In Paris, he said, he had taken a girl friend to a hotel and made love to her. Needing evidence, he persuaded the maid to write a letter beginning "My dearest Jean-Paul." Admiring and envious, the boys passed the letter around, and when he confessed it was a forgery, it only confirmed his reputation as a typical Parisian. Parisians could not be expected to tell the truth.[9] Self-righteous contempt mingled with envy-ing admiration. In his first year he succeeded in arousing the curiosity of the other boys. According to one classmate, "It was exciting to hear him talk. He knew how to get an argument going and keep the ball bouncing for hours."[10] But at least one other boy found he was "bad tempered, moody, quarrelsome, unpleasant to the other boys and thought himself superior."

He did not work hard. At home he was often slapped for refusing to make more effort;[11] in his second year at the school he felt that every-thing he could have contributed was being rejected. "I fought con-stantly with some of them [the schoolboys], who in fact were not so highly regarded by the others; there were some more tolerant friends who tried to save me from these battles."[12] Many of the boys, including most of his friends, were less friendly when others were present than when they were alone with him.[13] None of the boys seemed to like him as much as he liked them, and this combined with his misery at home to give him what he recalled as the unhappiest years of his life.

Most of the thirteen-year-old boys in the class had girl friends, even if they exchanged no more than kisses in dark corners. Thursday after-noon, when there was no school, was the usual rendezvous time. Without having spoken to her, Sartre set his sights on the pretty daughter of a ship's chandler who lived by the harbor. Although Gisèle was in great demand, his classmates offered to fix a meeting. When he arrived, as arranged, on the road overlooking the beach, Sartre saw her cycling along the path and jumped on his bike to follow. He was wearing a hat he had found in the road. "Why does he keep pestering me," she called out, "this old fool with his big hat?"[14] Possibly she also said something about the spectacles or his shortness. In different accounts of the incident Sartre put different words into her mouth, but fifty years later he remembered the snub. When his classmates told him that she must have been trying to hide her feelings, he was naïve enough to let himself be humiliated again, making him feel still more ugly and unpopular.[15]

Desperate to find favor with the boys, he joined in their persecution of M. Loosdregt, the French teacher, who had a large, colorful nose and found it hard to keep order. Sartre received numerous detentions, and three years later he used the teacher as his model for the sententious provincial schoolmaster in *Jésus la Chouette* (*Jesus the Owl*): "Your mother has entrusted you to my care, my young friend, I promised to make a man of you. But promise me in turn always to tread the path of honor. I hope you'll never have to do anything but follow my example."[16]

Equally unhappy at home and at school, Sartre crept into reading as into a refuge, often spending all day with a book during weekends and school holidays. He had always drawn more comfort from literature than from religion, and unbelief came forcibly to him one morning while he was waiting at the bus stop for two sisters who usually traveled to school with him. "You know what?" he said to himself. "God doesn't exist."[17] It was literature that could confer immortality.

DURING his first year at La Rochelle he wrote a novel starring Götz von Berlichingen, a hero like Robin Hood who uses evil for good ends.[18] During his next two years at the school he did little writing, though his enthusiasm for Roman history led him to start work on libretti for operas about Horatius Cocles and Mucius Scaevola.

Sartre's envy of his better-looking classmates made them seem like heroes whose friendship might redeem him from his own ugliness. Together with two of them, Pelletier and Boutillier, he courted a pretty girl, seeing her home from school and escorting her to the movies, where her mother worked as an usher.[19] In her presence the three boys behaved like equals, but when they were alone Sartre was treated like a slave, exploited and ruthlessly betrayed. He received numerous canings on account of Pelletier and Boutillier. He spent his pocket money buying them cakes, raising extra funds when necessary either by selling books stolen from home or by stealing from his mother's handbag. One night, cold in bed, he put his jacket on top of the blanket, and in the morning, when she shook him awake, the coins that fell out added up to seventy francs. He told her that he and his friends had taken the money from Cardino, whom they had beaten up for being fresh to them. Cardino was then persuaded to confirm the story in return for 40 percent of the money Mme. Mancy would return to him. Cardino then bought a flashlight with his twenty-eight francs, and when his mother found out how he had paid for it, she called on Mme. Mancy.[20]

Sartre's motives were similar to those he would later impute to the writer-criminal Jean Genet: "What does he really want? To *be like the others;* nothing more . . . The truth is that he is impelled by anxiety . . . For the child who steals and the child who masturbates, to exist is *to be seen by the adults,* and since these secret activities take place in solitude, they don't exist."[21]*

Joseph Mancy admonished his stepson severely, but the incident made little difference to their relationship. Trying to steer the boy into pursuing an academic career in mathematics or physics, Mancy was aware of his resistance, but he misjudged its strength. Later Sartre would trace the origins of his antiauthoritarianism to his first encounter with his stepfather. It is hard to overestimate Mancy's negative influence: "He was always the man I was writing against. All through my life; and the fact of writing was against him."[22]

In the disgrace that ensued after the stealing incident, Charles Schweitzer, who was now seventy-five, was the only one from whom Sartre could hope for sympathy. But when the old man dropped a coin in a La Rochelle store, the boy found himself pushed aside when he tried to pick it up. He was no longer to be trusted. Painfully the arthritic old man stooped to retrieve the money himself.[23]

Nor was there any prospect of winning his mother back, except briefly when he went into a clinic for surgery necessitated by an abscess in his ear. She stayed with him in the clinic, sleeping in a bed at right angles to his. When she undressed at night he watched through half-closed eyelids, thinking of the favorable impression she had been making on his classmates.

Unable to drag her back into paradise, Sartre used his intellectual prowess to distinguish himself at school. At the prize-giving ceremony in July 1919 he was awarded prizes in French, Latin, Greek, and mathematics.

* When italics appear in a quotation, they are always there in the source unless otherwise indicated.

In October 1919 he was moved up to the second form. When he wrote stories, he would show them only to her, never to Mancy, whose presence was a continuing provocation. To give himself a feeling of freedom, to strengthen his willpower, the boy forced himself into senselessly destructive actions. One day, lusting after a hat and eventually persuading his mother to buy it for him, he threw it under the wheels of a trolley car. For this she slapped him twice.

At the end of that school year Sartre won prizes in Latin and French, but because of the stealing incident and to protect him from "harmful influences," or to rid themselves of the constant reminder of their failure to win his goodwill, his mother and stepfather sent him to Paris, where Charles Schweitzer arranged for him to be admitted to the Lycée Henri IV. He found himself again in the same class as Paul Nizan.

After being a Parisian newcomer in La Rochelle, Sartre was now a provincial newcomer in Paris, and he was so anxious to be accepted by his classmates that he joined the choir for Mass in chapel on Sunday.[24] Afterward he went to the flat in the Rue Le Goff, where he made good use of his grandfather's library. Sartre spent Thursday afternoons and Sundays with his grandparents, who had moved down to the third floor. He slept there on Sunday nights, and the rest of the week he boarded. For the first time in his life he had uninterrupted contact with boys of his own age. In the dormitory he discovered mild homosexual inclinations: he enjoyed it when boys ganged up to take other boys' trousers off by force.[25] Nizan too was a boarder; their literary ambitions bonded them together, and Sartre turned to the novels Nizan enjoyed. While boarding school was intensifying Sartre's experience of personal relationships, Proust, Gide, Giraudoux, and Paul Morand altered his interpretation of them.[26] *A la recherche du temps perdu* seemed so real that Sartre and Nizan spoke about the characters as if they were alive: "What do you think M. de Charlus has done now?"[27]

While friendship with Nizan helped him to feel relaxed, the teacher, M. Georgin, encouraged him to think independently. "Find your own solution to the problem, your own answer to the question."[28] Sartre went to the Bibliothèque Sainte-Geneviève and began to take pride in his mental processes. His writing became more serious and less eclectic.[29]

The friendship with Nizan grew so close that the boys were nicknamed Nitre and Sarzan, as if they were interchangeable, while they looked so alike that they were sometimes mistaken for each other:

From 1920 to 1930 especially, at lycée and then university, we were indistinguishable . . . He never raised his voice . . . merely folded his hands

... letting his fearful remarks drop with a sly, deceptive calmness. At sixteen he proposed that we should be two supermen. He gave us Celtic names ... R'ha and Bor'hou ... We walked around Paris for hours, for days. We discovered flora and fauna, stones, and we were moved to tears when the first neon lights were switched on. We thought the world was new because we were new in the world ... We walked, we talked, we invented our own language and intellectual slang ... One night these supermen-at-large climbed the Sacré Coeur and saw beneath them a chaos of shining gems. Sticking his cigarette into the left corner of his mouth and grimacing hideously, Nizan said: "Hey, hey, Rastignac!" I repeated: "Hey, hey," as I was intended to do, and we walked down, pleased with the discreet revelation of our literary knowledge and the extent of our ambitions.[30]

As in his childhood relationship with his mother, Sartre was sharing values, confidences, giving and receiving emotional support. Nizan, who had established his superiority since arriving at the school, was incontestably the dominant partner. At sixteen he was something of a dandy. He was more successful than Sartre with girls, enjoyed an enviably close relationship with his father, and had a precocious vocabulary. "He could immediately master words he had just picked up ... He wrote better than I could and with his father's mournful eyes he watched himself write."[31] Nizan's father, who had been demoted to manager of a railway depot, was furious with himself for having been duped by promises about a privileged future and began launching into remorseful tirades. One night, bundling his clothes over his arm, he strode out of the house, threatening suicide. It might have seemed unenviable to be the son of such a man, but to the stepson of Joseph Mancy masochistic violence appeared more admirable than arid complacency.

A strong strain of negativity ran in both boys. "It had long seemed to me desirable," Sartre wrote, "to be and above all to appear very wicked."[32] This aspiration to decadence sometimes helped him to overcome his shyness. Though he lacked the aplomb and the verbal aggressiveness of Nizan, his impulse was still to seek the limelight. His ambition now was to become a jazz singer, and he was good enough to be appointed by his classmates "Satyre official," organizer of celebrations and jamborees.

In 1920 M. Georgin wrote: "Certainly there is good stuff in him,"[33] and in June 1921 he passed the first part of his *baccalauréat*. In France philosophy is taught in the senior class of lycées, and Sartre now came under the influence of M. Chabrier, who made philosophy seem "like knowledge of the world. All the sciences belonged to philosophy ... I thought that if I specialized in philosophy, I'd learn about everything I was going to discuss in literature."[34] Chabrier labeled him an "excellent pupil: intellect already forceful, adroit in examining a question but should be a little less self-assured."[35]

Certainly there is an astonishing maturity in the unfinished novel *Jésus la Chouette* and the story "L'Ange du morbide" ("The Angel of Morbidity"), written between the ages of sixteen and seventeen. The jaded, disconsolate, acid tone of Sartre's early fiction is dominant. The central character of the story is a twenty-five-year-old university teacher who wears a gabardine suit and a sullen expression. Needing strong ideas, he borrows other people's. Though his friends call him a superman and become his disciples, he is a virgin until twenty-two, when he makes love to his ugly landlady. The story's final sentence is: "He never wrote anything else and was decorated at the age of fifty-five with the Légion d'honneur, incontestable proof of bourgeois status."[36] Later Sartre will succeed better in fusing critical comment with narrative.

Believing himself to be at once brilliant and mediocre, Sartre endows his characters with the same qualities. The university teacher loves himself "with all the tenderness, all the goodness, all the infinite solicitude which replaces intellectual values in the mediocre." Sartre develops this theme through the imagery of disease; attracted to this by the example of Thomas Mann, he lends it a similarly bizarre glamour. The neighboring hotels have been made into clinics for the tubercular, and after many erotic fantasies about tubercular girls, the character awkwardly makes friends with one. The relationship remains platonic, but the messy, embarrassing, painful fits of coughing contrast with the vagueness and generality of the teacher's fantasies.

Wanting too, like Baudelaire, to cultivate literary beauty in bad soil, Sartre rebelled against the values his stepfather had in common with M. Loosdregt. Though he had internalized many of these values, Sartre was only fourteen or fifteen, he claims, when he came to believe that he must argue against himself. "What? I thought that? But it was idiotic to think that."[37] The habit he would never break was to reject everything he had once believed, a procedure that involved him in losing touch with the best of his own insights.

EDUCATION in France is elaborate and protracted: Sartre would still be a student at twenty-four, though he did no military service until afterward. But at eighteen he and Nizan were aiming at the Ecole Normale Supérieure, one of the most exclusive great schools, where standards are higher than at the universities. The ferociously competitive entrance examinations involved two years of intensive preparation after the *baccalauréat*, the examination usually taken at the age of eighteen. Instruction of the *hypokhâgne* and the *khâgne*—the first and second of these years —was reputed to be better at the Lycée Louis-le-Grand than at the Henri IV, where Sartre and Nizan were in any case no longer on good terms with the headmaster. After passing the second part of the *bac* in June 1922, Sartre took leave of the headmaster by spitting on his shoes.

In the autumn of 1922 the two boys started at the Lycée Louis-le-Grand, which Nizan has described as "a sort of large, pale-bricked barracks with sun-dials inscribed in gold, where nineteen-year-old boys could not learn much about the world by dint of living among the Greeks, the Romans, the idealist philosophers and the doctrinairians of the July monarchy."[38] What the boys felt, according to Sartre, was "an urgent need for action."

Boarders wore loose smocks, much like those of artists, and classmates remember Sartre's as being gray and ink-stained.[39] "We were depressed by our dirty uniforms, our torn smocks . . . We were especially overwhelmed by the atmosphere, this unbreathable atmosphere, always the same, emanating from the four walls of the lycée. We used up the time in sterile little disputes and rehearsals of the same old arguments, or in fooling about, spitting, fighting, dragging each other on the ground."[40] Their favorite game was a variation of hide-and-seek: the boy who was hiding had to find a place where he could smoke a pipe without giving himself away.

Sartre's life revolved around Nizan. The friendship was charged with an emotional intensity that was almost unbearable, especially for Sartre. During a long period of estrangement, from March to October 1923, he tried to control his feelings by starting an autobiographical novel, *La Semence et le scaphandre* (*Seed and Safeguard*). "I was hard, jealous, like a maniac lover, without being considerate or tender. Lucelles, independent and sly, found opportunities to deceive me." He betrays Tailleur, the narrator, by forming new friendships—with an Algerian Jew or a boy from Marseille. "He avoided me for days, and found me aggressive and morose, though suffocating in my inability to express my tenderness. . . . But when I'd just left him, I was trembling with joy because I had a friend and this friend was none other than Lucelles."[41] The name sounds feminine, while "Tailleur" is as close to "tailor" as "Sartre" is to "sartor." After this Sartre would never again take the risk of becoming so emotionally dependent on anyone, male or female. His subsequent sexual promiscuity was partly defensive: more than the vio-

lence of the La Rochelle schoolboys, which made him believe that brutality between males was unavoidable, the quarrel with Nizan made
Sartre emotionally cautious.

In the autobiographical novel the friendship between the two boys
flowers when they are allowed out of school for walks. "Outside the porter's lodge he adjusted my tie and playfully strangled me for a bit."
Other people are the enemy. "Each passerby made us feel strong.
Alone, each of us was impressionable, volatile, dependent on accepted
values. Together we were impervious. . . . Each outing was a sort of
battle against the civilians, and still more than classmates we were
brothers-in-arms."[42]

At the age of seventeen Sartre had lost his virginity to a woman of
thirty, a doctor's wife from Thiviers. When he told her that he was a
boarder, she asked whether he went out on Thursdays and Sundays.
She then arranged to meet him at a friend's flat, and without believing
that she was attracted to him, he understood what was expected of him.
Though he made love unenthusiastically, he had the impression she
was pleased, but they did not see each other again.

This first sexual experience failed to change the pattern of his life,
but when the shipbuilding yards in La Rochelle ran into financial
trouble, Mancy brought his wife to Paris, where they settled in the
Place de Clignancourt, near the Gare de la Chapelle, and Sartre moved
in with them. Having to cope in the evening with domestic oppression,
in which his mother sided with the domineering Mancy, he found it
harder to concentrate. His new philosophy teacher, M. Bernes, praised
his "active and alert mind" and predicted he would succeed but
warned him against "too much facility" and "excessive elaboration of
insufficiently clarified ideas." For the first year's philosophical disserta-
tion Sartre failed to win either of the first two prizes and came out only
fifth among the runners-up. The first runner-up was a boy who had
made friends with Sartre and Nizan, René Maheu, the son of a Toulouse schoolteacher. The three became inseparable.[43]

According to the history teacher, M. Roubaud, Sartre was "a little
confused" and achieved "uneven results." He did better in French and
Latin. While the lycée teachers did not encourage intellectual independence, Nizan, who was always inventing theories of his own, provoked
Sartre into competing and arguing. They liked to feel different from
other people: many of their moral and aesthetic ideas were formulated
when they were among crowds. At moments of discouragement they fell
back on "the theory of the witness," which they had evolved together:
they were temperamentally destined to be spectators of "the world's futile agitation." Other people could become passionate, but their role

was to observe, taking notes and using their psychological understanding.[44]

Lessons in philosophy consisted of little more than summaries of what the great philosophers had written, but for Sartre, thanks partly to Nizan and partly to the novels of Dostoevsky, philosophy and psychology were indistinguishable. His philosophizing was catalyzed by his finding an unused alphabetical index on the seat of a Métro train. Published by Midy Suppositories, with the company's name on the cover, it was intended for promotional distribution to doctors. Sartre kept it for jottings, grouping them alphabetically and juxtaposing philosophical reflections with aphorisms and fragments of fiction written to define a concept. For "soul" the entry is: "He looked into his soul as if looking at himself in a mirror: with the ardent desire to satisfy his longing to be beautiful (as he knew he wasn't), to be intelligent (which he certainly hoped to be) and his fear of finding himself ugly, mean. And he went from mirror to mirror, from introspection to introspection without ever being able to form an opinion based on an idea of the whole."[45] His definition of "love" is ingenious. "Desire consists of treating a woman as a means, not an end—love consists of treating a woman as an end, not a means." Under "art" he notes: "The secret is to dominate your art."[46]

Dostoevsky had seemed willing to share a secret that "transcended not only ordinary knowledge but scientific knowledge."[47] It followed that a writer should be a philosopher, should have a comprehensive view of all knowledge, should unveil "the truth about the world," should offer new insights and ideas.[48] Though he had found mathematics and natural sciences difficult, Sartre had faith in his intelligence and in his talent for reporting on the world he observed, though the truths he had to reveal were to be learned not by observing but by writing. "By combining words I'd gain real things." There were groupings of words that yielded a truth.[49]

Deeply serious in his ambitions, he was also drawn, if only defensively, toward comedy: conscious of his ugliness, he preferred to invite laughter rather than allow others to make him a victim. The clown is at least partly in control of his audience. When Nizan withdrew into his depressions, Sartre was the only one who could make him laugh, and during breaks between lessons the two friends would sometimes put on impromptu performances in their first-floor study. Standing in front of a table covered with a black cloth, Sartre would turn the handle of an imaginary phonograph; Nizan, squatting under the table, would mimic the nasal tones of a crooner. Or they would perform a dialogue consisting of archaic exclamations: "Si fait!" "Oui da!" "Parbleu!"[50] When they were together they were exhibitionistic, as neither would have dared to be alone. Acquired in the privacy of his grandfather's study, when he identified self-indulgently with the heroes of adventure stories, the habit of performing would remain central to Sartre's thinking: much of his writing has the rhythm of an extempore lecture.

There was no danger now that he would ever be mistaken for Nizan, who was taller and more stylish, while Sartre dressed carelessly, usually in a black shirt. Nizan had a musical voice and was given to long silences; Sartre's speaking voice was hoarse, though he could sing well, and he acted the extrovert. This too was a performance. He had resigned himself to the loss of his mother, while Nizan's facial neuralgia indicated that he was still unbalanced by his ardent love for a depressive father who considered himself a failure.

In their second and final year at the Louis-le-Grand there were over seventy boys in the class, but Sartre's commitment to philosophy deepened, thanks in part to his new teacher, M. Colonna d'Istria, a small, crippled man.[51] Required to write a long essay, "Consciousness of Duration," Sartre read Bergson's "Essai sur les données immédiates de la conscience," which is translated as "Time and Free Will." It was this that made Sartre choose philosophy as his main subject, believing that its focus was on mental processes and that it could help him to write Dostoevskian fiction. Bergson's reflections on duration and consciousness also prompted him to take a closer interest in "what went on inside the mind, in the way ideas are formed, how feelings appear, disappear, and so on." Sartre's intention was to become not a philosopher but a teacher of philosophy. The essay he wrote was little more than a summary of Bergson's essay, and Colonna d'Istria was unimpressed.[52] In the competitive philosophy exams held during the year Nizan and Maheu both achieved better results than Sartre. He did worst in French, badly in Greek, but better in Latin.

Generally he made a more favorable impression on his classmates than he did on the teachers. Georges Canguilhem has paid tribute to "his vivacity and good spirits ... He charmed his friends with his humor, loved jokes and wasn't above kicking up a shindy."[53] He was hyperactive, unable to settle down into sleep unless he put wax in his ears and a bandage over his eyes.[54] He talked willingly about his ugliness, but according to Raymond Aron, who was later a friend at the Ecole Normale, his face looked quite different when he was talking: "His intelligence wiped out the pimples and the bloatedness of his features. For the rest, small, strong-backed, tough, he climbed up

ropes, legs at right-angles, with an effortless ease which stupefied us."[55]
Soon after he started using the alphabetical index to record ideas, he
began to reflect on what he called contingency. At the cinema he
would see films in which narrative necessity linked all the elements
together. Everything irrelevant had been left out. But afterward,
walking out into the street, he would notice a startling absence of
any organizing principle. "People were moving about, they were anybody."[56]

It was at the same time that the idea of freedom began to excite
him. When they were younger, Sartre had argued with Nizan, contending that we are as free as we choose to be. But now Nizan
was considering whether to become a priest. "I tried to impose my
optimism on him, repeating that we were free. He did not answer, but
the faint smile at the corner of his mouth said a good deal about
this idea."[57]

And at the Louis-le-Grand, Sartre was asserting his freedom. If he
failed to win prizes or high marks, it was partly a matter of refusing to
gratify his stepfather by doing well. He skipped school so often that he
acquired a reputation for being invisible. Like Sartre, Berliac—Lucien's
friend in "L'Enfance d'un chef"—plays truant from school. He and
Lucien confide in each other, smoke English cigarettes, play Sophie
Tucker and Al Jolson records, compare notes on feelings toward their
mothers, and borrow books by Freud from the Bibliothèque Sainte-
Geneviève. Lucien starts feeling afraid to kiss his mother good-night. "It
was like carrying a volcano inside him."

Like Sartre, Lucien feels that to work hard at the lycée would be to
collaborate with his parents in their efforts to shape him into a bourgeois. "A good student enjoys working—I don't. I get high marks but I
don't enjoy working. Not that I hate working. I don't care. I don't care
about anything. I'll never get anywhere." Asking himself what he is, he
decides that he does not exist. His philosophy teacher tries, unsuccessfully, to reassure him that his doubts are proof of his existence. He
thinks of writing a treatise on nothingness, lets himself drift, wants to
take romantic moonlight walks, but his parents forbid him to go out at
night. He is glad that they will be disappointed to find that he does not
have any potential for being a boss in bourgeois society.

Sartre and his classmates also practiced another form of rebellion,
flirting with local working-class girls on Thursday afternoons in the
Jardins du Luxembourg. Many of the girls were willing to make love.
Sartre dated an eighteen-year-old who, like the doctor's wife, gave herself to him only once. But the park, the scene of his earliest humiliations
at the hands of other children, continued to appear in his sexual fanta-

sies. He had recurring dreams about a pretty blonde, wearing a little
girl's dress, playing by the Luxembourg pond, while he was bare-legged
and only a little older than she was. Even while he dreamed, the symbolism of the stick and the hoop were obvious to him. Perhaps his resistance to Freud was partly a determination not to confront the
traumatic aftermath of early rejections.

(3)

School for Superiors

SARTRE was nineteen in August 1924 when he came out seventh in the entrance examination for the Ecole Normale Supérieure. "I regained consciousness of myself as a free man, or at least one in the process of liberating himself."[1] "Many can say, as I do, that they have had four years of happiness."[2] In fact he spent five years there, not leaving until the summer of 1929.

The school was at 45 Rue d'Ulm, not far from the Sorbonne. Wide stone steps led up to an entrance hall, with the students' pigeonholes on the right. Beyond the paved courtyard was a garden with blossoming trees and a pool with a fountain and goldfish.

The principal of the school was the literary historian Gustave Lanson, who had taken over in 1919 when he was already sixty-two. Nizan looked down on him as a "little old man, patriotic, hypocritical and powerful, with a respect for soldiers." It was assumed that *normaliens* who did military service would be commissioned as officers, but discipline within the school was slack, though students were roused every morning at seven-thirty by the breakfast bell and had to sign the register if they came back late at night. They were not compelled to eat any of the meals in the refectory, where the food was so undesirable that most of them patronized the local bistros. Nor was much care taken about hygiene. The dormitory remained unaired and unswept, the crockery was badly washed, and, as if to discourage the boys from keeping themselves clean, the only running water was in a closet used for cleaning shoes and storing trash cans.[3]

Sartre and Nizan shared a study with portraits of Giraudoux and James Joyce on the wall. The two friends were at peace again, though Nizan sometimes went for days without speaking to Sartre.[4] Apart from René Maheu, their contemporaries included Jean Hyppolite, who was studying philosophy, Pierre Guille, a student of literature, and Raymond Aron. Aron had an extraordinary mixture of humility and pride. One of the most impressive students of his generation, he seemed destined to be a great philosopher. He had a quick, incisive mind, wit, eloquence, a natural authority, and such a formidable memory that he never needed to take notes. He was like a brilliant barrister with total mastery over his brief and a capacity for the effortless assimilation of new material. With his thin body, his bony face, and his hooded, twinkling eyes, he was at once aloof and available. His devotion to Sartre began at the ENS. Many people would later claim to be more friendly with Sartre than they actually were, but none would suffer more than Aron at not being able to continue a friendship with him, and no one could have given less provocation for being treated—as Sartre would treat him—like an enemy.

From the beginning, Sartre, Nizan, and Maheu gravitated into a subgroup consisting mainly of students who had been taught at the Henri IV by Alain (Emile Auguste Chartier). A philosopher and himself a product of the Ecole Normale, he encouraged his pupils to dismantle accepted values and beliefs, to challenge commonplace assumptions. He cultivated a Stendhalian lucidity, hated fanaticism, and enjoyed paradox. Even among the radicals, however, Sartre, Nizan, Maheu, and Guille stood out as a quartet that was ridiculed by the others and that accordingly became hostile,[5] but the whole Alain group was fairly brutal in its language, fairly violent in its behavior. Late at night the boys would hide at the top of the stairs to shout "Thus pissed Zarathustra" as they threw water bombs at boys who were returning in dinner jackets from an evening out.[6] But Sartre had a gentle side. At twenty, according to Jean Fabre, "he was the best and most generous companion imaginable ... Underneath the cynicism and self-disgust which he willingly displayed ... his secret was indubitably a great softness which he managed neither to acknowledge nor to disclaim."[7]

The Ecole Normale had been affiliated with the Sorbonne since 1903. *Normaliens* take the ordinary degree at the university, with complementary instruction at the Ecole, but Sartre scarcely ever went to the Sorbonne, except for the lectures by Bréhier on the Stoics. Apart from Sartre and Nizan, there were only three students of philosophy in the first year—Aron, Canguilhem, and Daniel Lagache—so the five saw a lot of each other.[8] Throughout his five years Sartre gave a good deal of time to psychology and, in his first year, together with Nizan, Aron, and Lagache, attended a course in pathological psychology given at the psychiatric hospital of Sainte-Anne by Georges Dumas, who was pleased to have four *normaliens* in his class. Sartre and Nizan were even able to earn money by taking part in experiments,[9] but Sartre still could not afford

the boxing lessons he would have liked to take at a local gymnasium.[10]
He worked extremely hard, pitching himself into what was to become a
lifelong habit of settling down to his books from nine in the morning till
one, and again from five in the evening till nine.

Of the philosophers he read in preparation for his exam, the ones
who appealed to him most were Descartes, Spinoza, and Rousseau. He
liked the rule Descartes had made for himself: "I have devoted only *very
few hours in a day to the thoughts that occupy the imagination*, and very few in a
year to those which occupy only the understanding, and I have given all
the rest of my time to the relaxation of the senses and the repose of the
mind, attempting thus to emulate those who looking at the verdure of a
forest or the flight of a bird persuade themselves that they are thinking
of nothing." We can infer from the advice Sartre gave to a friend in
1926 when he quoted these lines that he followed Descartes's rule in
a revised form: "The bird in flight must be *your* bird, the forest *your*
forest, and for that to happen you need not feel it but transform it
slightly."

It is difficult to assess the part played by the Ecole Normale in shaping a mind that had already matured to the level of sophistication
shown in the early fiction. If Sartre was to go on being educated until he
was twenty-four, the ideal education would have pulled him away from
the tendency that one of his teachers—M. Bernes—had detected during
his first year at the Lycée Louis-le-Grand: to write fluently on ideas he
had only partially digested. What he badly needed was a close and sustained relationship with a brilliant, sensitive, rigorous teacher who
could command his respect. But he was no good at making friends with
men in positions of authority, and the Ecole Normale was no good at
inculcating the habit of painstaking research into original sources;
Sartre was not deflected from his tendency to depend on insufficient
facts, insufficiently mastered. But he was already a virtuoso with words,
and with his attractive voice he would have the lifelong ability to spell-
bind an audience of one person, five people, or five hundred by speaking as if he were thinking out loud, while the verbal virtuosity already
made it dangerously easy for him to write as if he were speaking impromptu.

During his five years at the ENS he learned less from lectures than
from reading and conversation. Later in life, except with De Beauvoir,
he would seldom match his wits against intellects of a caliber comparable to his own. The company he enjoyed was that of girls and of men
who were both younger and intellectually inferior, but at the ENS he
was surrounded by brilliant young men of his own age, and, competitive as he already was, he cannot have failed to profit as much from ar-

guing with Nizan, Aron, and other friends as he did from his voracious reading. Between November 1924 and March 1925 he borrowed about a hundred and twenty books from the school's library, mixing philosophy with psychology and classics with modern literature. He kept going back to books by Plato, Kant, and Schopenhauer, also reading works by Shakespeare, Keats, Cervantes, Goethe, Pascal, Villiers de l'Isle Adam, Mallarmé, Nerval, Chrétien de Troyes, Spinoza, Descartes, Freud, Janet, and Hesnard. He took out three books by the psychologist Théodule Ribot, including *La Vie inconscient.* In April he read Bergson, Erasmus, Giraudoux, Lucretius, and Saint Augustine's *Confessions.* [11]

He was also reading Marx, without taking much in, and Freud, only to be annoyed by the assumption that consciousness was not autonomous. The reactions of the other students to Freud are parodied in "L'Enfance d'un chef" when Lucien and Berliac congratulate themselves on the size of their complexes. More seriously, Lucien feels enlightened about "this odd feeling of not existing; this protracted blankness in his consciousness, his sleepiness, his confusions, the vain attempts to achieve self-knowledge, attempts that met only a curtain of fog." [12] The friends got into the habit of interpreting their dreams and their gestures. Lucien throws himself greedily into psychoanalysis: it is a relief to find character situated below the level of consciousness. But whereas Berliac luxuriates in his Oedipus complex, Lucien sees in it "the sign of a passion for power which later he would like to use for different purposes." [13]

On Sundays Sartre would lunch with his mother and stepfather, seeing his mother on her own once every ten days or so until they moved to St.-Etienne, where Mancy was put in charge of the Le Flaive factories.

In his later interviews Sartre would claim that while at the ENS he gave up reading "classical literature" except for Stendhal. This is belied by the register of books he borrowed from the library. Throughout his five years at the school the range of his reading is most impressive. During his second year he took out books by Croce, Durkheim, Casanova, James Joyce, Goethe, Hugo, Nietzsche, Bertrand Russell, Strindberg, Wagner, Nerval, Zola, Maupassant, Marcus Aurelius, Epictetus, and Georges Sorel, as well as books on Cézanne, Van Gogh, and Goya. During his third year his reading included Beaumont and Fletcher, Jung, Piaget, Hegel, Croce, Fichte, and Hesnard. In his final year he borrowed fifteen books by Plato, as well as books about Plato and Socrates. He was also reading Descartes, Spinoza, and Kant, as well as Piaget, and though he did not have a high opinion of Léon Brunschvicg, the principal philosopher of the ENS, Sartre took out one of his books. [14]

At the same time Sartre came under the spell of the surrealists, who were mostly not much older than the students at the Ecole and were popular there. He emulated the surrealist indifference to beauty, read Breton and Eluard, trying to imitate the poems in his *L'Immaculée Conception* and doing surrealist exercises in style. He started thinking about madness in relation to surrealism. Having once believed that it was possible to hit on the truth through the arrangement of words, he mimicked the surrealist idiom. In "L'Enfance d'un chef" Lucien writes a poem with such phrases in it as "The great crabs wrapped in the mantle of fog" and lets himself be seduced by a surrealist, Bergère, after confiding to him that he has tried to commit suicide. Bergère diagnoses the boy's condition as "disorder" and tells him about Rimbaud's program for a systematic disordering of all the senses.

The estrangement between the two friends is caused by Berliac's jealousy when Bergère makes Lucien his lover; in actuality the estrangement from Nizan was caused by Sartre's failure to understand the crisis his friend was undergoing. Retrospectively Sartre would maintain that Nizan was authentically in rebellion against the school, which was "said to be normal and reputed to be superior" (Nizan's phrase). At the time it looked as though Nizan was a spoilsport, searching for help no one could give him. When he confided that he was afraid of dying, Sartre decided that since he gave way so readily to depression, his "moral health" must be inadequate. At one point Nizan disappeared for three days, to be found, drunk, with some strangers.[15]

In fact he was less self-involved than Sartre, more alert to the political situation, and profoundly troubled—as Sartre would be later—by the need to choose between *la vie intérieure* and political action. Sartre might later have reacted less violently against *la vie intérieure* if he had been less devoted to it now; it was his pattern each time he recanted to turn in obdurate hatred against the quality he had formerly loved. In *La Semence et le scaphandre* he declared his intention of writing only about his own experience; he equated it with the experience of humanity. The novel contains an account of the dealings he and Nizan had in 1923 with *La Revue sans titre,* in which Sartre, using the pseudonym Jacques Guillemin, published his story "L'Ange du morbide" and several chapters of *Jésus la Chouette.* Nizan's sense of isolation was exacerbated by brooding on the disintegration of Western civilization. Like many *normaliens* and young intellectuals of his generation—Aragon, for instance—he went on flirting with the idea of withdrawing into a religious order, but in the end he opted (like Aragon) for the PCF (Parti Communiste Français), goaded by the ineffectuality of the ruling Cartel des Gauches, an alliance of socialists and radicals more determined to fight against inflation than against unemployment and depressed wages.

The leader of the radicals, Edouard Herriot, was characteristic of the provincial bourgeoisie, patriotic and mediocre, the prototypical mayor of Lyons, while his supporters—shopkeepers, landlords, manufacturers—wanted a policy of laissez-faire. The socialists favored a tougher economic policy, but the party was hopelessly ineffectual. At the Socialist congress in Tours (December 1930) the party had been split by the vote in favor of affiliation with Moscow, and *L'Humanité*, founded by Jaurès in 1904, had been taken over by the Communist majority. Of the sixty-eight Socialists elected in November 1919 only thirteen had joined the Communist party. Caught between the radicals and the Communists, the Socialists preserved their identity only by cooperating with neither.

Sartre took little interest in all this, but to many of his contemporaries communism seemed the only socialism that had remained true to itself. Nizan detested half measures: in his fragmentary novel *Le Goût du définitif* his alter ego is intent on "rediscovering the truth that had been lost since he started, ten years ago, in the sixth form."[16]

Nizan was active in the Groupe d'Information Internationale, a student group, led by Georges Friedmann, with the aim of seeing beyond nationalist horizons, but Sartre stayed aloof both from the radical groups and from the reviews they published. The most important of these, *Philosophies*, had been founded "for the defense of the MIND, MYSTICISM and liberty. Our prime concern is for the renaissance of philosophy and for the creation of epic poetry. For us thought is an action."[17] The surrealists believed mysticism to be "the poetic solution of the fundamental problems."[18] The *Philosophies* group had been founded by Pierre Morhange, who regarded himself as a Rimbaudian visionary. Nizan became one of his five disciples, together with Friedmann, Henri Lefebvre, Norbert Guterman, and the aggressive, red-haired Georges Politzer, who formulated slogans and catchwords such as "The philosopher will take charge" and "spiritual dictatorship."[19] The group's idiom was literary and religious. When Simone de Beauvoir saw the magazine *L'Esprit*, which replaced *Philosophies* in 1926 (after a patron had withdrawn his backing), she recognized that the intellectual young socialists "were talking about soul, salvation, joy, eternity. . . . They were interested primarily in spiritual manifestations; for them economics and politics could only be subordinate." What capitalism had destroyed was "the sense of being"; men must rediscover "the eternal part of themselves."[20]

The surrealists were hesitating on the brink of commitment to communism: for Breton "one revolution or another, however bloody," was the only way "to escape, momentarily at least, from this fearful cage in which we go on arguing."[21] Students were confused by the ideological turbulence, torn between the incompatible insights of Einstein, Freud, Hegel, Marx, Lenin, Valéry, and Proust. "Pell-mell we went back to square one," wrote Lefebvre, "but we had access to means of reconstructing the world. The Russian Revolution reduced previous history to a *tabula rasa*, reconstructing society from top to bottom; we were out to emulate it as quickly as possible."[22] These ideas and pressures were to have a long-term effect on Sartre, but Nizan was more sensitive to the condition of Europe, which had not cured itself of the nationalistic thinking that had led to the world war: "How can we forgive the generations that were sacrificed for not having removed the need for useless sacrifice?"[23] Perhaps the Communist party could help mankind to obviate "an idiotic ending."

Though no less refractory than his friend, Sartre felt no urge to channel his dissident energy into politics. He needed confrontations to be more direct and personal, needed to find adult correlatives to the childhood pleasure he had taken in the idea of slapping kings in the face. The monarch in the Ecole Normale was Gustave Lanson. If Sartre was to gain enormously in self-confidence during his five years there, it was due less to what he wrote than to what he read, and it was less because he matured psychologically and intellectually than because he competed successfully against brilliant fellow students, excelling himself not only academically but as an entertainer—mimic, singer, actor, pianist. His most spectacular victory of all was in a battle that no one would have expected him to win against the dignified and distinguished Gustave Lanson, who was not going to escape with a slap.

It was not yet apparent to Lanson that this small student was dangerous, though he was obviously hostile. In March 1925, at the school's annual revue, *A l'ombre de vieilles billes en fleur*—the old faces in flower parodying Proust's young girls—Sartre played M. Lanson, who was seduced by the wife of a rich Brazilian, Dona Veraldes, played by Lagache. The allusion was to the international organizations that were recruiting many *normaliens* at this time. In the sketch the school was sent to conquer Brazil. In another sequence Sartre danced in the nude with a seminude Nizan. Sartre's skill in mimicking Lanson was formidable. "The student Sartre," reported *L'Oeuvre* in its issue of March 22, "sustained the role of M. Lanson brilliantly," and the review was illustrated by a photograph of Sartre in the impersonation.[24]

His strong streak of exhibitionism made him hanker for a life in which he could appear regularly in front of audiences: still cherishing the idea of becoming a jazz singer, he frequented the College Inn in the Rue Vavin. Though he had never been given piano lessons, he not only played competently but took pupils,[25] as well as teaching philosophy to first-year students who could not otherwise keep up with the work in class. His income from coaching enabled him to eat lunch and dinner in local restaurants, and he readily gave money away to friends, as he did throughout his life.

His ambitions were unbounded; he told a friend: "I want to be the one who knows the most things." Meanwhile he wrote a one-act comedy about a man who describes his death agony, *J'aurai un bel enterrement* (*I'll Have a Nice Funeral*). Instead of joining a political movement, he counted on liberating himself by becoming totally independent of other people. He had—intermittently at least—a clear vision of what he termed "moral health," which could be attained only by rejecting all social constraints, starting with those of morality. "If you are moral, you obey society; if you are immoral, you rebel against it, but on its territory, where you are certain to be defeated. You must be neither one nor the other but superior to all that."[26] The social aesthetic must be rejected. To covet goods in a shop window is to enslave oneself both to those who make them and those who sell them—imbeciles who exploit you.[27] In this context Sartre's first *acte gratuit* comes to seem less gratuitous, even if he had not, at the age of fourteen, understood why he wanted to destroy the hat that had seemed so desirable. In Paris the rejection of commercial culture was partly a matter of necessity: not being able to afford the goods that were so seductively displayed in the shops, he needed to feel he was rebuffing the seducers. He must not let himself be distracted from what was almost a quest for the absolute.

For most students, male and female, clothes on display in shop windows are desirable as a means of enhancing sex appeal. Sartre would have been incapable of rejecting the commercial subculture if he had not become more self-confident and more reconciled to his ugliness and his shortness. Until 1925, as he said in 1926, his appearance had made him "temperamentally very melancholy ... I have absolutely driven that out, because it's a weakness." He was determined to make himself tougher. By pursuing only objectives that were realistically attainable he could feel more free, stronger, and more passionate. It was easier to overcome scruples and not to be held back by pity. "I call this state moral health because it's like being physically very well and feeling strong enough to bend a street lamp with one hand."[28]

His faith in willpower was reinforced by an energetic but compulsive refusal to recognize himself as a victim of genetic accident. At times he felt jubilantly full of himself, bursting with pride in his future. Looking at self-important senior citizens, he felt vibrantly aware of his hidden powers, as if the spectacles, the squinting eyes, the unprepossessing face, the diminutive body were the disguise he had selected. "Confronted with men who are intimidating and revered," he later wrote to a girl, "you'll be able to think that these are marionettes you can manipulate."[29] It was his own secret strength he was thinking of. His childhood survived in a different form: the student Sartre was the great man of the future pretending to be just a student. This was the Ecole chapter of the autobiography he was living.

Though almost everything in his life was conniving at his feelings of superiority, Nizan, still ahead of him, was the first to win a girl. At the Ecole ball in December 1924 he had met a seventeen-year-old girl who was both beautiful and high-spirited. Henriette Alphen was descended on her father's side from a composer-conductor at the court of Napoleon III and on her mother's from the chief rabbi of Bordeaux; the family now lived in an apartment house on the Rue Vavin. Rirette, as she was called, would meet Nizan, Sartre, and Aron after lectures at the Sorbonne, and they would go into the Jardins du Luxembourg together or back to her flat for tea. She used to say that if she was not married by the age of twenty, she would take a lover so as to have children.[30]

Both Sartre and Nizan were spending a lot of time with René Maheu, who seems to have taken the lead in evolving a personal mythology out of Cocteau's *Potomak:* the three of them belonged to the Eugènes, the highest caste in the book, that of Socrates and Descartes. All their contemporaries were assigned to inferior orders, mostly among the Marrhanes, who loll about in the infinite, or the Mortimers, who slop about in the blue of the sky. The Catholic philosopher Gabriel Marcel and most contributors to the *Nouvelle Revue Française* were classified as belonging to the same species as the Cataboryx, a metaphysical animal that expresses itself in "borborygmic rumbles." The Eugène looks down on science, industry, and all universal moral systems: he tries to make his life into an original work of art.[31] The three friends could feel isolated, but not alone.

MANY of Sartre's paternal relations were still living in Thiviers, and in September 1925 he went there for the funeral of a cousin, the daughter of his aunt Hélène, his father's sister. At the funeral he met a beautiful girl of twenty-two with long blond hair and blue eyes.[32] They were both invited to dinner afterward at his aunt's house, but the conversation they wanted to have was interrupted by questions from doctors and lawyers. Leaving early, they went for a walk in the fields.[33] Simone-Camille Sans was the daughter of a Toulouse chemist who had implanted in her a strong taste for reading. Her sexual experiences had been plentiful and eccentric, involving amateur prostitution and orgies in fancy dress, held in a cellar. The twenty-year-old Sartre reminded her of Mirabeau, and for four days they were inseparable.[34]

Repeating the trick he had used at school in La Rochelle, he pretended there were already two girls in his life, but in his second letter to her, written early in 1926, he admitted that they did not exist. After the meeting in Thiviers, he and Simone-Camille—or "Toulouse," as he called her—did not meet for six months, but the relationship continued through correspondence. By the end of 1925 she was saying she loved him better than her mother, while he regarded himself as her fiancé, though in the surviving letters he uses the term only when he wants to reproach her.[35] Perhaps he would have been equally articulate in conversation, but it is doubtful whether he would have been so aggressive or so self-assured.

This correspondence gave him one of his earliest pretexts for an essay in autobiography. Since childhood, he told her, his main ambition had been to create—create anything, from a philosophical system to a symphony. But he was dissatisfied with everything he did, with each style he used. He was trying to create a new character for himself, devoid of the shaming sentimentalism that made him weep "like a calf" at plays, films, novels. He was ashamed of being cowardly and soft: "when a dog barks near me it can make me tremble with fear."[36] What gave him "this artificial attitude" she had noticed was the determined attempt to check tendencies that persistently reappeared: "I'm never genuine because I'm always trying to adjust, to recreate; I'll never have the pleasure of being able to act spontaneously."[37] It almost follows that spontaneity was one of the qualities he admired most in other men. Hankering after sincerity, he was confused by ambivalence toward the feelings that arrived of their own accord, dodging the formidable willpower that was on sentry duty; sometimes he found himself saying nothing or stammeringly saying the opposite of what he had intended or neutralizing the feeling by expressing it in awkward words.

He would have liked to make the four-hundred-mile journey to Toulouse every month to visit her, he said, but he had been quarreling with Nizan and had given up hope of any income from their collaboration on the translation of Karl Jaspers' *Allgemeine Psychopathologie* (1913). To earn money he was giving philosophy lessons to a boy, Albert Morel, who was preparing for his *baccalauréat*. He had formerly been tutored by Guille, who had recommended Sartre. Even so, he could look forward only to the Easter holidays, he told Toulouse, during which he would "wander through the streets without spending money—to economize and to be able to visit you—allowing myself twice a week the luxury of a three franc seat in the cinema."[38] He was reading Montherlant and warming to the "gauntleted cavalier" idea of love represented by Alban in *Les Bestiaires*.

After passing the first examination, Sartre found he could do little but "sit stupefied at my desk." His friends were dispirited, aimless. "They go wandering into each other's houses, where they silently eat lumps of sugar and cannot go away. . . . They would like to talk about their character and say those phony things one says when one is in this state. Only my presence stops them, for I hate feebleness and tasteless, facile confessions."[39] He also hated wishy-washy melancholy and reflection about the process of reflecting. He liked Alain's dictum: "To think is to want."[40]

Looking at the alphabetical index he had filled with philosophical notes two years previously, he felt ashamed: "I was so drastic about everything." He was slowly coming to feel more of a specialist, concentrating, for instance, on solving "a problem of pure psychology, a problem of detail."

He was thinking about writing a novel: it would be for her, he said. And he had started reading Charles Andler's six-volume biography of Nietzsche,[41] which developed his ideas about willpower and gave him the basis for a realistic adventure story modeled on the Wagner-Cosima-Nietzsche triangle, with himself in the Nietzschean position and Simone as Cosima. The novel, which he never finished, was to be called "Une Défaite." In each phase of Nietzsche's romantically turbulent life he would write a book, and though he died unknown, glory came afterward. Unlike Nietzsche, Sartre did not feel unloved, and, luxuriating in André Maurois's *Ariel,* he tried to read Shelley's life as prefiguring the way his own genius would flower.[42] He was thinking of himself when he made the hero of his novel say "I'm a genius because I'm alive . . . Oh, I wish others could experience my life as I do, overflowing, tumultuous . . . If only I could express it, tear it out of myself. Then I'd be in reality the genius I'm entitled to be. Only one man is alive for me: myself . . . and I cannot believe I am going to die."[43] This has affinities with the Rimbaudian ecstasy in Brecht's first play, *Baal.*

After six months without seeing Toulouse, Sartre raised the money to visit her in the Easter holidays, only to receive a telegram: "NOT FREE. POINTLESS TO COME SUNDAY." No letter followed, which infuriated him. "When one is not free, one frees oneself, that's all." Did he not deserve better treatment than this? "Who has made you into what you are, who is trying to stop you from turning into a bourgeoise or an aesthete or a great gawk? Who else cares about your intellect?" He gave her an ultimatum: either she must see him in Toulouse on Tuesday, April 13, at any time she chose, or she would never hear from him again.[44]

She gave in. They went to see a Chaplin film and stayed together until five in the morning. He felt more involved than he had in September, but she talked disturbingly about dances in Toulouse, and he was not sure whether to trust her. What if she had been putting on an act? He sat on a park bench with the pipe he had taken to smoking, fell asleep with it in one hand and a box of matches in the other. He was awakened by the old park caretaker. "Mechanically I lit my pipe, thinking it would be pleasant to spend a moment talking to this old man in the state of sad calm sometimes seen in certain heroes of novels after a moving scene (Myshkin for instance chatting with Rogozhin after the murder of Nastasya Filipovna—due allowance being made)."[45]

Sitting afterward in the Café Regina, waiting for the first train to Paris, he hesitated about whether to declare his love in a letter. He might make a fool of himself, but perhaps there should be a scene in the novel after Wagner's death: Cosima could meet Nietzsche again and show him that "this brutal female defiance which he was taking for strength was only wildness and weakness."[46] Toward Toulouse, Sartre had been alternating between overconfidence and fear of ridicule. "I wanted to be not the first but *the only* man you loved."[47] He had spoken to her in the movies about his "sad inner self that plays the fool"; perhaps she would understand him better by thinking of what Chaplin wanted to express through the Charlie character.[48] "I love you with a simplicity worthy of the old park caretaker."[49] In the train he felt very happy: "I love a little girl who loves me, who is exactly the little girl I need, I'm determined to come back before July to see her, I trust her, the landscape under the sun is pleasing."[50] Later letters would be full of promises. "I want to give you a mental attitude which at the heart of the most mediocre life will ensure that your life is not a failure, that you will not be a Madame Bovary but an artist, without regrets and without sadness."[51]

When Sartre's aunt Hélène arrived in Paris she upset his mother by revealing what was going on; Toulouse's mother had been writing to her about it. But when Sartre visited Thiviers to stay with his uncle Joseph, his father's brother, Toulouse made the hundred-and-thirty-mile journey to meet him. He noticed, though, that "love is the thing to be had from you most easily of all . . . you are prodigal with little secondary loves."[52] She should find a woman friend; there must be a woman she could like without loving her.

Back in Paris, the spring weather encouraged Sartre to luxuriate in affectionate possessiveness. "You're mine, and things are mine, and my love influences the things around me, and the things around me influence my love."[53] But she irritated him with the logicality of her letters. "Remember," he admonished, "that logic is the meal ticket of impotent intellectuals. Try to get ideas in other ways—*without reasoning*."[54] The five or six great philosophers he was studying, he said, were in no way impeded by self-contradiction. She must not indulge in self-pity or sadness. "Sadness goes with softness."[55] It also went with daydreaming, which was dangerous.[56] She should copy Descartes, refusing to spend much time on "thoughts which occupy the imagination." Melancholy could always be driven out by willpower. She could saw wood—"metaphorically, of course"—alter her posture, stop play acting, work at her novel. "Always be cheerful. If you really suffer one day, tell me. I've learned how to console people because so many—without my understanding why—have confided in me."[57]

AT the beginning of 1926 Nizan had been close to joining the Communist party, but in the summer he was hesitating about whether to leave for Aden, where he had been offered a job as tutor to the son of a businessman. Half ironically he wrote to solicit advice from men of letters, including Georges Duhamel, only to quote their replies mockingly to his friends,[58] who could not judge whether the letters had influenced him. Later Sartre would explain Nizan's decision to leave France by quoting from his novel *Antoine Bloyé:* "He would have liked to give up this existence . . . to become someone else, new, strange, who would be really himself . . . lost, like a man who has left no forwarding address but is still active and alive."[59] In Marxism, according to Sartre, Nizan found a justification for his hatreds and a way of reconciling the conflicting attitudes of his parents.[60]

The gap in Sartre's life was filled by Guille and Maheu, who became his inseparable friends. Secretive and sarcastic, Pierre Guille came from a Protestant family with peasant roots.[61] He was the most unambitious of Sartre's friends and the most empirical. With no desire to write, no interest in formulating theories (though he found Sartre's entertaining), he reserved his enthusiasm for food, wine, and the pleasures of the moment. Maheu was fair-haired, with blue eyes and the fresh face of a boy from the country, but he dressed elegantly and spoke with an irony that seemed to affect even the tone of his voice and the twist of his smile. The three of them paid frequent visits to Mme. Morel in her flat at the far end of the Boulevard Raspail. Born in Argentina of French parents, she was attractive, petite, plump, elegant, and vivacious. Her husband was a rich hypochondriac doctor who seldom left his draft-proof room. He encouraged her friendship with Guille, who had accompanied them to Anjou as tutor to their son. According to Simone de Beauvoir, the friendship remained platonic;[62] according to Sartre's letters to Toulouse, Guille became enamored of Mme. Morel, who gradually revealed her sexuality.[63] Guille spent all his spare time at the flat, where he had his own room, and Sartre sometimes spent the night there.[64]

Nizan's absence made it easier for Sartre to believe in his own intellectual prowess. In 1927 he would have to present a thesis for his *diplome d'études supérieures*. By the end of 1926 he had begun to evolve what he described as "a complicated theory about the function of the image for the artist," and he was already thinking of evolving a complete system of aesthetics.[65] He had felt, when he first read Bergson, that "the truth had come down from heaven": now he needed to "bring down some other truths."[66] While *normaliens* were given a thorough grounding in Aristotelian and mathematical logic, their philosophy teachers tended to assume that physical and mental phenomena could both be analyzed in terms of a common underlying reality. From the beginning Sartre disliked idealism, which effectively detached reality from the world, situating it inside consciousness. One pluralistic book that contributed to student resistance against the official philosophy was Jean Wahl's *Vers le concret* (*Toward the Concrete*). The ideas of Alain also helped to lay out an alternative track, and even on the question of images, Alain was refreshingly heterodox. It was puerile, he maintained, to believe that we could keep "copies of things" in our memory and riffle through them at our convenience.[67] Images did not exist; there were only perceptions and false perceptions.

Certain that images did exist and that they could be equated neither with sensations nor with ideas, Sartre embarked on an ambitious reading program, which reinforced his conviction that he had hit on an area mapped out inadequately by previous investigators. In Dumas's two-volume *Nouveau traité de la psychologie* he found an article by L. Meyerson defining an image as a perception that is "reconsidered [*repensée*] and rationalized."[68] Binet, in his 1903 *Etude expérimentelle de l'intelligence*, abandoned the position he had adopted in 1896 (*Psychologie de raisonnement*), but three years before he died in 1911 he was still thinking of images as "material elements."[69] Though Bergson had insisted that no solid fragments could enter the flux of consciousness and that inner life presented itself as a constant flow, a "multiplicity of interpenetration," he consistently thought of the image as an opaque thing that had "imprinted" itself in the mind. Sartre, who had no difficulty in digesting all this reading, had no hesitation in rejecting it; he would be the one to draw the first accurate map.

By the end of 1926 he had finished the first chapter of his Nietzsche novel, which he was now intending to call "Empédocle": he promised Toulouse that it would be ready by April 1 of the following year. In the first chapter the Wagner figure "plunges the unhappy little fellow into the depths of Contingency and manages to stupefy him by singing him the famous Song."[70] This was a celebration of contingency in verse. Together with Nizan, Raymond Aron, and Daniel Lagache, Sartre had also been planning to write a screenplay based on Jules Renard's 1892 novel *Poil de Carotte,* which had been dramatized in 1900. The story is about a sensitive, dreamy boy. Growing up in the country, he suffers at the hands of his bullying mother and his neglectful father. Eventually he learns how to protect himself. Sartre could identify with both phases of the boy's experience. "What we must place at the center," he said, "is the need for tenderness."

The fiction, the philosophizing, the letters to Toulouse, and (no doubt) the conversations with friends were all strongly didactic. Sartre believed in himself as someone who could stiffen the willpower of everyone prepared to take his advice. He claimed to have weaned one of his friends away from homosexuality. "As the desire did not come from deep inside himself . . . he'd have been very unhappy and probably destroyed."[71] Encouraged by his salvationist success, Sartre wrote dogmatically to Toulouse about the importance of gaining as much power as possible; she must make herself independent of society for the sake of her "moral health." He was not asking her to give up emotional pleasures. "You need to be sentimental (and I too make use of my sentimentality) but for oneself, not other people."[72]

It was probably in December 1926 that she came to Paris for two weeks. At the ENS ball she made a considerable impact. Henriette Alphen, after marrying Nizan, was to remember the ball as mixing the grand style with informality that smacked of ill breeding. Some of the students had invited well-born girls whose well-dressed mothers waited for them in the ballroom. She remembers Sartre as being pimply and blonder than he was later. The lampshade on his desk in the study he shared with Nizan was a pink voile undergarment, slightly yellowed, presumably given to him by Toulouse.[73] It was customary in the ENS for students to sport unorthodox lampshades. Though Sartre had borrowed money to entertain her in style, Toulouse was unimpressed by the hotel he had booked and the restaurants he chose.[74] Wanting her to stay on in Paris, he tried to find a job for her at a stationer's, but she had set her sights higher.

It was in April 1927, over eighteen months after he had met her, that he began to use the second person singular in his letters to her. In Paris, Maheu had been trying to convince her that Sartre was too complicated ever to be capable of loving simply and straightforwardly, but Sartre had found this out. "I will say—and at length—just the opposite at Toulouse." He was planning to spend four days there at the beginning of May. "I know that I have a crazy desire to squeeze you in my arms, my dear little girl, and that I am more attached to you than to anyone else in the world."[75] It seemed to him that when he was with a beautiful girl, her beauty, extending over both of them, became the dominant element. "I certainly had an appetite for beauty which was not so much sensual as magical. I would have wanted to eat beauty and incorporate it in me."[76]

More fragile than he wanted to admit, the attachment to Toulouse caused him much anxiety, but in May 1927 he was distracted from it by the unheralded return of Nizan in the middle of the night. "He came in without knocking. He was pale, grim, rather breathless. He said: 'You don't look very cheerful.' I answered: 'Neither do you.' At which we went off drinking and pronouncing judgment on the world, delighted that our friendship had resumed."[77]

Sartre still felt less oppressed than Nizan by the educational system, and altogether less desperate. But, together with three of their friends, they collaborated on organizing the large-scale practical joke that would carry Sartre's protracted duel with Lanson to its triumphant conclusion. During the hullabaloo in May about Charles Lindbergh's solo flight across the Atlantic the five students telephoned the evening papers to say that the disciplinary council of the ENS had unanimously decided to acclaim the pilot by making him an honorary pupil. The papers carried the story, and on May 25 *Le Petit Parisien* announced: "Lindbergh will be at the ENS this morning at 9:30." When one of the students, who bore a slight resemblance to the pilot, drove up in a taxi, he was greeted with an ovation from a crowd of about five hundred people. As he was carried triumphantly on the shoulders of the hoaxers, the crowd followed, and one old man kissed his hands. Reporting the successful impersonation, the newspapers referred scathingly to Gustave Lanson, who promptly resigned.[78]

The joke put a mask of frivolity on a dissatisfaction that was serious. "The tragic sense of life"—the phrase Miguel de Unamuno had popularized in 1913—was recurrent in student conversation. It pointed to the unresolved conflicts and problems that were being evaded by the complacent intellectuals in power. There was no question for Sartre of following suit when Nizan joined the party; that such a close friend could be a revolutionary struck him as "totally grotesque." Not even calling himself a socialist, Sartre professed to be glad that the Establishment existed. "I could use it as a target for verbal bombs."[79] Before the end of the year he would be summoned in front of the disciplinary council for publishing in the school's magazine a scathing attack on the French army and on the obligation of *normaliens* to do "special preparatory military service." He helped to organize an ironical petition in which students expressed their desire to give evidence of their patriotism, their respect for work and for institutions. They wished to dissociate themselves from anarchic fellow students by wearing uniforms and submitting to a stricter discipline. Newspaper reports missed the irony.[80] Sartre was nearly always glad to join in practical jokes and frivolous conversations. After supper he would often drink in the Triboulet bar, where serious discussion was prohibited.[81]

The most effective way of protesting against the established philosophy was to evolve an alternative, but this took time. The students were advised to read Marx in order to refute him,"[82] but they had no access to the Hegelian dialectic. Lecturers such as Lachelier, author of *Psychologie et métaphysique,* and Léon Brunschvicg, author of *La Conscience occidentale,* were indifferent or hostile to the Hegelian tradition, and there is no mention of Hegel in the extensive bibliography Sartre compiled for his work "L'Image dans la vie psychologique: Rôle et nature," though it refers to Freud, Jaspers, Piaget, and Babinski. Working with Nizan on correcting proofs for the translation of Jaspers' *Die Psychopathologie,* Sartre had been struck by the rejection of scientific etiology in favor of a studied reliance on intuitive guesses to make connections between discontinuous groups of facts. What emerged for Sartre was the possibility of "apprehending" an individual character without reference to universal principles or to analytical psychology as taught at the Sorbonne.[83] When he presented his thesis, he was awarded the mark "très bien." This was the first serious philosophical essay that would find its way into his mature work. It would be printed (in a revised form) as the first part of *L'Imagination* (1936).

During the summer he went on a vacation to Usson-en-Forez, in the Massif Central, where he had been invited to stay with the friendly Alfred Péron, one of Alain's ex-pupils. Sartre's relationship with Toulouse had cooled, and when he met Péron's cousin, the daughter of a grocer, he became unofficially engaged to her.[84] But the following year, when he asked his mother and stepfather to approach her parents, he was rejected. Nizan meanwhile was having better luck in his relationship with Henriette Alphen. When they married on December 24, 1927, the witnesses were Sartre and Aron.

IT was in 1927–28 that Sartre wrote *Er l'Arménien,* a hastily composed fiction derived from the story Plato tells about Er, the son of Armenius, at the end of *The Republic.* Ten days after his death in battle Er's body is still fresh, and on the twelfth day, coming back to life, he tells how he has watched judgment being passed on the souls of the dead, the good ascending to heaven, the evil being sent down to hell. Sartre was now trying to reconstitute certain philosophical ideas: he even tried to describe Plato's cave.[85] The conception was literary, and the narrative method was inspired by the classics, which had been simmering in him since he was ten. The young hero and his sister ascend to the realm of the gods, taking their petty bourgeois experience with them—Sartre's own, disguised as Greek. This action also involved a large-scale battle with the Titans.[86]

SARTRE, Guille, and Maheu were spending a lot of time with Mme. Morel. Maheu was studying philosophy; Guille was studying literature. Sartre discussed Proust with Guille, but their conversation was based more on what they had been doing, and when Sartre showed him and Mme. Morel some of what he had written, she laughed at "Une Défaite" and called Sartre "miserable Frédéric."[87] Nizan submitted the novel to Gallimard, but it was rejected.

Preparing for the 1928 *agrégation,* the examination that is decisive in the recruitment of teachers, Sartre wanted to show more originality than he had in either his essay for Colonna d'Istria or in his *diplôme d'études supérieures.* During one of Brunschvicg's seminars, held under the title "Nietzsche—was he a philosopher?," Sartre tried to explain the ideas he had formulated in his notebook about contingency,[88] and it was on this subject that he wrote in his *agrégation* paper. Students were ranked in order of merit according to the papers they submitted, and Aron was put in the top place, Sartre in the fiftieth. To the astonishment of his fellow students he had failed.

Returning after the summer vacation to Paris and to the necessity of spending a fifth year at the ENS to compete once again in the *agrégation,* he took a room at the Cité Universitaire. He also asked Aron's advice on the technique of succeeding.[89]

* * *

SARTRE'S name is featured among those of eighty-three *normaliens* who in November 1928 signed a petition against military training, and when *Les Nouvelles Littéraires* sent out a questionnaire to university students, Sartre's replies were quoted at length in the issue dated February 2, 1929. Comparing students of his generation to their predecessors he claimed: "We are unhappier but more likable."[90] More provocative still were the hints of a pessimistically nonconformist philosophy: "At the root of humanity I see only sadness and boredom." He attacked "the determinism which oddly attempts to create a synthesis of existence and being. We are as free as you like, but helpless ... the will to power, action and life are only useless ideologies. ... Everything is too feeble; everything carries the seeds of its own death. Above all, adventure—by which I mean that blind faith in haphazard and yet inevitable concatenations of circumstances and events—is a delusion."[91] The point is the same as the one he had made about the difference between necessity in a fiction and contingency in the street, but he had now found a tone commanding enough to make his seniors listen. He could also formulate incisive slogans against conventional morality. "Science is the outer surface of a ball," he declared. "Morality is the hole inside."[92]

EARLY in 1929 he received a note from Toulouse suggesting they should meet again. The previous year she had become the mistress of the famous actor Charles Dullin, who was in his middle forties. He had set her up in a ground-floor flat on the Rue Gabrielle and had taken her on as a pupil at the drama school attached to his theater, the Atelier. Sartre found her more sophisticated, less provincial, and their relationship resumed. In *La Nausée,* Anny, who is modeled on Toulouse, is an actress being kept by an old man who is no trouble.

Toulouse behaved with a studied outrageousness. In one performance at the Atelier she came on stage drunk and pulled off the leading actor's wig. Convinced that she was inspired by the devil, she was sketching out a collection of demonic stories,[93] and Sartre witnessed her midnight attempts at conversations with Nietzsche, Albrecht Dürer, and Emily Brontë. She claimed to have sufficient affinity with them for death to be no barrier. Their portraits stared out at her from the wall, and two enormous dolls called Friedrich and Albrecht were propped up in little chairs and dressed as for school; she spoke to them as if they were children. When she took Sartre to the Théâtre de l'Atelier, Dullin, who was playing Volpone, signaled that he was aware of her presence in the auditorium.[94]

(4)

The Beaver

IF Sartre had not failed his *agrégation* in 1928, he might never have had the relationship that was more important than any other in his life. In the summer of 1929 the twenty-four-year-old student met a twenty-one-year-old girl who was beautiful, friendly, exceptionally clever, and no taller than he was. A philosophy student at the Sorbonne, she had come out second in the June exams of 1927, beaten only by Simone Weil. The daughter of a Paris lawyer, Simone de Beauvoir had attended Léon Brunschvicg's lectures on the history of scientific thought and had responded positively to his idealism. The first left-wing intellectual she had met was Pierre Nodier, a member of the *Philosophies* group;[1] the second to make friends with her was an ex-pupil of Alain's.[2]

For a long time before she met Sartre, Nizan, and Maheu she had known them by sight. The first time Sartre was pointed out to her at the Sorbonne, he was wearing a hat and talking to a girl student. De Beauvoir noticed that he was not to be seen in her company for long: she was replaced by a prettier one, but this relationship was equally brief. Mostly the three boys went around together. De Beauvoir found Nizan's eyes intimidating; Sartre was reputed to be a drinker. Maheu seemed more accessible, and she struck up an acquaintance by sitting down to eat lunch at his table in the restaurant of the Bibliothèque Nationale; they discussed Hume and Kant. Unlike Nizan and Sartre, he attended Brunschvicg's lectures, and after the Easter holidays, their friendship developed. They told each other they were individualists, lunched regularly together on the first floor of a *salon de thé*, and went for walks.[3] But one Sunday when she saw him in the Jardins du Luxembourg wandering around the lake with Sartre, Maheu pretended not to see her.[4]

Sartre had already made up his mind to meet her. Thirty-six years later he said: "I've always thought her beautiful, even though she was wearing a hideous little hat when I first met her. I was dead set on making her acquaintance."[5] He dedicated a drawing to her—"Leibniz Bathing with the Monads"—and sent it via Maheu, who told her that Sartre and he were both amused by her husky voice.[6] But when Sartre asked to meet her in the evening, she let Maheu persuade her into sending her sister instead.[7]

After having to write an examination paper, "Liberty and Contingency," they had to prepare for the same oral in July, and the four of them arranged to work together on Leibniz at the Cité Universitaire. "I felt a bit scared when I went into Sartre's room; books were all over the place, cigarette ends in all the corners and the air was thick with tobacco smoke. Sartre welcomed me like a man of the world; he was smoking a pipe. Silent, a cigarette stuck in the corner of his crooked smile, Nizan scrutinized me through his thick spectacles as if he were thinking about me carefully."[8]

She went back every day. "Sartre took it upon himself to explain Rousseau's *Le Contrat social* . . . he was always the one who knew most about all the writers and every aspect of our syllabus. . . . I noted: 'He's marvelous at training intellects.' "[9] They worked all morning; in the afternoon, when Henriette Nizan arrived, they drove around Paris in the Nizans' car or went to the amusement park at the Porte d'Orléans. Sartre and Maheu would sing lustily—often songs of their own composition. A motet, for instance, was based on the heading of a chapter of Descartes's *Méditations métaphysiques*. Sartre would sing "Ol' Man River" and the current jazz hits. He liked playing records of Sophie Tucker, Jack Hylton, and Negro spirituals.[10]

Nizan was living with Henriette and her parents in the Rue Vavin. He introduced Sartre, Maheu, and De Beauvoir to Irish literature and the new American novelists. "He was abreast of all the latest fashions in the arts and even ahead of them. He took us to the dreary Café de Flore 'to get our own back on the old Deux Magots,' he said, gnawing at his fingernails like a mischievous rat." He was writing a pamphlet against "the official philosophies," and a book, "Marxist Wisdom."[11] The three men had eased themselves further than she had out of the bourgeoisie: they mocked at soulfulness of any kind and at *la vie intérieure,* deflating anything pretentious or precious or idealistic.[12] At first Maheu tried to demand preferential treatment, taking her to the cinema without the other two and renting a room at a small hotel in the Rue Vaneau, where the two of them worked abortively at translating Aristotle's *Nicomachean Ethics*. Maheu explained that he was different from his friends: *"They* always have to find a reason for everything, especially Sartre . . . Except when he's asleep, Sartre *thinks* all the time."[13]

On the evening of July 14, after eating dinner in an Alsatian restaurant, Sartre, Maheu, and De Beauvoir watched the fireworks from the lawn of the Cité Universitaire. Afterward Sartre, who had a reputation for munificence, took them in a taxi to the Falstaff in the Rue Montparnasse, where they drank cocktails until two in the morning.

On the day of the examination results she met him at the door of the Sorbonne. "From now on," he said, "I'm going to take you under my wing." He had won first place; she had come in second. Nizan had passed; Maheu, who had failed, left the same evening for Bagnoles-de-l'Orne without saying goodbye. He sent Sartre an express letter, conveying his good wishes to "Castor"—her nickname, the one mark Maheu would leave on her. The French word for "beaver," it alludes to her industriousness. "Beavers like company," Maheu told her, "and they have a constructive bent." He reappeared a week later but stayed only for a day. Sartre did not conceal his pleasure at having the beaver to himself, while she soon began to feel time spent without him was time wasted.[14]

At the oral exams he excelled himself, speaking with fearless fluency and enrapturing the jury.[15] She went to the Sorbonne with him, they went out with the Nizans, had drinks at the Balzac with Raymond Aron, who was doing his military service in the Meteorological Corps, and with Politzer, who had joined the Communist party. At the second-hand bookstalls on the banks of the Seine, Sartre bought her copies of *Pardaillon* and *Fantômas;* in the evening he took her to cowboy films. They sat for hours over coffee in bars and over cocktails at the Falstaff.[16] He conversed like no one else. His alert mind was abnormally free from prejudice and preconception. When they talked about her he tried, like no one else, to see her in the perspective of her own values. With other people she normally felt superior both intellectually and by virtue of living more intensely; she was now with someone who had copied into a notebook Hippias' boast: "I have never met any man who was my equal."[17] She had thought her desire to write was exceptionally strong, but here was a man who "lived only in order to write."[18] A year earlier he had wanted to marry; his current need was for freedom unrestricted by profession, possessions, family, or social roots. He would travel all over the world collecting experiences to nourish his writing. Believing the work of art to be an end in itself, he spoke of his "opposition aesthetics." A book depended on having something to attack.[19]

He was still in quest of salvation, hoping to earn immortality through literary merit, but he disliked the religious vocabulary that survived from her Catholic girlhood, though she was now as materialistic as he was. He appeared to be less interested in fame than in propagating truths that had been revealed to him; when he showed her his note-books, she soon came to accept his theory of contingency, but she was expecting his commitment to Stendhal and the specific to make gener-alization difficult for him. She recognized the clumsiness of his myth-making in *Er l'Arménien,* but he had so much determination, vitality, good humor, and self-confidence that his work could hardly fail to im-prove. Her own ambition was to tell the whole truth in a novel; it was disconcerting to find that Sartre, Nizan, Aron, and Politzer had all evolved more specific ideas for future books.[20] But now she had a part-ner. "He was the double in whom I found all my burning aspiration brought to incandescence."[21] When the summer vacation separated them at the beginning of August, she was expecting to share her life with him.

Instead of waiting to see her again at the end of the vacation, he trav-eled to Limousin, where she and her parents were staying in a turreted château that belonged to her uncle and aunt. Her cousin Madeleine was three years her senior. Sartre stayed at a hotel in Saint-Germain-les-Belles, and, to be discreet, they met outside the town. Assuming he would not be content to sit on the grass and talk, De Beauvoir suggested they should bring books, but he refused to read or go for walks. He was allergic to chlorophyll, he said. They met every day. At lunchtime she would go back to the château; Madeleine would conspiratorially leave cheese or gingerbread for Sartre in an abandoned dovecote; in the eve-ning he would dine among traveling salesmen at his hotel.[22]

De Beauvoir told her parents he was there to collaborate with her on a critical study of Marxism; they were more likely to approve of an anti-Communist enterprise. But on Sartre's fourth day in Limousin her father came striding across the field toward them. "Sartre, who was wearing an aggressively red shirt, jumped to his feet, looking bellicose. My father asked him politely to leave the area: people were gossiping; besides, there were hopes that my cousin would be married, and scan-dalous behavior was damaging to her reputation."[23] Not intimidated, Sartre stayed on for another week, but they met in a chestnut grove some distance away. After he left, the lovers exchanged letters daily.[24]

She returned to Paris in September; he came back in the middle of October, staying with his grandparents in the Rue St. Jacques. Charles Schweitzer was now eighty-five. Sartre met De Beauvoir every morning in the Jardins du Luxembourg. "It was late at night before we sepa-rated. We walked the streets of Paris, still talking—about ourselves and our relationship, our future life, our still unwritten books."[25] They were intending to change the world, but their only weapon would be books; "public affairs bored us."[26] Their vague optimism was characteristic of the French left during the autumn of 1929. Misunderstanding the international economic crisis precipitated by the American depression, intellectuals were waiting for capitalism to disintegrate. The National Socialists in Germany were not to be taken seriously, while the imminent collapse of colonialism was signaled by the Communist agitation in French Indochina and by Gandhi's popularity in India.[27]

Shortage of money did not obstruct what Sartre and De Beauvoir called their "radical freedom."[28] They compared themselves with Kant's dove: instead of holding the bird back, the resistance of the air supported its flight.[29] She was teaching psychology at a girls' school in Neuilly and paying rent to her grandmother for what had formerly been a drawing room in the old woman's fifth-floor flat on the Rue Denfert-Rochereau. Sartre, who was awaiting call-up, was earning nothing. The stores were full of goods they could not afford, and, unlike the Nizans, they had no car; they went for walks along the Bercy *quais* and by the Saint-Martin canal. They ate bread and pâté in De Beauvoir's room, had dinner in the Brasserie Demory, drank at the Falstaff, the College Inn, the Vikings' Bar, where mead cocktails were to be had, and the Bec de Gaz, on the Rue du Montparnasse, where one of the specialties was apricot cocktails.[30] They felt superior to the *beau monde*, which lived parasitically on a despicable régime. When De Beauvoir passed Fouquet's or Maxim's she felt that the real outsiders were the rich, "cut off from the masses, imprisoned in their luxury and snobbery."[31]

In Sartre physical and intellectual energy interpenetrated. He produced an inexhaustible stream of ballads, rhymes, epigrams, madrigals, mini-fables. Often he would improvise tunes for the verses he made up. He punned shamelessly, playing with assonances and alliterations. Borrowing from Synge and James Stephens, he elaborated a private mythology around the figures of the playboy and the leprechaun who kept misery at bay by cobbling tiny shoes. In the private language that the couple evolved, "our tiny shoes" meant the books they had not yet written. Neither was immune to depression, but they cheered each other up with caricature and self-parody. Their relationship, they decided, was a morganatic marriage, and when they dressed up for an evening of dancing at La Coupole or for a movie on the Champs-Elysées, they would be Mr. and Mrs. Morgan Hattick, an American millionaire and his wife.[32] If Sartre was accused of being a petit bourgeois, he could retort that, according to Marx, the bourgeois intellectual was capable of rising above the beliefs of his class.

Freedom was Sartre's ideal, but his immediate future was mortgaged. After eighteen months of compulsory military service he would have to face the teaching career he dreaded. Hoping to escape from Europe, he applied for a job in Japan as lecturer in French, starting October 1931, when his military service would be over.

He and De Beauvoir, he insisted, should both feel free to have other lovers. Adapting his philosophical terminology to his sexual convenience, he proposed: "What we have is an essential love; but it's good if we both experience contingent love affairs too."[33] On the afternoon of October 10, after they had watched Pudovkin's new silent film *Storm over Asia* with the Nizans, Sartre suggested that De Beauvoir and he should "sign a two-year lease." After two years of living together in the closest possible intimacy, they should separate for two or three years before living together again. They would never become strangers, but the relationship must not dwindle into a habit. Though she did not relish the prospect of losing him for two or three years, she accepted his proposal, and they promised never to tell each other lies or conceal anything.[34]

Ever since the defection of his mother in 1917, Sartre's appetite for symbiotic intimacy had been insatiable. In his friendship with Nizan he had been plagued by jealousy and frustrated by quarrels, separations, ideological differences, and above all by Nizan's reluctance or inability to share emotional experience. The closeness with De Beauvoir would be free from all these hindrances. No partner could have done more toward making the nonstop internal monologue (which he loved too much and therefore detested) into a constantly resumed dialogue. At once creative and highly critical, each of them could provide a constructive daily commentary on the life and work of the other.

For each of them, naturally, there was some loss of freedom, but she felt on the whole more liberated. She stopped trying to inhibit tendencies in herself when she noticed the same tendencies in him; he would weep at the movies, for instance. There were tears on his cheeks when the lights went up at the end of Al Jolson's *The Singing Fool*.[35]

She introduced him to her Polish friend Stépha Advicovitch and her Spanish friend Fernando Gérassi, an impoverished painter descended from one of the Jewish families driven out of Spain by the Inquisition.[36] Bald, round-faced and intense, he would later appear in *Les Chemins de la liberté* as Gomez. Sartre got on well with him until he left Paris with Stépha to settle in Madrid. Maheu had taken a teaching job in Coutances and paid only brief visits to Paris. Aron, who was finishing his military service at Saint-Cyr, sometimes drove Sartre and De Beauvoir out to Versailles for dinner. He had joined the Socialist party, which they derided as having been infiltrated by the bourgeoisie, but most of

Aron's arguments with Sartre were philosophical. Sartre refused to differentiate between the object he was viewing and his view of it. "I could not enjoy a landscape or a sky except by assuming that it was absolutely the same as what I saw. . . . Perception, achieved ceremoniously and respectfully, became a sacred act of communication between two absolute substances, the object and my soul." Essences and universals had been postulated, he maintained, to fend off a reality that other people found frightening.[37] Aron used to go on arguing until his opponent was trapped between two alternatives. "One thing or the other, *mon petit camarade*," he used to say. "Choose."[38]

SARTRE shared Nizan's enthusiasm for the movies, and, using a Pathé-Baby camera, they made several home movies. In *Le Vautour de la Sierra* (*The Vulture of the Sierra*) Sartre was a shepherd who used an umbrella to fight against the vulture (Nizan), who also used an umbrella. De Beauvoir and Henriette were shepherdesses. In another movie, made on the terrace of the Alphens' house in Saint-Germain-en-Laye, the two girls were prostitutes. They pulled off Sartre's shirt to reveal that he was wearing a scapular. During a heart-to-heart talk Christ offered him a cigarette and, but for technical difficulties, would have taken the Sacred Heart from his bosom to use it as a lighter.[39] The scenarios were modeled on fashionable surrealist films.

According to De Beauvoir, Sartre was being influenced by Guille, who, cheerfully averse to theorizing, maintained that life and ideas always contradicted each other. Thanks to Guille, she says, Sartre learned "how to collect experiences with an observant concentration unspoiled by afterthought." Guille made him more alert to nuances. Both men loved to dissect other people's behavior: "they could spend hours analyzing a gesture or a tone of voice."[40] Sometimes De Beauvoir, Sartre, Mme. Morel, and Guille would drive out along the banks of the Marne or into the woods around Saint-Germain or Fosse-Repose. They would eat in restaurants, drink cocktails in Montparnasse, see the new films, listen to Jack Hylton's band.[41]

AFTER four years of reprieve Sartre started his eighteen months of military service in November 1929. Call-up ended a phase of freedom in his life, but at twenty-four he was older than most recruits. For at least eight years his commitment to writing had been crucial; the rest of his life could take care of itself. Life, anyway, was a game already lost before you started playing.[42] Besides, his main duty, as a writer destined to be great, was to preserve his freedom. This he explained carefully to any girl who gave signs of incipient fondness.[43]

In the army, together with Guille, he opted for meteorology, and they were both sent to Saint-Cyr, where Raymond Aron, now a sergeant, was their instructor: they flicked paper darts at him during class.[44]

IN January 1930 Sartre was transferred to Saint-Symphorien, near Tours, about a hundred and thirty miles to the southwest of Paris. For the first time in his life he found that each day was an exact repetition of the previous one. "Consciousness is attenuated and the body, like that of a swimmer who knows he is caught in seaweed and lets himself go, drifts unresistingly with the current." Unable to calm his nerves by going out for walks, he wrote to De Beauvoir trying to describe his state of mind in the first phrases that occurred. "This terrifying prospect of the empty days ahead of me has given me a sort of nervous excitement which is precisely boredom."[45]

When his grandmother Schweitzer died at the age of eighty-four, she left him eighty thousand old francs—enough to buy him more of such luxuries as attracted him. He enjoyed expensive restaurants and getting around in taxis, but physical comfort could be inimical to the exertion he demanded from himself, puritanically determined as he was to exploit his potential to the full. He never read in bed, seldom sat in an armchair; he read in a hard chair with a straight back.[46] Nor would he invest the money. He disliked checkbooks and bank accounts. Now, as later, he carried a large roll of banknotes about with him and spent from it freely. The eighty thousand francs lasted only two or three years.

Suddenly a widower at the age of eighty-five, Charles Schweitzer badly needed someone to look after him. Mme. Mancy, who went to see him every day, found a housekeeper to run the flat for him, and when his schoolteacher friend came back from Algeria, she spent most of her time with him. He was still potent but, according to the servant, did no sexual favors for the woman who regularly masturbated him.[47]

On Sundays, De Beauvoir would sometimes catch the first train from Paris to Tours, bringing a supply of books borrowed from Adrienne Monnier's well-known library in her bookshop, which was patronized by many of the best known writers. Sartre had an insatiable appetite for what he called "entertaining rubbish." After cycling to meet her at the station, he would take her to the big brasserie, where a female orchestra performed, or to a café, or they would walk in the park or by the Loire.

He found it easy to articulate his visual impressions, but they disagreed about whether his feelings were as strong as hers. With his dislike of contingency, he claimed to set more value on what he called "emotional abstractions" than on disorderly physical reactions—the excessive emotionality that paralyzes communication. The writer must preserve a degree of detachment, he argued; while she often felt that "words have to murder reality before they can imprison it."[48]

Sometimes he would come to spend Sunday in Paris. When they met on the platform of a railway station, whether at Tours or the Gare d'Austerlitz, his greeting would often be "I've got a new theory." Each of his theories was an act of appropriation. The exciting world of appearances was there to be colonized. "Looking at the trees and the water, I told myself ecstatically: 'There's so much to do.' "[49] While De Beauvoir would search for the "underlying sophistry," he was still convinced that phenomena coincided exactly with one's knowledge of them.[50] He gained a great deal from using her as he had previously used Aron to test out newly formed theories in conversation. He would then adjust them.

Though he disliked Freudian psychoanalysis as denying the mind's autonomy, he went on reading psychological books. From introductions to Gestalt psychology he accepted the premise that mental processes cannot be reduced into elementary units since, from the outset, wholeness and organization are factors. The individual, he believed, was a synthetic totality, and inferences could validly be drawn from studying handwriting and physiognomy. He stared earnestly into the faces of De Beauvoir, her sister Hélène (who was known as Poupette), and their friends, trying to analyze what he saw.[51]

Meteorology and soldiering left him with plenty of free time. At Saint-Cyr he wrote poems. In one of them, "L'Arbre" ("The Tree"), he used the proliferation of a tree's branches to symbolize purposeless contingency—an equation he would repeat in La Nausée. But when Guille was invited to read Sartre's verse, he laughed.[52]

Sartre started another novel, based on the story of a girl he had never met, a friend of De Beauvoir's, Zaza Mabille, a lively, sensitive girl who had fallen in love with a normalien, Maurice Merleau-Ponty, who had been scared off by her disapproving family. The tension somehow engendered an illness, which eventually killed her. Guille found it funny when the unhappy hero's glance traveled toward the sea, "stroking the sunlight against the grain."[53]

Sartre persevered harder with a philosophical work he started at Saint-Symphorien. La Légende de la vérité (The Legend of Truth), like Er l'Arménien, had to be a story, partly because he was imitating Nietzsche, pitching his style somewhere between *Also sprach Zarathustra* and *Zur Genealogie der Moral*. Nor would he allow himself to theorize. Even his distrust of generalizations must not be expressed in generalized terms: everything must be demonstrated. In the new work he tried to correlate variations in the cognitive process with structural differences between social groups. "Truth is a by-product of commerce," he declared, and commerce was dependent on democracy. Science was a by-product of the assumption that people were interchangeable. In any society the elite rejected this view, producing ideas that were to its own advantage, but the truth was more likely to be found by outsiders who trusted only the evidence of their senses. Sartre saw himself as the writer who could save society from itself simply by recording his own impressions. The three legends were the legends of certainty (science), the legend of the probable (the abstract philosophy of the aristocracy), and the legend of the solitary man. Once again Nizan acted as middleman, submitting the essay to Editions de l'Europe, but it was rejected.[54]

From Saint-Symphorien, Sartre was sent to the Villa Paulovnia in the neighborhood of Tours, with two other trained meteorologists—a man from Toulouse who stole and a seminarian with smelly feet.[55] They went out at intervals to check temperature and humidity with instruments kept in a hut.[56] In the summer De Beauvoir came to stay for a month at the small hotel in Saint-Radegonde, on the banks of the Loire, ten minutes from the Villa Paulovnia. She spent the mornings reading in the open air, and after lunch she would climb the hill to meet him near the meteorological station. "At intervals of two hours he would go off to take an observation, and I'd see him waving a sort of miniature Eiffel Tower in the air."[57]

IN February 1931 Sartre learned that he had not been selected for the job in Japan. Disappointment soured the relief of being released from the army at the end of the month. A certificate affirmed that he had "maintained good conduct throughout his period of service" and that "he always served honorably and steadfastly."[58] Annoyance about having to stay in France was mollified when he was invited to substitute for a teacher of philosophy at Le Havre during the final term of the university year. Le Havre is only about a hundred and ten miles from Paris, but the teaching job offered to De Beauvoir was at a lycée in Marseille—over five hundred miles from Paris and still farther from Le Havre. The prospect of separation frightened her so visibly that Sartre offered to marry her: this would qualify them for a joint appointment, and, in the long run, he said, marriage need not seriously affect their way of life. Besides, it was silly to sacrifice oneself to a principle. But she knew him well enough to see that he was already close to panic at the prospect of losing what he cherished most—his freedom. The army had entailed only a temporary loss of the student liberty that he would forfeit permanently when he became a provincial academic.[59]

At one stage, when she had intended to marry her cousin, she had pictured herself as a mother, but "a child would not have strengthened the bonds that united me with Sartre; I did not want Sartre's existence to be extended and prolonged into someone else's."[60] She also felt so alienated from her parents that the idea of parenthood had been devalued. In any event, childbearing seemed less vital to her than literature, which was "a way of justifying the world by refashioning it in the pure context of imagination." But they did revise their pact, agreeing not to have any prolonged separation until they were in their thirties. Though he never believed De Beauvoir (as he had sometimes believed Nizan) to be his intellectual superior, this disadvantage was compensated by the possibility of discussing everything. In argument and in crticizing his work she could be formidable—he called her his "little judge"—but (unlike Raymond Aron) she never wanted to inflict defeat on him. She was as unreservedly on his side as his mother had once been.

Sartre was extremely lucky. No one could have been a better replacement for the mother who had been like an elder sister; no other woman could have been more undemanding than De Beauvoir while being so emotionally dependent, so devoted without demanding devotion in return. Something had survived from the devout Catholic childhood that had made her think of becoming a nun, but so had something from the ensuing adolescent rebellion. At the age of nineteen she had written in her diary: "I want my life to obey no other will but my own." This was aiming too high. She had internalized too much of what had been taught to her about virtue, chastity, and obedience, but she carried something of her defiance into submissiveness to a substitute religion in which Sartre and socialism were the twin gods. She had been bred and groomed for a socially impressive marriage to a respectable Catholic; her nonmarriage to Sartre was exemplary in a different way. The propriety she retained did not impress her parents, but it was impressive. She led a disciplined, organized, productive life.

Sartre, who once said, "She has the intelligence of a man and the sensitivity of a woman," was later to launch her on writing *Le Deuxième Sexe.* There was no limit to the amount of help they could give each other. She made excellent use in this and other books of his ideas, his categories, his attitudes, while he benefited from seeing them in both her life and her writing. His tendency to live as if he were drafting an autobiography he could tear up and rewrite at any moment was partly encouraged, partly curbed by the knowledge that he had the leading male role in the serial installments of her widely read autobiography. Her appetite for new experiences was keener than his, but they both needed to validate their experience not only by writing about it but also by having the other react to it verbally and write about it.

If, in the long run, De Beauvoir gave Sartre more than he gave her, it was not so much because he got more pleasure out of his infidelities to her than she did out of hers to him or because she wrote about him (both fictionally and nonfictionally) more than he did about her but because she translated his theories into her life. Her faith in him was complete; it was natural for her to change her mind when he changed his and to emulate his style of living even when she was not sharing his life. She even acquired something of the same indifference to possessions. She did eventually buy a car, and though he sternly reprimanded her for doing so, he afterward found it useful when she was willing to drive him around.

They also helped each other to keep their youthful idealism alive. In spite of his need for other women, he did most of his traveling with her, and when they were both in Paris they saw each other almost every day. They never tired of each other's conversation, and they liked being separate but together while working—sometimes in the same room, sometimes in different rooms of the same flat—like schoolchildren doing homework. Generally she would play the role of the caring older sister, making sure that he was not importuned too much by other people, that he did not go to bed too late or drink too much or smoke too much. It was difficult for her to find the right balance between strictness and tolerance, and to many friends and casual acquaintances she seemed overprotective; but however difficult he made it for her, he wanted her to go on playing the role he had given her. He wanted her to look after him.

PART II

FRIENDLY TEACHER

(1931–39)

⟨5⟩

Provincial Schoolmaster

WHEN Sartre installed himself in Le Havre for the spring term of 1931, staying at the Hôtel Printania, it felt as though he had moved into a grayer climate, shut off from the sun of promise that had illuminated childhood, boyhood, and youth. From confidential chats with his doting grandfather to candid conversations with De Beauvoir, from the writing of precocious adventure stories to confident student speculations about imagery, everything had helped him to believe in his future greatness. Fortified by the game he had played with Nizan, the idea of being a superman had never quite died away: everything he did was part of a rehearsal for the golden future. In Le Havre, though, he found that he was a provincial schoolteacher with no option but to let himself be integrated into a disciplinarian system he detested. He had arrived at a phase of life he had dreaded. Though allowing him to feel free, the Ecole Normale had insidiously destined him for confinement in a provincial intestine of the organism he had hoped to escape by living in Japan.

Social life in Le Havre was strongly colored by hierarchical snobbery. Controlling the cotton and coffee trade, the Protestant bourgeoisie dominated; it was known as "la côte" because of the villas it had built in more elevated positions. At the lycée the headmaster welcomed parents with a warmth proportionate to their social standing, while teachers who had not passed the *agrégation* were humiliatingly excluded from the board of examiners for the *baccalauréat* and from the annual outing to Caen. Sartre's position as a teacher at once distanced him from his own boyhood and put barriers between him and the schoolboys. But, hating hierarchy and instantly disliking his colleagues,[1] he did his best to demolish the barriers. "You saw this little fellow arriving, his hands in his pockets, no hat, which was unusual, smoking a pipe, which was very strange, then he immediately started talking without notes, sitting on his desk. We'd never seen that." He was liable to appear in his class-room "wearing a sports jacket, a black shirt and no tie; we understood straight away that this wasn't a teacher like the others."[2]

Psychology featured prominently in Sartre's philosophy lessons, and he chatted to the boys without the pomposity and condescension they had come to expect from teachers. When he was teaching philosophy he would often interrupt himself to question them on their own ideas. He was "vigorous, stimulating, amusing and serious at the same time." Intellectually he dominated them irresistibly, leaving an indelible mark. "He was generous in his marking, but kept his notebooks in a great muddle and wrote down marks at random."[3] He was "extraordinarily kind, simple, astonishingly amusing. He took many things seriously, but never his position as a master, or ours as pupils. . . . We had a rela-tionship with him such as we'd never had with an adult . . . a relation-ship without any of the usual barriers." He drank with them at local bars and cafés, played cards and Ping-Pong with them, joined in picnics on the beach, performed songs from operettas.[4] This unconventional behavior provoked disapproval from colleagues and complaints from parents, but he cheerfully ignored the headmaster's reprimands, and not only was his nonconformity tolerated, his temporary job became permanent. He gave free extra lessons to pupils who needed them, and at the municipal library he persuaded the librarian to be less strict about refusing the boys access to certain books.[5]

In the classroom Sartre would relax, sitting on a table and chatting with equal informality about philosophy and his own habits. He could make the bowl of his pipe shiny, he told them, by rubbing it against the side of his nose, where sweat collected. But some boys felt excluded from the clique he collected around himself. The boys he liked best were the most spirited and spontaneous; some of these would even get treated to meals in local restaurants.[6] He was already beginning to do what he would go on doing throughout his life—surround himself with what was almost a family of young friends who could enjoy a degree of inti-macy without ever being quite on an equal footing.

Among the teachers Sartre's three closest friends were Alphonse Bon-nafé, who taught Latin, French, and Greek, the gym teacher, Rasquin, and the English teacher, Isoré. Bonnafé was a good-looking man who boxed and told amusing stories. Once he and his girl went on a walking tour with Sartre and De Beauvoir. Bonnafé then suggested that they should give boxing lessons at a gymnasium in the town. He and Sartre persuaded about eight of the boys to come along, and when Sartre stripped to the waist and boxed with them, his smallness, which had handicapped him as a schoolboy, was advantageous in putting him on the same level as his pupils. But without glasses he found it hard to defend himself. Mostly the boys took care not to hurt him, but it was tempting for those who were jealous of his favorites to get their own back by delivering a hard blow to the head. When one boy, Albert Palle, did this, Sartre took it in good part, exaggerating his pain in a pantomime of distress.[7]

He loved boxing for the same reason that he had loved schoolboy fighting: it involved the whole body. He also fantasized about being able to fight any man and beat him.[8] At the gymnasium he worked out with a skipping rope and listened intently when Bonnafé gave him tips. Boxing helped him to know the boys better. Like Bonnafé, Rasquin was a good-looking man who told stories about sex and fighting. Though Bonnafé and Sartre made fun of him, Isoré was Sartre's usual companion for lunch at the restaurant that is featured in La Nausée.[9]

With only about sixteen hours of teaching to do each week and needing only about the same amount of time to prepare for it, he had plenty of free time. He spent most of it on trains between Paris and Le Havre, where he cultivated the taste for detective fiction that derived from his boyhood pleasure in adventure stories. He was interested both in the technique of structuring and in the way that dialogue could be charged with tension when loaded with clues to the mystery.[10]

WHEN he finished La Légende de la vérité, Nizan submitted it for him to the publisher Rieder, while an extract appeared in the June issue of the periodical Bifur. In the notes on contributors Nizan described Sartre as a young philosopher "at work on a volume of destructive philosophy."[11] During July, making a speech at a prize-giving ceremony, Sartre scandalized the conservative parents and teachers by championing cinema as an art, but his private interest was still in distinguishing between the sequentiality of films and the discontinuity of experiences in everyday life.[12]

He and De Beauvoir were planning to go on vacation together in Brittany during the summer, and in June they were briefly reunited with Stépha and Fernando Gérassi, who arrived in high spirits; Stépha was pregnant, and a provisional republican government had been formed after King Alfonso had fled from Spain in April. Fernando suggested that De Beauvoir and Sartre should spend their six-week vacation in Spain instead of Brittany. In Madrid they could stay with him, while the favorable exchange rate would make it cheap for them to travel inside Spain. Neither of them had ever been outside France, and after crossing the frontier, they spent their first evening wandering around Figueras, where they saw their first *guardia civil* and kept repeating: "We're in Spain."[13] Fernando had advised them to buy two first-class *quilometricos*—round-trip tickets valid for any route—and they went on to Barcelona. Instead of merely visiting monuments and museums, they tried to discover the secret of each city by noticing the smells, observing the light, tasting the local dishes, exploring the poorest districts. They spent their evenings in the Barrio Chino, where women signaled availability by dancing and singing on platforms in the open air.

Sartre enjoyed walking less than De Beauvoir did, and he was less voracious for new experiences; he would have been content to sit down after lunch, quietly smoking his pipe. Pipe smoking tended to make him want to settle wherever he was, watching passersby and talking through clouds of smoke. But when they visited the cathedral at Burgos, he was so attentive that he felt he had never previously looked hard enough at anything.[14]

In October, when *La Légende de la vérité* was rejected by Rieder, Sartre decided against offering it to other publishers. The teaching job left him with enough time to make a serious start on his literary work, and, obligingly, the experience that would be crucial to *La Nausée* occurred soon after the beginning of term. On October 7 he wrote to De Beauvoir about going to look at a tree:

> To do this, you need only push open the gate of a fine square off the Avenue Foch, then choose your victim and a seat. Next comes contemplation. Not far away from me, the young wife of a naval officer was explaining the hardships of a seafaring career to an aged grandmother, who was nodding her head as if to say: "That's life." . . . And I looked at the tree. It was beautiful, and I have no hesitation in setting down two facts vital to my biography: it was at Burgos that I understood what a cathedral is, and at Le Havre what a tree is. Unfortunately I'm not sure what kind of tree it was. You'll be able to tell me. You know those toys that turn around in the wind or when they're waved about. There were little green stems everywhere which played the same trick with six or seven leaves they had on top of them. A sketch is enclosed. I await your reply. After twenty minutes, having exhausted the arsenal of comparisons destined, as Mrs. Woolf would say, to turn this tree into something different from what it is, I left with a clear conscience.[15]

It was no accident that he had chosen a tree for observation. Later on, in *Les Mots*, he recalled his grandfather's advice: "It isn't enough to have eyes. You must learn to use them. Do you know what Flaubert did when Maupassant was a child? Sat him down in front of a tree and gave him two hours to describe it."[16] For the most famous sequence in his fiction Sartre would be indebted both to the grandfather he caricatured and to his archenemy, Flaubert.

He was intending to use the tree as a symbol of contingency in "Factum sur la contingence," which he had just started. (A *factum* is a text with a polemical purpose.) He wanted to illustrate his argument by describing the district where he lived. "Naturally everything was contingent there, even the sky, which, according to meteorological probability, should be the same above the whole town of Le Havre, but it isn't."[17] When he transformed the *factum* into the novel, which was first to be called "Melancholia" (after the Dürer engraving) and was later called *La Nausée,* the Hôtel Printania would be mentioned by name, and the view from the window of Antoine Roquentin's room seems to be identical with the view from Sartre's, though the author's mood blurs into the narrator's and into that of people on the railway platform. "This evening I'm quite relaxed, installed in the bourgeois world. My room faces northeast. Below, the Rue des Mutilés and the new railway yard. From my window I see at the corner of the Boulevard Victor-Noir the red and white flame of the Rendezvous des Cheminots. The Paris train has just arrived . . . A lot of people are waiting for the last train. They make a sad little group around the lamppost just under my window."[18]

De Beauvoir's advice was crucial in making him fictionalize the *factum;* there is no knowing what balance he would otherwise have achieved in it between generalization and specific detail, though some evidence is provided by an exercise book that probably dates from 1932. Bound in imitation leather, it had originally been used in the classroom. On the opening pages are names of pupils, marks, and essay subjects. The thirty-five pages of notes for the *factum* show he was still preoccupied with the relationship between fictional events and everyday experience. You never feel you're having an adventure; you never know which events will be causally connected to others. The feeling of adventure comes retrospectively.[19] His concern with duration was partly Bergsonian, while he was thinking of his own ugliness in relation to contingency: his features gave the appearance of having been "thrown together at random."[20] Other people's features combined harmoniously, but whenever he looked in a mirror he saw the squinting eye first and then features that "didn't combine to form a definite human face."[21] In *La Nausée* Roquentin will reflect: "I understand nothing about this face. Other faces have a meaning. Not mine."[22] Nothing is more familiar than your own face in the mirror, but scrutinize it at length and it becomes unfamiliar in a way that affects everything else; the price we pay for existential freedom is anguished realization of the world's total strangeness. As Alain Robbe-Grillet has said, some novels confirm the familiarity of the world, others assert its strangeness; *La Nausée* is extraordinary in capturing the transition from one mode of observing to the other.[23] Everything Roquentin sees in the drab provincial town, Bouville, is both nauseatingly unexceptional and vertiginously inexplicable.

Not that reassurance is to be found in memories of other places, and to discredit complacent bourgeois claims to knowledge based on experience Sartre will make the much-traveled Roquentin question whether the traveler knows any more about humanity than the philosopher who has never left his study.[24] The novel will demonstrate that middle-class professional males—bankers, lawyers, priests, doctors—have no right to make the claims they base on experience. "In fact experience = resignation. . . . No unconscious, no experience. Man is what he is in the present tense, and he's alone there."[25] Nor do historical events lead directly to particular results: the death of a soldier is caused by a set of circumstances, not by the supremacy of Napoleon.[26] Though he could not capitalize yet on these assumptions either in his fiction or in his philosophy, Sartre was beginning to consolidate a strategically advantageous position.

One reason he was attracted to biography was that he could look back from another man's life to steal an overview of his own. He would often forget what he claimed to have learned in the early thirties and formulated in 1939: "that one cannot put life into perspective while living it—it steals up on you from behind and you find yourself inside it." Nevertheless, in 1931 the half-submerged preoccupation with himself and autobiography was helping him to write a good novel.

He was also planning to question "the metaphysical reality of boredom . . . What is boredom? It is where there is simultaneously *too much* and *not enough*."[27] His notes on contingency differentiate between being and existing. "What is does not exist. For example an idea."[28] Most of his reflections at this time revolve around his concept of contingency. If nothing is necessary, it would be possible for everything to be different. "Nature is in the position of a person who would like to express himself through ideas but has only objects at his disposal." To this extent he could feel superior to whatever had generated the chestnut tree.

In persuading Sartre to write the book in narrative form, De Beauvoir suggested that it should be charged with the same kind of suspense they both enjoyed in detective fiction.[29] This was how the idea evolved of writing a kind of whodunit in which contingency would turn out to be the villain.

She went to Paris at every opportunity, sometimes creating extra opportunities by feigning illness, and she spent Christmas there. She had moved out of her grandmother's flat to settle into a cheap hotel on the Rue Gay-Lussac.[30] Each time they met he would show her what he had written. The exercise book contains notes for a diary to be kept by Roquentin, with a summary of entries for every day from February 3 to 14. Some of the notes are for incidents (for example: "walk in the park"), some for reflections ("contingency in me: in my limbs when I walk—incapacity for seeing myself whole").[31]

Since learning how to look at a cathedral or at a tree and how to avoid being misled by the arsenal of comparisons, Sartre had begun to observe people differently. Roquentin decides at the outset: "I must say how I see this table, the street, people, my packet of tobacco, because it's that which has changed."[32] Not that the change in Roquentin tallied with the change in Sartre, who was suffering much less severely from what he calls nausea, and it was easier to catch his alter ego in the act of looking than it was to catch himself. Though Sartre could imagine that he was watching Roquentin's eyes, he could not, writing in the first person, incorporate his observation of the character's observation—he had to dramatize it. But he could draw dramatic dividends from his inveterate insistence that an object was identical with his perception of it. Underlying some of the narrative is the preoccupation found in Sartre's work on the image: what is the relationship between the table or the street and the mental pictures we form of them? Sartre's habits of observing were altered by the activity of writing the novel: wandering through the provincial streets he would empathize with his character, asking himself how Roquentin would see a pair of suspenders or a seat in a tram.[33]

Sartre was lucky to have been given his first job in a provincial town; it was easier here than in Paris to regard himself as a solitary individual with no possessions, no roots in bourgeois society, and nothing to prevent him from discrediting its ideology. He seldom came in contact with the townspeople except casually in cafés or when he gave one of the lectures financed by the municipality and the library. He discoursed on James Joyce and other modern writers unfamiliar to the townsfolk.[34] The categories of their thinking, he concluded, prevented—or protected—them from coming into close contact with reality. What the bourgeoisie could not do for itself he would do for it—or against it. At the same time he was writing both for and against himself.

He was still a nonentity, and he needed to console himself by proving that everyone else was. No one escapes from muddy mediocrity into glamorous adventures.

SARTRE'S visits to Paris were frequent enough for him to keep in touch with many of his friends. Apart from De Beauvoir and her sister, Hélène, a painter, he saw Nizan, who was teaching at Bourg, forty miles from Lyon, and jeopardizing his career with publicity attracted by subversive political activities. Guille, who was teaching at Rheims, spent as much time in Paris as Sartre did, while Toulouse, who was now calling herself Simone Jollivet, had strengthened her position in Dullin's company. Staging a play she had written, *L'Ombre* (*The Shade*), Dullin let her star in it, but it was received with booing and hissing. When Sartre went to her flat in Rue Gabrielle a couple of days afterward, the doorbell had been disconnected. A few days later, when he was allowed in, she was swearing vengeance on the public.[35]

For the Easter vacation Sartre went with De Beauvoir to Brittany. Coaxed into a series of sight-seeing expeditions, he reacted to Chateaubriand's pretentious tomb by urinating on it.[36] Though the weather was rainy, he agreed to a twenty-five-mile walk around the hill of Saint-Michel d'Arré, which they climbed.[37]

Though he was coming, generally, to sympathize more with the Communists, he did not vote in the election of May 1932. The majority favored the Cartel des Gauches, which had been created in 1924 by Edouard Herriot, grouping together radicals and Socialists from the Section Française de l'International Ouvrière (SFIO). The Cartel favored rapprochement with Germany, though the Nazis were rapidly growing stronger, and as prime minister, Herriot was inept in his handling of both industry and agriculture. France had weathered the world economic crisis better than most countries, but unemployment was to reach 1,300,000 by 1933.

In June, when Sartre had ten free days, he spent them in Marseille with De Beauvoir, who took him happily to the restaurants around the old harbor and the cafés along the Cannebière. When the news arrived that she had been appointed to a job in Rouen, they were delighted at the prospect of working only forty-two miles apart. Knowing of their relationship, M. Parodi, the inspector general, had placed her considerately.[38]

Meanwhile Sartre spent a week with his mother and stepfather. Having been invited by Guille and Mme. Morel to go on an automobile trip through the south of Spain in August, De Beauvoir and Sartre met in Narbonne to make a preliminary trip to the Balearics, going on to Spanish Morocco. On their first morning in Seville they saw the mayor under military arrest in a black car. The streets were full of soldiers, and rifles were stacked on the pavements. A coup d'état was being attempted by General José Sanjurjo, the man who would be succeeded by Franco four years later as leader of the military junta. A crowd was surging through the streets, singing and bawling; firemen were being deliberately slow to put out fires started in exclusive clubs.[39] But Sanjurjo failed to rally enough support, and the republic was safe for nearly four more years.

In Cádiz, Sartre antagonized Guille by refusing to "waste time" on paintings by Murillo in the churches. The two couples had to separate. In Ronda, Sartre found nothing he wanted to see: "They're all aristocrats' houses."[40] But his radicalism was vulnerable: Guille could expose anomalies between the outlook Sartre had borrowed from another class and the bourgeois comforts he was patently enjoying. In Tarifa a boy of about twelve came up to the table where they were eating their fish dinner: "You're lucky. You can travel. I'll never get away from this place."[41]

Returning to France, Sartre and De Beauvoir asked to be dropped at Toulouse, where the other Simone showed them around. She was writing a novel about her adolescent sexual experiences, and she worked on the book every night, she said, from twelve to six.[42]

During the autumn term, having no teaching to do on Thursdays, Sartre would often spend the day in Rouen with De Beauvoir. Sometimes she would visit him in Le Havre, and, as before, they went to Paris every week, staying at the Hôtel de Blois. Toulouse introduced them to Dullin, who let them sit in on several rehearsals of *Richard III*. Nizan had spoken to De Beauvoir about another teacher at the school, Colette Audry, a friendly short-haired Trotskyist who knew Simone Weil and took Sartre and De Beauvoir to a film studio where her sister Jacqueline was working as a script girl.[43]

One Tuesday, in Rouen, Sartre had an attack of nephritis. He was in such pain and vomited so much that he had to see a doctor. But his resistance to pain was abnormal, or (as he preferred to have it put) his philosophical ideas were integral to his relationship with his body, and the doctor was astonished when he insisted that he had not been suffering. In *La Nausée* he gives Anny the same ability to block out awareness of pain. If pain is isolated, he maintained, it is only pain: it can be stopped from taking charge of the body.[44] The idea of self-control ap-

pealed to him so strongly that he tried increasingly to program his
mental and physical condition by using stimulants and sedatives; the
result was that he became less self-controlled.

He avidly read newspaper reports of crimes and trials, partly because
they brought bourgeois morality into question. He sympathized with
the Papin sisters, two maids who murdered their mistress (and inspired
Genet's play *Les Bonnes*). Crimes, said Sartre, were caused by the social
system and avenged by a primitively vindictive judicial system.[45] Fortu-
nately the end of capitalism was imminent: crowds of starving men had
marched on Washington, and bankrupt businessmen and financiers
were committing suicide.[46] Sartre thought of joining the Communist
party—once, for instance, after a dock worker, dressed in his blue overalls, was ejected from the Café Victor in Rouen after sitting down on
the terrace at a nearby table. Was it enough to go on supporting the
proletariat from the sidelines?[47] Though Sartre had read Marx's *Das
Kapital* and Marx and Engels' *Die deutsche Ideologie* while a student, he
had no contact with the workers—"an enormous, somber group which
lived Marxism"[48]—and it happened only gradually, over the next thirteen years, that Marxism "put all our acquired culture out of shape."[49]
The next conversion Sartre was to undergo had nothing to do with the
oppressed majority.

(6)

A German Credo

BUT for Raymond Aron, Sartre's life might have been quite different. If he had not applied to join the Meteorological Corps, his wartime experiences would not have been what they were, and his early fiction would not have been what it was if Aron had not introduced him to phenomenology. Since September 1932 Aron had been in Berlin, working at the French Institute there, simultaneously studying Edmund Husserl and writing a thesis. Sartre had not attended the lectures Husserl had given at the Sorbonne in February 1929, but he had subsequently felt attracted to phenomenology, and the turning point had come during an evening spent with Aron at the Bec de Gaz in the Rue Montparnasse.

The two men and De Beauvoir were drinking (apricot cocktails, according to De Beauvoir, and beer, according to Aron) when Aron said: "You see, *mon petit camarade,* if you're a phenomenologist, you can talk about this drink and that's philosophy." Sartre could not hide his excitement.[1] To succeed with the novel he was making out of his *factum* he needed a means of blending philosophical reflection with the direct transcription, factual or fictional, of personal experience. Phenomenology, said Aron, bypassed the familiar opposition between realism and idealism, affirming both the supremacy of reason and the reality of the visible world.[2] After buying Emmanuel Lévinas' *La Théorie de l'intuition dans la phénoménologie de Husserl* Sartre leafed hungrily through the uncut pages. He was soon certain that he needed to study phenomenology, and the helpful Aron, who had led him into meteorology, now arranged for him to study at the French Institute in Berlin for the year starting in September.[3]

So far, in his work on the novel, he had been open to influence from a variety of writers including Breton, Michaux, Silone, Moravia, Hemingway, Dos Passos, and Céline. De Beauvoir and he both knew passages of *Voyage au bout de la nuit* (*Journey to the End of the Night*) by heart. Céline had evolved a style of writing no less vivid than speech, and Sartre, says De Beauvoir, "finally gave up the stiff language he had been using in *La Légende de la vérité.*"[4] The influence of Dos Passos and Hemingway was still more important. A French translation of *The 42nd Parallel* had just been published, and Sartre would soon regard Dos Passos as "the greatest writer of our time."[5] Here at last was narrative that did not deny contingency: "Each event is a gleaming and solitary thing, which does not issue out of another—it looms up suddenly, adding itself to other things—something irreducible." Narrative, for Dos Passos, is adding up.[6] Proust, centering on subjectivity while relating both feelings and actions to past events, implied a causality; Dos Passos, adapting the techniques of American journalism, rejected *la vie intérieure*, crystallizing life into its social components, showing feelings as actions and actions as facts.[7] Dos Passos immediately made inroads into Sartre's conversations. With De Beauvoir he would try to reconstruct incidents as Dos Passos might have described them—the ejection of the dock worker from the Café Victor, for instance.[8]

Hemingway had an inimitable knack of making insignificant-seeming details significant without relying on subjectivism. Objects in his narratives were conspicuously solid, though he offered no more than would have been apparent to the character he was presenting. "Many of the rules we observed in our novels," says De Beauvoir, "were inspired by Hemingway."[9] American culture also filtered into their lives through jazz and Hollywood films. They missed few of the new films starring Greta Garbo, Marlene Dietrich, Joan Crawford, or Sylvia Sidney. The script might be poor, but the faces were beautiful.[10] They saw many of Walt Disney's *Silly Symphonies,* and Sartre did imitations of Donald Duck.[11]

They used their Easter vacation to discover London, where they were dismayed by the dreariness of the tearooms, so unlike continental cafés, but they explored the city and its suburbs, walking for hours through the streets until rain forced them indoors. They were amused by the bowler hats, umbrellas, and unsophisticated window dressing, while they liked the docks, the boats, the grimy storefronts in the Strand. They visited the National Gallery and the Tate, but Sartre had no desire to see the sights. Buildings, parks, paintings, tapestries had all been meticulously described, he argued, by writers of a previous generation, and, in the process, democratized. They could feel entitled to spend their time on slums. On their next trip to England, he said, he would visit Manchester, Birmingham, and other industrial cities.

In the evenings they went to the movies. Kay Francis' 1932 film *Cyn-*

ara gave them Ernest Dowson's line "I have been faithful to thee, Cynara! in my fashion," which Sartre was to go on using for years as a sweetener in conversations about infidelity.[12] In Canterbury he was as delighted as De Beauvoir with the cathedral, but in Oxford he balked at the arrogance of the undergraduates and refused to go inside the colleges with her.

Often she would resist his endless theorizing. She accepted the connection he made between English cooking and Locke's empiricism—both were founded on the analytical principles of juxtaposition. But when he generalized about London after a mere twelve days there, she insisted that reality defied verbal analysis, only to be told that if you wanted to impose your personal pattern on the world, it was not enough to observe and react.[13]

In March 1933 Henri Barbusse wrote in *Le Monde* that Hitler would not be able to save the German economy from the collapse that would lead the proletariat to recover its heritage. He was expressing the same naïve complacency that was endemic in the German Communist party. In France too the political impotence of left-wingers predisposed them to underestimate the danger. When the Association of Revolutionary Writers, which was formed in July, launched its magazine *Commune*, Nizan was coeditor with Aragon, but in his *Propos*, Alain feebly argued that it was better not to think about the possibility of war: to believe in it was to give one's tacit consent.[14] Sartre, who read the newspapers assiduously, reprimanded De Beauvoir for not taking enough interest in what was going on.[15]

In the classroom, though, he was more willing to discuss his theory of individual freedom than his ambivalence toward communism. He celebrated the end of the term by getting drunk with his pupils, finishing up with them in a local brothel. It was his first experience of brothels, but he was too drunk to remember what happened. When he talked about it afterward he would claim to have gone "upstairs on the back of a sturdy whore."[16]

The summer vacation gave him another chance to go abroad with De Beauvoir, and in 1933 they had no compunction about taking advantage of a bargain offered by Mussolini. Thanks to the Fascist Exhibition, foreign tourists could travel on the Italian railways at a 70 percent reduction. Sartre and De Beauvoir spent a fortnight in Florence and four days in Rome. But fascism had the country in its grip. Blackshirted party members had priority on the pavements; on the walls posters endlessly reiterated Fascist slogans. At night the streets were deserted. One night, when Sartre and De Beauvoir wanted to stay up till dawn, they were sitting by the fountain on the deserted Piazza Navona when, at about midnight, two Blackshirts ordered them back to their hotel. Disobediently they wandered through dark, empty streets for about three hours until they were stopped by a patrol in the Colosseum.[17]

But in Berlin, despite the uniforms, the Nazi posters, the abundant evidence of a militarist régime, the occasional glimpse of a Communist hiding from the Nazis, Sartre could personally enjoy more freedom than he'd had since starting military service four years earlier. At twenty-eight he could "rediscover the irresponsibility of youth":[18] it was like being a student again. Between his bouts of work—in the morning on Husserl, from about five-thirty in the evening on his novel—he would stroll through the streets, observing the behavior of uniformed thugs and intimidated Jews, but, unlike Christopher Isherwood, he did not feel this was what he ought to be writing about. Everyday observations need not be accorded priority, though he was responding positively to Husserl's insistence that the philosopher, discarding all preconceptions, must concentrate on phenomenological description.

At the Ecole Normale the philosophical teaching had been mainly concerned with theories of knowledge, and Sartre had been conditioned to accept "the illusion which is common to realism and idealism, according to which knowing is eating." This "alimentary philosophy" made the mind into a spider that "drew things into its web, covered them with white spittle and slowly assimilated them, reducing them to its own substance."[19] Husserl refreshingly insisted that objects could not be dissolved in consciousness and that consciousness was constituted by its refusal to be substance.[20] It was not self-enclosed, and if it tried to coincide with itself, it would only negate itself. Consciousness always needs to be conscious of something else—this is what Husserl meant by intentionality.[21] Phenomenology was a method of disregarding distractingly generalized hypotheses in order to concentrate on phenomena as experienced. Husserl's motto was: "To the things themselves." He had taken a good deal—including the term "intentionality"—from an Austrian philosopher who had exerted a beneficent influence on other novelists, including Kafka and Musil. Franz Brentano maintained that the philosophical task was purely descriptive. Sartre, with his admiration for Hemingway's straightforward accounting of physical action, was well disposed toward this attitude, which was conducive to vivid, ungeneralized writing.

It was easier in Berlin than it might have been in Paris to write a philosophical defense of the position he had unsuccessfully defended in arguments with Aron when Sartre had insisted that the landscape he saw was exactly the same as the scenery in front of him.

His aversion to the subject-object dualism was to persist throughout his life. "So far as I am concerned," he declared in a late interview, "there is no such thing as subjectivity; there are only internalization and exteriority."[22] After accepting Husserl's idea of a consciousness that perpetually transcends itself in favor of an object, Sartre went on in *La Transcendance de l'Ego* to argue that instead of being situated inside consciousness, the ego is out there in the world, an object of consciousness. It is not a concrete structure but a temporary product of reflection. It transcends any individual moment of consciousness; it consists of nothing more than a reflective synthesis of past and present mental impressions. This is to contradict Husserl, who insisted that the ego "is not a piece of the world."[23]

Sartre, who had always disliked the notion of "inner life," tries to destroy the equation of consciousness with self. The I which is aware, he maintains, is not identical with the me I am aware of. Even when it is conceived abstractly, the I is "always an infinite contradiction of the material ego."[24] Not that Sartre is concerned primarily about the self; his book is about consciousness, and his intention is to restore its transparency by cleansing it of personal subjectivity. But this encouraged a presumption of objectivity. In presenting his variations on Husserl's ideas Sartre is claiming the right to forget that they are his or Husserl's. He would have us believe that this is simply the way things are. But impersonal consciousness is consciousness without a subject, and this is no less unthinkable than consciousness without an object.

Dividing his day between work and solitary walks, Sartre missed De Beauvoir's company. He had lunch by himself in the Kurfürstendamm, ate in the evening with five or six of the other students at the French Institute, and sometimes went with them to the movies. He had been relishing the prospect of love affairs with German girls but soon realized that his German was not good enough. He had to make do with the wife of a French student who was living at the institute, a dreamy disorganized girl called Marie Girard. She was capable of being passionate but totally unambitious. He somehow guessed that her father had given her a traumatic experience: had he raped her? Angrily she denied it, but seven years later it would turn out that he had.[25]

Returning to Paris for Christmas was not altogether unlike returning after a term of teaching at Le Havre. Nothing in his life was more continuous than its discontinuity, though the stubborn regularity of his working habits generated a countercurrent of continuity. Even on vacation he would work two long shifts each day, and, spending his Christmas vacation with De Beauvoir, dividing the time between Paris and Rouen, he sketched out a story based on a teacher who had recently lost her virginity to a married writer: shapely but plain, the girl refused to accept the unmistakable indications that he wanted the affair to be brief. She became increasingly deranged, and when Sartre and De Beauvoir tried to help her out of a suicidal phase, she accused them of being involved in a conspiracy against her. Everything was a sign. After abandoning the story, he later made it into "La Chambre" ("The Room").

Back in Berlin, he resumed his routine of reading in the mornings and working in the evenings on the novel. Roquentin's narrative depends on the quality of his thinking, which depends on the quality of Sartre's, and this was changing under Husserl's influence, which was more stimulating than Bergson's had been. One crucial element in the phenomenological method was what Husserl called "Epoche"—a studied withdrawal from the "natural attitude" to observed objects. Normally we confuse the river we see with our knowledge that water flows downhill; the phenomenologist trains himself to "step back" from his knowledge of natural or scientific laws and to concentrate wholly on what is perceivable. Roquentin's observations often seem odd because the substructure of familiar assumptions has been deftly removed. The vision is that of a man who habitually steps back without being aware of doing so, and Sartre uses the symbolist trick of not naming things until after they have been described. "From time to time out of the corner of my eye, I see a reddish flash covered with hairs. It's a hand."[26] The narrative sometimes steps so far back from hands that they become independent animals. Roquentin's hand "shows me its fat stomach."[27] In the reading room, as the Autodidact makes a pass at the schoolboy, Roquentin watches their hands. The boy's "was resting on its back; slack, gentle, and sensual, it had the insolent nudity of a girl sunbathing after a swim. A hairy brown object approached hesitantly. It was a big finger, yellowed by tobacco. Next to this hand it "was as ungraceful as a male sex organ."[28] This forces us to visualize sharply.

Sartre was also benefiting (as a novelist) from his knowledge (as a phenomenologist) of the difference between the "indicative act," which is empty, and the "intuitive act," which is filled out. Intuition (in this context) is the action by which a consciousness fully confronts an object. It is not enough to have the object in mind. When Sartre learned in Burgos what it meant to look at a cathedral, he had started on the phase of development that led not merely to the experience with the chestnut tree but also to the appreciation of Husserl, who helped him to investigate hands with his consciousness and to describe them as if seeing them for the first time. He was also helped by Heidegger, who said: "The existent we have to analyze is ourselves. The being of this existent is my own."[29]

Phenomenology provided a credo that made Sartre confident he could rescue the novel from subjectivism, implicitly refuting Bergson and Proust. Hating the idea of being intellectually in anyone's debt, he always directed his harshest onslaughts against those who had helped him most. The musical phrase that recurs in Proust's novel, the refrain from Vinteuil's sonata, is parodied in the refrain from "Some of These Days," but, more uneasily, Sartre goes on to use the song as an intimation of what the artist can achieve. Sartre is more effectively ironic in handling Anny's (Proustian) belief in privileged moments, and he scores in his variation on one of Proust's favorite themes, the irreversibility of time, while Proust, himself a consummate parodist, is consummately parodied in the visions that place names induce in Roquentin. On the whole, Sartre's aggressive competitiveness is more a help than a hindrance: he is egged on to his best prose by an arrogant conviction that he can outflank Proust. Looking at the hawthorn bushes, Proust's narrator is convinced that if only he can recapture the impact they first made on him, he will solve the secret of life. Sartre, trying to convey what the stuff of life consists of, filters his own understanding of chestnut trees through Roquentin's jaundiced consciousness.

Though everything comes through this filter, the narrative makes authoritative statements about the nature of consciousness, the nature of existence, the nature of time, and the nature of emotion, simultaneously focusing on outward appearances and vividly characterizing social life in a provincial town. The tedium of Sunday, the regular customers in the restaurant, the people in the reading room are all brought powerfully to life. Husserl had led Sartre to a new way of uniting the subject with the object. Consciousness can define itself not by looking inward but by looking outward. Sartre would have been less successful if he had been less vindictive. In the middle of his essay on Husserl he pauses to gloat: "At last we have got rid of Proust." Temporarily, at least, help could be accepted in killing off one of the father figures who had been dominant for too long. Later it would be Husserl's turn, and later still Heidegger's, to be dismissed with a parting insult.

In 1931, when he sat down in Le Havre to look at the chestnut tree, Sartre had not yet studied either Husserl or Heidegger, but when he wrote the crucial episode in *La Nausée,* he was under the influence of both. For Heidegger the most important question was what Being is. Ever since Socrates and Plato had pushed philosophy toward analysis and rationality, thinkers had failed, he complained, to concentrate on the fundamental question: What is it that *is* in everything there is? Normally Being is hidden: we see only individual beings and objects, attaching names to them without asking the right questions. "We do not see the tree for the trees." Studied properly, anything "can become a clearing in which Being declares itself." Sartre, who had already looked quite hard at a tree, now did his best to make Being declare itself through one. "Normally," Roquentin is made to reflect, "existence hides itself. It's there, around us, inside us, it is *us,* you can't say two words without talking about it . . . but . . . if I'd been asked what existence was, I'd have said it was nothing."[30] Now, suddenly, it is to become something, but this something is different from the Being that had revealed itself to Heidegger, who believed that the best approach was one of radical astonishment and that the world was neither hostile nor nauseating. Sartre's stomach was more easily upset. In praising Husserl for saving philosophy from subjectivism, he insisted on the validity of emotion as a means of perceiving:

> Knowledge or pure "representation" is only one of the possible forms of my consciousness of this tree—I can also love it, fear it, hate it, and this intentionality—consciousness overtaking itself—is rediscovered in the fear, hate and love. . . . All of a sudden these famous subjective reactions . . . are only ways of discovering the world. . . . It's a *quality* of this Japanese mask to be frightening . . . not the sum of our subjective reactions to a piece of sculpted wood. Husserl has restored to things their charm and their terror.[31]

The analogy is misleading: a tree is not a piece of sculpted wood, but in *La Nausée* Roquentin is upset by Sartre's old anxiety about contingency. In a geometric form or in a work of art each part is (or should be) necessary in relation to all the other parts, but a real landscape (unlike a painted landscape) oozes with superfluity. Nothing is indispensable. "We were a heap of existing entities, embarrassed, unsure of ourselves, we hadn't the least reason to be there, none of us, each existing entity, awkward, vaguely uneasy, felt superfluous in relation to the others." Sartre hated nothing more than not being needed, and Roquentin even thinks of doing away with himself in order to get rid of at least one superfluous existence.[32] But in spite of being so miscellaneous, the entities all have Being in common. "It had lost the inoffensive aspect of an abstract category: it was the actual glue of things, this root was molded in existence . . . the diversity of things, their individuality was only an illusion, a coating. This coating had melted, leaving moist solids, monstrous and chaotic—nude, fearfully and obscenely nude."[33]

There may be a subterranean connection between Roquentin's attitude to the tree and Sartre's to the nude female body, threatening him with moist orifices and with contingent fertility. The root of the chestnut tree leads Sartre to the word that became so important to Camus: "Absurdity was neither an idea in my head nor a spoken word but this long serpent, dead at my feet, this wooden serpent . . . I realized that I'd found the key to existence, the key to my nausea, to my whole life. . . . I'd experienced the absolute: the absolute or the absurd. . . . In front of this great rugged paw, neither ignorance nor knowledge mattered: the world of explanations and reasons is not that of existence."[34] No less articulate than Heidegger, Sartre is less objective but more impassioned, and here he launches himself excitingly into the space between things and explanations. Though the originality of the novel pivots on its philosophical eclecticism, Sartre was not merely popularizing the ideas of Heidegger, he was dramatizing them.

In discovering Husserl he had undercut the conflict between idealism and realism by concentrating on description. Heidegger learned from Husserl but made the phenomenological inquiry into a more passive process in which the philosopher allows the phenomenon to speak for itself. In Greek, *phenomenon* means "that which will reveal itself," but it will reveal itself only if we listen attentively after freeing ourselves from preconceptions. While Husserl had not attempted to uproot Cartesian thinking, Heidegger insists that the central fact of human experience is Being-in-the-world. The observing ego is not separate from the observed world of objects and landscapes. Existence means standing outside oneself: Being is not encapsulated within the skin but spreads over the field of vision, which is a field of Being—*Dasein* (literally, "being there"). In Sartre's phrase, phenomena can interrogate emotions. Eager to refute the alimentary philosophy that made consciousness draw objects into its maw, Sartre pushed emotion outside subjectivity into description. "This blackness there, against my foot, it didn't look black, but more like a confused effort to imagine blackness made by someone who'd never seen it and couldn't stop himself, who'd imagined an ambiguous being on the far side of color. It *looked* like a color but also a bruise, or rather a secretion, a greasiness—and to something else, a smell for example, it based itself on the smell of moist earth, of moist lukewarm wood, a black smell spread like a varnish on this nervous wood an aroma of chewed fiber, sweetish."[35] As a novelist he could let his disgust goad his description into greater vividness, but what was valid as a method of working was not valid as a philosophical axiom.

Roquentin's nausea is obviously connected with adult commitments—with a fear, akin to Sartre's, of responsibilities that will drag him away from his boyhood freedom—and with sexual dissatisfaction. Though he is not sexually frustrated—the restaurateur's wife never says no—Roquentin seems unconcerned about what she looks like and lets his mind wander while he is making love.[36] But the novel does not explain his deficient emotionality as a result of past experience. Sartre wants to deny the past any power, but the book profits from the urgency of its fixation on the present. The narrative modulates skillfully between past tense and present tense, but the diary method helps to keep the camera aimed at the very recent past, while the movement from one moment of consciousness to the next generates an intensity that helps us to forget the relationship between one decade and the next. Almost nothing is said about Roquentin's parents or his childhood, while his decision to abandon his biography of De Rollebon functions as an assertion that no meaningful patterns are to be extrapolated from analysis of the past. There are no causal connections. One accident ensues on another. While Sartre appears to be more concerned with consciousness than Hemingway or Dos Passos, and his narrative tone could scarcely be more different from theirs, his premise is much the same: "things are exactly what they appear to be—and *behind* them . . . there was nothing."[37]

If everything is exhaustively described, nothing needs to be explained in terms of process. Looking at his face in the mirror, Roquentin sees something no longer human. "Brown wrinkles on either side of the feverish swelling of the lips, crevasses, molehills."[38] Features have become a landscape. Sartre's narrative, like Proust's, is carrying philosophical and psychological ideas in suspension, but Roquentin sets his face against the possibility of searching for lost time: "I will never find either this woman or that night. I lean over each second, I try to use it up; nothing goes by without my snatching at it, fixing it forever in myself—nothing, neither the fleeting tenderness of those lovely eyes nor the noises of the street, nor the false brightness of early morning; yet the moment passes and I cannot hold it. I'm glad it passes."[39] This is both anti-Proustian and anti-Faustian. At the same time Sartre anticipates the synchronic analyses of structuralism by insisting that nothing needs to be explained diachronically.

The presence of Heidegger in the novel is so strong that Sartre understandably wanted to deny it; we need to be suspicious of the chronology he has put on record. He was to complete the second draft of the novel before he left Berlin in July, but according to evidence planted in interviews and in the *Carnets,* he had made little headway with Heidegger by then. He had bought *Sein und Zeit* before Christmas, intending to switch after Easter from Husserl to Heidegger. But "I had been taken by Husserl. I was looking at everything in the light of his philosophy, which, besides, was more accessible to me because it looked Cartesian. I was 'Husserlian' and . . . I could not come to Heidegger till I'd used up Husserl. And, for me, to use up philosophy is to reflect in its perspectives, to evolve personal ideas at its expense until I get into a cul-de-sac. I needed four years to use up Husserl."[40] In April, he says, he had attempted to read *Sein und Zeit* but had given up after fifty pages, partly because of the difficult vocabulary and partly because commitment to Husserl was making Heidegger indigestible.[41] But Roquentin's reflections on existence suggest that Sartre had digested Heidegger rather well. Later on in life he was to claim that he did not read Kafka until after *La Nausée* was written.

This obsessive care in covering his tracks belongs to his complex about self-generation: in literature, as in life, he wanted to believe he had no progenitors. But he would later laud Mallarmé for insisting that all the ideas in our consciousness are old ideas, and already, in *La Nausée,* Sartre describes the Autodidact as disappointed when Roquentin pretends to be impressed with the originality of an entry in his notebook. Surely the idea can't be valid unless someone has already thought of it?

The strength of Sartre's negative feelings toward other novelists (Balzac, Flaubert, Proust) helps him to a scorchingly new tone, while the language is fresh and vigorous—neither rhetorical, like that of his plays, nor abstract, like that of his philosophical works. This abstractness is prefigured in *La Nausée* when Roquentin warns himself against flowery writing—"I need to clean myself up with abstract thoughts as transparent as water"[42]—and later, during the chestnut tree episode, when he complains that things exist too strongly. If only they could be drier, more abstract. Here a surprisingly strong nostalgia for a unified system, sanctioned by divine planning, combines with Sartre's horrified recoil from abundance, viscosity, fertility, pullulation, suggestively serpentine roots. Like a star actor who expects his prominence to be guaranteed by the script, Sartre wanted no part in crowd scenes. If nature is teeming with life, one small intellectual is unlikely to be missed (Someone's missing—it's Sartre!).

An inveterate townsman, uneasy in the country, he even projects his resentment onto the landscape. Things don't want to exist, Roquentin tells us. "Weary and old, they went on existing with bad grace, simply because they were too weak to die, because death could reach them only from outside; it's only melodies that carry their own death proudly inside them like an internal necessity."[43] The tension and the resonance come from direct confrontation with a mode of existence Sartre finds uncongenial. Subjectively but concretely he is dramatizing man's relationship with the planet, and he is writing better than he will later when he withdraws too far from landscape and townscape into hygienic abstraction.

In the confrontation with the tree no alien eyes stare back, but in the municipal gallery Roquentin feels challenged by the faces in the portraits. Looking at Olivier Blévigne, the merchant, he can find no fault in the handsome, unwrinkled features, but the gaze is implacably accusing. "His judgment transfixed me like a sword and raised doubts about my right to exist."[44] In later works Sartre will make Genet, Mallarmé, and Flaubert feel as children that they have been put in the dock by the challenging stare of bourgeois seniors. Like Roquentin, they have rejected the values their elders incarnate. Nor is Roquentin prepared to learn the lesson that another painted dignitary, Rémy Parrottin, is prepared to teach—about the admirable role of the elite. Roquentin's decision to abandon the biography comes immediately after his visit to the gallery, as if the complacent portraits have convinced him that the virtues necessary to fulfill his task are virtues he despises.

Sartre was now doing exactly what Raymond Aron had lightheartedly predicted—philosophizing while talking about an apricot cocktail. As Roquentin is staring at the chestnut tree or at the portraits, the philosophical points emerge casually but forcefully. We not only share the man's vision—we will never be able to shake it off. We are free to disagree with his redefinition of existence but not to forget it.

Sartre was better able to identify with Roquentin because he was writing out of isolation, separated in Berlin, as he had been in Le Havre, from the group that had surrounded him for so many years in Paris. And though his moods cannot be inferred directly from his character's, there is an obvious affinity, while Sartre's walks through Berlin contributed to Roquentin's through Bouville. Like James Joyce, writing in Paris about Dublin, or Günter Grass, recollecting Danzig in Paris, Sartre was reconstructing streets and scenes quite different from the ones in view. But unlike Joyce or Grass, he was pushed by distance toward abstraction, though carefully selected details evoke a distinctive atmosphere.

In February 1934 De Beauvoir arrived in Berlin; she had persuaded a doctor to certify that she needed two weeks of rest.[45] Sartre took her to the Romanisches Café and to "some debauched nightspots by the Alexanderplatz"[46] where she saw the inevitable transvestites. She also had her first taste of an ordeal that would be recurrent in her life: she had to meet Sartre's mistress and to give no sign of jealousy. When she was introduced to Marie Girard, De Beauvoir knew that her own relationship with Sartre was not in danger,[47] but it cannot have been easy to remain unemotional.

When her term ended in July he went to meet her in Hamburg so that they could tour Germany together before he settled back in France. German anti-Nazis were still expecting Hitler's régime to prove unstable, but there was evidence everywhere that it was establishing itself. In Hamburg the Nazis had demolished part of the red light district, leaving only a few streets. In Lübeck battalions of brown-shirted Nazis were parading through the quiet streets. Sartre and De Beauvoir had planned to visit Vienna, but after the news that Dollfuss had been assassinated, they opted instead for Munich, Nuremberg (which was festooned with swastika flags), Rothenburg, and the Königssee. Following Dullin's advice, they went to Oberammergau for the Passion play. It was the three hundredth anniversary of its first performance there, and the village was so crowded that they had to sleep on straw mattresses in a shed. Twenty thousand people watched the performance, which lasted for ten hours, with a two-hour intermission. Dullin would have approved of the "truthfulness that had nothing to do with realism."[48] Sartre liked the way Judas, on being given the silver coins, counted out loud from one to thirty.[49]

In Strasbourg they saw one of the first color films—*The Mystery of the Wax Museum,* with Fay Wray—and they were so pleased with the Alsace scenery that for three days they walked. They had no more baggage than could be carried in their pockets. Sartre sang songs he made up as he went along.

He and De Beauvoir were quite dissimilar in their reactions to tiredness: "She accepts her exhaustion and immerses herself in it, so that it becomes an agreeable and desired state, while I find the same fatigue disagreeable, because I do not consent to it, until I definitely feel I *can't* go on. There's a way of cleaving to oneself, which I don't understand. This has advantages and disadvantages."[50] It was a tremendous advantage to him when writing that he fought so stubbornly against fatigue, but on vacation with her he had to fight himself simultaneously on a number of levels. His tastes and instincts conflicted with hers. She was never happier than when tramping along difficult footpaths, filling her lungs with bracing air, and enjoying magnificent scenery, while he was subject to what he called "pre-fatigue, a disagreeable feeling of something that's going to descend on you."[51] Tiredness also afflicted him with physical symptoms—pimples, boils, blisters, raw skin.[52] Nor did he

like the country. As she said, "He abhors—the word isn't too strong—
the seething life of insects and the profusion of plants . . . he feels at
home only in towns, at the heart of an artificial universe consisting of
man-made objects. He likes neither raw vegetables nor milk which has
come straight from the cow. Nor oysters—nothing but cooked food, and
he always asks for bottled fruit rather than the natural product."[53]
In the chestnut tree episode of *La Nausée* he would make good use of
this revulsion he felt against the profusion of animal and vegetable life;
in *Les Séquestrés d'Altona* he would draw on his aversion to shellfish.
But in his friendship with De Beauvoir he was wrestling with his impulses in almost the same way as he fought against fatigue. His own
tastes must not be allowed to obtrude. The word "love" is inadequate
to explain the sacrifices Sartre was making. Like Flaubert, he was simultaneously proud and ashamed of his own sensitivity. Flaubert distanced himself from it by dramatizing it in the character of a woman,
Emma Bovary, who was unlike him, not only in her sex. More aggressive than Flaubert and more desperate, Sartre was a refugee from *la vie
intérieure.* Having tried to abolish privacy with his group of friends, he
found that it was easier with De Beauvoir. Both consciousnesses could
enjoy symbiotic transparency. Later on, in *Le Diable et le Bon Dieu,* Götz
will have a similar urge to be fused with a woman: without ceasing to
be himself he would like to *become* her.

Sartre and De Beauvoir separated at Mulhouse. Before returning to
Le Havre he went to spend two weeks with his mother and stepfather,
who had been having a great deal of trouble with Charles Schweitzer.
Now ninety, Schweitzer had been installed on the ground floor of their
house. After he had twice tried to throw himself out of a window and
had defecated in a cupboard at his eldest son's house, the family had
decided that he would be less troublesome if he were separated from his
woman friend, who was masturbating him (according to the servant)
until the blood came. Accordingly, the eldest son kidnapped him, and
when he had been installed with the Mancys, he made only halfhearted attempts to see her, but once, whether from genuine confusion
or senile malice, he made a pass at his daughter.[54]

(7)

Back to Bouville

SETTLING down again during the autumn of 1934 into the routine of teaching at Le Havre, where Raymond Aron had replaced him for the last academic year, Sartre found it more enjoyable than before.[1] One of his liveliest new pupils was Jacques-Laurent Bost, the youngest son of the lycée's Protestant chaplain, who had nine children. The eldest, the novelist Pierre Bost, was fifteen years older than Jacques-Laurent, who testified that the boys never felt their philosophy teacher was bored. Twelve of the seventeen pupils, he says, were genuinely interested, and they felt free to interrupt or ask questions. During the year of Sartre's absence, favorable reports on him and his teaching had been circulating, together with rumors about the incident in the brothel.

It was pleasant not to see Nazis in the street, but the French economic crisis was deepening: while unemployment rose to two million, rightists whipped up resentment against the foreign students who would soon be competing for jobs. In January 1935, 90 percent of the Saarlanders voted for reunion with Germany. Though Moscow was in favor of forming a common front, it was not easy for the PCF to change tack after years of rebuffing Socialist attempts at rapprochement. But as Laval's right-wing government showed its ineffectuality, Communists, Socialists and radicals gradually began to cooperate.

Accepting the consensus of friends that the novel was overwritten, Sartre went on pruning his prose until he was sidetracked by an opportunity to develop his ideas on imagery in response to a commission from Henri Delacroix, who was now editing a series for Alcan called Nouvelle Encyclopédie Philosophique. Eager to revise his thesis in a Husserlian perspective, Sartre started a book to be titled "L'Image" or "Les Mondes imaginaires." Summarizing theories about imagination evolved by Descartes, Spinoza, Leibniz, Hume, Taine, Bergson, and the Würzburg psychologists, only to dismiss them because they had all believed thoughts could be imageless, Sartre claimed that Husserl had made the first major contribution to a psychology of the imagination. He had understood how a remembered image, unlike a pickle that can be lifted out of the jar intact, is reshaped in the process, and feeling is always integral to the reshaping.

' Husserl did not establish any clear-cut opposition between perceiving and imagining: you are perceiving a Dürer engraving whether you see it as black lines on white paper or as a knight, Death and the Devil. But for Sartre perception is merely passive; interpreting belongs to imagination. From this premise he could go on to question the motivation behind the decision whether to form visual data into a perception or an image and to deny that the difference between the two could derive merely from intentionality. What was needed, he concluded, was a phenomenological psychology, and the conclusion was, of course, a beginning. He must write one.

He worked hard at "L'Image," but his routine did not preclude frequent meetings with De Beauvoir in Le Havre and Rouen. In Le Havre they wandered around the old docks, ate in a brasserie, talked in the Café Guillaume Tell, where Sartre did much of his writing. For the first few weeks he had enjoyed teaching after the year of solitude and freedom, but he now felt more ambivalent about the restrictions of having a job. In the café they talked about their prospects. Nothing new was ever going to happen. They would go on seeing the same friends, go on conducting the same scrupulously self-critical conversation.[2]

Much as he enjoyed writing, he was coming to depend on stimulants to screw himself into optimum productivity. At eight or nine o'clock in the morning he would start swallowing pep pills, which made it impossible for him to sleep at night without a sedative. He started taking four or five tablets of Belladénal at night and went on needing sleeping pills for the rest of his life. He also used them to lower his blood pressure when it became too high. It was no accident that he dreamed little—or usually forgot his dreams—from this time onward.[3] In one of his short stories, "Erostrate," he used a dream told to him by Jacques-Laurent Bost, and he liked girls to tell him their dreams, but he had few of his own.

In Rouen he played Russian billiards with De Beauvoir at the October fair and began to patronize the café-restaurant that would be featured in *La Nausée*. "A half dozen marble-topped tables bathed, summer and winter alike, in an aquarium light; the proprietor, bald and melancholy, did the serving; the menu consisted of little but eggs and tinned cassoulet."[4]

For the Christmas vacation De Beauvoir persuaded him to make an attempt at skiing with her. For ten days they stayed at a small *pension* in Montroc, above the Chamonix valley. A ten-year-old boy showed them how to turn, and, unconcerned with other people's reactions, they persisted, trying to teach themselves on the beginners' slope.

Back in Le Havre, teaching, working at "L'Image," and thinking about the novel, he became subject to fits of depression. In class, according to Bost, he would sometimes "turn icy; it did not last long—no more than about fifteen minutes. He would bite his nails and every so often he'd stare at the class, and, after a silence of perhaps forty-five seconds, he'd say: 'Just look at that sea of faces, and not a glimmer of intelligence anywhere.' "[5] Thinking about Roquentin's depressions could work therapeutically against his own, but these overlapped with those of the character. Bost once saw him despondently observing seaweed slapping against a rock with the same expression on his face as he had in the classroom when things were going badly or he was particularly disgruntled.[6]

In February 1935 he had his first experiences with mescaline. Knowing of his concern with images and anomalies of perception, his old friend Daniel Lagache, now an intern in psychiatry at Sainte-Anne, suggested that he could have an injection in the hospital to see what hallucinations it induced. They met at a bistro bar near the hospital, and Lagache introduced him to another intern, who was working with the drug.[7] It was not dangerous, he promised Sartre; at worst, one might behave rather oddly for a few days afterward.

In the hospital Sartre had to lie down in a dimly lit room. Objects began to change unspeakably in shape and size. When a doctor approached, his hand and his foot grew bigger, and then smaller as he went away. An umbrella hanging on the coat rack looked like a vulture, with its handle as neck and beak. Attacked by devilfish, Sartre was trying unsuccessfully to fight them off when he was called to the telephone. It was De Beauvoir. To her his voice sounded thick and blurred. Traveling with her in the train back to Le Havre he stared at the acornlike ornaments on her shoes, waiting for them to turn into giant dung beetles.[8]

In the morning the effects seemed to have worn off,[9] but for several days he was deeply depressed and unable to rely on his vision. A black spot danced constantly in front of his eyes. Houses seemed to have eyes and jaws; clock faces had the features of an owl. The symptoms, he assumed, would get worse: he believed himself to be suffering from "chronic hallucinatory psychosis," which, according to current belief, meant that within ten years he would be insane. One Sunday, when De Beauvoir and Colette Audry visited him in Le Havre, he made little effort to be agreeable or even to talk. Confiding in De Beauvoir about the symptoms, he rejected her assurance that he was not having psychotic hallucinations.[10] Working at his book and still insisting that consciousness could always differentiate between an image and an external object, he forced himself to look for what he could see, becoming distraught when he could not find it.[11]

Nor could he garner reassurance from doctors, who insisted that mescaline could not be causing the trouble. During the Easter vacation, at the Italian lakes with De Beauvoir, he was in high spirits for much of the time, but on their return to Paris he relapsed. Fernando Gérassi had an exhibition at the Galérie Bonjean, but Sartre stayed morosely in a corner throughout the vernissage. Sitting in cafés with De Beauvoir, or walking with her in the street, he sank into long silences. A doctor prescribed belladonna but advised him to continue working.[12] He was worst when alone, and he spent more time than usual in Rouen to be with De Beauvoir when she was not teaching; she provided a pupil to keep him company when she was.[13]

KNOWN as "la petite Russe," Olga Kosakiewicz was the daughter of a Russian nobleman and a Frenchwoman. Pale, blond, temperamental, tempestuously unpredictable, Olga sometimes won high marks, sometimes turned in poor work. A flood of tears in the classroom had prompted De Beauvoir to invite her out for a walk, and after finding she could talk more openly to the girl than to any of her older friends, she had started taking her out to lunch once a week at a brasserie, where Olga, who disliked eating and talking at the same time, would do neither. She and Sartre seemed to enjoy being with each other. She had, in common with Toulouse, something that De Beauvoir lacked—a combination of imperiousness and impetuosity. Probably Sartre had been unaware of missing it, but when he found it again he responded, and in *La Nausée* he pays tribute to it through his characterization of Anny. When she meets Roquentin again after not seeing him for four years her first words are: "Come in and sit down anywhere you like except in the armchair by the window."

Sartre's passion for Olga would last for two years, coinciding with an instability that seemed to "push out the limits of the probable." "I entered a world that was darker but less pale. As for Olga, my passion for her burned away my normal impurities like the flame of a Bunsen burner. I grew lean as a cuckoo and desperate: no more feeling relaxed."[14] He even began to worry about his waistline. During the year in Germany he had put on weight, and after his return to France he had only laughed when Guille had "taken my stomach in his hands, through my sweater, to show Mme. Morel that I had a big one."[15] At intervals he inspected his stomach in the mirror, weighed himself on machines outside drugstores, and tried to diet. One day Mme. Morel observed: "You like forcing yourself to do what you don't like doing." This was a constant in his behavior; it gave him the sense of being free. But he never persevered, never wanted badly enough to give up eating bread.[16]

One cause of his malaise was reluctance to grow up into what he called "l'âge de raison." No longer protected by a group of friends, he had to fend for himself in a society he hated, to be involved with headmaster, senior staff, colleagues, parents for whom he felt the same contempt he made Roquentin feel toward the *salauds* of the bourgeoisie.[17] The novel provided an outlet for his spleen, but his childhood confidence about his future greatness had boomeranged. Nizan's books were being published—*Cheval de Troie* (*Trojan Horse*) came out in 1935—but Sartre had not found a publisher even for *La Transcendance de l'Ego*.

On March 21, 1935, Charles Schweitzer died at the age of ninety-one. Five days earlier, Hitler, repudiating the disarmament clause in the Versailles Treaty, had introduced compulsory military service, causing panic in France. At the beginning of May a Franco-Soviet pact of mutual assistance was signed, which accelerated the rapprochement between the three left-wing parties. In July the three leaders, Edouard Daladier, Léon Blum, and Maurice Thorez, addressed a joint meeting of their parties, and on Bastille Day, July 14, Socialists, radicals, and Communists marched through the streets, waving tricolor flags, shouting slogans, and singing songs. Sartre and De Beauvoir watched but without wanting to join in.[18]

At the beginning of the summer vacation Sartre went on a Norwegian cruise with his mother and stepfather. At a fancy-dress ball on the boat he appeared in a black velvet dress of his mother's, wearing a blond wig with long pigtails. He met an aging American Jewish woman who was dressed as a man and found him charming. They talked in German, and when she wanted to dance, he used the style he had picked up from Olga.[19] The following morning, seeing him undisguised, the lady lost interest.[20]

His experiences on the Norwegian cruise led him to write a short story, "Soleil de minuit" ("Midnight Sun"). It was about a thirteen-year-old girl on a cruise with her parents. She had imagined that the midnight sun was only a red ball with no power to illuminate, but at midnight the boat passes an island, and the sunlight is strong enough for her to see the birds on it.[21] He also started a story based on the all-women orchestra that had performed at the café in Saint-Symphorien, but he torc it up after thirty pages.[22]

Returning from Norway, he joined De Beauvoir for a hiking tour. There was no possibility that he could ever take her on vacation with his mother and stepfather; De Beauvoir was never even to meet Mancy, but, without telling him, Sartre's mother often invited her out to tea. Sartre and De Beauvoir hiked through the middle of France, where he lost his only manuscript of the Norwegian story. He was always careless with manuscripts. Once he had written something, it belonged to the past; what he cared about was what he would write next. They followed the river Tarn through mountainous countryside, climbed the Aigoual, walked for hours over rough upland plateaus. They lunched on hard-boiled eggs and sausages in the open air. At Le Rozier they met Guille, who was also on a walking tour, with his attractive cousin, Thérèse. The four of them climbed rocks together, ate trout and *écrevisse*, paddled in the Tarn. As always, Sartre and De Beauvoir had planned their itinerary in careful detail. He preferred buildings to woods, and they visited châteaux, abbeys, villages.

All this time he felt convinced that a lobster was pursuing him, until one evening, on the way to Castelnau-de-Montmiral in a crowded bus, he announced that he was tired of being mad. After this he was consistently cheerful.[23]

HE was happy to be back with Olga, who put him into a state of almost permanent excitement. "For the first time in my life, someone could make me feel humble and disarmed. I wanted to learn from her."[24] Her consciousness seemed "naked and spontaneous, capable only of feeling, with violence and purity." She had more power than anyone had previously had to change his behavior patterns. With her he often stayed awake all night, going without sleep for forty hours. "At the same time and precisely because of this passion I began to lose faith in salvation through art. Art seemed useless in comparison with this cruel, violent and naked purity."[25] One conversation with De Beauvoir was enough to convince him that he was overstating the case against art, but a strong hostility to it was latent in him, and she was sucked by the force of his admiration into a deeper involvement with the impetuous young girl.

Despite the nine-year age gap, the two women saw more of each other in Rouen during term time than either of them did of Sartre. Like him, De Beauvoir admired Olga's refusal to hide her feelings. She valued emotions above ideas, "life values" above spiritual values. Sometimes she would go on dancing till she fainted from exhaustion. In 1935 she twice failed her medical exams; her mother and father, who throughout her childhood had seemed liberal and enlightened, now seemed treacherously authoritarian. At home in Beuzeville she was forbidden to smoke or stay up late, and her parents had decided to send her to a girls' boarding school in Caen. Without Sartre's encouragement De Beauvoir would not have intervened, but he had started an honors course in philosophy at Le Havre for male and female students, and she visited Olga's parents in Beuzeville to suggest that she and Sartre could coach the girl for her diploma. De Beauvoir, who had moved out of her hotel in Rouen, was renting a room in an old three-story building Olga had recommended, Le Petit Mouton, in an alley off the Rue de la République. Now Olga rented a room there herself.

Ivich, the girl in Sartre's *L'Age de raison* who is modeled on Olga, is the most vivid character in the novel. Mathieu, Sartre's alter ego, is not sure what he wants from her. Her face, largely hidden by fair curls, is broad, pale, girlish, and sensual. Other people think her pretty; Mathieu knows she is plain. "Mathieu stood at her side, ugly, importunate, forgotten. Yet he wouldn't have wished to be handsome: she was never more alone than when confronted with beauty . . . he could call her by her name or touch her shoulder, but she was out of reach, with her frail figure and her lovely hard throat; she looked painted and varnished, like a Tahitian girl on a Gauguin canvas—not usable."[26]

Olga could not concentrate on philosophy; when De Beauvoir asked her to précis a chapter of Bergson, she ate a pound of sweets and wrote none of the essay.[27] After two fruitless years of studying medicine, she was so scared of failing that she preferred not to compete; recrimination only increased her indolence. Sartre gave up trying to teach her, and by Christmas De Beauvoir followed suit. Both believed they could learn from her; living for the present, she could throw herself uninhibitedly into any experience—dancing, listening to a Gypsy violinist, or to her own heartbeats. When De Beauvoir recommended Stendhal, Proust, Conrad, Olga reacted to the characters as if they were real people. In De Beauvoir's room they played chess, drinking cherry brandy in inordinate quantities.[28]

Back in Rouen during 1936, after a Christmas skiing vacation with De Beauvoir in Switzerland, Sartre tried to monopolize Olga, clowning for her, making up songs and stories like a father half in love with his nubile daughter, and he grew jealous when she appeared to prefer the company of a good-looking young teacher. De Beauvoir tried to keep jealousy at bay while Sartre apprehensively watched Olga's changes of expression; no one must matter more to her than he did. Despising routine, braving lack of food or sleep, and questing in her immature, rebellious, capricious way after the absolute, Olga became so important to both of them that it irked their friends. Though they had no desire for a baby, they had once thought, momentarily, of adopting a distraught, half-drunk, charming girl they met in Montparnasse; now it was Olga who provided a passport back into adolescence. Singing, making up plays, intently analyzing the exact flavor of cassis,[29] Sartre was escaping from the age of reason. Once again he was a member of a trio, and this time, as the only male in it, he could usually dominate the triangular relationship, partly because he, like Olga, was less interested than De Beauvoir in the triangle as such. She was at a point that frequently disappeared from Sartre's field of vision, while the girl, amazed and happy to have so much power over both adults, found it easier to manipulate them separately.

As a writer Sartre had another setback when Alcan rejected the second half of "L'Image." Only the first half, which interested Sartre less, having less original thinking in it, would be published in 1936 under the title *L'Imagination*. The second half was not to appear until 1940, and then in a revised form, as *L'Imaginaire*.

For their Easter vacation Sartre and De Beauvoir took Olga to Paris, where they sat through two consecutive performances of Chaplin's first talkie, *Modern Times*. Sartre would later borrow its French title for his monthly *Les Temps Modernes*.

Ivich's brother in the novel, Boris, was modeled on the nineteen-year-old Jacques Bost. Sartre, who was coaching him for a teacher's diploma in philosophy, befriended him and brought him to Rouen. To distinguish him from his brother Pierre, they called him Little Bost. "To us," writes De Beauvoir, "he was an incarnation of youth. He had youthful grace, so casual it was almost insolent, and also a narcissistic fragility . . . Needing security, he sought adult company."[30] He was unambitious and unoriginal but lively, quick-witted, naturally stylish, droll, and rather charming. His party stunt was striking matches with his toes.[31] Like Olga, Bost was to some extent a surrogate child—not a girl to be protected and cherished but a male, gratifyingly unlike the surrogate father physically but with personality traits that appeared to have less connection with heredity than with Sartre's teaching. In the novel Boris has constructed his life around the ideal of liberty expounded by Mathieu in the classroom. Since the individual should be accountable to no one but himself, Boris conscientiously defies bourgeois morality by stealing. He challenges the assumptions of everyone but Mathieu and Ivich, who are above criticism.

Apart from "Soleil de minuit," Sartre's first story was "Erostrate," which he wrote during 1936, basing it partly on another student, Didelot, who was brilliant, illegitimate, depressive, and fascistic. One morning he drank coffee, wrote a letter to his grandmother, another to a girl friend, went into the bathroom and cut his throat with two razor blades. Still alive, he went onto the roof, shouted to warn passersby not to get in the way, and jumped.[32] The story is about a man who plans to kill people at random with his revolver, using the last bullet on himself. The narrative picks up Sartre's childhood pleasure at looking down on passersby from a vantage point high in a building; the story also prefigures the interest he would take in Jean Genet. Some sentences read like undiscovered Genet juvenilia, especially when the narrative alludes to the Papin sisters. The character lusts for the transformation that crime can bring, but what is most revealing is his ease in identifying with the antihumanistic viewpoint. As to Roquentin, fellow citizens are innately repulsive. There is something unpleasant about the way the human body is jointed, with "legs which open and close at will." (Sartre describes them as if they were shellfish.) The humanist loves "human flesh, people's appearance of being gravely wounded by education, and the way they seem to reinvent walking at every pace." Like *La Nausée*, the story exudes contempt for the values and activities of stolid middle-class citizens.

In contrast to the bourgeoisie, Olga behaved like the exiled aristocrat she was. De Beauvoir writes: "Together we hated Sunday crowds, conformist ladies and gentlemen, the provinces, families, children and all the humanisms. We liked exotic music, the *quais* of the Seine, barges, loafers, little bars with a doubtful reputation, the emptiness of nighttime."[33] Under the influence of phenomenology, Sartre tried to put the world in brackets, to jerk himself out of taking normal behavior for granted. One stratagem was to visit a mental hospital outside Rouen. Taking De Beauvoir, Olga, and Bost with him, he went to look at the blue-uniformed inmates, who were mostly stupefied with boredom.[34] Alternately flirtatious and withdrawn, Olga provoked Sartre by refusing to tether herself. This prerogative was meant to be his. They quarreled frequently, and one day, two hours after he had put her on the train to Rouen, she was told over the telephone that on the railway platform an angry little man had picked a fight with a much bigger man, who had blinded him in one eye. Now in the hospital, the little man had asked for her to be informed. In panic Olga rushed to tell De

Beauvoir, but it had been Sartre on the telephone, disguising his voice.[35]

Olga was like a sexy child trying to win the alliance of one parent against the other. About their relationships with Olga, Sartre and De Beauvoir argued endlessly, using phenomenological jargon. Olga often became violent, while Sartre, who prided himself on being stoical, lapsed into protracted gloom. During the Easter vacation, when they visited Toulouse, Olga pressed a lighted cigarette ferociously into her hand.[36] De Beauvoir used the episode in her first novel, *L'Invitée;* in *L'Age de raison* Sartre builds a nightclub scene to a climax in which Ivich slashes with a sharp knife at the palm of her left hand, opening the flesh from the ball of the thumb to the root of her little finger. Mathieu then outbids her by pushing the blade right through the palm of his hand.[37]

Dividing himself between the woman and the girl, Sartre felt safer with De Beauvoir, but the young blonde could arouse him to fury, ecstasy, or alarm. The first serious rift in his alliance with De Beauvoir resulted not from intimacy with Olga but from a quarrel with her and from the rapprochement between her and De Beauvoir that predictably ensued. While they were confiding in each other, he could confide in neither.[38] His partnership with De Beauvoir remained unsteady until July, when Olga rejoined her parents in Beuzeville. For the coming academic year he could choose between a job in Lyon, teaching a *khâgne,* and one in Laon, teaching for the *baccalauréat.* The Mancys pressured him to accept the Lyon offer, but he opted for Laon, which is much closer to Paris, where De Beauvoir had been offered a teaching job. Another reason was that since the Lyon job involved a promotion, he would have been expected to stay in it for several years; since the Laon job did not, he might well be moved to Paris at the next reshuffling.

(8)

Intimacy

In Laon, as at Le Havre, Sartre kept his distance from the other teachers. The most hostile was a M. Jollivet, master of the sixth form, who explained, threateningly, that he was "the leader of a group, Monsieur." At a ceremony held to celebrate the fiftieth anniversary of the lycée, one of the teachers would have to make a speech, and to ensure that Sartre did not stay aloof from school affairs, all eleven members of Jollivet's group voted for him. The likeliest of the other candidates was a literature teacher who also received eleven votes, but after Sartre, who had been forewarned of the danger, helped the headmaster's secretary to count the votes, it was announced that the literature teacher had received thirteen votes to Sartre's nine.[1] He was no less adamant than he had been at Le Havre in refusing to attend boring meetings, and one day in the common room he came to blows with a teacher who told him off for his absence from a *tableau d'honneur* meeting. The man was about his own age, and, going round and round the room, they went on fighting until another teacher came in.[2]

While his indifference to school affairs remained stable, his interest in politics went on growing. When the electoral victory of the popular front was followed by strikes in the aircraft factories around Paris, he and De Beauvoir contributed to the strikers' collections, infuriating Guille, who said they were helping to endanger the Blum experiment. In June they were pleased with the Matignon Agreement, which gave the workers collective contracts, wage increases, a forty-hour week, and paid holidays.[3]

Having decided to spend their summer vacation in Italy, Sartre and De Beauvoir were feeling elated despite the news of civil war in Spain. If the majority of the people wanted a republic, the minority of rebels must soon be defeated. On their way southward the lovers stopped at Grenoble, met Guille and his family at Guillestre, and continued with Guille to Marseille. In Rome, Sartre and De Beauvoir stayed at the Albergo del Sole for ten days. In Naples they booked rooms at a hotel near the station, in the center of the working-class district.[4] On vacation they took turns being "leader of the expedition." It was now Sartre's turn. They started off by exploring the prosperous-looking main streets. When they found the narrow alleyways off the Via Roma, he was outraged by the evidence of starvation so close to the expensive, sumptuous food available for elegant ladies and gentlemen in silk clothes, and he started a story called "Dépaysement" ("Bewilderment"). A ragged child picks up a piece of rotting watermelon from a fly-infested drain and starts eating it. In a cavelike room, open to the street, a woman is ill in bed.

> I could no longer see anything but flesh floating in a blue darkness, flesh to squash, suck, eat, moist flesh drenched with sweat, urine, milk. All of a sudden a man knelt down next to a little girl and looked at her, laughing. She laughed too. She said: "Papa, my papa." Then, raising the child's dress a little, the man bit into her grey thighs as if they were bread. I smiled. No movement has ever seemed so natural, so *necessary*.[5]

The incestuous cannibalism is described with a restrained violence that reflects the urgency of his need to invent an action correlative to the squalid vista of poverty. Like "Soleil de minuit," "Dépaysement" was written out of the feeling that objects, streets, landscapes contained secrets which could never be translated into words but that there must be a way of evoking three-dimensional reality without trying to detach a two-dimensional meaning from it. What was a garden like when no one was looking at it? He wanted to present glimpses of solid objects, combining a heterogeneous mixture of them in a brief action, rather in the manner of Katherine Mansfield.[6]

Unable to afford the funicular railway that carried tourists to the top of Vesuvius, he and De Beauvoir took a train to the nearest station on the Circumvesuvia and walked the rest of the way, despite the lava, slag, and ashes that made the going difficult. After visiting Capri, Pompeii, and Paestum they separated for two days while she went to Amalfi and he returned to Naples. Two sailors he met in a bar took him to a brothel where, in a circular room with mirrored walls, two naked women, neither of them young, performed *tableaux vivants* based on the frescoes in the Villa of the Mysteries at Pompeii. The women are featured in "Dépaysement."[7]

On the boat to Palermo, Sartre and De Beauvoir slept on deck; in the city they traveled in horse-drawn cabs to visit churches and palazzi. At Selina, Sartre tried to charm the lizards by whistling. On the ferry back to the mainland De Beauvoir was annoyed to see him reading newspapers instead of looking at the sunset. In Rome he was worrying about Spain, Hitler, and Olga; in Venice they decided to save money by not going to bed on their last night. After the cafés closed they sat on the steps of the Piazza San Marco, strolled beside the canals, watched the early morning barges, saw the market arcades being reopened. Afterward Sartre announced that he had again been pursued by a lobster.

They arrived back in Paris on September 14 so short of money that, shoeless, he had to wear his white espadrilles in the rain.[8]

In Laon he settled into an ancient hotel, comfortable but with a distinctive fusty smell.[9] Involved in teaching again he forgot about lobsters, and he could escape to Paris twice a week. De Beauvoir, who was teaching at the Lycée Molière in Passy, was living in a small room at the Hôtel Royal Bretagne in the Rue de la Gaîté. They met at the Gare du Nord and usually had a drink at a café near the station before going to Montparnasse, where they based themselves at the Café du Dôme.

When she was not teaching, De Beauvoir breakfasted there and stayed on to write, surrounded by German refugees and other foreigners reading papers or playing chess. The painter Ossip Zadkine and the writer Ilya Ehrenburg were among the regulars, while Giacometti was to be seen every evening wandering along the pavement, alone or with an attractive girl. De Beauvoir, like Sartre, found women more interesting to watch than men—models, artists' girl friends, minor actresses, bizarre women who talked to themselves.[10]

When Olga ran away from her parents, booking herself a room in the Royal Bretagne, she resumed her unsteady relationship with Sartre but not her pretense of studying philosophy. She got herself a job as a waitress in the Boulevard Saint-Michel, but the pointlessness of her work enervated her. When Sartre found he had decisively lost her to Jacques Bost, he took the defeat well, vengefully consoling himself by starting a friendship with her younger sister, Wanda, who was subject to the same temperamental unpredictability, whether through genetic inheritance or through a habit of copying her sister. Sartre's intimacy with Wanda and their commitment to each other developed rapidly but stopped short of lovemaking.

The defeat he did not take well was the rejection of his novel, which had been submitted by Nizan to one of Gallimard's readers. "I had put the whole of myself into this book and spent a long time working on it. To reject it was to reject me."[11] When he went with De Beauvoir to spend Christmas in Chamonix, he could not hold his tears back. "I had staked a great deal on the novel."[12]

As 1937 began, his relationship with Olga resumed, though he would never again be so important to her as Bost. It was now that Bost's novelist brother Pierre became helpful, going to see Gaston Gallimard, asking him to read Sartre's novel himself. Still more effective was the intervention of Dullin, who was an old friend of Gallimard's. Sartre's spirits were boosted sufficiently for him to continue work on "Dépaysement."

But his growing interest in politics did not help him to feel at peace. Puzzled by the Moscow trials, he questioned Nizan, who answered guardedly, not concealing his anxiety. In France a group organized by right-wing extremists was sending arms to Franco, who was also receiving help from Hitler and Mussolini, while Blum's Socialist government, like Stanley Baldwin's Conservative government, did nothing to help the republicans. When Fernando Gérassi came back on leave from fighting in Spain, he reported that the People's Army was underequipped, disorganized, and short of trained men. The individuals who joined the International Brigades were mostly useless. Simone Weil had crossed the frontier and asked for a gun but had been sent to work in the kitchens, where she spilled boiling oil over her feet.[13]

Sartre felt uneasy about not wanting to join the volunteers and ambivalent when Bost did want to; wasn't he too immature to fight? But shouldn't he have the right to decide for himself? Sartre spoke to Nizan, who put Bost in touch with André Malraux. Anxiety about Bost's future in Spain gave Sartre the idea for a short story, "Le Mur" ("The Wall"). Captured by the fascists, and sentenced to death, a boy and two men are in a cell waiting for daylight and trying to prepare themselves for the moment of facing the firing squad. A Belgian doctor, who spends the night with them, is unsympathetically interested in their physiological reactions. The boy, Juan, is the most hysterical—emotion as evasion; the narrator, Pablo, is the most clear-sighted, trying to use his imagination truthfully. Concern for Bost helped Sartre to project himself convincingly into the death cell. But Malraux was discouraging: only trained soldiers would be useful, he said.

Sartre's story "Intimité" ("Intimacy") was probably written at about this time. It seems to have been developed from fragments of café conversations that afford glimpses into other people's lives, as do the fragments Roquentin overhears in Le Rendez-vous des Cheminots. But identifying with the two girls and naming one of them Rirette, after

Rirette Nizan, Sartre is more sympathetic than he was in the novel. The basic situation is absurd: in spite of Rirette's encouragement, Lulu cannot bring herself to leave her impotent husband, Henri, for her lover, Pierre. The commonplace self-satisfaction and the vulgar sensuality of the two girls are brought ironically into focus, but the mimicry is so delicately accurate as to seem almost tender.

BEFORE the winter was over, De Beauvoir collapsed during a dinner party. She was taken home in a taxi and two days later was driven in an ambulance to a St.-Cloud clinic recommended by Mme. Morel.[14] The doctors diagnosed pulmonary congestion, but no doubt the tension with Sartre and Olga had helped to weaken her. Every day he took the train to St.-Cloud, and he found that his passion for Olga was evaporating: his need was for De Beauvoir. "I was nervous, unsettled. I looked forward each day to the moment of seeing her, and beyond that moment to I don't know what impossible rapprochement."[15] When she was discharged from the clinic Sartre arranged for her to be moved into a more comfortable hotel, where she was still bedridden during the Easter vacation. He looked after her, bringing her lunch from the Coupole and sitting at her bedside for hours.[16]

In her absence he had fun with Bost. They improvised games; one was to complete the *Paris-Soir* crossword puzzle without looking at any of the "down" clues. In April 1937 they shook hands on the oath that in September they would buy ragged clothes from a secondhand shop, dress like tramps, and set out with only ten francs each to live for a week by begging and stealing. Sartre felt secretly flattered whenever they planned such juvenile escapades; Bost said "we" and "us."[17] His charm was at its greatest when he put on performances just for Sartre, singing songs in English or improvising the role of a barman ejecting a drunken Sartre. Bost also elaborated on his baroque fantasies—in one of them he had twenty-seven girls, including De Beauvoir, her sister Poupette, Wanda, and their friend De Roulet's girl friend. After buying the Hôtel du Théâtre, he would install his mistresses there, one in each room. De Beauvoir would be allowed out to change her library books, but the others would all be confined to the hotel.[18]

In April, while De Beauvoir was recuperating in the Midi, Sartre suddenly found that, thanks to Dullin and Pierre Bost, success was no longer out of reach. The novel, Sartre was told, had previously been rejected on the assumption that it had been submitted for the monthly *Nouvelle Revue Française*, which was published by Gallimard and edited by Jean Paulhan. Sartre was summoned to the Gallimard offices, where

Paulhan asked: "Do you know Kafka? In spite of the differences I can think of no other modern literature for comparison with your book." He went on to ask for stories he could print in the *Nouvelle Revue Française.* In any case, Sartre could be quite confident about the novel: "Gallimard *can't* not take it." Sartre was then introduced to the philosopher Brice Parain, who was working for Gallimard and said the novel had at first reminded him of Dostoevsky, but he had found some of the sequences too protracted and disliked the diary form. Meeting Bost afterward in a café, Sartre put on an air of extreme dejection, throwing the typescript down on the table. Bost seemed shattered until Sartre told him it had been accepted.

When Gaston Gallimard read the book, his only objection was to the title, "Melancholia"; his suggestion was "La Nausée." De Beauvoir demurred, not wanting it to sound like a naturalistic novel. In any case, it would be published in 1938. Meanwhile "Le Mur" would appear in the July issue of the *Nouvelle Revue Française,* and he resumed work on the story "La Chambre," which derived not only from the experience with Louise Ferron, the psychotic schoolteacher, but also from the visits to the asylum in Rouen and from the delusions he had suffered after the mescaline injections. Pierre, who never leaves his room, is persecuted by flying statues, which make a noise like an airplane. The story is told from the viewpoint of three other characters—his mother-in-law, his father-in-law, and his wife, Eve, who goes on making love to him but intends to kill him before mental illness has reduced him to dementia. Accusing her of wanting to live solely by imagination, her father tells her it is wrong to enter into the delusions of the mad.

Happy that fame was at last on the horizon, Sartre did not intend to spend less time on writing letters, taking out girls, enjoying himself with friends. A long April letter to the convalescent De Beauvoir complains about the pressure on his time: "I love you very much but I absolutely no longer have time for being soulful [*les états d'âme*]."[19] Constantly hungry for the gossip integral to close friendship, he was spending a lot of time with Bost and Olga, seeing them separately more than he saw them together. Olga talked to him about Bost; he talked to her about Wanda. He talked to Bost about De Beauvoir, sometimes—and the joke may have been only an exaggeration of the truth—describing her as "a woman of steel," who scared him.[20] He was also seeing Poupette, writing to Wanda, trying to write every day to De Beauvoir. He was anxious about her: "You walk too much. You take risks . . . you're going to put too much strain on your heart."[21] The short story would have to wait until he could spare time for it.

In any event, her absence catalyzed a contingent affair with a friend of Poupette's who had also become a friend of De Beauvoir's. Toward the end of April, Sartre took her for a long walk through the streets of Paris. She was wearing makeup for the first time. When he took her up to his room and kissed her on the cheek, she kissed him on the mouth. After they had made love she said: "I almost enjoyed it." He presented her with a copy of "Erostrate" and took her back to her husband.[22]

If the affair—which he described in full detail to De Beauvoir—had any effect on his relationship with her, it was to strengthen it. His letters to her became more detailed and reminiscent of Kafka's letters to Felice in the diarylike reporting of day-to-day trivia. Reading a letter of hers that described how tears had come to her eyes, he found that tears came to his.[23] On May 11 he wrote that he was hurrying to finish the novel— he still called it his *factum*—to have it ready for her return.[24]

In July, when "Le Mur" appeared in the *Nouvelle Revue Française,* it caused a furor. Sartre received a great many letters, and he was no less pleased with the offer of a teaching job at the Lycée Pasteur, in Neuilly. After six years as a schoolmaster, six years of being exiled from Paris during the school year, he could at least work where he wanted to.

For the summer vacation he and De Beauvoir went to Greece with Bost. One day, when they were strolling through the slums near the Acropolis, urchins threw stones at them. They consoled themselves by thinking they were not really tourists of the kind the children took them for. Piraeus was full of beggars, who sat scratching their scabs, while a surprising proportion of the children were crippled, blind, or mutilated. Even the middle-class Athenians looked unhappy in comparison with the Italians.

They stayed at a hotel off Omonia Square. Bost was allowed to sleep on the roof without paying. They breakfasted on the pavement terrace outside a pâtisserie, explored the streets, the market, and the port, but gave most of their time to the Acropolis. After visiting the tiered amphitheater at Epidaurus they spent the night in the open air at the foot of the slope. Waking up there with De Beauvoir next to him was a memory Sartre would treasure.[25] Traveling on aging steamers and sleeping on deck, they visited Mykonos, Delos, and Syra, where they all slept on the roof of the hotel. After a long walk on Santorini to the ruins of Thera and the sanctuary of Stavrós, they arrived hot, exhausted, and bad-tempered at Emborio, urgently needing food and drink, but the streets were deserted, and the only woman they saw fled in fear. Eventually they lighted on a decrepit café, where they were served a tomato salad decorated with dead flies. The description of Argos in the first act of Sartre's play *Les Mouches (The Flies)* derives from this experience.[26]

After leaving Bost to sail from Piraeus back to France, Sartre and De

Beauvoir went on to Delphi, and spent three days on the terraced slopes of Mount Olympus, sleeping under a blanket in the open air. Relying on the itinerary De Beauvoir had prepared from the *Guide Bleu,* they had thought it would be easier to cross the mountains. Sartre, who was scared of dogs, had to fight off a fierce mongrel with a stick.

They went by bus to Sparta, and slept on the floor of a ruined palace in Mistra, where Sartre stole a skull from an ossuary. De Beauvoir wanted to climb Mount Taygetus (nine and a half hours up, five and a half hours down), but Sartre refused. They spent two days at a hotel in Mycenae; he would remember being alone there with her "under a beautiful staring sky, surrounded by these strange tombs and these rocks." Though their money was running out, they went north to Macedonia and waited in Salonika until Bost telegraphed their September salaries. They bought too little food for the journey back, and on the mailboat they were hungry in spite of the cakes and fruit given to them by the cooks. After two days together in Marseille, Sartre left for Paris, while De Beauvoir toured Alsace with Olga.

As so often before, a vacation with De Beauvoir had renewed their solidarity. "I haven't stopped feeling that there's an internal link between us," he wrote. "Whatever I thought, it seemed as though I was saying it to you or rather that you were thinking it with me. . . . I had the feeling of two consciousnesses melted into one."[27] Olga was jealous.[28] The Mancys were also being possessive: they wanted him to work in their flat and have lunch there.[29] Everything was reported to De Beauvoir in detail, with extensive quotations from conversations; though the letters were not intended as rehearsals for writing fiction, Sartre was training himself to select the most revealing phrases from what people said. For De Beauvoir, though she would have preferred not to share him with so many people, there was consolation both in reading the letters and in knowing that he needed to share the experiences with her.

THE Lycée Pasteur was a huge, red-brick building, which reminded Sartre's mother of the palace at Versailles. From Montparnasse he would be able to get there in twenty-seven minutes on the bus. When De Beauvoir came back from Alsace they moved into the Hôtel Mistral in the Rue Cels, between the Montparnasse cemetery and the Avenue du Maine, but he took a room on the floor above hers. "So we had all the advantages of sharing our lives, but none of the inconveniences."[30]

(9)

Breakthrough

IF Sartre had forgotten during the summer vacation how rapidly life was changing for him, Paris soon reminded him. He had been alive for thirty-two years without achieving any conspicuous success, but he could not fail to realize that he was on the threshold of fame. "I felt suddenly inundated with a formidable and profound youthfulness. I was happy and I found my life beautiful. Not that it had anything in it of 'the life of a great man,' but it was *my* life."[1] He was not playing a role, and he was no longer straining to keep pace with a flamboyantly passionate young girl.

Settling in Paris did not change his attitude to home or to possessions. He was not interested in owning or even renting a flat with furniture, a library, and ornaments in it. "I would always be ill at ease in a flat, quickly transforming it into a stable. And I have never kept anything for as long as ten years except a pipe and a pen." He would buy a new suit once a year and wear it all the time. Other possessions, including books, would sooner or later be lost, damaged, or given away.[2] He was always rather embarrassed by presents, feeling there ought to be some better way of accepting them, but he enjoyed giving to Wanda: though she never expressed thanks, the object visibly became precious to her—he could enjoy possessiveness vicariously.[3] In the same way he could enjoy other people's homes; he especially liked being in Mme. Morel's Rue Vavin flat and in Toulouse's at Montmartre—he enjoyed their domestic pride.[4] But he liked to write in cafés and claimed that no one would suffer less if private property were abolished.[5]

INSTEAD of starting another novel he settled down to a book on phenomenological psychology, intending to call it "La Psyché," but the only fragment that was later published—in December 1939—was then titled *Esquisse d'une théorie des émotions* (*Sketch for a Theory of the Emotions*). Taking an oddly narrow view of emotion, he equates it with responding unrealistically to external pressures. All emotions, Sartre maintains, are reducible to "the creation of a magical world, the use of our bodies as instruments of incantation." By magic he means self-delusion: unable to rearrange circumstances as we'd like to, we distort our apprehension of them; incantation distracts us into believing that what we desire is within reach.

Though masturbation is never mentioned, it seems to be his model for the way in which emotion pressures the imagination. He describes the object as if it were an absent lover: the image that is formed by the *acte magique* of imagination gives us the illusion of totally possessing something that, in reality, would yield itself only gradually to perception and then seldom in accordance with the perceiver's desires. If we succumb to the illusion, we are in a vortex that sucks us into crediting the imagination with a power it does not possess to change external reality; the image always produces confusion between desire and knowledge: "It may happen that we try vainly by our treatment of the object to give birth within ourselves to the belief that it really exists: we can temporarily camouflage but we cannot destroy the immediate awareness of its nothingness."

This is cautionary writing, addressed more to himself than to the reader, and in his distrust of the image we find the roots of Sartre's lifelong hostility toward *l'imaginaire*. Later he will refuse to discriminate between escapist writers and those who exercise self-discipline in the use of the imagination (Shakespeare and Stendhal, for instance). He will want the whole of literature to stand condemned, and he is already firing a broadside at all emotion: we fall back on emotion when we feel incapable of taking effective action. Fear works "to negate something in the external world by means of magical behavior"; at worst we faint, blotting out all awareness. He describes joy as "characterized by a certain impatience." We disport ourselves as if the object of our desires is already within reach. A man, told that a woman loves him, may start dancing and singing, "forgetting the judicious and energetic exertions that will be requisite if he is to deserve this love and develop it, to earn it through innumerable details (smiles, little attentions, and so on)." This quaint account of a lover's obligations is not what we would have expected from the author of *La Nausée*. In the characterization of Anny, who laughs unpredictably, gives peremptory orders and capricious answers, putting herself totally at the disposal of her moods, Sartre had seemed to be championing an engagingly feminine assertion of the vitality Roquentin would always lack. But the *Esquisse* might have been written by a Roquentin who had never met her: nothing in it accounts either for the emotionality that animates her or for the equally irrational emotionality that prompted Sartre both in his reactions to Toulouse or Olga and in his peremptory dismissal of emotion. His fastidious distaste for it is inseparable from a distaste for the body, which he does not want to represent as something passive, the involuntary victim of invasion by adrenaline. It is this extremist antideterminism which, joining forces with Sartre's unacknowledged emotionality, makes him insist that the nausea is not inside Roquentin: when he sees it on the walls of the café, on the suspenders of the men, he is inside it. The *Esquisse* reminds us of this when Sartre argues that to see an object as horrible is to achieve a passage to the infinite. "The horribleness is now in the object, in the heart of it. It is its emotive texture. It constitutes it. So, while the emotion lasts, an irresistible and definitive quality of the thing emerges. . . . Horribleness . . . is a revelation of the meaning of the world."[6] As philosophy this is nonsense; as a writer's credo it is useful. It leads to the success of the chestnut tree episode.

At the end of October 1937 the Spanish government retreated to Barcelona, and at the end of November, Franco began his naval blockade of the Spanish coast. Though newspapers carried photographs of corpses heaped on pavements after air raids on Madrid, Barcelona, Valencia, and Lerida, France and England nervously continued their nonintervention, while Hitler and Mussolini went on helping Franco. When Fernando Gérassi arrived on leave in Paris, he did not exempt Sartre or De Beauvoir from his scathing contempt: "Salauds de Français."[7]

In December, Italy withdrew from the League of Nations, and war had come to seem unavoidable by the time Sartre and De Beauvoir left to spend their Christmas vacation in the Mégève with Bost, who was expecting to be called up and to be killed at the front. In between skiing lessons Sartre and De Beauvoir read Pepys and Swift in translation.[8]

WHEN Sartre gave up "Le Psyché" after working at it for three months and writing four hundred pages, it was largely because it had been an obstacle to writing fiction. De Beauvoir was convinced that this was where his main talent lay. "Yes, you can execute little philosophical arabesques, but you'll never be a philosopher."[9] He now channeled his energy into his book *Le Mur,* which consisted of four short stories and one long one. "L'Enfance d'un chef" is more like a novel than any of his other stories, but implicitly it contradicts *La Nausée* by exposing causal connections between childhood events and adult personality in the imaginary biography of a hypothetical counterself influenced by the extremists of the right, by anti-Semitism, by surrealism, and by psychoanalysis, though the events of 1924–25, when Sartre was twenty, are confused (as Michel Rybalka points out) with those of 1935–38.[10] Sartre had once taken pleasure in his stepfather's regret that Poulou would never grow into a captain of industry or a businessman with a large staff. Like a character actor specializing in roles remote from his own personality, Sartre moved from his affectionate empathizing (in "Intimité") with two almost mindless girls to a more studied identification with a male who is physically dissimilar—above average height—and who is learning to exert his authority sadistically. As Michel Contat discovered, one of the models for Lucien Fleurier was a literary young man Sartre had known in about 1924. He "stuffed himself with pub poetry when it was fashionable, showed off a mistress, then, when his father died, leaving him the family factory, resumed the strait and narrow path." He told Sartre: "It's better to do what everybody does than to be like nobody."[11] The story intertwines strands from Sartre's past with strands of experience that might lead to the assumption of boss status in business or industry.

He had intended to visit Algeria with De Beauvoir in the spring, but just before the end of term she had a relapse, and when she recovered, there was time only for a short vacation in the Basque country. At Bozouls near Rodez she noticed that much of his hair was falling out. For him this was a "symbolical disaster." He had not been thinking about aging or the approach of death, but now, at thirty-two, he suddenly felt "as old as the world." He went on massaging his scalp vigorously in front of mirrors, afraid of premature baldness and of the aging process. At the age of twenty-two he had noted a saying by the early nineteenth-century Swiss writer Rodolphe Töpffer: "He who has not achieved fame by the age of 28 must give up the idea of glory." At twenty-two this had excited him, but at twenty-eight he was still unknown and unpublished. On their way back to Paris they stopped at Saintes and La Rochelle, where they walked around the harbor fortifications discussing "L'Enfance d'un chef." She wanted him to carry the story further, but his own instinct, which he followed, was to break off at Lucien's emergence into manhood.[12]

From March 21, 1938, *La Nausée* had been on sale in the bookstores,[13] and the reviews began to appear in May. In *Vendredi*, A. M. Petitjean saluted a novel "in which an enormous talent bursts out, in which everything evinces one of our greatest novelists."[14] Paul Nizan reviewed the book in *Ce Soir:* "M. Sartre could have been a French Kafka by virtue of his gift for expressing the horrors of certain intellectual situations, were it not that his thinking . . . is entirely foreign to moral problems. . . . There is no doubt that in M. Sartre we possess a philosophical novelist of the first order."[15] In the *Journal-Echo de Paris* Edmond Jaloux predicted that the novel "might well make a durable mark on the literary evolution of our epoch,"[16] and a longer review by Jaloux in *Les Nouvelles Littéraires* helped to establish Sartre's reputation: "It seems to me that no book has poured out for its reader such a quantity of disgust. . . . We get the impression of witnessing a visionary's walks through a world that is being created: everything is gluey, viscous, unshaped."[17] The twenty-five-year-old Albert Camus, writing in the *Alger Républicain*, declared: "Infinite talent is revealed by a flexibility natural enough to hold its own at the extremities of conscious thought and by a doleful lucidity. That is enough to make us love *La Nausée* as the first declaration of a singular and vigorous mind. We wait with impatience for future works and lessons from it."[18] The novel was in the running to win the prestigious Prix Interallié, while Sartre and De Beauvoir were excited at the prospect of being rich enough to fly from Paris to London.[19] The Interallié was finally awarded to Nizan for his novel *La Conspiration*, in which the name Sartre is given to a policeman. Reviewing it, Sartre asked: "Can a communist write a novel?" and answered: "I am not convinced that he can: he does not have the right to make himself the accomplice of his characters."[20]

"Le Mur" had appeared in the July 1937 issue of the *Nouvelle Revue Française*, which had begun to publish Sartre's critical work in February 1938, starting with a review of *Sartoris* which helped to establish Faulkner's reputation in France. "Here actions (putting on boots, climbing stairs, jumping on a horse) are not intended to characterize but to conceal. . . . From time to time, laconically, he reveals a consciousness. But it is like a conjuror who displays the box when it is empty."[21]

At the same time Sartre was planning his next novel, and in July, after De Beauvoir had left for a preliminary vacation in the Alps before the vacation they were to share in Morocco, he wrote to tell her: "I have all at once found the subject of my novel, its proportions and its title. Just as you wished: the subject is freedom." The title was to be "Lucifer." The book was to be in two parts called "La Révolte" and "Le Serment" ("The Oath").[22] The idea would grow into *Les Chemins de la liberté*.

Though unwilling to risk embroiling himself in anything that might come to resemble "l'affaire Olga,"[23] he began to flirt with an Atelier drama student, whose aunt, intending to reduce the girl's vulnerability, had increased it by warning her that he was said to be irresistible. Their first kiss was violent. She "sucked my tongue with the strength of an electric suction fan, so that it still hurts, and glued herself to me sinuously with her whole body. She seems very pleased with the way things are developing."[24] She would have been less pleased if she had known De Beauvoir was receiving detailed bulletins, with the reassurance "No vows are being exchanged."[25] He told the girl that he didn't know what to do with her: "You've arrived in my life like a dog on a putting green; I wanted to take you without having the least *need* of you, which is much more flattering. I've got three days to give you: let's take them and try to make the most of them."[26] She brought him back in contact with Maurice Merleau-Ponty, whom he had not seen since leaving the ENS. Merleau-Ponty, who was in love with the girl, called Sartre a *salaud*. Sartre's response was that he too loved her but, because of De Beauvoir and Wanda, had no space for her in his life.[27] They spent a night in bed together without making love but without going to sleep either. She was "Provençale as the Devil, full of odors and curiously hairy, with a little black fur at the small of the back, and a body that's quite white, whiter than mine. At first I was a bit surprised, almost disgusted by this rather violent sensuality and these legs which prick like an unshaven chin. . . . Her thighs are shaped like a drop of water, wider at the bottom than the top. . . . Very beautiful legs, a muscular stomach, absolutely flat, not the least shadow of a breast." In the morning she told him that she was jealous of De Beauvoir but not of Wanda. Sartre's bulletin ended with the assurance "I am extricating myself from all these storms to remain united with you."[28]

After two nights with the girl he reported that she had begun to love him passionately and that he was uncertain whether he had taken her virginity. "In any case that appeared to be a profoundly difficult and disagreeable job. You understand that I didn't sleep with her because you'd forbidden me to do that, saying: 'Don't get yourself into trouble.'" The jealous Merleau-Ponty now reprimanded Sartre for not sleeping with her, but she was saying that she loved him too much. One night she gave him "more than a very intimate kiss," explaining that normally the male sex organ horrified her but not his.[29] He didn't mind talking to her in the second person singular, he told De Beauvoir, because the girl was "Provençale and it goes well with her prunelike looks."[30] During their last night together he did take her virginity. She told him he wasn't hurting her but, a moment later, asked him to withdraw.[31]

De Beauvoir was not his only confidante. Meeting Mme. Morel at eleven on Saturday evening, he entertained her with an account of what had just gone on between him and another girl, an actress he had taken out to dinner at the Bouteille d'Or. She had wanted him to caress her arm while eating his cassoulet. Afterward she invited him to rub her stomach and her bosom. He could render her this service, he said, only between ten-thirty and eleven. Though she did not want to make love, she lay down on a divan, pulling him down on top of her. "Hug me. I want to feel very small, very small, very small." He soon got bored and said so, but they kissed before parting, and despite his verbal betrayal, they became lovers the next day. "Of all those who have honored me in recent months with their love, none has been so agreeable physically nor so touching in transports of passion."[32] But he went on seeing the drama student and wrote to tell De Beauvoir: "Only you can give me the impression of living in a new present, oh charmer of my heart and my eyes, bulwark of my life, my consciousness, my reason."[33]

His success with both girls was making him more demanding in his relationship with Wanda. Though he belittled her as having "the mental faculties of a dragonfly," he was no longer content with kissing her on the mouth and being halfheartedly reprimanded. She had a horror, she said, of kissing without making contact. Sitting on her sister's unmade bed in the room the girls shared in the Rue Delambre, she explained that she didn't know what sensuality was. This was a matter of great regret to her because it meant she would never have a complete relationship with him and never be an artist; without sensuality one could not hope to succeed in the arts. He comforted her and eventually kissed her, holding her down on the bed and climbing on top. She disengaged herself, and, angrily, he hurried away but not quickly enough; he could hear her vomiting in the lavatory. She had been drinking white rum and sherry.

One evening at a café near the Palais-Royal, where he had often taken Olga, he delivered an ultimatum to Wanda: the relationship would end unless they became lovers. She immediately promised to do everything he wanted but explained that she took no great physical pleasure in anything but contact and certain kisses, with him and with one other man.[34] When he and De Beauvoir left for Morocco, her virginity was still intact.

They had booked third-class tickets from Marseille to Casablanca, but they were switched to a second-class cabin by a friend who worked for the shipping company. From the depressing slums of Casablanca they went on to Bous-bir, where they met a heavily tattooed Arab woman who took them to her room, removed her flowing robes, rippled her stomach muscles, and smoked a cigarette through her vagina.[35] In

Fez they lost their way in the back streets and accepted help from a young man just as the sun was setting. When an old Moslem shouted a warning to them, their guide took to his heels.[36] They quickly retreated as the first lamps were being lit and chains were being secured to close the narrow streets on either side of them.[37]

Determined to sample the native food, they sat on the floor of a restaurant and used their fingers to eat pastilla, chicken with lemon, mechoui, couscous, and the marrow of gazelles' horns. Afterward Sartre was ill for two days.

In Meknes, where they were the only Europeans, Sartre smoked kief in a Moorish café. In Marrakech they watched snake charmers and sword swallowers, and they went for a three-day walking tour in the Atlas Mountains, sleeping in rest huts below the Berber villages and bargaining with peasants for unleavened loaves. Sartre entertained her with stories he improvised about a sergeant who hated flies and an Arab who could piss upward.

Traveling to the south by long-distance bus, they saw evidence of drought and famine. Starving villagers had tried to migrate northward, only to find the authorities had blocked the roads. In Ouarzazate the baggy-trousered hotel proprietor, coughing incessantly, described the typhus epidemic that had ravaged the country. Every day he distributed free boiled rice to local children. Some were blind or one-eyed; many were deformed. They squatted in the courtyard, dipping rhythmically with their hands into the large bowls—the point of the rhythm being that all should get an equal share.[38]

When Sartre and De Beauvoir arrived back in Marseille, Europe appeared to be on the brink of war. She decided to leave, as planned, for a walking tour of the Alps with Olga, but only after he had promised to wire her *poste restante* if the situation deteriorated. And at Gap, on September 25, she found a telegram telling her to come immediately. Hitler had demanded the surrender of Prague within six days. While she was one of the many who argued that any injustice was preferable to war, Sartre, who could have been called up at any moment, questioned the wisdom of appeasing Hitler. Restless, they went to the cinema a great deal and read each edition of the newspapers,[39] until on September 29, at Munich, Daladier and Chamberlain signed a pact with Hitler and Mussolini: Germany was to have the Sudetenland, but Czechoslovakia's remaining frontiers were to be kept intact.

Far from being unable to work, Sartre started on his novel and resumed "La Psyché." He would have preferred to express all his ideas through fiction, he told an interviewer, but "there are things which are too technical, demanding a purely philosophical vocabulary. So I see myself obliged, so to speak, to duplicate each novel with an essay."[40] He was also consolidating and formulating his ideas about the novel in critical essays and reviews, such as the one about François Mauriac, which begins by asking how the novel can create a world that stands up when its only material is words—*signifiés*. Saussure had used the world *signifié* in a different sense, referring to the meaning of the word, as opposed to its form, the *signifiant*. "How does it happen that Stavrogin comes to life? I don't imagine Stavrogin, I wait for him. I wait for his actions, for the end of his adventures. This opaque matter which I stir when I read *The Possessed* is my own expectation. It is my time."[41] Sartre was reminding both his readers and himself of what he had learned from reading and writing fiction—that movement in a novel is the movement of the reader's eye over motionless words.

> For the duration of my impatience and ignorance to be trapped, shaped and given back to me as the flesh of these invented figures [the novelist must know how to produce] a time similar to mine, in which the future is not formed. I must not be allowed to suspect that the future actions of the characters have been fixed in advance by heredity, social pressures or any other force. Psychological analysis is fatal; the novelist must present only emotions and unpredictable actions. He has no right to judge his characters except from the viewpoint of other characters. Mauriac's mistake is to instruct the reader instead of arousing his impatience.[42]

Sartre could channel most of his didactic impulses into his nonfiction, though his fiction was programmatic. He thought of it as a three-phase enterprise and went on to the end of his life talking about "*La Nausée*, the stories, the novels."[43] The object of *La Nausée* had been the same when the book had been conceived as a work of nonfiction: to expose the stuff of existence. The stories displayed the handling of that stuff by various individuals, who all had less affinity to Sartre than Roquentin had, while the novel was a more ambitious project. Thomas Mann had shown in *Buddenbrooks* that a huge fresco could be filled with contrasting characters, and this made Sartre think initially of a vast space with no predetermination in the narrative that would fill it.[44] He was now regarding himself as primarily a novelist. His intention was that the new novel should be a "continuation" of *La Nausée*. Roquentin would discover his liberty only on losing it—through enlistment—and on being demobilized he would be ripe for the pleasure of the *acte gratuit*, in line with Gide's Lafcadio in *Les Caves du Vatican* and the surrealists. He would rape and murder a woman. Nevertheless it was Sartre's aim, he said, to counterbalance the pessimism of *La Nausée:* "You will see existence rehabilitated, and my hero will act, will taste what action is like."[45]

AFTER catching Dullin's attention accidentally at an audition when she was reading cues for a friend, Olga discovered that she had talent as an actress, and she began taking lessons in mime from Jean-Louis Barrault. Saint-Germain-des-Prés was one of her haunts, and it was probably she who got Sartre and De Beauvoir into the habit of patronizing the Café Flore, which had served as the headquarters of the right-wing Action Française at the beginning of the century. Sartre could concentrate better in a café than at home. "It's a milieu of indifference, where other people exist without troubling about me while I don't worry about them. Anonymous drinkers who argue noisily at the next table disturb me less than a wife and children who would walk about on tiptoe so as not to disturb me." If a pretty girl came into the café, he'd watch her sit down and go on working: "She's passed like a movement of consciousness, no more."[46] By the time Sartre, De Beauvoir, and Olga formed the habit of spending their evenings at the Flore, it had become a rendezvous for film people, but they sometimes returned to the Dôme, where the clientele was slightly shabbier.[47]

In February 1939 *Le Mur* was published. Sartre had discarded "Dépaysement," though Paulhan liked it, but in addition to the title story the volume contained "La Chambre," "Intimité," "Erostrate," and "L'Enfance d'un chef." Sartre had been wondering whether to explain in a preface that he took no pleasure in degradation and that the book had its place in a scheme. While *La Nausée* defined existence, each of the five stories enacted a misguided attempt at escape.[48] No preface was included, but in the 1967 edition he explained what he'd had in mind. In "Le Mur" Pablo tries unsuccessfully to imagine his own existence after death. In "La Chambre" Eve tries unsuccessfully to penetrate her husband's madness. In "Erostrate" Paul Hilbert (an antitype of Roquentin and Sartre's most fanatical antihumanist) tries to reject the human condition by means of a monstrous *acte gratuit.* In "Intimité" Lola tries to throw a smoke screen between herself and the gaze she fixes on herself. Lucien Fleurier almost escapes from existence into contemplation of his rights, but the attempt fails because the rights do not exist. Each of the five escape routes is blocked by a wall: "to run away from existence is still to exist."[49] The resultant force of the stories might be negative, but Sartre intended to be positive in the fiction that would follow.

He sent a copy to his stepfather, who returned it with a note of the
oint at which he had stopped reading. Reviews were mixed. The play-
right Gabriel Marcel found the stories "distinctly superior to *La
ausée.*" André Rousseaux wrote an unfriendly review in *Le Figaro,* and
i *Le Temps* André Thérive condemned "a crudity so relentless that it
nacks of the obsessive."[50] One of the most complimentary reviews
ame from Camus in *Alger Républicain:* "A great writer always brings
·ith him his world and his sermon. That of M. Sartre wins converts for
ihilism but also for lucidity."[51]

Since returning from Germany four years earlier Sartre had read
Ieidegger's *Was Ist Metaphysik?* in Corbin's new French translation.
Jor was it coincidence that Corbin translated it at this time: there was
ow a potential public for it. It was not only that Heidegger's notion of
he "pathetic" made an impact, with his use of words such as Death,
)estiny, and Nothing; many readers needed tools for understanding
istory and destiny. Writing after the 1914–18 war—a period which
rought despair to those who had taken it for granted that it was "natu-
al" to be German—he advocated voluntary assumption of one's period.

.T this, the most creative phase of Sartre's development, reading and
·riting were almost inseparable activities. Just as consciousness (in his
iew of it) spontaneously reached out to passive objects, his creativity
eached out to books. Hemingway and Heidegger had both been wait-
ig patiently for his mind to alight on them, to draw them into his
·volving system. He did not at first talk about Heidegger to De Beau-
oir, but during the Easter vacation, while they were traveling through
·rovence, going by train and bus from one village to the next, they
ound themselves sitting on a stone bench at Sisteron, and here he told
.er about Heidegger's description of man as a "creature of distances,"
nd about the way that the world revealed itself to "maladjusted in-
truments."[52] The phrase "creature of distances" seemed to confirm the
dea of a fissure in the heart of consciousness. A man would not be what
.e is if there were no space between what he is and his awareness of it.

Though Sartre still took intense pleasure in De Beauvoir's compan-
onship and still benefited from having her as his resident critic, his suc-
ess was changing the quality of his partnership with her. At first they
.ad both been beginners, outsiders planning a raid on the citadel.
·here were no limits to their generosity in helping each other, but there
·ere limits to their intimacy, even as lovers. They continued through-
·ut their lives to address each other in the second person plural, and as
uccess made him busier, he made less effort to keep her in touch with

everything he was reading, writing, thinking, doing. Apprehensive that he was not giving her fulfillment as a woman, he found it easier to channel this anxiety into fiction than to keep the promise he had made to discuss everything with her openly. He was confused about his feelings toward Olga and uncertain whether De Beauvoir might be ambivalent about having a baby, even if she had assured him she did not want one.

To Mme. Morel it was by no means out of the question that they should have a child. "She is very insistent," wrote Sartre in July 1938, "that I give you a baby. 'To see what he'd be like,' she said. She will bring him up."[53] Here were two dangerous areas of ambivalence that he could neither afford to explore in reality nor afford not to explore in fiction. In *L'Age de raison* Mathieu and Marcelle have made the same pledge Sartre and De Beauvoir had made to discuss everything frankly. When Mathieu had committed himself to Marcelle, he had permanently renounced all thoughts of solitude—the cool thoughts shy and shadowy that sometimes slipped into him with the furtive vivacity of fish. He could only love Marcelle openly: she *was* his openness, his companion, his witness, his adviser, his judge."[54] In *L'Invitée* De Beauvoir makes her heroine feel as if nothing that happens to her is real until she has told her lover about it. "When he gives the moments back to her they are clearer, more polished, more complete." Each of them enjoyed giving moments back to the other, and though De Beauvoir was upset by Sartre's infidelities, she was glad to know he could not enjoy them fully without confiding in her. How much she gave back was up to her, usually she seems to have been generous. In *L'Invitée*, Françoise, De Beauvoir's alter ego, becomes so jealous of Xavière, the fictional Olga, that the action culminates in murder, but the fiction functioned as a safety valve, and till the end of her life De Beauvoir spoke of Olga as if the girl had been more her friend than Sartre's.[55]

Sartre, like Mathieu, was liable to feel "impregnated with humble gratitude"[56] when a friend held back from judging him, and Marcelle is doubly threatening because she could produce a child, who would have another pair of judging eyes. Like Sartre, Mathieu feels uneasy in the presence of children. "He had the sense of being engulfed by the child's eyes. 'Children are greedy creatures,' he thought, 'all their senses are mouths.' Pablo's expression wasn't human yet, but this was already more than life. It wasn't long since the child had come out of a stomach, and it looked like it: he was there, unsettled, quite small, he still had the velvety unwholesomeness of something vomited."[57] The nausea in the consciousness of the observer is fear of being observed. It is essential to prevent Marcelle's baby from being born. "There was the whole of a

ittle being, thoughtful and weasel-faced, devious and glum, with a
white skin, big ears and moles, with a handful of distinguishing features
you enter in passports, a little fellow who would never run through the
streets with one foot on the curb and one in the gutter . . ."[58] The curious mixture of affection and disgust is symptomatic. It is partly disgust
with life, though Mathieu also enjoys it, but marriage is a sacrifice of
freedom, so the fetus is sometimes a tumor and sometimes an inflammation, as if Marcelle had been stung at the bottom of her stomach.[59]

There was probably no autobiographical basis for the pregnancy,
and the unflattering portrayal may have been part of the design to dis-
ance Marcelle from De Beauvoir, but Sartre, addressing her through
fiction, was apparently aiming to discourage any lingering inclination
toward maternity. He also shared Mathieu's fear that even without
marrying he had been trapped into a relationship no better than a
bourgeois marriage. The pact of openness, he tells himself, works
mainly in her favor: "He especially liked talking about himself, dis-
playing his little crises of conscience, his moral scruples."[60] She intensely enjoys listening to all this, but he secretly fears that the
arrangement is working to her disadvantage, though he tells himself not
to worry about her. If anything were troubling her, she would tell him.
But would she?

Sartre was obviously uneasy about the growing imbalance in his relationship with De Beauvoir. Her love for him was so strong and so durable that there were no limits to her tolerance. He learned that he could
afford to be less scrupulous about keeping the pact and less considerate
in his behavior. This tended to make the relationship less exciting for
him. She had not learned what Proust could have taught her about
love: that it cannot survive without the pain of anxiety and the need to
conquer new territory. We love only what we do not entirely possess. De
Beauvoir made it obvious to Sartre that he entirely possessed her. His
need for her would continue throughout his life, but he needed her
more as a mirror than as a lover, and if she now started to go on vacations without him, it was because his craving for her physical presence
was dwindling. He had never felt the same urge as she did to escape
into the country at every opportunity, and he accompanied her neither
on her spring walking tour in the Morvan area nor on her June climbing trip in the Jura. Not that their relationship was harmed by disagreement about appeasement. It was already known that the Nazis were
killing Jews in concentration camps, but she still maintained that war
should be avoided at all costs: even if France was in danger of being engulfed like Austria, it would be absurd to condemn a million Frenchmen to dying. No, said Sartre, appeasement was making everyone into

accomplices of Hitler. War would be no worse than Nazi occupation o.
France. "I don't want Nizan's eyes to be gouged out with a coffee
spoon."[61]

When Colette Audry's Communist friends grumbled at her for wasting time with Sartre and De Beauvoir, she usually answered brightly
"I'm getting the man of tomorrow ready."[62] They had retained some of
their unrealistic youthful optimism about molding the cultural future
while their friends, emulating their fluctuating enthusiasms, helped
them to believe they were setting trends. Having been so largely deprived of family life during childhood, Sartre would need, throughout
the rest of his life, to be surrounded by an ersatz "family" of friends.
Invariably it was younger people who were recruited, with Sartre and
De Beauvoir in the quasi-parental roles, though he had more say than
she did over who was enlisted and who was expelled. "It's exhausting,"
complained Bost, "having to hold your opinions at the same moment as
you do."[63] Awareness of being imitated encouraged Sartre to change
positions even faster than he might otherwise have done. But if war
came, everything would change.

In May 1939 he took part in the international antifascist conference.
One of the writers he met there was Ilya Ehrenburg, who had returned
to the USSR and become more Stalinist since his days of frequenting
Left Bank cafés. In March the German army had occupied Czechoslovakia, Daladier had been empowered by the Assembly to accelerate
rearmament, Madrid had surrendered to Franco, and Poland had received a joint pledge of support from Britain and France. Sartre and De
Beauvoir had hoped to visit the USSR in the summer, but they decided
instead on a vacation in Portugal if the peace held. But when an invitation came from Mme. Morel to stay at her villa in Juan-les-Pins, they
decided to venture no farther. With her knapsack on her back De
Beauvoir set off alone on July 15 to hike southward; she would meet
Sartre in Marseille.

With the Wanda relationship neither consummated nor abandoned,
he was beginning a passionate relationship with a Polish girl, Bianca
Bienenfeld, another attractive friend of De Beauvoir's. She wrote to
him in July, enclosing her first letter in one De Beauvoir was writing to
him; in his reply he declared his love and promised to show her part of
his unfinished novel.[64] He wanted to share his future with her, he said:
"*Our* future is your future, there's no difference." De Beauvoir, he wrote,
lived "in a world where you are ubiquitous at the same time" and loved
Bianca more than she realized.[65] Bianca had suggested that she and
Sartre should tell each other everything, immediately, and he enthusiastically accepted the proposal. He loved her and thought about her all

the time.[66] Writing to her from Saint-Sauveur, where he was staying with his mother, he described his boredom. Until lunchtime he wandered from café to café. "I drink black coffees, but with dead flies floating in them, and I write my novel."[67] Having lost his suitcase on the way, he had nothing to read, and time seemed to pass very slowly. His mother couldn't enjoy his company in the presence of her husband but wanted Sartre to be there because Mancy wanted him to be there.[68] Dutifully he helped Mancy wash the car, but it had been stupid to think he'd be able to concentrate on writing.[69]

Wanda had agreed to go on vacation with him before he left for Marseille, and he took her to Avignon and then to Aigues-Mortes. Short of money, he had calculated carefully how much he could spend, but train fares were higher than he'd realized, and he had to balance his budget by economizing drastically. Instead of going to restaurants, they lived on fruit and sandwiches, sharing a bedroom to save money. In the evening she took forty-five minutes to get herself ready for bed, insisting on being alone in the bedroom all this while. At both Avignon and Aigues-Mortes they were staying at cheap hotels that closed at eleven, so he was reduced to taking long walks around the corridor. At Aigues-Mortes he aroused the suspicion of the night porter, who followed him, calling out: "Who's there?" He locked himself into the lavatory and read Nietzsche. But in the morning Wanda finally surrendered her virginity. Afterward she said she hated him and felt totally exhausted. All these details were reported to De Beauvoir in the bulletin he wrote later the same day.[70] But the relationship with Wanda developed pleasantly. They made love morning and evening. She seemed to enjoy it greatly but lay supine for fifteen minutes afterward, and, to feel fully alive, they both needed to quarrel violently as a buildup to reconciliation.[71]

Knowing that he concealed nothing from De Beauvoir, Wanda entreated him to make an exception of what she had told him about Olga. He gave his promise with no intention of keeping it. "You will benefit," he told De Beauvoir, "and so will I. I get the impression she's out to destroy the 'friendship' I have for you bit by bit. It's quite amusing."[72] At the same time Wanda was trying to cure him of his unhealthy indulgence in coffee and croissants. She would get up early and go out, naked under her overcoat, to buy fruit from the market, but after breakfast she would settle back to sleep. At about eleven he would furtively get up, wash, enjoy coffee and croissants in a café before calling at the post office to collect the letter from De Beauvoir that was usually waiting.[73] After reading her letters he tore up even the ones she wanted him to keep, but he took the risk of writing to her in the bedroom, and one day Wanda came in before he had finished. "You know my feelings," he wrote, "but I daren't write them down because it's possible to read up-side down."[74]

Elation at his literary articulacy (with De Beauvoir as his audience) was in competition with triumph as a seducer (with Bianca and Wanda as victims). Though he had a strong need, now as later, to be on intimate terms with women, he did not much enjoy making love. "I was more a masturbator of women than a copulator. . . . For me what mattered most in a sexual relationship was embracing, caressing, moving my lips over a body . . . I came erect quickly, easily; I made love often, but without very much pleasure. Just a little pleasure at the end, but fairly second-rate. I preferred being in contact with the whole body, caressing the body, in short being active with my hands, with my legs, touching the other person."[75] Even in bed freedom had to be experienced actively; an erection felt too much like something that happened to him. The indifference to lovemaking was partly incredulity that a woman could be enjoying his body. During his first important affair, the one with Toulouse, he was repeatedly told that he was ugly, and it seemed to him that during the act of love the woman's beauty was being enjoyed by both lovers. "Reciprocity was the thing I felt least; the fact that the other person could equally take pleasure in feeling my body."[76]

Throughout his life he was enormously reluctant to relax, to let go. Though he had a strong constitution, he felt at ease with his body only when it was in action, doing something for him. What remained from his childhood was not only his fantasy of himself as a man of action but the illusion of having—so long as he was doing something—a body quite different from the one he would have seen in the mirror. "The truth is that I saw myself as if I were the same size as anyone else."[77] He habituated himself to speaking loudly, addressing people taller than he was. "My imaginary body was the body of a strong military captain, of a Pardaillon in fact, that is to say a cloak and dagger hero. . . . And I've never stopped thinking that: it's been some sort of compensation for my shortness . . . which I've felt only abstractly."[78] The imaginary body, abstract at first, became more real: "I imputed greater value to the activity I felt in my hands, more strength, more power to activity in my body. If I pushed at a rock, my action was more violent and the rock heavier in the imaginary dimension than in reality."[79]

HE stayed with Bianca in La Clusaz before joining De Beauvoir in Marseille, where they took a room in a hotel overlooking the old harbor. In the evening, eating at a restaurant by the sea, they gave money to beggars without interrupting their conversation. In the morning, after breakfast, they read newspapers and wrote letters in the Café Riche, where they saw the Nizans, who were due to sail that evening with their children to Corsica. After the parents had bought their children a rubber boat from one of the big shops, they all ate a bouillabaisse together in a small restaurant by the harbor. According to Nizan, the tripartite agreement was being ratified, and Germany would soon be on her knees.

Afterward, walking along the quay with the children, they met Bost, who was now a second-class infantryman on leave after being stationed in the Ardennes. He'd been in Marseille since the morning, sitting in a brasserie, confident he would spot them sooner or later. They all had a drink at the Cintra before the Nizans left.[80] Sartre and De Beauvoir did not know they would never see Nizan again.

They went with Bost to Martigues, where they ate another bouillabaisse while rain pattered against the canopy above their heads. Watching gaily painted boats bobbing up and down, they discussed the future. The Germans were moving into Danzig, and Sartre would soon be called up. Was it better to return from the front blinded or limbless? When the rain stopped they went for a walk.[81] De Beauvoir was never to forget how Sartre looked, unable to relax, talking to Bost while sitting uncomfortably on blocks of stone with sharp ridges.[82]

They were waiting for news from Mme. Morel, who was coming from Cavallo. When she arrived she took Sartre and De Beauvoir to stay at the villa, which had been built by her father. Sartre wrote in the mornings, while De Beauvoir read. In the middle of the day they would go down to the sea, where he gave her swimming lessons. Though he was a good swimmer, he could not help believing that one day he would be dragged down by a sea monster with twenty-four legs and huge crablike pincers. Sometimes he would strike out for the shore in a panic.

After reading in the newspapers that the Supreme Soviet was about to make a nonaggression pact with Nazi Germany, Sartre and De Beauvoir, less certain than ever of the future and wanting a few days together, made an excursion into the Pyrenees. In the train from Juan-les-Pins to Carcassonne soldiers recalled from leave appropriated the reserved seats. "We're the ones who're going to get killed first."[83] At Foix, eating cassoulet and foie gras in a hotel, Sartre said that in the fourth volume of his novel, after hearing about the Nazi-Soviet pact, the Gérassi character would resign from the party and ask Mathieu for help, counterbalancing what happens in Volume I when he offers help.

In Paris, with the theaters, many shops, and many restaurants closed for the August vacation, the contrast between the *quartiers* had disappeared. "There was nothing but a totality which was Paris. A totality which for me belonged to the past." Making telephone calls, wandering through the streets, going to the cinema, Sartre found "there was this unpleasant feeling which is hope."[84] On August 31, the day before the Nazi army marched into Poland, he was still hoping: "With the state of mind the German people are in, it's impossible that Hitler's intending to start a war. It's a bluff."[85]

On the day Poland was invaded De Beauvoir traveled with Sartre to Passy and waited in the café by the viaduct while he visited the Mancys, who had been living in the Avenue de Lamballe since 1933. Learning that mobilization would start the next day, they went back to search for his kit bag and his army boots in the cellar of the hotel and then took a taxi to the assembly center, where he was told to report in Nancy the next day. At the Café Flore a tough-looking woman was quietly weeping, but most people seemed cheerful.[86]

Early the next morning, sitting with De Beauvoir outside a café in the deserted Gare de l'Est, waiting for the 7:50 train to Nancy, he did his best to convince her that as a meteorologist he would be in no danger.[87]

In the train he tried for the first time to make contact with soldiers. "I'd promised myself that I'd fraternize, but I can't. . . . I lack both fluency of speech and an agreeable manner."[88] On the train he finished Kafka's *Der Prozess*, which made him feel more than ever like a creature of distances. It was his body that felt impatient to arrive, his legs that wanted to be stretched, his gullet that was thirsty. "But I *myself*, finally, will never be in a better state than on this train."[89]

PART III

WAR

(1939–45)

(10)

The War Profiteer

"THE war has really divided my life in two,"[1] Sartre said, quoting Jules Romains: ". . . as if the whole of his personality had abruptly been transported from one environment to another. . . . Nothing internal or external could be perceived in the same way as before."[2] For eighteen months his normal life was to be held in abeyance as he served first as a soldier and then as a prisoner of war. He was assigned to the meteorological unit attached to an artillery division in Sector 108, just behind the front in Alsace. The unit was to be shuttled between several small towns near Strasbourg. He would be sent to Ceintrey, Marmoutier, Brumath, Morsbrunn, Bouxwiller, and then back to Brumath.

At three o'clock on the morning of Sunday, September 3, he arrived at the reception camp of Essey-les-Nancy, where he was told: "You're with Z11, but Z11 has already left." He was issued denims and a helmet, which were both too big for him. He wandered aimlessly about; no one could tell him anything about Z11. He slept on a straw mattress.[3] He was not happy to find himself at such close quarters with so many men, "coarse types who shit, wash, snore, exude maleness."[4]

After lunch, when he heard that war had been declared, he felt as if he were going to start his national service all over again. Depressed, he stretched out on his bed until a small spectacled corporal appeared at the door. "Is there someone called Sartre here?" The corporal, Jean Pierre, had two other privates in his meteorological unit—a fat, lazy-looking man of about forty, Müller, and a shrewd-looking, curly-haired Jew, Pieterkowski, who, to conceal his Jewishness, called himself Pieter. That night Sartre slept in their barracks room. In the morning a truck took them to Ceintrey, a village sixteen miles away. Thanks to Pieter, who was good at asking for what he wanted, they were billeted with one of the locals, an eighty-nine-year-old clergyman. The spectacled corporal, a nervous, guilt-ridden math teacher, allowed Pieter, who ran a hat shop, to take the lead and.to arrange for the four of them to have their meals at the house of a retired cook. It looked as though they would have nothing to do except make a couple of meteorological observations every day, and Sartre wasted no time in settling down to work on his novel; by Tuesday he had drafted twelve pages.

A man addicted to physical comfort might have found it impossible to concentrate while living the life of a soldier, but Sartre was enjoying his new life so much that he looked back with quizzical incredulity at the dread he had felt toward military service.[5]

The four soldiers were given two mattresses to put on the floor; Sartre shared with Jean Pierre, who neither snored as loudly as Müller nor roared like an animal, as Pieter sometimes did in his sleep. But Jean Pierre was a somnambulist. For years he'd been having a recurrent dream about being trapped under the debris of a house that had collapsed. "You are awakened ten times (I've never wanted to urinate so much) and in pitch darkness you grope your way ten times to the window, push the shutters aside and piss into the street."[6] He found it hard to live at such close quarters with the other three, but once it had struck him that Müller, the most irritating, was rather like a sea elephant, it was easier to put up with him. Sartre was so habituated to working in cafés that chatter and noises did not disrupt his concentration; by Friday he had finished his draft of Chapter 11 and started a clean copy. He could spend more time working than he had in Paris.[7] In letters to De Beauvoir he was apologetic about not feeling more depressed by their separation: "It's because the war *interests me*. It's like being in a foreign country I'm going to explore gradually."

On Thursday he learned that on Monday, September 11, the four of them would be assigned to the artillery in Marmoutier and not, as they had expected, the air force. Their work would consist of taking meteorological observations by sending up balloons about two feet in diameter and watching them through a theodolite. In the air force they would have had to follow the balloon for six kilometers; in the artillery it was only one kilometer. Calculations for gauging the "ballistic wind" were quite complicated, but he would still have plenty of time for his novel.

At a quarter to two on Monday morning the men were roused from their sleep. Wearing a helmet and carrying a rifle, a gas mask, and four packs each, "fifty or so men crept across the village in the black night like conspirators." They had a long wait for the train, and after watching "the grayness of dawn spreading over all these somnolent men," Sartre decided to keep a diary.[8] They arrived at Marmoutier, a charming old village, with green and pink cottages surrounded by orchards overflowing with fruit. They were put into a boys' school, where they slept on straw.

The village was cold, dark, and less than thirteen miles from the frontier. The next day they were given a room in the house of a woman who let them eat the greengages in her garden. There were no beds in the room, only two rather narrow mattresses; sharing with Pierre and using a knapsack as a pillow, Sartre often toppled onto the floor. Nor was there any furniture; he wrote his first letters sitting on a crate of equipment and resting his paper on a taller crate.[9] But they ate well. Though Müller, who was stingy, would have preferred to eat at the mobile canteen, Pieter persuaded him that the four of them should have their meals at a restaurant.

On Thursday, September 14, Sartre began his diary, and by Saturday he was thinking it could be published posthumously.[10] It soon became important to him. "It provides me with quite a little secret life on top of the other one, with pleasures, anxieties and regrets. I wouldn't have got to know even half of them without this little black leather object."[11] It was at risk, though, like the novel. If he tried to keep his writings with him, they might get lost or damaged; if he mailed them to De Beauvoir, they might go astray or arouse the suspicions of the censor. Probably it would be safer to mail the novel to her, fifty pages at a time.[12] Uncertain whether army life would always be so leisurely, he did more writing than reading.

On average he was producing five pages of the novel, four pages of the diary, and three letters every day. More stringently even than before, he rebuffed fatigue like a puritan resisting temptation. The feeling of exhaustion presented you with a choice—you could overcome it. In working, as when hiking with De Beauvoir, he needed to prove that his strength contradicted his size. He argues in *L'Etre et le Néant* that weariness does not depend on the difficulty of the journey or on how little sleep you had the night before. Although stubborn resistance to fatigue can, he admits, be symptomatic of an inferiority complex, the complex is itself a way of choosing yourself and choosing whether to succeed or fail. To tell yourself that you are ugly, he maintains, is not an objective judgment but a prediction that women will reject you.[13] He had no intention of achieving too little, either in his literary output or as a seducer.

One of his three daily letters was to De Beauvoir, and it was for her, he said, that he was keeping the diary. "You are on the horizon of all my thoughts. Everything I think or write or feel is for you."[14] This could not possibly be true. Obsessed though he was by his diary, bizarrely handicapping himself in the area that mattered most, in the core of his existence as a writer—as he would later admit to Pierre—he could confide nothing to the diary that he did not want De Beauvoir to read.[15] But, campaigning consciously and semiconsciously against the idea of the self, he had always inclined to deprive himself of privacy, as if to keep his ego permanently on a diet.

Since the age of sixteen, intimacy had never implied privacy. With Nizan, Guille, and De Beauvoir he had had "a life in which I constantly felt the whole tension of another presence, and hardened myself to support it. Living in a couple made me hard and transparent as a diamond; otherwise I couldn't have stood it. This is no doubt one of the main reasons my life has been so 'public.' " Because it seemed that his friends could see into his innermost thoughts, he felt constantly constrained to explain himself. It was more important to share ideas and emotions than to let them develop; in the diaries he was not so much conducting a self-analysis as forcing feelings and memories to the surface, while treating both like ideas he could manipulate. At the same time, the notion of confessional solidarity with De Beauvoir was a satisfying refuge from conversation with unstimulating fellow soldiers. The camaraderie of army life was inimical to egalitarianism: "I am now cured of socialism," he wrote, "if I needed to be cured of it."[16]

According to the diary, it was thanks to De Beauvoir that Paris still existed for him, and having a stronger sense than he did of what the war was, she was making it real for him. If he got six days of leave, he would spend them all with her; if he got eight days, he would devote two to Wanda, who sometimes wrote every day, sometimes lapsing from regularity.[17] Later he modified his plan: if he had eight days, three would be allocated to Wanda, but by pretending that he must see his mother and stepfather, he could give De Beauvoir two hours at lunchtime on each of the Wanda days.[18]

After the four men had been sleeping on the floor for fifteen days, Pierre managed to raise their standard of living, arranging for them to pay only six francs a night for a room on the first floor of the best hotel in the village. It might be possible for De Beauvoir to visit him, Sartre suggested, if she could obtain a pass and a safe-conduct, but he was not allowed to tell her where he was, and he did not know how much longer he would be there. On Tuesday, October 3, the order was given that they were to move. It looked as though they would be marched to Brumath, a training school twelve miles away, but Pieter complained of a hernia, and finally a truck arrived to take them. They were lodged in a barn with three orderlies, who had to sleep on the straw while the four meteorologists took the four beds. Their only job was to make meteorological observations and to telephone the artillery officers about the direction and force of the wind. According to Sartre, their balloons were liable to get lost behind chimneys, and the men, burdened with the theodolite, would have to run in pursuit. But, as Pierre has said in denial, there was never more than one balloon, and they could not have run while carrying a theodolite, which, as Sartre had previously written, took an hour to set up.[19]

There was no shooting in progress, and though he had to spend the day in the school hall that the army had taken over, he was free to work on his novel or write letters.

It was now ten years since he had agreed with De Beauvoir on their "two-year lease" after watching *Storm over Asia*. To celebrate the tenth anniversary of their "morganatic marriage," he had been intending to enclose a petal in his letter of October 6 to symbolize a bouquet, "but there are no flowers here, just manure." The anniversary fell on the tenth. "My love, you've given me ten years of happiness . . . My dear, dear love, I immediately renew the lease for a further ten years."[20] He did not inquire whether she wanted to renew it, and in later letters promised that the relationship with Wanda would not go on after the war;[21] he equated De Beauvoir with "all the tenderness and the poetic sense of life."[22]

The men moved out of the barn when they were billeted at the home of a warder in a lunatic asylum, but every morning there were rumors that the unit would be moved later in the day; every evening they were still there. In spite of the uncertainty, Sartre produced seventy-three pages of the novel in thirteen days,[23] and when Paulhan accepted his proposal for "Réflexions sur la mort," he started work on it. He was also writing an article on Gide and planning a volume of stories called "Histoires pour l'oncle Jules," based on the stories he had improvised for De Beauvoir in Marrakech.

His prewar life had vanished, but he was more than content with the opportunity war had brought for intensive literary activity. Expecting peace within a year or two[24] and not wanting to waste something so precious as war, he organized his time with a mixture of puritanic rigor and greed for the sensual pleasure of writing. He got out of bed at six or six-thirty, though reveille was not until eight. He breakfasted at the inn, starting at about seven to write his diary. He worked on his novel from seven-thirty to eleven, returning to the inn for a seven-franc lunch and reading while he ate. He had to be on parade in the courtyard of the town hall at one-thirty. After returning to the school, he would start writing again, distracted by impatience for the mail to be delivered at three. At about four he would start replying to letters, often going on till seven. Instead of eating dinner, he would drink a little red wine in his barracks room, working till about eight-thirty, when he would either sleep or go on guard duty, snatching spells of sleep on the straw.[25] Working fast on his first draft of the novel, he did not stop to make a clean copy.[26] He had to vary his routine according to observation duties, but these never took up much of the day, and sometimes he would volunteer for extra guard duty to gain additional writing time at night.[27] On October 24, a day he received no letters, he worked at the novel from eight in the morning till half past eleven and philosophized in his diary from twenty past one till twenty past five. By five he was feeling exhausted.[28]

In the same way that he had written in Berlin about Le Havre, he could write in Brumath about Paris, letting the distance help him toward a studied Husserlian withdrawal from the natural attitude. Uprooted from his Parisian routine, he made creative use of his self-criticism, projecting it into his characterization of Mathieu, who blames himself for not taking enough physical exercise, for not being politically committed, for indecisively letting time slip by. "He had never been able to sink himself completely into any love affair, any pleasure, never been really unhappy; it always seemed to him that he was somewhere else, hadn't yet quite been born. He was waiting. And all this time, gently, slyly, the years had come, they had seized him from behind. Thirty-four years."[29] Twenty-four years later, when Sartre accused himself in Les Mots of being unable to throw himself wholeheartedly into any task or passion or friendship, he appears to have forgotten leveling this accusation against Mathieu.

If Mathieu, at this stage of his development, feels inferior to Brunet, who has proved he is free by giving up his freedom to the party, the feeling derives from the more ambivalent attitude of the student Sartre toward his card-carrying friend Nizan. For Brunet every action is relevant to an overall design: "Nothing can now deprive my life of its meaning, nothing can stop it from being a destiny."[30] The contrast between the two men also parallels the contrast Sartre had drawn between events in a story and contingent events in actuality: his novel is about a man whose life lacks necessity. Mathieu incarnates "that total lack of attachment which Hegel calls terrorist and which is really the opposite of freedom. . . . Brunet incarnates 'the spirit of seriousness.' "[31] From the age of twenty-five he has been committed, whereas Mathieu had lapsed into what is virtually a bourgeois marriage. "You are married, Mathieu," says Daniel, "you live like a bourgeois."[32]

Sartre, in the army, was writing fiction from an extraordinary vantage point. He felt closer to De Beauvoir than when they were together.

"There is only one of us," he wrote, and "My dear little one, today I'd willingly give a finger to see you for five minutes and *tell* you that I love you."[33] But in her absence he was completely free—even free to accuse himself via the novel of being involved in a bourgeois relationship with her. By temperament Sartre was a mixture of *bon viveur* and ascetic, with no great sexual appetite. In one letter he spoke happily of his "monastic life with comfort, central heating and running water."[34]

The self-accusation derives partly from the banter he provoked by using his money to enjoy bourgeois comforts. While most of the men were sleeping on straw mattresses, Pieter used his influence to find a room Sartre could share with Pierre in a private house, where the landlady even provided eiderdowns.[35] Needing the companionship of a partner, Sartre used Pierre to fill part of the gap created by De Beauvoir's absence. Though he did not share Sartre's passion for breakfasting, Pierre was seduced into a routine of setting the alarm clock for six instead of seven and cycling out into the cold for the sake of two fat sandwiches and a glass of chicory juice at the inn, the Rose.[36]

The companionship of Pierre and Pieter was unlike any Sartre had known. He entered energetically into protracted conversations with both men, wrote about them at length in his diaries, and used them in *La Mort dans l'âme,* where Charlot Wroclaw is modeled on Pieter and Sergeant Pierné on Pierre. When the three of them were sharing sleeping quarters with Müller, it had been Müller, not Sartre, who had been the odd man out. Because Müller smelled so bad, none of them wanted to share a mattress with him,[37] and his habits were particularly offensive. He failed to wash out pots and mess tins; after telling him off for this, Sartre suspected that Müller was taking his revenge by stealing letters.[38] Generally Sartre enjoyed a feeling of solidarity with Pieter and Pierre against Müller, who was shamelessly greedy. When others offered him their unwanted meat, he would eat up to seven portions a day.[39]

Conversations with Pieter and Pierre had their effect on the philosophical thinking behind Sartre's existentialism. When Pieter gently reminded him that he must "take people as they are," his impatient reaction was: "Yes, but I know in my bones that people aren't; they do."[40] This thinking had one of its deepest roots in an obstinate rejection of fatality and passivity. Wanting to believe in a maximum of autonomy, he had no relish for the accidental *données* of existence: spontaneity of consciousness and strength of will had to compensate for everything that was determined, including face and body. He even wanted to believe that he had chosen to be alive at this time. No one could have predicted that the years 1918–39 would acquire a new meaning from the war, but "I should take it as my destiny, should understand that in *choosing* this period for myself, I was choosing myself for this war." He had chosen even the time he was born—concretely, not in the metaphysical sense of choosing a character.[41]

In Brumath he was well placed to analyze the impression Mathieu has in Paris—"that he was somewhere else." None of Sartre's intentions had led him here, and he looked back ironically at his past ideas of the future: "Où sont les avenirs d'antan?" Where are the futures of yesteryear? In the novel Mathieu is made to remember crucial moments in his past—smashing a valuable vase at the age of seventeen, fighting with another boy at the age of sixteen, and, after forcing him to eat sand, dedicating himself to freedom: "He had made a bet that his entire life would resemble this extraordinary moment." The novel would have been quite different if Sartre had written it as a civilian. Caught up in his peacetime routine, he had been anything but introspective, and there is some autobiography but little self-portraiture in his previous fiction, if we discount juvenilia. His interest in himself was still geared to his future, and if he was now going all out to characterize himself in detail, it was with an eye on what he wanted to become. The war had pushed him into the wings; when he went back onstage, it would be in a different role. The image he used in the diary was of a snake sloughing its skin, and he felt entitled "to look at this dead skin, this brittle image of the snake that will be left behind, and to take stock."[42]

Thinking about his life as if he were constantly revising an autobiography, he felt that his earliest self had been shaped by childhood decisions. Mathieu remembers early moments "with their private future, like a little personal heaven, quite round, above them, and this future, it was himself, just as he was at the moment, slack and maturing, they had rights over him, bridging all this time that had elapsed, they sustained their demands, and he often felt a desolating remorse because his unconcerned and cynical present was the old future of those past days."[43] Like the leisureliness of childhood, the leisureliness of army life was conducive to living autobiographically: notes for the unpublished chapters could be dramatically revised.

Combined with the disruption of his normal routine, the diary writing encouraged his tendency to think with his eyes, spying on himself to catch inclination unawares. But he did not intend to go on watching himself when the war ended: "I will no longer keep these diaries, or if I do, I will not talk about myself."[44] All the more intensive for having a time limit imposed on it, the experiment in self-observation led him to new theories about what he came to call "authenticity." It also deepened his habit of philosophizing, his technique of translating in-

rospection into ontological generalization. Philosophy gave him an al-
ernative to Proustian subjectivity.

In the same way that the alphabetical index had served as a recep-
acle for insights, encouraging the seventeen-year-old philosopher, his
iary worked like a midwife on his existentialism: the "little black
eather object" was bringing the ideas to birth. He had masses of ideas,
e wrote on October 26, and Pieter was calling him a "war profiteer"
ecause he capitalized so much on the leisure of military life.[45]

The leisure was being shared—imaginatively—with De Beauvoir.
eparation was making their literary relationship more intense: quite
part from the long, regular letters he was writing, her presence was
ehind the diary, which she would read, and the novel, on which she
would be more than an editor if less than a collaborator. He was more
ndependent in his philosophizing, but he was beginning to hunger for
er presence. At this distance he could no longer take her love for
ranted. In 1937 De Beauvoir's collapse had suddenly reduced his need
or Olga; now De Beauvoir's absence was steadily increasing his need
or her.

By the middle of October he was impatiently puzzling about how to
ell her what to do and where to come. He must not arouse the suspi-
ions of the censor, who had obliterated several passages in one of his
etters to his mother.[46] "By the way," he wrote to De Beauvoir on Octo-
er 15, "you don't tell me how Emma received Bernard and René Ul-
mann when they rang her bell; I hope she didn't play the same trick as
ast month when Maurice Adrien and Thérèse Héricourt, who had
one there specially, couldn't get in."[47] Emma was a character he had
ust invented; her mother, he suggested, would probably have no objec-
on if De Beauvoir took her to the Midi on November 1. The capital
nitials of the other invented names spell Brumath; De Beauvoir would
nderstand that he wanted her to come there on November 1. On Octo-
er 21 he explained that he had just had a letter from Emma, who
ould probably receive De Beauvoir in November. "You'll be able to
ee quite a lot of her although she has her work: in the morning at
leven and till about one and then in the evening at above five, when
he comes out of the office. . . . She tells me she'll be pleased to see
ou."[48] Four days later he was again urging her to visit Emma. "The
ar hadn't started when you last saw each other, which means you
ever shared thoughts and feelings about this war. I want the war to
elong equally to both of you."[49] In another letter he promised that
mma would give De Beauvoir a hundred and thirty pages of his novel
nd the first of the black notebooks, which he had entrusted to her.[50]
ust before the end of the month he sent her a sketch map of Bru-

math—saying it was a map of Quimper—and instructions about how to find Emma.[51] After meeting De Beauvoir in the turban she had taken to wearing, Wanda had described her as looking "beautiful, like young Hindu in a turban";[52] Sartre now asked her to wear the turban when she went to see Emma.[53]

Arriving in Brumath too late in the evening to make contact, De Beauvoir booked into an uncomfortable hotel, set her alarm for seven and went to the Taverne du Cerf, expecting to find him eating his breakfast. He was not there, but she wrote him a note and, outside the headquarters, found a soldier who promised to deliver it. A few minutes later Sartre appeared in air force uniform with a "a horrible mossy beard which does not suit him."[54] The cafés were out of bounds, so they went to her room in the hotel for an hour. He then had to report for duty, but reappeared at eleven, clean-shaven. He tried to arrange for her to stay at his lodgings by telling the landlady that his wife had arrived. The woman knew he was not married, but the word "fiancée" persuaded her to provide a separate room. They had dinner in the crowded Lion d'Or, which smelled of sauerkraut. In the morning, before going off to make meteorological observations, he gave her a hundred pages of *L'Age du raison,* which she read approvingly, noting down her reservations about Marcelle. At lunchtime he went off with two soldiers to find a room he could share with her. His theory about the war was that it would be modern, with no real fighting in it, just as modern painting had no real subject matter. Before she left on November 5 for Paris they had read and discussed each other's diaries: literature was giving them at least an approximation to sharing each other's life.

He wrote to her the next day, saying he'd been "profoundly and peacefully happy."[55] He was astonished at how much she had given him, but above all, "your presence, quite alone and quite naked and your little face and your tender smiles and your little arms around my neck . . . I'd be able to live with you no matter where."[56] He resumed writing to her every day, and the letter of November 8 ends: "Your little husband loves you."[57] Wanda, jealous when he wrote to her about De Beauvoir's visit, wanted to visit him too,[58] but rumors were circulating that they would soon be moving from Brumath.

De Beauvoir had made him see that Marcelle was the least convincing character in the novel. In her he had departed further than with any of the other characters from the real-life model, but, impressively objective, De Beauvoir's criticisms had nothing to do with herself or their relationship. It was for the novel's sake that he set about remodeling Marcelle, a task that was disappointingly time-consuming.[59] He knew too that he must not say too much about liberty in the first volume, and he was worried that a chapter full of action might make readers intolerant of "poetic mud" in the next.[60]

Eager to write a play, he was impatient to have the novel out of the way.[61] He also wanted to write more philosophy, especially after being awakened so often in the night by the need to urinate; by thinking philosophically to distract himself from his discomfort, he had arrived at a new idea about the will. As he had explained to De Beauvoir, the will needed passive resistance; this insight could be combined with Spinoza's idea that consciousness and will were identical. Using his diary to take stock of moral ideas he had propounded since the age of seventeen, he started to sketch out a morality. Nietzsche had understood that the death of God created an urgent need for a new system of values; Sartre, who felt able to provide one, knew his outlook had changed radically since he wrote *La Transcendance de l'Ego*. His stoicism had collapsed, and he had been propelled toward his new position by the war, by Arthur Koestler's *Spanish Testament*, an account of experiences in a death cell during the civil war, by Antoine de Saint-Exupéry's novel *Terre des hommes* (1939, translated as *Wind, Sand and Stars*), and by *Verdun*, the sixteenth volume in Jules Romains's twenty-seven-volume cycle *Les Hommes de bonne volonté* (1932–47, *Men of Good Will*).

Sartre called his new ethic a "morality of complaisance." "We have come some way since the time we were rationalist, Cartesian and anti-existentialist."[62] What should be the aim of human activity? It should aim at itself, he answered. "Human reality can and should be its own end because it is always on the side of the future—it is its own reprieve."[63] He did not mean to equate morality with social utilitarianism or with the individualism that mistakes the individual for an end. For Husserl reality is neither a fact nor a value but a relationship between a fact and a value. Consisting primarily of consciousness, it is nothing if not consciousness of being. It is free, but total freedom exists only for the man who takes responsibility for the existence of human reality. Consciousness does not have an origin outside itself, and it projects itself into the future to be its own foundation there. This possibility of being one's own foundation is the source of all values.[64]

To *accept* everything that happens is both excessive and inadequate, but we should understand that nothing can happen to us except through ourselves, and we must take responsibility for everything exactly as if we had willed it. We must always move forward from the event as if it had been given to us by decree and as if the object were to find out what progress we could then make.[65] This is an exciting idea, and his new philosophy made an impact when he explained it to friends; a clerk called Selzer[66] said he had changed completely, thanks to Sartre. Leaving home, three months before, he had been desperate, but he now felt almost serene: he had accepted the war as an event in his own life. "He is nervous," wrote Sartre, "and in thanking me, he stammers. I've nervous too and drink milk . . . Always this strange impression that none of this is meant for me, that I'm playing a part, that I'm basically a wretched charlatan who's deceiving everybody."[67] He was worried that the novel, belonging partly to an earlier phase of his thinking, muddled Husserlian and existentialist ideas of liberty.[68]

He had little difficulty in getting up between six and half past. After a leisurely breakfast at the Rose and the first meteorological observation of the day, he was free to work from about nine. He had lunch with Pieter at the Ecrevisse, and after the second observation he was free to work again.[69] At the Ecrevisse the radio would sometimes be switched on in the room adjoining the dining room, and toward the end of November he caught the strains of jazz mixed with the clatter of plates and the buzz of conversation: "That suddenly made a poetic and cruel Paris loom up before me in exactly the way a jealous, exiled lover might think of it as surrounding his mistress."[70] The feeling was only momentary, but he made use of it in a letter to Wanda and then confided to De Beauvoir: "I pretended it was of her that I was jealous."[71] In fact the only pretense seems to have been in making out that the jealousy was faked. He was afraid that Wanda might be having an affair, possibly with the actor Roger Blin,[72] though even if she was, Sartre believed her to be "caught up in my destiny, like a louse in a head of hair."[73] He spent less than 20 percent of the day, he said, worrying about her; the rest of the time was devoted to thinking happily about De Beauvoir and to working.[74]

When the division was moved to Morsbrunn, twelve miles away, Sartre was expecting it would stay there about seven weeks. They left at four in the morning of December 5, on a truck that, three hours later, pulled up outside a rather dilapidated hotel on a hill less than half a mile outside the village. Inside, crammed with soldiers' packs, haversacks, and military paraphernalia, the hotel looked more like a headquarters than the peaceful school at Brumath had, and the bedrooms smelled of mushrooms. The flowered wallpaper was dirty and torn.[75] Sartre had been hoping for a room of his own, but he had to share with Jean Pierre. He was immediately given a job as a telephone operator, working in a large room bustling with officers, some leaving, some arriving. At first he felt proud to be in charge of the imposing apparatus, which had little black shutters and about twenty plugs on cables, but after twelve hours of nonstop work his head was aching, and he still had to spend the night on a couch next to the switchboard. He wrote his diary in the pauses between operating it and overhearing conversations about the war, which still looked as though it might fail to develop. He started, between interruptions, to read Flaubert's *Education sentimentale,* but hated the gallantry and refinement of the period; he also complained that the book was stupid and badly written.[76]

His routine at Morsbrunn gave him less time for the novel. He found an isolated café he could use as a sanctuary between seven and half-past-eight for reading, drinking coffee, eating bread and butter.[77] He should have made three meteorological observations every day and taken responsibility for the telephone one day in every four and for sweeping out the rooms and making up the fires one day in eight.[78] But to give him more time for writing, Pierre took over all his duties every third day for a month.[79] He wrote to De Beauvoir: "I'm quite absorbed by the atmosphere of this place and by my morality; nothing outside matters more than you do."[80] In another letter he wrote: "I'm quite alone with you."[81] Her visit had worked on him like a time bomb, and the move to Morsbrunn, he told her, had killed his passion for Wanda; it was exactly as if she no longer existed.[82] He signed the letter "Your little husband,"[83] and in another letter to De Beauvoir he claimed to dislike writing hypocritically to Wanda about how much he loved her.

By the middle of December he had resumed work on the novel, starting the final chapter, which consisted mainly of dialogue.[84] He was expecting to have it finished before he went on leave early in the new year. He would bring the diaries to Paris, so that De Beauvoir could read about his new conception of nothingness, which had occurred to him while he was reading Kierkegaard;[85] he also had new theories about violence and bad faith.[86]

At the party on Christmas Eve he sang the Toreador's Song from *Carmen,* making the other soldiers join in the chorus,[87] and before the year was over he finished the novel, but after writing the word "Fin" he tore up the three final pages and threw them into the coal bucket. His dislike of writing endings never expressed itself more clearly. He had to rummage for the fragments of paper and carefully stick them together.[88] His intention was to call the second volume "Septembre" and to make a start on it within a couple of days. Instead he began on the short stories, "Histoires pour l'oncle Jules," and on a bloodthirsty play, "Prométhée," full of rape and massacre. He felt so pleased with this that he sang "The Man I Love" during a meteorological observation, making the theodolite shake.[89] But he soon tore up both the stories and the play.[90] He was writing even more prolifically than at Brumath, where he had produced a hundred and fifty pages of the novel during September and October. The capsules of ink in his fountain pen were lasting only a day and a half,[91] and within two days he filled eighty-one pages of his diary.[92] Knowing that the evening was the best time for writing, he lived on bread and chocolate for three days to save the time he would have spent on going out to a restaurant.[93] Nor was he willing to waste time on washing or shaving. He let his beard grow[94] and acquired a reputation for being dirty. Pierre was told: "Your chum's famous in the division."[95] He felt he had appropriated more freedom than ever before, and he made experiments that struck his companions as silly. "Today I won't smoke. I'm going to prove that I'm free."[96] But he was pleased with his progress: "It seems to me that I'm on the way, as biographers say round about page 150 of their book, 'toward finding myself.' "[97]

But Sartre did not try to live in accordance with his new philosophy; the only role it had in his life was to cheer him up when he was feeling depressed,[98] and it was gratifying to believe he had explained the singleness of the world for the plurality of consciousnesses and had conclusively overcome the dichotomy between realism and idealism.[99] Contingency was favoring him: having none of his philosophical books with him, he had to rediscover Husserl and Heidegger by thinking the problems out without consulting them. In this way he liberated himself from them, using the techniques of phenomenology and existentialism, to develop his own ideas about perception and existence. "The war and the sense of being, in spite of everything, a bit 'lost,' have given me courage."[100] But how could he keep the novel abreast of his thinking? It worried him that many of the best ideas in it had been elaborated out of Heidegger's ten succinct pages on historicity.[101]

Impatient to go on leave, Sartre was especially looking forward to eating omelettes again and to being with De Beauvoir. He had promised to divide his time between her and Wanda, but he had also been writing regularly to another woman—probably Bianca—and he did not want her to know he was going to be in Paris. To continue his correspondence with her he gave Pierre carefully numbered letters, one of which was to be mailed each day. On the eighth day Pierre was to send her a telegram.[102]

Not wanting to be seen in the streets of Paris wearing a uniform and "looking like Punch," he arranged for De Beauvoir to collect some of his civilian clothes from his mother's flat so that he could change as soon as he arrived.[103] When his eleven days of leave started on February 4, he felt highly privileged to resume the life he had once taken for granted.

Scarcely any men were to be seen in the streets, except for the old and the infirm.[104] Night life had fizzled out; nightclubs looked moribund. "Let's not go to the Chantilly," Wanda said, "it's too cold there."[105] In peacetime he felt distanced from other people by the way they were all looking forward to events from which he was excluded; now everyone's life seemed to have been adjourned. One evening, waiting for De Beauvoir outside a café in the Champs-Elysées, he felt all the more alive for having been uprooted from this dead city, where "this new, felt-lined discretion had given the cafés in the evening the secretive look of brothels."[106] At Le Jockey, with Wanda, it seemed to him that they were no less in love than other couples who were dancing but that he was not available: he could not stay. But "it's much easier to live decently and authentically in war than in peace."[107] He had been more authentic in camp, he believed, than he was being in Paris.[108]

Wanda's reactions to his diaries could hardly have been more different from De Beauvoir's. Though in many ways an extremely private person, De Beauvoir had a strong drive to publish nearly all her documentation of her own existence and of his. She was more proprietorial literarally than sexually. The ontological insecurity of both Kosakiewicz sisters took a different form. Olga was so averse to being written about that De Beauvoir gave her less space in the autobiography than she would have liked to. Less histrionic offstage than Olga, Wanda was more exhibitionistic, but when Sartre told her that he was intending to publish his diaries, she was incredulous and disapproving. How could he expose something so intimate? In fact they were published only posthumously, and their authenticity has been impugned by Jean Pierre, who maintains that Sartre's diaries were confiscated in the stalag by a German officer and that the published volumes were written after his return to Paris. This is unlikely. Some of the later volumes may have been confiscated and irretrievably lost, but after going on leave to Paris, Sartre is unlikely to have taken the early volumes back to the camp, and it would have been out of character for him to spend so much time on faking something that was not even intended for immediate publication.

Early in the morning of February 15 he changed back into uniform. But in Paris he had employed a civilian tailor to remake his uniform, and putting it on, together with his new pair of puttees, he felt cleaner than he had since the beginning of the war.[109] As he boarded the train, which was filled with soldiers returning from leave, De Beauvoir joined the line of wives and girl friends waiting for a final kiss on the high step outside the carriage door. She was the first woman to leave, walking away fast.[110] Sartre was not returning to Morsbrunn: the unit had moved to Bouxwiller, but his immediate anxiety was caused by the other soldiers on the train. They were terrified of a spring offensive.

At Bouxwiller, Sartre could work during the mornings and evenings in the Hôtel du Soleil, a large, ill-named café where he always felt cold. On the first floor was a big room that had been used in peacetime as a movie house. It had a lot of chairs in it, a Ping-Pong table, and about fifteen tables with patterned tablecloths and vases of flowers on them. About fifty soldiers would be sitting around, reading, writing, and playing cards, while a radio provided music.[111] Looking around him, he felt no desire for personal contact. "Collectively they touch me somewhat, but if I consider them individually, most of them shock me either by their attitude or their way of speaking. . . . I don't like men—I mean the male of the species. . . . In short, for me there is a half of the human race which scarcely exists."[112]

Though he had felt, when he was with Wanda at Le Jockey, that he was in love with her, his memories of her evaporated quickly; he told De Beauvoir that she was more vivid in his memory.[113] He felt guilty about giving Wanda a little knife De Beauvoir had given him,[114] and he was still suspicious that Wanda was involved with another man,[115] but when she found out about the letters he had written in 1938 to the drama student, he was frantic with anxiety. The girl showed the letters to a friend of Olga's, Marcel Mouloudji, a scruffy writer who spent much of his time at the Flore and occasionally acted in films. Mouloudji told Wanda about them, letting her form the impression that Sartre's affair with the girl was not over when his affair with her began and that to impress the girl he had told her Wanda was in love with him. To pacify Wanda, Sartre sent her a vicious letter he had just written to the girl; Wanda was invited to read it before mailing it to the girl in the unsealed envelope he sent her.

I never loved you. I found you physically pleasing, though rather vulgar, but I have a certain sadism which your vulgarity actually attracted. . . . In your romantic brain you staged a beautiful comedy about love which was reciprocated but frustrated by a vow taken previously, and I didn't interfere, because I thought separation would be easier for you to bear . . . I wasn't enjoying myself much with you. My letters, which were an exercise in impassioned writing that afforded a good deal of laughter to the Beaver and me, did not entirely deceive you at the time.[116]

At first Sartre was pleased with his stratagem, calling it a "stroke of genius" and explaining to De Beauvoir: "I'm becoming tougher with people."[117] In his strenuous efforts to reassure Wanda, he wrote: "You know quite well that I'd trample on the whole world (including the Beaver) . . . in order to stay on good terms with you."[118] Confessing this betrayal to De Beauvoir, he apologized, saying he had never known how to lead his sexual life or his emotional life: "I quite profoundly and sincerely consider myself to be a *salaud* . . . a sickening sort of academic sadist, a wage-earning Don Juan." He promised to have no more casual affairs,[119] but he did not plan to give up the practice of deceiving: during his next leave Wanda would be made to believe that he was in Paris for five days fewer than he was actually there; this would give him more time with De Beauvoir.[120] "My little one, my charming Beaver, I swear to you I'm absolutely honest with you. If I weren't, there'd be nothing left in the world in face of which I'm not a liar—I would lose myself."[121] At the beginning of the affair with Wanda he had decided to sacrifice her at the slightest sign that De Beauvoir wanted him to and in the meanwhile to sacrifice the others to her.[122] "I promise you there will be no more affairs for a long time (a long time after the war, of course, or it would be too easy). . . . All that was always a matter of seducing, I can see that clearly now I'm writing it down, and once the good woman was seduced, I was quite astonished to have her on my hands."[123] All this was over. "Not only you but my *relations* with you are precious to me. And so far as any sort of 'conjugal' seduction is concerned," Wanda would be "amply sufficient."[124]

These were not the only plans he was making for his postwar life; he would apply his new morality and would involve himself in politics. To conform to his idea of "authenticity," he must take responsibility for his situation in life. He could not have known how fashionable his ideas would become, but, in an unposted letter, he declared his intentions: "As for politics . . . I shall go alone into this soufflé, I shall follow no one, and those who want to follow me can follow me." It was important, he went on, to protect the younger generation from coming out of the war with guilty consciences, and no one was better equipped to protect them than their seniors, who had fought at their side.

On March 15 the unit was moved from Bouxwiller back to Brumath. Again he was to work in the school building but this time on the first floor. The next day, Saturday, he went back to the Rose. The two barmaids were still there, the sleepy redhead, Jeannette, and the fat, promiscuous brown-haired Alice, who was now married to a soldier.[125] Most of the soldiers were received by the civilians in Brumath with open arms, "but I play no part in the game: no one recognizes me . . . except the large old woman at the Rose, who squeezes my hand cordially."[126]

The day before the move he had received from De Beauvoir's sister Poupette the first third of his novel in typescript. Rereading, he found the theme did not emerge clearly enough. Mathieu was lacking in unity and the chapters were insufficiently connected. What worried Sartre most was that too little of the past was visible behind the present of each character. The reader should know, he decided, where Mathieu came from, where he had taught, how he had met Boris and Ivich.[127] One solution would be to write a prologue set in 1928, ten years before the main story begins. The reader would meet Ivich, Mathieu, and Marcelle long before they meet each other. "That will give roots to my character and this will enable me to lighten the rest of the text."[128] By the middle of March he was devoting ten hours of each day to the prologue.[129] He was now expecting the novel to be ready by October and to be six hundred pages long. "I've always considered abundance a virtue."[130]

After just over two weeks in Brumath he had to leave again. In Paris, when he showed De Beauvoir his new prologue, she had no difficulty in persuading him to scrap it. He talked at length about the philosophy he was evolving. She remembered a damp evening when they were strolling around the Gare du Nord: "I had an impression of incurable desolation; I had wished too fervently for the absolute and suffered its absence too much not to recognize in myself this useless reaching toward Being."[131]

Chatting with her about his philosophical theories, he netted ideas for developing them, and some of her reactions gave him ideas for Mathieu. Revising the novel when he was back in Brumath, he profited from the criticisms of his "little judge." "It's for you I write when I revise, much more than when I invent."[132] Before the book went to the printer she would be given carte blanche to make cuts.[133]

Wanting to write an essay on Malraux, Sartre read or reread his novels, noticing how characters tried to absorb into the bloodstream of their willpower the circumstances they could not control.[134] "He irritates me because he is too much like me: he's like John the Baptist to my Jesus."[135] They were both writing on the assumption that "the age of fundamentals is being resumed . . . Reason needs to be founded all over again." This is how a character puts it in *L'Espoir;* to Sartre it seemed that people were finally understanding what Nietzsche had said about the need for new principles in a world without God.[136]

Sartre's main relaxation was playing chess. In Brumath, on average he'd play six or seven games a day, sometimes nine. When he played in the afternoon, he could plead that it was better to write in the morning when his mind was more lucid. At the end of April, when he played two games simultaneously, he claimed to have won both.[137] But he never admits to being beaten by Pierre, while Pierre claims to have won an average of one game in three.[138]

After eight months of not having a room of his own, Sartre acquired one on the thirtieth, when he was installed in the Hôtel Bellevue. "It's a dainty little room with marbled wallpaper, a bed, a little table, a jug of water and washbowl, a bedside table and a flower vase. I'm ecstatic."[139] The more imposing hotel the officers had taken was infested with bed-bugs, so the men, hoping to avoid a swap, went around scratching themselves.[140]

But the pleasantness of the new room ceased to matter when a letter arrived from Wanda: she was ill and alone, with some kind of lesion. "My God," she wrote, "how I want you to come, to come at all costs." Without knowing how serious the illness was, Sartre responded by offering to marry her. He would then get three days of leave; apart from deserting, there was no other way he could come. De Beauvoir must have been astounded by his letter of May 12. Less than six months earlier he had signed himself "Your little husband," and only three months previously he had assured her that from the beginning of the Wanda affair his intention had been to break it off "at the slightest sign" that De Beauvoir wanted him to. He now explained that the marriage would be "purely symbolical": it would mean that he was committed to Wanda and that from now on he would do all he could for her. It would be a nuisance, though, having to conceal the marriage from his mother and stepfather, who were bound to find out eventually, and it would be unpleasant for De Beauvoir. To compensate, he would spend a whole day with her, telling Wanda that since Germany had just invaded Holland, soldiers were being allowed only two days of compassionate leave instead of three. Or perhaps De Beauvoir would prefer not to be in Paris this time while he was there; it might be more sensible to stay with Mme. Morel at La Pouèze, a village near Angers where she had settled.[141] This superficial considerateness must have been extremely hurtful. While telling De Beauvoir that he was about to marry another woman he was implying that he had never stopped taking her point of view into account. He obviously assumed that even when he was married to Wanda, De Beauvoir would be no less available than she had always been, except during these three days when she might prefer not to be in Paris.

He was soon regretting the offer of marriage. Even if Wanda was already better, she was quite capable of responding: "Marry me all the same—at least we'll have three days together." After instructing De Beauvoir to find out about the illness,[142] Sartre received two letters from Wanda, who was not seriously ill. "In these circumstances I think it is pointless to marry her; I shall write to tell her that it would serve no purpose." His letter to De Beauvoir ends: "We are *inseparable*." After his act of betrayal, his confidence was strikingly arrogant, but he was not wrong.

ON May 12, 1940, the Germans invaded Holland and Belgium, but Sartre's unrealistic optimism was unchecked: "They will overstrain their resources in defending such a vast front."[143] He told Pierre off for being pessimistic.[144] But though the "phony" war was becoming real, the texture of their lives was not changing. Meteorological observations four times a day and, for Sartre, agitation over the novel. Was it lacking in vitality? Refusing to be thrown off-balance by the Wanda episode, his "little judge" was asking for a new scene between Mathieu and Daniel. He gave himself a month to finish the book, and, working on it now, had no feeling of manipulating puppet strings,[145] but he was impatient to start a philosophical book about nothingness.[146] Even when he heard that some of his diaries, which De Beauvoir had lent to Bost, might have been lost, it scarcely worried him; what counted was that they had led him to the idea of nothingness, which was still alive in his head.[147]

"Somewhere in the North," he wrote to De Beauvoir, "not only the country's destiny is being decided, but mine and yours."[148] But he still had no part in the action. "I am not serving any purpose."[149] The war was helping him to ruminate and regroup memories. "It's true that one becomes more profound."[150] The sound of gunfire was audible almost constantly, and defeatist rumors were circulating. What if the Germans were to win? "Oh, but in any case they won't treat France the same as Poland. Life would still be livable."[151]

By May 19 Sartre learned that the Germans had taken Laon. He instructed De Beauvoir to leave Paris for La Pouèze and to send the Kosakiewicz sisters to Laigle. "Think how atrocious it would be for me to know Paris was being bombarded, besieged or surrounded and to know you were inside it."[152] How were they going to celebrate the end of the war "if one of your little legs is missing or perhaps the whole head?"[153] He felt completely free and completely helpless. He went on working at the novel, but he was losing momentum. He played chess, read thrillers. "There are moments when, like you, I feel it's maniacal and obstinate to write while men are dying like flies in the North and while the whole of Europe's fate is at stake, but what can I do?"[154]

On May 14 the Dutch army surrendered, and the advancing Germans broke through French defenses near Sedan. Except for two days when Sartre was too depressed to write, he went on with the novel, though it was impossible to think about publication or to believe that people would eventually read the book.[155] He had been purged of the vanity that had ensued on the success of *La Nausée;* he felt as "pure" as when he was writing it; "and besides it's *against* the breakdown of democracy and liberty, against the defeat of the Allies—symbolically—that I'm performing the act of writing."[156] Though he went on planning the rest of the novel—the entire action of the final volume could take place when Mathieu was on leave[157]—he felt cut off from any future, especially any literary future.[158] While the German army advanced, Sartre played chess.[159]

France could no longer be expected to win the war; "neither do I think we'll lose it: I think nothing, the future remains closed."[160] On June 10, the day Italy declared war on France and Britain, the radio reported that a battle was raging to the north of Paris. "All the same I worked well today, the Mathieu-Marcelle chapter is finished." He was expecting an armistice and the return of peace.[161] With enough good will they would find that life could be lived without cowardice, though not without humiliations. At least they would see each other again soon, "and that gives me, in spite of myself, a kind of joy."[162] The Germans had reached St.-Dizier in the Marne, while the French army was retreating to avoid being cut off. The radio gave the impression that an armistice was imminent, that America was certain to stay neutral. Pieter tried not to show that he was terrified.[163]

During ten chaotic days of retreating they stopped at Haguenau, in the extreme northeast of France. When they arrived there on June 10, the evacuated town had been empty for a month. In the classroom of a Catholic girls' school Sartre found exercise books that stopped at May 10. For five days the men had seen no newspapers, heard no news on the radio, received no letters. They did not know when they would leave or where they would go. It was Wednesday, but the closed shops made it look like Sunday, except that flourlike dust was accumulating on goods in the windows. The streets were deserted.[164] In 1942 when Sartre reproduced the experience for the Geneva-based review *Messages,* he used the title "La Mort dans l'âme," but it is not merely the phrase that links the episode to the third novel in his series, it is the necessity of coming to terms with a reality that felt like fantasy or fiction.

They were moved back to Breschwillers and then back to Padoux, in Lorraine. With the German army approaching, French soldiers were drawn into arguments with pro-German Alsatians. Sartre's unit was moved from village to village until the men were abandoned by their officers, who walked off into a forest carrying a white flag. Of the two hundred officers from the headquarters only the commandant and two others stayed with the men, the commandant's reason being that he was too drunk to run away.[165] The sergeants also stayed. When Sartre was taken prisoner on the morning of his thirty-fifth birthday, June 21, 1940, he felt as if he were acting in a movie. He had slept in a peasant's house on the village square. He dressed quickly. A gun was firing at a church, where a few French soldiers were holding out. He found himself among a large group that was being marched by armed Germans to a gendarmerie barracks. He was shut up in the attic with a lot of men he knew. They had to sleep on the floor. They were left there for several days without enough to eat; he was sometimes dizzy with hunger.[166]

The next day the eighty-four-year-old Marshal Pétain, who for six days had been in control of the French administration, concluded an armistice with Germany. It was agreed that French troops captured in Germany would stay there till the end of the war. Sartre was sent to Baccarat, between Strasbourg and Nancy. Four days before the armistice was signed, Charles de Gaulle, a tank expert who had been serving as undersecretary of state for war, flew to England and broadcast an appeal: all Frenchmen who wanted to continue fighting should contact him. The British government recognized him (in August) as leader of the Free French movement, but by then the armistice had been ratified by the French National Assembly, which met at Vichy in July. Plenary powers were given to Pétain, but in his Vichy régime, which was to survive until 1944, the real power was wielded by the astute Pierre Laval, an opportunist who, convinced that the Allies would lose, made no effort to help them, though he did secure more independence for France than was allowed to any other defeated country. Only the northern and western half of France was occupied by the Germans, while the Vichy government was allowed to keep an "armistice army" of a hundred thousand men.

"My captivity," Sartre wrote on July 8, "is limited to camping." The prisoners were sleeping in tents. He was with Pieter and Pierre still, and they were still being kept so short of food that, physically enfeebled, Sartre felt stupefied and somnolent. Time slipped past as if he were dreaming. Even when the supply of food improved, he was depressed by the extreme cold and by his fellow prisoners—"stupidity, meanness, jealousy, idiotic tricks, coprophilia etc. I've assumed some authority over the men around me, but one loses all desire to laugh."[167] For five weeks he let his beard grow, and despite the danger of lice—hundreds of men had them—he scarcely ever washed, becoming even dirtier than he had been at Brumath. He walked around with much the same expression on his face as when he was with his stepfather. The ersatz coffee they were given at six in the morning was made from roasted barley. They were fed at eleven in the morning and five in the afternoon with bread and soup made from barley, cabbage, or pork. At six in the evening they had to parade in columns. Otherwise they were free to do what they liked. On sunny days men would sunbathe, stark naked, on blankets in the courtyard. "The paradox of our situation is that it's both impossible and easy to live in it."[168]

Sartre was hoping to be liberated before the end of August, but by July 22 he had resumed work on the novel, had started to write *L'Etre et le Néant*,[169] and had soon generated so much momentum that at night, as in the camp at Morsbrunn, he felt impatient to resume work in the morning.[170] But he was reminded of his identity when a spectacled habitué of the Café Flore asked him whether he was related to Sartre the author. He now began to wash and shave again.[171]

None of De Beauvoir's letters appeared to have been censored, but he could write to her only on postcards or by smuggling a letter to be mailed outside the camp through the civilian postal system. He promised that as soon as they were reunited, they would start living together.[172] He was anxious about Bost; he also asked for news of Nizan, Guille, Maheu, and Aron, who, as a Jew, might be in danger. Pieter, who was not expecting to survive, had become almost unapproachable.[173] Without trying to spend much time with him, Sartre forged ahead with his work. He had been moved into a big unfurnished room with fourteen other men. Incessant rain confined them indoors, where everything had to be done on the floor—sleeping, reading, writing[174]—but Sartre had completed seventy-six pages of *L'Etre et le Néant* by August 12.

(11)

Stalag

In the middle of the month he was transferred to a prisoner-of-war camp, Stalag XII-D, which was on a hilltop at Trier, near the Luxembourg border. For ten months he had worn a uniform without once catching sight of the enemy until the day he was captured. When he had tried to picture German soldiers in Left Bank cafés, he had failed,[1] but now, in daily contact with the Germans, he felt an exhilarating solidarity with the French prisoners. They were all at risk together, though the only immediate danger was of being kicked or slapped. Infuriated by their indolent disobedience, the adjutant, who was nicknamed Pilchard, dealt out slaps galore, and other Germans followed his example.

Far from feeling humiliated, Sartre was oddly excited by the daily violence. One evening, trying to creep into his hut after curfew, he found a flashlight shining in his face. "The sentry began to shout, threatening me with his bayonet. I knew he had no intention of bayoneting me in the stomach but he was thinking about stabbing my thighs: he was waiting for me to turn my back on him. I turned slowly, never had I been so vividly and clearly aware of all this impotent meat collected at the base of my back. In the end I received a hard kick which threw me against the door. I was still laughing as I went into the hut." When he told the others why he was laughing, they joined in.

Among the prisoners were Poles and Czechs, who made fun of the retreating French army. The Czechs had not forgiven France for watching passively in March 1939 when Hitler's armies occupied Czechoslovakia; the Poles were equally contemptuous, and according to a Russian deserter, the French were all rabbits.[2]

Pierre and Pieter were among the prisoners, but Sartre preferred the companionship of a more intellectual group clustered around an officer, Captain Bourdin, who had effective control over the infirmary, where he arranged for Sartre to be used as an interpreter and to be quartered in a room with two other prisoners. As at Baccarat, he was free to move about inside the camp. Some of the priests and chaplains knew his work or at least his name, and he offered, if they could gather an audience for him, to give a lecture. About twenty prisoners assembled and, talking without notes, he discoursed on the treatment of death in the work of Rilke, Malraux, and Heidegger. The prisoners were more attentive when he raised the question of whether the women of France would now prefer German soldiers, who had proved their courage, to Frenchmen, who had not.[3]

After about three months he lost his job in the infirmary, but, not wanting to work in the fields, managed to get himself classified as an artist. The "artists" included professional and amateur musicians, actors, boxers, and wrestlers. They were paid a salary by the Germans, and they had a hut of their own. To keep fit he joined the boxers and wrestlers in their regular morning workouts—first for thirty minutes, later for forty-five.[4] Hanging up on the wall of the hut were guitars, banjos, flutes, and trumpets provided by the Germans so that the "artists" could keep up the morale of the prisoners by giving concerts, and there was a piano, on which the Belgians played swing, rather in the style of the College Inn.

There was also a little theater where, twice a month, on Sundays, a performance was staged for the fifteen hundred prisoners in the camp. The man who had been put in charge of the actors, Chaumis, thought he had seen a play by Sartre, who did not contradict him and was then commissioned to write scripts for the troupe. None of these was staged,[5] and Sartre spent most of his time in conversation with the priests, who all came from the bourgeoisie. Now, with easier opportunities than ever before or after for fraternizing with working-class men, he chose not to. He had a genuine love for the tough vulgarisms of working-class speech, but his liking for the people was generalized and theoretical. Except when eating or sleeping, he scarcely spent any time in the hut. He sat at a long table, writing or reading, and when he was with the priests, they discussed such questions as the Virgin Birth. He made friends with a Jesuit called Paul Feller, the abbé Henri Leroy, Marius Perrin, the Basque abbé Etchegoyen, and a Dominican, Père Boisselot. Perrin was interested in phenomenology, and Sartre began to tutor him, patiently translating, sentence by sentence, from a copy of Heidegger's *Sein und Zeit* that had been procured from a Benedictine in a monastery at Trier. After coming across a copy of Claudel's *Le Soulier de satin* in the artists' hut, Sartre asked the priests to help him find a cast without drawing on the troupe of actors. Feller had a good voice, as did Marc Bénard, a journalist and painter from Le Havre. Though the enterprise was abortive, it prepared the ground for one that was not.

When the priests were planning Christmas celebrations, Sartre not only offered to join the choir that would sing hymns, carols, and the Pilgrims' Chorus from *Tannhäuser*,[6] he suggested they should return to the old custom of complementing midnight Mass with a mystery play. By writing scripts for the troupe he had convinced himself that he had talent as a playwright. Would the priests let him create a play that would not, strictly speaking, be Christian but would be suitable for Christmas performance? They were easily persuaded—partly because, underrating his toughness, they scented an opportunity to convert him.

Abandoning the Heidegger sessions with Perrin, Sartre set to work on a script, bearing his actors in mind. He would use Feller, Abbé Leroy, and Marc Bénard, as well as actors from the troupe, and he would play a part himself. By introducing a chorus, he would involve a large number of prisoners. Three weeks before Christmas the script was still unfinished, but the play was already in rehearsal; the best way for the actors to learn their lines was by rehearsing them.

Bariona, ou Le Fils du tonnerre (*Bariona, or the Thunder's Son*) is set on December 24 in a village about seventy-five miles from Bethlehem. Sartre situated the action on the edge of the Nativity story: a man would set out to kill the Christ child, a well-meaning man, prompted by concern to avert delusion and submissiveness. His plot would be abandoned, but the change of plan would itself constitute a climax in the play. Directing the actors himself, Sartre copied what he'd watched Dullin doing in rehearsal but without being so rude. The priests assumed that he'd had professional experience as a director,[7] while the response of the actors to the script indicated that he had not overestimated his talent as a playwright.[8] He could create tension, even in scenes between minor characters whose only function was to retail information about offstage events. He could translate philosophical ideas into impressive theatrical rhetoric, could make the audience sympathize with the characters while structuring his storytelling so that the climaxes made considerable impact.

As in *L'Age de raison,* he introduced many of his own preoccupations—both philosophical and private. Bariona, the village chief, is, like Mathieu, an alter ego, a man with strong feelings about liberty and with no wish for offspring. The German occupation of France is reflected in the situation of the village, which is being squeezed by the fiscal ruthlessness of the Romans; rebellion would be suicidal, but why not inaugurate a defiant religion that will eventually depopulate the Roman Empire, leaving it without soldiers or slaves? "We shall set an example throughout Judea and I hope it is the origin of a new religion, the religion of nothingness, and that the Romans stay masters of our deserted towns . . . by the God of Vengeance and Anger, by Jehovah, I swear never to have a child."[9] Bariona will be unable to keep this oath—his wife is already pregnant—but Sartre kept it.

Influenced by Giraudoux and by Cocteau's adaptations of Sophocles' *Antigone* (1922) and *Oedipus Rex* (1922–25), Sartre introduced an ironical narrator, a chorus that used contemporary language, and a series of anachronisms. One of the shepherds plays a harmonica; characters talk about factories and capitalism. But this was not whimsicality: Sartre was using the Nativity to camouflage a message about the possibilities of resistance in occupied France. To the words "Peace on earth to men of goodwill" Bariona replies defiantly: "I shall not ask for grace or express gratitude. I shall bend my knee to no one, I shall put my dignity into my hatred, I shall keep an exact record of everything suffered by me and by others." He tells the villagers that God himself "can do nothing against this pillar of granite, against this irresistible column, man's freedom." Before the play could be performed, the script was censored by the Germans, but no objections were raised. This is not so odd as it seems. With the success Sartre had achieved before the war, and with the interest the German commanders were taking in French intellectuals, they are unlikely to have been ignorant of his identity. But their policy was to clamp down only on pro-Jewish and anti-German sentiment. If the intellectuals were gagged they would appear to be hostile and dangerous; to let them speak out was to blur the difference between coexistence and collaboration.

Pilate was played by Marc Bénard, who also designed the set. Sartre appeared as one of the three kings, Balthazar, who protests when Bariona tries to stop the villagers from going to worship the newborn Messiah. "Look your misfortune in the face," Bariona exhorts, "for the dignity of man lies in his despair. . . . For man, you see, is always more than he is. . . . Wherever a man is, he is always elsewhere. . . . To the man who hopes everything is smiles and the world is given like a present." Heidegger's phrase "creature of distances" was still at the forefront of Sartre's mind.

He was clever enough to make *Bariona* neither too much like nor too much unlike a religious play. The climax is a conversion, not to Christianity but to optimism in a situation no less dispiriting than that of occupied France. Sartre made his point obliquely. Bariona plans to strangle the Christ child in order to save his villagers from a creed of submissiveness. In the manger he again meets Balthazar, who again argues with him. Skillfully, Sartre divides his message between the two characters. Though the baby is now surrounded by worshipers, says Balthazar, they would all abandon him if they knew he would neither drive out the Romans nor put a stop to human suffering. But Bariona existentializes Christianity: "Christ is here to teach you that you are responsible for yourself and your suffering."

Playing Balthazar, Sartre acted so persuasively that one member of the audience, misunderstanding the play's meaning, was subsequently converted to Christianity. The applause of the prisoners, which was enthusiastic and sustained, gave Sartre his first taste of direct contact with a big audience. He had found a way of preaching in his own style, of rousing the prisoners with a pungent mixture of hope and existentialist pessimism. You are alone, he was saying, you have only yourself to rely on. He had hit on a way of carrying his teaching beyond the classroom and of using words to share—not just with De Beauvoir but with a public—his own pride in being alone and alive.

At the end of the performance he joined in the celebration of the Mass, singing canticles and responses with the choir.[10] To Perrin this seemed to bode well for his salvation, but the communion Sartre was enjoying was not religious. At the stalag he had rediscovered collective life, satisfying a need that had been starved since he left the Ecole Normale. "What I liked at the camp was the feeling of belonging to a crowd. Uninterrupted contact, night and day, talking directly to equals."[11]

Since being captured, he had not been able to keep up the flow of daily correspondence with De Beauvoir; but they went on exchanging letters. It was worrying that no news had come from Nizan—the priests noticed that he mentioned his friend more often than his mother—and eventually he learned that Nizan had been killed at the front on May 6. Sartre stopped talking about him, but gave no indication of what he felt, and resumed his readings of Heidegger with Perrin, appearing punctually every morning at ten. Discussing the sixth chapter, "Die Sorge als Sein des Daseins" ("Care as Being of Existence"), Sartre confided his intention of writing a book on the subject. Sometimes Perrin would let his attention wander to the lice on Sartre's pullover. He noticed that Sartre never killed them, though he often said he had no respect for what was called "life."[12]

The idea of escaping from the camp had been in his mind for a long time. Before Christmas, wanting to tell De Beauvoir that she could expect to see him in Paris soon, he wrote that Poulou would shortly arrive there. Prisoners did escape, and postcards arrived containing coded messages to say they were safely home or had made contact with De Gaulle.[13] Some escaped with help from postal workers, who smuggled them in with the mail to a garage on the edge of Paris but charged several thousand francs for the service.[14] A cheaper means of escape offered itself when the Germans began to release civilians imprisoned because they had been mistaken for servicemen. Some could prove their civilian status by showing their reservists' paybooks, while others could fake civilian status: a group of prisoners were forging reservists' paybooks. Perrin, who was involved with this group, produced a document certifying that Sartre suffered from "partial blindness of the right eye, causing difficulties in orientation."[15] Convinced by Perrin that he could pass himself off as a man who would have been rejected at the medical, Sartre offered to coach the priest in how to simulate the symptoms of epilepsy, so that they could escape together.[16] Eventually, though, Perrin decided to stay on in the camp; Sartre would escape alone.

But the freedom Sartre wanted was not the freedom he had enjoyed before the war. Mathieu had been under pressure from Brunet and from his brother to prove himself free to surrender his freedom—whether to the PCF or to an unwanted marriage. Sartre would commit himself to neither, but he was determined to take action against the Nazis; for too long people who valued freedom had left the initiative to others who did not. "One can't belong to a party: they're all rotten, including the Communist party."[17] "If I joined a party, it would be through a generosity that was all too self-conscious to be moral. The Communist party is right to distrust intellectuals."[18] A new political party should be formed, the Party of Liberty, open to everyone who would commit himself to the ideal of freedom for all.[19]

An opportunity of early escape was provided by an ex-poacher known as Braco, a wizened little man who had killed his wife after finding her in bed with a lover. One day in March he brought Sartre and Perrin an undated letter from the stalag authorities with a message in German to the guard: "Please allow bearer and two accompanying prisoners to pass." It had not been forged but had been picked up by Braco after a farmer had used it and thrown it into a ditch without even crumpling it up. Every day local farmers came into the camp to sell their produce. With the aid of a man, half Luxembourger, half Alsatian, who had trading relationships with the Germans and sometimes dealt in clothes, civilian outfits were acquired for Sartre and the two men who would accompany him. They would wear their stalag uniform until they were outside the camp, with a change of clothes inside the bags they would carry, following Sartre, who would be dressed as a farmer. Perrin watched them leave the camp: "The 'civilian' walked in front, his gait relaxed and heavy, a briefcase in his hand, like every self-respecting German. From the distance he looked like rather a prosperous farmer.... The prisoners followed, side by side, stooping under their luggage. I don't think they raised their eyes once.... I presume that the 'farmer' preserved the appearance of a bad-tempered animal and that he made the right impression, for the barrier was raised almost at once."[20]

Subsequently the Communists would try to discredit Sartre by alleging that the escape had been staged: the Germans had made a bargain to release him because he had promised to work for them. Though this slur can be dismissed, one problem remains. After *Bariona* they could hardly have failed to realize he was the Sartre who had written *La Nausée,* and if they had wanted to recapture him in Paris after his escape, it would not have been difficult. But it would be more advantageous to have him at liberty. If he was one of the intellectuals who could function freely under their régime, he would be helping to demonstrate that it was not oppressive.

(12)

In Occupied Paris

As soon as he arrived in Paris, he went into a café, where it was daunting to see how far apart the customers were sitting. "Suddenly I was afraid—or nearly—I couldn't understand how these squat, bulging buildings could contain such deserts; I was lost: the scattered drinkers seemed further away than the stars."[1] Habituated by the stalag to close physical proximity with fellow prisoners, he no longer had the right to put his hand on a man's leg or greet him with friendly abuse.[2]

He was reunited with De Beauvoir toward the end of March. He left a note at the Hôtel Mistral, where she was living: he would be at the Café des Trois Mousquetaires. He waited there two hours and then went for a walk, leaving a note with a waiter who knew her. When he came back she was waiting for him.

It was not easy to resume their relationship. He was a stranger to the *modus vivendi* that had evolved between the Parisians and the German occupiers. Dubbed "King Otto I" by Céline, the German ambassador, Otto Abetz, an attractive, cultured, urbane Francophile, used his position to construct a nexus of friendly relations with distinguished French socialites, intellectuals, and artists, as well as intimate relationships with French actresses. At the German Institute thousands of people enrolled for the German-language courses, while many of the best known actors and writers (including Barrault, Cocteau, and Céline) were often to be seen in the building.[3] A German victory seemed inevitable. Wanting a maximum of collaboration and a minimum of resistance—in both senses of both words—the Germans set out to be tolerant. Writers and artists would have been reluctant to stop working, even if they had not needed to earn money. The Germans aimed for a maximum of cultural continuity; the risk of anti-Nazi propaganda was balanced by the advantage of involving French intellectuals in complicity. Though paper was in short supply, Abetz ensured that Paris publishers received generous allocations, while the literary censor, Gerhard Heller, rarely used his powers of veto.[4]

Sartre was disturbed to hear that De Beauvoir had signed a declaration that she was neither Jewish nor a Freemason. Questioned about goods sold on the black market, she confessed to buying tea from it.[5] Sartre had arrived in Paris with a purpose: he was going to organize a resistance movement.[6] He was planning to form a group that would find grass-roots support all over France;[7] it had not occurred to him that a number of resistance groups might already exist.

He moved into the Hôtel Mistral but, as before, took a room of his own, a squalid room with a lavatory in the corner. Without troubling to get himself demobilized—he would have had to report at Bourg, in the Free Zone—he was able to resume teaching at the Lycée Pasteur in Neuilly when the summer term began, and the inspector general, Davy, promised that in September he could teach the *khâgne* at the Lycée Condorcet.

As a teacher Sartre now tried to be unobtrusive, and this was disappointing for the boys. Rumors had reached the Lycée Pasteur about the friendly prewar Sartre who had perched tieless on a table as he chatted entertainingly, sometimes letting the boys sit on the steps of a staircase instead of at their desks in a classroom. He was still a good teacher, positive and clear, but he never discussed the war or his experiences in the stalag, and he would round off each lesson by dictating a summary of what he had just said.[8]

In September 1939 he had written that he was "cured of socialism," but the name he now chose for his group was Socialisme et Liberté. To recruit members he sought out former pupils, and met Merleau-Ponty, who had served as an infantry officer.[9] Merleau-Ponty had also come under the influence of Husserl and was already at work on the book that would be published ten years later, *La Phénoménologie de la perception.* He immediately joined Sartre's group, as did Bost, who had recovered from his wound and was able, even under these austere conditions, to enjoy civilian life in Paris. The first meeting of the group was held in De Beauvoir's room at the Hôtel Mistral. Merleau-Ponty and Bost attended, as did the anthropologist Jean Pouillon, two *normaliens* called Jean Cuzin and Jean Desanti, Desanti's wife Dominique, and a few of their friends. Desanti was in favor of attacking prominent collaborators, including Marcel Déat, formerly a socialist minister but now leader of the pro-Nazi Rassemblement Nationale Populaire, but the consensus was in favor of moving more slowly: they would recruit more supporters by forming cells of five people, each member having the responsibility of finding five new members. They would also collect information, which would be publicized by circulating pamphlets and a news bulletin, to be edited alternately by a Marxist and a non-Marxist.[10]

For Sartre there was almost nothing that could not be formulated epigrammatically, and in the first bulletin he argued that if Germany won the war, it would be the function of the Resistance to make sure that she lost the peace. Many other groups had been formed, but in the spring of 1941 there was little organized resistance, partly because the PCF had been following the Comintern directive to support Stalin's policy toward Hitler. In 1940 numerous Communist students were already rebelling against the party line, and many of them joined in the demonstration of November 11 at the Arc de Triomphe, but during the spring of 1941 there would not have been more than fifty men in Paris capable of using weapons against the Germans. Georges Politzer was one of the few intellectuals who took initiatives that helped an effective resistance to emerge. Another was Charles Tillon, who contacted veterans from Spain able to train men to become instructors in the use of weapons.[11]

There were also right-wing groups, and Sartre made contact with one of these, the Pentagon. He also met Jean Cavaillès, a philosophy teacher who had started a resistance movement at Clermont. Members of Sartre's group were extravagantly incautious: Bost carried a duplicating machine through the streets; Pouillon regularly carried pamphlets in his briefcase.[12] But in one way they were less at risk than other groups: since they had all known each other for some time, it was unlikely that an insider would denounce them to the Germans.

The most quixotic of all Sartre's activities for Socialisme et Liberté was to write a draft of about a hundred pages for a French postwar constitution. Assuming that current actions could make sense only in the perspective of a plan for the future, he used Proudhon and Marx as his models in formulating proposals for a utopian France in which objects would be valued according to the quantity of work that went into making them, while each group of workers and tradesmen would be represented in a democratic parliament. The document was destroyed when the woman who was smuggling it to the Free Zone in the south, nervous of being discovered with it on the train, flushed it down a toilet.[13]

London was being blitzed, and in May the House of Commons had been hit by a bomb. In North Africa, Rommel's army was advancing, and the Vichy government promised naval help to Germany. In June the Nazis invaded the USSR, and although this provoked an Anglo-Soviet alliance, the German army had little trouble in piercing the Stalin Line and taking Smolensk, making it look as though Hitler's invasion of Russia would be more successful than Napoleon's. In France persecution of the Jews was stepped up. They were forbidden to carry on any business activities, schools were limited to a quota of Jewish pupils, foreign Jews were interned and deported, and anti-Semitic propaganda was intensified, though most Parisians stayed away from cinemas showing German films such as *Jud Süss* (*Jew Süss*).[14] The Communists had already been under attack in the press; after the USSR entered the war, they were liable to be arrested as public enemies.

Resistance intellectuals mostly refused to write for the press, which came under Nazi scrutiny, but Sartre, acting against De Beauvoir's advice, accepted the offer of a regular column in the weekly *Comoedia*, which was being revived under the editorship of a journalist, René Delange, who claimed that the paper would be independent and unaffected by censorship. Sartre was eager to write about Melville's *Moby Dick*, and his piece appeared in the issue dated January 2, 1941; but once he had seen the paper, he refused to go on writing for it.[15]

Theatrical activity continued in Paris. Barrault staged Aeschylus' *Suppliant Women* at the Roland-Carros stadium with music by Honegger. Olga played a small part in it, which gave Sartre the idea of writing a play with a good role for her. This time he would have a bigger audience than for his stalag play. He would again be writing as a victim to fellow victims, using history and myth as a code for smuggling inflammatory ideas across the frontiers of censorship.

THERE was nothing to stop him from taking a summer vacation with De Beauvoir. Provided that you went without luggage, it was easy to cross into the Free Zone, and while they were there, he could get himself demobilized. But his main object was to make contacts for Socialisme et Liberté. De Beauvoir already had a bicycle; Sartre was given one by her friend and former pupil, Nathalie Sorokine, who stole bicycles. Jacques Bost lent them a tent and camping equipment. Parcels could be sent into the Free Zone, so they forwarded the bicycles and luggage to a priest who had escaped from the stalag to Roanne. They booked railway tickets to Montceau-les-Mines; at a café there the proprietor could put them in touch with someone who would smuggle them across the border. They sat waiting in suspense all afternoon until a woman of about forty, dressed in black, sat down with them and offered, for a fairly small fee, to take them across. She would be in greater danger than they would. When it was dark they followed her in silence across fields and through woods. Sometimes she would signal them to stop moving. Eventually they were in the Free Zone. They spent the rest of the night at an inn, where they were given mattresses in a room they shared with six other refugees and a baby. In the morning they caught the train to Roanne.

They picked up their bicycles and pedaled about twenty-five miles before staying overnight at a hotel. Riding on, they spent the next night in a field outside Mâcon. They soon became expert at pitching and striking the tent, but as Sartre was less enamored than De Beauvoir of the open-air life, they usually camped near a town or village so that they could breakfast in a bistro.[16]

At Bourg, on August 23, Sartre was given a certificate of demobilization, though not without being reprimanded by the French officer for faking entries in his service book. With De Beauvoir he went for walks over the hills around Lyon and saw American films in the movie theaters. At Saint-Etienne he showed her the house that had belonged to his family. He preferred bicycling to walking but sometimes pedaled so slowly that he fell off. "I was thinking about something else," he would explain.[17] It seemed odd that in the middle of a war they should be cycling peacefully along hill roads in the Cévennes, but Cavaillès had given him some addresses, and he made contact with one member of the Resistance, a *normalien* called Kahn.

They cycled down to Marseille, found a room near the old harbor, and repeated walks they had taken on previous visits. At a café in Porquerolles, Sartre began to work on the opening scene of his play *Les Mouches (The Flies)*. After his classical education he was more at home with Greek myth than with biblical history, and the first theatrical experience he remembered was seeing Mounet-Sully as Oedipus.[18] After searching for Gide at his home in Cabris, Sartre was directed by his daughter Catherine to look for him at a hotel in Grasse. When Sartre asked for advice, Gide, misunderstanding his intentions, told him the story of a married Dutchman who, finding himself to be latently homosexual, had come to ask Gide for an address.[19] The conversation with André Malraux was no more productive. At his villa in Saint-Jean-Cap-Ferrat he fed Sartre Chicken Maryland and advised him that no action could usefully be taken.[20]

In Grenoble, Colette Audry told them about a village near Châlons where it was easy to make arrangements for crossing back over the border. About twenty people, all with bicycles, followed a guide along narrow woodland tracks to a road with barbed-wire fencing all along it: they had to wriggle under the wire. Sartre and De Beauvoir had spent all their money. A draft was waiting for them at Auxerre, but traveling through Burgundy they were tormented by hunger. From Auxerre they returned to Paris by train but left again to stay with Mme. Morel. They

returned to Paris in time for the start of Sartre's first term at the Lycée
Condorcet, where he was to go on teaching until 1944.[21]

DURING the summer, relations between the Germans and French had
deteriorated. The Communists had organized a riot near the Porte
Saint-Denis, and two demonstrators had been shot. A German soldier
had been killed; a Frenchman had tried to assassinate Laval and Déat.
There had been sabotage on the railways, and the Germans were
operating a reprisal system, shooting several hostages—usually Communists or Jews—when any member of the Wehrmacht was killed; in
October the death of two German officers was avenged by shooting
ninety-eight Frenchmen and imprisoning twenty-seven in concentration camps.

German armies had occupied most of western USSR and the
Ukraine, but the retreating Russians burned the land they were surren-
dering. After the attack on Pearl Harbor, America had entered the war,
but in the Pacific the Japanese had been winning a series of significant
victories. In this perspective it was hard for Sartre to go on believing, as
he had in the stalag, that he had a historical function as an organizer of
resistance. Other groups were disintegrating. The Communists were
better organized, while the non-Communist left was no longer so critical of the Stalin-Hitler pact; to Sartre the advantages of a common
front were obvious, but party members distrusted "petty-bourgeois intellectuals," and even some of Sartre's friends believed the rumor that
his release from the stalag must mean he had agreed to work for the
Germans as an *agent provocateur*. In his group morale plummeted as some
members defected, and a young woman, a former student of De Beauvoir's, was deported after joining a similar group. In the end Sartre and
Merleau-Ponty decided to dissolve the group, which had accomplished
nothing. Sartre would concentrate on his play.[22]

During the hard winter, though they were by no means well off,
Sartre and De Beauvoir helped to support Olga, Wanda, Bost, and
Nathalie Sorokine, who was living in a small hotel on the Rue Delambre. Even the cheapest restaurants were now too expensive for
them, and finally, at the age of thirty-five, De Beauvoir resigned herself
to cooking regular meals—an effort she would have to sustain for three
years. At the Hôtel Mistral she moved into a room with a kitchen attached to it, borrowing saucepans, casseroles, and crockery from her sister's studio. She made careful use of the coupons in their ration books
and searched diligently for unrationed foods such as cabbage, beets,
pasta, and dried vegetables. But there was little in the shops, and they

were often hungry. Even this did not interfere with Sartre's obsessiveness as a writer; De Beauvoir found it harder than he did to work with an empty stomach but easier to give up smoking. He would search in the gutters and under the seats of cafés for cigarette butts he could use to fill his pipe.

Their pride was sapped, and though some comfort was to be had from the sense of solidarity with the thirty-five million people who could no longer feel that their country was their own, he also experienced, more shamingly, an involuntary solidarity with the Germans who were sharing "the unanimous life of a big city."[23] The uniformed foreigners in the streets did not seem hostile. Clutching briefcases and hurrying to their offices, or getting lost and asking help in imperfect French, or sitting in cafés sipping lemonade, they caused embarrassment without provoking hatred. At night it was different. Just before midnight, running footsteps on the pavements belonged to Frenchmen hurrying to observe the curfew; after midnight the footsteps were all German. Frightened yells were sometimes to be heard. "There was no one in Paris without a relation or a friend who had been arrested or deported or shot." As Sartre said, it seemed as though there were hidden holes in the city, which was gradually being emptied through them, as if seized by an internal hemorrhage that had now revealed itself.[24]

Along with goods that had disappeared from the shops, laughter had dwindled in everyday conversation. No tourists were to be seen in the streets and few cars. Many stores, cafés, and bars had closed; their proprietors had disappeared or been deported. Hotels and movie houses had been requisitioned by the Germans. There were plinths without statues, unilluminated advertisements, public gardens disfigured by zigzag trenches and reinforced concrete pillboxes.[25] There were no pictures in the Louvre, no English or American books in the bookstores, no wine from the Free Zone—the shops displayed only dummy bottles of Meursault and Saint-Emilion.[26]

No apparent attempt was made to monitor what Sartre taught his pupils in the lycée, but the boys could not be sure whether they would ever take their examination. His job was to prepare them for the future; no one could know what the future would be like.

ORDERS had been issued that everyone was to take shelter when the air-raid siren sounded, closing stores and offices. In Paris these orders were ignored. English and American bombs were being dropped elsewhere in France, but not here. Like his compatriots, Sartre felt ambivalent toward the damage, destruction, and death: these had to be welcome insofar as they were weakening the Germans.[27] Since coupons were needed for shoe repairs, De Beauvoir, who was permanently wearing her turban and troubling less about her appearance, took to wearing wooden-soled clogs. She and Sartre saw little of their former friends except the four who had become almost members of their family—Wanda, Olga, Bost, and Nathalie. Nor did the six see each other at the same time. De Beauvoir testifies: "When I was chatting at the Flore with Olga (or Nathalie), when Sartre went out with Wanda, when Nathalie and Wanda were talking together, none of us would ever have sat down at their table. We always had and would always keep a predilection for conversation *à deux*."[28] Sartre and she had abandoned Montparnasse. Usually they would breakfast at the Café des Trois Mousquetaires, where the radio was always turned on loudly, and in the evening meet at the Flore, where nothing was to be had except ersatz beer and coffee.

Sartre would spend a good deal of the day at either the Flore or the Coupole, packing a subversive message into the story of Orestes. "The drama I'd have liked to write was about a terrorist who, by ambushing Germans, becomes the pretext for the execution of fifty hostages."[29] After the ambush, resistance fighters could save the hostages' lives only by giving themselves up; the play argues that they should neither do this nor feel guilty about causing the deaths of innocent people. Sartre also wanted to show how absurd it was to accept defeat as a punishment France deserved. Pétain was preaching submissiveness. "You are suffering," he had told the French people on June 17, 1941, "and you will still go on suffering for a long time, because we have not yet expiated all our faults."[30] The press was echoing this dismal message. No counterargument could have been published openly, but Sartre could reiterate in his play the point he had made in *Bariona:* even the gods are powerless to interfere with human freedom.

Giraudoux had already retold the story in his 1937 play, *Electre.* When he brought the gods into the action he usually deprived them of dignity and power; Sartre followed suit. The way Jupiter befriends Aegisthus, the usurper, parallels the way history has favored Hitler, while Thebes, infested with flies, represents Paris under German occupation. As in *Bariona,* the social situation is one in which the oppressed citizens appear to have little freedom, but a hero can show them how to preserve their integrity by rejecting the role of helpless victims and accepting responsibility for their situation. In Aeschylus' *Oresteia* only superhuman powers can rescue Orestes from his guilt. But Sartre's Orestes follows Heidegger in believing conscience is the will to accept the guilt that is inescapable. While the occupying army makes it impossible to fight for the future except by putting other people's lives at risk, Orestes is exemplary because he can ignore the Pétainist arguments of Jupiter and Aegisthus, the proto-fascist god and king who try to scare him away from Thebes or bully him into acceptance of the status quo.

Like Mathieu, and like Sartre, Orestes at first finds freedom troublesome. He feels no urge to avenge the death of his father. What can these people have to do with him? A king should share the memories of his people, and after growing up in exile, Orestes has different memories. Electra's attitude is more rebellious. Reviling the god who has allowed the people to condone the murder and accept the rule of the usurper, she is waiting impatiently for her brother, while Clytemnestra feels scared. The queen represents the docile conformism of occupied France: "For fifteen years we have kept silent, and only our eyes betray us."

The usurper, Aegisthus, has little appetite left for living: "Almighty God, who am I unless it is the fear that other people have of me?" Orestes is uniquely dangerous because he knows that he is free, and, as Jupiter admits, "Once freedom explodes in a human soul, the gods can do nothing against that man." Aegisthus is killed onstage, Clytemnestra offstage, but the killer Orestes has chosen to become is quite different from his sister in his reaction to the doglike Eumenides. Though she has taken no part in the killing, she is so overwhelmed with remorse that she cannot stand up to them. While Gide had often dramatized the challenge of individualism to religious authority, and in *Amphitryon 38* (1929) Giraudoux's Alcmena had taught Jupiter that the gods could not manipulate human relationships, Sartre generates greater theatrical electricity out of Orestes' defiance:

I *am* my liberty. You had scarcely created me when I stopped belonging to you. . . . Suddenly liberty burst on me and went through me. Nature jumped backwards. I was ageless and felt quite alone in the middle of your well-meaning little world, like a man who has lost his shadow; there was nothing left in heaven, neither good nor evil. Nor anyone to give me orders . . . For I, Jupiter, am a man, and each man must find his own way. Nature hates men, and so, god of the gods, do you. . . . As for me, I don't hate you. What have I got to do with you or you with me? We'll pass each other, like boats in a stream, without touching.

Before leaving Argos he displays his pride in the crime, which is his *raison d'être*. "You can neither punish me nor reprimand me, and that's why I make you afraid. Yet I love you, my people, and it's for you that I

killed." This is very much a resistance Orestes, a destroyer who does not
see it as his duty to stay with his people as their ruler.

AT Christmas, Sartre and De Beauvoir traveled to stay with Mme.
Morel in La Pouèze, taking their bicycles in the train to Angers, and
cycling the final fourteen miles. They were given more meat than
they'd had in Paris, but dinner invariably consisted of apple fritters.[31]
Mostly they stayed indoors, enjoying the luxurious log fires, chatting
with Mme. Morel, who no longer came to Paris, and reading, though
bookstores were no longer full of exciting new publications.

Back in Paris, De Beauvoir stayed on in the Hôtel Mistral, but Sartre
moved several times. His longest stays were all in hotels close to the
Jardins du Luxembourg—the Hôtel Welcome, in the Rue de Seine, the
Grand Hôtel de Paris, in the Rue Bonaparte, and the Hôtel Chaplain,
in the Rue Jules-Chaplain. But De Beauvoir was not left alone in the
Mistral. Nathalie moved there from the Rue Delambre, and when the
sirens sounded, she hammered on De Beauvoir's door, begging her to
shelter in the Métro station. But De Beauvoir was confident the Allies
would never bomb the center of Paris.[32]

The Mancys still had the flat in Passy, where Sartre visited them a
good deal. His relationship with his stepfather had been improved by
the war and the hostility they shared toward collaborators.

Before Easter, Marc Bénard was released from the stalag. He was living at Le Havre in a big house belonging to his father-in-law, a successful lawyer; Sartre and De Beauvoir were invited there during the
Easter vacation. The old port of Rouen and the suburbs of Le Havre
had been badly damaged, and when they arrived at the house, which
was on high ground near the port, Bénard's father-in-law told them
what a good view he had of RAF raids and how exciting it was when a
bomb hit a gasoline refinery. Later on, walking with Bénard to the old
Quartier Saint-François, Sartre and De Beauvoir found nothing left of
the sailors' dives or the slate-fronted houses they had liked so much.

Served in handsome dishes, the dinner consisted of Swedish turnips.
Afterward, while they were sitting around the radio listening to the
BBC news, the hum of British bombers became audible.[33] Without
moving from their chairs, they listened to both the broadcast and the
sound of dropping bombs—a whistle followed by a loud explosion close
by. The radio voice sounded closer than the bombs, though only a few
hundred yards away houses were being pulverized, and in the morning
they saw shrapnel in the garden.

Leaving Le Havre, Sartre and De Beauvoir crossed the Seine by ferry. The rest of their vacation was spent in La Pouèze. They returned to Paris by train, carrying eggs with them, and from now on the indefatigable Mme. Morel sent them two or three food parcels every month. But the mail was slow, and the roast pork in the first parcel had maggots in it. De Beauvoir did not throw it away, and each time a stinking parcel arrived, she cooked as much as she could of the meat, using herbs to disguise the taste.[34]

Since the beginning of February, Jews in the Occupied Zone had been forbidden to change their addresses or to go out after eight in the evening. From June on they were ordered to wear a yellow Star of David. There were few survivors among those who obeyed, but many disobeyed, especially in Montparnasse and Saint-Germain-des-Prés. Even after the decree of July 15, which forbade Jews to enter restaurants, movie houses, or any public buildings, they were still to be seen in the cafés. Rumors were circulating about Gestapo roundups, and French Jews were being interned in a camp at Drancy; thousands were deported to Germany. Many went into hiding in the Free Zone; many were caught while trying to escape. At the end of May, Sartre learned that Politzer had been tortured and shot.

Sartre has been criticized for not joining the Resistance and neither protesting against what was happening to the Jews nor helping individual Jews in danger. True to his pattern of discontinuity, he had swung from organizing his own underground resistance movement to the generalized hymn about liberty that could be sung safely through a play. Jean Wahl was disappointed that he remained silent when all Jewish teachers in France were fired.[35] Vladimir Jankélévitch suggested that all Sartre's postwar political activity was "a kind of unhealthy compensation, a remorse, a quest for the danger he did not want to run during the war."[36] It would have been easy to put himself at risk in 1942. For him, as for others, the question of how to balance the danger against the usefulness of the contribution he could make was a delicate moral question which changed its center of gravity as it gradually became apparent that the Germans were not going to win the war. Optimism was reinforced by ulterior considerations: the masters of the future would be impressed unfavorably by good-conduct marks awarded during the occupation.

Resistance to the Germans gathered momentum slowly. Inside France the most important leader was Jean Moulin. After escaping from the Vichy zone into Portugal, he made his way to England, where he met De Gaulle, who at the beginning of 1942 had him parachuted back into France, where he made contact with leaders of underground networks and many intellectuals who were now involving themselves in sabotage work. Sartre took minimal risks in 1942, even managing to keep his job at the lycée when other teachers, suspected of anti-Nazism, were dismissed, but in 1943 he swung to the opposite extreme. At the end of May, Moulin organized the first meeting of the Conseil National de la Résistance, aiming to coordinate militant and intellectual movements. Sartre's name was not mentioned at this meeting, but, eager to become more involved, he volunteered for action when he met the secretary of the committee, Pierre Kaan. Committee members, though, were suspicious of him as a writer whose work had been published and staged during the occupation.[37] He now put himself at risk again by contributing to underground papers, *Combat* and *Les Lettres Françaises,* but it is doubtful whether he did much more than this after the disbandment of Socialisme et Liberté in the autumn of 1941.

BASICALLY the Vichy government was antirepublican and authoritarian, blaming the defeat of France on the decadence that had ensued after the 1789 revolution. Pierre Laval, who had emerged in the autumn of 1940 as the main spokesman for Vichy France, was eclipsed by the Anglophobe Admiral Darlan, who acted as chief minister from February 1941 to April 1942, when his policy of military collaboration with the Germans failed to win him their trust, and it was on Hitler's orders that Laval was reinstated as chief minister in April 1942. By shrewd maneuvering he managed to stop France's commitment to Germany from going any deeper, while sabotage continued, regardless of the notices on the tiled walls of Métro stations reminding the French people about the savage reprisals. The closest male relations of offenders would be shot, their wives deported, their children interned. As part of a drive to drum up support among intellectuals, a collaborationist bookstore was opened in the Latin Quarter, but it was wrecked by a grenade. Students staged anti-German demonstrations, and some youngsters advertised their Anglo-American sympathies by wearing zoot suits and long hair, carrying umbrellas and taking an exorbitant interest in swing music.

Sartre made no attempt to publish his novel, but he was eager to have his play produced. It was rejected by Jean-Louis Barrault, who had been playing Hamlet at the Comédie Française, but Dullin was sympathetic, though he had been losing money at the Théâtre de la Cité—the new name for what had been the Théâtre Sarah Bernhardt. (A theater could not bear the name of a Jewish actress.) With the crowd of extras it entailed, *Les Mouches* would be an expensive play to mount, and when Dullin thought he had found a rich backer, the man turned out to be a penniless con man.[38]

With no prospect of a production until the new season began in the autumn, Sartre did not want to stay in Paris through the summer, and he left with De Beauvoir and Bost for a cycling vacation in the Free Zone. Once again it was easy to cross the border illegally. They had been given an address in Sauveterre, near Avignon, and after a guide had appeared on his bicycle to lead the way down a country lane, they had lunch in Navarrenx, where the inn was crowded with refugees, mostly Jewish. Sartre, De Beauvoir, and Bost went on to tour the Pyrenees together, but one advantage of having Bost along was that Sartre could stay behind writing while the other two went out on expeditions. They went to Lourdes, and when the two of them walked from the Col du Tourmalet to the top of the Midi de Bigorre, they left Sartre sitting in a field with a writing pad on his knees. Despite the strong wind, a great many pages had been filled by the time they got back.[39]

It was an exhausting and uncomfortable trip. Unable to find hotels, the three of them often had to sleep in barns, and when they tried to cycle uphill they could feel how undernourished they were. For lunch they could usually buy fruit and tomatoes in a village, but meat was scarce, and they mostly dined on soup and some unattractive vegetable dish. At Foix, Sartre and De Beauvoir parted company with Bost, who wanted to visit friends in Lyon before returning to Paris; but after being caught while trying to cross the border, he was imprisoned for a fortnight at Châlons.

Sartre and De Beauvoir made their way through Provence to Marseille, sometimes stealing grapes from vineyards they passed. In the Marseille movie theaters American films were to be seen, and they stayed in the town for several days despite the food shortage. The expensive restaurants were still open, but only rationed food was on sale in the stores. Hunger reduced Sartre and De Beauvoir to eating moldy bread spread with a ferocious garlicky ersatz mayonnaise made without eggs. Afterward they would suck tasteless red or green ices.[40]

After cycling across the Larzac plateau they went on to Pau by train but then had to waste a day waiting for their bicycles to arrive. They cycled on to Navarrenx, where they found nothing to eat. A friend of De Beauvoir's family was living about twelve miles away, but Sartre refused to go with her. She was given a loan and a generous lunch, but when they arrived at Dax he was weak with hunger. The only food they could buy was a plate of lentils. They bought tickets for Angers so that they could go on to La Pouèze, where they tried to revive themselves by taking a shower. But in the dining room, after eating a few spoonfuls of soup, Sartre collapsed. He stayed in bed for three days. De Beauvoir had lost sixteen pounds in weight, and she was covered with a rash.[41]

They stayed for a month in Mme. Morel's eccentric household, which consisted almost entirely of old women. Dr. Morel had been in bed since the beginning of the war. His room was illuminated only dimly, by a night-light. He would lie motionless for days, and he was liable to attacks, which would bring on profuse sweating. An elderly maid, Joséphine, looked after him. There were also a bald octogenarian housekeeper, Nanette, who had worked for the Morels in Paris, and an eighty-two-year-old humpbacked woman, who lived on the second floor of the house. On the ground floor was an elderly Russian princess. She was stone-deaf and never left her room, which she shared with a small long-haired white dog. Mme. Morel's Briard collie bitch was kept on a chain because she was dangerous to children and small animals, but while Sartre and De Beauvoir were there she broke free and disemboweled the white dog. The ancient princess sobbed for hours.

Sartre could not easily be persuaded to go out for a walk or a bicycle ride; his inclination was to stay indoors reading and writing. He was working simultaneously on the sequel to *L'Age de raison* and on *L'Etre et le Néant,* the gigantic philosophical treatise that had been growing out of the ideas assembled in his army diaries. Each of the new books profited from having evolved alongside the other; *L'Etre et le Néant* was written fast, on the basis of thinking he had already done. Neither book would have been what it was but for the German occupation, which gave a new edge and a new resonance to Sartre's passion for liberty. In *Les Mouches* he had highlighted the freedom inalienably available to the man who refused to view himself as a criminal or a sinner; *L'Etre et le Néant* centers on the freedom of the individual to choose—and especially to choose himself—within a historical situation that appears to enslave him. "My birth makes me a worker, a Frenchman, a hereditary syphilitic or a tubercular";[42] but I must "obey Nature in order to command Nature." Sartre endorses Descartes's advice: we should "try to conquer ourselves rather than fortune." While our freedom of action may be restricted by various obstacles, we are free to form the perspective in which they reveal themselves as limitations. In Sartre's terms, "a free For-itself can exist only in a resistant world. . . . Success is not important to liberty."[43] But there are no accidents in life. "If I am enlisted in a war, this war is *my* war; it is in my image, and I deserve it."[44] Unless I opt out by deserting or committing suicide, "everything happens as if I carried the entire responsibility for this war. . . . To live this war is to choose myself through it, and to choose it through my choice of myself. . . . So *I am* this war which concludes and limits and explains the period which preceded it."[45]

Similarly in the new novel, *Le Sursis* (*The Reprieve*), Boris is made to reflect that he is lucky in comparison with young men killed in street accidents or dying of cholera. He had known that war was coming, and his parents "had put him into the world for this war: they had brought him up for it, had sent him to the lycée, to the Sorbonne, they had given him culture . . . they had spared no expense to make sure he would be a fine corpse, fresh and healthy. . . . It's my war. It's what made me, and I made it: we're inseparable. I can't even imagine what I'd be like if it hadn't been due to break out."[46]

Sartre's characters have to be heroic in their willingness to shoulder responsibility for contemporary history, and later on, his existentialism would win popularity by implicitly promising to raise its adherents to the same level of heroism by making them fully accountable; choosing themselves, they were volunteering to take responsibility for their epoch. Each decision would have a cosmic dimension: abandoned by God, humanity depended on each individual.

In his January 1939 essay on Husserl, Sartre had written rhetorically about the horror and charm of the world phenomenology had restored—the world of artists and prophets, "frightening, hostile, dangerous, with havens of grace and love." It is not through any Proustian immersion in subjectivity that we can find ourselves; "it is on the road, in the town, in the middle of the crowd, a thing among things, a man among men."[47] This panache continues into *L'Etre et le Néant,* which equates consciousness with choice, choice with action, and freedom with passion, without ignoring frustration and suffering. Human reality, writes Sartre, is "by nature an unhappy consciousness with no chance of escaping its unhappy state."[48] It is constantly hungry for the physical existence it can never achieve. This is dramatized in the novel when Mathieu, leaning over the parapet of a bridge, feels envious of the stone. "It was there enormous and solid, enclosing in itself the squashed silence and the compressed darkness which are the interior of things. It was there; a plenitude. He would have liked to grapple onto this stone, melt into it, fill himself with its opacity and repose. But it could be of no help to him: it was outside, permanently."[49] Consciousness is equated with lack and with nothingness. The For-itself is always in flight from the In-itself and always in pursuit of it. Neither could exist without the other, but they are structurally incompatible. Here the influence of Husserl and Heidegger had not so much displaced as reinforced that of Bergson, who had characterized human reality as something which can be defined only as movement into the future. We are free when our actions emanate from our whole personality and when we take off into the future, but spontaneity is inhibited when consciousness feels like a thing.[50] Sartre is indebted to Bergson for this crucial equation of consciousness with flight into the future. The assumption is that, like movement, it has no corporal existence, no physical constituents.

In his fundamental division of Being into two orders, the For-itself and the In-itself, Sartre ignores the problem of animal consciousness (and animal elements in human consciousness); while assuming, as in *La Transcendance de l'Ego,* that consciousness is independent of self, he feels entitled to disregard the question of how consciousness is rooted in the brain. "Nothing of what I see comes from me," he declares, "there is *nothing* outside what I see or what I could see." Jacques Lacan was later to take over this assumption in his dictum "I am not where I think, and I think where I'm not." In *L'Etre et le Néant, as in La Transcendance de l'Ego,* consciousness is transcendence, a project in which the For-itself goes beyond itself, but in the new book Hegel is accused of letting epistemological and ontological optimism hush up the scandal of the plurality of consciousness."[51] Sartre, like Marx, is substantially indebted to Hegel's analysis of the relationship between the Master and the Slave, but Iris Murdoch is as unfair to dismiss *L'Etre et le Néant* as "a lengthy footnote to *The Phenomenology of Mind*"[52] as George Steiner is to dismiss it as a footnote to Heidegger's *Sein und Zeit.*[53] Unlike Hegel, Sartre recognizes that there is no reciprocity between Master and Slave, no common measure "between what I am for him, what he is for me, what I am for myself, what he is for himself."[54] The relationship between the self and the other is quadrilateral, and Sartre is at his best in characterizing it. He had always felt abnormally vulnerable to the gaze of other people—a weakness that is the source of great strength in his writing—and in the army, having to survive without privacy, he became even more concerned with our awareness of the way other people are aware of us. It feels as though the other person has stolen my being from me, and this is welcome insofar as it tends to stabilize me in objective existence, but I have no control over the image he forms of me. If I look at someone who is looking at me, I see only his eyes, not his look. Forming an image of him, I make him into an object which I possess. Since I build my subjectivity on the collapse of his, conflict is inevitable, involving both sadism and masochism. I am a slave insofar as I need someone else to constitute me as a body but I turn his aggression against him when I make him into an object.[55]

Many of Sartre's key terms (including Being, Nothingness, Transcendence, For-itself, In-itself, and Facticity) derive from Heidegger, but this is not to say that Sartre uses them in the same sense. His Nothingness is different from Heidegger's concept of an active or nihilating nothingness (*das nichtende Nichts*), while *Sein und Zeit* characterizes Being as something impersonal that is simultaneously close to us and remote from us, simultaneously hidden and revealed. Heidegger identifies phenomenological truth with revelation of Being, maintaining that every philosophical question pivots on the question of existence, but, as he explains when he dissociates himself from Sartrian existentialism in his "Brief über den Humanismus" ("Letter on Humanism," 1946–47), he never equated existence with "the actuality of the *ego cogito*." He had not been referring to "the actuality of subjects who act with and for each other" but to "ecstatic dwelling in the nearness of Being." What Sartre means by Being is closer to what Heidegger means by *Dasein*— the conscious being of the questioner who has power to organize his impressions of the world. When Antoine Roquentin confronted the chestnut tree, he was grappling with what Heidegger calls the truth of Being. But Sartre's wartime experiences tended to make him think of the individual as surrounded only by other adults and things—a world without children, animals, or plants.

He criticizes the asexuality of Heidegger's *Dasein,* but his own explanation of sexuality ignores animal impulses and presents sexual appetite as independent of physiological structure. Since our organs do not derive from the ontology of consciousness, he insists, the same must be true of sexual desire:[56] what I want to possess is the subjectivity of the other. I need her to make herself into an object that I can act on. I try to strip her body not only of clothing but also movements, making it—and making myself—into flesh as consciousness slides toward consenting passivity. In fact, most men do not try to strip the woman's body of movements, but Sartre takes his own sexuality as the norm. He is also untypical in his revulsion against the animal instincts that take control:

> Suddenly the one who desires turns into a heavy tranquillity which is frightening, his eyes stare and seem half closed, his movements are clogged with a heavy, sticky sweetness . . . and when one fights against this desire, it is the languor one is fighting. If the resistance succeeds, the desire, before vanishing, becomes distinct and clear, like hunger. . . . One will feel lucid, but with heavy head and a pounding heart.[57]

Desire is a lack of being,[58] a feeling that arises from the For-itself's need to rediscover its being, which has been estranged by the other.[59] Sartre's obsessive voluntarism has generated a puritanic animosity against sexual abandon: Thou shalt be free, but Thou shalt never let go.

In his view all human appetites and activities are tributaries of the stream toward being. Even the acquisitive impulse derives from this source. Ownership is primarily a symbolical or magical relationship. What I secretly want is the world—I want to be it and to possess it; the object I desire is merely representative.[60] I am the objects that belong to me. Without them I am nothing but a nothingness that possesses. Through ownership I rediscover a form of being that tallies with the being I have in the eyes of other people, and property serves as a defense against them. "What is mine is myself in nonsubjective form insofar as I am the free foundation of it."[61] Destroying and consuming are variant forms of possessing. In destroying an object I establish my appropriation of it, at the same time as stopping it from brandishing its impenetrability at me; this is what Charles does in *Le Sursis* when he smashes the mug that the nurse has given him as a souvenir. She is less generous than she seems. In *L'Etre et le Néant* Sartre argues that underneath all giving is an urge to destroy, which is basically an urge to possess. To give is to enslave. I force the recipient to preserve this part of myself that I no longer want.[62]

Even smoking can be analyzed similarly as an acquisitive and destructive activity. Rhythmically annihilated as I breathe, tobacco represents the world, which, symbolically, I am destroying and incorporating. The argument has circled back to nothingness. What I am is a lack of being, and what I lack is the being that exists all around me. This is what I want. "So my freedom is choosing to be God—a choice which is translated and reflected in all my activities."[63]

> Every human reality is a passion in that it tries to lose itself in order to become a foundation for being and at the same time to form the In-itself which escapes contingency by being its own foundation, the *Ens causa sui*, which religions call God. The passion of man, therefore, inverts that of Christ, for man loses himself as man so that God may be born. But the idea of God contradicts itself, and we lose ourselves in vain. Man is a useless passion.[64]

This is his conclusion in *L'Etre et le Néant*.

Throughout the book philosophy overlaps with psychology. For nearly twenty years—from his study of psychological books while at the Ecole Normale to his study of his fellow soldiers' behavior—nothing had interested Sartre more than the functioning of human consciousness. The vitality of both his fiction and his philosophy is nourished by insights that come from the same stockpot of observations and reflections. Neither of the new books could have been written without Husserl and Heidegger, but eclectic though he was, Sartre was also stubbornly critical, and in *L'Etre et le Néant* it soon becomes obvious that he had been unable to forgive Heidegger for not taking consciousness as his starting point. In the Introduction, gravitating away from Husserl toward Heidegger, Sartre seems to be penetrating to a deeper ontological level, but he makes only a perfunctory case for "fullness of being." For consciousness to operate, he argues, something must be there for it to focus on, and he subsequently concerns himself less with the nature of being than with the contrast between what he defines as its two modes—the For-itself and the In-itself. Everything devoid of consciousness belongs to the In-itself, while the For-itself is equated with what Heidegger calls nihilation. Underneath Sartre's radicalism is a bedrock of Cartesian conservatism. Conditioned by his philosophical training, he goes on taking the *cogito* as the starting point, while for Heidegger the central truth is the truth of Being.

No less than *Bariona*, *L'Etre et le Néant* is the product of a period in which France was occupied by the enemy; one of Sartre's needs was to console himself and his readers by emphasizing the freedom available in an anthropocentric universe. For Sartre, man is the only god in a godless world; for Heidegger, we are not "in a situation where there are only human beings" but in one "where principally there is Being."[65] Though Heidegger's periphrastic and repetitious glorification of Being may appear to lack philosophical sophistication, he is cogent in his attacks on Sartre's simplistic adherence to the Cartesian *cogito*, his humanism in which man is the sole source of meaning, and his uncritical use of such terms as "man," "existence," and "essence." More cautious in its use of language, Heidegger's philosophy is more durable, less obviously a product of its period.

Temperamentally, Heidegger is more individualistic. Language is the key to understanding, and after analyzing the etymology of "existence," he reminds us that man should stand out into the truth of Being. *Dasein* should not let itself be held down by the chatter and mediocrity of public life, by mass existence, which levels off genuine possibilities. Nevertheless Heidegger is closer to Marx, for whom "social man" is "natural man," than is the Sartre of *L'Etre et le Néant*. Involving himself with the problem of alienation, Marx, according to Heidegger, "recognizes the essential importance of the historical in Being."[66] In 1947, when Heidegger wrote his "Brief über den Humanismus," Sartre had not yet proved himself capable of a fruitful dialogue with Marxism.[67]

He was still involved in a dialogue with theology. Like the ending of *L'Etre et le Néant*, which affirms the futility of "choosing to be God," *Le Sursis* demonstrates that we can neither possess the world as a totality of being nor look at it from any extraterrestrial viewpoint:

If you tried to stand face to face with the planet, it would crumble into fragments, nothing would be left except consciousness, a hundred million free consciousnesses, each of which would see walls, the glowing end of a cigar, familiar faces. Each would construct its destiny on its own responsibility. But if you *were* one of these consciousnesses, you'd be reminded by scarcely perceptible prompting and modifications of your place in the colony of polyps. The war: everybody is free but the chips are down. It's there, it's everywhere, it's the totality of all my thoughts, all Hitler's words, all Gomez's actions, but nobody is there to do the adding up. It exists only for God. But God doesn't exist. Yet the war exists.

The novel is cleverly centered on a double irony. In September 1938 it looks as though war is unavoidable. The politicians sidestep it by sacrificing Czechoslovakia to the Nazis, but the evasion of the crisis has little bearing on the ontological issues, which are the issues that matter. The mirage of war forces the characters to confront themselves, confront each other, confront their environment. What they discover is not a mirage, and it is only the most myopic who are happy about the cowardly compromise made in Munich.

The novel also clarifies the contrast between Mathieu and Daniel in terms of Mathieu's recognition that he is nothing and Daniel's stubborn belief that he is something. In *L'Age de raison* Mathieu had been made to say "I am not . . . one is never anything." This reminds us of Sartre's 1939 expostulation to Pieter: "I know in my bones that people aren't; they do." At this level his thinking is anti-Heideggerian, and his emphasis on action is in accordance with his insistence on the insubstantiality of consciousness, which he defines in *L'Etre et le Néant* as "the being which has in its being consciousness of the nothingness of its being."[68] The characters in *Les Chemins de la liberté* are trying—most of them in what Sartre calls bad faith—to catch up with their own being, to coincide with themselves in a solid, thing-like existence. Daniel wants "to be a pederast in the same way that an oak tree is an oak tree"; in *L'Age de raison* he had assumed that freedom was to be found in doing the opposite of what he wanted. After trying and failing to drown his beloved cats he had tried and failed to edge Mathieu into freely sacrificing his freedom by marrying the pregnant Marcelle. When Daniel marries her himself he fails to make himself as unhappy as he had expected to be. In desperation—but without realizing how desperate he is—he turns to religion, inverting the Cartesian *cogito* into "I am seen, therefore I am" and luxuriating in the belief that God is watching him. "I no longer have to bear the responsibility for the clammy proceedings of my body: he who sees me brought me into existence; I am as he sees me. I turn my nocturnal, eternal face toward the night, I stand up straight, like a challenge."[69] Though Georges Bataille was not a theist, Daniel's arrogant abjection was modeled partly on the addled mysticism of Bataille's book *L'Expérience intérieure,* which Sartre reviewed at length in *Cahiers du Sud.*[70]

Daniel is guilty of "bad faith," which, for Sartre, is primarily a matter of hiding the truth from oneself. He analyzes a variety of strategems for doing this, developing his attack on psychoanalysis by arguing that the notion of the unconscious mind makes it possible to tell lies without feeling like a liar: one postulates involuntary self-deception.[71] Daniel confesses he is evil; the apparent sincerity is only a camouflage for escaping responsibility by denying freedom. Sartre's hostility to Freud is above all a refusal to admit any limitation on individual freedom.

In his attack on François Mauriac, Sartre had criticized him for acting as Thérèse's accomplice by sharing her freedom, relaying her thoughts at the same time as pronouncing judgment on her, taking a godlike viewpoint and assuming divine power in prescribing her destiny. If novels were entirely fictional, the novelist would invariably be giving his characters their destiny, but in *Le Sursis* Sartre does his best to make history take responsibility. With the action set in 1938, history can be shown to reprieve all those called up for military service. The impending war touches them, but history cannot quite be persuaded to take over the role of omniscient narrator, though it does help Sartre to move on to a more experimental technique derived partly from Dos Passos, partly from Virginia Woolf. Instead of being interconnected through personal relationships, the narrative threads remain separate, the object being to show contrasted individuals all caught up in the same historical situation. In *L'Age de raison* most of the action consists of thoughts developing, moment by moment, in the consciousnesses of Mathieu, Daniel, Boris, and Ivich, while there are only six other important characters—Marcelle, Lola, Brunet and his wife Sarah, Jacques and his wife Odette. In *Le Sursis* the cast of characters is bigger. Much depends on simultaneity, and within eight days (Friday, September 23, 1938, to the following Friday) we move—often unaware of the transition until after we have made it—from one character to another, one place to another. Central Europe is in turmoil. The narrative jumps like a film from incident to incident: the heads of state meeting at Munich and privately preoccupied with trivialities; an illiterate shepherd unable to defend himself against con men who want his money and noncommissioned officers who want to humiliate him; a rich Jewish businessman trying to forget his Jewishness; a Czech schoolmaster looking at the swastika flags on the balcony opposite. Another character, Philippe, is based on Baudelaire, whose stepfather became a general.

Like the poet in Sartre's biography of him, Philippe is immature, self-destructive, emotionally fixated on his stepfather. To convince himself that he isn't a coward, the boy protests against the war by shouting in public places. Some of the sequences involving Mathieu, Daniel, and Boris are quite long; other sequences are succinct, with situations developed no more elaborately than in a short story. Though the construction is actually careful, the structure gives the appearance of being determined only by the calendar progression from one day to the next in a frightening European crisis.

D. H. Lawrence believed that form in the novel pushed the writer toward telling the truth; Sartre believed it helped to fend off the truth. In *La Nausée* Roquentin was, as a biographer, exploiting the power of narrative to give us an illusion of freedom from contingency, while Sartre worked hard to stop the form of the book from neutralizing all the nauseating odors exuded by his images of formlessness. In *L'Age de raison* the problem was different because it was the first volume in a series; the narrative could remain open-ended. And in *Le Sursis,* which is formally less conventional than any of his other fictions or plays, he develops an idea latent in the essay he wrote in 1938 about Dos Passos' simulation of historical time in 1914: "Big disturbances—war, love, a political movement, a strike—disappear, crumble into an infinity of little odds and ends which one can just line up, side by side." The example Sartre quotes is Dos Passos' dramatization of the armistice: at the beginning of November rumors begin to circulate, and then, one afternoon, Major Wood, bursting into the office Evelyn shares with Eleanor, kisses both girls.

In *Le Sursis,* when the shepherd is ejected from a fashionable restaurant, Sartre appears to be remembering the incident in 1932 when a worker in overalls was ejected from a Rouen café. Afterward he and De Beauvoir had speculated about the way Dos Passos might have described the incident, and in the 1938 essay on Dos Passos, Sartre introduces a brief parody in which two friends express their passionate hatred of war: "Paul declared that he'd rather do anything than fight and Jean said that he agreed and they both got excited and said they were happy to be in agreement. When he got home, Paul decided to see Jean more often."[72] Already one of the seeds for *Le Sursis* had been planted.

Well written and well constructed, the novel is consistently impressive—while *L'Etre et le Néant* is more uneven. In many of its best passages the prose tends to be rhetorical and loosely metaphorical; in the worst, it is abstract, repetitious, and disfigured with sub-Heideggerian jargon. But the best parts could have been achieved neither without an unscientific imprecision nor without the co-presence of the worst parts. *L'Etre et le Néant* is not a footnote to *Sein und Zeit* but an answer to it, an alternative attempt at a twentieth-century metaphysic, a comprehensive explanation of existence. Searching for a feeling that could reveal something essential about existence, Heidegger, prompted by Kierkegaard, singled out anxiety. "What gives rise to anxiety," writes Heidegger, "is being-in-the-world as such."[73] Pitched headlong into life, we find ourselves face-to-face with the absurdity of the human condition, or, as Heidegger prefers to put it, "*Dasein* finds itself face-to-face with the nothingness of the possible impossibility of its own existence."[74] The anxiety this produces is the anxiety Sartre had tried to translate into the nausea that is not inside Roquentin: he is inside it. Glutinously, the world is vomiting its plenitude at him as it overflows with contingent existence.

Sartre's allergy to the glutinous sap of *Natura naturans* also had its effect on *L'Etre et le Néant*. Insisting on the need for a psychoanalysis of *things,* he argues that the world consists of potentialities which do not belong to the In-itself.[75] Inspired by Jacques Audiberti's phrase "the secret blackness of milk," Sartre suggests that if there is a secret meaning in snow, it will turn out to be an ontological meaning.[76] If you are disgusted by what is glutinous, this can be explained only by its combination of physical and moral qualities.[77] In relation to the In-itself, stickiness has a symbolic value that is identical with its psychic meaning. It appears as "the outline of a fusion of the world with myself." "It is like a leech sucking me."[78] *La Nausée* left us free to keep Roquentin's vision at arm's length as that of a neurotic; here the personal allergy is integral to the philosophy.

The underlying fear seems to be one of being devoured, as in Sartre's fear of shellfish with claws. His nervousness that an octopus might attack him in the sea is indicative of the same phobia. One day he might get sucked under. The anxiety may have extended—in a milder form—to the fluids encountered in the orifices of the female body. Though he preferred women's company to that of men, he seems to have assumed a polarity between consciousness (which he pictured as active, alert, male) and flesh (inert, flabby, clinging, female). If consciousness is to preserve its freedom and its capacity for penetration, it must express itself in prose as beautiful and hard as steel; at the end of *La Nausée* it is clear that Roquentin is better off without Anny if he is going to write a novel. In *Le Sursis* Boris' escape from the clinging Lola echoes Mathieu's escape in *L'Age de raison* from the pregnant Marcelle. When he finally beds the more androgynous Ivich in *Le Sursis*—almost a rape, coinciding with that of Czechoslovakia—the usual Sartrean polarity is preserved but reversed: the viscosity is male, while a female consciousness holds on to its independence: "A glutinous perturbation like blood invaded Ivich's thighs and stomach, it slid into her blood, I'm not a girl who gets raped, she opened, let herself be stabbed, but while shivers of ice and fire rose up to her chest, her head stayed cool, she had saved her head and she yelled at him in her head: 'I hate you.' "[79]

Camus's first novel, *L'Etranger* (*The Outsider*), had been published in the middle of June 1942, and by September, when Sartre reviewed it, it had already been hailed as "the best book since the armistice." Camus's essays, *Le Mythe de Sisyphe,* intended for simultaneous publication with the novel, had been delayed, mainly because the German censor vetoed the chapter about Kafka, and the book was not published until mid-October, but copies were ready earlier, and Sartre had read it before he wrote his essay in September.

If Camus had been influenced by *La Nausée,* the influence worked negatively: thinking Sartre placed too much faith in language and lucidity, Camus veered toward silence. "A man is more of a man," he wrote in *Sisyphe,* "by virtue of what he keeps silent about than of what he says." In *L'Etranger,* Meursault cannot, as narrator, be made to keep silent, but he does not understand the story he tells, while his girl friend, Marie, when she gives evidence in court, feels that she is being compelled to say the opposite of what she thinks. For Camus, knowledge could be attained not by reasoning but only by means of a leap to faith. Temperamentally he was more religious than Sartre and more optimistic, believing man could assert his innocence against the absurdity of his condition. Sartre was quick to recognize Meursault as an innocent and to understand that what Camus meant by absurdity was disconnection between human yearnings for unity and the insuperable heterogeneity of the environment. "If I were a tree among trees," says Camus, perhaps remembering Sartre's chestnut tree, "this life would mean something, or rather this problem wouldn't, because I'd be part of the world. I'd *be* the world which, at the moment, I'm opposing with my whole consciousness."[80] Without mentioning Sartre's name he says: "This 'nausea,' as a contemporary writer calls it, is also the absurd." People secrete the inhuman. When you see a man telephoning inside a glass booth, his incomprehensible dumb show makes you wonder why he is alive. For Sartre absurdity was contingency raised to the power of the absolute: the key to Roquentin's nausea was the wooden serpent, the root of the tree, the purposeless abundance of natural fecundity. Camus's absurdity is closer to alienation. He did not share Sartre's aversion to viscosity or to the moist areas of the human body; he took more pleasure than Sartre in sex and in the sensation of being alive. He hated the limita-

tions of human intelligence, but he also hated emotional pretentious-
ness. If Meursault incarnates the "grace of the absurd" (to use Sartre's
phrase), it is partly a matter of rejecting all pious pretenses, emotional
and traditional.

Like Sartre, Camus had studied philosophy, but he was less of a philosopher, and while Sartre portrayed a consciousness that was restlessly
moving outward toward the world, Camus cultivated a prose style that
implied passive receptivity. Events are recorded, never in the past tense,
always in the perfect or the present, as if there is no connection between
them, no causality. Sartre noticed the indebtedness to the laconic prose
of Hemingway, who never used long sentences. In Camus's novel, as in
Hemingway's stories and novels, each of the short sentences refuses to
profit from the momentum generated by the previous sentence. Each
one is a new beginning.[81] But whereas Hemingway always wrote in this
style, Camus was affecting it. He had another, more poetic style. The
trick he was playing in *L'Etranger,* complained Sartre, was to introduce
a glass wall between the reader and the characters; the wall was transparent to events but opaque to their meaning.[82] The discontinuity between the sentences implied a discontinuity between actions that were
not really discontinuous. This is to ignore the fundamental fact that one
function of the narrative style is to characterize the narrator: it is
Meursault whose vision ignores continuities. But Sartre insists that in a
novel it must be obvious that time is irreversible; *L'Etranger* was not so
much a novel as a moral fable, reminiscent of Voltaire.[83]

(13)

The Future Reappears

IN the autumn of 1942 it began to seem possible that Germany would be defeated. In Africa the British Eighth Army, under its new commander, General Montgomery, was forcing Rommel's army to retreat, and on November 8 the Allies landed in French North Africa under the leadership of General Eisenhower. France lost its Free Zone when the Germans hurriedly occupied it in order to defend the Mediterranean coast, but from now on it was exciting to read the newspapers. Each day could bring news that meant the Third Reich was closer to collapse. Meanwhile the Vichy government became more vindictive toward Jews, foreigners, and those suspected of helping the Resistance. Trainloads of victims were deported.

Once again it was possible to believe in the future, but when Sartre and De Beauvoir arrived back in Paris for the autumn term, they could not settle down into a comfortable routine. Her hotel room had been let to someone else. After several days searching in Montparnasse and Saint-German-des-Prés for another hotel room with a kitchen, she found a dilapidated room with peeling walls in the Rue Dauphine. She hired a handcart to shift her possessions, and Nathalie helped her to push it through the streets of Paris to her sordid new home. The kitchen had a water closet in it; the bedroom had an iron bedstead, a wardrobe, a table, two wooden chairs. The prostitute who lived on the same floor left her four-year-old son to sob on the landing whenever she had a man with her. Mice would soon gnaw through a wooden partition to get at the lentils and dried peas in De Beauvoir's cupboard; rumor had it that large rats were breeding all over Paris. When Marc Bénard and his wife came to dinner, they were unable to hide their dismay at the squalor. The meal consisted of potato pie and carrots.[1]

It was an uncomfortable winter, with coal shortages and power cuts. Candles were scarce too, and when Sartre and De Beauvoir were not teaching, they spent most of their time at the Flore, which was illuminated by acetylene lamps whenever the electricity failed. In order to get the warmest table, next to a stovepipe, De Beauvoir would arrive soon after the café opened at eight in the morning. Picasso was a regular customer, as was Jacques Prévert. As soon as the air-raid sirens sounded, the café had to close. Most of the customers were hustled out into the street, but a few of the regulars, including Sartre and De Beauvoir, were allowed to wait for the all-clear in a room on the second floor.[2]

For the Christmas holidays they went back to La Pouèze, where they listened excitedly to BBC news programs. On December 29 the German thrust toward Stalingrad was defeated at Kotelnikovo, and the good news continued after Sartre and De Beauvoir returned to Paris for the beginning of the term. At the Casablanca conference, held during the second half of January 1943, President Roosevelt demanded unconditional surrender. Toward the end of the month Berlin was bombed by daylight for the first time, and at the beginning of February the last German troops in Stalingrad surrendered. A couple of weeks later, Laval, who had for some time been recruiting work parties for Germany, issued a new decree: all the young men who reached call-up age between 1940 and 1942 must serve for two years with the Service du Travail. Many escaped to join the Maquis.

A number of anti-Nazi committees were being organized by the Communists, who were recruiting prominent non-Communists for them, and early in the year Sartre was invited through François Billoux, a Communist he had known in the stalag, to join the Comité National des Ecrivains (CNE), which had the poet Paul Eluard as its president. Members included Mauriac, Paulhan, Claude Morgan, and Jean Guéhenno. At the meetings Sartre, according to Morgan, would try to avoid making divisive proposals.

In the spring Dullin started rehearsing *Les Mouches,* directing, as well as playing the part of Jupiter, with Jean Lannier as Orestes, Olga (calling herself Olga Dominique) as Electra, and with Wanda in a small part. A newcomer to professional theater at the age of thirty-seven, Sartre learned a great deal from watching rehearsals. Without asking for cuts or revisions, Dullin could make dialogue less rhetorical by telling the actors: "Don't play the words, play the situation."[3] Later Sartre would tell himself: "Don't write the words, write the situation." Dullin, who had worked with Jacques Copeau, maintained that Dionysian violence should be presented with Apollonian restraint. As Sartre testifies, "intangible richness arose out of poverty, violence and bloodshed were suggested with serenity, and, evolved with patience, the union of these opposites . . . contributed an astonishing tension which had been missing from my play."[4] Not that the course of rehearsals ran smoothly. Jean Lannier was inexperienced, as was Olga, who would burst into tears when Dullin lost his temper.[5]

The dress rehearsal was held in the afternoon, when the electricity was less likely to be cut off than it was in the evening. While Sartre was standing in the foyer, Albert Camus came up to introduce himself.[6] Attractive and well built, he looked athletic; in his native Algeria he had been a football star.

When the play opened on June 3, it was impossible for the audience to miss the political meaning of Orestes' speeches about liberty, but most of the critics prudently ignored it. In *Paris-Soir* Jacques Berland complained that Sartre was more of an essayist than a playwright,[7] while another reviewer accused him of "flogging a humanity he detests."[8] In *Les Lettres Françaises* Michel Leiris wrote an unsigned panegyric, remarking on the play's political implications,[9] but, as Dullin wrote later, "It rapidly became a complete flop; the box office was pathetic."[10] Undeterred, he put the production back into his repertoire when the theater reopened in October after the summer recess. The play was given about forty performances.

By staging *Les Mouches* Dullin was helping Sartre almost as much as when he urged Gallimard to publish *La Nausée*. Using all the means at their disposal—newspapers, radio, movies, placards—the Nazis and collaborationists were projecting a humiliating image of the French people. Had it not been for Dullin, the only platform for Sartre's defiant ideas on human freedom would have been *L'Etre et le Néant*, which attracted little attention when it was published in the summer. At the theater, even if audiences were small, the play was upholding the option of freeing oneself from a historical trap by committing an atrocious act and taking full responsibility for it. Zola had said that the novelist must "kill the hero" in order to show "the ordinary course of average lives"; Sartre's slogan was: "No more characters; the heroes are freedoms caught in a trap like all of us." His paradoxical assumption is that we have no freedom except to be free.

Like the theater, French cinema had been lamed but not paralyzed by the occupation. In December 1940 the Germans had established the Comité d'Organisation de l'Industrie Cinématographique (COIC), which had expelled all Jews from the industry and banned trade unions. Many films were clogged with collaborationist propaganda, but myth, symbolism, and historical drama were still viable modes. Though Cocteau and Jacques Prévert went on working in motion pictures, most of the scenarios submitted to the studios were mediocre, but the director Jean Delannoy, who in 1943 had directed Cocteau's *L'Eternel Retour*, a reworking of the Tristan and Isolde story, arranged for Sartre to be signed up by Pathé. When he left Paris for his summer vacation, he was already being paid a retainer, and it seemed he might soon be earning enough to give up teaching.[11]

De Beauvoir had left earlier for three weeks of solo cycling in the country. Sartre traveled by train to meet her in Uzerche, thirty-five miles from Limoges. With the manuscript of *Le Sursis* in his saddlebag, they cycled together in a leisurely way, putting on plastic yellow capes when it rained. At Beaulieu a storm blew up while they were eating in a hotel, and they came out to find the bicycles had been blown over and the saddlebags carried off in a stream of yellowish water. The manuscript was floating in the gutter. It was easy to dry it out, not so easy to restore the passages where the ink had smudged.[12]

Even the best hotels were serving only vegetarian meals, and real coffee was scarce. Eggs, which were sometimes to be had from farms, could be taken to restaurants, so that the meal could be fortified with an omelette. Sometimes they slept in barns, and at Conques they slept in a schoolroom on palliasses. At Vaour, spending the night in a stable, they were attacked by bugs. After cycling to Toulouse, they adjourned to stay for the last part of August and the whole of September with Mme. Morel at La Pouèze, where the main pleasure was listening to BBC news programs. Mussolini had been overthrown in July, and on September 8 General Eisenhower announced that Italy had signed an armistice. On September 9 the Allies landed at Salerno, while in the east the Red Army was advancing steadily.

Sartre worked on *Le Sursis* at La Pouèze, but after they returned to Paris, put it aside in favor of a new play. The initiative came from the owner of a pharmaceutical factory near Lyon, Marc Barbezat, who at his own expense published an elegant literary periodical, *L'Arbalète*, which he printed on a hand press. It appeared twice a year. He had just married Olga Perret, a young actress who had played Clytemnestra in *Les Mouches,* and the intention was that Sartre's script would contain parts for her and Wanda, who was now attending Dullin's classes. Barbezat, who offered to finance the production, wanted a play that could tour the country.[13]

Sartre began to write a short play with a single set and only two or three characters. To obviate complaints about the relative size of the roles, he decided that none of the three principal characters, a man and two women, would ever leave the stage. But he also added a fourth character, who has only a small part. After playing with the idea of keeping them in a cellar throughout a prolonged bombardment, he decided to put them in hell. He called the play *Les Autres* (*The Others*), and it was published under this title in *L'Arbalète* (No. 8, Spring 1944). The title was later changed to *Huis clos:* a legal term for "behind closed doors," this is usually translated as *In Camera* or *No Exit.*

The script was written in a fortnight, and the absence of rhetoric shows how much he had learned from watching Dullin rehearse. *Huis clos* is Sartre's first play in which the statement is made through the action and the situation. Again his basic concern was freedom. Hell would have been of little interest to him unless he had found a way of using it to imply the opposite of imprisonment. Though the dead can do nothing to change their lives, Sartre wanted, as in *Le Sursis,* to attack the bad faith of men such as Daniel who live as if they have no control over their behavior. They are "encrusted in a series of habits, of customs. . . . This is a living death."[14]

One of the play's roots was in Sartre's wartime experience of being unable to escape from the hellishly intrusive gaze of other people. The play is a three-dimensional metaphor exploring this deprivation while fleshing out points Sartre had made in *L'Etre et le Néant* about being-for-others. Hegel had treated this as a necessary stage in the growth of self-consciousness: "I need the other as a mediator between myself and me" (as Sartre put it in *L'Etre et le Néant*).[15] In hell (as he portrays it in the play) there are no mirrors: each of the three main characters depends on the other two to reflect an image. Had there been only two people in the room, they might have become lovers, but the gaze of an excluded third person is bound to be less flattering.[16] In a triangular situation—as Sartre had found with De Beauvoir and Olga—each is tortured by the other two: hell consists of other people.

Without knowing much about Camus, Sartre invited him to direct the play and to act the only important male part. Their second meeting took place at the Flore. According to De Beauvoir, who was with them, Camus had charm and a boyish sense of humor; he would address Pascal, one of the waiters, as Descartes.[17] After a slow start the conversation gathered momentum when they talked about Francis Ponge, a former surrealist and a Communist, who was now active (unlike Sartre and Camus) in the intellectual Resistance. The conversation went on to theater. As a student in Algiers, Camus had formed a theatrical group, Le Théâtre du Travail, and from 1936 onward had worked as adapter, producer, director, and actor. After balking when Sartre came out with his offer, Camus let himself be persuaded. Soon the production was under way. A former pupil of Sartre's, R. J. Chauffard, who was working for Dullin, was cast in the small part of the waiter, and Camus started rehearsing in De Beauvoir's hotel room with Wanda, Olga Perret, and Chauffard.

Camus had not yet settled in Paris, though he had worked there for a couple of months in 1940 for *Paris-Soir* and had spent a fortnight there in January 1943, returning on June 1, the day before Sartre met him at the theater. De Beauvoir describes him as a simple, cheerful man, laconic but capable of enthusiasm. The idea of editing a monthly review emerged as Sartre became increasingly impatient for the future to begin. At cafés, restaurants, dinner parties, conversation during the final years of the war bristled with plans for the future.

Sartre's main friendships were with Camus, Michel Leiris, and Raymond Queneau. Formerly, as a surrealist, Leiris had powdered his face white and painted landscapes on his bare scalp. With his shaven head and the formality he affected in dress and manner, he had always seemed intimidating at meetings of the CNE, but he and his wife, Zette, turned out to be friendly. Soon Zette was helping De Beauvoir buy meat, and at dinner parties the Leirises were frequent guests, as were Queneau—another former surrealist—and his wife, Jeanine. Queneau had not yet started to write for the movies, but since the thirties he had been playing with the dichotomy between spoken French and the literary language. Sartre wanted to have a review of his own, with his friends on the editorial board.

Rehearsals of the play stopped when Olga Perret was arrested, suspected of working for the Resistance. Frustrated, worried, restless, Sartre made himself concentrate on the first of his scripts for Pathé, *Les Jeux sont faits* (translated as *The Chips Are Down*). Once again he tried to float a Resistance message in a bottle that would drift past the censor, but the screenplay was rejected by Pathé. The film was not made until 1947, when Delannoy directed it with Micheline Presle as Eve. In *Huis clos* the three characters can watch what is happening on earth, while the space they occupy has no terrestrial location, even though it looks just like a drawing room furnished in a Second Empire style. In Sartre's screenplay the Paris occupied by the dead overlaps with the Paris occupied by the living, and he writes some effective sequences in which living and dead characters are simultaneously visible to the audience, though the dead are invisible to the living. Those who have just died find it hard to remember that they can't intervene.

As a screenwriter Sartre was energetic and inventive, with the same flair he showed in the theater for involving the audience emotionally with the characters, but this film is marred by melodrama and by the obligation he felt to put a love story in the center of the action, though it was clever not to let Eve and Pierre meet until they are dead. Eve had been a rich woman, married to André Charlier, secretary of the militia; Pierre had been the leader of a revolutionary movement trying to over-

throw the vicious military régime of the Regent. She has been poisoned
by André, who married her for her dowry and now has designs on her
younger sister; Pierre has been shot by a traitor. Though dead, they are
sufficiently in love to qualify for a twenty-four-hour resurrection. If they
can prove themselves capable of remaining together as lovers, they will
be allowed to stay alive. Like Brecht (in *Puntila*), Sartre shows how social barriers make it hard for a rich middle-class girl to settle down with
a proletarian lover, but in the screenplay the barriers are not insuperable. The main obstacle to love is revolutionary commitment to freedom. Knowing of the Regent's plan to liquidate the resistance
movement, Pierre cannot abandon his comrades; risking his second life,
he loses it.

When the script was rejected, Sartre knew that he would have to go
on teaching his *baccalauréat* classes at the Lycée Condorcet. So short of
money he was nearly always hungry, he was glad to earn a bit extra by
lecturing to Dullin's students on the history of theater; *L'Etre et le Néant*
would bring in only negligible royalties. De Beauvoir had been accused
by her collaborationist headmistress of corrupting a minor and had lost
her teaching job, but she got work on the national radio network. To
steer herself into nonpolitical territory she proposed a series about traditional festivals from the Middle Ages onward. With help from Bost
she pieced together old ballads with material she found in the Bibliothèque Nationale.[18]

By the beginning of 1944, when she went off with Bost but without
Sartre to ski in Morzine, it looked as though the war would soon be
over. The Russians had recaptured two-thirds of the territory taken by
the Germans, and on January 20 the RAF dropped 2300 tons of bombs
on Berlin. Cologne, Hamburg, and other German cities had been attacked no less ruthlessly, while, in France, it was not only factories,
ports, and railway junctions that were bombed. Nantes was devastated,
and even the suburbs of Paris were under attack. The Resistance had
become more active, and rumors were circulating about German
reprisals. Sometimes it was said that the entire male population of a
village had been shot. On March 4 twenty-two "foreign terrorists" were
killed. They had been condemned to death on February 18, and photographs of the young faces were posted up on the walls of Métro stations.

Sartre was now a member not only of the CNE but also of the Comité
National du Théàtre, and he was averaging three meetings a week.
Many of the writers involved saw each other frequently, and when a
panel was formed to award the Prix de la Pléiade, which had just been
founded by Gallimard, Sartre's fellow judges were Eluard, Malraux,
Camus, Paulhan, Blanchot, Queneau, Roland Tual, and the novelist

Marcel Arland, with Jacques Lemarchand, the novelist and drama critic, in the chair. The prize of 100,000 francs was awarded to Mouloudji for his novel *Enrico*. For Sartre, possibly, literary merit was not the only criterion: he liked to champion emergent proletarian culture heroes. Mouloudji, who was not so well qualified for this role as Camus, would soon be dropped, and Genet, whose potential was greater, would be picked up.

A celebration lunch for Mouloudji was organized at the Restaurant Hoggar, where De Beauvoir's lamb chop consisted entirely of bone and gristle. Hunger was such a familiar feeling and food such an overriding preoccupation that Picasso made it the theme of his play *Le Désir attrapé par la queue* (*Desire Caught by the Tail*). When Michel Leiris arranged to give a public reading of the play, Camus rehearsed the actors. Leiris, who had done the casting, had appropriated the main part, Big Foot, for himself. Sartre was Round End and De Beauvoir the Cousin. Picasso's mistress, Dora Maar, played Fat Misery.

Picasso was in the audience, as was the young Spanish actress Maria Casarès, who fell under Camus's spell as he read the stage directions with calculated monotony,[19] rapping on the floor with a walking stick to indicate each change of locale. The readers stood up each time they had to speak. The Leirises' drawing room was too small to accommodate the audience, which included Georges Braque, Jean-Louis Barrault, Armand Salacrou, Georges Bataille, and Jacques Lacan. De Beauvoir was complimented by Picasso on her appearance, which was enhanced by Olga's red angora sweater and a necklace of Wanda's.[20] Those who stayed after midnight had, because of the curfew, to stay till dawn; Mouloudji sang "Les Petits pavés," Sartre sang "Les Papillons de nuit" and "J'ai vendu mon âme au Diable."

Eager to continue the mood of celebration, some of the friends went on to organize a series of "fiestas," as Leiris called them. The first was held in March at Georges Bataille's flat, where the musician René Leibowitz was in hiding; for the second fiesta Bost's mother lent them her villa in Taverny.[21] They drank and they clowned. Queneau and Bataille dueled with bottles; Camus and Lemarchand played tunes on saucepan lids; Sartre conducted an imaginary orchestra from a closet.

Over Easter, while Sartre and De Beauvoir were in La Pouèze, Paris was bombed: the RAF had started attacking railway stations. When they returned from La Pouèze, the Gare du Nord, the Gare de l'Est, and the Gare de Lyon were not functioning.[22] Life became more chaotic, with food still scarcer. In the evening the Métro stopped at ten; at theaters and movie houses fewer performances were given.[23] In April the Allies dropped 81,000 tons of bombs, mainly on Germany; in Italy the

German army was retreating rapidly throughout May. But Jews were being packed off to Germany in sealed trains, and Nathalie lost her lover, a nineteen-year-old Spanish Jew, Jean-Pierre Bourla. Sartre tried to console De Beauvoir with an ad hoc theory: every life is complete at its end, and death is no less absurd at the age of eighty than at the age of nineteen.[24]

THROUGHOUT his life Sartre was to strike up remarkably few friendships with men of his own age. Bost had graduated from being a pupil to being a member of the family, but it was never a relationship between equals, whereas with Camus, Sartre could have a great deal of fun. Though less subversive than Sartre, Camus was in some ways still like a tough Algerian street urchin, and they could tell each other obscene stories while De Beauvoir and Maria Casarès or Camus's wife, Francine, tried to look shocked. Later Sartre would describe him as "probably the last good friend I had."[25] The friendship was to be short-lived, but it was highly enjoyable, not only for both men but for their other friends. Bost, for instance, benefited. His ambition was to be a journalist, and after reading his book on his experiences in the infantry, *Le Dernier des métiers*, Camus published it in the collection he was editing for Gallimard and sent Bost to the front line as a war correspondent. He willingly gave jobs to other protégés of Sartre, and De Beauvoir attests that when they opened *Combat* in the morning "it was almost like reading through our personal mail."[26] It was Camus who involved Sartre in writing for the underground paper *Combat* from the spring of 1944.[27] Part of Camus's appeal was that he did not belong to the bourgeoisie, but as a proletarian culture hero he was soon to be eclipsed.

One afternoon in May he was with Sartre and De Beauvoir at the Flore when a man with close-cropped hair and thin lips came across to introduce himself. "You Sartre?" he asked. He looked like a boxer, a lightweight. He was Jean Genet. Cocteau, who had discovered him in prison, was claiming him to be the greatest writer of the age, and Barbezat had published a section of *Notre-Dame des fleurs* in *L'Arbalète*. De Beauvoir describes Genet as a good listener, but Sartre, five years later, complained that he could not remember discussing anything with Genet except Genet. "My passion is to understand people and his to remain in ignorance about them."[28] Genet had charm and boldness of judgment, but he was intolerant of anecdotes and small talk. When De Beauvoir took him up to admire the view from the penthouse terrace of her hotel, his response was: "What the devil am I expected to make of *that?*"[29] Nor was he a man they could invite to their fiestas.[30]

Sartre would not begin to write about Genet until the beginning of 1950, but it was in 1944 that he wrote *Baudelaire,* the first of his three biographies. "If we don't regress continually," he said later about Flaubert, "to the author's desires and objectives, back to the total enterprise ... we'd just be making the book into a fetish ... like a piece of merchandise, considering it as a thing and not as the reality of a man, objectified by his work.[31] The key question—How much can we know about a man?—had to be answered in terms of the individual. By 1971 Sartre would assert: "Every man is utterly knowable,"[32] and in his study of Baudelaire he claims: "Each event reflects back the irreducible totality that he was from the first day to the last."[33] Long before he started to use the word "totalize" Sartre committed himself to a biographical accounting in which each fact is a figure in a column that can be added up. Though Antoine Roquentin had given up hope of understanding the Marquis de Rollebon, Sartre was to devote a major part of his working life to biography, but none of his biographies is conventional in approach. His strong tendency toward the synchronic looks forward to the structuralists and backward to Bergson, who had insisted on the unity of the personality, which must be apprehended intuitively or empathically. Instead of detailing the succession of events, Sartre refused to concern himself with the way Baudelaire developed. His eccentric assumption is that the only crucial decision in Baudelaire's life was made at the age of seven, when his mother remarried, and the child chose his destiny. According to Bergson, we exist more in space than in time, and we live more for the external world than we do for ourselves. Sartre writes of Baudelaire's personality as though it had, throughout his adult life, a consistency determined by this childhood decision. Trying to construct a detailed portrait of the man, Sartre cantilevers speculatively out from the writings and the known biographical facts. He makes the unfounded suggestion that Baudelaire would have preferred meat cooked in sauces to broiled meat, preserves to fresh fruit.[34] Sartre does not mention that these are his own preferences.

The book is important as an attempt to repudiate what might have struck Sartre as part of his own psychological destiny. Like Lucien in "L'Enfance d'un chef," and like Flaubert, Baudelaire was an antitype. Traumatized by his mother's second marriage, Baudelaire took refuge in *la vie imaginaire.* Writing with a ferocity aimed partly at conventional literary values but mainly at the part of himself he was determined to slough off, Sartre castigates Baudelaire for being immature, morbidly narcissistic, masochistic, dishonest, obsessive, onanistic, and exhibitionistic. The charges are all the more serious for Sartre's assumption that we can choose what we want to be. Baudelaire is therefore held to be "fully and lucidly responsible" even for his syphilis, for his failure to achieve financial independence, and for his emotional dependence on his mother. Instead of evaluating the poetry, Sartre condemns the man for his defective manliness. Like the unforgivable Flaubert, Baudelaire had chosen to be an effeminate artist rather than a man of action. As if reminding himself to avoid that pitfall, Sartre condemns Baudelaire's literary achievements as useless, treating the poems as if they were no more than an appendage of his dandyism, pieces of literary self-indulgence, written not to help humanity but to reflect his own image. Instead of trying to change the world or even to change himself, Baudelaire merely tries to see himself as if he were someone else and, because this is impossible, depends, like an addict, on the disapproval of his stepfather and his mother. Their judgment makes him into an object. In Baudelaire self-hatred and narcissism coalesce as he chooses to live in bad faith. This is Sartre's Baudelaire; not only was the real Baudelaire quite affectionate toward his stepfather, he was also active on the barricades and championed social reform.

Sartre had brainwashed himself into believing that poetry was altogether undesirable—only prose could be useful. But four years previously his attitude to poetry had been different. "I'm furious not to be a poet," he wrote in 1940, "to be so heavily fettered to prose."[35] This was his reaction a fortnight after composing a twenty-three-line poem, only to feel that it should be reduced to five lines.[36] Pleased that his prose sometimes approximated to the poetic, he ruefully tried to analyze why poetry was beyond his range: "There's something tangled in me, a secret shame, a cynicism learned too slowly, and then also a lack of charm; my feelings haven't found their language, I feel them, I reach out a timid finger, and the moment I touch them, I change them into prose. The choice of words betrays me. If I start, if I find a poetic phrase, it's subverted by a word that slips in, a word that's too pointed, too plain; the movement of the phrase is rhetorical."[37] Even while writing this he was hoping that when he reread it he would "discover in stupefied amazement that I'd just created with my prose the beautiful object, the ship in the bottle, I was vainly asking of poetry."[38] Hopes of this kind would linger long after he started to denounce poetry as useless.

THE third fiesta was held at Toulouse's flat, where the huge circular drawing room opened onto a garden. The hall and the rooms had been decorated with flowers, ribbons, garlands, knickknacks, but Toulouse had drunk too much during her preparations, and the guests were welcomed by a nervous Dullin. Camus arrived with Maria Casarès, who was rehearsing his play *Le Malentendu*. The others included the Salacrous, the Queneaus, Olga Kosakiewicz, Bost, the Leirises, and students from Dullin's drama school. When Dullin recited some of Villon's ballades, Jeanine Queneau responded by barking like a dog until Olga tapped her reprovingly on the nose. At three in the morning Toulouse made her appearance, wearing rouge on her eyelids and blue eye shadow on her cheeks. Unsteadily she danced a paso doble with Camus. The party lasted till daylight, and when Sartre and De Beauvoir, with Olga and Bost, were walking through the deserted Place de Rennes, they saw placards on the station wall: no trains would run until further notice. Later on in the day it was announced over the radio that English and American troops had landed in Normandy. Sartre and De Beauvoir drank ersatz gin outside the Flore, celebrating the future.[39]

By the time Olga Perret was released, plans were under way for a production of *Huis clos* at the Vieux-Colombier, and Camus, who felt unqualified to direct stars, had withdrawn. The production was entrusted to the actor-director Raymond Rouleau, who cast his wife, Gaby Sylvia, as Estelle, with Roger Vitold as Garcin, Tania Balachova as Inès and R.-J. Chauffard still in the part he had started to rehearse, the waiter. For Sartre these interpretations of the four roles were definitive.[40] The first night was scheduled for June 10. The performance went well, and the audience was amused at the idea that in this hellish hotel the lights would stay on all the time: "We have unlimited electricity." The play was presented as part of a double bill; what followed was a comedy which was so boring that not all the audience stayed. It was understandable that the theatrical manager, Anet Badel, should decide to reverse the order of the two plays. But he failed to alter the programs or the posters. Claude Morgan was one of those under the impression that Sartre had written the comedy.[41]

Soon afterward, Jean Vilar, who as codirector of a touring company, Le Roulotte, had been staging plays by Strindberg, and had been organizing a series of lectures on the theater, invited Sartre to give one of them. The audience included Cocteau, Camus, and Barrault, who all asked questions; fashionably dressed ladies afterward approached Sartre for his autograph.[42] When Cocteau came to *Huis clos* with Genet, Sartre and De Beauvoir met them after the performance. Cocteau dominated the conversation, complimenting Sartre on the play before expatiating on his own theatrical experiences. Afterward they walked down the Rue Bonaparte to the *quais*. Watching searchlight beams in the sky and flares flashing, Cocteau maintained that the poet should hold himself aloof from the follies of war and politics.[43]

It was hard to remain aloof from the Nazis' final acts of vengeance. At Oradour-sur-Glane thirteen hundred people were burned alive, in their homes or in the church. Rumor had it that in the Midi children had been seen dangling from butcher's hooks, which had been pushed through their throats. Because of his involvement with *Combat,* Sartre was in danger after a member of the network confessed names to the authorities. Camus advised him to go into hiding, and after staying for a few days at the Leirises' flat, he went to Neuilly-sur-Clermont with De Beauvoir. They stayed for three weeks in the village *auberge-épicerie,* eating and working in the public bar to the sound of billiard-balls clicking and villagers chatting as they drank and played cards.

On August 11, hearing that the Americans had reached the outskirts of Chartres, Sartre and De Beauvoir set off on their bicycles for Paris, determined not to miss the liberation. Told that the Germans were retreating along the main road, they took a side road to Chantilly, where they boarded a train, which came to a halt after a few miles as it was machine-gunned from the air by an RAF plane. Sartre and De Beauvoir were among the passengers who, as the plane zoomed away, rushed for shelter to the nearest ditch. From the front cars ambulance attendants carried out bodies on improvised stretchers. Some of the passengers refused to go back on the train, but Sartre and De Beauvoir resumed their journey.

In Paris, finding the Métro was closed, they cycled to register at the Hôtel Welcome. At the Flore they met Camus, who had taken over as editor of *Combat,* and was preparing for its first public issues. He said the leaders of the Resistance had agreed that Paris should liberate itself. It was clear that this would cost lives, but nothing else was clear. What was happening, in fact, was that the American Third Army had begun to surround the city, but with the intention of isolating it in order to avoid the destruction and bloodshed of a siege. Inside the city an uncoordinated insurrection had already begun, with Communist partisans working at cross purposes with De Gaulle's FFI (Forces Françaises de l'Intérieur). Camus commissioned Sartre to write a detailed account of the liberation for serial publication in the paper.

The electricity had been cut off, and there was no food on sale. The police had disappeared from the streets, and on August 16 the gas was cut off. At the Hôtel Chaplain, Bost built square tins into a stove that could be fueled with newspapers, but it was hard to cook spaghetti on it, and the room filled with smoke. Rumors were circulating. Shooting had been heard inside the prisons; arrests and deportations were still going on. The worst fear was that the whole of Paris would be blown up when the Germans left: people were saying that mines had been laid under the whole area surrounding the Palais de Luxembourg. In fact Hitler had ordered that Paris should be destroyed, but the Francophile Abetz disobeyed.

In the afternoon of August 18, German army trucks packed with troops and boxes drove northward up the Boulevard Saint-Michel, but in the morning the swastika flag was still flying from the Palais du Luxembourg. De Beauvoir saw a platoon of German soldiers emerging from the building to march down the Boulevard Saint-Germain. Before they turned the corner the Germans loosed a parting volley of machine-gun fire at pedestrians. People were carried away on stretchers; a concierge came out to scrub the blood off the steps. After Sartre had left for a committee meeting at the Comédie Française, De Beauvoir walked to the Leirises' flat, and from there she saw the French flag flying from the *préfecture*. Progressively, resistance was being mobilized inside the city. Parisians were recapturing their own public buildings, and the FFI had been firing on the Germans, who often took revenge on innocuous civilians. Friends kept calling Sartre up excitedly with news and rumors. In the evening he was at the Hôtel Chaplain with De Beauvoir and the Leirises when some boys rode by on bicycles shouting that the Germans had asked for a cease-fire.

In the morning it was being said that the Third Army was only three or four miles from Paris. The French tricolor had appeared in windows. In the Carrefour Buci shoppers were picked off by gunmen on the roof of a hotel. After storming into the building, FFI soldiers emerged with a dozen Japanese prisoners. Laughing savagely at them, the crowd pounced. Some of the Japanese had their trousers pulled off and their bottoms spanked before they were driven away in a police car.[44]

Sartre spent the day wandering around the streets of the *quartier*. It would have been safer to stay indoors, but the best way to write the article for *Combat* was from firsthand experience. "I describe only what I've seen. . . . It begins like a holiday and, today still, the Boulevard Saint-Germain, deserted and intermittently swept by machine-gun fire, keeps an appearance of tragic solemnity."[45] In the afternoon loudspeaker trucks drove around with the announcement that all fighting had stopped, but shots were still to be heard, and alarmist rumors were circulating. One woman said that if a single shot was fired, the Germans would bombard Paris: their guns were already trained on the city.[46]

More men were joining the Resistance fighters; women were cooking for them in improvised canteens. German army trucks were ambushed openly in the streets; while men sat fishing on the Seine, freedom fighters were sheltering behind balustrades along the *quais*. But German trucks and armored cars were still driving about, and according to one rumor, German tanks were approaching to shell the buildings along the *quais*. Columns of German armored cars were still firing at pedestrians, and at the corner of the Rue Saint-André-des-Arts, De Beauvoir saw a pool of blood. FFI fighters were shouting "Stop" and "Go" to tell pedestrians when it was safe to cross the road.

On August 21 the Comité Parisien de la Libération issued fighting orders. Citizens of Paris must use methods of all kinds to stop the enemy from moving: "Cut down trees, dig anti-tank pits, set up barricades." The idea was to drive the remaining soldiers into surrender, though the Germans, who still had large forces in the area, could have quashed the insurrection savagely. As soon as Eisenhower, who was in command, learned of this call to the barricades, he changed his plans, sending General Leclerc's army to advance on the center of the city.

In the first public issue of *Combat,* which was distributed in the streets the same day, Camus's editorial supported the call to arms: "It's by fighting the invaders and traitors that the FFI are reestablishing the Republic in our country." An unsigned text on the same page was titled "From Resistance to Revolution," and this slogan would appear daily under the masthead of the newspaper. "We know what our orders are," wrote Sartre in one of his articles. "Hit a German over the head and take his revolver, get hold of a gun, with the gun get hold of a car, with the car take an armored car and a tank. This has raised more than one smile among the cynics of the Resistance, and yet the program is being realized, point by point, under my eyes."[47]

Barricades had been erected in the Place Saint-German-des-Prés and along the boulevard. Liaison officers cycled up and down the Boulevard du Montparnasse telling citizens to help with the barricades. Fewer German tanks and armored cars were to be seen in the streets, but snipers were shooting from rooftops, and while Sartre and De Beauvoir were listening in the Salacrous' flat to the BBC announcement that Paris had been liberated, gunshots were still to be heard. In the evening, when De Beauvoir was on her way to dinner at the Hôtel Chaplain, a passing cyclist shouted that General Leclerc had reached the Place de l'Hôtel-de-Ville. As Sartre and De Beauvoir arrived at the Carrefour Montparnasse, bells began to peal all over Paris. A bonfire was lit in the middle of the road, and, joining hands, they all danced around it, singing, until an approaching German tank dispersed the crowd.

At six o'clock in the morning of August 24 Leclerc's troops marched in columns to the Avenue d'Orléans, with crowds cheering on the pavement, the excitement surviving the snipers' shots that still rang out. A few collapsed bodies would be carried away, but the crowd would go on cheering. The streets were draped with flags; girls threw their arms around soldiers' necks. The next day Sartre, together with other members of the Comité National de Théâtre, watched from a balcony in the Hôtel du Louvre as De Gaulle marched down the Champs-Elysées, followed by police officers, soldiers, and freedom fighters. When shooting started, the FFI mistook the committee members for militiamen and opened fire. The writers retreated inside, unhurt.

Sartre and De Beauvoir were having dinner with Genet, the Leirises, and a uniformed American friend of theirs when a solitary German plane began to drop bombs: the Halle aux Vins was destroyed, as was a house in the Rue Monge. And that was not the end of it. Sniping continued, rocket bombs fell on the suburbs, but the uniforms in the streets were American. These were soldiers who chewed gum and parted their fingers in the V sign.

The excited crowd dealt out only a rough justice. Had the shaven-headed old woman been any more of a collaborationist than those who had insulted her?[48] So long as the occupying forces had been there, moral issues had been clear-cut, but with liberation came inhibiting ambivalences. In the first public issue of *Les Lettres Françaises* Sartre wrote: "We have never been more free than under the German occupation."[49] What had created a feeling of community was the need for silence. Faced with the possibility of betraying members of the Resistance to the Nazis, each Frenchman had been responsible to the community and to himself. "And the choice each man made of himself was authentic, because it was made in the presence of death, since it could always have been made in the form 'Rather death than . . .' . . . So the question of liberty itself was posed and we were at the edge of the deepest knowledge man can have of himself."[50]

A pamphlet had been printed—probably in 1943, when the Communists were campaigning for unity of action—denouncing Sartre, Montherlant, and the novelist Alphonse de Chateaubriant as collaborationists. For Sartre, as for Henri in De Beauvoir's 1954 novel *Les Mandarins,* the choice appeared to be between siding actively with the working class and becoming an object of hatred. "Unless he could prove it was not so, he was an enemy for hundreds of millions of men, an enemy of humanity. He didn't want that at any price."[51] Sartre had no intention of joining the party: he wanted to be a useful—if critical—ally.[52] After refusing an invitation to write for the Communist weekly *Action,* partly because it had attacked Malraux unfairly, he was surprised to come under attack himself. Though his existentialism had made little impression as yet on the public, the Communists were quick to see that it might emerge, dangerously, as an alternative to communism. Sartre's response to the attack was an article published in *Action* at the end of December under the title "A propos de l'existentialisme: Mise au point" (definition of terms). Though he was trying to be conciliatory, this did not improve his relationship with the Communists.

HUIS CLOS was translated into several foreign languages. In London it was banned from the stage by the Lord Chamberlain but was broadcast four times by the BBC. In Paris it was due for revival at the Vieux-Colombier in September, and Sartre went on writing for the movies, taking the idea of *Typhus* from the epidemic that had broken out during 1938 in Morocco shortly before he and De Beauvoir went there. Though his scenario remained unused until 1953, when Yves Allégret directed *Les Orgueilleux (The Proud Ones),* Sartre could now count on earning enough from the movies and the theater to give up teaching. When he applied to the university for leave of absence, he was within six months of his fortieth birthday. A writer of his talent, versatility, and energy might have expected to turn professional sooner, especially after discovering in the army how prolific he could be. But *L'Age de raison* and *Le Sursis* were still unpublished, and unlike Brecht, who was able during his wartime exile to stockpile unproduced plays, Sartre was not temperamentally suited to writing for his desk drawer. Instead of turning back to fiction, though, immediately after the liberation, he worked on the essay he had intended to call "La Situation des juifs en France." The title was changed to *Réflexions sur la question Juive,* but the main thrust was against the anti-Semites rather than in favor of the Jews. During the occupation it had been embarrassing to see Jews wearing yellow stars; it was obvious that well-meaning non-Jews who took off their hats to them were humiliating them no less than people who ignored them. After the liberation, Jewish survivors were coming back to their homes, but, as if anxious not to offend the anti-Semites, French newspapers kept almost silent about the gas chambers.

Angered by this cowardly discretion, Sartre made up his mind to speak out, though he did not yet know when or where he would publish his polemic. The black American writer Richard Wright had told him: "There is no Negro problem in the United States, there is only a white problem." In France, Sartre declared, there was no Jewish problem, only a problem of anti-Semitism. It is the anti-Semite who makes the Jew; the question to ask was not "What is a Jew?" but "What have you made the Jews into?"[53] Though Sartre's polemic is well intentioned, his thinking is superficial. Thirty-five years later he will admit to Benny Lévy: "I wrote without any documentation, without reading one Jewish book. . . . I wrote what I thought."[54]

More important, his premises are more anti-Semitic than he realizes. One commentator has noticed that the word "Aryan" occurs seventeen times in the essay, and only five times is it in quotation marks.[55] Sartre has not dissociated himself from the racialism implicit in this Nazi word. He has no quarrel with the assumption that the Jew is congenitally different from the non-Jew. For the Jew, he maintains, authenticity is to live out fully his condition as a Jew. Refusing to feel ashamed of his "own kind," he must accept the obligation to live in a situation that is unlivable. He must take pride in his humiliation. Though Sartre is dutifully condemning anti-Semitism as an irrational passion, a lower-middle-class snobbery, he is doing nothing to contradict the grossly prejudiced remark he had made about the Jewish soldier he befriended: "Rationalist Jews like Pieter are inauthentic insofar as they consider themselves to be men first of all, not Jews."[56] The satire on the Jewish businessman in *Le Sursis* is acceptable: he is going out of his way to deny his Jewishness. But how would Pieter or anyone else behave if he tried to live out his condition as a Jew before living out his condition as a man?

It was not until November that Sartre submitted his two novels to Gallimard, using the title *Les Chemins de la liberté* for what he was then planning as a trilogy. He dedicated it to Wanda. The foreword tells us that the three volumes will cover the years 1938–44, bringing the characters to the liberation of Paris "but perhaps not to their own liberation." He explained the stylistic difference between the first two novels: in 1937–38 it had still been possible to retain the illusion of having an individual existence in a watertight compartment; in September 1938 "the partitions melt." But he was trying to write a "heroic novel," he said, promising that the characters who seemed most cowardly would prove themselves in the third volume to be capable of acting heroically.[57]

PART IV

SEARCHING FOR
A THIRD WAY

(1945=57)

(14)

Making a New Start

WHAT Sartre did not know was that thanks to the melting of the partitions he was going to let four years go by before he worked on the third novel. He was swept away from his literary moorings by the vast tide of euphoria that surged out of the Liberation. Damaged cities could be reconstructed, but there could be no revival of national self-confidence until a new foundation was built for moral, cultural, and intellectual life. Seeing this, the PCF understood that it needed intellectuals as allies. "The ambition of our party," said a member of the Central Committee, Roger Garaudy, at the tenth congress, "is to be the animator of France's intellectual and moral renaissance."[1] This did not seem unrealistic. The right had been discredited by its opportunistic collaboration with the Nazis; the party had gained prestige from being identified with the cause of resistance. In coordinating anti-Nazi militancy it had genuinely played an important role; its objective now was to dominate progressive forces by coordinating them without waving its political banner. Front organizations with non-Communist names (such as the CNE) were given non-Communist presidents as figureheads but were kept under careful control, while the youth organization, Jeunesses Communistes, was dissolved in 1945 to be replaced by the Union de la Jeunesse Républicaine de la France.[2] Intellectuals were at first easy prey because the Resistance had encouraged the feeling that the sword was mightier than the pen, and their appetite for action was still keen. Private creativity could stay in abeyance till the writers had played their part in shaping the future of France.

Like other left-wingers inside and outside the party, Sartre had no notion in 1945 of how envenomed the struggle for dominance was to become. What seemed important was that work should be done collectively. He was glad to invest time and energy in a monthly review that would involve him and De Beauvoir in collaborating with a group of friends to wield an influence that was simultaneously political and literary. An obvious space for the new review was created by the disappearance of the *Nouvelle Revue Française,* which had continued during the occupation and was therefore banned. One sign of Sartre's overoptimism about the possibility of editorial cooperation between politically opposed writers was his idea of inviting both Malraux and Camus to join his editorial committee; not wanting to work under his leadership, both refused.

Camus's refusal must have been especially disappointing. Reading *La Peste (The Plague),* which was not yet published, Sartre had forecast that "the principal characteristic of French literature of the future can probably be discerned in the somber and pure work of Camus."[3] Dr. Rieux was particularly appealing as a man fighting with severely limited resources against an irresistible natural force, a rebel against the vicious intractability of the natural world. He was modestly asserting the preeminence of the human spirit, said Sartre, while Camus, modestly but more effectively than any other writer, was carrying the heroic spirit of the Resistance into postwar literature. "It is this belief in action which is austere, modest and useful that distinguishes the generation of Camus from the generation of Malraux."[4]

When the editorial committee was formed in September, political standpoints were hardly less heterogeneous than they would have been if Malraux and Camus had accepted the invitations. Those who joined Sartre were De Beauvoir, Leiris, Merleau-Ponty, Jean Paulhan, Camus's associate Albert Ollivier, and Raymond Aron. Paulhan had helped to found the clandestine *Lettres Françaises;* Aron had come back after living since 1940 in London, where he had coedited a review, *La France Libre,* which had not found favor with the Gaullists. Briefly Sartre's friendship with Aron flickered back into life. Aron's daughter Dominique had the impression that he was her family's "best friend," and it was taken for granted that she would go on vacation with De Beauvoir.[5]

Sartre, as he said, rose above his disgust only when he could "rally support for a solid organization"—what he was trying to do during the war with Socialisme et Liberté. But it was no longer realistic to believe that antifascist feelings would be enough to unite those he wanted to fight under his new banner. In the discussions about a title, Leiris, still surrealistic in his inclinations, proposed *Grabuge (Squabble),* but they settled on the more neutral name *Les Temps Modernes,* partly because of Chaplin's film, partly because of the emphasis on commitment to the present.

Almost a year was to elapse before the first issue appeared, though it had been under discussion since the middle of 1943. Paper was in short supply, and quotas were allocated by Jacques Soustelle, the minister of information, who was not impressed by the editorial committee; hadn't Aron been an anti-Gaullist? Resigned to the prospect of a long delay, Sartre was not sorry to leave Paris when an opportunity arose to visit the United States. Wanting to publicize the American war effort in France, the Office of War Information in Washington arranged for a group of French journalists to be invited. "I have never seen Sartre so elated," writes De Beauvoir, "as the day Camus offered him the job of representing *Combat*."[6] Here was his first chance to make contact with the culture that had produced jazz, Chaplin, Dos Passos, and Hemingway. Afterward it was arranged that he would also represent *Le Figaro*.

Hemingway was now in Paris, and it was through Nathalie Sorokine that Sartre met him. She had formed a relationship with Hemingway's younger brother. When Ernest Hemingway came to Paris as a war correspondent he stayed at the Ritz and invited his brother, who suggested that Nathalie, Sartre, and De Beauvoir should go along with him. They were shown into a big, ugly bedroom with two brass bedsteads in it. On one of these was the large body of Hemingway, who was wearing pajamas and a green eyeshade. He had influenza. On a table within reach was a collection of empty and half-empty whiskey bottles. Hemingway levered himself up to clasp Sartre in a bear hug. "You're a general," he said. "Me, I'm only a captain. You're a general." The subsequent conversation was fueled by a great deal of drinking. Sartre left, exhausted, at about three in the morning; De Beauvoir stayed till dawn.[7]

She was disappointed not to accompany him to the States, and in *Les Mandarins* Flora knows what it means when Henri pretends to be sorry that she is not going with him to Portugal. Had he really wanted her to go along, he could have arranged it, and he knows she knows he no longer loves her, though they still make love and still exchange loving declarations. She accommodates herself gladly to his needs. "You wouldn't be yourself," Flora says forgivingly, "if you weren't wishing for new horizons, new nourishment . . . It's enough for me to be necessary to you." She knows that this eager subordination of her needs to his is itself a source of irritation to him, but there is nothing she can do. What De Beauvoir could do was keep her unhappiness under control by using it in her fiction.[8]

It was a cold December in which physical discomfort was exacerbated for both of them by his anxiety about whether he could get the papers he needed for the American trip. In the middle of the month the Germans began their offensive in the Ardennes, and Sartre was worrying about Bost, who was at the front. By Christmas Eve the attack had been halted, but it was hard to feel festive. Sartre and De Beauvoir spent New Year's Eve with Camus, who was living with Francine in Gide's flat on the Rue Vaneau. Pointing to one of the least talkative guests, Camus said he was the model for Meursault in *L'Etranger*. According to Herbert Lottman, this was most likely Pierre Galindo, a phlegmatic, heavy-set, tough-looking man who had probably been in a fight with Arabs on a beach and had befriended Camus in Algiers.[9]

On January 12, 1945, when Sartre and seven other journalists left for America on a military plane, he was flying for the first time. It was midnight when they arrived at La Guardia Airport, and no one was there to meet them or to warn the customs men not to be rude.[10] Eventually Sartre was driven to the Plaza Hotel.[11] The next day, a Sunday, he wandered through the streets of New York trying to discover the character of the unfamiliar city, but it seemed to have no character. "What I was looking for, no doubt, was a European city."[12] He had been expecting boulevards with cafés like the Flore. Skyscrapers had once seemed to symbolize America's fabulous wealth and to represent the architecture of the future,[13] but they looked bewilderingly unlike buildings for people to live in,[14] while "the numerical anonymity of the streets and avenues" made him feel there was no reason to be in one place rather than another.[15]

Though his lumber jacket caused some embarrassment to his hosts,[16] his first dispatch, cabled on January 22 to *Le Figaro,* described the warmth of his reception. Feeling little gratitude to Camus, Sartre had no scruples about sending all the best articles to *Le Figaro* and only the second best to *Combat.* He went on, deliberately undiplomatic, to report conflicts between French supporters of Pétain and De Gaulle in America, alleging that money had been provided either by the State Department or by tycoons for a newspaper that had harmed the interests of France. On January 25 *The New York Times* published a dispatch from its Paris correspondent accusing Sartre of wanting to undermine Franco-American friendship, and six days later it published a letter attacking him and naming the paper as *Pour la Victoire.* He replied in the issue of February 1, accusing the Paris correspondent of plucking quotations out of context.[17] This was not the kind of publicity the Office of War Information had wanted, and it seemed that Sartre might be sent ignominiously back to France,[18] but the scandal was soon forgotten.

The French journalists were flown from one big city to another, guided around factories, supplied with statistics, taken to look at bridges, buildings, dams. "We'll have seen more steel and aluminum," Sartre complained, "than human beings."[19] In New York he found

Stépha and Fernando Gérassi, who introduced him to the sculptor Alexander Calder. Among the French refugees he met were André Masson, Fernand Léger, Yves Tanguy, Claude Lévi-Strauss, and the former leader of the surrealist movement, André Breton. In Hollywood Sartre found Henriette Nizan, who was earning her living by writing subtitles for French films. She told him about the PCF's campaign of vilification against her dead husband. In the South he discovered that 90 percent of blacks still had no vote.

Soon he was involved in a relationship that became surprisingly important. Dolores Vanetti had worked as an actress in Paris. She was intense, vivacious, clever, with a striking resemblance to De Beauvoir. She had been working for the Office of War Information since it started broadcasting in French, and when the eight journalists arrived for a series of interviews, Sartre was last in the line as they filed into the recording studio. He stumbled against something, accidentally or deliberately dropped his pipe, and got into conversation with her as he picked it up. Constantly amazed at how lively and entertaining he was when he concentrated his entire, formidable energy on pleasing her, she became his guide to New York, translating newspaper articles for him, pointing out famous faces—Stravinsky, Garbo—in the Russian Tea Room.[20] Later he would say that she had "given America" to him.

Writing to De Beauvoir at the beginning of the forties, he had promised not to have any more casual affairs for a long time after the war. The war was not yet over, but he was deeply involved in an amour that would jeopardize his relationship with her more seriously than his love for either of the Kosakiewicz sisters had. However badly hurt De Beauvoir had been by his offer to marry Wanda, it had made little if any difference to their subsequent intimacy. He still wanted to talk or write to De Beauvoir about more or less everything that happened, still confided in her about his feelings toward other women. But Dolores was a more formidable challenger, and though the proprietorial challenge was ultimately to be defeated, the affair was a turning point in the relationship with De Beauvoir. Without fully honoring their pact, he had usually respected it; it was now that he denied her even a literary share in his emotional life, and his dependence on her would never be the same. From now on, letters to her would be shorter, more infrequent, and less informative.

On March 10 President Roosevelt received the French journalists. "What is immediately striking," Sartre wrote, "is the deeply human charm of this long face, at once delicate and hard, the eyes gleaming with intelligence. A kind of generous warmth is apparent: something open and communicative, which combines oddly with the slightly ferocious sharpness of the jaws."[21] Five weeks later the President died at the age of sixty-three. He was succeeded by Harry Truman.

Sartre was not accustomed to cities in which the streets are not primarily places for walking, and sometimes he felt like a parcel being picked up and delivered.[22] One reason for the anti-Americanism he developed was that he witnessed the pressure put on Americans to conform before he witnessed the pressure put on Russians. Education, both in colleges and extramurally, struck him as being directed at teaching Americans how to be more American,[23] and New York looked like "the most conformist city in the world."[24]

Sartre was to stay in the States for about four months.

ONLY nine days after he left France, his stepfather died, at the age of seventy, but not wanting her son to sacrifice his opportunity of seeing America, the widow had not told him the news. She was now sixty-three. In the summer Sartre took her on a vacation with him in the country. By then the Allies were in control of Germany, which had been divided into four zones, and during the second half of July, Stalin, Truman, and Churchill were demanding the unconditional surrender of Japan. But the peace began to turn sour before it had even begun. On August 6 an atomic bomb was dropped on Hiroshima and, three days later, another on Nagasaki.

Before the second slaughter Sartre had rejoined De Beauvoir to spend a month at La Pouèze, where, overcoming his outrage, he settled down to work on his play "Les Vainqueurs" ("The Victors"), later retitled *Morts sans sépulture* (which is translated as *Men Without Shadows*). Though his plays did more than any of his other writings to win him success, fame, and money, he never invested as much emotional energy in them as in his philosophy or his novels. A major motive was to provide roles for the women who were emotionally and financially dependent on him. "Les Vainqueurs" gave Wanda her first big opportunity as an actress; she established herself professionally under the name Marie-Olivier.

In his essay on occupied Paris he had equated the limits of individual freedom with powers of resistance to torture and death; in the play he shows men and one woman defining themselves in terms of their ability to resist pressure. The torturers and the victims are all French. The situation is straightforward and potentially melodramatic: Vichy militia are trying to extract from freedom fighters information about the whereabouts of their leader, Jean. He turns up during the action in the school attic, which is being used as a prison, but his captors are still ignorant of his identity. The woman, Lucie, is his lover, and the youngest of the freedom fighters, François, is her fifteen-year-old brother. The boy is so likely to crack under torture, betraying Jean and other comrades, that she consents when the others decide to strangle him, while one of the older men, Sorbier, commits suicide because he believes the torturers would get the better of him. Lucie is raped by her captors, and the others are not only tortured but humiliated, demoralized, crippled by guilt feelings. Sartre shows that the militiamen are motivated less by the wish to extract information than the need to humiliate the patriots, depriving them of their right to feel superior. Later, in *Qu'est-ce que la littérature?*, Sartre will describe explicitly the quasi-sexual intimacy in which the torturer is symbolically gratifying his hatred of all mankind, while the victim, by pushing himself to his limits, comes to terms both with his torturer and with his self-hatred. Torture is communion in which two freedoms meet in the destruction of the human.[25]

Sartre's continuing preoccupation with torture depends partly on his understanding that in forcing himself to work the way he did, he was both torturer and victim. He was coming to terms with his self-hatred by pushing himself to his limits. Left with little interest in living, the freedom fighters in the play are not yet free to die. Not only are they physically imprisoned, they are imprisoned by their own liberty, which forces them to go on making decisions. In a sense they are, as the title suggests, already dead. They have no chance of escaping or of being released, but so long as there is life in them, they have to go on using their freedom.

Chief Existentialist

AFTER spending a month at La Pouèze, Sartre and De Beauvoir could enjoy their first postwar summer vacation: they visited Bruges, Antwerp, and Ghent. They did not know that in returning to Paris they would be returning to fame, but the fashion for existentialism surged up suddenly. Sartre's article "A propos de l'existentialisme: Mise au point" had been published in *Action* on December 29, 1944, and in the issue dated June 8, 1945, he had been reviled by the Marxist sociologist Henri Lefebvre as an idealistic subjectivist manufacturer of weapons against communism. Sartre did not want to be associated with a body of ideas that would look like an alternative to Marxism. In his "Mise au point" he had written: "Class struggle is a fact: I accept it unreservedly," and after Lefebvre's article appeared, he tried to repudiate existentialism. At a colloquium organized by the publishers Editions du Cerf—a firm controlled by the Dominicans—Gabriel Marcel described him as an existentialist, but Sartre retorted: "My philosophy is a philosophy of existence; existentialism—I don't know what it is."[1]

In the early autumn he stopped trying to repudiate the label. In September *L'Age de raison* and *Le Sursis* made their long-delayed appearances. Though the earlier novel reached back to the beginning of the war, it belonged, so far as the public was concerned, to the latest phase of Sartre's existentialism, which seemed to offer a possibility of moral and cultural rehabilitation.

Together with the material damage inflicted on France by the German occupation, by the Allied bombing, by the fighting and sabotage as Hitler's armies retreated, the people had suffered a profound loss of self-confidence. For more than four years they had been divided, but not cleanly into two halves; between the Resistance fighters at one extreme and the collaborators—uniformed and un-uniformed—at the other there had been a wide spectrum of attitudes. Everyone had made compromises, sometimes by remaining passive—failing to help Jews or failing to stop a neighbor from denouncing a Resistance network. Everyone had taken risks, but criteria were quantitative—how much risk, how much to be gained? For the unstable majority it had been impossible even to hope wholeheartedly and consistently. When a German victory seemed inevitable, many wanted it to come quickly; once it became obvious that Germany was going to be defeated, people started to destroy evidence of their cooperation with the Nazi authorities. The same people were demonstrative in celebrating the victory of the Allies.

The one commodity in plentiful supply when the war ended was guilt feelings. Hungry, cold, impoverished, disoriented, people were uneasy about the past, apprehensive about the future. Cultural and educational continuities had been broken by the book-burning Nazis with their rabid anti-Semitism and their bigoted views on what constituted decadence. It was obvious that in France prewar values would never be reinstated in their old forms, and morale would have to be boosted before the people could be rallied to the task of clearing away debris and reconstructing. Of all the French intellectuals the diminutive Sartre might superficially have looked least like the one capable of becoming a leader, but in fact he was well equipped for the role. Nothing could have qualified him for it better than the private disposition that had generated his ideas. What people wanted to believe was that they could afford to forget the past and make a fresh start. Sartre had been inclined all his life to disregard the past and let the present take its tinge from his appetite for the future. In *Les Mouches* he had already hit out against the pessimistic Pétainist view that the defeat of France had been divine retribution for moral degeneracy. Sartrean existentialism mingled optimism with responsibility: each of us chooses the historical context in which he lives. If this idea had been formulated cynically to secure a maximum of popularity for Sartre, it could not have been more effective. What he was offering the French people was a chance to accept a share of the blame for the immediate past at the same time that they affirmed their willingness to take charge of the immediate future. They must commit themselves morally and politically. Those who had not taken part in the Resistance could feel solidarity with those who had; those who could not believe in God could believe, religiously, in the human race. The occupation had shown that morality and politics could not be kept apart; Sartre was a political moralist with no allegiance to any party or any church. He would force his followers to be free.

His popularity is partly explained by De Beauvoir's description in *Les Mandarins* of the impact Robert makes as a speaker.

Behind the words he spoke, this friendship he offered us was a certainty:
men are not condemned to hatred, to warfare ... Day after day I saw
him bent over his desk, eyes bloodshot, back hunched, alone and doubt-
ing himself: it was this same man five thousand people were applauding.
What exactly was he to them? At once a great writer and the man of the
vigilance committees and the antifascist meetings; an intellectual committed to the revolution without denying his nature as an intellectual
... he did not offer a program, he gave us tasks. And these were so urgent we couldn't fail to perform them: victory was assured by its very necessity.[2]

Sartre was neither unaware of his power over audiences nor unex-
cited by it. Reality was at last confirming both his childhood fantasies
and the semiadolescent fantasies of impassioned conversations with De
Beauvoir about their future as cultural reformers. If Sartre was capable
of being a leader, a shaper of public opinion, a shaper of France's future, he must stop thinking of himself as just a writer. A review would
provide a channel of communication through which influence could be
exerted, and in sharing editorial decisions with colleagues he would be
sharing his thinking. If consciousness and the self were not identical,
why shouldn't experiments be made in nonindividual thinking? The
symbiotic relationship with De Beauvoir had succeeded, at least partially, in breaking down barriers of privacy. Only intellectual intimacy
would be involved in exchanging editorial ideas with a committee, but
unlike writing a book, editing *Les Temps Modernes* would depend on collective thinking. Or so it seemed.

But it was hard to think clearly in the euphoria induced by sudden
fame. De Beauvoir too was floated into prominence. *L'Invitée,* her novel
about the triangular relationship with Olga, had been accepted by
Gallimard in the summer of 1942 and published in the spring of 1943.
Her second, *Le Sang des autres* (*The Blood of Others*), a story about the Resistance, came out in September 1945, just before Sartre's two novels.
But it was the huge vogue for existentialism that made her famous as
her name and her face kept appearing alongside Sartre's in newspapers.
Publicity established them as a couple, and it made no difference when
the first issue of *Les Temps Modernes* appeared with Sartre's "Présentation" dedicated to Dolores.

Written with formidable evangelistic cogency, it made the case for *la
littérature engagée.* If the Commune of 1871 had been followed by repression, Flaubert and the Goncourts were to blame "because they did
not write one line to prevent it."[3] But "we"—and the word invited his
readers to feel at one with him—will take responsibility for the future:
"we make it ours, we want no other future."[4] Looking back critically at

his childhood ambitions, he condemned the authors who wooed posterity; his concern would be with the present and the immediate future: "It is our task as a writer to expose the eternal values implicit in these social or political debates. . . . What is absolute, what a thousand years of history cannot destroy, is *this* irreplaceable, incomparable decision which [a man] makes at this moment about these circumstances. To sum up, our intention is to unite and to produce certain changes in the society that surrounds us."[5]

The gibes at Proust are cheap and unfair. "A pederast, Proust thought he could use his homosexual experience to describe Swann's love for Odette; a bourgeois, he presents this feeling of a rich, idle bourgeois for a kept woman as the prototype of love." Proust is denounced as an "intellectualist" and an "accomplice of bourgeois propaganda" who had helped to spread "the myth of human nature." Sartre's main target was the fallacy that emotions can be independent of their social context, and in his polemical excitement he did not care if he coarsened subtler arguments he had advanced in calmer moments or if he made pronouncements his editorial colleagues would not have backed. His antiliterary extremism was at odds with the appointment of René Etiemble as the review's literary critic, but after starting his monthly articles for *Les Temps Modernes* in October 1946, Etiemble continued them until 1952. He was a serious littérateur who only later became famous as the author of *Parlez-vous Franglais?*

Sartre in his opening manifesto promised that the new review would not serve any of the political parties, though it would take up a position in relation to political and social events, helping literature to recover its social function. In another article, "La Fin de la guerre" ("The End of the War"), Sartre again invites the reader to join in taking responsibility for the future: the atomic bomb, by giving humanity the chance to exterminate itself, has brought us new freedom and new responsibility. Each day we will have to decide that we want to survive.[6] The issue contained an article by an ex-pupil who had joined the PCF, Jean Kanapa, and one by Jean Pouillon, who sneered at the reforms that could be effected constitutionally; he condemned "revolution by law" as an attempt "to prolong what it pretends to abolish." It was clear that the review was committed to the ideal of democracy; it was not clear how its relationship with communism would develop.

On October 24 Sartre lectured on existentialism in Brussels, and, four days later, speaking to the Club Maintenant in Paris, he took as his title "L'Existentialisme est un humanisme." Women fainted—partly, perhaps, because of oxygen shortage—and he could scarcely make himself heard. In the lecture he described T. E. Lawrence as an existentialist, but this passage is suppressed in the published text.[7] The next day, interviewed for the magazine *Paru*, he claimed to want no disciples,[8] but in the coming months he would be fêted, quoted, emulated, discussed, attacked. The short-lived weekly *Terre des Hommes* published a response by Gide to the "Présentation" in *Les Temps Modernes*. Other prominent intellectuals joined in the controversy: Gabriel Marcel condemned Sartre's existentialism as negative;[9] the Christian essayist Pierre Emmanuel denounced it as "une maladie de l'esprit." Many Communists attacked it. Henri Lefebvre called it "a phenomenon of rottenness altogether in line with the decomposition of bourgeois culture," but Francis Ponge was ready to pay tribute to a philosophy that had not yet expressed a morality. In the streets Sartre was endlessly photographed, endlessly followed, endlessly accosted by strangers. When he walked into a café, people would welcome him, wave, shout.[10] Communists attacked him for keeping young people away from Marxism; gossip columnists denounced him for preaching despair.

Camus battled to stop himself from being bracketed with the existentialists, while Sartre dissociated himself from Camus's "philosophy of the absurd." What Camus meant by absurdity was the disjunction between man's reasonable expectations and the irrationality of the world, whereas Sartre, when he spoke of the absurd, meant contingency.[11]

The vogue for existentialism promoted *Les Temps Modernes*. Though the review may have been read only superficially by most of the "existentialists" who bought it, it went on ticking loudly as the politico-literary conscience of the new movement; it was also a public dressing room in which Sartre could be seen struggling to adjust his priorities. At editorial meetings the discussion ranged freely, like a conversation, over heterogeneous subjects, and his main function was to pick out the ones that should be treated in the review.[12] He left his editorial committee to sift articles submitted and do routine work, but his decisions shaped the contents while the review was to exert a strong influence—not always an obvious one—on his decisions about how to divide his time. What should his priorities be? His philosophy was pulled away from ontology and psychology toward sociology and what he began to call anthropology. Though he denied there was any such thing as "human nature," he often expressed belief in the possibility of defining "the essence of man," while his interest in politics had been gaining ground steadily. But alongside the opportunity for collective thinking, the review offered him power he could never have exerted as a private individual. The objectives stated in his "Présentation" are ambitious: "to change man's social condition and the conception he has of himself."[13] Redefining and reshaping should be inseparable parts of the same process: the researcher was not so much a scientist as a catalyst; bourgeois analysts might posit the possibility of scientific detachment in research on human affairs, but the humane researcher got caught up in the chemistry. The anthropologist should not try to remain uninvolved in the society he was observing. Maintaining that while men have in common their "metaphysical condition," they consist of "irreducible totalities." Sartre pledged that the new review would contribute "to the constitution of a synthetic anthropology."[14] The question he had not faced squarely was whether he wanted papal authority over the new anthropology or whether he was prepared to settle altruistically for a modest editorial role, holding the balance between philosophers, psychologists, and trained anthropologists who could be commissioned to contribute essays.

Though Marcel Mauss, the author of *Essai sur le don,* had introduced the term "social anthropology" in France during 1938,[15] "ethnography" had been the word generally in use. At the Collège de France, where Mauss held a chair from 1931 to 1942, his subject was called sociology. His 1925 book *Essai sur le don,* which focused on systems of exchanging gifts in preindustrial societies, was seminal: Lévi-Strauss, Sartre, Merleau-Ponty, and Michel Leiris all came under its sway. For *Les Temps Modernes* Leiris was a key figure. It was natural that he should be: he was not only closer to Sartre than Merleau-Ponty, he was closer to anthropology than Sartre. His book *L'Afrique fantôme* had been based on a 1931 expedition led by Marcel Griaule, a professor at the Sorbonne, to French West Africa. Perched between anthropology and literature, Leiris' writing was exemplary and progressive. Dissociating himself from the patronizing ethnographers who tried to remain detached from the primitive societies they studied, Leiris insisted that there must be give and take between investigator and society. He also anticipated Lévi-Strauss's thesis that linguistic models can be employed in studying the unconscious processes behind the symbolic systems a society uses. Lévi-Strauss credits Leiris with initiating in his literary work the study of unconscious structuring in vocabulary; but linguistics was going to be kept out of the new review, although Merleau-Ponty lectured on Saussure at the ENS in 1948–49.[16] According to Lévi-Strauss, linguistics was the key to positive knowledge of social facts, but Sartre never accepted this. Without naming Saussure in his *Esquisse d'une théorie des émotions,* he had spoken of the "signifier" and the "signified," but he had little interest in the study of language, and he was not open to influence from Merleau-Ponty on this subject, though politically Sartre accepted him as mentor.

Merleau-Ponty's political influence was soon to drag Sartre away from his promise of nonalignment. In the fourth issue of *Les Temps Modernes* (January 1946) Merleau-Ponty proclaimed that their intention was to "rediscover Marxism on the road of contemporary truth and in the analysis of our times." "In short," he wrote, "we must carry out the policy of the Communist party."[17] Not yet trusting his own political judgment, Sartre uncritically accepted Merleau-Ponty's. "He showed me what my own thoughts were." The two men were vastly different— by temperament Merleau-Ponty was more withdrawn, more academic. They never became friendly, seldom ate meals together; Merleau-Ponty relayed to the readers of *Les Temps Modernes* ideas that were taken to be Sartre's. Articles that were signed "T.M." were written by Merleau-Ponty. He always wanted Sartre to read them before they were published, but Sartre gave his approval in advance,[18] under pretext of involving both himself and the readers in thinking that was done more collectively than individually. The journalist, he would write later, "does not create thoughts in his readers—this might disunite them—he *uncovers* their thoughts for them: but not the thought of each one in each one—the thought of all in each one."[19] Sartre was trusting Merleau-Ponty to uncover the thought of all in him. The ideal is transparent collectivity: the barriers of individuality are to be knocked aside.

All this is unrealistic, but the euphoria helped Sartre to achieve one of his greatest successes: he popularized the concept of *la littérature engagée*. The phrase did not catch on abroad until the middle fifties, but in France there were many who shared Sartre's quasi-nostalgic attitude to the occupation, when the one luxury generally available had been the simplicity of political decisions. Writing in clandestine papers at the risk of his life, the writer had been in a position comparable to that of Osip Mandelstam and Anna Akhmatova in the USSR after the revolution or to that of dissident writers in Communist countries today. Commitment is automatic when the writer is risking his life or his liberty. To Sartre, French and English literature of 1918–39 seemed inflationary: words had been thrown around like paper money unbacked by hard currency.[20] The writer should be fully immersed in each statement he made; writing was an action that could have and should have practical consequences.

He believed in the power of *Les Temps Modernes* to alter the *Zeitgeist* by reflecting it. "An anecdote reflects an entire era as much as the contents of a political constitution. We would track down meaning, we would tell the truth about the world and our own lives."[21] It was easier to campaign idealistically for consensus among "us" than to preserve harmony among the coeditors, but the success of the review was assured. It had become fashionable, and no sooner had the third issue arrived in the bookstores than, confidently, Sartre absented himself from Paris for four months.

To get himself invited back to America he had been in touch with universities there. He was missing Dolores. On December 12 he embarked on a Liberty ship, a military cargo boat that would take eighteen days to cross the ocean. Under the aegis of the Relations Culturelles Françaises he made star appearances at Harvard, Princeton, Yale, and in New York and Canada. During the first half of 1946 he lectured a lot on the situation of French literature but did surprisingly little writing, except for a screenplay that was nourished by his antipathy to the United States. It approximates in several ways to an apologia for Stalinism—he even drags concentration camps into the plot, though the action is set in a small country based partly on Cuba. Its capitalist neighbor, by threatening invasion, makes it impossible for the revolutionary leader to nationalize the oil industry. Sartre's original title for the screenplay was "Les Mains sales" ("Dirty Hands"), the title he used later for a play on the same theme. The 1946 screenplay pivots on the friendship between two members of the Central Committee: Lucien is an almost saintly journalist, who refuses to have any traffic with violence, while Jean, after leading the revolution, shoulders responsibility for governing the country. Once it had looked as though Lucien could act as Jean's conscience, restraining him from violence, but Lucien dies in one of Jean's concentration camps. Sartre's point is that violence cannot be dismissed as unnecessary. In one sense Lucien is a parasite. In an almost credible showdown Jean tells him: "Yes, I've got blood on my hands. But I saved you from having it on yours. . . . You think I wouldn't have preferred to keep mine clean?" Jean is not just a tyrant: genuine love of the people makes him detest poverty even more than the violence he uses to get rid of it, but as he grows to detest himself, he falls back on heavy drinking. Sartre eventually settled on the title *L'Engrenage* (*In the Mesh*)—an allusion to the trap that ensnares not only Jean but the new revolutionary leader who condemns him to death and starts simultaneously on the slide that will tumble him into the same oppressive violence.

Since 1938 Sartre had never let so much time go by with so little literary activity. During January he described his daily routine in a letter. He would rise at nine, linger over his toilet and breakfast till eleven, lunch with Dolores or with admirers, wander till six in the streets of New York, "which I now know as well as Paris," meet Dolores again, and drink with her in a bar till two in the morning. From Friday afternoon till Sunday afternoon he would stay inside her flat to avoid being seen by the porters; she had not yet entirely separated from her husband. Sartre was short of money, spending at least a day on writing each lecture, which brought in only fifty dollars, while he was at first earning nothing from journalism.[22] But he was soon to receive an advance of 300,000 francs on the Broadway production of *Huis clos*.

He had intended to return by boat, leaving at the end of February, but he was offered some lucrative lectures in Toronto, Ottawa, and Montreal during the second week of March, and he did not want to leave Dolores. He had never departed so far from his working routine for the sake of Toulouse, De Beauvoir, Olga, or Wanda, and by February he was describing Dolores as the woman he knew best after De Beauvoir. Though timid, she was capable of becoming so passionate that it scared him, "but when she's happy, she can be as open and innocent as a child."[23] When Columbia University offered him a job, he told her he wanted to marry her and stay there for two years. Even if she had been free to marry, she would have been skeptical about whether he would be wise to settle in the United States for so long unless he could conquer his reluctance to learn the language.[24] They compromised by agreeing to spend two or three months together each year. He stayed until April, gave a course of lectures on existentialism in Switzerland during late May and early June, and left Paris again, later in the month, to lecture in Italy. After returning to Paris in April he told De Beauvoir that Dolores was deeply in harmony with him. When they went out together they always had the same instincts, he said, about when to stop, when to go on. Disconcerted, De Beauvoir asked explicitly whether Dolores was more important to him than she was. His answer was noncommittal: "She's enormously important to me, but you're the one I'm with."[25]

He had missed some dramatic political developments. In January 1946, when De Gaulle had resigned as the head of the provisional government, a coalition was formed, and a decision had to be made about the constitution. In the elections held in October 1945 for a Constituent Assembly, the Communist party and the SFIO (Section Française de l'Internationale Ouvrière) had won an overall majority, and, unlike the Christian Socialists of the MRP (Mouvement Républicain Populaire), they favored a single-chamber system. A second chamber might act as a curb on radical legislation. It was decided to hold a referendum.

While posters were going up on the billboards exhorting voters to say "Yes" or "No"—De Gaulle emerged from retirement to recommend a "No" vote, while the Communists campaigned vigorously for a "Yes"—Sartre succumbed to mumps. The doctor smeared his face and neck with a black ointment, and soon he was well enough to receive visitors in bed; his room was always full of people willing to risk infection. Wearing a pointed nightcap over the helmet of bandages on his swollen face, he looked bizarre; by the beginning of May he could discard these, but his face was still swollen, with a pimple on his nose. Sartre had no desire to vote. What mattered, according to him, was to know which side one supported; it would be best to vote Communist and to vote "No." In *Les Temps Modernes* Aron and Ollivier had both written articles in favor of voting "No"; this caused a furor at *Combat,* where most journalists were voting "Yes."[26]

In May, Sartre took De Beauvoir with him on the Swiss lecture tour, which was organized by the publisher Skira. Articles about atheist existentialism proliferated in Swiss newspapers and magazines, many of them attacking Sartre as a corrupting influence, an apostle of conscienceless freedom. In Geneva he had an audience of over a thousand. He went on to Zurich, where *Huis clos* was being staged.

In Lausanne, after lecturing in a large, packed movie theater, he was taken by the organizers to drink in a bar, where the man who sat down next to him was a young Austrian historian, André Gorz, who had read all his books. Fascinated by the "novelty and complexity of his thought,"[27] Gorz had adopted his terminology and had formed the impression that Sartre possessed an answer to every possible question. But in the bar, brushing cigarette ashes off his vest or spilling wine on someone else's sleeve, the diminutive philosopher seemed more human than any of his surrounding admirers. His gestures were generously expansive. "Cigarette in hand, he raised his whole arm to the shoulder, so that to approach him was to risk a blow from his elbow."[28] He seemed to have a huge appetite for living and a horror of abstract ideas; his philosophy corresponded to a strong personal need.

SARTRE and De Beauvoir frequently had meals with the sculptor Giacometti and his wife, Annette. He talked, often obscurely, about his progress from his first thick statue to his later attenuated figures, and he talked, more entertainingly, about women, especially when Annette was not with him. He would describe the adventures he had had in brothels, looking for women who were slightly ungainly, slightly ugly.[29] One evening, drinking in a small group on the terrace of La Pergola, Giacometti, after staring admiringly at Sartre for some time, brought the conversation to an astonished silence by saying: "Sartre, you're beautiful."

With a friendly laugh Sartre answered: "I think there are quite a few things you can say about me, but that I'm beautiful—sincerely, I don't think so."

Giacometti insisted: "You're beautiful."

"Okay, fine. I'm beautiful."

"You're like Hamlet. Yes. You always think Hamlet was a tall, thin guy, and so on, eh? No, me, I'm sure he was a little fellow who drank beer, eh? A fat little man with hair like yours and eyes like yours. Very beautiful."[30]

In Paris, during June, Sartre met a young man, Jean Cau, who had written to him earlier, asking for help in finding a job. Sartre now decided to offer him one—as his secretary. At first there was little for Cau to do except fend off admirers, but it was not yet clear whether Sartre's work load would increase after the dissolution of the editorial committee at *Les Temps Modernes*. Aron and Ollivier had resigned in June 1946, and nearly eight years were to elapse before a new editorial committee would be named on the cover. At first Sartre's name appeared there alone as editor; Merleau-Ponty, who in practice was not only political editor but *gérant,* or editor in chief, stolidly refused to accept any front-page credit. With him at the helm, politics was certain to be given prominence, but Sartre did not try to bring the literary policy into line. He was content for Leiris to be poetry editor and for René Etiemble to have freedom of expression, though his literary values were anything but Sartrean. The literature that appeared in *Les Temps Modernes* during its first six years was oddly heterogeneous—poetry by Beckett, Char, Ponge, Queneau, and several black poets, including Aimé Césaire, prose by Kafka, Faulkner, Ignazio Silone, Michel de Ghelderode, Nathalie Sarraute, Maurice Blanchot, Jean Genet, Leiris, Violette Leduc, Marguerite Duras, Boris Vian, Robert Merle, and Nelson Algren. Sartre was palpably undecided about both literary values and the value of literature. During the next twelve months, while he wrote *Qu'est-ce que la littérature?* partly to make up his mind, he still let the literary pages of the review float free from the conclusions he reached.

Lecturing in Italy, he found it was possible to have a better relationship with the Italian Communists than with the French: in Milan the self-educated novelist Elio Vittorini was friendly—he was editor of *Il Politecnico,* which had published a translation of Sartre's "Présentation"—but Sartre's Italian publisher, Bompiani, who belonged to the extreme right, found his author's speechmaking so embarrassing that he reneged on the agreement. Vittorini set up a meeting with Arnoldo

Mondadori, who was glad to take Sartre over and arranged for him to stay with De Beauvoir at luxurious hotels in Venice and in Rome. There they made friends with Silone and Carlo Levi, who had written *Cristo si è fermato a Eboli* (*Christ Stopped at Eboli*).

Returning to Paris, Sartre finally had to confront the problem he had sidestepped by absenting himself in America and Italy. His political navigator, Merleau-Ponty, was using a map drawn according to principles that contradicted those of *L'Etre et le Néant*. Since writing it, Sartre had edged toward envisaging a society without masters or slaves: instead of exploiting each other, men would unite to exploit the natural world. But he could give up neither his faith in freedom nor his belief that consciousness had no material foundation. He therefore balked at Stalin's *Dialectical and Historical Materialism*—still, apparently, his main source. He quotes from it three times in "Matérialisme et révolution," while the references to Marx appear mainly in the footnotes, which were not added until 1949; but it was already apparent in 1946 that he was more in sympathy with what Marx wrote before he came under the influence of Engels, who maintained that nature proceeded dialectically. The idea was anathema to Sartre: if a determining pattern was built ineluctably into the processes of nature and history, and if all the activities of consciousness were conditioned by social and economic circumstances, men were not free.

Sartre regarded dialectical materialism as a mythology; it was understandable that Communists should be nervous about a philosophy founded on human freedom. Their need was for discipline, and to insist that man was already free was to imply that revolution was unnecessary. Nevertheless, Sartre argued, his own philosophy, centering as it did on action, was more suitable for revolutionaries. Action was resistance against the stubborn impenetrability of the universe; the revolutionary act was the free act par excellence. A new ideology would protect the Communists from the danger that the myth of materialism would suffocate the revolutionary project. He was thinking of his own future philosophical projects when he prescribed what the "business of the philosopher" should be: "to make the truths contained in materialism hold together and to construct, gradually, a philosophy which suits the needs of the revolution as closely as the myth does."[31] After the publication of "Matérialisme et révolution" in the June and July issues of the review, his relations with the Communist party deteriorated still further.

The wartime arrangements about dividing his leave between De Beauvoir and Wanda had heralded a pattern of scheduled promiscuity. In December 1945 he had started an affair with Boris Vian's wife, Mi-

chelle, who had long silky blond hair and a happy smile; she was vivacious, warm, open, and behind the effervescent enthusiasm was a wide
knowledge of books and music. Her taste in both was more catholic
than Sartre's, and she loved poetry. The affair was kept secret, and
when Sartre was away from Paris he wrote to her care of Cau, who
handed the letters to her. Sartre now had at least three other women—
Dolores, the tolerant De Beauvoir, and the jealous Wanda[32]—but with
Dolores on the far side of the Atlantic, he was free to divide leisure and
vacations between Michelle and the other two.

In his summer writing he expressed his feelings about racism in
America. A new play was needed to make up a double bill with *Morts
sans sépulture,* which was going to be revived during the autumn at the
Théâtre Antoine. Skillfully and rapidly Sartre constructed *La Putain respectueuse* (*The Respectful Prostitute*), a play in two scenes, set in Alabama
and based on the well-known Scottsboro case of 1931. In the play a
well-meaning prostitute agrees to give false evidence against an innocuous black man in order to protect a well-born white man who has
drunkenly shot another black. The girl, Lizzie, is helpless against the
rhetoric of a distinguished-looking senator, the boy's uncle, who convinces her that his nephew's life is worth more to America than that of
the black. In the climactic scene Lizzie, who has a revolver, thinks of
shooting Fred, the senator's son, who, after sleeping with her, has tried,
insultingly, to bully her into saving his cousin's life, and, no less insultingly, blames her for the lust he felt while, as a member of a lynch mob,
he shot another innocent black. The characters are all stereotypes, and
to any Americans in the audience it would have been as obvious as it
was to *The New Yorker*'s correspondent Janet Flanner that Sartre had no
firsthand experience of Southern-gentleman lynchers.[33] But when Lizzie, unable to shoot Fred, accepts his offer to set her up as his mistress,
the audience is trapped into wanting an act of violence, which the play
withholds.

IGNORING the recommendations of the Communist and Socialist majority, the voters rejected its constitution, but in the elections of November
10 the Communists won 186 seats, the MRP (Mouvement Républicain
Populaire) 166, and the Socialists 103, which caused a political dead-
lock. Camus's position was still a long way from De Gaulle's, while
Merleau-Ponty, who had earlier been troubled by the prewar Moscow
trials, was provoked into defending them. To refute Arthur Koestler's
book *The Yogi and the Commissar,* Merleau-Ponty started, in October
1946, on a series of articles, *Le Yogi et le prolétarien* (*The Yogi and the Prole-*

tarian), arguing—more or less as Sartre had in *L'Engrenage*—that politics was inevitably immoral; no régime could be innocent of violence. The important question was whether Communist violence could help to humanize humanity. Generally Merleau-Ponty tended to equate morality with bourgeois moralism; for Sartre, who felt no qualms in supporting him, the basic dichotomy was between ideas and actions. Traditional morality belonged to the cerebral world of his grandfather; to be effective, any political leader must dirty his hands.

SARTRE was now so secure in his intellectual and emotional independence that he could afford to share a home once again with his mother, and he seems to have made the decision without any rigorous self-questioning about motivation. Was he trying, twenty-nine years later, to reverse the defeat he had sustained when she became Mme. Mancy? It was she who suggested they should live together again; she had suffered a loss almost as great as his when marriage put an end to their close relationship.

For five years, since escaping from the stalag, he had been living in hotels and working in cafés, owning no furniture or ornaments. Now he settled into the small flat she bought at 42 Rue Bonaparte, on the fourth floor, with a view of the Place Saint-Germain-des-Prés. The best room in the flat became his, but it had to serve as both study and bedroom; for sixteen years a narrow couch became his bed at night. On the wall between the two windows he put a reproduction of Dürer's *Melancholia,* and facing the desk was a picture Fernand Léger had given him. Having accumulated no possessions while living in hotels, he now began to buy books from the shops in the Rue Bonaparte and the Rue Mazarine; he grew possessive about his Bibliothèque de la Pléiade classics. The shelves were soon thickly lined. From his window he could see the church and the Café des Deux Magots. Mme. Mancy kept the drawing room and a small bedroom for herself; Eugénie, the old housekeeper, slept in the bedroom at the back. Mme. Mancy enjoyed saying: "This is my third marriage,"[34] and she confused visitors by calling Sartre "Poulou."[35] The flat changed the rhythm of his life: he was on the move less, and he would play the piano almost every evening before his final stint of writing.

When Jean Cau (who was never given a key to the flat) rang the bell in the morning, he would sometimes hear piano duets being played, but the music would stop and Mme. Mancy would withdraw to her room. Cau worked on a folding table that became the dining table whenever Sartre and "ma petite maman" had lunch together. Cau, who was never asked to do any research, answered the telephone, made out the checks, ran errands, filtered demands on Sartre's time. Some of these were rejected by Cau, some were passed on to Sartre, who rejected most of them himself. "I haven't got time to talk to that idiot." "I'm not going to let those fools bore my ass off." "Why should I waste time on that moron?"[36] The language was no more violent than the desperation to defend precious working time. In the 1953 play *Kean*, the actor's relationship with his secretary, Solomon, is closely modeled on Sartre's relationship with Cau.[37] Solomon's main duties are to protect his master from unwanted visitors—including creditors—to restrain his financial fecklessness—discouraging him from acts of reckless generosity—to make practical suggestions about how to drum up credit for the needs of the moment, and, not least important, to be available as *raisonneur* and confidant when no one else is around. Though less exhibitionistic than a star actor, Sartre disliked being alone, even when writing, and it was more fun to behave unreasonably in the presence of a secretarial stooge who reliably argued from a commonsensical standpoint.

Cau's daily stint for Sartre ended at lunchtime; in the afternoon De Beauvoir came to the flat and worked at the other table in the same room.[38] Because they were habituated to working in cafés, neither of them was much distracted by the other's presence.

At the end of October, Sartre attended a meeting convened by Koestler at André Malraux's flat in Boulogne-Billancourt. Koestler's proposal was that since the French League for Human Rights was dominated by the Communists, intellectuals should take the lead in creating a new organization. The chief spokesman for the project was Manès Sperber, a former emissary of the Comintern, who had defected during the trials. Camus supported the project, but Malraux was so skeptical and Sartre so hostile that the idea was dropped.

Sartre had first met Koestler at the Pont-Royal during October when the small, dark, intense, thick-haired, French-speaking Hungarian had come up to introduce himself. Later, at the flat in the Rue Bonaparte, Koestler told him: "You're a better novelist than I am, but not such a good philosopher."[39] Sartre nonetheless took to him and made a formal offer of friendship. It was Koestler who at first demurred, and they quarreled during a drunken evening at Camus's flat when Sartre abused an American journalist as being an enemy of freedom and Koestler in turn denounced Sartre as an apologist for Stalin's terrorism. Koestler afterward wrote an apologetic letter to Sartre, who replied warmly and at great length.[40]

One evening Sartre, De Beauvoir, Camus, Francine, Koestler, and his pretty English wife, Mamaine, had dinner together, went on to a little dance hall in the Rue des Gravilliers and then to a nightclub, the Schéhérazade. Lugubriously maintaining that friendship was incompatible with differences of political opinion, Koestler accused Sartre and Camus of trying to compromise with the Soviets but conceded that for Camus, as for him, friendship mattered more than politics. Although Sartre was due to lecture the next afternoon at the Sorbonne, they went on at four in the morning to a bistro in Les Halles, where they drank a great deal. Koestler threw a crust of bread, which hit his wife in the eye. Sartre was sometimes giggling, sometimes weeping. De Beauvoir, in a state of drunken depression, suggested as they walked back across a bridge that they might just as well throw themselves into the Seine. After a couple of hours' sleep Sartre drugged himself with orthodrine to prepare his lecture, which was on the responsibility of the writer.[41] He spoke about violence, saying that in the modern world nothing could be done without it; what the writer must condemn was useless or excessive violence.[42]

A week later, when *Morts sans sépulture* and *La Putain respectueuse* opened at the Antoine, Sartre was giving subtler support to violence with a case history which suggested that nothing else could clean off the racism that was corroding the American system of justice. Mainly because of a municipal councillor who was campaigning to have the play banned, its title was censored by the Métro authorities. On posters in the subway stations it had to be announced as *La P . . . . . respectueuse*. But on the first night it was the torture sequences in *Morts sans sépulture* that caused a scandal. One woman stood up and shouted "Disgraceful!" In the front rows people even came to blows. Aron's wife, who had almost fainted, left with her husband during the intermission.[43] The torture scene had to be modified: instead of having his nails pulled out onstage, Sorbier was merely beaten with truncheons.[44] Press reactions were generally unfavorable: Sartre was accused of writing Grand Guignol and of reviving old hatreds, but after a hundred performances the double bill was still playing to enthusiastic audiences.[45] The Communists mostly supported *Morts sans sépulture* but condemned *La Putain respectueuse* for showing a black man trembling with fear.[46]

Later on in the month De Beauvoir left for a lecture tour of Holland, where, after a week, Sartre joined her. Together they looked at paintings by Rembrandt and Vermeer. What moved Sartre most was a beautiful red brick wall on one of the canvases. On the train to Utrecht he was still analyzing *why* it was so beautiful, and the experience led to the theory of art he put forward in *Qu'est-ce que la littérature?*, which he

began to write a few weeks later,[47] taking a more favorable view of the
aesthetic experience than he had in *L'Etre et le Néant*.

His own involvement was more complex than ever before. With his
novel held in suspense, he was open to the influence of all the writing he
was publishing in *Les Temps Modernes*—literary, political, psychological,
anthropological. In February and March 1946 the review had published extracts from Leiris' *Biffures* (*Crossings Out*), a volume in his autobiographical sequence. Leiris' interest in the exchange that occurs
between writer and reader derived from Mauss's *Essai sur le don;* and
Sartre, looking at Dutch paintings, became acutely aware that, like the
reader, the viewer is making a collaborative contribution. Studying
Van Gogh's painting of a red path, you follow it farther than the
painter took it; in Dostoevsky's *Crime and Punishment* you have to create
your own Raskolnikov. Through art, Sartre now suggests, it is possible
to achieve a fusion of subjectivity and objectivity, a reconciliation
between the Self and the Other. The goal of art is to recover the world
as it is, but as if the willpower of the reader were bringing it into existence.

Qu'est-ce que la littérature? was prompted by Sartre's need to test how
his thinking about literature was being affected by pressure from current events, from editorial experience, from his anthropological program. His tendency was always to blur the question "How much can
we know about a man?" with "How much can we know about man?,"
but the blurring took different forms. The activity of writing was, for
Sartre, a natural movement toward answering both questions, but the
activity had become different from what it was when, as a schoolteacher
in Le Havre, he tried to redefine the quality of existence in *La Nausée* or
when, as a soldier and as a prisoner of war, he had almost unlimited
leisure for making notes and for redrafting chapters. Now that he was so
busy, what had emerged, alongside his devaluation of poetry, was an
aversion to polished prose. Prose should be serviceable, lucid, work-
manlike, but not crafted too painstakingly. Time should not be wasted
on rewriting the same sentence to make it more beautiful. This principle was in conflict both with his early realization that truth could
emerge from an arrangement of words and with his habit of making
epigrams for all occasions. But he was always attracted to principles
that went painfully against the grain. From now on his practice as a
writer was inconsistent: the work he regarded as literary was constructed in a different way from the philosophical or political or jour-
nalistic work, which was written more hurriedly, often with the help of
drugs to accelerate the process of translating facts and ideas into written words; for the "literary" work he would never drug himself, though

he kept a thermos of strong tea on his desk and consumed about a quart each morning.[48]

The review provided an immediate outlet for anything he wrote, but contributing to it was not so much a matter of taking a fresh initiative as of answering criticism, modifying statements already made, responding to challenges that came in different forms and at different angles— from Merleau-Ponty, from Communist attackers, from friends who were less radical. Quarrels exploded around him almost daily, sometimes arising from political differences, sometimes from aggressively boyish competitiveness. On one drunken evening Camus and Koestler agreed to race on all fours across the Place Saint-Michel. Koestler arrived first on the far side but Camus accused him of cheating. In the fight that ensued Koestler gave Camus a black eye.[49]

In December, Sartre went with De Beauvoir to a party given by Boris and Michelle Vian. Merleau-Ponty and Bost were among the guests. When Camus arrived he accused Merleau-Ponty of trying to justify the Moscow trials in *Le Yogi et le prolétarien.* After Sartre joined in, supporting Merleau-Ponty, Camus walked out, slamming the door. Sartre and Bost pursued him into the street, but he refused to come back.[50]

Hanging over Sartre all this time was the shadow of his unfinished novel sequence. In America, during February 1946, he had been intending to complete it on his return to France,[51] but other demands on his time proved irresistible. The day after the party he lectured on oppressed minorities in America. Before the end of the month he had joined the French League for a Free Palestine, an organization associated with Zionist terrorist groups. In *Qu'est-ce que la littérature?* he condemned British policy in Palestine and attacked Flaubert (who claimed that he used the word "bourgeois" to mean "anyone who thought basely") for failing to notice that the bourgeoisie was a class of oppressors. Flaubert's prose turned its back on reality, said Sartre, while the destructiveness of the surrealists was no more than the culmination of a negativism that had permeated literature since the eighteenth century. Not that Sartre, who had equated consciousness with nothingness, was hostile to negativity. What literature should be, he maintained, was a synthesis of negation and movement toward a future order. "In short, literature is essentially the subjectivity of a society in permanent revolution."[52]

Qu'est-ce que la littérature? was to be published in *Les Temps Modernes* between February and July 1947. He dedicated it to Dolores, who was due to arrive in Paris during January while De Beauvoir was on a lecture tour in the United States. When she arrived there, she met Dolores, who had not yet left and was, De Beauvoir writes, no less charming than Sartre had made her out to be. Before embarking, Dolores wrote to declare her intention of trying to procure from him an invitation to settle in France. She knew Camus and, in March, managed to make peace between the two men. Sartre did not invite her to stay permanently, but at the beginning of May he asked De Beauvoir to stay in the United States for an extra ten days as Dolores was extending her stay in Paris. De Beauvoir spent the ten days with the novelist Nelson Algren, first in Chicago, then in New York. The affair has its counterpart in *Les Mandarins.*[53]

IN the spring of 1957 General de Gaulle decisively reentered French politics. When, twelve months earlier, his admirers had formed the Gaullist union, he had ostentatiously held aloof from it, but on April 7, 1947, he called for the formation of a Rassemblement du Peuple Français (RPF). This was to be a party against parties, or, in effect, a union of non-Communists. Though the RPF rapidly gained support, the PCF, which had won over many supporters from the Socialist party, had not given up hope of taking control. But it found itself in difficulties as inflation led to agitation for wage increases and to strikes, which it ambivalently supported, although it was part of the government. In May the Socialist prime minister, Paul Ramadier, reacted by dismissing the Communist ministers, effectively creating an alliance of Socialists and MRP against the Communists. In June the situation was further complicated when General Marshall made his crucial speech on American economic aid to Europe. "The generosity of an ogre," Merleau-Ponty called it. Few other non-Communists opposed it, but Sartre sided with Merleau-Ponty.

It was in this tense situation that Sartre published "Le Situation de l'écrivain en 1947," the hundred-page final section of *Qu'est-ce que la littérature?* Like Brecht, he was assuming that only frivolous writers want to spend time on an unpolitical love story. Unlike Brecht, Sartre had an extremely subtle and philosophical mind, which he intermittently subordinated to the need for hard-hitting polemic. The success of *Les Temps Modernes* encouraged him to feel as confident of holding his audience's attention as he had in the classroom; he was no less liable to chat while writing, to rake stimulating insights together in a random way, often repeating himself and scarcely troubling about structure.

Merleau-Ponty's influence was pulling him toward Marxism, while the tendency to think anthropologically encouraged him to view literature in its social context, focusing particularly on reciprocity between writer and reader. *Qu'est-ce que la littérature?* claims that literature can realize its full essence only in a classless society. Flaubert, Baudelaire, and the symbolist poets had been content to ignore the oppressed masses who did not read their work; to function fully the writer must align himself with the majority. The surrealists, having no readers among the proletariat, had been parasites on the class they had insulted: "their revolt remains on the margin of the revolution."[54] The Resistance had given Sartre a glimpse into the possibility of addressing himself to the whole community; more damagingly, it had addicted him to for-or-against partisanship. What the writer should do, he now argued, was use the mass media to convert the reader's goodwill into an active ambition to change the world.[55]

But he went on to repeat the question he had asked ten years earlier about Nizan's novel: Is it possible to be a Communist and remain a writer? Sartre's answer was unequivocal: "The politics of Stalinist communism are incompatible with the honest practice of the literary profession."[56] The party was currently trying to impose on its intellectuals "two contradictory conservatisms: materialist scholasticism and Christian moralism."[57] Like Nazism, Gaullism, and Catholicism, French communism was mystifying its adherents; the duty of the writer was not to deplore the inadequacy of language but to use language in a campaign to liberate the victims of mystification.[58] The end does not justify the means—in L'Engrenage he had suggested that it did—and the party must not be allowed to go on "lying to its own troops."[59] By now he knew there was no chance of taking effective political action as an ally of the PCF—hence his emphasis on the practical value of the action that the writer could take in "demystifying."

But it was difficult to use Les Temps Modernes for exploring tensions between his ontological thinking and his political stance. If the review was to be effective it must build a consensus among readers, but Sartre, who went on giving Merleau-Ponty a free rein, could not always achieve consensus in himself; there was too much dissension between what he called "the myself I am for the Other" and "the myself I am for me."[60] In 1939 his diary had given him "quite a little secret life on top of the other one"; now, starting to write notes for his book on ethics, he found himself communing mainly with the self he was for him. His public self was more exposed than when he had promised, at the end of L'Etre et le Néant, an ethical sequel. If he broke the promise, it was not through shortage of time. The notebooks he filled during 1947–49 contain more words than L'Etre et le Néant, but in their scrupulousness and in their criticism of dialectical materialism they have more of an affinity with his diaries than with either his published journalism or his published philosophy.

In spite of having *Les Temps Modernes* and a large following of young "existentialists," Sartre felt isolated. He was under constant attack from the Communists. *Pravda* had denounced existentialism, and in his book *L'Existentialisme n'est pas un humanisme* Jean Kanapa condemned the self-styled existentialists as fascists and enemies of mankind, while anti-Communists and non-Communists were alienated by Sartre's support for the party and his continued opposition to the Marshall Plan.

IT was under these pressures that he wrote his notes on ethics, struggling not only with the conflict between his existentialist ontology and his political inclinations but with the still greater problem of how to reconcile politics with morality. In 1944 he had told an interviewer that morality was his "dominant preoccupation";[61] the notebooks show that until 1949 he kept returning to the problem of goodness in a world where God had "fallen into time."[62] In ostensibly putting God at the center of the universe, man had put himself there: eternity was seen as a perpetuation of judgments about virtue and vice, whereas modern ideologies tended to subordinate man to historical movements.[63] But historical processes were far more complex than dialectical materialism made them out to be.[64] There were periods in which history was destiny for a nation or a class:[65] in the feudal period no dialectic had been at work; disunity had constantly been suppressed.[66] Sartre could see how God had often been manipulated into working for the preservation of the status quo,[67] but it was absurd to argue, as Lenin did, that anything which helps the revolution is morally good.[68] Far from being justified by the end, the means can destroy the end,[69] while violence, though often perpetrated in the name of freedom, destroys the freedom of other people,[70] and lying, though it is the inverse of physical violence, is also destructive. The impossible ideal of violence is to force the liberty of the other person into wanting what I want him to want.[71]

ACQUIRED when he was a schoolteacher, the habit of taking long summer vacations was to persist. He would usually leave Paris in July, as if the term had just ended, returning in October, as if a new academic year were about to begin.[72]

In July he and De Beauvoir were invited to London for the production of *Men Without Shadows* and *The Respectable* [sic] *Prostitute* at the Lyric Theatre, Hammersmith, directed by the twenty-two-year-old Peter Brook, who self-confidently told Sartre: "You've got a surprise coming." The surprise was that a scene had been cut. He and De Beauvoir stayed only four days but took time to wander through the blitz-scarred streets.[73]

In August they flew to Copenhagen, where they visited the Tivoli and the sailors' dives, drinking aquavit into the small hours. They went on to Sweden, disembarking in Helsingborg and spending three days looking at canals and lakes before they went on to Stockholm. They visited the Drottningholm Theatre and one night saw the aurora borealis. From Stockholm they went northward, traveling alternately by boat and train to Lapland, staying for several days at Abisko in a hotel surrounded by a forest full of reindeer.[74]

(16)

Democratic Revolutionist

AN individual fighting to end the Cold War was almost like Camus's Dr. Rieux fighting the plague, and any political action, whatever its purpose, was liable to increase the tension instead of reducing it,[1] but in October 1947, while De Beauvoir was in Chicago with Nelson Algren, Sartre started a series of programs for radio. Alphonse Bonnafé, his old friend from the school at Le Havre, took the initiative through his father, a close friend of President Ramadier. The series, which was called *La Tribune des Temps Modernes,* was to be broadcast weekly, with contributions from Sartre's colleagues on the review.

The first broadcast was transmitted on October 6, and the second followed after a gap of a fortnight, with contributions from De Beauvoir, Merleau-Ponty, Pontalis, and Bonnafé, with R.-J. Chauffard playing the part of a typical Gaullist. Sartre derided the idea that war was inevitable, arguing that there was little to choose between the two great powers and comparing the Rassemblement's posters with those of the Nazis. Pontalis complained about General de Gaulle's contempt for the masses, while Bonnafé compared him to Hitler.[2] The broadcast provoked furious reactions. To a comment by Sartre on the general's physique Paul Claudel riposted: "Is he satisfied with his own?"[3] Condemned by right-wing newspapers for his disrespect toward the great liberator of France, Sartre was attacked on the radio by two well-known Gaullists, General Guillain de Bénouville and Henri Torrès, who challenged him to a radio debate. In the studio, before the broadcast, they attacked him insultingly, while the embarrassed Raymond Aron, who had been invited to take part, remained silent, unable to support either the enraged Gaullists or the comparison of De Gaulle with Hitler.[4] Sartre remained silent too. Listeners must have been puzzled: the only voice to be heard was that of Torrès, who said Sartre's attack on De Gaulle deserved nothing but public contempt. Aron's silence, which

Sartre took for betrayal, precipitated the rupture that had long been inevitable between the two old friends.

Conservative newspapers became less hostile after Sartre's attack on the Communists in the broadcast of October 27. Three more programs followed in November, but on December 3 Ramadier was displaced by the MRP leader Robert Schuman, who immediately suppressed the broadcasts scheduled for December.[5] Later on, after hearing rumors about his "quarrel" with Sartre, Aron, together with Manès Sperber, called at Sartre's flat, hoping to make peace. "Fine," said Sartre, "we'll have lunch together one of these days." But they never did.[6]

In November and December the PCF encouraged a new wave of strikes, but these failed, in spite of the party's hold on the trade union movement and on the majority of industrial workers. After so many Communist ministers had been dismissed, the new defeat made the party look ineffectual, intensifying the feeling of many malcontents on the left that what was needed was a new socialist movement. In November, Sartre was one of those who signed an appeal addressed to "all the world's democratic and social forces." The main concern was for peace. A divided Europe was dangerous because the USSR and the United States were each nervous about the other's influence; a united Europe would be more reassuring to both.[7] The other signatories included André Breton, Camus, and David Rousset. A fat former Trotskyite, with several missing teeth and a black patch over one eye, Rousset had written *L'Univers concentrationnaire*, an impressive book about surviving in Nazi camps. Koestler, who was not involved in the appeal, was prophesying that the Communists would seize power in France, and Europe would fall into Stalin's hands. Sartre, De Beauvoir, and Camus were with him and Mamaine one night at a Russian nightclub when they all got very drunk on vodka and champagne. Koestler, suddenly furious at Sartre, who was flirting, deliberately outrageous, with Mamaine, threw a glass at his head. Outside on the pavement Koestler hit Camus, who had affably put a hand on his shoulder. Leaving Mamaine to take care of her husband, Sartre and De Beauvoir climbed into a car with the bewildered Camus, who, drunkenly lamenting the destruction of a friendship, sent them into frightening lurches as he drove along, weeping.[8]

Koestler considered Gaullism to be the least of the available evils. He was in a bar one day with a Gaullist journalist who teased De Beauvoir by pretending that Sartre had promised to support the Rassemblement after being offered substantial incentives. Koestler merely laughed, but she failed to see the joke, and later, when Koestler, meeting her with Sartre in the street, tried to arrange a meeting, Sartre, after hesitating, refused: "With opinions that diverge so widely, people can't even see a film together."[9] This ended the friendship that had begun with Sartre's formal initiative.

Once again Sartre and De Beauvoir spent Christmas with Mme. Morel at La Pouèze, where he settled down to write *Les Mains sales*. As in the screenplay *L'Engrenage,* the central conflict is between a man who believes he can keep his hands clean and a leader who knows he can't; less eager than he had been in 1946 to justify Stalinism, Sartre can empathize better with both men. Hugo is a young bourgeois intellectual, intent on proving himself as a man of action. But he finds that commitment to the party is incompatible with honesty. Hugo is sufficiently self-obsessed to go around with photographs of himself as a child. If he represents the self Sartre was trying to reject, Hoederer represents his fantasy of what he might have been—a man of working-class origin, ignorant of literature, with a warm love of mankind and a mature political wisdom, a man of action motivated by genuine concern for the welfare of the majority. In contrast, the other leaders of the PCF are unimaginative, cold, and misanthropically ruthless in carrying out orders from Moscow.

In an article published in November 1947 Sartre had condemned psychological drama for its blindness to "the willpower, the oath and the hubris which form the virtues and vices of tragedy." What theater should show is "a character creating himself, the moment of choosing, of the voluntary decision that commits him to a moral code and a way of living." To "bring the whole man into play" the dramatist should build situations that force the characters to choose between alternatives, one of which can lead to death. Freedom is "revealed in its highest form" when it consents to lose itself so that it can affirm itself. "The most dramatic situations leave men with only two ways out, and the play is good if in choosing the way out they choose themselves."[10] It is in this sense that Sartre's plays are heroic. The freedom fighters in *Morts sans sépulture* do not choose to die and do choose themselves, which exposes the bad faith of the fascist collaborators who kill them. In the final sequence of *Les Mains sales,* Hugo must either accept personal responsibility for obeying the order to kill Hoederer or continue as an uncritical servant of the party, which has recently shifted to the policies for which Hoederer has died. Hugo's life has been cowardly: but for sexual jealousy, he would never have found the courage to shoot the older man. In his heroic death he assumes full responsibility both for his unheroic life and for the ill-judged orders he was belatedly obeying.

Unfortunately Sartre's dramaturgical principles join forces with his predilection for melodrama. The final sequence, which culminates in

Hugo's decision that he is "not fit for salvage," is theatrically cruder than the earlier development of the relationship between the two men.

Sartre's sources for the characterization of Hugo were not exclusively autobiographical; he was also thinking of former students on the rebound from middle-class families toward the party and of a story De Beauvoir had told him after meeting one of Trotsky's former secretaries in New York. Trotsky's murderer, when taken on as another secretary, had lived for some time in the well-guarded house at close quarters with the man he was going to kill.

While Sartre had been in the Netherlands with De Beauvoir during November 1946, his handwriting had been analyzed by a graphologist; the character of Hoederer is discussed when Hugo and his wife, Jessica, are in his room looking at various objects and studying his handwriting. The role of Jessica was one of Sartre's most generous gifts to Wanda, but the character's pert waywardness makes her reminiscent of Ivich. The writing derives more from Olga than from her sister, while the slangy style of the dialogue generally derives from the way Sartre had always carried on conversations with friends.

The case against moral purity is the same case that was made in *L'Engrenage,* but Hoederer makes it more forcefully: "It's not by refusing to lie we'll get rid of falsehood; it's by going all out to get rid of class barriers. Purity! That's an ideal for fakirs and monks. You intellectuals, you middle-class anarchists use it as an excuse for doing nothing. . . . Me, I've got dirty hands. Right up to the elbow. They've gone deep into shit and blood. So what? Think anyone can rule without hurting?" He is more tolerant, more humane, and more realistic than either the orthodox Communist bosses or the renegade bourgeois intellectuals, and he is vindicated by the central irony of the play, which shows how the party swings round to his ideas after killing him for them. This is more resonant than the point Sartre had made in *L'Engrenage* when he showed that François, caught, as Jean was, between the revolutionary demands of the people and the military power of the neighboring capitalist country, had no option but to make compromises. Sartre had not intended to engineer a powerful anti-Communist weapon, but one of the themes in *Les Mains sales* is that actions, once committed, can boomerang into consequences at odds with the original intentions. The play turned out to be a boomerang.

EXISTENTIALISM was at the height of its fashion, and Sartre was hardly less attractive to sightseers than the Eiffel Tower. Tour buses would drive slowly past Les Deux Magots in the hope of giving passengers a passing glimpse.[11] But the vogue had little to do with his ideas. There was even an existentialist way of dressing—black shirts, black pullovers, black trousers—derived, absurdly, from the fascist style,[12] though the popularity of jazz had been swelled by the removal of the Nazi embargo on black American culture. "Le swing" had secretly been enjoyed during the occupation in cellar bars, and as the need for secrecy vanished, the appetite grew. During April 1947 a cellar nightclub called the Tabou opened in the Rue Dauphine, with Boris Vian playing the trumpet, a young red-haired prizewinning poet called Anne-Marie Cazalis receiving the customers, and, later on, a beautiful young actress with long black hair, Juliette Greco, as chanteuse. Greco had never considered herself to be a singer, and Sartre encouraged her to make the transition, helping her to choose lyrics and giving her one he had written for *Huis clos* and eventually cut. To provide new music for it he introduced her to the composer Joseph Kosma, who went on to collaborate with her successfully.[13] The newspapers gossiped a great deal about the Tabou, especially about the brawling which went on, their implication being that Sartre's philosophy encouraged orgies. Far from being regulars at the Tabou, he and De Beauvoir went there only twice.[14]

WHEN he took De Beauvoir to Berlin in February for the opening of *Les Mouches,* he was courted by the Americans, but he kept his distance.[15] Back in Paris, knowing he had power to make himself useful, he gave evidence at the trial of a former student, Robert Misrahi, a member of the Stern Gang, the Zionist terror group. He had been found in possession of arms. Thanks partly to Sartre, who said he had been a good student, Misrahi was let off with a fine. "The duty of non-Jews," said Sartre, "is to help the Jews and the Palestinian cause."[16] "The Palestinian cause" did not mean then what it means today.

IN *Les Mains sales* Hoederer advises Hugo that instead of trying to prove himself as a man of action he should do the work for which he is best qualified: "Your talent is for writing. . . . A good journalist is more valuable than a bad assassin." Sartre was arguing against his own deepseated compulsion to prove himself as a man while equating masculinity with action and femininity with art. But instead of listening to his own advice he began to involve himself in practical politics. Though he had attended many of the meetings that led to the manifesto of November 1947, he had not sat on the organizing committee, which consisted of David Rousset, Jean Rous, and Georges Altman, editor of *Franc-*

Tireur, which had about 300,000 readers, mainly in the working class. Rousset was the prime mover. The Rassemblement Démocratique Révolutionnaire was founded at the beginning of 1948, and when Sartre joined in February, his presence was expected to be decisive in rallying support. But he no longer had as much pull on public opinion as in the early days of existentialism. The intention was to create a genuinely democratic alternative to a party that was democratic in neither structure nor procedure: the PCF made no attempt to find out whether its policies coincided with what its members wanted. Stalinism, said Rousset, had nothing to do with socialism.

In February 1948 the committee of the RDR published an appeal in the papers attacking both capitalist democracy and Stalinism. "For us, means are not less important than ends. . . . We will have nothing to do with this double dealing that consists of practicing, in the present, unworthy means which are known as such, for the sake of securing, in the future, a noble end."[17] At a press conference held on March 10, with Sartre and Rousset among the speakers, the RDR offered itself as a rallying point for the militants of leftist parties. The object was to "organize democracy," putting Europe "in the forefront of the struggle for freedom." When the RDR's first public meeting was held, nine days later, about a thousand people crowded into the Salle Wagram. Sartre took issue with those who attacked the workers' "sordid materialism." Hunger was a sign of solidarity. "You are never hungry alone. When a man's hungry, he's hungry with all the comrades of his class, with people who receive the same wages."[18] Since the RDR was not a party, members of other parties could not be stopped from joining, though leading Communists were quick to denounce Sartre and Rousset as agents of the government and Wall Street, while the SFIO threatened to excommunicate any member who joined the RDR. But when the left wing of the SFIO split, nearly 20 percent of its Socialist separatists, Action Socialiste Révolutionnaire (ASR), did join the new movement.

In the first issue of *La Gauche,* the RDR's paper (published fortnightly and later monthly), Sartre wrote that their prime objective was to link "revolutionary claims" with "the idea of freedom."[19] In an interview, he explained that he did not want reforms but a bloodless revolution, retaining the freedom that capitalism claimed as its *raison d'être* but extending it to everybody.[20] Camus contributed to *La Gauche,* pleading for "democracy without catechism";[21] Merleau-Ponty also gave his allegiance to the RDR, though halfheartedly, not believing in force of numbers as a means of putting pressure on the PCF. Though he was a founding member of the executive committee, he never attended meetings.[22]

Sartre's involvement with the new movement did not prevent him from seeing a good deal of Jean Cocteau, who agreed to take a hand in the staging of *Les Mains sales* when it was in rehearsal at the Théâtre Antoine. According to rumors that were circulating, the play would have the effect of restoring Sartre's popularity.[23] The production was by Pierre Valdé, "amicalement supervisée" (as the program has it) by Cocteau. François Périer played Hugo, with André Luguet as Hoederer. Sartre was absent from the first performance, lecturing at a Masonic lodge in the hope of enlisting members for the RDR.

The Communist papers attacked the play viciously: *L'Humanité* called Sartre a "nauseous writer," a "Third Force demagogue," and an "understudy for Koestler," while Marguerite Duras wrote a spiteful review in *Action*. Later on, Ilya Ehrenburg would complain in *Les Lettres Françaises* that during a witch hunt against the Communists Sartre had "joined his fate with the fate of Jules Moch [a Gaullist minister], with the fate of Mr. Dulles [the US secretary of state], of Mr. Churchill and the others who have inspired the crusade."[24] But the force of the play was irresistible. In Paris the original production ran for nearly eighteen months. As a printed text it became Sartre's most popular fiction in France: by the end of 1978, 1,892,000 copies had been sold, compared with 1,670,000 of *La Nausée*.[25]

THE new novel, *La Mort dans l'âme*—the third in Sartre's sequence and the last he was to complete—reflects a situation and an attitude that had changed since he completed *L'Age de raison*. In 1945 he had promised that Mathieu would finally liberate himself from his past. "He will find love and get himself on the right track. He'll commit himself freely, which will give the world a meaning for him."[26] In the 1948 novel Mathieu's final scene coincides with the defeat of France. The soldiers have been abandoned by their officers; the country is on the point of capitulating. For the routed, disorganized, dispirited men the question of whether to continue fighting is not a question of honor or patriotism. It is a moral choice but not one that can be made rationally. If they go on shooting from inside buildings, the Germans may decide to burn down the village, kill women and children. If Mathieu joins the small group of soldiers who intend to fire on the advancing Germans from the tower of the church, he is probably condemning himself to die for no good reason—an absurdity that makes him feel exultant. "I'm deciding that death was the secret meaning of my life, that I have been living to die. I'm dying to prove that it's impossible to live. My eyes will close to the world, put it permanently out."[27] Mathieu sees what looks like a toad crawling toward the town hall—a German with a grenade in his hand. Mathieu kills the man. "For years he'd been trying to act. In vain. His actions had been stolen from him, one by one; he had been soft as butter. This time nothing had been taken away. He'd squeezed the trigger, and for once something had happened."[28]

Though he does not dissociate himself from Mathieu's attitude—which is in line with the feeling Boris had in *Le Sursis,* that he'd been put into the world for *his* war—Sartre is not content to end the novel on this note. As the Germans advance, bombarding the church tower with a cannon, Mathieu is left shooting from the parapet. The image has roots in Sartre's childhood feelings on looking down from a high window; at his vantage point, with a rifle in his hand, Mathieu is also in the same position as Erostrate in Sartre's short story. The reader assumes that Mathieu cannot survive, and in the last section of *La Mort dans l'âme* he does not reappear. The sequence is set in a stalag, where we see that Brunet, the dedicated Communist, still has a greater sense of purpose than any of the other prisoners. Even here he can work energetically for the party, and soon, finding that some prisoners are already comrades, while others can be indoctrinated, he is creating a cell. But whereas Sartre in 1940 had felt a compassionate and sometimes passionate solidarity with fellow prisoners in the stalag, Brunet is interested only in the ones he can use, despising the others as a bunch of *salauds.*

Sartre introduces a new alter ego, Schneider. (This, the German word for "tailor," is reminiscent of the name "Tailleur" Sartre had used in *La Semence et le scaphandre,* playing on the Latin word *sartor.*) Schneider voices misgivings about Communists who are robotlike in obeying orders. It is here that Sartre introduces the phrase "la mort dans l'âme." When Brunet blames the French soldiers for their defeat, Schneider loses his temper: it is the leaders who are to blame both for the defeat and for ensuing demoralization. "He's stuck there, he's fallen out of the world, out of history, with dead ideas. He's trying to fight back, to rethink the situation. But with what? He's only got old-fashioned tools for thinking with. You've put death into his soul."[29] *La Mort dans l'âme* is Sartre's title for the novel, but the English translation is called *Iron in the Soul.*

Sartre was working simultaneously on the novel and on his notes about morality, which reflect the same disenchantment with Communist orthodoxy. Leaders, he complains, who lie to achieve unity are like the priest, the oppressor, or the psychoanalyst who claims to understand his patients better than they understand themselves.[30] Brunet is doing his duty as a good party member, but "duty," like "goodness," needs critical redefinition. Following Nietzsche, Sartre sees duty as "the

violence of other people, but internalized."[31] When I obey the call of
duty, I am submitting to the voice of someone else, who refuses to take
account of the current situation, other people's intentions, temporality,
means. "Someone else is incessantly repeating: 'I don't want to know.'"
Duty is alienated liberty, depersonalized.[32] Enslaving himself to the
PCF, Brunet is enslaving his followers and enjoying his power. Sartre's
attitude has changed substantially since Mathieu felt envious of the
purposeful Brunet.

As in *Les Mains sales,* Sartre is incensed less by Moscow than by the
PCF. "The party will reestablish itself without you," Schneider tells
Brunet, "and on principles you know nothing about. You could escape
and you don't dare, because you're afraid of what you'll find down
there. You, you've got death in your soul."[33]

From Sartre's belief in existentialist freedom of choice it followed
that the French soldiers had chosen to be defeated, and he shared their
humiliation. Writing in 1948 about his experiences of eight years earlier, he found it easier to be compassionate. The bewilderment, boredom, and frustration of the men are vividly dramatized, and he extends
a retrospective literary sympathy to his Jewish friend, Pieter. When
Pieter gave up hope, Sartre found little to say, but Mathieu tries to
console Charlot, who retorts: "You'd have to be a Jew . . . Otherwise
you can't understand . . . It's not me that's scared, it's my race inside
me."[34]

The critic Geneviève Idt has noticed how Sartre uses the novel to
continue an argument with Malraux and Camus.[35] In *L'Espoir*
Malraux's faith in revolutionary art is asserted through a conversation
between a Spanish painter and an American journalist; in Sartre's
novel, visiting an art gallery with an American journalist, Gomez realizes that he is no longer a painter: "I've gone blind. . . . It would be necessary not to have shot human beings."[36] Calling Sartre's novel "a reply
to *La Peste,*" Geneviève Idt compares the two sermons of Camus's Father Paneloux with the sermon of the Pétainist priest in Sartre's stalag,
a sermon based not on the attitude of the priests Sartre knew in Trier
but on proclamations by the Vichy government. While Camus focuses
on change of attitude in an individual priest, Sartre is generalizing, as
he had in *Les Mouches,* about collaborationist defeatism; but whereas
Camus's sympathy for the ordinary people was vague, Sartre is admira-
bly specific in dramatizing the feelings of defeated soldiers.

Some of his ironies rest on the absurdities of squabbles in which private trivialities upstage major political events. On the day the German
army enters Paris, Ivich complains furiously to a waiter about ersatz
coffee; a French soldier fastidiously washes his shirts in the river. During

May 1948 events in Paris were full of anomalies not much less absurd: as Sartre complained in a letter, the newspapers were paying more attention to the British Princess Elizabeth, who was in France on a visit, than to the hardships of Jewish survivors, who were being prevented by the British from settling in Palestine. (As early as May 1948 Sartre favored the creation of a Jewish state.) To make it easier for himself to bring the past alive, he often transposed experiences from the present. The novel opens with a heat wave in New York during June 1940; in May 1948 Paris was as hot as it normally is in July: "We're living in our shirt sleeves; we're sleeping naked."[37]

During the spring, vacationing with De Beauvoir at Ramatuelle, near Saint-Tropez, he'd been able to write undisturbed; back in Paris, working at the novel, the ethics, and a book on Mallarmé, which was lost after several hundred pages had been written,[38] he wrote as usual in two shifts—from nine in the morning till two and from five till nine—but it was seldom without interruptions. Twice a week he had meetings with the regular contributors to Les Temps Modernes, and while De Beauvoir was with Nelson Algren in the United States, Guatemala, and Mexico, Sartre enjoyed an affair with a young American reporter whose current task was to write bulletins on Princess Elizabeth's doings in Paris. Far from being repelled by her preoccupation with royalty, Sartre liked the girl's involvement in her job. It was obvious that "la petite," as he called her, would never matter to him as much as Dolores did, but she came regularly to the flat in the Rue Bonaparte at about five, so exhausted after a day of pursuing the princess that she flopped down on his bed and slept deeply for a couple of hours. She could play the violin, and he enjoyed accompanying her on the piano. They played Schubert. They would spend the night together, either in her flat or in his—his mother liked her—and it would be painful to end the affair, but for De Beauvoir, he promised, there would be no upsets when she returned in June. On the contrary, he was looking forward to telling her all about the affair and to taking her on a trip in August.[39]

They went to Algeria, spending the first two weeks in Algiers, but they slept in separate hotel bedrooms. They could now afford to explore coast roads in taxis,[40] but it was no longer so easy for them to enjoy togetherness in a foreign country.

THEY returned to find pessimistic Parisians predicting war between America and the USSR. In June the Russians had blockaded Berlin, and supplies were still being airlifted in; Yugoslavia had been expelled from the Cominform for hostility to the USSR. On September 1 the creation of the North China People's Republic had been announced by the Communists. Would the US intervene to support Chiang Kai-shek against Mao Tse-tung, concentrating American troops in the East and leaving Europe to be overrun by the Russians? In March, France had joined with Britain and the Benelux countries in a treaty of mutual assistance, but the Atlantic Pact had not yet been signed, and Sartre would go on fighting to keep Europe neutral. The world, he believed, would be cut permanently in two if Robert Schuman aligned France with the US.

On September 12 a courageous American eccentric, a former bomber pilot, Gary Davis, proclaimed himself a citizen of the world, renounced his US citizenship, and started a sit-in at the headquarters of the United Nations in the Palais de Chaillot. In October, after he had been evicted by the police, he was supported by a "council of solidarity" that included Camus, the philosopher Emanuel Mounier, André Breton, and Richard Wright, who had settled in Paris. There were press conferences and rallies; in December one of these drew twenty thousand people, but Sartre refused to join in. All his energy for political agitation went into campaigning for a neutral Europe and against colonialism. On November 18 he told a Morocco audience: "Those who oppress you oppress us for the same reasons."

He was in no mood to get rich on Broadway royalties. Under the title *Red Gloves* an unauthorized adaptation of *Les Mains sales* had opened during November in New Haven with Charles Boyer as Hoederer. When Sartre protested, he was told by his publisher, Nagel, that he had already made five million francs. The advance booking so far amounted to $280,000. But Sartre vetoed the production.

The play's success in Paris did help to reinstate his reputation, but relatively few of his admirers wanted to follow him into the RDR. In Paris the movement had only 830 members by the end of 1948, though about 4000 people crowded into the hall when a "day of studies" was held on December 13 in the Salle Pleyel, while, according to the *Franc-Tireur,* another 2000 were turned away. With "internationalism of the spirit" as their main theme, the speakers included Sartre, Camus, Rousset, Breton, Carlo Levi, and Richard Wright. They might have recruited more support if they had seemed more united, but Sartre, more pro-Russian and anti-American than Rousset or Camus, was maintaining that the Soviet camps had no major political or social importance.[41] The meeting failed to reverse the trend, which would continue throughout 1949: thousands of people flocked to hear the star speakers at rallies, but membership remained low.

In January 1949 the principal battle of words was fought after Victor

Kravchenko, a former Russian government official who had defected, published a book, *I Chose Freedom*, which drew attention to the existence of Soviet labor camps. He sued *Les Lettres Françaises* for suggesting that the text must have been written by agents of the American government. Sartre and De Beauvoir attended a session of the trial, at which pro-Communist witnesses sent from Moscow confronted anti-Communist witnesses sponsored by the Americans. The trial was important mainly for its revelations about the labor camps. It would no longer be possible to deny their existence; the choice was between affirming it and remaining evasively silent.

THIS, for Sartre, was to be a long-term problem; the immediate problem at the beginning of 1949 was how to respond to Georg Lukács, who was in Paris for the publication of his book *Existentialisme ou marxisme?* At his lectures and press conferences he called existentialism an "indirect apologia for capitalism."[42] Sartre retorted that Lukács was himself a "crypto-existentialist."[43] The two writers never met.

Sartre's more serious formulations were being made in the notebooks. Wanting to work on ethics and on the final novel of his tetralogy, he left Paris with De Beauvoir for the south of France. She had picked an isolated hotel on the Esterel coast, but feeling unsettled there, they moved on to Le Cagnard, high up in Cagnes. As usual they had separate rooms; they stayed for three weeks.

He was going to call the novel "La Dernière chance," but he completed only about seventy pages. Mathieu reappears in a stalag after two months in the hospital; Sartre loops back to his memories of prison camp during the winter of 1940–41. Eight years later this experience still seemed crucial. "Listen," says Mathieu in one draft of the fragment, ". . . once I was an individual, and then I learned that truth chased after me, and in the end I experienced something extraordinary. The comradeship of defeat . . . In defeat you get the impression that men can find their own salvation."[44] Emerging from the hospital, Mathieu feels like a new man: "Mathieu was not yet a prisoner, he had just been born."[45] This places a gauche emphasis on the feeling of renaissance. Solidarity with his fellow prisoners had given Sartre the sense of having a new self, and nostalgia for this feeling was to haunt all his efforts to compromise with the one political party that could claim to represent the working majority. The isolation of Schneider corresponds both to the isolation of Paul Nizan after he left the party and to the postwar isolation of Sartre, who could never bring himself to join it. In wanting to help Brunet when, like a sheepdog, he is herding like-minded lambs together, Schneider is motivated less by conviction than by need for comradeship. But Brunet, like Hugo in *Les Mains sales,* finds that during his imprisonment the party line has changed, making nonsense of everything he has dutifully done. When Chalais, one of the PCF bosses, arrives in the stalag, Brunet is reprimanded: the men he has indoctrinated may turn to Gaullism; he should have denounced De Gaulle and Pétain together with the imperialism of the bourgeois democracies, and he should have praised the love of peace in the working masses.[46]

Sartre felt ambivalent toward men who, unable to think for themselves, succumbed to indocrination. One of the soldiers tells Mathieu: "In the camp you're never alone, not even for a shit." The sentence refers back to the disappearance of privacy that Sartre had at first hated and then began to love as he came to feel at one with the men. While he cannot forgive the leaders who manipulate the defeated soldiers, making them feel ashamed and inadequate, he cannot forgive the men for being duped so easily. In the fragmentary fourth volume Brunet furiously intervenes when two of his loyal followers are beating up Schneider, who, according to Chalais, is liable to denounce them.[47] Sartre had been told how Nizan suffered at the hands of former comrades when he left the party; even his wife was ordered to denounce him.[48]

Writing in his notebooks about stupidity, Sartre refers mainly to the mindlessness that puts people at the mercy of political charlatans. Fools give up their human reality and their liberty to the deceiver, who offers to take responsibility for their decisions. This man is transformed into a god;[49] Brunet and Chalais acquire godlike powers over their devotees. The fool lets other people steal the world from him, building his future out of their past, thinking slowly what they have already thought quickly.[50]

On the other hand, cohesive pressure is indispensable if solidarity is to be mustered against oppression. Sartre tries hard in the notebooks to analyze what oppression is. As in *L'Etre et le Néant,* he uses Hegel's model of the master and the slave, but he goes beyond it, dividing the oppressed into four groups—children, the ignorant, the stupid, women—and he finds that oppression can exist in three situations: when a society excludes some of its members from a culture or system of values it has created; when a class or group, put into an almost intolerable position, cannot count on the free will of other people to rescue it; when there is forced labor.[51] The oppressor makes himself into destiny, as the parent does for the child.[52] Usually oppression is viewed in a political, social, and economic perspective, but Sartre's standpoint is ontological: "It is precisely the character of enslavement that Hegel failed to see: all you enslave is a freedom; you enslave it because it is freedom . . . the purpose of the enslavement is not the utilization of a labor force but the diminution and appropriation of a freedom by the other."[53]

Huis clos had illustrated the argument advanced in *L'Etre et le Néant* about rivalry between the freedoms of two individuals. Friendship is an exchange of favors; in a business or professional relationship the customer or client pays, but the slave, having nothing to offer, pays with his person.[54] His work reflects not his own image but only his master's, so the purpose of his work is stolen from him.[55] In the morality of slavery, as in the morality of duty or devotion, I choose the other as preferable to myself.[56]

These reflections on oppression lead Sartre to ideas about revolution and violence irreconcilable with what he had written earlier in the notebooks, when he had argued that revolutionaries always have a bad conscience because they are fighting not just against a status quo but against themselves and against an established right.[57] He had also maintained that all violence is in bad faith. To refute Trotsky's argument about the justification of the means by the end, he had argued that the means can be wrong, not because it is immoral but because it can destroy the end.[58] Violence often conceals a desire for the destruction of the end by the means.[59] Violence is invariably grounded on the assumption that a latent order will emerge when the ill will which masks it has been destroyed. Sexual desire involves violence to the extent that the desired person is transformed into an object,[60] while the rapist is using violence in the conviction that there will be no future: the violent triumph of desire will freeze the end forever in the absolute.[61]

We do not know how much later Sartre's later notes on violence and revolution were written; what seems crucial is that in the interim he had come under the influence of Genet and the books he published between 1944 and 1948, especially the autobiographical novels *Notre-Dame des fleurs* and *Querelle de Brest* and the directly autobiographical *Journal du voleur*. These books suggest that a glamorously unglamorous counterworld is constructed by criminals. "What I call violence," writes Genet, "is passive courage infatuated by danger." In pursuit of evil he has embarked on adventures that lead to prison, where he feels as secure as a monarch in his palace. "My talent consists of the love I feel toward the state of imprisonment. . . . My courage consists in annihilating all the usual reasons for living, and then making up new ones." In this perverse panache and apocalyptic bravado, as in this style of living and writing, the rhythms and attitudes of Rimbaud are unmistakably echoed.

Not that Sartre was a reader who would easily let himself be overcome by intoxicating prose rhythms. The main appeal of Genet was that he suggested a way out of the ethical maze. After five years of making notes without discovering how to organize them, Sartre had almost arrived at the moment of asserting his freedom deliciously by deciding to leave the book unwritten. As a writer Genet was not logically convincing, but as a man he had allowed himself to be taken over by the idea other people had of him, and the story of his life taught Sartre a new way of chasing goodness out of evil. Genet had chosen to let himself be possessed. Unlike the dutiful slave, the pious worshiper, and the loyal party member, all victims of the manipulator who steals their humanity, making them prefer the other to the self, Genet reverses the negative into a way of living. Caught by the community in an impossible system of values, he restructures his derelict life as an abrasive celebration of its impossibility. Instead of becoming an object, the slave discovers his subjectivity in what the masters call evil. He chooses to be in the wrong, and, erecting no alternative system of values, submits to self-loathing. He feels murderous, not just toward others but toward the other that he has internalized. The project is suicidal. Since the future is controlled by the master, the slave recognizes himself only in the passing moment of rebellion. He dismisses the future and all the retribution it holds for his present assertiveness. By accompanying Genet this far along a non-Marxian road toward abjection, Sartre has made himself a partisan of rebellion. The status quo is intolerable, and no ethics can be established until after a revolution more public and positive than Genet's.

AFTER three weeks in the south of France, Sartre and De Beauvoir returned to a Paris torn by disagreement about the Marshall Plan and the Atlantic Pact, which was to be signed on April 4. To emphasize its aggressive implications the Communists launched a "peace movement," and Picasso's white dove was conceived as a symbol for the rally to be held at the Salle Pleyel on April 30. The RDR announced a counterattraction on the same date—an International Day of Resistance to Dictatorship and War. On the sixteenth the leaders of the two movements held a meeting, but compromise was impossible. Visiting the United States to make contact with American trade unions and raise funds, Rousset should have anticipated that left-wingers would accuse him of accepting money from the CIA. He exacerbated the split in the RDR by writing an article conceding that the Atlantic Pact was "not a measure of war" and denouncing the Communist régime as representing "the fiercest social reaction since the disappearance of Nazism."[62] On April 30 the morning meeting was held at the Sorbonne, where the big lecture hall was filled, and in the evening about ten thousand people packed into the Vélodrome d'Hiver, but Sartre was absent from the speakers' platform. Together with Merleau-Ponty and Richard Wright, he sent a message: he wanted nothing to do with an event that would encourage anticommunism. Implacably hostile to the Atlantic Pact, he held that Europe should remain neutral and that it would not even keep its cultural autonomy if it accepted economic help from America. It did not matter whether French culture survived; what he wanted was a united socialist Europe, economically and culturally dependent on neither the United States nor the Soviet Union.[63] Instead of campaigning for this, the RDR was being betrayed by Rousset and by Altman, who was defending American policy in the *Franc-Tireur*. When Sartre demanded a national conference, so that members from all over France could state their views, Rousset objected that it would cost too much. Eventually, when Sartre subsidized it personally, an extraordinary conference was announced for June 30. He spoke out at it against the April rally, and the majority supported him, but this meant that there was no future for the movement. "Breakdown of the RDR. Serious blow. New and definitive apprenticeship to realism. You can't create a movement."[64]

(17)

Communist Values

EARLIER in 1948 Sartre had been persuading Dolores not to settle in Paris, but he was glad to spend his summer vacation with her while De Beauvoir shared hers with Nelson Algren. Sartre and Dolores went to Guatemala, Panama, Curaçao, Haiti, and Cuba, where they spent an evening in Havana with Ernest Hemingway and his wife, who was disappointed that the two writers "talked like businessmen."[1] In Haiti, Sartre was intrigued by the voodoo ceremony he witnessed[2] but appalled by the poverty. "Haiti throws itself passionately on everything that evokes French culture . . . and among the rich Antilles, this black republic is the only one to be dying of hunger."[3] Throughout the trip his relationship with Dolores was deteriorating: he was finding her company less enjoyable, while she was finding him depressive, remote, grumpy.[4]

In August, staying at La Pouèze with Mme. Morel, he worked for twelve hours every day, alternating between his notes on ethics and a preface for the Gallimard collection of Genet's works. After writing about 360,000 words on ethics, he had arrived at an impasse. "All I know," he wrote in a letter, "is that I'd like to create a morality in which evil is an integral part of good."[5] He had not yet abandoned the book on ethics; when he did, much of the accumulated material would be shifted into the work on Genet. Such transpositions are typical of Sartre: the whole of his work can be read as an inconsequential series of installments in one enormous, unfinishable book. Ostensibly a biography, *Saint Genet* is largely a discourse on the nature of good and evil. Genet is more than a pretext but less than the whole subject. The Sartrian monologue is like a dialogue between the philosopher who generalizes about Being and the biographer who, instead of chronicling events, tries to give a comprehensive account of how a mind works. The universe, Sartre complained, "has the derisory fate of manifesting itself *through* a particular consciousness and above all *to* a particular consciousness. All its 'there is' is suspended in my finitude."[6] Focusing on Genet's finitude, he presents an anthology of insights into good and evil.

The crucial point is that in a world debased by alienation no ethical principle can be validated. From condemning violence as a means which contaminates the end he had come to accept Marx's contention that war is good if it serves the interests of the proletariat and bad if it does not. There can be no morality without freedom, and freedom has been cut in two. True morality is not a prohibition of evil but a concrete totality that synthesizes evil with good. Sartre was above all a moralist, and if he was shifting toward a more dialectical mode of thinking, the tendency began from a need to think dialectically about ethics. But his reflexes were Kantian. His habit, as Raymond Aron had noticed, was to judge other people less according to their actions than their intentions, "and he ended up with an irrevocable judgment, good or bad, based on the ulterior motive he imputed to the person."[7]

While working on Mallarmé in 1948–49 he produced about 2000 pages of notes and 500 pages of a book. Though both were subsequently lost, except for fragments, he gave Mallarmé more attention than any other poet: "Mallarmé is our greatest poet. Passionate, wild . . . His commitment seems as complete as possible: social as well as poetic."[8] On the surface Mallarmé could hardly have been less passionate or wild. He was a diffident, polite schoolteacher who concealed his feelings and kept people at a distance, but his thinking was subversive.

According to Nietzsche, the desire to create, like the desire to destroy, can spring either from overflowing Dionysian vigor or from *ressentiment,* the malice of the underprivileged, outraged by the well-being of others. The man of *ressentiment* avenges himself on reality by burning his image into it. The poets dominant during the second half of the nineteenth century all, according to Sartre, made themselves into agents of the counterrevolution by cultivating incomprehensibility and contemplating nothingness. It was easier to abolish the universe than to touch the established order.[9] From the Parnassians to the symbolists, French poets did nothing but flatter the bourgeoisie by holding up to it a mirror that threw back only an aristocratic image.[10] The values of a defunct nobility informed the preciosity of the poets, who refined the negative image that the property-owning class needed to have of itself. But there was no reciprocity between readers and poets, whose ideal was to annihilate the world and recreate it through words.[11] "The terrorism of politeness," Sartre called it. An extremist, Mallarmé was chosen by the negative poetry of his period as its means of committing suicide.[12] In the biography of Flaubert, which he would start in 1954,

Sartre imputes to him the same diabolical project of trying to make the world unreal, tossing it into the void of *l'imaginaire.*

In writing about Mallarmé like this Sartre pays little attention either to his development or to what differentiates him from other poets. Nihilism is presented as all-embracing. Sartre's objective in this abandoned book is to write in the perspective of his synthetic anthropology, combining Freudian and Marxian insights, without forgetting Marcel Mauss. Trying to visualize the relationship between poets and public as a single series of transactions, Sartre perceives the bourgeoisie emulating aristocratic orgies in ritual destruction of worldly goods, while the poets belong to a secret fraternity whose initiation rites involve suicide and rebirth.[13] Anthropology's archetypal patterns dominate the imagery. Though some of Sartre's insights are valid, the generalizations dull the critical acumen, while the biography (insofar as we can judge it from the fragments) fails to bring its subject to life. As in *Saint Genet,* Sartre's basic question is: How does a man make himself into a writer? As in *Saint Genet* and *L'Idiot de la famille,* the facts are tailored to fit the new myth Sartre is creating. When he asserts "From the first day Mallarmé saw in his wife the image of his own desolation" or that his grandmother "loved him with a phony lucidity, sniveling and grumpy,"[14] we are given no evidence and no sources. Sartre's method in *L'Idiot de la famille* will be the same. No substantiation, no footnotes. He has done the thinking for us; here are his conclusions. The myth is very much the same myth as in *Saint Genet;* we will meet it again in both *Les Mots* and in *L'Idiot de la famille:* the decision that will shape the writer is made by adults during the victim's childhood. The boy is withered by a glance:

> The child knows that they are his truth. "You will be a civil servant [*administrateur*] like your father." This time he embraces his janitor destiny with a glance. . . . Under his eyes his future personality, unfolded, acts out his future career in dumb show, parades its dull vicissitudes in front of him. These tics will be his. What am I saying? They are there already. Family life is a gallery of mirrors; the child, the man, the dotard are reflections which change places. In them he sees his future, in other words the family's past, incessantly repeated.[15]

This is the leitmotif of Sartrian biography.

ONCE again a peaceful period of writing outside Paris was followed, when Sartre returned, by a busy period, full of interruptions and political decisions. No longer believing that anything could be achieved through the RDR, he had come closer to Merleau-Ponty's view of the role they should play.[16] If they entered the political arena, they would appear as either allies or rivals of the PCF; instead they should limit themselves to exerting influence through *Les Temps Modernes*.[17] When he resigned from the RDR on October 12, Sartre was inflicting a fatal wound on a movement that could not in any case have survived for long. His departure, reported *Le Monde,* evidenced the RDR's failure to resolve its internal quarrels.[18]

In the controversy that exploded at the end of the year about Soviet labor camps Sartre wholeheartedly supported Merleau-Ponty against Rousset, whose expostulations against the camps were serialized in *Le Figaro Littéraire* during November. The defense of the Soviet Union that appeared in the January 1950 issue of *Les Temps Modernes* was written by Merleau-Ponty but signed jointly. While some apologists for the Soviet régime were denying the existence of the camps, Merleau-Ponty admitted it and tried to explain why Russian workers did not find them intolerable. Many "young heroes" and "gifted bureaucrats" no doubt assumed that the prisoners were "lunatics, antisocial people, men of ill will." And whereas German concentration camps had not been part of a movement toward classlessness, the USSR was "broadly on the side of the forces that are fighting against the familiar forms of exploitation." This was the great commonplace of pro-Soviet apologias: the repulsive present is justified by the happy future. Merleau-Ponty went on to affirm: "We have the same values as a Communist," and Sartre, no longer believing that the means can undermine the end, agreed that the Soviet Union should not be compared critically with capitalist countries; if there were anomalies in the Soviet system, the Russian proletariat could be trusted to get rid of them at the right moment.

Though his intellect was no less subtle than André Gide's, Sartre was less scrupulous in stamping on doubts about the Soviet Union. Gide, his senior by thirty-six years, had already been through the whole gamut of disillusionment with the West, optimism about the Soviet alternative, disillusionment with it. Appalled during his long African expedition (1925–26) by the white exploitation of the blacks, Gide returned to become a champion of victims and underdogs all over the world. Having started, like Sartre, as an impassioned advocate of individual liberty, he had changed his mind. "The triumph of the individual is the renunciation of individualism." Communism seemed to promise "a new and better form of civilization." Like Sartre, he felt ashamed of his bourgeois privileges, guilty at having a place in the lifeboat while most people were left to swim or drown; in 1932 he wrote that he would gladly sacrifice his life for the success of the Soviet Union. But when he visited the country in 1936 he saw a dictatorial state ruthlessly imposing uniformity of style and uniformity of opinion on a helpless people. The workers were being exploited but so deviously that they did not know whom to blame. Gide's conclusion was that the spirit of communism was no longer different from the spirit of fascism. In his 1936 pamphlet *Retour de l'URSS* he ridiculed the argument that deportations, exploitation, and undemocratic government were provisional measures, indispensable if the gains of 1917 were to be preserved. Essentially this was the argument Sartre and Merleau-Ponty were using fourteen years later.

Contemporary history, though, was throwing up criticism of the Soviet system. After Marshal Tito's defiance of his Russian overlords, Yugoslavia had been expelled in June 1948 from the Cominform, but in July, Tito had received a vote of confidence from the Yugoslav Communist party, which was subsequently purged of its Cominform supporters.

The PCF was hostile to Tito, but Sartre, writing a preface for a book by Louis Dalmas, *Le Communisme yougoslave depuis la rupture avec Moscou* (*Yugoslav Communism Since the Break with Moscow*), comes out strongly in support of Yugoslav dissidence. Soviet policy could be defended as corresponding to "the objective requirements of the situation" in the USSR, but Lenin had promised that the Soviet Union would give disinterested aid to states on the road to socialism, so that their economic unity could be reestablished without domination. Was there any reason to think Tito had been more despotic or terroristic than the Politburo?

IN June, Sartre met Koestler and Mamaine, who were in the neighboring compartment on a night train to Berlin, where they were to attend a congress for cultural freedom. When Koestler invited him to share the food and drink Mamaine had brought in a basket—the train had no restaurant car—Sartre accepted gladly, though Koestler felt sure he would have refused if De Beauvoir had been with him: "minus her he behaved like a schoolboy on vacation."[19] But she was the traveling companion he liked best of all—having spent his last summer vacation with Dolores, he was planning to take a spring vacation with De Beauvoir in Italy or Egypt.[20] Michel Leiris suggested that instead they should visit black Africa to investigate what was happening, especially on the Ivory Coast, where the RDA (Révolution Démocratique Africaine) had been brutally repressed. De Beauvoir was eager to see the Sahara, so they planned to start in Algiers, going on to Hoggar, Gao, Timbuktu, Bobo-Dioulasso, and Bamako.

They stayed for several days in Ghardaïa, where Sartre agreed to give a lecture, and then drove in trucks across the Sahara, stopping sometimes for twenty-four hours, sometimes just for a night. They spent over a week at Tamanrasset,[21] in spite of a hotelkeeper who let himself into De Beauvoir's bedroom and tried to seduce her.[22] They flew over the Niger to Gao, a town built of mud, where, following the sound of tom-toms, they found a wedding being celebrated with dancing in a court-yard.[23] Two days later Sartre succumbed to fever. With a temperature of 104, he took so much quinine that he lost his sense of balance, and, unable to see or hear, stayed in bed for two days before flying on to Bobo-Dioulasso. One of the native districts was controlled by the RDA, but although their arrival had been reported in the local newspaper, none of the rebels made contact, probably because the PCF had been trying to discourage them from meeting him.

In the evening they flew to Bamako, where they again failed to make contact with the RDA, though they stayed for several days before moving on to Dakar. Exhausted, they spent two weeks recuperating in Morocco before going back to Paris, where Sartre found Dolores had installed herself. His attempts to dissuade her had not been forceful enough. But he was no longer emotionally involved, and he knew she would be more demandingly proprietorial than Michelle. The moment had come for partial withdrawal and negotiation. Wanda, who was having little success as an actress, had been glad to accept his offer of a regular income, parts in all his plays, and meetings at regular intervals. But to Dolores it seemed insulting when he offered a flat, an income, and scheduled times for togetherness. The relationship, which had lasted for five years, ended in a clean break.

After this his partnership with De Beauvoir was never again to be seriously threatened by any of his affairs. The relationship with Michelle would continue to the end of his life; some of his future mistresses would be beautiful, some of his intimacies extremely intense, but no other woman would ever bring him so close as Dolores had to sacrificing De Beauvoir, who would remain his resident critic and his chief partner in conversation. Above all, she would go on looking after him. Dolores had tried persistently, as other women would try later, to expropriate him from De Beauvoir, but the partnership, which had lasted since 1929, would continue till shortly before his death. He and De Beauvoir even gave the impression of thinking jointly. They could complete each other's sentences.[24] In company he talked much more than she did, but she always looked as if her ideas were in complete harmony with his. Nevertheless they went on addressing each other as "vous."

IN September 1950 the Korean War broke out. In 1945 Korea had been split into two halves, with the Russians occupying the northern half and the Americans the southern half. In August 1948 a republic had been proclaimed in the south, with Syngman Rhee as its president; four weeks later a republic was proclaimed in the north, and it assumed the right to sovereignty over the whole country. The danger of civil war was obvious, especially after the American occupying forces were withdrawn in June 1949. After a number of provocations along the border, the northern Communist forces invaded the south on June 25, capturing Seoul, the capital, within three days.

It was being said that China would detonate a world war by attacking Formosa. People lined up outside groceries to stockpile canned food. Some of Sartre's friends, including Francine Camus, spoke of killing themselves when the Red Army entered France, and her husband tried to persuade Sartre not to stay.[25] Merleau-Ponty joked about working as an elevator man in New York.[26] For Les Temps Modernes, he insisted, the only possibility was to keep silent about politics. It was obvious that the USSR had encouraged the invasion of South Korea: Stalin was no less an imperialist than the Western leaders.[27] Sartre did not see the need for silence, but he did not try to overrule Merleau-Ponty after accepting his political judgment for so long. "I was swimming in uncertainty."[28]

AT the beginning of 1951, finding it harder than ever to make headway with his ethics, he started a new play, constructing it around the same moral point he now considered crucial: that good and evil are not opposites. Le Diable et le Bon Dieu (The Devil and the Good Lord) carries its central character to the conclusion: "On this earth at this time, good and evil are inseparable." Götz von Berlichingen (1480–1562) was a warrior knight who reluctantly fought on the side of the peasants during the rebellion of 1525. He wrote an autobiography that was not published until 1731,[29] and Goethe's play Götz von Berlichingen mit der eisernen Hand (published 1773, produced 1774) portrays him as a champion of freedom. Sartre had been only twelve when he started to write a novel about Götz, but the new impulse came from a conversation with

Jean-Louis Barrault, who summed up the plot of Cervantes' 1615 play *El rufián dichoso* (*The Blessed Scoundrel*) about a bandit from Seville who throws dice to decide whether he should go on doing evil. He ends up as a saintly friar in Mexico.

The argument for canonizing Genet in the biography is that a man can approximate to saintliness by embracing all the evil projected on him by ostensibly virtuous people. Sartre compares Genet to Marcel Jouhandeau, who, in novels published in the twenties and thirties, had made a cult of abjection: "Only passion or vice throw you into the same destitution as saintliness. I believe that it's only when man is at this point of finding himself abandoned by everything and by himself that he is closest to grace—I mean to being worthy of it."[30] This is the pattern Sartre imposes on Götz, who makes his appearance in the play as a bastard outsider (like the young Genet) and swings perversely into a piety motivated not by reverence for God but by rage at his unforgivable absence.

Though Sartre was not intending to allegorize Genet's options in the play, its main issues relate closely to the issues in the book, while Sartre's Götz is ensnared as helplessly as his Genet in the trap contrived by traditional morality. Because the sixteenth century was more theocentric than the twentieth, the warrior knight can be shown (more clearly than the modern criminal can) to be taking up positions determined by attitudes to God. A professional soldier, Götz is a killer, and the peasants suffer from his ruthlessness. Sartre makes the Brechtian point that when war grows out of a quarrel among the rich, it is the poor who get killed.

Also at the back of Sartre's mind were Luther's reactions to the peasants during the wars of 1524–25.[31] The repression was ferocious, and the peasants ended up in a worse state than before. Sartre was trying to write a "play of crowds," in which the main characters could be understood and judged through their effects on the groups they galvanize.[32] But, evolved for heroic drama, Sartre's dramatic technique was inadequate. He was facing many of the same problems that Brecht had faced with *Mutter Courage*. Both plays differ from Shakespeare's history plays in containing no onstage battle scenes; both try to graft a moral and political argument onto a historical situation; both try to convey the illusion that armies are fighting, towns are under siege, citizens are being massacred. But Brecht is more successful than Sartre in suggesting the background of violence and in splicing action tightly into dialogue. Remembering what he had learned from Dullin—to write the situations, not the words—Sartre does his best to avoid static arguments, but he makes his points verbally, in rhetorical harangues, sometimes in analytical discussions and in aphorisms that are occasionally reminiscent of Oscar Wilde. "What's boring about evil," complains Götz, "is that you get used to it. To invent you have to be a genius. Tonight I hardly feel inspired!"

Like Sartre's Genet, this Götz is driven to extremism in good and evil but not by passion or sadism or masochism. Götz is activated by the nonstop argument he carries on with himself and with the absolute. God, he says, is the only enemy worth fighting. Like one of the Marquis de Sade's characters, he perpetrates outrages in order to submit the human condition to a laboratory test: Is it possible that wholesale cruelty will go unpunished? Once it is clear that no retribution is forthcoming, the only remaining hope is that God will be embarrassed: "I am the man who makes the Almighty uncomfortable. In me God feels horrified at himself."

Told by Heinrich, an ex-priest, that it is impossible for anyone on earth to do good, Götz finds the challenge irresistible, and, drawing more directly on Cervantes' play, Sartre writes a dice-throwing sequence in which Götz cheats in order to lose. He wants to pay the forfeit, which is to live altruistically. As he forces himself to act lovingly toward his fellow creatures the play becomes more than ever like a dramatized debate. Comedy is uneasily balanced against sentimental melodrama when he embraces a leper, though the action swings ironically against Götz when the leper shows more interest in being presented with an indulgence.

The two women in the play, Catherine (the role created for Wanda) and Hilda, are little more than foils to Götz, while Heinrich and the peasant leader, Nasty, are incarnations of opposing viewpoints, Nasty representing approximately the attitudes of the Communist party, while Heinrich exemplifies Sartre's habit of contradicting former principles. Heinrich is intended to embody a refutation of the idea that people are always free to choose. He "cannot choose either the church, which has abandoned the poor, or the poor, who have abandoned the church. . . . He is *totally conditioned* by his situation."[33] This tendency to argue through a play makes for bad drama while increasing the autobiographical value of the text. Sartre was also projecting his own problems on his hero, writing almost enviously about a man who never experienced any difficulty in moving forward from ideas to actions. Sartre could be described exactly as he described Götz—"an adventurer whose failure will never make him into a militant, though he will form alliances with militants throughout the rest of his life. . . . Götz's failure is to some extent that of anarchism; also that of paternalism, the anarchism of the masters."[34]

Until the outbreak of the Korean War and the dissolution of the RDR, Sartre had not been politically impotent, but he now felt he was in an impossible situation. What would he do if France really was overrun by the Russians? If he stayed it would be dangerous not to collaborate, but he could not picture himself living in South America with other rich refugees.[35] In the meantime he was free to write about freedom, but his writing was of no interest to the enslaved majority: if it was not intelligible to "the Hindu dying of starvation" it was worthless.[36] No longer struggling against nausea and alienation like Kafka's "hunger artist," Sartre was frustrated in his lust for solidarity with the rest of humanity. Though Götz gives away his estates to found a community based on love and brotherhood, he is jealous of Hilda, who has the knack of making people love her, while he, lacking her simplicity, feels uncertain whether he genuinely loves the people or merely wants them to love him.

The secret subject of the play is Sartre's sense of being isolated and of lacking warmth. The whole of his quest for power was ambivalent: he wanted it for his own sake but also because he believed empirically what he denied philosophically—good was not inseparable from evil, and he could use his power to do good. One reason he admired spontaneity so much in others was that he had tried unsuccessfully to cultivate it in himself. According to Cau, "All his generosities are in his head: they don't correspond to anything but moral signals, codes worked out cerebrally. His friendship is not warm but dry, like his voice, like his laugh."[37] The generosity was partly aggressive—a means of dominating; the detachment was partly defensive and partly necessitated by the isolation. "I killed God," says Götz, "because he separated me from men, and now his death is isolating me still more effectively." When he throws in his lot with the rebels, Nasty will not accept him as a common soldier, a man among men, but only as a leader. Like the heroes of Sartre's childhood reading, Götz is an adventurer; he ends up wanting to fight on the side of the peasants but needing both to conceal his atheism from them and to terrorize them. Sartre was an intellectual adventurer who would never succeed in making himself as indispensable to the party leaders as Götz was to Nasty, but, like Götz, he was caught between the impossibility of cultivating his own garden, indifferent to historical movements, and the impossibility of being honest in public. When he started writing *Le Diable et le Bon Dieu* Sartre, who had been

reading extensively about the French Revolution, wanted to incorporate in the play a comprehensive view of society, and he evolved a character called Dosia to represent the aristocracy.[38] Eventually he scrapped
Dosia, introducing a banker who could put forward some of the same
arguments. But because there is no rival figure of temporal authority
(while the figures of spiritual authority are feeble and the women mere
foils), Götz's only real conflict is with himself, while the offstage battles
fail to function as an objective correlative to it.

Sartre seems envious of the way violence comes naturally to the man
of action. Götz kills with no more compunction than a writer has in
crossing out a word. But Götz is most destructive when he tries not to
be: giving his land to the peasants, he is making slaughter inevitable,
and in the final moment of the play, when he kills a peasant to establish
his authority over the others, he is reflecting the latest phase in Sartre's
thinking about violence. It is indispensable.

As soon as Sartre had finished drafting the play, Simone Berriau,
who was still running the Théâtre Antoine, arranged for him to read his
script to Louis Jouvet. The first act is extremely long, and at the reading her husband kept dozing off, as did their friend Yves Mirande,
while Jouvet, who knew he did not have long to live—he was suffering
from a cardiac illness—listened impassively, making no comment even
at the end. He found the play blasphemous but asked his confessor for
permission to direct it.[39] This granted, they began to discuss casting.
The obvious choice for Götz was Pierre Brasseur, the heavyweight actor
who had done so well in Barrault's film *Les Enfants du Paradis* (1945) and
on the stage in the 1948 revival of Claudel's *Partage de Midi*. Hilda
would be played by Maria Casarès, with Jean Vilar as Heinrich.

The production was scheduled to open in May. To escape interruptions while finishing the script, Sartre decided to leave Paris. De Beauvoir wanted to go skiing, so, with Bost, they left for Auron, in the
Alpes-Maritimes, where Sartre stayed in his room writing while the
other two skied. Sartre and De Beauvoir went on to Saint-Tropez, and
from there back to Ramatuelle, where Brasseur visited them to discuss
the character.[40]

When rehearsals started the final scenes were still unwritten, and
Sartre did not try to conceal his contempt for Brasseur and Jouvet,
while they were frustrated by his uncooperativeness and infuriated by
his high-handedness. To everyone else it was obvious that the play was
too long, but instead of cutting he added to the text, and instead of attending rehearsals he sent Cau as his emissary with the new dialogue.
Brasseur was provoked into writing drunkenly abusive letters: "I'm fed
up with you, Sartre, you're a cunt. I'm fed up to the teeth. I shit on your

play with my piles. With a great bunch of piles I shit on your stupidity." Sartre read only part of the letter. "He repeats himself too much when he's raving."[41]

Brasseur refused to learn Götz's soliloquy in scene 9, which incorporates material from St. John of the Cross. Never averse to eclecticism, Sartre also borrowed a remark of Savonarola's ("The Church is a harlot"), repartee taken from Clement VII ("You are a bastard." "Yes, like Jesus Christ"), and a paraphrase of a statement by a Cluniac monk, quoted in Huizinga's *The Waning of the Middle Ages*. Odo of Cluny makes the point that if men were endowed with vision like the lynx of Boeotia, penetrating to the entrails, they would never want to embrace the mucus, bile, gall, and excrement that lies hidden under the skin of a lovely woman.[42]

WHEN Camus came to pick up Casarès from rehearsals, they would sometimes have a drink with Sartre,[43] but little was left of the friendship between the two men. The ailing Jouvet, who had been fairly passive during rehearsals, left for the country without even waiting to watch the first performance, but the play was a success. The run, which began on June 7, 1951, continued until March 1952, though critics and apparently audiences were confused, misinterpreting the final moment when Götz knifes the peasant soldier who refuses to fight under his leadership. He is not returning to the gratuitous pursuit of evil; all it means is that he has recognized the impossibility of suiting his actions to his ideals. As Francis Jeanson put it, "Götz's itinerary has seemed to exhaust all possible forms of idealism."[44] The blind forces of history always dragoon the individual into betraying his conscience as he chooses between turning his back on the current situation and trying to control it.

The royalty income solved Sartre's financial problems, but he was ill at ease, worrying that the Korean War might develop into a world war. Nor could he even commit *Les Temps Modernes* to an unequivocal position: he described the review during "the interregnum of 1950–52" as "a ship without a captain."[45] The war had isolated the PCF from the rest of the left, and if the review was drifting, it was drifting toward the isolated position occupied by the party. Merleau-Ponty would have preferred to repudiate the party, but for Sartre this was out of the question. "It's impossible to take an anti-Communist position without being against the proletariat." On the other hand, it would be impossible to take a pro-Communist position without reneging on the promise he had made in his "Présentation" that the editors should belong to no party and no church; the idea had been to investigate problems without any predetermined commitment to their solution. Merleau-Ponty, when he had forced political silence on the review, had been honoring this principle; Sartre was willing to jettison it. But from the beginning he had never wanted to keep the editorial reins in his hands. To do that he would have had to spend much more time in Paris.

In the middle of July he left again with De Beauvoir. First they flew to Norway. From Oslo they crossed the Telemark; then, cruising in a ship, Sartre showed her the scenery he had enjoyed sixteen years earlier with his mother and Mancy, and from the deck they watched the midnight brightness of the sky, which had inspired his story "Soleil de minuit." Next they spent ten days in Iceland, went on to Edinburgh, and visited the Hebrides. Traveling across Scotland, they were oppressed by inhospitable hotelkeepers who refused to provide a table for writing in the bedroom. ("If you want to write, go into the writing room.")

After a fortnight in London[46] they returned to Paris, where Sartre resumed meetings at his flat on alternate Sunday afternoons for contributors to *Les Temps Modernes*. The orientation toward the party was confirmed by the enlistment of new left-wing collaborators, Guy de Chambure, Bernard Dort, and two journalists with a philosophical background, Claude Lanzmann and Marcel Péju. Both had jobs on newspapers rewriting other people's articles. Lanzmann was an attractive man from a provincial Jewish bourgeois family. Olivier Todd describes him as a mixture of Malraux, Proust, and the novelist Roger Vailland.[47] Péju had interviewed Sartre about *Le Diable et le Bon Dieu* for *Samedi-Soir*,[48] and Sartre was pleased with what he wrote. A degree of unanimity began to emerge, but the new orientation meant that a breech with Camus could not be postponed much longer. Before he had completed *L'Homme révolté* (*The Rebel*) in July 1952, it was arranged that a chapter—the one on Nietzsche and nihilism—would be excerpted in *Les Temps Modernes*. It appeared in the August issue with no indication that the book was out to attack the Communists. Comparing the idea of revolution with the actions it had triggered, Camus argued that the utopian end could not justify the violent means. Hegel is condemned for equating reason with fate, Marx trounced for assuming that the class struggle is powered by the force of reason, while the PCF is found guilty of ruthless deference to Moscow and ruthless indifference to the individual. Camus makes the point Sartre had already made in *Les Mains sales* about the slaughter of those who are out of step with party policy, whether they are slightly ahead or slightly behind, but he attacks Sartre for failing to produce a moral philosophy that could transform existentialist *Angst* into a positive rebelliousness. Sartre is accused—not quite fairly—of jumping into an uncritical acceptance of historical determinism as interpreted by the party. But behind Camus's book was something even more deeply inimical to Sartre's present position. Both writers had been changed by the sense of crisis during the occupation; in Sartre the change was permanent, and he no longer wanted to relax into a literary career. Camus, who did want to, intended *L'Homme révolté* as his final statement about political philosophy.

The book was published in October and was generally acclaimed. *Le Figaro Littéraire* called it Camus's most important work, while *Le Monde* pronounced it the most valuable book to have appeared since the war.[49] Even if he was displeased to receive praise from the extreme right, Camus was more disconcerted by the protracted silence of *Les Temps Modernes*. What was happening at the fortnightly editorial meetings was that De Beauvoir was regularly reminding the others, who had all read the book, that it had to be reviewed, but none of them liked it, and the general feeling was that Camus, instead of studying Marx and Engels, had relied on résumés of their work and had failed to understand it.[50] When Sartre asked for a volunteer to review the book, no one spoke up, and eventually the job was given to the twenty-nine-year-old Francis Jeanson, who had fought with the FFI (Forces Françaises de l'Intérieur) in North Africa and Germany and had written a book about Sartre, *Le Problème moral et la pensée de Sartre*, to which Sartre had contributed a preface.

To write *Le Diable et le Bon Dieu*, Sartre had put aside his biography of Genet, but in thinking about Götz he had never stopped thinking about Genet, though less concerned to write objectively about either man than to use him as an exemplar for an intricate system of generalizations: the extremes of good and evil meet, while for the hero, as for the saint, the only way to earn social esteem is by self-destruction. It is easy to move from soldiering to saintliness: you internalize the process of dying and slow it down. Refusing to explore or enjoy the environment, you sacrifice everything to God. Sartre could see close parallels between the career of his Götz, the strategy of Genet, and the strategy of anyone who, instead of venturing into an active relationship with the world, tries to transubstantiate it into language. Sartre is fascinated by the way Genet uses words onanistically to destroy and transfigure. His books consist of "words which clash, which burn themselves up," becoming "an index of the rigorously impractical operations to which he has devoted his life. Thanks to language, Genet can lend a being to nothingness and remain restlessly in the domain of shadow, that's to say of evil."[51] The landscape is dissolved, while the characters are, as Genet says, "pretexts for my iridescence, then for my transparency, finally for my absence; these boys I describe evaporate. Nothing remains of them except what remains of me. . . . I exist only through them, while they are nothing, existing only through me."[52]

Sartre keeps comparing Genet with Mallarmé, who recognized the " 'universal determinability' and the 'absolute negativity' of consciousness. He too was going to pass this 'blanket condemnation on everything which is perceptible.' "[53] Sartre was still concerned with the problem of mental digestion: the individual consciousness cannot stomach the glutinous proliferation of external reality. In the 1939 essay on Husserl he had used the spider image to attack the illusion that consciousness devoured objects.[54] This analogy makes the process of perceiving seem more repulsive than the object perceived; but in the chestnut tree episode the ugliness was in the object, and Sartre, who has never felt entirely at ease with the physical environment, welcomes Genet as an ally, equally allergic to it: "He hates matter. Excluded, he looks at the goods of this world through a pane of glass, like poor children looking at cakes through a shop-window. . . . Matter is the unintelligible, the unforgivable outrage; it represents his impotence and the reality of his exile."[55] It is as a refugee that he settles in literature. He dislikes things but relishes the words that represent them; hates flowers but loves their names.[56] Again and again Sartre comes back to characterizing language as something that dissolves reality in order to reconstitute it, destroys the world in order to reproduce it. Quoting Maurice Blanchot, he equates language with "the flight of being into significations, the evaporation of the significations, in short, annihilation," but at the same time it inscribes nothingness in being. Like the surrealists, Genet operates a war machine that recuperates non-being while dissolving reality—we get many repetitions of this phrase, and many variations on it.[57]

In Qu'est-ce que la littérature? Sartre had castigated the surrealists for their lack of social commitment; he condones that of Genet, who is judged by a new set of criteria. Mauriac had been roundly condemned for manipulating characters like puppets instead of giving them leeway to make decisions of their own; Genet once said to Sartre: "My books aren't novels because none of my characters takes a decision on his own."[58] Instead of recognizing this as a limitation, Sartre praises the desertlike desolation of Notre-Dame des fleurs: "All his characters are inert, tossed about by fate; the author is a savage god who gets drunk on human sacrifice."[59]

Does this god allow himself to be seen? His words not only burn themselves but burn him, and the Genet phoenix that emerges is a fantasy, no less factitious than his seductive murderers and brutish pimps. "To compose," writes Sartre, "is, for him, to recreate himself."[60] Less critical than he seems and always attracted to self-generation or regeneration, Sartre raises no objection; in fact he carries the process one stage further, burning the phoenix to conjure up a new one. Like Sartre's studies of Baudelaire and Flaubert, *Saint Genet* is not so much a biography as an elaborate, brilliant, inaccurate display of how another consciousness functions. Not content with leaving out most of the biographical facts, Sartre distorts the ones he introduces: "Between his years at the Mettray reformatory (he was fifteen) and his first burglary (he was twenty-five) ten years pass without marking him."[61] Later we are told that these ten years were "astonishingly full: he becomes an apprentice, runs away, gets caught, placed in a bourgeois household, he steals, he's sent to Mettray, he escapes again, he begs, travels round France, joins the Foreign Legion, deserts, escapes to Barcelona, lives by begging and prostituting himself in the Barrio Chino, steals again, leaves Spain and goes everywhere, Italy, Poland, Czechoslovakia, Germany, stealing and crossing frontiers illegally."[62] No one could be unmarked by all this, but Sartre, still fixated on the notion that a single choice, made in childhood, determines the future, distances himself scornfully from the biographers who would have built several colorful chapters out of these adventures.

Genet describes himself as having been homosexual before he started stealing; Sartre contradicts him without adducing any evidence. The primary disorientation was due to oppression, he says; Genet must have identified himself as homosexual after being bullied into identifying himself as a thief. "This first violation was the gaze of the other person, which took him by surprise, penetrated him, transformed him permanently into an object. . . . An actual rape can register in our moral conscience as an iniquitous yet irrevocable condemnation, and, inversely, a condemnation can be experienced as a rape."[63] Here, as Douglas Collins has pointed out, Sartre was following Angelo Hesnard's 1948 book *L'Univers morbide*, which condemns the "moral rape" that forces children into an alien discipline.[64] Sartre had started reading Hesnard at the Ecole Normale, borrowing the books *Relativité* and *L'Inconscience* in his first year and taking both out again in his third. He was excited by the idea of the homosexualizing gaze of the Other: he had already written, in "L'Enfance d'un chef," about the intrusive adult gaze that can take the boy from behind, as in buggery. "Lucien invented a new game: in the morning, when he took his bath alone in the bathroom like a grown-up, he pretended that someone was watching him through the keyhole. . . . Then he turned his back to the door and squatted on all

fours to make his bottom stick out ridiculously."[65] It is almost as if
Sartre had been waiting since 1937 for a subject such as Genet, whose
life was arguably changed by a single traumatic moment of "moral
rape."

Sartre may have been unaware of how much he was identifying with
Genet, although, in an awkwardly defensive footnote, he attacks the assumption that a critic is likely to be revealing more about himself than
about his subject.[66] Sartre tries to keep himself out of the picture, not
even confessing that he too was caught stealing in childhood. But the
affinity goes deeper. Like Baudelaire, Genet had been rejected by his
mother, and he revenges himself in fantasy: he imagines vomiting on
her hands.[67] In the novel *Pompes funèbres* the burial of the illegitimate
child may represent "the perpetual funeral of the child Genet."[68] Sartre
could be describing himself—or anyone—when he says: "Genet is so
made that all his feelings have double and triple depth. The liveliest,
the freshest passion is at the same time a pretext for reliving the decisive
moments of his childhood."[69] In *Les Mots* Sartre will alienate his childhood; in many ways he comes closer to himself when writing about
Genet, not least when he discusses Genet's technique of coming to terms
with disaster by persuading himself that he willed it.[70] More philosoph-
ical-minded and less overtly self-involved than his subject, Sartre generalizes this compulsion, not contending that he wanted everything which
happened to him but that we are all responsible for our situations.
Sartre's doctrines about choice have neurotic roots.

Even when he describes Genet's technique of writing while in prison,
Sartre is inadvertently describing his own while at liberty: "When the
masturbator changes into the artist, it is still to act on himself; let's remember that he throws himself into writing as if into stealing or making love—frenziedly, doped by orthodrine tablets, and he doesn't put
his pen down until he's finished. ... He hurries toward the moment
when he will write 'The End' at the foot of the final page, and when
he'll have *nothing else to say* because he will have *said everything."* There is
no knowing whether Sartre used stimulants while writing *Saint Genet*,
but, like *L'Etre et le Néant* and the notes on morality, the book was obviously written in a headlong rush, with a strong urge to leave nothing
unsaid. Sartre's 573-page book can be described by applying his own
description of Genet's fictions: systematically it develops in the realm of
the imaginary all the possibilities latent in the actual situation—especially those that have not been realized.[71] *Saint Genet* is an analytical
work, but it also belongs to the "realm of the imaginary," even if the
experience of writing it helped to dissuade Sartre from devoting time to
imaginative literature. To him Genet incarnated "solitude pushed into

passion."[72] If we want to reconcile the object and the subject, Sartre concludes—and no one has wanted this more urgently than he did—we must, if only once, "realize this latent solitude which eats into our acts and thoughts."[73] In warning the reader, Sartre was revealing his own fear.

The interaction between Sartre and Genet was far-reaching, but there was no reciprocity, no exchange of gifts equal in value. Genet was the loser: writing, for the first time, the biography of a living writer, Sartre stopped him in mid-career, crushing the artist under a massive and premature monument. Genet wrote no more books and only three more plays. After reading the typescript he expressed his reaction by trying to throw it into the fire. The relationship between the two men deteriorated sharply, and it is hard to believe that Genet's abdication from literature was due more to the suicide of Abdullah, a boy who loved him, than to Sartre's book. To Cocteau, Genet complained: "You and Sartre have made me into a statue. . . . I'm another person and the other person has to find something to say." Cocteau's verdict was: "Jean has changed since Sartre's book. He seems at the same time to be conforming to it and running away from it."[74]

Where Sartre was most unlike Genet was in his evangelism: his task, he believed, was to construct an ideology that would help people understand the world and how to behave in it.[75] He researched voraciously, recommending books to De Beauvoir, but his priorities were changing: work had come to matter more and friendship less. Fantasies about fame had once been a source of excitement; the reality of fame brought more power than pleasure. He was determined to stay in the public eye and to make full use of the power, but the quality of his writing was deteriorating because, mixing with people less, he was observing less and theorizing more, while, busier than ever, he tended to read only books relevant to what he was writing while he spent less time in cafés and cinemas. This had been one of his main pleasures, but now tiresome strangers would accost him. He was also spending less time with De Beauvoir; Olga and Bost were not in Paris; since Dullin's death Toulouse had been living an isolated life.[76] At home Sartre chained himself to a heavy working routine.[77] Jean Cau, the man who regularly saw him at work, describes him in nonhuman images—bullock, monster, mule, machine—while the people around him are "satellites."[78]

(18)

Under Oath to Hate

SARTRE was involving himself more deeply in an alliance with the PCF, but it was not he who took the initiative. The party had consistently opposed the war in Vietnam, which had been in progress since 1946. France was unmistakably losing: by now much of the country was controlled by the Vietminh. A French sailor, Henri Martin, had volunteered at the end of 1945 for the campaign in Indochina against the Japanese who had gone on fighting when their country surrendered. He was sent to Vietnam, where he found himself pitted against the Vietnamese. Three times he applied unsuccessfully for a transfer. After being sent back to France at the end of 1947, he was assigned in 1948 to Toulon, and in 1949 he began to stick up leaflets, which he wrote himself, protesting against the war in Indochina. Arrested in May 1950, he was condemned by a court-martial to five years' imprisonment.

When a committee was formed to campaign for his release, Sartre joined it after being approached by Claude Roy, a Communist who had never been unfriendly, and by Jean Chaintron, an old working-class militant. After signing an appeal addressed to President Auriol, Sartre was received by him, and the President agreed that the sentence was excessive but said he could offer no remission so long as the Communists went on campaigning for it.[1] Sartre then undertook to collaborate on editing a book about the affair.[2]

It was not until later that Camus was invited to join the campaign, but in February, when the French League for the Rights of Man arranged a meeting to protest against the death sentence passed in Spain on a group of labor leaders, he selected the speakers, and Sartre was one of them.[3] But, refusing to join the Henri Martin campaign, Camus said that "the values of liberty would only be compromised and confused with other values if defended in Les Temps Modernes and associated with those who approve of it." The review's silence about L'Homme révolté was still unbroken, and in April, at a café on the Place Saint-Sulpice, when

"Poulou" with Anne-Marie. It was easy to win praise from his mother. He was fair and rosy-complexioned, with plump cheeks and curls. Endless photographs of him were taken; his mother retouched them with crayons.

Sartre started at the Ecole Normale Supérieure in August 1924 and left in 1929, when he was twenty-four. "Many can say, as I do, that they have had four years of happiness there."

Sartre as a private soldier looking through a theodolite at a meteorological balloon held by his corporal, Jean Pierre, somewhere in Alsace during the first nine months of the war.

Sartre at the age of thirty-seven working as a schoolteacher at the Lycée Condorcet (1942).

Paul Nizan (1905–40). "That such a close friend should be a revolutionary struck me as totally grotesque."

Sartre in 1939. He had never been able to sink himself completely into any love affair, any pleasure, never been really unhappy; it always seemed to him that he was somewhere else, hadn't yet been quite born. He was waiting. And all this time, gently, slyly, the years had come, they had seized him from behind. Thirty-four years.

Simone de Beauvoir in 1955. Thirty-six years after he met her in 1928
Sartre said: "I have always thought her beautiful."

Left: Wanda Kosakiewicz, who used Marie-Olivier as her stage name. "You know quite well that I would trample on the whole world (including de Beauvoir) . . . in order to stay on good terms with you."

Below: Sartre and de Beauvoir with Boris and Michelle Vian, who were still married when Michelle's affair with Sartre began in December 1945. She remained a close friend until he died in 1980. But when they went on holiday together she was left on her own most of the day while Sartre worked to the same routine as in Paris.

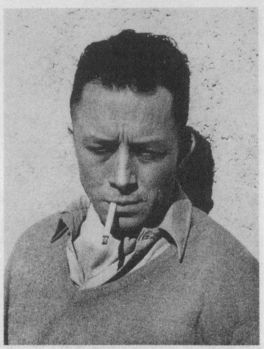

Right: Albert Camus (1913–60). With Camus Sartre could have a great deal of fun; in some ways he was still like a tough Algerian street urchin. They could tell each other obscene stories while de Beauvoir and Maria Casarès or Francine Camus would appear to be shocked. Later Sartre would describe him as "probably the last good friend I had."

Below: Sartre at the Pont-Royal with (left to right) Dolorès Vanetti—"She's enormously important to me" —Jacques-Laurent Bost, an ex-pupil who was the model for Boris in *Les Chemins de la liberté*, Jean Cau, who was Sartre's secretary for twelve years, and Jean Genet (1907–86).

Left: Sartre and de Beauvoir
with Claude Lanzmann, who
joined the editorial committee
of *Les Temps Modernes* in 1952
and became her lover but
remained on good terms with
Sartre.

Below: Sartre in June 1957 with
François Mauriac (1885–1970).
"God is not an artist and
neither is M. Mauriac."

Left: At the Théâtre de la Renaissance during rehearsals of *Les Séquestrés d'Altona* during September 1959. Serge Reggiani, who played Frantz, is on the right at the front; Evelyne Rey (Johanna) is on the left. Sartre was to become one of the most important men in her life, while she was to become—until her suicide—one of the most important women in his, a mistress, like Wanda, for whom he wrote plays.

Below: Sartre with Arlette Elkaïm in January 1965 after adopting her as his daughter. She was nineteen when they met in March 1956, and she soon became his mistress. When he died intestate, Arlette was left with full copyright control over everything he had written, including his letters to de Beauvoir, which were published illegally.

Sartre with Tito in Yugoslavia during 1960.

Sartre in March 1968 addressing a meeting held to protest against the war in Vietnam.

Above: Sartre in court during
February 1970 waiting to
appear as a witness at the trial
of Roland Castro.

Right: Sartre outside the
Renault works at Billancourt
in October 1970, speaking out
against the suppression of
La Cause du peuple and the
Geismar trial. "The
intellectuals should be the
allies of the people. . . .
Geismar, the man on trial, he
is the people himself."

Above: Daniel Cohn-Bendit
(right), who became friendly
with Sartre during the 1968
student rebellion, acts as his
interpreter at a Stuttgart press
conference in December 1974
after they have visited Andreas
Baader of the Baader-
Meinhof gang in Stammheim
prison. Sartre is already almost
blind. Sitting on the other side
of him is Klaus Croissant,
Baader's lawyer.

Left: Accompanied by André
Glucksmann (left) and
Raymond Aron (center) Sartre
is leaving the Elysée, where
they have been received by the
President, Giscard d'Estaing,
together with other delegates
from the committee organizing
relief for the Vietnamese "boat
people."

Above: The crowd surrounding Sartre's hearse on 19 April 1980 as the cortège moves toward the cemetery in Montparnasse. Eight days later the coffin will be disinterred for cremation at Père-Lachaise.

Right: A chair has been brought for Simone de Beauvoir's graveside farewell to Sartre.

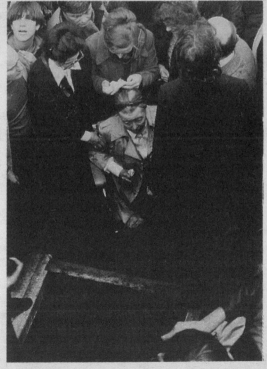

Camus talked derisively about hostile reviewers, Sartre was too embarrassed to reply.[4] Jeanson was already at work on his critique. "He'll be the harshest," Sartre had said, "but at least he'll be polite."[5] Meeting Camus in the street, Sartre warned him that the review would be unfavorable; he seemed so perturbed that Sartre invited him to write a reply.[6] The review turned out to be even harsher than Sartre had expected, and he persuaded Jeanson to tone it down,[7] but it was still unequivocally hostile. Published in the May issue under the punning title "Albert Camus ou l'âme révoltée" (". . . or the Revolted Soul"), it accused Camus of rejecting history in favor of ineffectual moralizing; the book was described as a "pseudophilosophy of a pseudohistory of 'revolutions.' "[8] Deeply depressed—he had lost all appetite for life, he said—Camus went on hesitating about whether to exercise his right of reply.[9]

Now that Michelle Vian had separated from her husband, her affair with Sartre came out into the open, and in May they drove to the south of France with De Beauvoir and Bost, who shared the driving. They were at Saint-Tropez when Merleau-Ponty arrived there with his wife. The two men argued but with no hope of reaching any agreement: Merleau-Ponty was moving decisively away from the left while Sartre was becoming more radical. Not that he would ever cease to be preoccupied with literature. He continued his work on Mallarmé before returning by train to Paris for some meetings.[10] He soon left again for three weeks in Italy with Michelle, but for most of the time she was on her own: Sartre worked no less hard on vacation than he did in Paris.[11]

They were in Rome when he heard about the demonstration of May 28 in Paris. In April, General Eisenhower had resigned as Supreme Allied Commander in Europe and had been succeeded by General Matthew Ridgway, who had taken over from General MacArthur in Korea when he became critical of American policy. In August 1951 Ridgway had broken off armistice talks, accusing the Communists of violating the agreements on demilitarization. When he visited Paris in May 1952, the PCF organized a demonstration, which became violent, and the police pitched in brutally. The next day several leading Communists were arrested, including Jacques Duclos, leader of the Communists in the National Assembly. Two pigeons were found in his car, and he was accused of espionage on the assumption that they were carrier pigeons; in fact, he had been intending to eat them. At the same time the party's newspapers were seized. A protest strike was organized for June 2, and after it failed, Sartre was furious when the right-wing press reacted in the way anyone would have expected it to react—saying that the working class had lost faith in the party. "The last connections were

broken," wrote Sartre, "my vision was transformed: an anti-Communist is a swine, I can see no way out of that, and I never will. . . . After
ten years of brooding about it, I had reached breaking point, and I
needed only a gentle push. In the language of the church, this was a
conversion. . . . I swore against the bourgeoisie a hatred which will die
only when I do."[12] If the workers had failed to support the strike, he argued, their motives must be personal: their inaction did not amount to
a criticism of the party. He was also under the influence of Henri Guillemin's *Le Coup du 2 Décembre.* "It's a book which mattered to me: the
documentation Guillemin provides showed me how much shit there
can be in a bourgeois heart."[13]

Besides telling the story of Louis Napoleon's 1851 coup d'état, which
changed the French constitution, Guillemin marshals extracts from letters, diaries, newspapers, and magazines as evidence that after the easy
defeat of the communist riots in June 1849, what the rightists wanted
was not a republic but a dictatorship.

Sartre's explosion of hatred was partly against himself: he spoke of
wanting to break the bones in his head.[14] He was too angry to stay in
Italy. "I had to write or suffocate."[15] Returning to Paris, he worked feverishly at *Les Communistes et la paix* (*The Communists and Peace*). "In two
weeks," De Beauvoir told her sister, "he's gone for five nights with no
sleep, and during the other nights slept only four or five hours."[16]

Of all the turning points in his life this was probably the most important: if commitment as defined in *Qu'est-ce que la littérature?* had already been making him into a different kind of writer, he was now
passing the point of no return. The creative momentum gained from
writing three novels and seven short stories had petered out before his
fourth novel, *La Mort dans l'âme,* was written. Though the outbreak of
war had boosted his creativity, it had been impossible to publish either
L'Age de raison or *Le Sursis* during the occupation, and there is no knowing how his career might have developed if they had not been delayed
until 1945. Though both novels made an international impact, they
had lost most of their relevance to current politics and to his current
thinking. But even if he had kept more of his creative momentum, he
would probably have been floated into a different kind of activity by
the surge of popularity brought to him by the vogue for existentialism.

Fame meant power, and for about seven years after the end of the
war it was by no means absurd to believe that he might have a key role
to play in saving the world from a new war. He was convinced that
everything depended on keeping Europe neutral. Later it would be apparent that he had overrated both his own influence and the militancy
of the two great powers, but it is easy to see why he could not have settled

down to cultivate his fictional garden. Even after he had failed both in his opposition to the Atlantic Pact and in his efforts to create inside France a democratic, revolutionary alternative to communism, it was clear that for a man so capable of public-spirited hatred there would be plenty of other battles to fight. He always had more to do than could possibly be done in the time available, and though he did not succeed fully in any of the major political or philosophical or literary tasks he set himself, the sum total of his achievements was to be enormous.

The paradox was rooted in the most fundamental of his personal problems—what was he? What should he be doing? He was permanently uncertain about whether he should be taking the advice he made Hoederer give Hugo—"Your talent is for writing"—or whether he was justified in leaving his desk littered with unfinished work while he set out on another journey to see socialism on the advance or colonialism being exposed for the evil it was or while he accepted yet another invitation to let his name and his face be used in publicizing another political cause of obvious importance. People were really suffering. He could give real help in fighting oppression. If he enjoyed the publicity and the popularity, did that detract from the value of his contribution? Or was he still fixated on the notion of earning his salvation through good works? Or motivated by deep-seated anxieties about not being a man of action and not being needed? Or was he deliberately overcrowding his life to give himself an excuse for not finishing the work that in any case he would have been unable to finish adequately, however much time he had at his disposal?

Did he even ask himself these questions as he plunged into overcommitment? The more hectic the activity, the less danger there would be of having time to brood about motivations. From 1952 till his death in 1980 he never tried (as Camus did) to reduce his political commitments and his output as a writer of politically loaded books in order to leave more space for self-examination, creativity, and literature. His only major literary objective would be in line with that of *Qu'est-ce que la littérature?*—to condemn nineteenth-century writers, especially Flaubert and Mallarmé, for failing to help the working class.

A man who complains that there is shit in the bourgeois heart is a man too angry to be concerned with expressing himself elegantly or even logically. Sartre's rage was genuine, and it gave him a burning sense of urgency. It also carried him to an extreme position, close to the one Lenin had taken on the relationship between the party and the proletariat. For Marx the proletariat—because its sufferings were universal—was the universal class that would lead the world to revolution; though Lenin went on claiming to believe in "the spontaneous awakening of the masses," he wanted the party to take the lead by making the proletariat conscious of itself. In *Les Communistes et la paix* Sartre will equate the party with the movement that unites the workers by carrying them toward revolution. Without the party they remain amorphous, impotent.

In the first of the three long essays he published under this title he denounced his former ally Georges Altman and ridiculed the ideal of the RDR—a democratic alternative to Stalinist communism. "Where is the majority that will carry it into power?"[17] Having joined in attacks on the party as being democratic in neither structure nor procedure, Sartre now turned all his polemical artillery against its critics. Abandoning his principle of preserving a neutral position between the two power blocs, he gave his allegiance to the Soviet Union, which "wants peace and proves it every day."[18]

When the first essay appeared in the July issue of *Les Temps Modernes* it was obvious that he was steering the review to the left. If he remembered his initial promise of nonalignment, he would not have worried. He was at one of his many crises of believing with all the fervency of the convert that until now he had been totally wrong but now he was totally right. For Sartre nothing was more thrilling, more enjoyable, than the moment when a project or a system of belief collapses to reveal amid the ruins the basis on which a new one can be built. In May 1949 *Les Temps Modernes* had protested against the Soviet system by proclaiming: "There is no socialism when one citizen out of twenty is in a camp." In 1952 the system was unchanged, but Sartre, no less than the PCF, was now supporting it. In *Drôle d'amitié* he condemned the bullying PCF militant he had admired in *L'Age de raison*, but he never turned his critical artillery against Soviet party henchmen. The Communists welcomed his support; Kanapa applauded his courage and generosity,[19] but René Etiemble disliked the new line and Sartre's new friends, especially Claude Roy, whom Entiemble called "a Stalinist Nazi."[20]

When Camus finally wrote his reply, in a letter dated June 30, he addressed himself to Sartre, calling him "Monsieur le Directeur." He was weary, he said, of receiving "lessons in effectiveness from critics who have never pointed anything but their armchairs in the direction of history."[21] Complaining about the feebleness of Jeanson's review, Camus called him "a bourgeois Marxist" who wanted "a revolt against everything except the Communist party and the Communist state." Sartre was furious. "I'm going to answer him in any case," he told Jeanson. "You can if you want to."[22]

Sartre did not know when he wrote his letter that he'd never see Camus again, but he did know that their friendship was dead. "Many things brought us together, few divided us. But these few were still too many."[23] The letter begins angrily, accusing Camus of "dull self-importance" and of carrying a "portable altar" around with him, as if the value of his book had been divinely guaranteed.[24] Later on, the polemic becomes more guarded. Claiming he is not a Marxist—a claim that by then was highly equivocal—Sartre admits to being bourgeois, just like Camus and Jeanson,[25] but Camus, wanting to destroy the party without having anything to offer in its place,[26] is guilty of a "quietism" that refuses to distinguish between the oppressors.[27] The heat of Sartre's argument remains intense, but the language becomes flat. "The iron curtain is only a mirror, and each half of the world reflects the other half. Each turn of the screw here corresponds to a turn of the screw there, and finally, here and there, we are the screwers and the screwed."[28]

He goes on to write generously about Camus's achievements in *L'Etranger* and during the Resistance. "You personified the conflicts of the era, and you subsumed them through your ardor for living them. You were a *person,* the most complex and the richest: the last and most welcome of Chateaubriand's heirs, and the zealous defender of a social cause."[29] Since then Camus had detached himself from contemporary history: "Only half of you is still living among us. . . . You are no more than an abstraction of revolt."[30] Sartre ends by inviting Camus to write back, but if he does, there will be no answer to this answer. "I refuse to fight you."[31]

Sales of *Les Temps Modernes* had never been higher. Since *Les Communistes et la paix,* each edition had been selling out within a few days and selling out again when reprinted. Agog at the quarrel between the two star writers, readers were hoping Camus would reply, but he did not. In his diary he wrote: "They admit sin but refuse grace. . . . Something in them, ultimately, aspires to servitude."[32]

AT the end of July Sartre traveled by train to Milan, where De Beauvoir was waiting for him, and together they drove in her car through Cremona, Ferrara, Ravenna, Urbino, and Bari. In Sicily they visited Agrigento and Syracuse. They drove back to Rome, then on to continue their exploration of Italy. She wanted to see as much as possible; he wanted to write the second part of *Les Communistes et la paix.* They compromised but not without quarreling.

In this second part Sartre tries to substantiate his contention that the party is the exact expression of the working class. "What it represents in their eyes is their aspirations, their inclinations, their wishes," carrying these to the highest level of efficacy.[33] The isolated worker is a subhuman; he achieves humanity only by refusing to be what he is, by rebelling against his situation, by acting in unison with fellow workers. Indispensable to this is the organization the party provides; it is only through collective struggle that the proletariat can come into existence as a proletariat.[34] It must therefore be regarded not only as interdependent with the party but as inseparable from it. There can be no question of working-class spontaneity: "It's a matter of an Order which makes order prevail and issues orders."[35] Though Sartre has come around to an unequivocally Leninist position, the rapport between leaders and led is described, in the manner of *L'Etre et le Néant,* as if it were a one-to-one relationship. Diffuse sovereignty is concentrated in the leader and reflected to each member of the group, who, in obeying, functions as a repository of sovereignty. Acting in unison through the collective dimension, everyone is a leader. Like Trotsky, who once wrote "Our 'truth' of course is not absolute,"[36] Sartre did not always quite believe in his own arguments.

It was inevitable that the quarrel with Camus would soon be followed by a quarrel with Merleau-Ponty. Though he had resigned in 1950 as political editor, he was still editor in chief, and he found it hard to work with the extremists, such as Claude Roy, whom Sartre was using as his adjutant. Though they were not named members of the editorial board, Sartre, as he later admitted, was letting himself be prodded by them into moving further leftward.[37] Merleau-Ponty, who had been meticulous in submitting all his contributions to Sartre, was annoyed when Sartre failed to show him the second installment of *Les Communistes et la paix* until it was in proof. Sartre was feeling guilty about his past deference to Merleau-Ponty's political leadership and about the silence they had preserved since the outbreak of the Korean War in 1950. With the enthusiasm of the convert, Sartre was determined to speak out decisively, and, upset though he was, Merleau-Ponty neither provoked a quarrel nor stated his views in an article. He regularly attended the fortnightly editorial meetings, but he arrived late, left early, and kept his opinions to himself. Had he been more outspoken, Pouillon and Pontalis, already uneasy at Sartre's new radicalism, might have rallied to Merleau-Ponty's support.[38]

INTELLECTUAL life in France tends to be schismatic, and even if Merleau-Ponty, who was a colleague of Lévi-Strauss at the Collège de France, had remained on better terms with Sartre, it is unlikely that he would have been able to cement an alliance between the two men, though a good deal of Lévi-Strauss's work was published in *Les Temps*

Modernes during the early fifties. Listing "books which have advanced knowledge" in "Le Réformisme et les fétiches," a contribution to the February 1956 issue of the review, Sartre pays tribute to the "ethnographic works" of Lévi-Strauss, books by Henri Guillemin, the historians Georges Lefebvre and Marc Bloch, and the art criticism of Pierre Francastel, but in calling Lévi-Strauss an ethnographer, Sartre was implicitly laying claim to anthropology as his own territory while resisting Lévi-Strauss's attempts to differentiate his anthropology from traditionalist ethnography. Like Leiris and Sartre, Lévi-Strauss was hostile to both colonialism and the noninterventionist anthropology that had grown up under the old system. The anthropologist is naturally drawn to territories where an old culture has been defeated though not extirpated, but he is professionally predisposed to being more of a cultural conservationist than the anticonservative Sartre.

As imperialism ran into one crisis after another during the fifties, Sartre gave more time—and more space in the review—to the injustices of the old system and the brutality of the colonial oppressors. In 1946 the French use of torture in Madagascar had already been exposed in Roger Stéphane's reports.[39] During the fifties the allocation of space in *Les Temps Modernes* reflected not only Sartre's shift of interest from literature to politics but his lack of interest in language. Merleau-Ponty, as he concerned himself less with left-wing politics and more with linguistics, flirted with structuralism, accepting the view that all cultural phenomena belong to a single order, that language is not transparent, and that political action needs to be based on accurate understanding of the symbolic systems a society is using. But Sartre, after his brief flicker of interest in the Saussurian terminology, turned his back on the structuralists, recognizing them as rivals and believing that he could fight them more effectively by ignoring them than by confronting them directly. He would make indirect assaults on positions held by Lévi-Strauss and Roland Barthes but mostly without mentioning them or structuralism by name. Intellectual controversies now engaged less of Sartre's interest than political confrontations.

In the autumn he supported several left-wing protests. In the middle of October, after Alain Le Léap, left-wing secretary general of the Communist-dominated union Confédération Générale du Travail (CGT), had been arrested for "demoralization of the nation," Sartre protested in *Libération* and *Ce Soir*.[40] In the middle of November he signed the "Manifesto Against the Cold War" prepared by the CNE. Four days later, no longer wanting to seem critical of the party, he banned a production of *Les Mains sales* in Vienna. He had been involved since the summer with the peace movement, and in December, when it was announced that a World Congress for Peace was to be held in Vienna, he decided—either on his own initiative or at the suggestion of Aragon—to attend, dismissing the arguments of the editorial board, which tried to dissuade him.[41] Nearly all the delegates from the West were Communists. Making a speech on December 2, Sartre said that the only way to campaign for peace was to campaign with the Communists; anticommunism was a no-man's-land obstructing collaboration between all those who sincerely wanted peace.[42] He was given a standing ovation, and on December 23, when a meeting was held at the Vélodrome d'Hiver to report on the congress, two of the speakers were Sartre and Jacques Duclos, who sat next to each other.[43] Sartre was at his most naïve. Since he had come of age, he said, three events had suddenly given him hope—the popular front of 1936, the liberation of France, and the Vienna congress.[44]

JUST before the year ended, after lecturing at the University of Freiburg, Sartre went on to visit Heidegger, but spent only half an hour with him,[45] and described him as looking like a retired colonel. "The old man of the mountain, that's what he is." Afterward, climbing into his reserved railway compartment, Sartre found it was full of roses sent by Heidegger. As soon as the train had pulled out of the station he threw them out of the window.[46] Sartre's debt to Heidegger was immeasurable and therefore intolerable. Since the critique of his existentialism in Heidegger's 1947 "Brief über den Humanismus," Sartre had moved in the direction it had prescribed, exploring the historical dimension of Being and entering into a more fruitful dialogue with Marxism. Had he wanted or managed to enter into a dialogue with Heidegger, it could have been profitable, but he could tolerate only dead masters, and in *Questions de méthode* Jaspers is absurdly selected as the representative of existentialism, the case of Heidegger being implausibly dismissed as "too complex for treatment." Without *Sein und Zeit* Sartre could have written neither *La Nausée* nor *L'Etre et le Néant*, but the Sartre who met Heidegger wanted to turn his back on the Sartre of the thirties and forties.

Nor was he the same Sartre who had once read Marx, Lenin, and Rosa Luxemburg. The experience of rereading them after his "conversion" was quite different, and he felt bolstered in his new-found faith. As Merleau-Ponty preserved his silence, refusing to challenge this faith, it seemed inevitable that one of the other moderates on the editorial committee would soon throw down the gauntlet, but none did. It was Sartre himself who provoked a confrontation. After a number of spirited discussions with Claude Lefort, a former Trotskyite, a friend of Merleau-Ponty's, and a regular contributor to the review, Sartre invited him to formulate his arguments in an article. The article, which focused on Sartre's equation of the party with the working class, accused him of "counterrevolutionary Stalinism." In reply Sartre reiterated the points he had made in *Les Communistes et la paix.* "The party is distinct from the masses only insofar as it is the union of the masses. Through this union they create their identity." Though he had never been in the party himself, Sartre accused Lefort of bad faith in not showing his solidarity with the proletariat by joining; instead he was trying to "anchor himself in the intellectual bourgeoisie."

Either Sartre was angry or, more probably, the acrimonious tone was calculated to make it impossible for Merleau-Ponty to preserve a neutral silence. He threatened to resign unless a particularly offensive paragraph was cut.[47] Lefort's 30-page article and Sartre's 59-page reply appeared together in the April issue;[48] Merleau-Ponty's resignation followed in May after a further piece of provocation. Above an article by Pierre Naville about the "contradictions of capitalism" Merleau-Ponty wrote a caption pointing to Naville's silence about the "contradictions of socialism." Sartre removed this caption. In an impassioned argument over the telephone the two editors charged each other with abuse of power, and Merleau-Ponty never again had anything to do with the review.[49] Péju was invited to take over from Merleau-Ponty, but, modestly, he called himself general secretary of the review. He was more anti-Stalinist than Sartre and more resistant to pressure from the PCF, which frequently proposed writers and articles. Sartre, who gave Péju a free hand to say no, seemed glad not to be the one who was refusing. Nor did he try to stop Péju from publishing in the review an article he had written about Slansky (Rudolf Salzmann), the secretary general of the Czech Communist party, who had been tried for treason in November 1952 and executed.[50] (He would be rehabilitated in 1963.)

In June, Sartre was in Venice with Michelle Vian when the American government executed Julius and Ethel Rosenberg, two scientists accused of atomic spying. It was two years since they had been condemned to death, but the evidence was so unconvincing that even the Pope had joined in the international clamor for their reprieve. On the day their execution was announced, Sartre and Michelle were to meet De Beauvoir and Claude Lanzmann, who were vacationing together. Lanzmann arranged for *Libération* to publish an article on the Rosenbergs by Sartre, who shut himself up in his hotel room and gave vent to his anger by writing as if innocent people had never been executed in the Soviet Union. In January nine doctors (seven of them Jewish) had been accused of plotting to murder Zhdanov and had been tortured; their innocence had been revealed later. In Stalin's persecution of the Jews, hundreds of innocent people were vanishing, and Sartre's silence on the subject was so audible that François Mauriac took him publicly to task for it, but the killing of the Rosenbergs made him angry enough to work all day on his article. In the evening he read it to De Beauvoir, Lanzmann, and Michelle Vian, afterward rewriting it in the light of their comments.

> This is a legal lynching which covers a whole people with blood and glaringly exposes once and for all the bankruptcy of the Atlantic Pact and your incapacity to assume the leadership of the Western world. . . . You've allowed the United States to become the cradle of a new fascism . . . fascism is defined not by the number of its victims but its way of killing them . . . you have quite simply tried to stop the progress of science by a human sacrifice . . . your country is sick with fear.[51]

Aron's comment was that this text belonged to the literature of hyper-Stalinism.[52]

IT was in 1953 that Sartre began spending his summers in Rome, and it was there in July that he made his adaptation of *Kean ou Désordre et génie* (*Kean, or Chaos and Genius*), a play written for the nineteenth-century actor Frédérick Lemaître. It dates from 1836, and it was credited to Alexandre Dumas *père*, though most of the writing appears to have been done by a journeyman playwright named De Courcy, in collaboration with Lemaître. In 1951, during rehearsals of *Le Diable et le Bon Dieu*, Sartre had talked about *Kean*, and in March 1953, while he was at Saint-Tropez, Pierre Brasseur had asked him to rewrite it. Had the play been staged in its original form, it might have made the audience laugh, like a recent production of Hugo's *Hernani* that Sartre had seen. Both *Hernani* and *Kean* are good examples of heroic melodrama—a form that attracted him—but he especially liked *Kean:* its hero belongs (as Francis Jeanson has pointed out) to Sartre's line of affectionately portrayed bastards—Orestes, Hugo, Genet, and Götz.[53] He could identify with bastards, as he could with the actor "who never stops 'acting the part of himself.' " A great actor can, as Sartre put it in his program notes, "talk to the audience about his art, his private life, his difficulties and his misfortunes, but according to the rules of his profession: discreetly, modestly, that's to say by slipping into someone else's skin."[54] This is exactly what the creative writer does. "It's simultaneously a marvelous gift and a curse: he is his own victim, never knowing who he really is, whether he's acting or not." In his complicated sex life Sartre had often, during conversations with willing women and suspicious men, stepped into the no-man's-land between sincerity and deception. Though he claimed, in an interview, that conversations with Brasseur had taught him how "the actor sometimes puts on an act to deceive himself,"[55] the conversations must have reminded Sartre of himself. He could also project his hatred of the bourgeoisie onto Kean, who had "become an actor in order to escape from his resentment against society, and brought it to a kind of revolutionary force."[56] In Sartre's private behavior there were occasional manic outbreaks of rebelliousness, but a great actor more often looks like a man of action than a writer can.

Sartre liked the optimistic ending of the original play[57] and preserved all the scenes in the last act. He remodeled the consumptive heroine, Anna, who in the original play finds her cure in theater, and he made her rival, the countess, more coquettish. He tightened and deepened Kean's speeches about the glory and abjection of being an actor, and he pruned the sentimental rhetoric, but *Kean* is by no means an original play. It was to open on November 14 at the Sarah Bernhardt, with Brasseur directing as well as playing Kean. Wanda appeared as Anna with Claude Gensac as the countess. Audiences were enthusiastic.

SARTRE was still intending to finish his novel, but his intentions were compromised by his restlessness. Dislike of the political status quo sharpened his need to keep escaping from Paris. After a brief return he left again, this time for a summer tour with De Beauvoir, using an Amsterdam hotel as base. They visited museums, drove out to explore the banks of the Rhine and the Moselle, went to see what was left of the stalag on the hill above Trier where he had been a prisoner thirteen years earlier. All they found was rusty barbed wire and a few huts.[58] Alarmed to hear that Lanzmann had been in a car crash outside Cahors, they left to visit him in the hospital there. He was not badly hurt, and as soon as he recovered, the three of them went driving together, first around the Lot and the Limousin, later around Toulouse and the forest of Grésigne. Both men were tolerant of De Beauvoir's relationship with the other. Finally, alone with Sartre, she toured Brittany.[59]

As usual Sartre worked hard while on vacation, and when the book he had edited on Henri Martin was published at the end of October—by then Martin had been released—he said that his working time was being divided between his book on ethics and an autobiography.[60] The ethics had been abandoned in 1949, and though he subsequently returned to it from time to time, it is unlikely that he was intending to publish it. The autobiographical project was more serious. *Les Mots* was not published until ten years later, but most of it, Sartre says, was written in 1953.[61] His original title for it, "Jean-sans-terre" (John Lackland, the nickname for the English king John), puns challengingly on the title of Proust's autobiographical novel *Jean Santeuil,* which was not published until 1952. " 'Sans-terre' ", said Sartre, "meant: without inheritance, without possessions. That meant what I was."[62] Though it was to be abandoned later, this title points to a characterisic that was crucial. Like Genet, who swallowed the label other people had stuck on him when he became the "thief" they anathematized, Sartre made it a virtue to own nothing. In childhood he had never suffered deprivation but never felt he was in his own home with his own possessions around him; in adult life he defiantly continued in the same track. His pipe was indisputably his, but living first in hotels and then in his mother's flat, he owned neither the building nor the furniture he used. His bed was not his, and he kept few of the books he read. A private joke was involved in choosing the title "Jean-sans-terre," and after developing a negative relationship with Proust in so many of the motifs of *La Nausée,* Sartre must have been amused to read in *Jean Santeuil* that the creative writer, B, thinks it would have been pleasant to live as a philosophy teacher in a small provincial town, playing cards every evening at the café and drinking bock.[63]

Sartre's conversion had led him to a new crisis in his ambivalence toward the written word. No one can ever have taken a more sensuous pleasure in the act of penning words on paper, no one can have agonized more over indulging himself by retreating into *l'imaginaire.* Sartre felt he was preserving the present moment in the aspic of literature instead of fusing his consciousness generously with that of the group. Even when writing an activist article about a current political situation, he was failing to take direct action. But to someone so fond of the expression "loser wins," every defeat was potentially a victory; couldn't a retreat into autobiography be an advance? He could show that as a child he had been "completely mistaken about the meaning of life," show himself to have been "the plaything of circumstances," explain why it had seemed so important to become a writer.[64] Or as he put it in a later interview, "I grew up in a period when the greatest teachers of thinking were, after all, Gide and Proust, a period in fact of subjectivism and aestheticism."[65] What he intended to show in "Jean-sans-terre" was that he had been "constantly in a hurry to change, uncomfortable inside my own skin, uneasy with other people."[66] The book was not going to be limited to an account of his childhood: "I wanted to write my whole life from a political viewpoint, that's to say my childhood, my youth and middle age, giving it a political meaning in terms of my arrival at communism."[67] The book was going to be quite long—possibly two volumes, or at least one thick one.[68] But after drafting the childhood section, "I haven't at all written the childhood I wanted to write."[69] "It struck me as unbalanced. There's no reason to drag an unfortunate creature through the mud just because he writes."[70]

SINCE the death of Stalin (March 5, 1953) and the appointment of Khrushchev in September as first secretary of the Central Committee, it had been hard to predict how the Cold War would develop. A fortnight after Stalin's death, the West German Bundestag had approved the agreement about establishing a European defense community, but it was not yet in existence, and at the beginning of 1954 Sartre was taking every opportunity to denounce the idea. At the end of February he went to Knocke-le-Zoute in Belgium for a conference between Eastern and Western writers organized by the Russian-born novelist Elsa Triolet, Aragon's wife. Brecht, Anna Seghers, and Carlo Levi were there, together with several Soviet writers, who invited Sartre to Moscow in May. After the conference had agreed on the text of an appeal to prepare the way for a much larger meeting, Brecht caused consternation by proposing they should incorporate in the appeal a protest against the American atomic test (March 1) at Bikini in the Marshall Islands. Instead the signatories pledged themselves to make their works consistent with their "will to peace" and to "combat war" in their writing.

Sartre's contribution was to go on with *Les Communistes et la paix* in *Les Temps Modernes*. The third installment had its roots in the intuitive judgment that had made Sartre link the events of December 1851, as Guillemin described them, with the arrest of Jacques Duclos. Sartre draws interestingly on reading he had done during the last few years about the French Revolution and French nineteenth-century history, consulting books of memoirs and books on agriculture. Had the mentality of the rightists changed since 1851? If the strike of June 1953 had failed, there must be a historical explanation for the workers' apathy, and, stimulated by Guillemin, Sartre began to search for it.

In writing social and economic history he is polemical and unscholarly. Before the rising of 1848, he says, there had been only two classes in France—the bourgeoisie and the animals; the humanity of the workers had been denied. During the June days, when General Cavaignac led troops against the Paris workmen, fifteen hundred people were shot; in 1871, during the week of the Commune's defeat, twenty thousand people were shot. "Everywhere else the working class is starved; only in France has it been bled. The proletarian of 1886 sells his labor to the men who have killed his father or his older brothers."[71] Sartre musters evidence to show that class war has been waged, literally. "The secret of the working class is that it holds the French bourgeoisie to be a gang of criminals."[72]

He writes about the bourgeoisie as if it had a collective consciousness and as if its collective will had consistently been articulated in the government's economic policy. Successive governments, he says, concerned less to enrich France than to weaken the proletariat, have deliberately depressed the economy. "Economic Malthusianism" is his term for the underproduction designed to demoralize and impoverish the workers. The unskilled are especially vulnerable, being interchangeable. Strike action is therefore ineffectual unless organized on a large scale, while the division of the proletariat between skilled and unskilled workers makes it easier for the bourgeoisie to retain control. If the proletariat (unlike the bourgeoisie) has no collective consciousness, working-class unity can be achieved only when imposed from outside.[73] The masses have no defense except through mass action; they must be organized into one movement, into obeying one word of command.[74] "When everything is linked, Malthusianism and misery, inflation of prices, rearmament and Marshallization, to reject the Communist Party's policy is to carry out that of the government."[75]

There is no space in *Les Communistes et la paix* for the sympathy Sartre had shown in "La Dernière chance" toward men too "stupid" to resist indoctrination. His sympathy for the abused soldiers in his novel derived from experience; his sympathy for factory workers is more perfunctory and theoretical. "Each man perceives the existence of his neighbors in the form of the collective rhythm to which he must adapt himself . . . the semiautomatic machine is the instrument *par excellence* for massification."[76] "Massification" involves dehumanization. "To the extent that massification engenders at once isolation and interchangeability, it gives birth to imitation as a mechanical relationship between the molecules."[77] Though the values of the working class are valid for the whole of humanity, the only valid viewpoint is that of the most deprived. The masses are the object of history.[78] The militant works to transform the "masses object" into the "proletariat subject." His aim is "to liquidate their granular structure in favor of an organic unity."[79] Here Sartre is laying himself open to a charge that was to be leveled against him two years later by Merleau-Ponty: "If the workers are nothing, not even proletarians, until they create the party, the party rests on nothing which has been established—not even the history they have in common."[80] Sartre, says Merleau-Ponty, was falling back on the model he had evolved for *L'Etre et le Néant*, equating the activist with the active For-itself and the masses with the inert In-itself.

Sartre's essay, which occupied eighty-eight pages in the April 1954 issue of the review, appears to have been written in less of a hurry than the first two essays: it is carefully thought out, and it has more research behind it than most of his political writing. Though he seldom mentions his sources, he quotes a great many statistics, and he had delved deeply into the history of the French working-class movement. Generally he had been doing too much, and his blood pressure was too high. The doctor recommended a long rest in the country,[81] but Sartre habitually ignored doctors and until leaving for the Soviet Union at the end of May, kept himself extremely busy, hitting out energetically at government policy. An editorial note published in the May issue renewed his attack on the atrocities perpetrated in the Indochina war. "If it is forbidden to call Bidault [the foreign minister] a criminal, we shall call him a very guilty man; if we are prevented from speaking of the blood on his hands, we shall speak of the scales over his eyes."[82] Sartre also wrote prefaces for the catalogue of a Giacometti exhibition and for Cartier-Bresson's book of photographs taken in China. He wrote a protest in *Libération* about the banning of the Soviet ballet ("Next year, M. Lamiel, Ulanova will still be dancing, but you will no longer be President of the Council").[83] He attended a meeting organized by the CNE in a suburban Renault factory, where he spoke to the workers about torture as described by Julius Fucik in his book about Communist militants in a Czech prison during 1942–43.[84] Working on the Cartier-Bresson preface, Sartre had to stay up for several nights, and on the way to Moscow he stopped in Berlin to make a speech at a meeting held by the peace movement.[85]

From the window of his Moscow hotel bedroom he watched the parade in Red Square celebrating the anniversary of the Ukraine's integration into the USSR in May 1923. The program arranged for him was strenuous. The sight-seeing included visits to the university and to factories. At the dacha of the writer Konstantin Simonov he had to survive a four-hour banquet with wine from Armenia and Georgia as well as twenty toasts in vodka. He traveled by train to Leningrad, where he was driven around the city for four hours, and after an hour's rest, he had to spend four hours in the Palace of Culture. The next day, which was no less full, ended in an evening at the ballet. After returning to Moscow, he was flown to Uzbekistan. He was scheduled to travel with

Ilya Ehrenburg to Stockholm for a meeting of the peace movement, but instead he was taken to a hospital[86] and detained for ten days, treated for hypertension and an excessive intake of alcohol.

After he returned to Paris on June 24, still exhausted, he gave *Libération* an enthusiastic report of his impressions. The interview was published in five installments under such captions as "Freedom of criticism is complete in the USSR and the Soviet citizen is continually improving his condition in the bosom of a society making nonstop progress."[87] "I met a new breed of men." It was impossible "not to think of them as friends." In the USSR, he reported, one was "conscious of the incessant and harmonious progress in both private life and social life. Individual and collective interests coincide." Except for some reservations about Soviet architecture, he was blandly uncritical about the USSR, and when the journalists Pierre and Hélène Lazareff, who had been in Russia at roughly the same time, reacted less enthusiastically in *France-Soir,* Sartre tried to discredit them in one of the *Libération* interviews,[88] while at some level, perhaps, he was trying to refute André Gide. Sartre was aware that there was as much oppression and deviousness in the Soviet Union, and as little justice and democracy, as in 1936, but the truth mattered less than the commitment to befriend Communists. Twenty years later Sartre would claim that what had been printed as a series of interviews with him had actually been written by Jean Cau: "I gave him a certain number of main points." Sartre now conceded that what he had seen in the USSR "did not fill me with enthusiasm. . . . I had a lot of reservations."[89]

Recuperating in Italy with Michelle, he tried to work on his autobiography but made little headway.[90] An event, though, that vastly strengthened his positive feelings toward Italy was a meeting with the veteran leader of the Communist party, Palmiro Togliatti, who had worked with Gramsci. They had started the weekly *Ordine nuovo* together in 1919 and then had founded the national Communist party in 1921. Unlike Maurice Thorez, the French leader, Togliatti was not stolidly submissive to Stalinism. For the next ten years his ideas would be filtered sympathetically to French leftists through *Les Temps Modernes,* especially after 1956, when Togliatti formulated the principle of "polycentrism." Instead of having a single center, international communism should have several—Moscow, Peking, Havana, and so on. The idea was anathema to Thorez, who in any case would not have wanted Rome to be seen as the center of European communism.

One meeting was enough to make Sartre think of Togliatti as his friend, but he did not stay long in Rome. Repeating the pattern of the previous summer, he returned to Paris, only to leave again in De Beauvoir's car for a second trip with her. In the Strasbourg hotel where they spent their first night he still seemed exhausted. "For a long time he stayed sitting in his chair, hands on his knees, back slumped, eyes blank"; in the restaurant where they had dinner, he told her that literature was shit.[91]

They drove through Alsace and the Black Forest to Munich and Salzburg. By now he was feeling energetic enough to start working again. After a week of excursions to the surrounding countryside, revisiting the lakes and mountains, they went on to Vienna, where he had banned the production of *Les Mains sales.* The contract had been signed without consulting him, and after intervening to ban the production, he told a press conference how the play had been exploited by the anti-Communists.

IN December he accepted the vice-chairmanship of the Franco-Soviet Association, which was closely linked to the Comintern, and in February 1955 spoke at a meeting commemorating the victory at Stalingrad. The British and the Americans, he declared, had been given too much credit for winning the war: it was the Soviet victory at Stalingrad that had made the Normandy landing possible and necessary. One lesson to be learned from it was that "it would be dangerous to differentiate between the Russian people and its leaders." Their popularity was demonstrated by the courage and goodwill of the soldiers. "The people have created their régime and they are inseparable from it." A second lesson was that France needed to go on being Russia's ally; it would be absurd to rearm Germany against the country that had sided with the French in both world wars.[92]

Though Sartre was unstinting in the time he lavished on left-wing causes, he had no intention of abandoning biography, and he was launched on the biggest of all his projects by a conversation with Roger Garaudy, who had been on the PCF's Central Committee since 1945. Garaudy maintained that to understand an individual or a group, the Marxist perspective was indispensable.[93] Why had no one written a Marxist biography? Sartre became excited. Why shouldn't Marxism take over psychoanalysis? After all, an individual's upbringing could condemn him to repeat the history of his family or the history of society.[94] In *Saint Genet* Sartre had already attempted a comprehensive statement about one man, dovetailing Freudian and Marxian insights, but Flaubert, the writer who filled Sartre with the most stimulating mixture of love and hatred, would provide a better focus for investigating the damage inflicted by a characteristic bourgeois family. It had long been inevitable that sooner or later Sartre would start a biography of Flaubert; the interesting question is whether it was inevitable that he would leave it unfinished. During the spring he did some research, quickly completing a first draft.

Early in 1955 he took another working vacation, driving down to Marseille with De Beauvoir and Lanzmann. A summit conference of Britain, France, the US, and the USSR was to be held at Geneva in the early summer, and in the climate of détente Sartre felt anxious about the influence of the right-wing press. In the play *Nekrassov* his object was to undermine anti-Communist propaganda. He was remembering his pledge at the Belgium conference to "combat war" in his writing; he may also have been remembering the practical joke at the ENS in 1927, when a student's impersonation of Lindbergh forced Lanson to resign. In the play a confidence trickster impersonates Nekrassov, a Soviet minister, making it seem that he has defected, and in their mindless crusade against communism the directors of a Paris evening newspaper lap up the information he feeds them. This is the most Shavian of Sartre's plays, with no semblance of free will in the characters, who are mostly caricatures, brusquely manipulated according to the needs of the far-fetched plot. Like *Le Diable et le Bon Dieu, Nekrassov* is designed to express an attitude toward society, but Sartre's dramatic technique derived from the bourgeois theater he wanted to reject. As a theatrical storyteller he was far from incompetent, but, wisely, he had never attempted comedy or farce. A good satire could have been written about the relationships between management and journalists in the right-wing papers, but not by Sartre. He was uncertain about how to divide the focus between the confidence trickster and the newspapers, while anger made him heavy-handed.

Again he gave his play to Simone Berriau for production at the Théâtre Antoine; again the script was unfinished when rehearsals began. The director was Jean Meyer, who had worked mainly in the Comédie Française. Michel Vitold played the confidence trickster, with Chauffard as a police inspector. Wanda had a role as the Communist daughter of an anti-Communist journalist. The atmosphere at rehearsals was overcast by political disagreement as well as by the usual arguments about the exorbitant length of Sartre's script. Several of the actors withdrew. The date of the opening had to be postponed more than once, and public controversy broke before the premiere on June 8. On that evening a hostile tract was distributed by a group calling itself the "free circle of Russian studies." Though the Communist papers supported the play, most of the reviewers were hostile, and the production ran for only sixty performances.

In one way Sartre benefited from the short run. Michel Vitold, who had played Garcin both in the 1944 premiere of *Huis clos* and in the 1946 revival, as well as directing *Morts sans sépulture* and *La Putain respectueuse* in 1946, had an insatiable appetite for Sartrian drama. Whetted again, it made him want a third go at Garcin, though the play had been revived only two years previously at the Comédie Caumartin, with Gaby Sylvia. For the 1955 revival Vitold had Judith Magre as Inès, while Claude Lanzmann's beautiful sister, Evelyne Rey, was Estelle. Together with her husband, the writer Rezvani, and her lover, Claude Roy, Sartre was to become one of the most important men in her life, while she was to become—until her suicide—one of the most important women in his—a mistress, like Wanda, for whom he wrote plays. She never ceased to be touched and surprised by his combination of humility and gratitude on receiving sexual favors.[95]

AT the end of June he traveled with De Beauvoir to Helsinki for an eight-day congress of the peace movement. There were representatives from all over the world. During one of the lunch breaks Georg Lukács started a discussion about liberty, telling Sartre, who listened politely, about the historical conditioning of the individual.[96] But the writer who behaved most like a cultural commissar was Ilya Ehrenburg, who instructed Sartre not to be too militant about the US when making his speech: the Kremlin wanted conciliation.[97] Speaking on the twenty-sixth, the fifth day of the conference, Sartre obediently appealed for cooperation between the US and the USSR and for economic aid to underdeveloped countries. Peace and liberty were synonymous; nations must respect each other's independence.[98]

CARTIER-BRESSON's photographs of China had served as an introduction to the country; in the early summer Sartre and De Beauvoir received an invitation and finally went in September, arriving on the sixth, to spend two months there. In the USSR the name Sartre was not completely unknown; in China, after reports in the newspapers that he had written a life of Nekrassov, people assumed he was the biographer of the nineteenth-century Russian poet.[99] The People's Republic of China had been proclaimed on October 1, 1949; on October 1, 1955, nearly four weeks after his arrival, Sartre watched the anniversary parade in Peking; he was presented to Mao Tse-tung but with no chance of having a conversation.

The population of China was 600 million, and even to the visitor from the West the country's poverty was immediately apparent, though the predominant impression was one of cleanliness and health. If until shortly beforehand, conditions had encouraged vermin and the spread of disease, while the majority of people had been undernourished and inadequately dressed, the revolution had established hygiene and stability. Sartre was impressed by the prevailing calm and the moderation of the army, which appeared to be totally in control. The revolution, he concluded, had "begun by ridding China of inflation, misery and rising prices, insecurity, anarchy and local despotism."[100] But stability was not stasis: "The present reality of China is its future. . . . One of us was saying: 'In China you feel already dead.' This is often true, because the most tangible reality is a future which the young will see, and we certainly shan't."[101]

Having spent a day in Moscow on the way out, he and De Beauvoir stayed there a week on the way back. Compared with the socialist reconstruction in China, the rebuilding in the USSR looked highly mechanized.[102] They visited monasteries, churches, schools, and theaters, seeing Gorki's *The Lower Depths* and Mayakovsky's *The Bedbug*.[103] At Simonov's suggestion Sartre addressed a conference of Soviet critics about the critic's role.[104]

FRANCE'S Algerian troubles had begun in November 1954 when the nationalist Front de Libération Nationale (FLN) launched an armed insurrection. Algeria was legally integral to France—under the interior minister's jurisdiction. Only about 10 percent of the nine million people in the country were white, but as in South Africa, the minority dominated. The Arabs had few legal rights and little economic power. The injustice of the situation was obvious, but in France not even the Communists advocated Algerian independence. The left favored reforms, but government policy was to crush the rebellion by military force.

Les Temps Modernes had been critical of French colonialism in North Africa before the rebellion, and in October 1955 the editorial sided with the rebels: the Algerians associated French rule with repression, racism, and torture. Sartre warned Péju not to go too far in supporting the FLN,[105] but the November issue came out explicitly in favor of Algerian independence. By then a group of intellectuals had started an information center, which published evidence that rebels were being tortured, while thousands of Arabs had been interned in camps.

At the beginning of 1956 it did not look as though the war would drag on for more than six years. In the elections of January 2, 1956, the left-wing Front Républicain gained a majority, and making his inaugural speech on January 31, the new Socialist premier, Guy Mollet, called the war "cruel and insane." Four days earlier, at a protest meeting in the Salle Wagram, Sartre condemned France for using the nineteenth-century economic machinery of colonial exploitation; the only possible line of action was to support the Algerian fight against tyranny.[106]

When a young friend who was doing his military service had been drafted to Morocco, Sartre advised him not to desert. "You must go there and work. Do agitprop among your soldier comrades."[107] But in Algeria, Sartre favored desertion. Camus took the opposite line: he supported the French presence in his native country. This damaged his prestige among progressive intellectuals and posthumously damaged his worldwide reputation. In the United States, for instance, his stock was to sink in the sixties as Sartre's rose. Sartre was least popular there when aligning himself with the PCF, as he was doing in 1956.

But in 1956 he was condemning himself for having supported the RDR. The distance he had traveled ideologically since his involvement with the RDR was apparent when Pierre Hervé, a leading Communist intellectual, published a short book, *La Révolution et les fétiches,* attacking the party bureaucracy and making points similar to those Sartre had made during 1948 in *Entretiens sur la politique,* condemning the party's dogmatism and its undemocratic procedures. As if to demonstrate its intolerance of internal criticism, the PCF expelled Hervé on February 14, 1956. Sartre's article, which is dated four days earlier, makes the point that Hervé was exposing himself to the risk of expulsion in "addressing himself to a popular front of the future," and it maintains that if Hervé is making a mistake, he is making it in good faith. His expulsion "would be deplorable."[108] "He's an idealist? A reformist? Undeniably. But we all hope his opponents will discuss it [the book]."[109] Marxism does not need to be on the defensive now that the bourgeoisie is on the retreat: "Faced with Marxism, its ideas die without the Marxists' having to raise a little finger."[110] This was the moment for Marxism to expand, outflank the last bourgeois philosophies, interpret them, "smash their shell and incorporate their substance."[111] Georges Politzer had formulated a Marxist critique of psychoanalysis, proposing an alternative, "concrete psychology" based on economic determinism. "Since the very interesting studies by Politzer, psychology has been stagnant."[112] Sartre took the opportunity of mentioning that he was at work on a biography which would bring psychoanalysis inside a Marxist framework.

But the painstaking intellectuality of his approach did not stop him from betraying intellectuals during his love affair with the party. His panegyrics made it look as though he was on the point of joining: "Transported by history, the Communist Party manifests an extraordinary objective intelligence. It makes few mistakes; it does what it must do; but this intelligence—which gets confused with *praxis*—is not often embodied in its intellectuals."[113] What was needed was a living Marxism, free from the dogmatism that inhibits movement; it should have been possible for philosophers, economists, "ethnographers," psychologists to undertake specific research and then contribute their findings to the party. As it was, Marxism, instead of developing, was repeating itself; "Marxism has stopped."[114]

In retrospect the PCF's expulsion of Hervé looks all the sillier for coinciding with Khrushchev's astonishingly explicit condemnation of Stalin's "bloody crimes" at the twentieth party congress. The Kremlin's slow movement toward tolerance seemed to have gathered momentum, and suddenly, three years after the dictator's death, the word "Stalinism" could be used, like a trash can, for collecting everything that did not match the new décor. Stalin could be blamed for the "cult of personality" and for the assumption that armed conflict was inevitable. It was not. Imperialism could wither peacefully away; each nation had the right to find its own route to socialism.

It is possible that Sartre actually wrote his article after the expulsion and after Khrushchev's speech but retrospectively dated it February 10 to make it look as if he had anticipated both. Sartre's plea for an expansionist Marxism is oddly in tune with Khrushchev's attitude, and even if the article followed the speech, Sartre was much faster than the PCF to pick up Moscow's cue. At the end of March *L'Humanité* reprinted a *Pravda* attack on Stalin, but there was nothing conciliatory in the speeches at the PCF's national party congress in Le Havre, and speaking in Grenoble, Duclos defended Stalin,[115] as did Courtade in *L'Humanité*, putting the blame on Beria. When the Trotskyite Pierre Naville attacked Sartre in March, he seemed to be expressing the views of the party. His articles, which appeared in *France-Observateur*, denied that Marxism had stopped and condemned Sartre's equation of it with the party. Sartre replied in *Les Temps Modernes* (March-April), and Naville wrote a second piece in *France-Observateur* (April 19). In July, speaking at the fourteenth party congress, Garaudy mentioned Sartre's article but denied that Hervé's deviancy had been provoked by party dogmatism.[116] Hervé quickly wrote a new book, *Lettre à Sartre*, claiming Khrushchev as an ally.

Dividing himself between political controversy and journeyman writing, Sartre was working between November 1955 and May 1956 on a screen version of Arthur Miller's play *The Crucible,* which linked McCarthyite witch-hunting in the US with witch-hunting in seventeenth-century Salem. Marcel Aymé's adaptation, which had been produced in the theater under the title *Les Sorcières de Salem,* irritated Sartre, who not only made the social and political issues more explicit but introduced a strong element of class conflict, building up the role of the deputy governor, Danforth. Raymond Rouleau, who had directed the play, also directed the film, playing Danforth himself and using the same actors who had played the leading parts—most effectively—on the stage: Yves Montand (John Proctor), Simone Signoret (Elisabeth), and Mylène Demongeot, who had taken over from Nicole Courcel as Abigail. For the screenplay Sartre received six thousand francs from the producer, Bernard Borderie.[117]

In March he met a nineteen-year-old Jewish Algerian girl, Arlette El Kaïm, who had written to him from Versailles, where she was studying *L'Etre et le Néant.* She was writing a thesis on injustice for the competitive entrance examination to the Ecole Normale Supérieure in Sèvres. Although his affair with Evelyne Rey had begun only a short while earlier, Arlette was soon to become sexually involved with him.

At the end of the month he went to Venice for a colloquium organized by the Société Européenne de Culture, an organization founded six years earlier to establish rapport between intellectuals from eastern and western European countries. Britain was represented by Stephen Spender, J. D. Bernal, and Alan Pryce-Jones. When Sartre took his seat he noticed on the empty chair next to him a card with the name Merleau-Ponty on it. When Merleau-Ponty arrived, late, during a speech, he tiptoed behind Sartre, touching him lightly on the shoulder and then smiling.[118] One of the British speakers was so naïve that Sartre and Merleau-Ponty were equally exasperated, and they spent some of the evenings together, though never alone and not without a certain awkwardness.[119] During the session on March 26, when Merleau-Ponty spoke about the "thaw," Sartre insisted that the Communist half of the world was no more frozen than the Western half. We too should be asking ourselves how we are going to unfreeze, and we had no right to ask "people in possession of a cultural ideology such as Marxism to accept a truth belonging to another ideological system without trying to see how that truth can be integrated into Marxism."[120] It was too easy for us to forget that all our ideas were conditioned by bourgeois ideology.[121] The two men argued at some length: while Merleau-Ponty favored coexistence and mutual tolerance, Sartre maintained that "coexistence can only be a dynamic movement of integration."[122] Discussing psychoanalysis, Sartre argued that in Marxist hands it could become "a disci-

pline allied to sociology and economics"; Merleau-Ponty retorted that
first the Marxists would have to take psychoanalysis seriously, without
devaluing it or calling it a bourgeois ideology. Sartre maintained that it
was a bourgeois ideology and could cease to be one only if released from
its limits and negations by being absorbed into a totality.[123]

Throughout the spring and early summer the thaw seemed to be
proceeding. In April, Khrushchev dissolved the Cominform and, together with Marshal Bulganin, the Russian premier, paid a ten-day
visit to Britain. In June, Marshal Tito's visit to Moscow was followed
by a Soviet-Pakistani trade pact, but by the end of the month the cau-
tion of the PCF seemed to be vindicated. The rising of June 17, 1953, in
East Berlin had occurred just over three months after Stalin's death,
when the thaw had hardly begun; it led to the June 1956 risings in Poland and Hungary, and these led to the end of the thaw. In Budapest,
Matyas Rákosi, who had served Stalin loyally, had remained as first
secretary during the liberalizing régime of Imre Nagy (1953–55) and
had regained control of the country in 1955. Criticism of Rákosi culminated toward the end of June, when journalists who had been
branded as "bourgeois" were being rehabilitated, while intellectuals
were clamoring for freedom of expression and the return of Nagy. In
Poland the shortage of food led to disturbances. On June 28 thousands
of metalworkers in Poznan went on strike, demanding bread. When the
police fired on the crowds, forty-eight workers were killed. According to
the PCF, the riot had been provoked by foreign agents.

Sartre made no public comment before leaving Paris for his summer
vacation with Michelle, De Beauvoir, and Lanzmann. Setting off in two
cars, they drove to Venice, where they stayed two days before going on
to Belgrade. In Yugoslavia collectivization had caused widespread
hardship, which was obvious even when driving along country roads
between Belgrade and Skopje.[124] After crossing the frontier into Greece,
Sartre and Michelle stayed in Salonika, while De Beauvoir and Lanzmann went on to Athens. Michelle drove Sartre to Rome, where the
others eventually joined them. The four of them spent a few days together in Naples, Amalfi, and Paestum, and when Lanzmann took the
train back to Paris, the others stayed in Rome, remaining there till the
end of October, reading in Italian newspapers about events in Poland.
In September the Poznan trial began, accompanied by riots and demonstrations. Sentences were lenient, but the people, no longer unable to
hope for democracy and independence, went on pressing for the withdrawal of Soviet troops, for workers' management in industry, for the
slowing down of collectivization. Wladyslaw Gomulka, who had been
forced to resign as leader of the Polish Communist party in 1948 and

had been released from prison in 1955, regained a place on the Central Committee, where he demanded the dismissal of all pro-Soviet leaders. Khrushchev was in Warsaw as Russian tanks began to bear down on the city; Gomulka was arming workers and preparing Polish troops to fight against the Russians when Khrushchev abruptly decided against violent confrontation, leaving Gomulka in control of the country.

In Hungary violence was not avoided. Rákosi had been dismissed in July, but when Andras Hegedüs, who had replaced Nagy as premier, was offered the job of first secretary, he declined: it would have required a "ruthlessness and militancy I did not possess."[125] Lenin said that the precondition for a successful revolution is present when popular discontent coincides with a failure of confidence in the ruling class. This was true of Budapest. In October, hungry for the freedom that was within reach if only the Soviet overlords behaved as they had in Poland, students began to demonstrate. Soon they were joined by armed factory workers, and so many Hungarian soldiers sided with the rebels that the Soviet commanders, unable to control the rising, signed an armistice. Hegedüs, who had been living in dread of a popular uprising, was flown to safety in Moscow, while Nagy, who was reinstated, asked for Hungary to be given the same neutral status as Austria. If only the West had supported him, the Kremlin might have given in, but a presidential election campaign was under way in the United States, while Britain and France were preoccupied with the Suez Canal, which had been seized in July by the uncompromising Colonel Nasser, just over a month after he had been elected president of Egypt. At the end of October, while Soviet troops were invading northeastern Hungary, French and British planes were dropping bombs on Egyptian airfields. On November 2 the Hungarian government renounced the Warsaw Treaty and appealed to the United Nations, but two days later, when Soviet forces attacked Budapest, Nagy had to take refuge in the Yugoslav Embassy.

Sartre's loyalty to the Soviet Union did not evaporate overnight. "If the USSR is worth no more and no less than capitalist England, then there is really nothing for us to do except cultivate our garden."[126] On his return from Italy, Sartre was appalled by the reaction of the PCF, which had congratulated the Soviet Union on its action, while party newspapers used such phrases as "dogs of the fallen classes" and "Versaillais" to describe the Hungarians who had attempted a "fascist putsch."[127] Sartre finally committed himself on November 4. In an interview with *L'Express* he condemned the Soviet aggression as "a crime," which "had been made possible and perhaps necessary (from the Soviet viewpoint) by twelve years of terror and imbecility. . . . What the Hungarian people is teaching us with its blood is the complete failure of socialism as merchandise imported from the USSR." America should not have tried to interfere with the construction of socialism in the "satellite" countries, but the main culprit was Khrushchev. Without being able to raise Soviet living standards, he had catalogued in detail the misdeeds of "a holy personality who has represented the régime for so long." The Kremlin was now being run by "a group (army "hawks," old Stalinists?) which is outdoing Stalinism after denouncing it." Sartre was breaking off his relationships with the Soviet writers who didn't (or couldn't) denounce the aggression against Hungary and with the present leaders of the PCF. "All their comments, all their actions are the outcome of thirty years of lying and sclerosis," while the reports in L'Humanité were "repugnant lies." For Sartre it would never again be possible to have relations with the leaders of the PCF, though he had no quarrel with "all the sincere and honest men of the left, even those who stay in the party."[128] He resigned from the Franco-Soviet Association but stayed in the peace movement and in the CNE, though he was not satisfied with the wording of the protest produced by the Communist president, Aragon.[129]

Sartre was now released from the hidden embarrassment involved in giving unqualified support to the PCF, as he had for nearly five years. Instead of completing Les Communistes et la paix, which had appeared in Les Temps Modernes with "A suivre" ("To be continued") at the end of the third essay, he published "Le Fantôme de Staline," which is better than any piece of political journalism he had previously written. Disciplining himself into voicing no public disapproval of the USSR, he had battened down a great deal of energy, which was now released in a vigorous attempt to understand the causes of the Hungarian rising and the Soviet reaction. Confronting truths he had evaded, Sartre struggled openly with the difficulties of taking a position. The tension is apparent in his prose, which is less flabby and less rhetorical than in Les Communistes et la paix. He is still writing too quickly, but he approximates more closely to reproducing the flow of his thinking.

For help in reconstructing what had happened in Hungary he was indebted to François Fetjö, author of La Tragédie hongroise ou Une Révolution socialiste antisoviétique, which came out before the end of the year, with a preface by Sartre praising Fetjö's objectivity in the book and in his many articles about Hungary. Ignoring the will of the Hungarian people, the Soviet Union had "criminally overindustrialized" the country while collectivizing agriculture.[130] In Russia the revolutionaries had understood that socialism was inseparable from economic planning: a balance had to be struck between the long-term interests of socialist construction and the natural appetite of the working class for a higher standard of living.[131] But it had been a mistake, characteristic of Stalinism, to impose homologous economies on all the "people's democracies" of Central Europe, and in Hungary the Soviet intervention had been followed by a general strike, which showed the world that the Red Army was the enemy of the Hungarian workers.[132]

Hungary was still in ferment while Sartre was writing—in the resistance, which continued till mid-December, between twenty and fifty thousand Hungarians were killed—and before the essay was published in January 1957, Sartre added a footnote to challenge the decision by the new premier, János Kádár, to quash the workers' councils: "What is this socialism which is bent on destroying organs of control elected by the proletariat?"[133] Writing about the worker in bourgeois society, Marx had argued that his revolutionary force came from "the contradiction between his human *nature* and his actual life, which is the manifest, decisive and total rejection of that nature."[134] In Hungary overindustrialization and enforced collectivization had produced a contradiction that was no less ferocious. The Kremlin had loosened its undemocratic grip on Poland; why not allow Budapest a "Hungarian Gomulkism"?[135]

Though he knew how simplistic it was to hold Stalin personally responsible for everything that had gone wrong with the Soviet system, Sartre was quick to exploit the new words "Stalinism" and "de-Stalinization." Dictatorship, he argued, might have been unavoidable while the Soviet Union was in danger of being destroyed by Western nuclear bombs, but not now when the Kremlin could negotiate from a position of strength.[136] The Hungarian rising could have been avoided if Nagy had been recalled in 1955 or even at the beginning of October 1956; what had made it inevitable was the "explosive mixture in the bosom of the party itself of a Stalinism that is still aggressive with partisans of de-Stalinization."[137] Temporarily the neo-Stalinist faction had gained control.[138] What angered Sartre most was the damage that had been done to the cause. Instead of exploiting the opportunity to win popularity, Nagy and the Kremlin had made the Red Army look oppressive.[139]

On November 7 Sarte and De Beauvoir signed a letter affirming friendship for the USSR and for socialism but condemning the use of guns and tanks in Hungary. Socialism could never be achieved at bayonet point. The letter was also signed by Vercors as well as by leading French Communist intellectuals—Claude Roy, Roger Vailland, J. F. Rolland and Claude Morgan.[140] On the following day the directing committee of the CNE (including Sartre and Aragon) issued an open appeal to Kádár for the protection of Hungarian writers. But in the

Soviet Union intellectuals were supporting the régime. Thirty-five Russian writers publicly condemned the French writers' protest. When the national council of the peace movement met in December, Sartre and other non-Communists managed to pass a resolution calling for the Russian troops to withdraw.[141] But he was still as hostile as ever toward the anti-Communists. What should the French *gauchistes* do? Unity without the PCF was impotence; unity against it could lead to fascism; unity with it was impossible. Unless a new popular front could be formed, there would be no way of saving France from its "colonial cancers," its Malthusian economy, and its involvement in NATO.[142] In the meantime, the way to work constructively was to work for the de-Stalinization of the PCF.[143]

On November 21 Rolland was expelled from the PCF, while the other three members who had signed the letter were publicly censured and subsequently kept under close surveillance. In March 1957 Roy's membership was suspended. *L'Humanité* welcomed the Kádár government: "Popular power is reestablished solidly."[144]

PART V

TOWARD REVOLUTION

(1957–68)

(19)

Back to Philosop~~h~~

SINCE the beginning of 1952, when he had taken his oath of lifelong hatred against the bourgeoisie and had agreed to work with the PCF on the Henri Martin affair, Sartre had written little except *Les Communistes et la paix, Nekrassov,* and a quick first draft of the Flaubert biography. In his confrontations with Camus, Lefort, and Hervé he had expressed himself through long essays in *Les Temps Modernes,* but never before had his motivations been so unliterary. His priority had been to protest, to campaign, to condemn, supporting the FLN and the ideal of world peace as presented at international conferences organized by the Communists, while denouncing NATO and the European Defense Community.

Now, after condemning the repressive Soviet action in Hungary, he became more tolerant neither toward colonial repression nor toward the United States. His support for the FLN was to continue, but for nearly six years he did not visit the Soviet Union. He was no less concerned with Marxism, but, never unambitious, he was intending to change it. Between the 1954 conversation with Roger Garaudy and the March 1956 confrontation with Merleau-Ponty at the Venice conference, Sartre had gone on thinking and talking about a Marxist takeover bid for psychoanalysis, and this intention underlies the two major books he was yet to write, his *Critique de la raison dialectique* and his Flaubert biography. He was not exactly retreating into writing. He was still campaigning but on different ground.

Strongly in sympathy with the opposition inside the Communist world, he often encountered Polish intellectuals in Paris, and during November he was invited to the Polish Embassy, where he met the editor of the review *Twórczość,* Jerzy Lisowski, who was planning a French issue. He invited Sartre to write about the situation of existentialism in 1957. Henri Lefebvre had been asked to discuss developments in French

. Sartre had been feeling inclined to associate the word "exis-
__ism" with "a past, peripheral cultural fashion, not unlike a par-
_cular brand of soap,"[1] but he agreed to write an essay, which he called
"Marxism and Existentialism." His play *Les Mouches* was currently
being rehearsed in Poland, and he attended the premiere in January
1957. The February-March issue of *Les Temps Modernes* was a Polish
issue, collecting articles, reports, and verse published in Polish papers
since 1954: "Here we finally see what should exist, what can exist today
and will exist tomorrow—a communism freed from Stalinism."[2]

In France the government was hardly troubling to deny that Algerians were being tortured, raped, plundered. There were executions
without a trial, ruthless and arbitrary reprisals against the civilian population. Over a year had passed since the abbé Gau, an MRP deputy,
had made a speech in the Assembly denouncing police methods as
"worthy of the Gestapo." In 1956, when the FLN leader Ahmed Ben
Bella had been kidnapped in a Moroccan plane by the French secret
services, Premier Mollet had retrospectively given his approval. By
1957 about 400,000 French servicemen were being deployed in Algeria
to maintain the peace, venting on the unfortunate Algerians the spleen
that had accumulated out of frustration and defeat in Vietnam. The
French government made only perfunctory attempts to discipline the
army; the real power was in the hands of the settlers' leaders and their
administration, controlled by the unscrupulous minister-resident Robert Lacoste. In the second week of April, Sartre described French
methods of "pacification" in "Une entreprise de démoralisation," an
article commissioned by *Le Monde*. He seized the opportunity of reaching a wide public, cogently accusing the French people of complicity.
When the article was rejected, he published it in *Les Temps Modernes*.[3]
Though he had always been anticolonialist, he was not so closely in
touch with the Algerians as Francis Jeanson, who had distanced himself
from Sartre after "Le Fantôme de Staline," considering it to be too
anti-Soviet. Jeanson had worked in Algeria during the war and had
many Moslem friends.[4] Siding wholeheartedly with the FLN, he started
a clandestine paper, *Vérités pour* . . .

Sartre was in the process of trying to make himself into a humanist.
Fifteen years later he would say: "Today the new style of intellectual
must give everything to the people."[5] Sixteen years earlier he had admitted: "I don't like men—I mean the male of the species. . . . For me
there is a half of the human race which scarcely exists."[6] Now, at the
age of fifty-one, he was always ready—at once self-denying and indulgent toward his appetite for self-denial—to leave his desk for a demonstration or a political meeting. He was less ready to leave it for long

sessions of gossip with friends in cafés. To the end of his life he would go on spending a great deal of time with the female of the species, but he was no longer interested in writing novels or short stories about personal relationships. In biography and even in autobiography his aim was to look beyond the individual to the social pressure. Talking in June 1957 about the book which was to become *Les Mots,* he said that he was trying to view himself as a member of a group. "My own experience can be significant to the extent that it can be that of a crowd of people who resemble me . . . intellectuals of the Third and Fourth republics. . . . In what you see as something rich and original I am constrained no longer to see anything more than one manifestation among others of a certain intellectual of a certain type."[7] It is hard to picture a crowd of people who resemble Sartre, but he was trying to escape from self-involvement, at the same time indulging a drive he had in common with Tintoretto: "that diligent and almost sadistic violence I call the full employment of oneself."

With his phenomenal energy and his greedy, sensual enjoyment of writing, he produced what he knew to be an abnormal number of written words almost every day, but the love of writing was coupled with a hatred of artistically remodeled sentences. Prose should just communicate the ideas that were in the head. Like Tintoretto, Sartre was imprisoned by his greed to exploit his talents, but while Tintoretto "*always* finished everything, with the terrifying application of a man bent on completing his sentence, no matter what else he does,"[8] Sartre would assert his freedom by leaving work unfinished.

In Sartre, as in Brecht, the writings of Marx and Engels encouraged the spread of self-dislike into passionate campaigning for an escape from the self, together with a generalized revulsion against the idea of individuality. In "Le Fantôme de Staline" Sartre attacked bourgeois individualism: what bourgeois man respects in himself and claims to respect in other people is the value of the individual personality, whereas Soviet man subordinates his identity to the group, avoiding the "vices of bourgeois personalization." Tintoretto is praised in Sartre's 1957 essay for being competent to paint in a variety of styles, those of Veronese or Titian for instance, and for training assistants and members of his family to collaborate with him. Some of the paintings that bear his name are the work of "a strong collective personality."[9] In the summer, writing a preface for André Gorz's *Le Traître,* Sartre compares the book with an experiment to determine whether "I did it" can accurately be said of any action. Who is speaking? Who has acted? Rimbaud insisted: "Je est un autre." In Gorz's book language appears to be speaking by itself, and when the word "I" is pronounced, the glimpse of a speaker is

no more than a mirage.[10] Like Genet, Gorz appears to himself as someone else.[11]

Growing as it had from Sartre's abandoned notes for an ethic, his
book on Genet is more philosophical than sociological, but the massive
biography of Flaubert, begun in 1954, pulls the social and intellectual
background into the foreground. The contrast between Flaubert's
mother fixation and the father fixation of Baudelaire (who was born
during the same year—1821) is attributed to the difference between
their environments. With her aristocratic connections, Flaubert's
mother represented a class of ownership verging on liquidation, while
his father, who had roots in the peasantry and the countryside, used
wealth to buy land; Baudelaire came from an urban family of share-
holders.[12] This may fail to prove Sartre's point, but he argues convincingly that the Marxist biographer cannot afford to reject psychoanalysis
when it helps "to establish how a child lives his family relations inside a
given society."[13] Psychoanalysis also provides a means of moving from
generalization and abstraction to individual particularities. Engels had
tried to dismiss these as irrelevant to the course of history, which would
have been no different, he said, if Napoleon had never been born. But
Sartre's intellect is seen at its formidable best in the cerebral acrobatics
he performs on the tightrope stretching between the biographical fact
and the totalizing movement.

The word "totalize" recurs frequently in his work from 1957 onward,
but the idea goes back to 1942. In Le Sursis he was already asking what
would happen if you tried "to stand face-to-face with the planet." During a world war the war is "the totality of all my thoughts, all Hitler's
words, all Gomez' actions, but nobody is there to do the adding up."
The paradox is that the whole war has a tangible existence, though
none of us can come into contact with more than a fragment of it. In
the absence of God, there is no witness. When Sartre started to use the
word "totalize" he gave it a number of overlapping meanings. To
totalize is to synthesize a plurality into a unity, but sometimes he makes
"totalization" synonymous with *praxis* (activity directed at an object),
treating all work as an attempt to make a new synthesis out of existing
elements. Detotalization follows when the synthesis proves to be unfinished.

In Le Sursis the totalizer was contemporary history, and Sartre tried
to make it take over the narrative function; in a biography the writer
must concern himself with the "total individual": between the individual and his background, conditioning is reciprocal. Each statement of
Robespierre's, each habit, each circumstance will yield its full meaning
only if viewed in the context of his political attitude and his social posi-

tion. But the relationship between circumstance and behavior does not emerge clearly in a biography based on a linear narrative of actions: "a life develops in spirals, constantly passing the same points at different levels of integration and complexity."

Sartre makes a good case in favor of reclaiming psychoanalysis for Marxism in spite of the blurring between the two questions "How much can we know about a man?" and "Is there any such thing as a truth about man?" Used like this, the words "thing" and "truth" are almost meaningless, while the word "man" is a vague synthesis spanning Neanderthal man, medieval beggars, African pygmies, and French intellectuals. But Sartre was driven by the urge to reduce human history to a single, explainable entity; this is the motive behind *Questions de méthode,* which he evolved from the essay for *Twórczość* on Marxism and existentialism. Expanding it and adapting it under the new title for French readers, he published it in *Les Temps Modernes,*[14] where it took its natural place, as a battle in his campaign to found a synthetic anthropology independent of Lévi-Strauss's structural anthropology.

Since publishing his essay "L'Analyse structurale en linguistique et anthropologie" in August 1945,[15] Lévi-Strauss had frequently used the words "structure" and "structural" in titles of essays and papers. The collection of these in *L'Anthropologie structurale* did not appear until 1958, but Jean Pouillon had supported Lévi-Strauss in *Les Temps Modernes,* writing in 1956 that although he was not the first to emphasize the structural character of social phenomena, his originality lay in taking it seriously and "calmly deriving all the consequences from it." Without being explicitly antistructuralist in *Questions de méthode* or in *Critique de la raison dialectique,* Sartre declared his intention of founding an "anthropologie structurelle," the difference in spelling pointing to its difference from Lévi-Strauss's. The only question Sartre wants to raise, he says, is whether we are in a position to construct a theory "of man as he structures himself historically." To formulate the question like this is arguably to beg it by putting "man" and "himself" in the singular, but Sartre's combative object was to annex the word "structure" for chronological progression, when the method of the structuralists was to sidestep historical change, looking only at resultant structures. While Sartre was drafting *Questions de méthode* he realized it was going to lead into a much bigger work, and a few weeks before publishing the first volume of his *Critique de la raison dialectique* he said that he had been struggling for fifteen years to "lay the political foundations of anthropology."

As a Marxist he wanted to believe that dialectical materialism offered a complete interpretation of history—that all the contradictions, conflicts, heterogeneities, anomalies could be subsumed in a single totalization. Sartre is simultaneously concerned to provide Marxism with an adequate theory of knowledge—both Marx and Lenin had worked without one—and to combat Heideggerian existentialism, which consistently makes Being its point of departure. Sartre insists that history is the history of human initiatives. What emerges as the crucial problem is how to map the jungle of obscure interconnections between historical movements and individual actions.

The philosophical concern with history is less academic than political. If there is no God to face the planet, history has either to make itself or to be made. Writing about the future in which the "universal class," the proletariat, will lead the world to revolution, Marx said: "Its goal and its historical action are irrevocable and visibly traced out for it in the very circumstances of its life." This implies either determinism or scientism: the future of the class is either predestined or predictable from objective analysis of evidence already available. Sartre had consistently rejected determinism, but how are we to define the space in which choices are made? As Merleau-Ponty noticed, Sartre had always been reluctant to acknowledge a middle ground between subject and object, whether between men and things or between men and others, and the new phase of Sartrian thinking seems to be indebted both to Merleau-Ponty and to the early thinking of Georg Lukács. In his 1923 book *History and Class Consciousness,* which he later repudiated under pressure from Stalinist orthodoxy, Lukács made an abortive but courageous effort at what Merleau-Ponty and Sartre attempted much later—to rescue Marx from the rigidities of the Marxists by analyzing the complexity of reciprocal relationships. In Merleau-Ponty's restatement of the argument in his 1955 book *Les Aventures de la dialectique* the viewpoint is phenomenological. To regard consciousness as a centrifugal movement without opacity, he says, is to relegate history and the social to a series of instantaneous observations. If there is an interworld of human relationships, a residue of history, between men and things, the individual can no longer be held responsible, as in Sartrian existentialism, for choosing the whole contemporary environment, and it is easier to recognize that all action is partly symbolic, reaching not only for a practical result but for the meaning it has as gesture.

In the *Critique* Sartre would make a large-scale raid on the historical interworld; his immediate concern in *Questions de méthode* is to separate the basic truths of Marxism from the dogmatic superstructure while curing himself of habits formed after his "conversion" of 1952. He had to disentangle his thinking from compromises he had made for the party's sake. "I considered that true Marxism had been completely twisted, falsified by the Communists."[16] Marxism, he said, "possesses theoretical bases," but "no longer *knows* anything."[17] (Sartre likes to follow an abstract collective subject with a personalizing predicate.) "For the majority of Marxists, thinking is pretending to totalize, which provides a pretext for substituting the universal for the specific."[18] "The method is identical with Terror in its inflexible refusal to *differentiate.*"[19] These are ferocious criticisms, but Sartre, who only five years previously had declared "I am not a Marxist," now maintains that no anti-Marxist idea can be anything more than the revival of a pre-Marxist idea. Marxism is the only valid philosophy for our time. He quotes approvingly Garaudy's claim: "Today Marxism forms the only system of coordinates which makes it possible to situate and to define a thought in any area—from political economy to physics, from history to ethics." A philosophy is "first of all a particular way in which the rising class becomes conscious of itself," and there have been few real philosophies since the seventeenth century, if philosophy is to be "simultaneously a totalization of knowledge, a method, a regulative Idea, an offensive weapon, and a community of language, if this 'vision of the world' is also an instrument which ferments decaying societies, if this particular conception of man and society becomes the culture and sometimes the nature of the whole class."[20] According to Sartre, there have been only three philosophies in this period: "that of Descartes and Locke; that of Kant versus Hegel; and Marxism." "It is impossible to go beyond them until man has gone beyond the historical moment they express."[21]

So what about existentialism? It should be ranked not as a philosophy but as an ideology. "It is a parasitical system living on the margin of knowledge which at first it opposed but into which today it seeks to be integrated."[22] The appearance of self-critical modesty is specious; behind it is an arrogant appropriation of work done by precursors. Sartre is personifying existentialism as if Kierkegaard, Heidegger, Jaspers, and Gabriel Marcel had all been generals, with him as commander in chief. The allegation that existentialism at first opposed knowledge is characteristically loose—Kierkegaard set himself up against Hegel, but so did Marx; Sartre now wants to lead the deserting existentialists back to the headquarters of Marxist knowledge. Encapsulating the history of Western philosophy in shamelessly inaccurate generalization, Sartre is simultaneously proposing that the new role of existentialism should be to counteract abstract generalization: "Marxism has reabsorbed man into the idea, and existentialism seeks him everywhere *where he is,* at his work, in his home, in the street."[23] This echoes the exciting rhetoric that had been inspired by Sartre's early infatuation with Husserl.

That Sartre wants to outflank structuralism is clear when he claims that the "regressive-progressive method" can "integrate sociology and history in the perspective of a materialistic dialectic."[24] He claims to be deriving the method from a study by Henri Lefebvre of a rural community.[25] The first step is to see what Lefebvre called the "horizontal complexity" of a society; we describe what is currently visible—habitat, family structure, agricultural and mechanical techniques, and so on. Each of these has its history, and this is what comes under observation in the second phase. Nervous that things might sound too simple, Lefebvre calls this the analytico-regressive phase and tells us that we are now concerned with "vertical complexity." We then proceed to synthesis. With the understanding we have acquired of the past, we return to the present in what Lefebvre terms the "historical-genetic" phase. This approach is what Sartre calls the "regressive-progressive method." No less expert than Lefebvre in introducing terminology which obfuscates a simple procedure, he explains that we move backward into the determining set of political, ideological, social, and economic circumstances and then forward into analyzing the project by which man internalizes these forces and then externalizes them while producing himself in the world as an organized totality. Misled by the marriage between his own jargon and Lefebvre's, Sartre seems to be forgetting that he has already used the terms "regressive" and "progressive" when discussing Freudian psychoanalysis in *L'Etre et le Néant:* "By a regressive psychoanalysis one climbs back from the considered action to one's ultimate potentiality; and by a synthetic progression one goes down again from this ultimate potentiality to the considered action, grasping its integration in the total form."[26]

In the forties Sartre had complained that "the dimension of the future does not exist for psychoanalysis."[27] He was less unfriendly now to Freudianism but hostile to structuralism. His anthropology has a wider range, he claims, dealing not just with structures that have already been evolved but with the process of evolution. In 1949 Lévi-Strauss had already formulated his own definition of history and anthropology in terms of progressive and retrogressive movement: "The anthropologist goes forward, striving to attain, through the conscious, which he never forgets, more and more of the unconscious; whereas the historian advances, as it were, backward, keeping his eyes fixed on concrete and specific activities from which he withdraws only to review them in a fuller and richer perspective."[28] For Lévi-Strauss "the solidarity of the two disciplines is a true two-faced Janus," while for Sartre the historian is the dominant partner. But he now writes with a certain awkwardness, which reflects itself in the use of language that is significantly more jargon-ridden than the language of *L'Etre et le Néant.*

The postwar popularity of existentialism had grown out of its exciting redefinition of freedom: instead of being hemmed in by contemporary history we are responsible for it. In relegating existentialism to a subordinate position in the Marxist system, Sartre is also reducing human freedom to a mere gleam on the horizon. He quotes *Das Kapital:* "This reign of freedom cannot begin until there is an end to the work imposed by necessity and external finality."[29] Sartre goes on: "As soon as there is a margin of *real* freedom *for everyone* beyond the production of a livelihood, Marxism will have lived out its span; a philosophy of freedom will replace it. But we have no means, no intellectual instrument, no concrete experience to enable us to conceive of this freedom or this philosophy."[30] This is a violent *volte-face,* which allies Sartre with Marx's assumption that oppression has nothing to do with human aggression and that under a different social structure injustice could be eliminated. But Sartre no longer seems to want a revolution. Progressing on a spiral such as the one he describes, his thinking has arrived at a new level without moving away from its stubborn core of disbelief in evil human impulses. In *Saint Genet* and in *Le Diable et le Bon Dieu* he had brought good and evil close together; in abandoning his notes toward an ethic he had denied the validity of moral standards in our oppressive society. In *Questions de méthode* he was assuming that we do have access to truth about man, but he made no serious attempt to erect a distinction between philosophical truth and truth in reporting on impressions. Whereas Gide had been scrupulously honest after his return from the USSR, Sartre, after his first visit to Moscow, had told expedient lies, and even now, after unbuckling the straitjacket, he was dangerously close in writing a philosophy for the rising class to equating truth with what serves the cause.

ALL through 1957 *Les Temps Modernes* was keeping up its campaign against the failure of the feeble French government to enforce justice in Algeria. Women were being raped, people were disappearing, others were being arbitrarily arrested. Suspects were being tortured with electric prods, having their bones broken, having their nails torn out. The French army and the French settlers, the colons, were directly responsible for these outrages; the government was indirectly responsible in failing to keep its forces under control. But there was no stability at the center. Intent on staying in power, Guy Mollet, who was squandering half a million troops on the Algerian war, came increasingly under attack from the moderates while increasingly trying to stop French papers from publishing the facts. Between April 11 and May 2 *France-Observateur* was twice suppressed. But Mollet's government collapsed in May, and in June *Les Temps Modernes* reprinted the articles that had provoked the seizure of *France-Observateur*.[31] Mollet was succeeded by Maurice Bourgès-Maunoury, a radical, who formed a new government during the second week of June, but it survived for only ten weeks. During the year *Les Temps Modernes* was impounded four times in Algeria but not in France until November.[32]

In the July-August issue, reviewing Albert Memmi's double-volume *Portrait du colonisateur* and *Portrait du colonisé,* Sartre argued that colonialism depended on a system of production which divided humanity into two classes. "For some people privilege and humanity are inseparable: they make themselves men by the free exercise of their rights; for the others, the lack of rights sanctions their misery, their chronic hunger, their ignorance, in short, their subhuman status."[33] The dehumanization of the oppressed recoils on the oppressor, who has to overcome all compassionate impulses for the sake of the system. "In short, he 'dehumanizes' himself in turn."[34] The system was not even economically advantageous to the colonial power: France would eventually be forced to abandon the Algerian war as too expensive.[35] Sartre's forecast, of course, was accurate.

In December he was one of the left-wing intellectuals to testify at the trial of Ben Saddok, who had assassinated the former vice-president of the Algerian Assembly. Ben Saddok's lawyer, Pierre Stibbe, wanted Camus, who had just won the Nobel Prize, to read a passage from one of his essays at the trial, but Camus's mother was still in Algiers, and he refused to put her at risk by involving himself. Jacques Soustelle, who had been governor-general of Algeria since the beginning of 1955, appeared as a witness for the prosecution. Sartre, who was one of the last to speak, argued that the young man's action was not a terrorist attack but a political murder; during the Resistance similar killings had been applauded as heroic.[36] At dinner with De Beauvoir and Lanzmann, Sartre, who for some time had been allowed no alcohol, succumbed to the need for whiskey and soon became agitated, saying that to please the right-wingers on the jury he had spoken as if he disapproved of terrorism.[37] The next day Ben Saddok was sentenced to life imprisonment.

The fall of Bourgès-Maunoury in October had been followed by thirty-five days of chaos. In November a new government—the twentieth of the Fourth Republic—was formed by Félix Gaillard, a young radical who had been finance minister. Struggling energetically against the economic crisis, he raised taxes, devalued the franc by 20 percent, and borrowed heavily. But the Tunisian president Bourguiba refused to cooperate with him against the FLN, who were operating successfully from bases inside Tunisia, and on January 16, 1958, sixteen French soldiers were killed on the Algerian side of the border near the small Tunisian village of Sakhiet. A French bomber then attacked the village, killing sixty-nine people, including twenty children. Not daring to antagonize the army by condemning the raid, Gaillard merely offered to pay compensation to the Tunisians. "He has made us all into accomplices," Sartre declared in "Nous sommes tous des assassins," published in the March issue of *Les Temps Modernes*.[38]

In February there was a huge demand in French bookstores for a firsthand account of torture in Algeria, *La Question*, by Henri Alleg, Communist editor of the newspaper *Alger Républicain*, which had been suppressed in September 1955. In November 1956 Alleg had begun to publish the paper illegally. Arrested by French paratroopers in June 1957, he had been imprisoned for a month. Still fascinated by the rapport between torturer and victim, Sartre reviewed Alleg's book for *L'Express*, pointing to the anomalies that were exposed: thugs could enjoy the convulsions of a man being electrocuted but couldn't bear the sound of his screaming; torture was being used to destroy in the Arabs the qualities that Europeans most admire—courage, willpower, intelligence, loyalty.[39] *L'Express* was seized by the police, and when Sartre's review was printed as a pamphlet it was immediately impounded.

The violence infected Paris. Policemen were being shot in reprisal by Algerians, and on March 13 the police demonstrated in front of the Chambre des Députés. De Beauvoir found she was recoiling from French military uniforms as she once had from swastikas, while Sartre's work on *Critique de la raison dialectique* was activated partly by the need to distract himself from what was going on.

> He did not work in his usual way, pausing, crossing words out, tearing up pages, starting them all over again; for hours at a stretch he rushed from one sheet of paper to the next without re-reading them, as if possessed by words his pen couldn't catch, even at this gallop. I would hear him crunching corydrane capsules to maintain the impetus . . . by the end of the afternoon he was exhausted, his concentration shattered. His gestures were uncertain and he would often say one word instead of another.[40]

Corydrane was a mixture of aspirin and amphetamines. Until it was prohibited in 1971 it was on sale at pharmacies. Advertised as a tonic, analgesic, and antipyretic, it was effective as a stimulant and was popu-

lar among students and intellectuals, who found it increased their productivity. The recommended dose was one or two tablets in the morning and again at midday; Sartre was taking about ten at a time and,
before the book was finished, twenty. As he put it, he "abused drugs a
great deal" for twenty years, but most of all while writing the *Critique*.
Besides corydrane he was taking orthodrine; a container would last him
a day. "As soon as one passed a certain point," he told De Beauvoir,
"one began to be destroyed, and the risk was a reality. . . . One liked destruction as such, one liked having blurred ideas which were vaguely interrogative and which then disintegrated. . . . It also meant that one
could drop dead, but there was no knowing when." He needed to test
how far he could push both body and mind. He reached the stage of
having no skin left on his tongue. For a time he was partially deaf.

There is a case, of course, to be made for narcotic inflation of the
mental marketplace. Imaginative writers, from Coleridge and De
Quincey to Rimbaud and the surrealists, had provided a distinguished
precedent. What is odd about the case of Sartre is that though he wrote
philosophy while stoned, he took care to keep his mental faculties intact
while writing fiction. "I felt that in a novel the way one chose and jux-
taposed words and formed phrases—in short, the style—and then the
way one analyzed emotions made it a prerequisite that one should be
absolutely normal." While he was writing the *Critique* (or so he said sixteen years later), "I thought I had in my head . . . all the ideas I was
putting down on paper. . . . A container of corydrane meant: these ideas
will be analyzed in the next two days."[41]

When Sartre indulges in the painful pleasure of recriminating
against an earlier self he is liable to exaggerate, but here the internal
evidence supports the self-accusation. From any point of view, the *Critique* (with or without the second half he left unpublished) forms the
climax of his philosophical writing. His object was to restructure the
entire foundation of Marxist philosophy, to demonstrate the dialectical
unity in both external reality and knowledge. Had he succeeded, history would have been shown to have a single meaning, while analytical
reason would have been discredited as conducive to atomistic thinking
that advanced the interests of the bourgeoisie. Nothing could have
mattered to Sartre more than to accomplish this vastly ambitious enterprise, but he was bizarrely determined not to use his full powers as a
mental athlete. Instead of keeping himself in a fit state to look up passages in the Marxist philosophers and in his own earlier writings, to
check facts, sources, quotations, statistics, he was content to rely on his
drugged memory and to take evasive refuge in the kind of abstraction

that infuriated Engels when Marx resorted to it. Like *Die Heilige Familie*, the *Critique* would be of no interest to the general public.

The writing, especially in the published volume, is muddled, long-winded, repetitious, and jargon-ridden, the jargon being used inconsistently, while the philosophy rubs up indigestibly against long sections that are more political, historical, economic, sociological, and polemical. Sartre also transposes material from his draft for the Flaubert biography. During his fifteen-year struggle "to lay the political foundations of anthropology," the project, he said, had grown "like a generalized cancer." Not knowing what to do with the ideas that presented themselves, he had put them down in whichever book he was working on, but they were "all in place now"—or so he claimed a few weeks before the first volume was published. The second, he said, would be out within a year.[42]

Insofar as the *Critique* bases itself on the "regressive-progressive method," the first volume is regressive; the second was scheduled to deal progressively with the history of humanity, proving that it had a single meaning. The first task Sartre sets himself is to survey the historical interworld by sketching out a general theory about the evolution of groups and the relationships between them. Relationships between individuals are ignored, though he promises in the Introduction that he will carefully "follow the threads of Ariadne" from individual *praxis* to collective action. In the second volume he will analyze Stalin's régime as an example of individual leadership in relation to collective need, but in the volume he published, the individual disappears from historical categories. A man's understanding of his own life, Sartre argues, must reach the point of denying its distinctiveness to find its dialectical intelligibility in the history of humanity.[43] After concealing itself in the accumulating facts of what is happening, the dialectic reveals itself in making them comprehensible.[44]

To cope with the historical interworld, the concept Sartre introduces is reciprocity. He is following Lukács and Merleau-Ponty, but he follows halfheartedly; he has not shaken off the conviction that between one consciousness and another the relationship must be one of struggle for subject-object domination. His emphasis is not on consciousness but on *praxis*, and *praxis* brings men into relationship either with other men or with things. Sartre portrays both kinds of relationship as taking place in a world of scarcity. Because materials are in short supply, we compete instead of collaborating. Ignoring sexual rivalry and the shortage of physical beauty, he assumes that life could be less competitive and qualitatively better if material supplies were more abundant. As it is, there can be no social justice, only a vicious cycle of oppression. "Everyone struggles against an order which crushes his body really and materially, while he sustains and strengthens the order by resisting it."[45]

Nor can any form of social contract provide a basis of justice. Like Marx, Sartre takes the state to be a product of the class system, while reciprocity is possible, he says, only when rebellion brings a group together. In an oppressive society there can be no freedom without violence. Sartre contrasts seriality (exemplified by people in a bus line—bored, passive, indifferent to each other) with the group-in-fusion, which is collectively active. When the Bastille was being stormed, everyone in the crowd was behaving in a new way, he says, not as alienated, not as an individual, but as an individual incarnation of "the common person." In *Les Communistes et la paix* he had written unrealistically, as if this kind of cohesiveness existed between the party and the proletariat. Everyone, he said, is a leader. As a description of the crowd that marched on the Bastille this phrase would be less inaccurate—people were united by a common purpose which led to immediate action—but it is revealing that Sartre should have come to believe in collective violence as the only available form of human freedom. The man who had once admitted to disliking the male half of the human race and who in the stalag had shunned the company of working-class soldiers was now glorifying the common people when herded together in righteous lust for vengeance.

After launching himself in impassioned championship of individual freedom, Sartre had already made his most extraordinary *volte-face* when he allied himself in *Questions de méthode* with Marx's contention that no freedom can be available until "there is an end to the work imposed by necessity and external finality." In an oppressive society there can be no liberty without violence, no hope without terror: "the structures of freedom and reciprocity" take on their full meaning only when they appear in the "practical material movement of terror." Though the idea of a social contract is inadmissible, the individual who pledges himself to the group has "freely consented to the liquidation of [his] person as free constituent *praxis*." Those who betray the group deserve to be lynched. "I am a brother in violence to my neighbors. . . . Violence is the actual power of this lateral reciprocity of love."[46]

This contradicts Sartre's entries in his wartime diaries about the pointlessness of trying to sacrifice future freedom: an oath was an "empty incantation," "an avowal of distress . . . I cannot choose my subsequent choices." On the other hand, the equation of violence with the "lateral reciprocity of love" is reminiscent of the freedom fighters in *Morts sans sépulture* when they kill the fifteen-year-old François, who might have cracked under torture and betrayed their beloved leader. Though Sartre was already thirty-five when the German army marched into France, the occupation had been intellectually formative: the Resistance had tended to sanctify violence. But to offer the group this much power over the individual in peacetime is to reject liberalism no less contemptuously than Brecht did in *Die Massnahme* (*The Remedial Measure*). In this 1930 play the agitators renounce their names and their personal identity, becoming "blank leaves for the Revolution to write its orders on." When one of them follows his own impulses instead of obeying orders, he is shot by his comrades, but they shoot him lovingly.

Like Brecht, Sartre was now committed to an all-out battle against the individual ego. The *Critique* often refers to "the common person" and makes frequent use of Marx's phrase "the accidental individual." During the spring and summer of 1958 Sartre's political conviction had been hardening around the core of ambivalence that was already merging discomfort with himself into hatred of the self. Pascal had said: "Le moi est haïssable" ("The self is detestable"). Sartre had questioned whether "I did it" can ever be said accurately. Nor was he by any means the only anti-individualist among progressive French intellectuals. Lévi-Strauss claimed to be "nothing but the place where my work is done." Sartre, who had been more creative, was at his worst in writing based, uncreatively, on the implicit denial that his knowledge centered on his experience.

Writing about Lucien, Mathieu, or Götz, he was writing about himself; in the *Critique* he was trying to view himself as a member of a class and to view the class with the detachment that might come from taking a wide-angle view of its conflicts. One of the books most important to him during the war was Jean-Léon Jaurès' four-volume history of the French Revolution. And if Sartre keeps coming back to this subject, it was mainly because the revolution had crystallized the French bourgeoisie while sweeping the individual into successive tides of collective movement. Dissatisfied with the human condition, Sartre had once yearned for the unambiguous existence of a thing—Mathieu wishing he could be a stone. Another stratagem for escaping from the self had been to view consciousness as impersonal, with individuality as its object, not its subject. The new alternative was to believe that the individual disappears as soon as he understands his connection with the "cultural field" which consists of a "synthetic bond between everyone."[47] When he described swearing as "a regulatory and totalizing *praxis*,"[48] he was thinking of June 1789, when the Third Estate, the representatives of the commoners in the Estates General, finding that they had been shut out of their meeting place, adjourned to the royal tennis court and vowed to go on meeting until they had established a constitution. But the effort to think anonymously in the plural leads to obscure writing about activity in which the subject is collective and the action singular. "Common *praxis* is *dialectical* . . . ," he asserts. "It totalizes the object, pursues some total aim, unifies the practico-inert field and dissolves it in the synthesis of the *common practical field.*"[49]

Together with "scarcity," "the practico-inert" is one of the key concepts in his explanation of why freedom is available only to the insurrectionary group. The practico-inert is the area that contains the residue of past *praxis*. As Sartre sees it—taking, as so often, a literary model—work consists of "imprinting" one's image on inorganic materiality, or, to put it less clearly, the worker is realizing himself by externalizing interiority. This leads Sartre back to Hegel, who believed that alienation inevitably accompanied objectification. During the process of objectifying himself in his work, the subject becomes something other than himself. He loses out in both his involvement with things and his involvement with other people, who appropriate his product, thievishly adapting it to their own uses. So just as there is no existing without *praxis*, and no *praxis* without objectification, there is no objectification without alienation. The worker who leaves one factory job for another is merely defining the limits that confine him, while confirming his destiny, which is to be exploited. "All men are slaves insofar as their life unfolds in the practico-inert field and insofar as this field is always conditioned by scarcity. . . . The alienation of the exploited is inseparable from that of the exploiters."[50]

Undeniably, Sartre's attitude is complicated by his emotional hostility to things. Like the chestnut tree, objects are unforgivable. Though the *Critique* is never rhetorical in the manner of *L'Etre et le Néant,* it uses highly charged emotional language to denounce them. We are victims of "violence, shadows and witchcraft"; we have to fight against "the evil actions of material which has been worked on." But this time he has no Roquentin to pick up the bill; it is Sartre himself who is telling us that objects persecute us.

If it had not been for the corydrane, his emotionality would be all the more surprising in a manifesto for a new rationality. Marx would never have maintained that dialectical reason and analytical reason were mutually exclusive, but in *Questions de méthode* Sartre had already made a highly unreasonable demand for an alternative rationality. "Because no one has been prepared to establish this rationality in experience, I state factually: nobody in the East or West writes or utters a sentence about us or our contemporaries which is not a flagrant error. . . . Our present ideas are false because they have died before us. Some stink of carrion, while others are clean little skeletons; it's all the same thing."[51] This is to carry the hyperbole of platform rhetoric into serious philosophizing, and in setting out to invalidate analytical reason, he was once again undertaking a Herculean task he would have to abandon. He is, as Lévi-Strauss complains, undecided about whether analytical reason is sometimes admissible as a necessary component of dialectical reason. Totalization, claims Lévi-Strauss, has been taken for granted by anthropologists since Malinowski, but for them it is only a point of departure. Once the philosopher, using dialectical reason, has constituted a totality, it is for the scientist to do the serious work of analyzing it.[52] The penultimate chapter of Lévi-Strauss's book *La Pensée sauvage* made its first appearance in *Les Temps Modernes,* and the final chapter, an attack on Sartre's *Critique,* derived from seminars in which Jean Pouillon participated.[53] Before launching his attack, Lévi-Strauss admits that he has been using Sartrian terminology with the ulterior purpose of leading the reader to this point; none of the criticisms he makes in the chapter is more damaging than the incidental reminder of how the terminology, like the concepts, has failed to pass into general usage, even among philosophers or sociologists. But Lévi-Strauss surrenders the word "anthropology" to Sartre, reverting to "ethnology" for his own work.

Their rivalry is a fight between two champions who each has the same ambition—to update Marxism. Lévi-Strauss agrees that *praxis* "constitutes the fundamental totality for the sciences of man."[54] But while both were influenced by Mauss's *Essai sur le don,* Lévi-Strauss believed that Sartre had misunderstood Mauss and that between *praxis* and practices there is always a conceptual scheme. What Lévi-Strauss wanted to contribute was a theory of superstructures, an explanation of the way matter and form come together in structures. The problem of infrastructures could be relegated to the historian.[55] Unfortunately the two leaders of the rival anthropologies were each content to score debating points against each other without direct confrontation. Even if collaboration was out of the question, discussion was not. *Les Temps Modernes* could have made a more important contribution to French intellectual life. So averse to the idea of leadership that he was incapable of being a good editor, Sartre was also too busy, absent from Paris for too much of the year, and insufficiently committed to the editorial function. Altogether, in thirty-five years of directing the review, he scarcely did any editing; he took full control over only one issue. Merleau-Ponty had given his services generously and self-effacingly;

perhaps to protect himself against the aftereffects of generosity, Sartre made the gesture and the effort of editing the issue dedicated to his former colleague's memory.

The review might have developed differently if Merleau-Ponty had been more aggressive and preferred confrontation to withdrawal. Of the others the one intellectually best qualified to arbitrate was Pouillon, but he was neither strong enough personally nor in a position of sufficient strength. The core of the problem that Sartre and Lévi-Strauss should have confronted has been summarized by Howard Davies: "Sartre can tolerate the concept of structure only as a configuration of *praxis* and practico-inert within the group, while Lévi-Strauss fails to explicate the relationship of *praxis* and structure."[56] Davies also makes the point that Les Temps Modernes missed a good opportunity to test the theory of ensembles Sartre had advanced in the *Critique:* the review could have investigated political developments in primitive societies.[57] Much later—in 1966—Pouillon would edit an issue devoted to structuralism, contending in his own essay that coordination between the two anthropologies is feasible: "structural" refers to structure as syntax, while "structurelle" refers to structure as reality. But neither Sartre nor Lévi-Strauss contributed to the issue. Oddly enough, friendship continued between Lévi-Strauss and De Beauvoir, who accepted his advice not only on Le Deuxième Sexe (1949) but on La Vieillesse (1970).[58]

NOT that events in France were conducive to healthy intellectual controversy while the political crisis continued. In February 1958, after the bombing of Sakhiet, Gaillard, the ineffectual premier, resigned, and for five weeks none of the candidates for the succession was able to form a government. Trying to steep himself in work, Sartre dosed himself recklessly with corydrane, which exacerbated his restlessness. He had always tended to move a great deal, swinging his arms so much as he walked that his shoulders seemed to be rolling, but during his fifties he was becoming more fidgety. In De Beauvoir's flat he paced about so much that she had an extra piece of carpet put down to conceal the threadbare patch he had made.[59]

By May 5 President Coty was making overtures to De Gaulle, who seemed willing enough to take over, but on May 8 Coty approached Pierre Pflimlin, a liberal. The colons were outraged, while the generals warned the president that the anxieties of the army could be allayed only by a government firmly committed to keeping Algeria French. In spite of this, Pflimlin managed to form a government on May 13. This triggered an insurrection in Algiers. With De Gaulle's supporters active among them, demonstrators occupied the government building. The army, which could have stopped them, assumed control. Pflimlin's government nervously ordered General Salan to take charge in Algiers, but it seemed possible that he would be strong enough to take charge in Paris too. People were terrified of the paratroop regiments: at any moment the sky might be full of parachutes, meaning civil war had begun. But the mood of the army was unpredictable: if the generals had attempted a coup, would their men have supported them?

We do not know how much De Gaulle did to precipitate the demand for him in Algiers. There were limits to his popularity in the army; officers who had supported the Vichy government did not regard him as their friend, but they had no alternative leader, and when Guy Mollet's SFIO opted for him in preference to an alliance with the Communists, his return became inevitable, though it was still possible to throw obstacles in his way. Sartre's article "Le Prétendant" was published in *L'Express* on May 22. "The solitude of this man, shut up in his lofty grandeur, prevents him in any case from becoming head of state in a republic. Or—what amounts to the same thing—prevents the state he will control from remaining a republic."[60]

On the evening of May 27 De Gaulle said that if he was not given power within forty-eight hours, he would seize it. It was not an idle threat: the army was behind him. The next day Sartre and De Beauvoir joined a massive anti-Gaullist demonstration from the Place de la Nation to the Place de la République. When the "Marseillaise" and the "Chant du Départ" were sung, Sartre jointed in lustily, glad to be part of a group-in-fusion.

Even now he was capable of adjusting the mental shutters for writing, but pushing the *Critique* aside, he worked on the play he had promised Simone Berriau for the autumn season at the Antoine.[61] In February, at a round-table discussion with Adamov and Michel Butor after the opening of Adamov's play *Paolo Pauli,* he had spoken up for plays dealing with current political events: "Today these are the only plays which make it possible to revitalize the theater."[62] His own new play was going to be about a Frenchman who had tortured Algerians. Three years earlier, after *Nekrassov,* he had announced that he had nothing further to offer the bourgeois public, but now, provoked into writing about torture, he wanted to reach the biggest possible audience.

After days of rumors that the paratroopers had landed, fears of civil war were unallayed. There were demonstrations and counterdemonstrations, shouts of "Vive De Gaulle" and of "No fascists in France," processions and counterprocessions, with placards and flags. But the sixty-nine Socialist deputies had been cowed into supporting De Gaulle, while President Coty threatened to resign unless De Gaulle was put in office. Sartre's protracted campaign against him had been like an adult repetition of his campaigning at the Ecole Normale against Lanson, but this time the unacceptable father figure, the embodiment of authoritarianism, was invincible.

(20)

Freudian Interlude

DESPONDENT though he was, Sartre was not too depressed to have a meeting on May 31, 1958, with the American film director John Huston, who in 1946 had scored a big success with a stage production of *Huis clos* on Broadway. He had later flirted with the idea of basing a film on *Le Diable et le Bon Dieu*, and he now invited Sartre to script a Hollywood film about Freud. Ever since 1945, when he had directed *Let There Be Light*, a sixty-minute documentary film for the U.S. Army Pictorial Service about battle neurosis, Huston had wanted to make a Freud film, and now that Ernest Jones had completed his biography—the three volumes appeared in 1953, 1955, and 1957—it seemed to be the right moment. Huston's idea was to center the film on the early part of Freud's career, building a thrillerlike suspense around the founding of psychoanalysis.

It was not just financial need that made Sartre accept the commission, though he had just borrowed twelve million old francs from his mother to pay taxes. His expenses were around 1,800,000 francs a month, though of this only about 300,000 francs were spent on himself, the rest going to his clan of dependents, including his mother, Michelle, and Wanda. The film would bring in $25,000, but like the exorbitantly generous Kean of the play, he would not have been prepared to atone for his munificence by accepting jobs he considered unworthy. His reaction to Huston's offer meant that he at last felt ready for a serious confrontation with Freud. Even at the Ecole Normale, where he had read widely in psychology, he had opted mostly for disciples and anti-Freudians, reading little by the man himself. Perhaps the motive was the same as Freud's for refusing to read Nietzsche—fear of being influenced. But Sartre's attempt to sidestep Freud had been unsuccessful. The biographies of Baudelaire and Genet are nothing if not Freudian in their approach, and now, after proclaiming psychoanalysis to be com-patible with Marxism, Sartre welcomed the paid opportunity to study the great man's life and work. Nor was the idea of a film unattractive; if we discount the adaptation of *Kean,* Sartre had never written fiction based on biographical fact, but he would not have undertaken to write about Freud in any other way.

He was also glad to have an assignment that would distract him from the uncontrollable political situation. After a brief period without cory-drane he was taking it again. "I'm not sad," he told De Beauvoir, "but I'm asleep. It's like a morgue."[1]

The day after he met Huston the death sentence was passed on the Fourth Republic when the National Assembly elected De Gaulle as premier. Sartre took part in another hostile demonstration the same day, but nothing could stop the sixty-eight-year-old general from con-solidating his power, though he had no formula for solving the Algerian problem. He was quick to visit Algiers, and on June 4 he assured the rebels he had understood them. His main concern was to make himself acceptable.

Sartre reacted in accordance with his usual pattern. He would have achieved nothing by staying in Paris; on June 16 he left for three months in Italy. De Beauvoir had left Paris two days earlier for Milan, where he joined her. Dining in the Piazza del Duomo, he told her it was a long time since he had felt so calm.[2] They moved on to Venice, where they stayed for a fortnight, visiting Ravenna and Spoleto before settling in Rome on July 4. Simone Berriau was planning to stage his new play in October, and Sartre tried to work at it in the hotel but made little headway, even after breaking his rule about not using corydrane when writing creatively. The only result was that he sometimes scribbled il-legibly, sometimes produced sentences that were either meaningless or irrelevant.[3] To make himself concentrate he was using the air condi-tioner to keep his room extremely cold, though outside the heat was a hundred degrees.

His idea was to show how an ex-soldier, by refusing to talk about his Algerian experiences, causes the disintegration of his family.[4] Sartre completed a draft of the first act, but when he showed it to De Beau-voir, she told him it was like a drama by Sudermann.[5] In her diary she wrote: "He's in no mood to write 'fiction' these days. He's doing it only because he's contracted to."[6] Anxiety that he might have difficulties over censorship was another deterrent, and he failed to finish the play.

But he did start studying Freud. He was never reluctant to jettison premises basic to earlier work, but it was not clear at the outset how flagrantly he would contradict his anti-Freudian writing. Sketching out the scenario that would consist of ninety-five typed pages and would be ready by the middle of December, he found himself telling a story in a way that accorded neither with the assumptions of the *Critique,* which reduces the individual to an air bubble caught between social pressures, nor with those of his early fiction, which represents the self as incessantly being recreated by ongoing consciousness, as if the past can have no casual hold over the present.

On the other hand, he was not turning his back on Marx, who had struck an oddly Freudian note in a passage Sartre loved to quote from in *Der 18. Brumaire des Louis-Napoleon* (1852): "Men make their own history, but not in any way they please; they make it under circumstances not chosen by themselves but directly encountered, given and transmitted from the past. The tradition of the dead generations weighs like a nightmare on the brain of the living. Just when they seem to be revolutionizing themselves and things, creating something unprecedented . . . they nervously conjure up the spirits of the past." Freud, who discovered that it was possible to exorcise the spirits of the past by analyzing the nightmares, used to derive general principles from self-analysis and from case histories. For Sartre too, or at least for the Sartre of 1958, singular experience could lead to universal conclusions, even if the individual is only a singularized universal.

In the first paragraph of his synopsis he sums up what the film is to be about: "A man undertakes to understand other people because this seems the only way to understand himself, and he realizes that his researches on other people and on himself can be conducted simultaneously."[7] The film would show how Freud, like a detective, collected from patients clues that helped to solve the problem of his own fixation. This theme had a special appeal to the author of the *Critique*. Rejecting the idea of objectivity based on scientific detachment, Sartre held that the dialectic reveals itself only to an observer situated in interiority, to an investigator whose inquiries are integral to his personal experience as well as being a project aimed at modifying the universe. Analyzing his own dreams alongside his patients' neuroses, Freud changed the history of human thought by discovering the truth about himself.

In Rome, Sartre did his preliminary reading and his preliminary thinking. Only the first volume of Jones's biography had appeared in a French translation, but this is the one that deals with the period Huston wanted to cover, ending with the breakthrough that ensued on the death of Freud's father in 1896. Jones's book had an immediate effect on Sartre's attitude, making it much easier for him to identify with Freud, who turned out to be diffident, obstinate, and fractious. He refused to advance his own career by kowtowing to orthodox medical opinion. His hostility to the Establishment even had certain affinities with Sartre's. A Jew in an unmistakably (if patchily) anti-Semitic city, Freud was torn between the dream of passing unnoticed among gentiles and the drive to avenge himself by subverting their whole system of thinking. In Sartre, as in Freud, a secret wish to be someone else, or at least to be more like other people, had developed into a violent compulsion to make the others more like him by imposing his ideas on them. Both men were driven by painfully irreconcilable feelings of love and hatred toward the culture that had grown up out of Western civilization. Though Freud was more bourgeois than Sartre in his style of living and less outspoken in his criticism of the bourgeois family, in psychoanalysis he built a weapon that was to disrupt its stability more than anything Sartre wrote.

Sartre soon found that his reading of Freud brought him uncomfortably close to his own experience. He would have no choice but to be an observer situated in interiority. For Freud the weakness of his father had been problematic; for Sartre the early loss of his father had not been the boon he made it out to be; and Freud's immature reliance on father substitutes was easily comprehensible to a man who had grown up in the home of an autocratic grandfather. There is an unmistakable resemblance between Charles Schweitzer and Sartre's version of the authoritarian Dr. Meynert, who, after accepting the young Freud as his protégé, ferociously rejects him as soon as he begins to make decisions for himself.

Sartre decided early on that the film would be structured around the relationships with the father and the surrogate fathers. Unable to model himself on the feeble Jakob Freud, Sigmund becomes inordinately dependent on doctors who are paternally supportive and sometimes bullying. One, Breuer, gives him financial help; one, Fliess, is Freud's junior, but he is sufficiently dominant and charismatic for this not to matter. The patriarchal Meynert is the first to encounter resistance, but to arrive at maturity Freud has to achieve independence from them all. This he can do only after the death of Jakob. The synopsis suggests two possible beginnings for the film, and in one of these Freud's offscreen voice is heard saying: "It all began with the death of my father." At the end of the film the voice would say: "I knew very well that it was all over. I was on my own . . . I was forty-one. It was my turn to play the role of father."

This theme is skillfully interwoven with that of Freud's reactions to his female patients. It is unconscious aggression against Jakob that makes him willing to believe that thirteen of his patients have been victims of paternal rape. He wanted to degrade the image of paternity; eventually he realizes that he has been listening to fantasies which tell the truth not about what happened but about the desires these women kept secret from themselves. This is how Freud discovered infantile sexuality.

After spending nearly a month with De Beauvoir, Sartre traveled with her to Pisa, where he met Michelle Vian and took her to Rome. There, line by line, she gave him an oral translation of the second and third volumes in Jones's biography of Freud. Before the end of August, though, he promised Jean-Jacques Servan-Schreiber, who had founded the weekly *Express*, to put the screenplay aside for long enough to write three articles about the referendum to be held in France on the new constitution, which had been drafted by De Gaulle's legal adviser, Michel Debré. The object was to strengthen the executive, separating it from the legislature while maintaining an independent judiciary. The draft was amended by a parliamentary committee chaired by Paul Reynaud, who in 1940 had succeeded Daladier as premier. It was published on September 4 and then submitted to the referendum, which was to be held on September 28. Sartre's first article for *L'Express* was written in Rome and shortened in Paris by De Beauvoir and Servan-Schreiber. It appeared in the newspaper on September 11 under the title "La Constitution du mépris" ("The Constitution of Contempt"). Attacking De Gaulle for blackmailing his country, Sartre called on the French to reject the constitution.

He arrived back in Paris on September 16, but on the twentieth, about to start on his second article, he succumbed to a liver infection. He had been feeling exhausted even before the train journey from Rome, and in the afternoon he looked too feverish and weak to write, but he worked for twenty-eight hours with little interruption, and when De Beauvoir left him at eleven on Monday evening he started another twelve-hour stint. By Tuesday afternoon he gave the impression of being deaf and blind, but he went on to make a speech at an anti-Gaullist meeting.[8] The article was called "Les Grenouilles qui demandent un roi" ("The Frogs Who Want a King"). Sartre analyzed the failure of the Fourth Republic, which had survived for less than thirteen years. It was already apparent, he said, that far from introducing the necessary reforms, De Gaulle was continuing the abuses which had been rightly denounced. But three days later, when the referendum was held, 79 percent of the voters supported the constitution.

"It's rather awful," De Beauvoir wrote in her diary, "to be against a whole country; you feel as though you're already an exile."[9] No longer needing to brace himself for fighting, Sartre had to recognize that he was ill. He kept losing his sense of balance, had attacks of dizziness and nonstop headaches, but instead of consulting a doctor, he dosed himself with optalidon, belladénal, and corydrane. On October 2, putting down a wineglass while lunching with Simone Berriau, he missed the edge of the table by several inches. She immediately telephoned a doctor, Professor Moreau, who diagnosed fatigue in the left ventricle of the heart and recommended complete rest. He prescribed certain drugs and promised the apathetic patient that he would soon be more animated. But he must not drink or smoke. Sartre did not entirely ignore the doctor's instructions but refused to rest. Sometimes he felt better, but sometimes, as on October 13, he had difficulty in both walking and talking, while his handwriting and spelling had deteriorated alarmingly. The headaches persisted, and in comparison with his old self, he was still lethargic, stiff-necked, wooden in his movements, uncertain in his speech, and puffy in the face. His moods were unpredictable—fits of violent irascibility punctuating an ominous tranquillity.[10]

De Beauvoir knew she must intervene but did not know how often or how firmly. When she found him at his desk, fighting off exhaustion to keep the pen traveling across the page, she risked an explosion of anger each time she entreated him to rest. Sometimes he would answer, "All right, five minutes," and then sleep for two or three hours. Once she persuaded him to cancel an appointment with a girl friend, who was reduced to tears when she saw how badly he had jumbled the words together in the scribbled message. When De Beauvoir spoke to Professor Moreau, he warned her that though Sartre was only fifty-three, he could be dead within six months if he went on "racing against the clock." She then approached Simone Berriau, who agreed to postpone the play until the following autumn. Sartre received the news with an apathetic smile, more worrying to De Beauvoir than a fit of temper. But he did begin to work less.[11]

The first parliament of the Fifth Republic was to be elected toward the end of November 1958. In the campaign even Guy Mollet supported De Gaulle, who shrewdly maintained that he was not to be seen as the leader of a particular party. But the new Gaullist party, the Union for the New Republic (UNR), won 206 of the 549 seats, while the Christian Democrats and Independents had won 249, so he was not going to need any help from the socialists.

OF Sartre's earlier books the one contradicted most blatantly by the Freud synopsis is *L'Etre et le Néant,* in which Sartre had denounced the error of picturing consciousness as a territory in which barriers could be erected: in the 1917 *General Introduction to Psychoanalysis* Freud compares the unconscious to an anteroom with a doorman who decides which visitors will be admitted to the adjoining reception room. Inaccurately, Sartre had taken this spatial differentiation between conscious and unconscious to be no different from the distinction Freud later introduced between ego and id. The pro-Freudian position Sartre adopts in the synopsis is all the more remarkable for being based on the early stages of Freud's development. Sartre's philosophy of liberty had seemed incompatible with the idea that consciousness could be betrayed from within by forces that remained unknown. He had admitted the existence of self-deception but attributed it to *mauvaise foi*. Now, at the opposite extreme, he was to complain about Huston: "What's tiresome is that he doesn't believe in the unconscious."

In the synopsis Sartre makes the reactionary Dr. Meynert contend that consciousness is always transparent: "Besides I don't waste time spying on myself. I'm as transparent as spring water."[12] But Sartre sides with Freud, who notices that Meynert keeps pulling at his mustache and chewing it while tapping the left side of his nose with his forefinger. The body speaks in a code unintelligible to Meynert's consciousness.

In both the 95-page scenario and the 800-page screenplay Sartre was to construct from it, fact and fiction are judiciously fused. The patient who features most prominently is the beautiful Cecily Körtner, who has spells of paralysis in which her fists are clenched and her arms held as if she is about to lift something. Freud will eventually decode this: she would like her mother to go away so that she can be the one to save her father from falling. She is also punishing herself for desiring her father and to distract herself from guilt feelings over her mother's suicide attempt. Cecily is based mainly on a patient of Breuer's, "Anna O.," or Bertha Pappenheim, whom Freud never treated and probably never met. When she developed a hysterical pregnancy in 1892, Breuer broke off his treatment, and much of Sartre's action is based on hypothesizing what might have happened if Freud had taken over the case. He also interpolates an affair between Cecily's father and a pretty governess; this is borrowed from Freud's case history about "Dora," which was written up in 1901.

It was in 1896, the year of his father's death, that Freud introduced the term "psychoanalysis," but to tell the story Huston wanted him to tell, Sartre needed to conflate events that spread over ten years. Breuer started to treat Bertha Pappenheim in 1890, and though Freud began to analyze his own dreams in 1895, it was not until 1897 that he embarked on the self-analysis which was to last three years, culminating in the discovery of infantile sex and the Oedipus complex, though both were prefigured in the correspondence with Wilhelm Fliess. Some of these letters had been published in *The Origins of Psychoanalysis,* and the relationship between the two men is dramatized in the screenplay, which hints tellingly at the erotic element in Freud's feelings for the domineering young doctor. As Freud saw, if only belatedly, the female side of his personality had responded to Fliess's flamboyant masculinity. But it was not only because he was writing for Hollywood that Sartre held back from looking closely at Freud's way of dealing with his femininity. Though there was a lot of transference in his long friendship with Fliess—the correspondence continued from 1887 to 1904— Freud's failure in the "Dora" case was primarily a failure of transference. Still inexperienced as an analyst, he was rigid and aggressive in resisting the emotional pressures of the eighteen-year-old girl. With Fliess he was relaxed enough to let his female side come into play; with "Dora" he was not. In contrast, Sartre could relax happily with young girls—even if the therapeutic benefits were one-sided—but he was incapable of sustaining an affectionate friendship with a man.

In the screenplay the death of Jakob Freud coincides with Sigmund's breakthrough in curing Cecily, and he is finally able to acknowledge his aggressiveness toward the inoffensive old father: "His sweetness disarmed me. I'd have liked Moses to be my father. The Law!" Sartre could have made a parallel statement starting with "His absence disarmed me." He makes Freud tell Breuer: "I took all these fathers to protect me against myself, and I gave myself no respite because I hadn't destroyed them. You all fascinated me, and I wanted to kill my father in you." Sartre would have wanted neither to understand why he found it so easy to identify with a man who had a self-effacing father nor to recognize anything Oedipal in his refusal to forgive his stepfather for taking possession of the mother who had once been like a cuddly sister. Though Sartre had never needed counterparts in his life to such tyrants as Meynert, Breuer, and Fliess, he had quickly learned to use his writing as a weapon against men in stronger positions. With fiction such as "L'Ange du morbide" he attacked teachers, using philosophy to demolish the formidable Brunschvicg. Sartre had also surrounded himself with a "family" of younger friends, had played a semipaternal role to a long line of loving younger women, from Olga to Michelle Vian and Arlette El Kaïm, while fictionally killing off parents and father figures in *Les Mouches* and *Les Mains sales*. Freud had needed bullying surrogate fathers. "You see, Fliess," he says in the screenplay, "people like me need to be tyrannized. I don't know why."

Sartre had reacted in the opposite way to the paternal vacuum. He had been able, even as a student, not only to manage without paternal guidance but to profit from his contempt toward authorities. And though he needed, like Freud, to cram an abnormal amount of work into each day, he needed no prodding from outside. The tyrant had been securely internalized. And while Freud had been devaluing his father by believing the stories of his hysterical patients, Sartre, who had acquired an equally strong grudge against his mother, was devaluing the parent-child relationship, not only denouncing the family but committing sacrilege against it by seducing all his surrogate daughters. Soon he will even go to the extreme of adopting a young mistress as his daughter.

Sartre's declaration of war on the father figure meant that he had to live permanently under siege. He was in constant fear of being influenced, and when he was, he had to deny it, even to himself. The fear of influence was so anguishing, the defense system so overdeveloped, the belief in making fresh starts so compulsive that he refused to learn anything even from what he wrote himself. In the screenplay he could exploit the understanding he had acquired of his own self-destructiveness by exposing the self-destructiveness of Freud, who goes on smoking in spite of his cough. But Sartre went on making ashtrays overflow with the stubs of Boyards and gave complete freedom to his other self-destructive tendencies, including the compulsion to go on overworking throughout the autumn and winter.

After completing the synopsis on December 15, 1958, he resumed work on the *Critique*. In the same way that he had once been obsessed by the contrast between lived experience and adventure stories, he was now struggling to explain the relationship between the individual moment of experience and the history in which moments have at most a symbolical value: each particularity is representative of the total reality. Dialectical reason was attractive because it seemed to offer him a means of uniting each moment, as experienced, with the historical totalization: a relationship must be established between each of history's component events and its overall meaning.

His assumption is that human activity always sets up a tension between itself and everything in the past that has gone into making the status quo. Hunger is a need that forces me to rearrange the universe, however slightly: an apple, which grew, is absorbed into a digestive system. In orienting ourselves toward the future, we disturb the past. As a writer Sartre had discovered that the reality of the mountain can be conveyed by a story about a pilot flying over it, the desert realized in an account of the traveler whose life it threatens, though neither the mountain nor the desert takes any action. In the same way, history is an adversary that goes on absorbing and negating human initiative. This idea should have educed vivid writing, but, hamstrung with abstractions, Sartre mostly fails to bring his subject matter alive except when writing about the French Revolution. His trite remarks about factory workers obviously derive from hearsay: in Husserlian terms these are "empty" intuitions.

Superficially it might seem odd that, dividing his time between screenplay and book, he was content to put so much good writing into dialogue destined for Hollywood and so much bad writing into what should have become his greatest philosophical work. Though there are sentimental and melodramatic lapses in the screenplay, the general level of the writing is high. Sartre, defying his principles, is allowing himself to write well. In the *Critique* he was conscious of writing badly. He would later say that the book could have been better written had he taken time to make cuts and revisions. The narrow escape from a heart attack had warned him to be careful how he allocated time, and this sharpened his ambivalence toward good writing. If he was helping to jerk contemporary Marxism out of its somnolence, he was doing something important, but to write imaginative literature or to spend time on polishing his prose was to shut himself off from other people in the present, to abdicate from the possibility of putting pressure on the future.

It was not long since he had given up all his lingering hopes of completing "La Dernière Chance." He said in 1959 that one of his main reasons for starting *Les Séquestrés d'Altona* had been frustration at failing to finish his novel: "I can't express the ambiguities of our period in this story, which is set in 1943. On the other hand, this unfinished work weighs down on me: I find it hard to start another novel without having completed this one."[13] He had little incentive, anyway, to start a new one, believing he had outgrown his literary ambitions: "I had transposed religious needs into literary longings . . . writing is an escape, a sign of weakness."[14] But the play would present both Wanda and Evelyne with a bouquet of opportunities.

Looking back on the writing he had done before he was forty, he associated it with his childhood fear of death. Just as a Christian could use earthly life to prove himself worthy of immortality, a writer could merit posthumous glory. But Sartre, looking skeptically backward at his bids for immortality, could exploit his insight in the screenplay. Freud is compulsive about arriving early whenever he has to catch a train. The phobia has roots in early childhood. His first train journey took him from happiness in Freiberg to poverty in Vienna. After trains had come to represent death and misery, his fear of death was transposed into fear of missing trains. In Sartre's synopsis the phobia is established in an early sequence and cured on the final page. The instincts of the artist were still functioning in Sartre long after he had decided to stop functioning as an artist.

Without explicitly repudiating *L'Etre et le Néant,* he was indicating that he now believed desires and memories could be pushed down into the unconscious. Much of the plot turns on this. One male patient has suppressed his patricidal impulses. Cecily Körtner's strabismus—it must have amused Sartre to inflict his own ailment on a beautiful woman—derives from an experience she did not want to remember with her father's corpse, and she has repressed her memories of how he died in a brothel and of a quarrel about the pretty governess who was dismissed by his jealous wife. When Sartre accepted the commission, he had not known how deeply it would involve him. Though the screenplay was never to be made into a film—it was too long for Huston, and television companies have so far ignored it—it deserves to be taken as a piece of writing no less serious than Sartre's biography of Baudelaire. It is no less thoughtful, while the texture of the writing is no less rich. Considered alongside Sartre's three biographies, it emerges as more straightforwardly biographical than any of them, and though Freud is not canonized, he is treated no less respectfully than Genet. He is not given the heroic treatment Huston probably wanted, but in contrast to the other doctors, who are shown to be doctrinaire, self-involved, pompous, reactionary, and prejudiced, Freud has the courage to look openmindedly at the clues that present themselves in clinical practice. Initially a weak man, he gains strength through his determination to find out the truth.

Like Freud's, Sartre's life was full of quarrels, and for two years he had not been on speaking terms with Francis Jeanson, who had disapproved of his reaction to the Soviet intervention in Hungary during 1956. Since the beginning of 1958 Jeanson had been campaigning for the Algerian rebels by editing *Vérités pour* . . . , the clandestine monthly. One of the women in Jeanson's network was a friend of Evelyne Rey, who had no difficulty in persuading Sartre to resume contact with his former colleague, and as soon as the two men saw each other again, Sartre was pledging full support. "You know I'm one hundred percent in agreement with the action you're taking. Use me in any way you can." He immediately gave Jeanson an interview for the June issue of his monthly. The French people, he said, "have no other defense in this country, which is turning fascist and ruining itself bit by bit, than to acknowledge frankly their new but profound solidarity with the Algerian fighters."[15] Jeanson also involved Sartre's *Temps Modernes* colleagues in pro-Algerian activity. De Beauvoir agreed that her car and her flat could be used; Péju and Lanzmann offered to shelter Algerians; Leiris gave money.[16]

IT was in Rome, when Sartre again spent the summer there, that he settled down to finish his play, transferring the action to Altona, a district of Hamburg, and transforming the Frenchman who had tortured Algerians into a German who had tortured partisans during the war. Sartre also developed a motif he had introduced in the screenplay: Freud is called in to see Charles von Schroeh, a man who for six years has never stepped outside his room. He sits on a kitchen stool with thin red tape around his legs. He believes that only the tape is stopping him from going out and killing someone in the street. But when Freud hypnotizes him, it emerges that the fantasy of killing a stranger disguises his impulse to kill the father he despises.

In the screenplay, despite numerous references to anti-Semitism, Sartre makes little effort to show that individuality is, as he had contended in the *Critique,* an unimportant by-product of social forces. Though the new play follows the script in centering on the father-son relationship, it follows the *Critique* in trying to look at contemporary history as it might be viewed by a future historian and in demonstrating that choices derive not from the willpower of a private individual but from the economy. The father, head of a Protestant family ennobled by Wilhelm II, is a leading Hamburg shipbuilder who has tried to remain politically uncommitted. Without supporting the Nazi party, he has had dealings with its leaders, having sold them land that has been used as a concentration camp. Frantz, like Götz, is a man caught between two traditions. Educated to be imperious, he has resented the superior manipulative power of the father, who can extricate him from any difficulty. Even when Frantz tries to rescue a Polish rabbi who has escaped from the concentration camp, the father can still protect him but not the rabbi. The experience of seeing the Jew beaten to death is crucial: "Two leaders—either one must kill the other or become his wife. I was Hitler's wife. The rabbi was bleeding, and I discovered at the heart of my impotence I don't know what acquiescence. I have supreme power. Hitler has made me an Other, implacable and holy, made me himself."

Once again De Beauvoir came to spend a month in Rome with Sartre. Again he showed her what he had written of the play, and again the "little judge" found that her advice had helped him greatly. He went on working at it while she was there, and when he gave her his draft of the final act, in which a family council sat in judgment on

Frantz, she was again reminded of Sudermann. Sartre's original idea, he told her, had been for a confrontation between father and son. As soon as he reverted to this, they were both satisfied with the result.[17] The scene shows that Frantz is what he has been made—not so much by his father (who, like the father in "L'Enfance d'un chef," has groomed his son to be a leader) as by the shipbuilding business. "My poor child! I wanted you to run the firm after me. It does the running. It chooses its men. Me, I'm not needed any more. I own it, but I'm no longer in command. As for you, little prince; it rejected you from the first moment. Why should it need a prince? It trains and recuits its own managers." Imbued with his father's talents, passions, and appetite for power, Frantz has been prepared for a life that existed only in the pre-war world. Impersonal forces gave birth to the frustration behind the personal need for violence, the need to torture.

Sartre is building his play toward a powerful final climax in which father and son, like lovers, commit suicide together. When Frantz was eight the father used to say: "We must get you ready for the war. We're going to drive really fast." And they drove, at speed, over the Devil's Bridge. This is how they will die, while the two women who are devoted to Frantz—his incestuous sister (played by Wanda) and his brother's wife (played by Evelyne Rey)—listen to one of the tape recordings he has made during thirteen years of self-imposed solitary confinement in his room, defending his century against the crabs who, for him, represent posterity and sit in judgment on Germany. They are the totalizers; they also incarnate the old shellfish phobia. *Huis clos* had centered on a man caught in limbo between two women and needing to be judged; Frantz has created his own limbo, but his need is not dissimilar—to have judgment passed on him. This was Sartre's need, and in what was his last serious attempt to offer himself as a creative artist to the judgment of critics and theatergoers, his underlying motives were bizarrely muddled. He was helping two mistresses, who were both beautiful, both desperate for success, both unable to sell themselves in the theater except when he wrote parts for them. He needed money. He wanted to give himself a final chance to rework motifs that had always been important to him: the loving attempt of the sister, Léni, to enter a man's madness echoes the futile attempt of the wife in "La Chambre"; in *Morts sans sépulture* he had already made an imaginative effort to probe the motivations of the torturer.

The title of the new play, *Les Séquestrés d'Altona*, echoes Sartre's title for his 1957 essay on Tintoretto, "Le Séquestré de Venise." Like the painter who used his sons as apprentices, Von Gerlach produces a dynasty of shipbuilders, while both families incarnate bourgeois puri-

tanism during the decline of a formerly aristocratic republic. This subject matter seemed to promise an opportunity to combine Marxian
with Freudian insights. As in the Freud screenplay, Sartre no longer
denies the possibility of defining or understanding a personality by dig-
ging up memories from the past. In his overanxiety to show how behavior is conditioned by memories of the past, he goes to such lengths as
introducing gauchely filmic flashbacks, using part of the stage for a
straightforward reenactment of past events. The effect in the theater is
clumsy, and throughout most of the action the treatment of mental imbalance is less convincing than in the screenplay, partly because
Frantz's abnormal behavior seems contrived. Too much depends on argument, and Sartre fails to splice the Marxian and the Freudian together. The screenplay had been authentically Freudian, taking its
shape, like Freud's case histories, from a progressive movement toward
enlightenment, maturity, and health; the play is informed with a non-
Marxist pessimism, and its movement is toward death and defeat.
Frantz's apologia for the twentieth century is founded on self-deception, and in the final monologue Sartre comes closer than ever before to
affirming that there is such a thing as human nature and that it is evil:

> The century would have been good if man had not been kept under sur-
> veillance by his merciless age-old enemy, by the carnivorous species
> sworn to his destruction, by the malignant, hairless beast, by man. One
> and one make one, that's our riddle. The beast was hiding, we saw his
> look suddenly, in the naked eyes of our neighbors. Then we struck, pre-
> ventively, in legitimate self-defense. I took the beast by surprise, I struck,
> a man fell, in his dying eyes I saw the beast, still alive, myself.

This is fine theatrical rhetoric, but it is only through statement, not action, that Sartre can clarify what he wants to say about violence; the
resonance of this prose derives from a combination of strong feelings
about Algeria and deep fears about the next world war.

After the month with De Beauvoir in Rome, Sartre had moved on to
stay for a few weeks with Arlette El Kaïm in Venice. Starting the vacation in one of the grandest hotels, they ran short of money and moved
to a noisy *pensione* near the station. It was here that he worked on the
final sequence. When he performed Frantz's monologue for her she
thought it too melodramatic for the rest of the play, but she was misled
by his declamatory performance.[18]

He had told an interviewer that he wanted the audience to condemn
the characters as being the same sort of people who worked during the

occupation at the Gestapo headquarters in the Rue des Saussaies.[19] In fact, he generates considerable sympathy for all but one of the characters—the younger brother, who is cowardly and calculating. Wanting Frantz to appear as "a victim insofar as one is ready to excuse him and a criminal insofar as one is ready to condemn him,"[20] Sartre delays until the fourth act the revelation that he has been a torturer.

He was still revising Frantz's final speech when the play went into rehearsal, with François Darbon directing a cast headed by Serge Reggiani as Frantz and Fernand Ledoux as the father. As usual, there was trouble during rehearsals; as usual, the main sticking point was Sartre's obstinacy over cuts; as usual, De Beauvoir attended rehearsals and acted as intermediary, not only encouraging him to cut but helping him to make the cuts, though, as usual, she was in a difficult position, understanding the extent to which his plays had their roots in his relationships with other women. The actors were having trouble learning their lines, and the opening had to be postponed until September 23, but the play was still far too long when it opened. It was only after the first night that Sartre submitted, agreeing to drastic cuts that took nearly half an hour off the running time. Even now his motivation was suspect. Pressure from the theater manager, Véra Korène, no doubt played a part, but he was in a hurry to leave Paris with Arlette, and he did not even wait for the reviews.

He had been invited to Ireland by John Huston, who had not yet read the Freud screenplay. To escape from American taxation the fifty-three-year-old film director had rented an enormous Georgian house in County Kildare, sixty miles southwest of Dublin. He had been there since 1952.

From his bedroom Sartre could see a seemingly endless expanse of fields with cows and horses in them. The producer of the film was to be Max Reinhardt's son Wolfgang, who was staying at the house and helped Sartre make cuts. The other guests were a random mixture. After inviting people he hardly knew, Huston would pay little attention to them. Reinhardt's mistress, Mrs. Phillips, did more than their host to put the guests at their ease. Huston, who enjoyed doing the opposite, once left Sartre and Arlette alone with a major who spoke no French. Hoping to start a conversation in English, the major said: "Churchill is funny when he speaks French." The only response Sartre managed was "Ha, ha!" Arlette, who knew English, was too shy to talk, and the three of them waited in embarrassed silence until they were called for dinner.[21]

De Beauvoir wrote to Sartre, enclosing reviews of the play, which were much more favorable than he had expected. Reggiani's performance was singled out for praise, while production and décor came under attack.

Huston talked a great deal about *Let There Be Light,* his 1945 film about shell-shocked soldiers. He had seen men coming off boats in large groups, some mute, some amnesiac, some paralyzed, some shaking. He often said that shooting this film had been like a religious experience, and one evening he showed it to his houseguests, together with his 1944 film *The Battle of San Pietro.* Sartre found both films mediocre and propagandist, but when the lights came up afterward, Huston's eyes were wet with tears. In *Let There Be Light* he had filmed army psychiatrists hypnotizing victims of combat neurosis, and Huston, who enjoyed showing the prowess he had acquired as a hypnotist, offered to demonstrate on "the Arab girl." He had formed the impression that Arlette was there as Sartre's secretary. Her English was good, and after each working session she typed out a translation of Sartre's notes and suggestions. Huston had no difficulty in hypnotizing her, but after seeing her succumb, Sartre offered himself as a subject, and this time Huston had to admit failure.

Sartre was equally resistant in other ways to this tall, tough, equable man who usually found it so easy to charm and to dominate. Sartre had no personal experience of Hollywood directors. Hollywood films had been a major source of pleasure throughout his life—he went to the movies, on average, once a week with Michelle, in addition to his movie-going with De Beauvoir and with other girl friends—but trying to work with Huston was quite unlike working in the Paris theater with directors who were impressed by his intellectual standing and respectfully tolerant toward long monologues. Huston, who liked action, simplicity, and having his own way, soon aroused Sartre's antipathy. Writing to De Beauvoir, Sartre reported that Huston had used himself up. "The man has emigrated. I don't know where. He's not even sad: he's *empty,* except in moments of childish vanity, when he puts on a red dinner jacket or rides a horse (not very well) or counts his paintings or tells workmen what to do. Impossible to hold his attention five minutes: he can no longer work, he runs away from thinking."[22]

Huston had written successful screenplays of his own and had often worked collaboratively with other screenwriters, but he had never encountered anyone like this Frenchman, who, while he talked, made notes of his own ideas and who got up so early that he had usually written about twenty-five pages of dialogue by the time Huston appeared, around ten-thirty.

He noticed how heavily Sartre was relying on pills and generally formed a most unfavorable impression: Sartre was "a little barrel of a man and as ugly as a human being can be. His face was both bloated and pitted, his teeth were yellowed and he was wall-eyed. He wore a gray suit, black shoes, white shirt, tie and vest. His appearance never changed. He would come down in the morning in this suit, and he would still be wearing it last thing at night. The suit always appeared to be clean and the shirt was clean, but I never knew if he owned one gray suit or several identical gray suits."

The routine of work was interrupted when Huston came down one morning to find Sartre with a swollen cheek. He had an abscessed tooth, but when Huston suggested driving to a dentist in Dublin, Sartre opted for a local Galway dentist and made no fuss when the man pulled out the tooth.

Sartre stayed in the house, St. Clerans, for ten days, but the only point on which the two men were agreed was that Marilyn Monroe would be the ideal Cecily. According to Huston, Sartre judged her to be the finest actress alive. But neither man acquired any respect for the other. Sartre was not amused when Huston claimed that in his unconscious there was nothing,[23] while Huston found Sartre totally unwilling to be flexible. "I've never worked with anyone so obstinate and categorical. Impossible to have a conversation with him. Impossible to interrupt him. You'd wait for him to catch his breath but he wouldn't. The words came out in an absolute torrent. It happened once that, exhausted by the strain, I walked out of the room. The buzzing of his voice followed me a moment, and when I came back, he hadn't even noticed I'd gone out." Sartre's version of the story is different: several of them had been in a smoking room, talking, when Huston abruptly walked out. Sartre struggled valiantly to keep the conversation going.[24]

The most obvious of the problems was the length of the script, which would have run, according to Huston, for five hours. Sartre was not unwilling to rewrite, and after returning to Paris he went on working at it, making substantial changes. In several of the new sequences Viennese anti-Semitism came into sharper focus, but instead of shortening the screenplay, he made it longer, rather as if he were writing for the Paris theater.

The film was eventually shot with a hybrid script. In 1947, two years after he had scripted *Let There Be Light* for Huston, Charles Kaufman had drafted a screenplay about Freud. Wolfgang Reinhardt collaborated with him on revising this, and they incorporated some of Sartre's material. But he did not allow his name to be used, and during shooting still more changes were made in the text as Huston introduced dialogue of his own, adding to the confusion of Montgomery Clift, who played Freud, with the nineteen-year-old Susannah York as Cecily. According to Huston, "Much of what Sartre had done was in our version—in fact it was the backbone of it. In some scenes his dialogue was left intact."[25]

(21)

Unofficial Ambassador

THE sixties began with the death of Camus. On January 4, 1960, he was in a car with Michel Gallimard (Gaston's nephew), Michel's wife, Janine, and her eighteen-year-old daughter, Anne. They were on their way back to Paris from the south of France. Michel was driving the Facel-Vega, not going fast. They were on the *route nationale*, just outside the village of Villeblevin, sixty-eight miles from Paris, when the car swerved off the damp road, hit one of the roadside plane trees, and crashed against another. Camus was thrown backward and killed instantly as his head hit the rear window, his skull fractured, his neck broken. The cause of the accident is still unknown. Perhaps an axle broke, perhaps the steering went out of control. The two women survived, but Gallimard died six days later from a brain hemorrhage.[1]

As soon as Claude Lanzmann heard the news he telephoned Sartre, but it was De Beauvoir, alone in the flat, who answered the telephone. When she hung up, throat tight, lips trembling, she ordered herself not to cry. "He no longer meant anything to me." But throughout the evening she, Sartre, and Bost spoke of almost nothing but Camus. Sartre's homage to him appeared in *France-Observateur* on the seventh. "We had quarreled, he and I, but a quarrel is nothing, even if you never see each other again. It's simply another way of living together, without losing sight of each other in this narrow little world which is given to us. . . . In this century and against history he was the representative and the present heir of that long line of moralists whose work perhaps constitutes what is most original in French literature. . . . Camus will always go on being one of the main forces in our cultural realm and representing, in his own way, the history of France and of this century."[2] Sartre was obviously trying not to contradict what he had written in his angry reply to Camus's *Temps Modernes* letter, but quite apart from the immediate illogicality ("never see each other . . . without losing sight of each other") there is a contradiction between "Only half of you lives among us and you are tempted to withdraw altogether" (August 1952) and this funeral tribute to Camus for always putting "the political act in question." Whereas Sartre's letter had charged Camus with letting his morality turn into moralism—"Today it is only literature, perhaps it will be immorality tomorrow"—the *France-Observateur* article makes the opposite point. However much you disagree with Camus, he is a moral force you have to reckon with. For Sartre the contradiction was unavoidable, but there was no dialectical escape route.

WHEN Sartre was invited to Cuba, he was not at first eager to go, though he knew it would not be the Cuba he had seen in 1949 with Dolores. It was in April 1958 that Fidel Castro had declared total war against Fulgencio Batista's government, and in January 1959 the president had fled to Dominica. Manuel Urrutia had been appointed provisional governor, but Castro had strengthened his position by purges and by postponing the elections. Sartre and De Beauvoir were invited by Carlos Franqui, editor of the biggest Cuban newspaper, *Revolución*. Eventually, persuaded, they left in February 1960, wanting firsthand experience of a revolution that was still in progress.

Unlike China, Cuba was small enough for direct and frequent contact between leaders and people. In a luxurious, air-conditioned hotel, the Nacional, Sartre had a bedroom larger than his Paris flat.[3] The Havana Hilton had been renamed the Havana Libre, but the twenty or so expensive hotels were all thriving. He strolled with De Beauvoir for hours in the streets. In the working-class districts the poor seemed neither better nor worse off than formerly; other areas looked more prosperous. There were plenty of deluxe restaurants, and the brothels, which had been closed after the revolution, had reopened.[4] But the country was visibly in the hands of the rebels. "Beards and long hair are still the insignia of the 3000 pioneers of the revolution."[5] The average age of government ministers was twenty-nine.[6]

They met Che Guevara, who received them at midnight for coffee in his office at the National Bank. "I'm first of all a doctor," he said, "then something of a soldier, and finally, as you can see, a banker."[7] He had exerted himself to acquire the technical knowledge a state banker needs.[8] The revolutionary leaders seemed to be managing on little sleep. When Castro arranged to pick up Sartre and De Beauvoir at their hotel, he arrived punctually at a quarter to eight in the morning and had to wait ten minutes for them. He then announced that he would take them to see several beaches, including Varadero, the best known, sixty-two miles from Havana. This was a tour of inspection Castro had been planning to make anyway, needing to revive the island's tourism.

Several times the car was halted by groups of peasants clamoring for Castro to look at villages under cooperative construction. Like a tired but loving father, he seemed unable to refuse any demand for his presence and attention. Eventually Sartre asked whether people had the right to anything they demanded. Castro's answer was: "A man's needs give him his fundamental right over other people." "And if he asks for the moon?" "If someone asked me for the moon it would be because someone needed it." Humanism, Sartre pursued, should be founded on need. "That's the only humanism there is," Castro agreed. "We have to demand from each man everything he can give, but I'll never sacrifice this generation to the next. That would be abstract."[9]

Finally invited to Castro's home, Sartre and De Beauvoir were driven to the marshes of Cienaga de Zapata. A motorboat took them across a canal that was being dredged. They slept in a long hut with a corrugated iron roof and reinforced concrete walls. On either side of the central corridor were about twenty mattresses on double-decker bunks. Castro, his brother, his family, and his guests would sleep in the same space. Before supper Castro went outside with a shotgun, took aim, fired into a muddy pond. A large fish floated to the surface, stomach upward.[10] Generally Castro was friendly and warm, though anxious about the way Sartre would report on his impressions in France. It would be better, Castro suggested, to avoid the word "socialism."[11]

Almost every day the newspapers published photographs of Sartre and De Beauvoir with Castro and Che. Che came out with one sentence Sartre would often quote: "It's not my fault if reality is Marxist."[12] Introducing a talk by Sartre on Cuban television, Castro told viewers he was their friend. After this, people stopped him in the street and passing taxi drivers shouted: "Sartre, it's Sartre!"[13] But what pleased him most was the endemic gaiety. "It's the honeymoon of the revolution," he said.[14]

Having promised to write a preface for a new edition of Paul Nizan's book *Aden-Arabie,* he worked on it in the mornings after breakfasting with De Beauvoir on strong black coffee and pineapple. Addressing himself to the younger generation, he incorporated such phrases as "In a society which reserves its women for the old and the rich ..."[15] Although Sartre could not have predicted the 1968 rebellion, he was starting to sow seeds for it. Explicitly blaming himself for having failed to rebel, as Nizan did, at the Ecole Normale, Sartre was implying that anything less than rebellion was ineffectual. In January he had given two interviews, one to the seventeen-year-old Patrice Cournot, editor of a review for the young, *Le Semeur*,[16] and the other for the first issue of *Les Cahiers libres de la jeunesse*,[17] in which he told the interviewer that the idea of justice was neither indispensable nor useful. No one could be free unless the whole world was, and life would not be human until everyone had enough to eat. The preface to *Aden-Arabie* is more self-accusing. Belonging, as he did, to a generation that had betrayed its youthful ideals, how could he give advice to the young? How could he say "Be Cubans, be Russians, be Chinese, or if you prefer, be Africans?"[18] Men of his age had no advice to give, but Nizan could still speak to the young: "Yesterday he was our contemporary; today he is theirs."[19] Speculating on what Nizan might have told them, Sartre echoed the conversation with Castro: "You are dying of modesty. Dare to desire. Be insatiable. . . . Don't be ashamed to want the moon. You should have it."[20] In leaving for Aden, Nizan had rejected everything he had been given in France, where he had felt constrained and manipulated. He had left to inspect the damage done by imperialism.

In blaming himself for not following Nizan into political commitment while at the Ecole Normale, Sartre was blaming himself for not having already reached conclusions he was to reach much later. "Before Sartre," as Merleau-Ponty sums it up, "Nizan lived this pan-tragism, this flooding anguish which is the flux of history."[21] Where Nizan saw an unhappy human intermingling, a reciprocity of suffering, Sartre had then seen only the mutual estrangement of subject-object relationships. But Merleau-Ponty is right to be suspicious of the mature Sartre who blames his immature self for not knowing better. What he does not admit now is that he did know something then which he has since chosen to forget: that beneath its objectivity, Communist thought is "secretly flabby and humid," that "the Communist negation, being positively inverted, is not what it says it is."[22] Sartre had suspected from the beginning what Nizan did not discover until the Nazi-Soviet pact—that it takes courage to join the party and cowardice to remain a member. Sartre was surely wrong to assume that if Nizan had survived, the Resistance would have brought him back into the Communist ranks.

On the return journey Sartre and De Beauvoir spent eight hours in New York, where the Cuban attaché had organized a press conference at the Waldorf so that the Sartrian truth about Cuba could immediately be disseminated.[23] After arriving in Paris, Sartre turned down an opportunity to chat with Khrushchev at a meeting of writers and journalists but took De Beauvoir to a reception held for the Soviet leader at the embassy. In her simple black dress the placid Nina Khrushchev contrasted sharply with the overdressed Gaullist ladies in their elaborate hats.[24]

The incongruity between Sartre's personal popularity and the popular indifference to his major work was never more apparent than during the spring of 1960. In March, when he lectured on theater at the Sorbonne, speaking for over two hours without a break, the students gave him a huge ovation and surged around him as he walked to his taxi.[25] But while his preface helped *Aden-Arabie* to make a big impact on students and the general reading public, the *Critique,* which was published in May, attracted little excitement, except from the Communists and from the right-wing reviewers, who savaged it. The drive to work on the second part had only the most exiguous connection with any image of how readers might react.

Most of the 781 typed pages were probably written between Sartre's return from Cuba in March and his departure for Brazil in September, but he was no further than page 20 when he slipped into his old habit of rashly promising a separate work to cover ground he would not be able to cover in the present one. He would write another book about conflict, he said, demonstrating the full truth of dialectical materialism.[26] Prepared though he always was to write at enormous length, Sartre was already half aware that he would reach no conclusion, and despite the number of unredeemed promises he already had on his conscience, he went on making them, like a gambler asking for credit.

He starts the second part of the *Critique* with a new effort to keep a promise made in the first. The dialectic, he had said, must "proceed *from individuals* and not from some sort of supra-individual ensemble."[27] He had soon afterward lost sight of the individual, doing what he condemns Hegel for doing—arguing aprioristically that both individuals and collectives are part of a totalization which produces them and goes beyond them. While a battle is being fought, thousands of consciousnesses are active, but history ignores them. When Sartre now tries to identify imaginatively with the individual soldier, the writing is briefly reminiscent of *Les Chemins de la liberté,* but the concrete is soon displaced by the abstract as he reiterates the question he still sees as crucial: Is totalization possible without an extraterrestrial totalizer or does history disintegrate into "a plurality of individual histories?"[28]

Boxing is then made to serve as an analogy for social conflict: Are the two boxers collaborating on a common project while lashing out at each other? They are gathering up the aggressions of the audience, he argues, and *"boxing as a whole"* is present in each blow they exchange; both men belong to "the world of boxing," which has conventions, as well as rules. But he writes about this "world" as if he has not seen much of it, and his attempt to portray two boxers is halfhearted because his interest in them is half abstract. They are not individuals; they are manifestations of the concrete universal that is incessantly producing itself as the animation and temporalization of individual contingency.[29] Conflict, which is unity fighting against itself, pits *common individuals* against each other. When he concludes that one "enveloping totalization" has been present throughout the boxing match, this seems to have little bearing on the separate consciousnesses of soldiers on a battlefield. It is not enough to explain that competing subgroups always express the workings of a wider dialectic.

Nor does he ever look critically at Marx's contention that the history of every society is the history of class conflict. Even boxing is explained in terms of class. Capitalism domesticates violence by coercing the underprivileged into realizing their aggressions against each other. The historian, like the policeman, needs witnesses, but in violence there are only participants, so the evidence is suspect.[30] Many good points, like this one, emerge sporadically, but the argument is hopelessly unstructured, partly because Sartre's political objectives are at odds with his philosophical objectives. He needs to believe that his thinking can contribute to contemporary socialism; it may be helpful, in the future, to leaders of progressive movements if he can explain how the Bolshevik revolution led to Stalinism. Also wanting to clarify his own ideas on this question, he devotes four hundred pages to it, with his misgivings about the Soviet bureaucracy visibly sharpened by his exhilarating experiences of the close relationship between leaders and led in Cuba. In the Russian Revolution, as in the French, the cause of terror had been loss of contact with the people.

Was it conceivable, he asked, that Soviet society could be controlled by "a group of impecunious, unprivileged revolutionaries who refuse all titles?"[31] The question, he suggests, may be connected with the question of whether divergent pressures and interests inside revolutionary Russia had coagulated into a single, comprehensible history. He analyzes Soviet history from the conflict between Stalin and Trotsky during the twenties to the revival of anti-Semitism in the early fifties. First he argues that the conflict between the two leaders was not the result of personal incompatibility but the totalization of a "contradiction in the party's common *praxis*."[32] Trotsky's urge to revolutionize Europe was defeated by Stalin's more realistic concentration on building socialism in one country. For this he needed a united work force, even if he had to "destroy the workers as free practical organisms and as common individuals."[33] Elites were created in both the proletariat and the bureaucracy; the oppression extirpated by the revolution was replaced by new oppression, necessary to unify the work force; forced collectivization and terror reduced the peasantry to resentful impotence.

The new generation of Soviet peasants has internalized the terror.[34] In Soviet society, each local *praxis,* each singular destiny is an incarnation of the totalizing *praxis.*[35] Discussing collectivization, Sartre shows himself to be aware of the misery it caused but unsympathetic. Human suffering vanishes in his abstract summary of "this irreversible temporalization which in history will take the name of Stalinism."[36] Sometimes his use of jargon is in what he would once have called bad faith.

Stalin is described as "not just an individual": he incarnates and singularizes the practical totalization that constitutes this moment of Russian history.[37] An inflexible leader was needed, but could someone else, with a different temperament and a different past, have avoided the purges, the show trials, the labor camps? Though Stalin's brutality is condemned, together with the "absurd cultural isolation" into which he led the Soviet Union and the "endless lies about the condition of the European worker,"[38] Sartre argues that Stalin's personal aggressiveness is inseparable from aggressions necessary to the historical situation: "If the process of planned growth could be directed by an angel, *praxis* would proceed with the maximum objectivity. The angel would never be blind, spiteful or brutal: it would always be what it has to be." But a fallible human being is liable to do too little or too much and then go too far in the opposite direction. Stalin's policies did not tally with the "objectives and demands of socialization," but they were inevitable "insofar as this society in its first phase demanded to be controlled by one individual."[39] Though Sartre rejects Plekhanov's doctrine that the function forms the man, he also rejects the psychological explanation of historical events. In the French Revolution, Robespierre's inferiority complex did not cause the terror, which was necessary because he and his colleagues had to invent a practical externalization of the dangers they had internalized.[40] But Sartre had not set out to contradict Marx's assumption that the mode of production is always the decisive factor, and the amalgam of evidence and argument was pulling the book away from its objective—to show that history was intelligible as a totalization without a totalizer. Nor could Sartre resolve the difficulty with the formulaic assertion that history integrates accidents and contingencies, that each event, however private, should be considered as an incarnation.[41]

It is understandable, of course, that he should have chosen to reexamine the Bolshevik and French revolutions without asking himself whether they provide the most useful illustrations of the way history moves. Was it necessary or unnecessary for slaughter and totalitarian bureaucracy to displace revolutionary idealism? He believed that *praxis* is invariably deformed because the men behind it invariably "become other men involved in achieving other objectives by other means."[42] Human activity is helplessly absorbed into the practico-inert. Men "realize themselves in the process of objectifying themselves, and this changes them."[43] The new phrase Sartre introduces for this process is "totalization of envelopment," and he maintains, neither lucidly nor convincingly, that "all individual behavior represents the reproduction of the social totalization of envelopment under the forms of an enveloped totalization."[44]

When he goes on to speak about the "circularity of counterfinalities," he virtually invents a historical unconscious. Our autonomy is undermined by "totalization of envelopment," which produces an environment that deflects the course of our actions.[45] All the elements in the practical field, including the agents, are conditioned by the totalization of envelopment.[46] Though Sartre is now writing, in his characteristic jargon, no less deterministically than Hegel, he is at least penetrating more deeply than he did in Part 1 into the questions he had raised at the outset as crucial. "If the dialectic is possible," he had said, *praxis* must be explained as an experience of freedom and of necessity, while swarms of individual destinies must appear in history as subject to a totalizing movement.[47] When Part 1 patently failed to fulfill these conditions, how could he have been content to leave Part 2 unpublished, even if it succeeds only partially?

The decision not to publish must mean that he was aware of the extent to which he had fallen short of his objectives, but he could not have fulfilled them just by writing about revolutionary conflict and the conflict that follows revolution. He would have had to deal with power conflicts in bourgeois society and to demonstrate that the history of the world was a single history, not a proliferation of separate histories. He might also have been forced to question the extent to which he had been misled by a tendency he shared with other French intellectuals— to treat the history of France as if it were coextensive with the history of Western civilization.

He had set himself an impossible task; he was addicted to the impossible. Since 1948 he had stood no more chance of changing the PCF from outside than of keeping Europe out of the Atlantic Pact or creating a new alliance between Marx and Freud. Without completing any of his major projects he was making ever-increasing demands on his phenomenal stamina. His style of living was precariously balanced between contradictory demands. He was traveling dutifully around the world in response to invitations prompted by the publicity he could bring, while, in the time that remained, he went on living the half-life of a writer. He was fond of saying: "You have to choose: live or tell stories."[48] He no longer wanted to tell stories but refused to choose. During the last twenty years of his life he was going to give at least as much time to travel, political journalism, and agitprop as to philosophy, literature, and biography, but when he was in Paris he spent most of the day in his untidy study. A young writer who visited him for the first time in March 1961 observed: "Literature had overrun the room. The bookshelves could not accommodate the books: there were piles on his desk, on chairs, on the floor, together with files, typescripts, notebooks, as well as pipes, packets of Boyard cigarettes, overflowing ashtrays, boxes of matches. Scarcely anywhere could you see an inch of the wood of the furniture."[49]

When he abandoned the *Critique* it was in order to concentrate on *L'Idiot de la famille*.[50] His addiction to the impossible was so helpless that even after abandoning a book, he would still go on for years, as he had with his ethics and his novel tetralogy, half believing that he might bring himself to do more work on it. Eight years later he would still be hoping that the second part of the *Critique* would eventually appear, though he spoke of what he had intended as if the intention belonged to the past: "I was going to end by studying the unity of objects in a society completely rent asunder by class struggle, and considering several classes and their actions to show how these objects were completely frustrated."[51]

DURING the second week in May 1960 he accepted another pretext for pushing work aside by reverting to his role as unofficial ambassador. He went to Yugoslavia at the invitation of the writers' union. Two of his plays, *Huis clos* and *Les Séquestrés d'Altona,* were being performed in Belgrade, and he went to see both productions; he was received by Marshal Tito, and he lectured to students at Belgrade University.

In the middle of June he appeared as a witness at the trial of Georges Arnaud, a journalist who had been arrested in April for "failing to denounce a malefactor." The malefactor was Francis Jeanson, who had invited correspondents of all the main foreign newspapers to a meeting about Algeria. Held by a military tribunal, the trial had a large audience of left-wing intellectuals; giving evidence, Sartre denounced the Algerian war and the repression in France: "Now we have no platform except the courts."[52] The overcrowded room was so hot that he left with De Beauvoir almost as soon as he had given his evidence. Arnaud, who was convicted, received a suspended sentence.[53]

Before his visit to Cuba, Sartre had been invited to visit Brazil, the likeliest candidate for revolution among the Latin-American countries. He now felt more inclined to accept the Brazilian invitation; according to progressive Brazilians, it would be helpful not only to the Cubans— for the fate of Cuba depended on Latin America—but also to the French left and the Algerians if an authoritative French voice were raised in Brazil to promote Castroism and to contradict pronouncements of De Gaulle's minister of cultural affairs, André Malraux.[54] Sartre and De Beauvoir decided to spend three months in Brazil, but before they left in mid-August, he had begun to formulate reasons for feeling hostile to almost everyone in France except the young. Writing the Nizan preface and reflecting on the men of his own age who had settled down into amoral materialism, he had felt a strong desire to distance himself both from them and from the *gauchistes* who had been so ineffectual in protesting against the war in Algeria. The younger generation, he told an interviewer, was not going to be content with "verbal action." "It is only the young who have responded to mystification in the right way—that's to say with violence. For me the only true men of the left in France today are twenty years old."[55] After this it was natural for Sartre to join forces with the signatories who pledged themselves to civil disobedience in the "Manifesto of the 121." "Their fates are linked too. The victory of the FLN will be the victory of the left." The other 120 dissidents included Marguerite Duras, Simone Signoret, Pierre Boulez, André Masson, Claude Lanzmann, and Claude Roy.

By the time he left for Brazil, Sartre, who had recklessly gone on overworking, was suffering from a deep-seated depression and from shingles.[56] He and De Beauvoir were met at the airport by the forty-eight-year-old Jorge Amado, the pioneer of the politically committed novel in Brazil. He introduced them to many of his hospitable friends and took them to Bahia, where he had grown up. Seventy percent of the population there was black. In the covered marketplace he bought Sartre and De Beauvoir necklaces and bracelets made of colored seeds, pottery, earthenware figurines, black-faced dolls, musical instruments, knickknacks. Remembering the marrow of gazelles' horns in Morocco, Sartre was nervous about the native cooking, but De Beauvoir sampled some of it.[57] At Recife an entertainment had been prepared for them, with blacks disguised as Indians dancing sophisticated ballets;[58] they attended two voodoo ceremonies,[59] and a *candomblé,* a religious ceremony amalgamating Haitian voodoo with African ritual and Catholic liturgy, combining incense with the sacrifice of chickens. In the streets at night, young foot-boxers fought with razor blades attached to their ankles.[60]

Sartre and De Beauvoir visited Copacabana and Rio, where they saw the work of young Brazilian architects, pupils of Le Corbusier. Of the three million inhabitants nearly a quarter were living in huts made of planks, iron sheeting, and cardboard on derelict land that was marshy or rocky. In the religious rituals of this depressed and undernourished subproletariat drugs were used to induce delirium, and in their trances initiates would inflict burns and wounds on themselves.[61]

De Beauvoir had read in Freyre's *Maîtres et esclaves* (*Masters and Slaves*) that in northeastern Brazil girls used to marry at thirteen, while at the height of their beauty, which had already begun to fade at fifteen; to his embarrassment, Sartre sometimes found himself ogling well-developed girls, forgetting how young they were.[62]

At his lectures audiences were responsive, especially when he talked about Cuba.[63] In Recife and Bahia he discussed Algeria without openly attacking the French government, but in a press conference at the university in Rio he replied candidly to questions about De Gaulle and Malraux. From then on the press paid attention to him, and when his book on Cuba, *Huracán sobre el azucar* (*Hurricane on the Sugar*), which had been hurriedly translated, arrived in Brazil, a mass of people turned up at the autographing session in a brightly decorated hall.[64] He had authorized Spanish, Portuguese, and English translations of the book, which was based on his articles in *France-Soir*, but he did not want it to appear in French.

When he and De Beauvoir flew to São Paolo, they were met by a crowd at the airport and found that a Sartre society had been formed at the university; in Rio they were given the rank of honorary citizens.

In France, Jeanson was due to be tried by a military tribunal. Sartre had promised Jeanson's lawyers to make a surprise appearance as a witness, but the date of the hearing had been postponed to September 7, while he was still in Brazil, and when Lanzmann telephoned him there, he said that all he could do was send a message to be read out. He dispatched a three-line telegram confirming his "total solidarity" with Jeanson's network, but even when the disappointed lawyers managed to offer him a free return flight, he refused to come, resisting the pleas of Lanzmann and Péju over the telephone and saying that he still had shingles. The most he was prepared to do was let Péju write a letter in his name. What Péju then wrote was strongly worded: "During the resistance, teachers at the Sorbonne did not hesitate to relay messages and make contacts. If Jeanson had asked me to carry suitcases or hide Algerian militants, and if I could have done it without endangering them, I would have done it without hesitation." The accused were in the dock "as our delegates. What they represent is the future of France. And the ephemeral power which is preparing to judge them no longer represents anything." Péju's draft was retouched by Lanzmann and typed. A forged signature was added, and since there was no authenticating envelope, the letter was presented to the tribunal together with Sartre's telegram.[65]

To the defendants Sartre's absence looked like a cowardly betrayal, but the letter caused a scandal. In *Le Figaro* Thierry Maulnier wrote that the only logical step for Sartre to take now was to join the ranks of the FLN with a gun or a bomb in his hand.[66] One deputy asked for legal action to be taken against him.[67] The minister of information accused him of representing "an anarchic and suicidal dictatorship wanting to force itself on a perplexed and decadent intelligentsia."[68]

Meanwhile Sartre and De Beauvoir went on touring Brazil. In Brasília they met the architect responsible for it, Oscar Niemeyer, who used them as his audience for a conversation with himself: "Is it possible to create socialist architecture in a nonsocialist country? Obviously not."[69] With Niemeyer and Amado, they met the president, Kubitschek, who considered Brasília to be his personal achievement.[70]

The end of their Brazilian trip was nightmarish. Ill with what was diagnosed as typhoid, De Beauvoir was taken to a hospital for tropical diseases in Recife. Depressed in his hotel, Sartre was drinking Scotch and taking phenolbarbital to avoid sleepless nights. Rumors reached them that Sartre would be arrested as soon as he arrived in France. He could buy no French newspapers, but finally a long-delayed letter from Lanzmann brought him up to date with events. The 121 signatories of the manifesto had been banned from broadcasting on radio or television. On October 1, police had seized the new issue of *Les Temps Modernes*. Five thousand war veterans had marched down the Champs-Elysées shouting "Kill Sartre." Lanzmann's advice was that instead of returning to Paris they should base themselves in Barcelona.[71]

Wanting to spend a few days in Havana on the way to Europe, they first had to make the thousand-mile journey back to Rio. In Cuba the honeymoon of the revolution was already over; they had the impression of less gaiety, less freedom.[72] In an interview he gave later to a Hungarian journalist Sartre complained: "I have the impression that in Cuba there is now interference with diverse literary tendencies."[73] But his misgivings would have no effect on the help he had already given to Castro by acting as his spokesman both in Brazil and in the West.

(22)

"Kill Sartre"

THEY flew to Madrid and then to Barcelona, where Bost and Jean Pouillon met them at a hotel near the cathedral. Thanks to the letter Sartre had encouraged Péju to forge but had not yet read, he had been much vilified in the press. Over the telephone Lanzmann now advised him and De Beauvoir to drive home: if they flew, it might cause brawling at the airport, and possibly they would be arrested.

When they arrived at the frontier the official told them he was under orders to advise Paris. Some of the 121 signatories were in prison; others had deliberately inculpated themselves for the sake of publicity. Eager to get themselves officially charged too, Sartre and De Beauvoir were surprised to encounter procrastination. An examining magistrate reported sick; after a new date had been fixed, a pretext was found for postponing it. Sartre had been condemned to stay at liberty. "You don't arrest Voltaire," said De Gaulle, who may have been forgetting that Voltaire had spent nearly a year in the Bastille.

But Sartre and De Beauvoir did not escape with impunity. At restaurants other customers made them feel like public enemies, while Sartre received so many insulting and threatening calls that he stopped answering the telephone except when friends went through the routine of letting it ring once, hanging up, letting it ring once again, hanging up again, and then letting it ring till he answered.[1] In the evenings when he was with De Beauvoir they dined frugally in her studio, eating ham and listening to the phonograph.[2] For both of them social life depended mainly on the small surviving "family" of friends, including Bost and Olga, and on the *Temps Modernes* team, which met in the morning twice a month at De Beauvoir's flat.[3] But Sartre, though he had given permission for a statement to be written in his name, was unable to forgive the man who had made him so unpopular. Péju was fired.

The review went on reporting truthfully about events in Algeria and acts of vengeance against Muslims in Paris. An article by Lanzmann summed up what he had learned from a secret file about psychological and physical torture involving electrodes, burning, broken bottles, hanging, strangling.[4] Though De Gaulle was well aware that the FLN was unbeatable and that none of the European countries could hold onto their African colonies much longer, he could not be sure that the French people would think him indispensable once the war was over, and he was apprehensive about provoking the powerful reactionaries who insisted on keeping Algeria French. In handling the generals he was cautious, conciliatory, but in November 1960 he had finally announced that without waiting for peace with the FLN, he wanted to give Algeria its own laws, institutions, and foreign policy. A referendum was to be held in both France and Algeria at the beginning of 1961. For the colons the end was in sight, and like the Germans during the last weeks of the occupation, they reacted viciously. General Salan created the Organisation de l'Armée Secrète (OAS), which assassinated Muslims and European sympathizers, first in Algeria and then in France, counting on terrorism to delay settlement in Algeria. One of their main weapons was the plastic bomb. Not that the FLN held back from terrorist attacks. Both sides were fairly arbitrary in choosing targets.

Like other writers for *Les Temps Modernes* and other members of the "121," Sartre campaigned for a "No" vote in the referendum. As he told *L'Express,* "the question posed links self-determination with the establishment of provisional institutions in Algeria, aimed at giving power to a hypothetical third force between the 'ultras' and the FLN. . . . To vote 'yes' is to refuse to wake up, to go on dreaming."[5] But De Gaulle won a massive majority.

In April, Sartre left Paris again, traveling with De Beauvoir and Bost to Antibes, where they heard about Castro's Bay of Pigs victory over an ill-judged attempt, backed, apparently, by the Americans, to invade Cuba. Sartre and De Beauvoir visited what had once been Mme. Morel's villa: it had been made into a clinic and was surrounded by tall buildings. On April 21, four days after the abortive invasion of Cuba, there was a rising in Algiers, led by four retired generals (Salan, Challe, Zeller, and Jouhaud). Paratroopers of the Foreign Legion took over most of the public buildings, government representatives were arrested, and a state of siege was proclaimed. What the rebels wanted was a guarantee that Algeria would stay French. De Gaulle, who had made himself president, announced a state of emergency, and his prime minister, Debré, broadcast a panicky appeal to the nation, asking people to go to the nearest airport and reason with any paratroopers who landed. In the meantime all the bridges of Paris had been blocked with buses.

In the morning twelve million French workers were on strike, but on April 23 De Gaulle addressed the army, asking the men to disobey their leaders. Consisting largely of national servicemen who were worried that their demobilization might be delayed, the army obeyed the president, and within five days the rebellion had collapsed. But to be sure of keeping Algerian affairs under close personal control, De Gaulle continued the state of emergency until the end of September.

Sartre and De Beauvoir were still in Antibes on May 4 when Merleau-Ponty died suddenly of a heart attack. Sartre threw himself into work. Without even troubling to reread his earlier essay on Tintoretto, he settled down to write on the painting *Saint George and the Dragon,* which he had often seen in London. As before, he emphasized the claustrophobia he sensed in Tintoretto's paintings. The volatile Venetian firmament could be depicted but must be placed firmly out of reach. Humanity must prove itself innocent or be found guilty "under the bituminous lid of a leaden sky."[6]

The unease in the essay is partly Sartre's unease at the situation he was in, but he did not try to make things easier for himself. The Nizan preface had displayed the pleasure he took in condemning himself; already at risk as the most famous of the "121," he gambled against himself more dangerously in the provocative interview he gave *France-Observateur* in the middle of May. The "terrorism of the rich" was counterproductive, he said. The strategy was to make it look as though a breakdown in negotiations would lead straight to civil war, but since the assassinations were increasing people's impatience for peace, the terrorists were helping France to wake up out of her lethargy.[7] After this he began to receive threatening letters. Anticipating a bomb attack on his flat, he settled his mother in a hotel, moving in temporarily with De Beauvoir. He was working—rather too frenetically and using too much corydrane—on an essay about Merleau-Ponty, who although his junior by three years, had been a father figure politically, and in his book *Signes* had defended Sarte against his morbid tendency to condemn himself. But he went on attacking himself both in the essay and in the overdoses of corydrane, which were affecting his hearing. Sometimes he was so deaf by the afternoon that he could not hear when the doorbell rang.[8] Feeling more than usually in need of the therapeutic Roman summer, he was planning to leave with De Beauvoir on July 19. At seven-thirty in the morning they were packing the last of their suitcases when the telephone rang. A plastic bomb had exploded in the entrance hall of 42 Rue Bonaparte but had done little damage.

In Rome they gave themselves a less arduous routine than usual, sleeping in communicating rooms, rising late, listening to music on De

Beauvoir's transistor radio before going down for coffee and newspapers. The morning stint of work would be followed by a car ride into the center of Rome and a walk, the afternoon stint by dinner in the Piazza Santa Maria in Trastevere or at one of their other favorite restaurants, and finally a drink on a terrace with a view of Campagna.[9] But the news was conducive to neither relaxation nor work: clashes between French and Tunisians; slaughter in Bizerta, followed by De Gaulle's refusal to evacuate it; the building of the Berlin Wall.

SINCE the first proposals for a compromise peace between France and Algeria, one of the loudest voices raised against the idea was that of Frantz Fanon, a Martinican doctor, great-grandson of a slave, author of *Peaux noirs, masques blancs* (*Black Skins, White Masks*) and *L'An V de la révolution algérienne* (*Year 5 of the Algerian Revolution*), and a member of the provisional revolutionary government of Algeria. He had been influenced by Sartre's *Critique*—especially by the discussion of terror—and after he had invited Sartre to write a preface for his new book, *Les Damnés de la terre* (*The Wretched of the Earth*), the first chapter, "De la Violence," had been published in the June issue of *Les Temps Modernes*. Fanon was convinced that since colonialism depended on violence, counterviolence was the only possible answer.

After Sartre had agreed to write a preface, Fanon came to Rome, although, two years earlier, when he was in a hospital there, he had escaped only just in time when an assassin found the way to his room. After he and Sartre had lunch together, the conversation went on until two in the morning, and when De Beauvoir pleaded that Sartre needed sleep, Fanon's response was: "I don't like men who hoard their resources." He told Lanzmann: "I'd give twenty thousand francs a day if I could talk to Sartre from morning till night for two weeks." As it was, they talked almost nonstop for three days. In the Algerian war, Fanon, who had been supplying the guerrillas with drugs, had trained terrorists in how to resist torture and how to keep calm when planting bombs or throwing grenades.[10] According to De Beauvoir, Fanon's face would express less anguish when he described the "counterviolence" of the blacks and the vengeance of the Algerians than when he spoke of Congolese mutilated by Belgians or Angolans by Portuguese—faces battered to flatness, lips pierced and padlocked.[11] He accused Sartre of not doing enough to expiate the crime of being French: how could he go on trying to live normally? The two men talked again when Fanon came back to Rome, ten days later, on his way to Tunis, but this was to be their last meeting. Already ill with leukemia, Fanon would be dead before the end of the year. As soon as he left Rome, Sartre started on the preface, writing less feverishly than during the early summer in Paris. "I am recomposing myself," he said.[12]

In 1947 he had been unambivalently hostile to violence: perpetrated in the name of liberty, it deprived people of their liberty.[13] The 1951 play *Le Diable et le Bon Dieu* showed that his attitude had changed, and *Saint Genet* argued that without violent resistance and militancy the oppressed majority could never come fully alive. In 1959 he had written the *Critique*, with its apologia for terrorism, which had influenced Fanon, and now, in his preface to *Les Damnés de la terre*, his most outspoken defense of violence is couched in an impassioned declaration of solidarity with the Algerian rebels. Violence must come as the Third World throws off the yoke that had been violently imposed by imperialism. "Our victims know us by their wounds and their fetters. . . . You, so liberal, so human, who love culture to the point of preciosity, you pretend to forget you have colonies and that massacres are carried out in your name."[14]

Fanon was no more than a catalyst, but the Algerian experience had produced a chemical change in Sartre's thinking. His political horizon had broadened. The urge to show that the PCF had left the French proletariat in the lurch was displaced by the urge to show that the oppressed peasantry of the Third World was being left in the lurch not only by the bourgeois imperialists but by the Western proletariat. What he had seen in Cuba and Brazil changed his perspective on what he knew about Algeria. The true revolutionaries of the sixties, he believed, were to be found in Asia and Africa, where the dividing line between working class and middle class had not been obscured. The wretched of the earth had nothing to lose by rebelling, and in France, where neither the party official nor the *embourgeoisé* proletarian was ready to befriend the dark-skinned victim, university students were less complacently self-involved. When *Les Damnés de la terre* was published, they read in Sartre's preface that violence was the only cure for "colonial neurosis." The native would discover his lost innocence when his rage boiled over. By shooting a European he could destroy both the oppressor and the part of himself that had been oppressed. Even in France culture was being reconstituted according to the image that the colon had of it. The outbreaks of violence in Paris showed that "the time of wizards and fetishes" would continue until common sense was fighting on the same side as the rebels, whose "counterviolence" was a reassertion of human values.

Since 1940, when the diary-writing Sartre had found a tension between the secret self and the self other people saw, he had given himself a long and necessary training in resistance to internal tension. He was willing to collaborate with such disparate men as John Huston and Frantz Fanon. Comfortably distanced from the violence that had spread from Algeria to OAS bombings in Paris, he and De Beauvoir were enjoying the Italian summer while, articulated between the covers of one book, the alliance between Sartre and Fanon helped to encourage violence and to create *tiers-mondisme* (orientation toward the Third World) in the French revolutionary young. On them his influence was to continue with only minor fluctuations until the 1968 rebellion, but his standing as an intellectual was to be seriously damaged by the success of the structuralists. Distracted by his activism and complacently aware that Lévi-Strauss, Barthes, Foucault, Derrida, Lacan, and the writers, such as Jean Ricardou, associated with the review *Tel Quel* had all been influenced by his strong opposition to essentialist determinism and by his insistence on the disunity of the self, Sartre underestimated these writers. He attempted neither to keep abreast of their work nor to use *Les Temps Modernes* as a forum for debate. Generally his tendency was to avoid one-to-one confrontations—written or oral—with intellectual equals, and he failed to learn, except superficially, from what ought to have been a cautionary experience at the beginning of the sixties, when, for once, accepting an invitation to lecture at the Ecole Normale, he had committed himself to a confrontation with Louis Althusser. An Algerian and a party member, Althusser taught at the Ecole Normale and wanted his structuralist Marxism to have a scientifically antihumanist basis. He had not yet published *Pour Marx,* but his ideas already had great appeal for the students. According to Regis Debray, then a student at the ENS, Althusser emerged as the more dialectical of the two thinkers: "He said that the Sartrian *cogito* was difficult to sustain inside a Marxist problematic of history."[15] Though the experience strengthened Sartre's inclination to avoid such debates, he was not prompted to make his position less vulnerable by using stucturalist Marxism as a perspective for updating the ideas he had advanced in his *Critique.*

In Italy he was equally remote from OAS violence and French intellectual debate. In the sea at Anzio he saw an ancient Egyptian galley floating on the waves: *Cleopatra* was being filmed, with Elizabeth Taylor. Sitting next to Sartre in the ruins of the little theater at Tusculum, De Beauvoir felt nostalgic for the tranquillity of their early vacations: "If we've got another twenty years to live, let's try to enjoy them." But they had to confront open violence in Paris on their return. In September, after De Gaulle had entered into serious negotiations with the

FLN, the OAS tried to assassinate him, and in both France and Algeria plastic bombs were becoming almost commonplace. By the end of 1961 there had been six hundred explosions, and an arrested OAS agent was found to be carrying a list of three thousand addresses due to be bombed during 1962.[16] In Paris the police had been clubbing Algerians to death on the streets in full view of the public; corpses were said to have been found hanging in the Bois de Boulogne; others, mutilated, were reported found in the Seine. Ten thousand Algerians had been herded into the Vélodrome d'Hiver as if it were a camp.[17] On October 17 an Algerian demonstration was murderously suppressed, and on November 1 all Algerian rallies were banned; in response, Sartre was one of those who organized a silent demonstration by French intellectuals in the Place Maubert. In jails throughout France, Algerian prisoners and French sympathizers had just begun a hunger strike. Sartre made a speech; a plastic bomb was thrown, but no one was seriously hurt; people started a sit-down on the pavement, and some were arrested; the demonstration was given good coverage on the radio.

In *Les Temps Modernes* much of the space was given to exposure of what was going on, but the October issue was devoted to Merleau-Ponty. In the first version of his own essay on Merleau-Ponty, written during July 1961 in Rome,[18] Sartre comments on the references in *Signes* to him and Nizan, but in the published version, which is quite different, no mention is made of what Merleau-Ponty had said about them. While Lacan contributed to the memorial number of the review, Lévi-Strauss was left to pay his tribute independently. He did this by dedicating *La Pensée sauvage* to his dead friend.

After the failure of the RDR in 1949 Sartre had intended to play no further part in organizing political groups, but he now decided to join forces with the mathematician Laurent Schwartz and Jean-Pierre Vigier to form the League for Anti-Fascist Movements. Vigier, a Communist who was advocating rapprochement with the non-Communist left, had taken the initiative, asking Sartre and other prominent intellectuals to sign a pamphlet denouncing the OAS and racism; Sartre wanted to go much further—taking action in support of the Algerian rebels and condemning what seemed virtually to be an alliance between the government and the OAS.

Knowing he was likely to be on the hit list of the OAS assassins, who were active again, he tried to take a room in a hotel, only to be rejected by the nervous manager. In the end Sartre's new secretary, Claude Faux, rented a furnished flat in his own name; Sartre and De Beauvoir both moved in. The flat was in an unfinished building on the Boulevard

Saint-Germain, with rubble on the staircase. Noisy builders worked all day, and so little light came in from the narrow Rue Saint-Guillaume that they always needed electric lights on.[19]

On November 18 a demonstration against fascism and racism was organized, mainly by the young Communists. A crowd of about eight thousand turned out in support, and, with De Beauvoir, Sartre paraded behind a placard proclaiming "Peace in Algeria." By faking breakdowns, car drivers delayed the police cars that were racing toward the demonstrators, but when the procession reached the Boulevard Haussmann, the police, savagely using outsize truncheons, caused a stampede. Faux, who was trapped in the police charge, saw one demonstrator with the flesh hanging away from his face.[20]

During another anti-OAS demonstration, on December 19, the police charged at the leaders of the procession, beating up those who were carrying placards. Many people were seriously hurt.[21] Sartre tried to immerse himself in work on Flaubert.

In January 1962, hearing a nearby explosion at about two in the morning, he took it to mean that the OAS had discovered where he was living. Smoke was drifting from the Rue Saint-Guillaume, broken glass was falling onto the pavement, planks had been blown out into the street. Police cars and a fire engine arrived. The shirt store on the corner had been demolished by a plastic bomb, but it turned out that the target had been the proprietor, an Algerian-born Frenchman who had refused to collect funds for the OAS. Only three days later another plastic bomb exploded at 42 Rue Bonaparte—on the floor above Sartre's flat. It had destroyed both flats as well as the bedrooms on the floor above. Sartre's front door had been blown off, and his Norman cupboard smashed. From the third floor upward the staircase was hanging out through a vast hole in the wall. Inside the flat the floors were littered with papers, doors had been blown off their hinges, walls and ceilings were covered with soot.[22] Many of Sartre's unpublished manuscripts disappeared.

Shortly afterward his mother received a telephone call from Mme. Morel, who had not been in touch for a long time. She said nothing about the bomb. "Of course, you know, I'm in favor of Algeria staying French."[23] On the other side of the balance, Sartre received a warmly sympathetic letter from his uncle Albert Schweitzer. He wrote back: "Each time I see your name among those who are campaigning against atomic war, I feel how close I am to you."[24]

After the explosion Sartre was given police protection that could not fail to put him in greater danger. Two policemen stood outside the house during the day and went off duty in the evening; the bombers worked at night, and few nights passed without the noise of bombs exploding.[25] Sartre and De Beauvoir moved into a large apartment building overlooking the Seine on the Quai Louis-Blériot, not knowing that two OAS killers were hiding there. The danger increased when *Djamila Boupacha* was published—a book coauthored by De Beauvoir and an Algerian lawyer, Gisèle Halimi, about an Algerian girl who had been viciously tortured. This immediately provoked threatening telephone calls.[26] On February 8, during another anti-OAS demonstration, the police charged the crowd. When some of the demonstrators tried to escape into the Charonne Métro station, the police tore up metal tree guards to throw at them. Five adults were killed, and a boy of sixteen. The official explanation was that the crowd had "crushed itself." The trade unions arranged to make the funeral into a mass demonstration. All the workers in Paris went on strike, and with no public transport running, the traffic was immobilized by jams while a crowd of about 700,000 demonstrators converged on the Père Lachaise cemetery.

But it was no easier to collaborate with the Communists than it had been in the forties. Strongly opposed to what it ought to have wanted—radical action among the masses—the PCF insisted that there should be no opposition to the government, only to the OAS, and that membership in the league should be limited to intellectuals. Sartre had to let them change its name to Front for Action and Coordination Among University Teachers and Intellectuals for an Antifascist Movement (FAC). In March, when Sartre gave a lecture about Algeria in Brussels, he had an audience of 6000,[27] but, as before, his popularity made the Communists fearful that he might be instrumental in creating a rival political force. When he was to address a meeting of the FAC at the Mutualité, a bomb warning was issued, which reduced the size of the audience to about 2000.[28]

"Collaboration with the Communist party is both necessary and impossible," Sartre told *La Voie Communiste*: "The party wants to shut the sympathetic intellectuals up into a ghetto." In effect the PCF had steered the working class away from politics: "Steam is let off on the social level, but the political conflict is no longer discussed."[29]

At the beginning of March a conference opened at Evian to negotiate peace with the FLN, and on the nineteenth both sides ordered a ceasefire. Special privileges were to be accorded the Europeans in Algeria, but about 750,000 of them decided to emigrate. A referendum was held in France on April 7, but before the July referendum in Algeria there was a recrudescence of violence. European women drove their cars into Muslim children; public buildings were blown up; the OAS fired on people lined up for tickets to leave the country. Muslim districts were

bombarded; unemployed Arabs were machine-gunned in front of labor
exchanges. Two dozen deaths on average were reported daily in the
newspapers. Torturers escaped with impunity, while deserters were
ferociously punished.[30]

SINCE the Liberation it had never been more unpleasant to live in Paris,
and Sartre was impatient to resume his traveling. It was eight years
since he and De Beauvoir had been in the USSR, where they arrived on
June 1, in response to an invitation from the Union of Soviet Writers.
Living standards appeared to have risen. The women were dressed
more brightly, displays in store windows were more appealing. But the
labor camps were still in existence.[31] The interpreter assigned to Sartre
and De Beauvoir was Lena Zonina, secretary of the union's French section. She was a beautiful thirty-nine-year-old woman, with dark eyes in
an oval face. She was from a Jewish family, highly intelligent, and, as
Sartre was soon to discover, passionate. He would return to the Soviet
Union eight times within just over four years; she was not the least important of his reasons.

With De Beauvoir he met Voznesensky, attended one of his poetry
readings, and saw Andrei Tarkovsky's film *Ivan's Childhood*, which
Sartre ranked alongside Truffaut's *Les 400 Coups* as one of the best postwar films. In Leningrad they saw a production of Brecht's *Gute Mensche
von Sezuan* in the style of Stanislavsky.[32] With Dorosh, a writer, and his
wife, a physics professor, they spent two days in Rostov.[33] In Leningrad
they saw Dostoevsky's house and drank vodka to the memory of Pushkin on the spot where he had fought a duel.[34] In Moscow they accepted
invitations to the houses of writers and intellectuals, and Sartre met
Khrushchev. On the way back to France they stayed in Poland. In
Warsaw they were driven around the town by a French-speaking Communist, Lissowski, they met the writer Kazimierz Brandys and Professor Jan Kott, who had translated Sartre's plays into Polish; in Cracow
they saw the university, the cathedral, and the castle.[35]

Within little more than a fortnight Sartre was back in the USSR to
take part in a world congress for peace and general disarmament. He
gave a speech under the title "The Demilitarization of Culture." Even
Kafka, he said, had been exploited during the Cold War: banned in the
Soviet Union, he was championed in the West as an enemy of the bureaucracy characteristic of the Eastern bloc.[36] What Khrushchev had
said about peaceful competition between the two blocs should also
apply to culture. Some of the more liberal Soviet intellectuals responded enthusiastically to these arguments; encouraged, Sartre would

go on working like a diplomat with no state behind him but with détente as his objective.

DEVIATING from his normal routine, he made an autumn trip to Rome, where he began to sketch out a new play based on Euripides' *Alcestis,* about a queen who offered to die in place of the king, Admetus, when he said he was too busy to die, having to rule his country and to win a war. In his version Sartre wanted to imply the story of female emancipation. When Alcestis returns, spared by Death, her husband is held in contempt as a man who would let a woman die for him. The French for Alcestis is Alceste, which led to a confusion in *Le Figaro.* On November 20 it was announced that Sartre's next play would be about a "neomisanthropist," a character who would remind audiences of Molière's Alceste.[37]

At the end of December he went back to the Soviet Union with De Beauvoir—the third visit within six months. He wanted to explore the possibility of setting up an international community of writers. Ilya Ehrenburg was friendly, as were Voznesensky and other intellectuals, while the cultural thaw appeared to be progressing. Solzhenitsyn's novel about the camps, *One Day in the Life of Ivan Denisovich,* had been published by *Novy Mir; Pravda* had printed Yevtushenko's poem *Stalin's Heirs,* which asked for extra guards around the tomb of the former leader to make sure there was no resurrection. Sartre and De Beauvoir went to see the large exhibition of modern painting and sculpture at the Manezh, but after Khrushchev's visit to it the cultural atmosphere began to change. He ferociously denounced formalism and abstraction; in an ominously anti-Semitic speech his propaganda chief Ilyichev attacked "ideological coexistence."[38]

After returning from the USSR with De Beauvoir on January 13, 1963, Sartre settled down to work on *Les Mots.* Of all his books this is the one that can most easily be read quickly, but it is also the most devious; a superficial reading yields only a fraction of what went into the making of it. Though he wants it to look as though he has written down everything he can remember about his childhood, he has none of the passion most autobiographers have for resurrecting their past. He could have questioned his mother and his uncles about what they remembered; he could have searched for old photographs and tracked down what he had written himself about childhood when his memories were fresher—in letters to Toulouse, for instance, and in his 1940 diaries. But the autobiographical commitment failed to pull him away from his usual habit of writing as if all the necessary facts were already in his

head or from his indifference to his past writings, which he tended to
dismiss as if they were unreal, like past events. At the beginning of 1962,
while moving out of his flat, he had forgotten to take the manuscripts
from the big cupboard on the landing—a memory lapse that was highly
profitable for the landlord—and when he had the chance to buy back
two volumes of the war diaries De Beauvoir had lent to Bost (who had
lost them when wounded and unconscious), Sartre refused. A dealer in
secondhand books was offering them for the same price as a collector
was willing to give. But why should he pay for what he had written
himself?[39] And why should he exert himself to research his own childhood? Was it not his—a possession to manipulate in any way he
wished? His instinct was not so much to repair the damage time had
inflicted on his memories as to complete the demolition; if he was still
haunted by ghosts from the past, perhaps they could be exorcised by
the book.

(23)

Writing Is Neurosis

SARTRE'S motives for writing an autobiography were mixed, if not confused. The need for money bulked quite large. To invest as much time as he had since 1954 in traveling, unremunerative political activity, and such unremunerative books as the *Critique,* he had borrowed money from Gallimard as an advance on his next book but without agreeing what the next book was to be. An English publisher was now trying to commission a new work from him, but after letting himself be persuaded that his obligation was to Gallimard, he went back to the autobiography abandoned in 1953, shortly after his "conversion" to communism, when he had been "close to regretting" his commitment to literature.[1] "Madness" and "neurosis" were the words he now used for what was generally called "vocation," but in the new version of the book he tried to be less severe with his young self: "Action too has its problems and one can be led to it by neurosis. . . . Salvation is no more to be achieved through politics than through literature."[2]

During his friendship with Nizan they had, despite their atheism, gone on planning how to earn their salvation; Sartre is still doing this now, and he never freed himself from the fear he had dramatized in *Les Séquestrés d'Altona* about being judged in the unpredictable future. But though he is unguarded in his use of such words as "neurosis" and "salvation," the autobiography is motivated partly by the need to defend himself against the danger of being seduced by the idea of posterity—he plants the addiction among childhood fantasies—and partly by the fear of having gone too far toward Freudianism.

First of all, though, he tried to go even further, inviting Pontalis to psychoanalyze him. How was this to be taken? A surrender to what he had recently called a bourgeois ideology? A dangerous stratagem, like that of a boxer feigning weakness? He was prompted, he said, more by curiosity about psychoanalytic method than by a need for analysis.

Pontalis was too canny to fall into the trap. After knowing Sartre for twenty years he valued the friendship too highly to jeopardize it by accepting him as a patient. Nor was he entirely clear about Sartre's motives. Perhaps he felt challenged in a new way by the Jewish doctor who had fought so hard against father figures before becoming a patriarchal archetype. Perhaps he relished the prospect of psychoanalytical sessions in which the golden brain dueled against Freudian insights. Sartre did not look for another analyst when Pontalis refused to take him on, but he did conduct a kind of self-analysis in Les Mots, as if he could manage no less easily without an analyst than without a father. Pontalis construed his original title, "Jean-sans-terre," to mean "Jean-sans-père."

Les Mots is a monologue that makes gestures toward duologue. The voice we hear is always that of the well-known fifty-eight-year-old writer, sitting in a room that overlooks a cemetery. Ostensibly the main character in the narrative is Poulou, but no young boy, however precocious, would be capable of the ideas imputed to him by the mature writer. The first person refers sometimes to Sartre, sometimes to Poulou, but abrasive adult comment is regularly insinuated into the narrative: "I liked to please and wanted to give myself baths of culture; I recharged myself every day with holiness."[3] "I take society to be a strict hierarchy based on merit and power."[4] "I never stop creating myself; I am the giver and the gift."[5] The present tense (lost in Irene Clephane's English translation) belongs to the stratagem of infiltrating mature reflections into an immature mind; the claim of self-generation, which is regularly reiterated throughout the book, belongs to Sartre's obsessive denial of parentage—the mother is presented as a sister figure—while the idea of being giver and gift has obviously less to do with Poulou's attitudes than with Sartre's wish to substitute an anthropological for a psychological perspective.[6] The book contains many echoes of Mauss's Essai sur le don; this is the most undisguised.

One of the main points is that the child was putting on an act, developing the role he was expected to play in the family. But Sartre uses none of his dramatic skill to make us identify with the child as he picks up the adults' hints about the behavior they want. This is partly inability to identify and partly refusal. Not wanting us to sympathize with Poulou, Sartre is driven by his hatred for his own childhood and for the idea of childhood most adults have. He digresses into an anecdote about an American friend in a dogs' cemetery. "Outraged, he kicked out at a cement dog and broke its ear. He was right: to love children and animals too much is to love them as an alternative to men."[7] Sartre did not love children or animals enough, but not because he loved men too much. The book is informed by hatred of the bourgeois family. As he said in a prefatory note when *Novy Mir* published an excerpt from the book, "I do not hold the child responsible but the period which had formed him. And above all I detest the well-worn myth of childhood perfected by the adults. I'd like this book to be read for what it really is: the attempt to destroy a myth."[8]

It is also an attempt to create a myth about self-creation and freedom from guilt.

> Among the Aeneases who carry their Anchises on their back, I cross from one bank to the other alone and detesting these progenitors mounted invisibly on their sons throughout life; I left behind a young corpse who had no time to be my father and who today might be my son. Was this bad or good? I don't know, but I subscribe willingly to the verdict of an eminent psychoanalyst: I have no superego ... the hasty retreat of my father had supplied me with a very incomplete Oedipus complex: no superego, agreed, but no aggressivity either. My mother was mine, no one disputed my quiet possession of her. ... Against whom, against what would I have rebelled? Never did the whim of another claim to be my law.[9]

This bland denial of his superego is never explicitly contradicted by the narrator, but the narrative has already begun to contradict it. The bearded patriarchal grandfather is compared with God the father and with Moses. Charles Schweitzer rules despotically over his daughter, who is not allowed to return later than ten in the evening, even when she goes out to dinner, while he implants such a ferocious superego in Poulou that fifty years later his conscience still speaks in his grandfather's voice, "this recorded voice which wakes me up with a start and pitches me toward my table. I wouldn't listen to it if it were not my own."[10] No superego? Not agreed.

In the myth Sartre creates about the origins of his literary neurosis, the grandfather is the villain who implants it. The book is divided into two halves, "Reading" and "Writing." The first half, which centers on Poulou's experience with stories and books, ends with the sentence: "I was saved by my grandfather: he threw me, without wanting to, into a new imposture which changed my life."[11] Between the ages of nine and ten, we are told in the second part, the boy becomes entirely "posthumous"; the imaginary child turns into a real knight errant whose exploits will be real books. The mother buys exercise books for him to write stories in; the boy comes to believe he has two voices: one dictates what the other should say. He is learning how to achieve immortality by turning himself into books; for centuries he will sit indestructibly on other people's shelves. "My bones are leather and cardboard, my parchment flesh smells of glue and mildew. . . . I'm taken, opened, spread out on a table, opened with the flat of the hand and sometimes made to crack."[12] The mother says: "This child will write"; the grandfather, feeling the boy's skull, confirms: "He's got the bump of literature,"[13] but advises him to become a teacher. Famous writers have died of hunger, it is better to choose a second calling.

> If Charles had called out from afar, opening his arms: "Here's the new Victor Hugo, here's the budding Shakespeare!" I should today be an industrial designer or a teacher of literature. He was careful not to: for the first time I was facing the patriarch . . . this was Moses dictating the new law. My law. He had mentioned my vocation only to underline the disadvantages: I conclude that he was taking it for granted . . . I did not doubt for an instant that this was my lot; I tell myself at the time: "That's all there is to it" and "I'm talented."[14]

Of all the characters in the narrative Charles Schweitzer is the liveliest. The brightest sequences have the frozen vividness of snapshots, and Charles never comes to life more than when he is striking poses, as if for a camera. Photographs of him fill the house. He is the victim of two recently discovered techniques—photography and the art of being a grandfather, as outlined by Victor Hugo in *L'Art d'être grandpère*. A reactionary old man, he had stopped reading new books in 1885, the year of Hugo's death. Now he only rereads. As a teacher he values novels only for their vocabulary; as a translator he lives by cutting dead men into slices. But is this the real Charles Schweitzer or just a caricature grandfather, a figure in an antibourgeois myth? Though Sartre told Leiris that he wanted to write the autobiography as if he were a historian or a biographer of someone else, the real Charles Schweitzer was progressive both in his "direct method" of teaching language and in his attitude to literature. In *La Vie et les oeuvres de Hans Sachs* he attacks "la littérature de la bourgeoisie," which he defines as "now purely didactic, now morose and corrosive." Sartre's characterization seems to be based partly on his grandfather but partly also on Victor Hugo's book.

As in his novels, which contain more pastiche and parody than is immediately apparent, Sartre is writing anti-literature, a book designed to invalidate previous books. *Les Mots* mocks Gide's autobiographical *Si le grain ne meurt* and involves a complex pattern of contrasts between low culture and high culture, comics, films, and boys' adventure stories versus the classics of literature. The classics are discreditable because they have served to bolster middle-class complacency, while their champion, the grandfather, is disconcertingly similar to the archetypes of bourgeois paternalism satirized in *La Nausée:* incarnated in a gigantic bronze statue, Gustave Impetraz clutches a top hat in one hand, resting his other on a pile of folio volumes, which is reassuring to black-clad housewives, who can regard him as guardian of the values they grew up with.

This is only one of the dialectical axes in the book, which is structured around contrasts. Constantly moving between the present and the past, the narrative treacherously cultivates the appearance of chronological progression. Sartre is either forgetting or counting on the reader to forget the caveat embedded so deeply in the narrative of *La Nausée*. "To make the most banal event become an adventure, you have—and you have only—to start making it into a story."[15] Surrounded by your own and other people's stories, you look at your life through them and live it as if you were telling it. Though exceptionally alert to this tendency, Sartre was exceptionally prone to it. Had he tried to tell the truth about his attempts to cope with it, while trying, without any conjuring tricks, to test how far he could reconstruct himself by making his past into a narrative, the autobiography might have been a superb totalization, but he is too contentious, too manipulative.

In *La Nausée* he makes Anny uninterested in the details of what happens to Roquentin; she cares only about his "eternal essence." In his autobiography, as in his biographies, Sartre, more aprioristic than existentialist, concerns himself with the eternal essence of his subject but camouflages his indifference to facts and chronology. In *Les Mots* his dating is vague and inaccurate. We are left in uncertainty about when the crucial commitment was made to becoming a writer—sometimes it is lodged between the ages of seven and eight, sometimes between eight and ten, and he asserts confidently that he was seven when his golden curls were cut off, which (as we have seen) contradicts what he had told Toulouse.[16] But this incident is climactic in the first half of the book, as it could not have been if he was only five at the time. What the story needs is a mythical moment of disenchantment when the idyll of childhood beauty dissolves into realistic awareness of his ugliness. He is betraying himself by telling the story, but his technique is to let one level of self-betrayal overlay another. The resemblance to Genet is nowhere stronger than in this habit of treachery. In a curious footnote he writes: "Be satisfied with yourself and other self-satisfied people will love you; tear your neighbor to pieces and your other neighbors will laugh. But if you punish your soul, all the other souls will cry out."[17] No autobiography has hit out more vindictively at the author's soul; but not content with betraying himself, Sartre betrays the habit of self-betrayal. The reader is left wondering whether at the end of the book he is meant to agree that Sartre has no superego or to recognize that the narrative has undermined its starting point.

When Sartre's mother read the book she was so upset that she said: "Poulou has understood nothing about his childhood," and to put the record straight, she sat down to write her own memoir. She is not portrayed unsympathetically in *Les Mots;* as characterized, she has a great deal in common with Lucien's mother in "L'Enfance d'un chef" and with Flaubert's mother in the biography. But it is not her that Sartre is trying to betray: it is himself.

The premise of "Jean-sans-terre" is visible when he says that he had inherited neither property nor any sense of destination from his father. But the grandfather gives him his vocation. "He flung me into literature by the efforts he made to guide me away from it."[18] Docile, unmasculine, malleable, the little boy is trapped into writing for the sake of writing. The fifty-eight-year-old Sartre is more tolerant—and more amusing—when he describes how the boy fantasized about being a man of action, rescuing heroines from vengeful Janissaries with curved swords. But he convinces himself that even his adult habit of leaving work unfinished had its roots in his boyhood. As a child he wrote fast, hated rereading his stories, lost some of the exercise books that fell on the floor, saw no point in finishing a story when the first episodes were missing.[19]

The style of *Les Mots* is grounded in ambivalence. The prose is quite different from that of the *Critique.* "The sentences are among the most carefully polished I've ever written. And I took time on it. I wanted there to be implications in every phrase, one or two implications. . . . It was full of tricks, stratagems, belles-lettrism, almost wordplay." He claimed that the reason he wanted the book to be literary was that "it was in some fashion a way of saying goodbye to a certain kind of literature. . . . I wanted to be literary in order to show the error of being literary."

His intention was to bring the autobiography up to middle age and then to concentrate on political writing.[20] He wrote a long essay on Patrice Lumumba, the Congolese leader, whose assassination ended his short career of advocating nonviolence,[21] but the autobiographical project would be cut short, and for the next fifteen years the bulk of Sartre's working time would be given to Flaubert. On the other hand, the writing of *Les Mots* may have fed Sartre's disinclination to think of himself as a writer and bolstered his willingness to undertake commitments that took him away from his study.

In the summer he and De Beauvoir accepted another invitation from the Union of Soviet Writers—this time to a congress of COMES, the Community of European Writers, which had been set up in 1958 to encourage détente. The president was the poet Giuseppe Ungaretti. Held in Leningrad, the meeting was attended by writers from all over Europe, including Angus Wilson, Nathalie Sarraute, Alain Robbe-Grillet, Hans Magnus Enzensberger, and Tibor Déry.[22] But Khrushchev had reverted to a more Stalinist cultural policy since he had vilified the progressive art exhibited at the Manezh, and Ilya Ehrenburg was under attack. Khrushchev believed he had exerted a harmful influence on Sartre, encouraging him to leave the party; it was useless to point out that he had never joined it.

At the congress other Soviet writers tried to show their loyalty to the leadership by attacking Proust, Joyce, and Kafka. Afterward Sartre and De Beauvoir were among the delegates Khrushchev received at his country house in Georgia. When his guests had been shown the new swimming pool, surrounded by a glass wall that disappeared at the touch of a button, they were harangued about the evils of capitalism and the beauties of socialism. At lunch Khrushchev scarcely spoke, and the non-Russian guests afterward had to sit in uncomprehending silence for forty-five minutes while Aleksandr Tvardovsky read a poem. Apparently Khrushchev had been visited earlier in the day by Maurice Thorez, who had denounced the anti-Communist lunch guests.[23]

From Moscow, Sartre and De Beauvoir went on to the Crimea, where they stayed for a week before continuing to Georgia and Armenia. Lena Zonina spoke no Georgian, and when a dinner party was given for them by the president of the writers' union, who also acted as a *tamada,* or master of ceremonies, everything he said had to be translated first into Russian and then into French.

Sartre and De Beauvoir returned to Paris in September, and in November left again to visit Czechoslovakia. There too they were guests of the writers' union. Since their 1954 visit the cultural climate had obviously improved. Kafka's books were on sale, as were many foreign books in Czech translation, including some by Sartre and De Beauvoir. In Prague, Antonin Liehm, Sartre's translator, acted as their guide and interpreter, along with the writer Adolf Hoffmeister, who had been ambassador in Paris at the end of the forties. At a press conference, where one of his interlocutors was Milan Kundera, Sartre attacked the idea of decadence as an obstacle to communication between Eastern and Western intellectuals. In Leningrad, Freud, Kafka, and Joyce had been denounced, but these three writers, said Sartre, had helped to make him into a Marxist.[24] From Prague they went on to Bratislava. Later Sartre published one of Kundera's stories in *Les Temps Modernes.* According to Liehm, Sartre's influence had contributed to the relaxation of pressure on Czech intellectuals.[25] In Prague he took part in a debate about decadence, gave a talk on the radio, attended the Czech premiere of *Les Séquestrés d'Altona;* he also gave three lectures—in Prague, Bratislava, and Brno.

WHEN *Les Mots* was published in January 1964, it was widely applauded. Many critics assumed that Sartre had made peace with literature, but in an April interview he said: "In comparison with the death of one child, *La Nausée* isn't up to scratch." This provoked a good deal of controversy,[26] but the remark needs to be seen in the perspective of what he had already written in the Fanon preface about Western culture: the only true culture was the revolution.[27] The Western intellectual should not be allowed to use cultural monuments as a justification for a civilization that had been murderous toward the colonized population: in the past the Parthenon, Chartres cathedral, the Rights of Man, and the swastika had all served as floats on the fishing line,[28] but this period was over. What had to come now was violence. It may have been anomalous for Sartre to concern himself with autobiography so soon after advancing this argument, but his life had long been full of anomalies. He said that his object in measuring a book against a child's death had been to question what significance literature can have in a world where people are starving, but the remark shows he was as eager to disparage his first great literary achievement as he had been in *Les Mots* to disparage his childhood. Sartre's method of moving forward was to move violently against his earlier self, rather like an angry Jewish father turning his back on the grown-up child who has married out of the faith. Sartre could never quite afford to let his self-hatred catch up with him, but he gave it carte blanche to play against his past.

This partial acceptance of Freudianism had done nothing to make him feel warmer toward writers or friends who had influenced him in the past, and he had not been in touch with René Maheu since the thirties. But Maheu had been director of UNESCO since 1962, and when it organized a colloquium under the title "The Living Kierkegaard," to be held in Paris during April, Sartre was invited to give a lecture. Though Kierkegaard had been the first philosopher to use the word "existentialism," Sartre had previously had little to say about him, and the invitation constituted a challenge, partly because Kierkegaard was such a champion of individuality, partly because he had laid so much stress on the insignificant accidents of his life. Looking at him in the perspective of the *Critique,* Sartre would have to question both how much of his private experience had entered into history and how much of this man could be known. Like Freud, Kierkegaard believed that self-knowledge was the passport to knowledge of others; unlike Sartre, he detested the masses: his existentialism was a program for attaining existential subjectivity while rising above the men who had let themselves be made into things.

At the colloquium, held in the UNESCO auditorium, recorded messages from Heidegger and Jaspers were played. Sartre was such a star attraction that an uninvited group of students arrived from the Sorbonne. "We're philosophers too." Some sat on the floor, others squeezed onto benches where well-dressed UNESCO luminaries crushed closer together.[29]

Kierkegaard, said Sartre, had a special relationship with history—"As the Kierkegaardian adventure unfolded, it revealed itself as known in advance"[30]—and, like Nietzsche, he made philosophy coextensive with the personal experience of the philosopher. Wanting to designate himself a transhistorical absolute, he ceaselessly fabricated himself by writing. His life was crystallized around the problem of the relationship between history and lived experience: how much of this is recuperable? Kierkegaard had been formed by a series of biographical accidents, but what was their historical meaning? Sartre uses the term "singular universal" for the significance acquired as the insignificant accidents are subsumed. Man is the creature who transforms his being into meaning.[31] Kierkegaard was "perhaps the first to show that the universal enters history as a singular, insofar as the singular institutes itself in it as a universal."[32] In this dialectical formulation Sartre was preparing the position he would take in his Flaubert biography.

He would often make elaborate preparations for a lecture, knowing that some of the work would filter into a book. After accepting an invitation to speak on morality and society at another colloquium—this time in Rome during May at the Istituto Gramsci—Sartre wrote about two hundred pages of notes.[33] Proceeding from the premises of his *Critique,* he attacked ethical imperatives, social customs, and moral norms as attempting to curb the individual's freedom to produce himself as a subject and as imposing a predetermined future that belongs to the past. Each social system produces moral-seeming pressures that are conducive to its own survival but give no clue about the behavior that will be requisite after its demise. Capitalism cannot determine the future of the working class.[34]

INVITED to join the celebrations in Kiev for the one hundred and fiftieth anniversary of the Ukrainian poet Shevchenko's birth, Sartre and

De Beauvoir hesitated because an anti-Semitic pamphlet had been published by a professor at Kiev. Finally, urged by their friends to accept, they left Paris at the end of May. From Kiev they went on to Moscow, where more modern apartment houses were being built and the number of taxis had doubled in twelve months, while food was more plentiful.[35] Next they visited Vladimir, Tallinn, the capital of Estonia, Leningrad, and Novgorod. After a few more days in Moscow they flew back to Paris on July 10, to stay only briefly before leaving for another Roman summer.

Sartre had abandoned his version of *Alcestis,* but he began to work in Rome on what was to be his last play, an adaptation of Euripides' *The Trojan Women.* He had become interested in the play during 1961 when a performance of a literal translation had impressed an audience that obviously favored negotiations with the FLN. Euripides was hostile both to war and to colonial expeditions, but the play struck Sartre as more like an oratorio than a tragedy, and he gave a sharper dramatic edge to the conflicts.[36] He also sharpened the denunciation of colonialism. And, as in *Les Mouches,* he emphasized the weakness of the gods, who will disappear alongside the humans.

After being in Paris when Maurice Thorez died on July 12, Sartre was in Rome when Palmiro Togliatti died at the end of August. Like the two parties they had led, the two men were vastly different. It was Sartre's misfortune not to live in a country where the party was led by such a man as Togliatti. The statement he had sent to the PCF was polite but cool, paying tribute to Thorez's intelligence, energy, courage, and persistence.[37] But after attending Togliatti's funeral, Sartre wrote enthusiastically in *Les Temps Modernes* about "the man who has forged with his own hands a party of men who are tough and free ... my friend Togliatti."[38]

At the beginning of the autumn Sartre was approached by an Italian acquaintance, the philosopher Enzo Paci, who surprised him by asking for a text of the speech he would make when he was awarded the Nobel Prize for Literature. This was his first intimation of the judges' decision. *Les Mots* had brought him back into the international literary limelight. His decision to reject the prize was not quite immediate. Some people urged him to accept, but when De Beauvoir canvassed opinion among students and friends she was confirmed in her feeling that he ought to refuse. One of those consulted was Nizan's daughter, now married to Olivier Todd. What concerned Sartre deeply was the political implications of the decision he had to make. The prize had been given to Pasternak in 1958 but never to any nondissident Soviet writer; to Camus but not to any Western Communist—not even Neruda. Were the Swedes trying to show that Sartre could be aligned with the right? On October 15 an article appeared in *Le Figaro Littéraire* written by the Swedish correspondent: Sartre might be this year's winner. The next morning he wrote to warn the Swedish Academy that he did not want the prize. His letter was received but ignored, and on October 22 the prize was awarded to him. He was having lunch with De Beauvoir in a café near her flat when a journalist came over to tell them the news. Not wanting to use the French press as his means of conveying a refusal to the Swedish Academy, Sartre made a statement to a Swedish journalist, who passed it to Stockholm through Gallimard's representative. Translated back into French, the statement then appeared in *Le Monde* and other newspapers. The writer should not make himself into an institution, it said: his attitude toward Venezuelan guerrillas, for instance, should involve only him, not those who awarded him the prize. In any case, Sartre did not want an award that could be offered only to Western writers or Soviet dissidents: "It's regrettable that the prize was given to Pasternak before Sholokhov, and that the only Soviet work to be honored should be a work published abroad and banned at home."[39] As soon as the statement was released, Sartre was pursued by crowds of journalists. He took refuge, thoughtlessly or disingenuously, in De Beauvoir's flat, where they had no difficulty in tracking him down.

The scandal lasted for months, and many well-known writers joined in. Gabriel Marcel called Sartre a "licensed corrupter."[40] André Breton diagnosed "a perfectly gauged political action, a propaganda operation in support of the Eastern bloc."[41] A Marxian ideologist, Kostas Axelos, wrote that Sartre could have lived as readily under Hitler as under Stalin.[42] Sartre's worldwide fame was enhanced more by the rejection of the prize than it would have been by acceptance, but what embarrassed him were letters from people asking him to accept the prize and pass on the money (26 million old francs) to them.[43]

SARTRE'S relationship with Arlette Elkaim (as she now styled her surname) had progressively become more important. A keen amateur musician, she had learned to sing and to play the flute and the piano. After lunching with her at the Coupole he loved to sit down at the piano in her flat and accompany her or play duets or sing to her, accompanying himself.[44] He spent a good deal of time there, sleeping there on average perhaps twice a week. At the end of January 1965 he applied formally to adopt her as his daughter, and in March permission was granted.

Most people would have expected him to want De Beauvoir at least as his literary executor, if not as his heir. To adopt Arlette was to make her both—a betrayal in line with the offers of marriage to Dolores and Wanda. For a lifetime of devotion De Beauvoir's reward would be to see the youngest of her rivals given unchallengeable ownership of everything Sartre had written, everything he had possessed.

If the gesture was partly symbolic, the symbolism was complex. By a legal act Sartre was approximating to the realization of a fantasy he had entertained throughout his life. The relationship between Frantz and Léni in *Les Séquestrés d'Altona* consummates the incest already hinted at in the relationships between Boris and Ivich and between Orestes and Electra. Arlette was not a younger sister, but by adopting a young mistress as his daughter he was aiming a sacrilegiously mocking blow at the institution of the family while acting out a variation on a favorite fantasy. Also behind the gesture was a mixture of generosity and aggression. It was an act of solidarity with the underprivileged. Arlette was in four ways an incarnation of victimization: she was a woman, she was Jewish, she was Algerian, she was lacking in self-confidence. As Sartre's adopted daughter she would be given a new identity, which would certainly bring civic and financial security, together, possibly, with a greater degree of emotional and ontological security. Assured of wealth and power in the future, she might immediately feel more secure. At the same time, if Jankélévitch was right in thinking that Sartre still had residual guilt feelings toward the Jews, here was a grandiose gesture of atonement. It was also a magnificently impertinent but practically effective way of forging a permanent link with a mistress, more original and more defiant of convention than the nonmarital pact with De Beauvoir.

As an act of aggression it was directed mainly against her: she had been insufferably loyal for unconscionably long to a man who could not bear to be in anyone's debt—not even a woman's. In spite of her involvements with Algren and Lanzmann, she had nearly always been available. Loyal, discreet, unselfish, steady, cool, disciplined, a good organizer, she had succeeded extraordinarily well in replacing the lost mother and deputizing for the sister he had always wanted. Though she enjoyed saying "we" about herself and Sartre, she was not proprietorial. But she was still emotionally dependent. She had once said to Henriette Nizan: "If Sartre died, I wonder what I'd do. Perhaps I'd commit suicide." But as an act of vengeance against her the adoption of Arlette was open-ended. There was no need to decide yet about whether to leave a will or whether to appoint De Beauvoir as his literary executor.

Whatever he did, the world would go on thinking of her as the woman who had shared his life. But if he made no will, Arlette would inherit everything, including his literary estate.

LES Troyennes was due to open at the Théâtre National Populaire on March 10 in a production by the Greek film director Michael Cacoyannis, who had just made *Zorba the Greek*. Influenza prevented Sartre from attending rehearsals, and when he saw the production with De Beauvoir only a few days before the opening, he was appalled. The music (by John Prodromides) made much of the text inaudible, and the choruses had been badly choreographed. Sartre persuaded Cacoyannis to cut some of his theatrical effects, but it was too late to make any radical changes.[45]

It was the Algerian war that had first prompted the idea of adapting the play, but the Vietnam War had been worsening during the summer of 1964 while he was working on it. In February 1965 the American air force bombed North Vietnam, and on March 8 thirty-five hundred U.S. Marines landed in the south. Sartre had been due to give a series of lectures in April at Cornell University on Flaubert and on ethics. Continuing the work done for his contribution to the 1964 colloquium in Rome, he had written notes extending over several hundred pages, but in March, to protest against the intervention in Vietnam, he rescinded his acceptance of the invitation. Earlier his Cuban friends had been encouraging him to go: he could tell the Americans about Cuba. Since the raids they had been saying: "What do you want to do there?"[46]

At the beginning of May he sent a long telegram to the organizers of a teach-in on Vietnam at Boston University: he hoped they would have more success than French intellectuals had had in opposing the Algerian war; in any case, their activities would show the world that the rising generation in America disapproved of its leaders' policies.[47]

(24)

Halfway to Revolution

DURING the run-up to the presidential elections of December 1965 it was obvious that the PCF was impotent against De Gaulle's authoritarian leadership. The need for a social-democratic party was obvious; the chances of uniting the left were remote. Since the 1920 Congress of Tours, hostility between Communists and Socialists had been interrupted with short-lived alliances, but in 1963 hopes of rapprochement dwindled in face of the initiative taken by Gaston Defferre, mayor of Marseille and temporarily a presidential candidate, as he made a strong effort to unite all the non-Communist socialists into a new federation. Except that he was operating from inside the party system, he was attempting almost exactly what David Rousset and Sartre had attempted fifteen years earlier, but Sartre had moved on too far to approve or offer support. In two interviews with *Le Nouvel Observateur* Sartre admitted that the left was moribund but declared that it could not be revived by such "defeatists" as Defferre, who offered poison labeled as medicine. The right would be the only possible beneficiary of any attempt to form a coalition that excluded the Communists.[1]

It was not only that Sartre had moved further to the left since the days of the Rassemblement Démocratique Révolutionnaire; his horizons were different. After his encounters with Castro and Fanon, after countless conversations with politicians, intellectuals, dissidents, militants, students in Italy, Cuba, China, Egypt, Israel, Brazil, the Soviet Union, and Eastern Europe, he was more cosmopolitan in outlook. In France he was less interested in party politics, more oriented toward the students, addressing himself primarily to them as the only true socialists and the only people genuinely concerned with Third World victims of colonialism. This probably tended to make French students more like what he took them to be.

Though the main explosion was not to occur until May 1968, the pressure was building steadily. The student population, only 175,000 in 1958, grew to 330,000 by the summer of 1964, and little had been done to adjust the antiquated educational system. Everyone who passed the *baccalauréat* was entitled to a place at a university, but almost 50 percent of the students were dropping out by the end of the first year. Attempts were being made to recruit more teachers. Four new universities had been created (at Amiens, Orléans, Rheims, and Rouen), while in Paris extensions of the Sorbonne had been built—faculties in the Rue Censier and on the Quai Saint-Bernard, residence halls at Orsay and Nanterre. But unhappiness about overcrowding, poor facilities, shortage of money, inefficient administration, and sexual segregation in the residence halls was compounded by anxiety about future employment. One reason for the popularity of the student union, the UNEF (Union Nationale des Etudiants Français), which had 100,000 members by the summer of 1964, was that students felt alienated from a system which did not meet their needs. The men who had power—De Gaulle, the professors, the bureaucrats (French universities were controlled directly by the state)—seemed old, traditionalistic, remote, dictatorial, unsympathetic.

In 1964 the minister of education, Christian Fouchet, produced his plan for a two-tier system in the universities: some students would stay for only two years. This provoked both hostility and resistance. UNEF campaigned in the streets for a uniform student grant, winning support from both students and the general public, while the union was pushed further to the left, partly by pressure from a hostile government, partly by internal pressure from the militant radicals.

This double movement was characteristic of what was happening in the mid-sixties; the growth of militancy was fomented by unsympathetic efforts to impose discipline. The government, the Catholic Church, and the PCF were unwittingly collaborating to provoke the rebellion. In failing to stop the police in May 1968 from dealing viciously with students who were protesting peacefully, the government was to go on making the same mistake it had already made, along with the Church and the party, which had both expelled dissidents from youth organizations. These grievances could not be contained by discipline. From 1963 onward the militants who dominated the Catholic student union, Jeunesse Etudiante Chrétienne (JEC), and the Communist student union, Union des Etudiants Communistes (UEC), took over the leadership of the UNEF.

The new secretary-general of the PCF was Waldeck Rochet, a man of Burgundian peasant origin, more flexible than his predecessor, Thorez, but not flexible enough for the dangerous situation. The defeat of Defferre's plans for a federation and his withdrawal from presidential candidacy made a Communist-Socialist alliance look feasible again, and Rochet pledged the PCF to support Mitterrand in the election, expelling the UEC rebels who objected. Sartre was the ally of these rebels, who had been inspired by the ideas of Togliatti, filtered to them through *Les Temps Modernes*. His supporters in the UEC were known as the *italiens*, and at the congress of 1963 they won control of the union. After this, Sartrian ideas and terms were noticeable in its manifestos.[2]

This was not the only way in which Sartre's ideas were influencing the students. One of the key figures was André Gorz, who since 1956 had been working to steer the review into vociferous support for revolutionary movements adapted to local conditions; from 1961 onward the articles he introduced conducted a tough campaign against "neocapitalism." Scrutinizing the French educational system in contributions to the review he showed his faith in the revolutionary potential of the economically oppressed students, and when he started writing regularly for *Le Nouvel Observateur*, using the name Michel Bosquet, he had a platform from which he could address a larger public. *Les Temps Modernes* meanwhile, with the aim of appealing to militant student readers, commissioned leaders of the UNEF to write on student *gauchisme*,[3] and in 1964 Gorz published his book *Stratégie ouvrière et néo-capitalisme:* since poverty could no longer be counted on to act as a sufficient incentive to revolution, the concept of alienation should be used to radicalize the better-paid workers, creating solidarity between them and the underpaid proletariat. Sartre not only encouraged Gorz but helped directly to promote the idea of a new working class, privately subsidizing Serge Mallet while he wrote *La Nouvelle Classe Ouvrière,* which appeared in 1963. Pierre Belleville's book *Une Nouvelle Classe Ouvrière* was published the same year in the *Temps Modernes* collection.[4]

Politics was more prominent than ever in Sartre's motivation, but this made it still harder for him to decide on how to allocate his time. Since 1963 China and the USSR had been dangerously at loggerheads, and the hostility was exacerbated by the Soviet refusal to help the North Vietnamese with ammunition. Both the Russians and the Chinese were due to attend the peace congress at Helsinki in July, and when Ehrenburg, who was briefly in Paris, asked Sartre to come along so that he could speak up for the Russians, he was uncertain whether his presence could really have much effect, but it was not an invitation he could refuse. He went to Moscow with De Beauvoir at the beginning of July, planning to fly from Leningrad to Helsinki for a couple of days in the middle of the month. Khrushchev had been replaced in October 1964 by Brezhnev and Kosygin; when Sartre and De Beauvoir arrived in Moscow the cultural situation seemed more relaxed. Kafka's work was still unavailable but Pasternak's was on sale again. Solzhenitsyn's stories were coming out in *Novy Mir,* and Tvardovsky had issued a manifesto asking writers to speak their minds openly. Sartre and De Beauvoir traveled to Lithuania and Pskov, where they visited Pushkin's estate. In Moscow and Leningrad they were free to do as they pleased, but in other towns they were received by delegations of writers who were reluctant even to let them take a walk by themselves.[5]

In Helsinki, on July 13 and 14, 1965, the Chinese delegates, who applauded none of the speakers except the Vietnamese, accused the Russians of deviationism, revisionism, and a return to capitalism. Ehrenburg not only lost his temper with the Chinese but got upset with Sartre, who seemed to be siding with them when he asked for total solidarity with the North Vietnamese and proposed a motion to demand the immediate withdrawal of all American troops.

In Moscow, acting on Ehrenburg's suggestion, Sartre sent a letter through the writers' union to Anastas Mikoyan (president of the USSR since July 1964) asking him to pardon the young Jewish poet Brodsky, who had been accused of "parasitism" (a charge normally used only against prostitutes) and sentenced to five years of forced labor. Shortly afterward Brodsky was pardoned.[6]

But in October, Andrei Sinyavsky (who used the nom de plume Avram Tertz) and Yuli Daniel (who called himself Arzhak) were arrested and charged with publishing anti-Soviet works abroad. When Sartre and De Beauvoir went to Rome at the beginning of October for a COMES meeting, they found Tvardovsky, Ehrenburg, and other Russian writers alarmed at this new development. Defying the censor, who had condemned them to silence, some Soviet writers were circulating work in typescript, and it looked as though the authorities were about to clamp down on all this clandestine activity.[7]

The theme of the congress was "The European Avant-Garde Yesterday and Today," and when Sartre made his speech on October 6, he launched a surprising attack on what he called the phony avant-garde: Solzhenitsyn, James Joyce, Céline, Breton, and Robbe-Grillet, he said, were concerned "simply to exploit all the possibilities of a given language, experimenting with the limits of the language or introducing a new mode of reading." All these writers were basically "traditionalist" and were carrying on a "dialogue with the dead." Genuinely avant-garde writers did not just play with language; they created it, giving it to the people. Today it was only outside Europe, Sartre concluded, that avant-garde writing could thrive.[8]

Had he been living in Italy, Sartre might have felt less isolated, but in the perspective of De Gaulle's France, Europe appeared to be tainted with Americanism. In an interview with Mikis Theodorakis, addressing himself to the Greek left, which had staged demonstrations during the summer, he attacked American investment in European states: "For you, as for us, these objectives are inseparably linked: democracy, national sovereignty, autochthonous culture."[9]

If De Gaulle won the election of 1965, he would have another seven years as president. His popularity had been seriously lessened by the antistrike legislation and the austerity programs designed to build up gold reserves and pay for nuclear weapons. But when Defferre withdrew from the race, François Mitterrand was unchallenged as the left's candidate, and it was obvious that he stood no chance against De Gaulle. In the November issue of *Les Temps Modernes* the editorial was mainly negative toward Mitterrand, but on the day before the elections Sartre issued a statement: "To give Mitterrand your vote is not to vote for him but *against* personal power and *against* the drift of socialists to the right."[10] On the first ballot De Gaulle failed to win an absolute majority, and in the second, a fortnight later, he polled only 55 percent of the vote.

HAD Sartre tried to keep the promises made when *Les Temps Modernes* was launched, the review would have forced him to keep in touch with intellectual life in Paris. During 1965 Lévi-Strauss, Foucault, Barthes, Lacan, and Althusser had all published major books, but Sartre, though his own reputation was in decline, still took no initiative to define his position in relation to structuralism. In the November 1966 issue of the review Jean Pouillon was to make a valiant, if belated, effort to show that Sartrian ideas were not incompatible with it, but Sartre himself replied polemically and superficially when interviewers questioned him on the subject. In a 1965 interview with Pierre Verstraeten he defined the signifier as the speaker and the signified as the object, accusing the structuralists of a literary positivism that sank pessimistically to the level of Flaubert: the function of the "literary object" was to compensate for the inadequacy of language.[11] In an interview about "anthropology" for *Cahiers de Philosophie* he attacked the structuralists for trying to abstract structure from historical *praxis:* the linguistic model was misleading because it led toward a separation of the "practico-inert" from the historical forces that constituted it.[12] And in an interview with Bernard Pingaud he baldly condemned Lévi-Strauss, Lacan, Althusser, and the *Tel Quel* writers as unhistorical and neoposi-

tivistic. They were all guilty of approaching philosophical and historical problems with a scientific method.[13]

Too busy to engage seriously with the issues, Sartre could not protect
his reputation, which was eclipsed. No longer living the professional life
of a Paris intellectual, he was no longer felt to be in the avant-garde. If
he had been spending more time in Paris, he could have defended himself better, but this is not to say that he would have done so. Though his
popularity mattered to him enormously, changes in intellectual fashion
did not.

His increasingly frequent, increasingly protracted absences from
Paris, where his life consisted mainly of interruptions, helped him to
make headway with the Flaubert biography, while he spurred himself
once again with reckless doses of corydrane. Since boyhood he had felt
more affinity with Stendhal but more stimulated by Flaubert, who
seemed like a cautionary nineteenth-century paradigm of everything
Sartre might have become had he not put himself under oath to hate
the bourgeoisie and had he not resisted the lure of *l'imaginaire*. If he still
had lingering regrets about his undeveloped talent as a novelist, he
could fight them by characterizing Flaubert as an idiot who became a
genius while propelled pathologically into a creativity that was no more
than an alibi for passivity, an escape from reality. Henry James observed that in making Emma Bovary "the victim of the imaginative
habit" Flaubert must have been "far from designing or measuring the
total effect which renders the work so general, so complete an expression of himself."[14] But the book, for James, is a masterpiece, fortified by
Flaubert's ability to project his "irritated sensibility" into hard facts.
Sartre cannot forgive his incapacity for hard action.

As so often before, the question of literary tradition is evaded. Is the
work of Homer, Sophocles, Shakespeare, Molière, Tolstoy, Dostoevsky,
Kafka to be dismissed as imaginative and therefore valueless? Once
again the two main questions are "How did this man become a writer?"
and "Does his life have a single intelligible meaning?" Sartre had already been worrying at the second question when he wrote *La Nausée*.
Roquentin tells himself that however reasonable his hypotheses about
Rollebon appear to be, "they are simply a way of unifying my pieces of
information—not a glimmer comes from Rollebon's direction. Slow,
lazy, disagreeable, the facts adapt themselves reluctantly to the order I
want to impose, but it remains outside them."[15] His conclusion is that
"fictional characters would be more convincing or in any case more entertaining." The Sartre of the sixties offers *L'Idiot de la famille* as "a true
fiction," but he is obliged to assume that all the necessary illumination

is coming from Flaubert's direction, while his approach to both questions is conditioned by the period in which he finally arrives at the project that has so long been inevitable.

After abandoning the *Critique,* he gave himself up to long sessions of intensive work on Flaubert. The promise he could not redeem in the *Critique* was to explain the relationship between the individual and history; he now tries to compensate by explaining the relationship between one individual and history. The personal pressures that shaped Gustave Flaubert must be shown to have impersonal sources; correspondences must be found between public events and private crises. If Sartre devotes an inordinate amount of time to Flaubert's juvenilia, postponing *Madame Bovary* for one of the two final volumes he will never write, it is because he is working less as a literary critic than as the psychoanalyst of a dead patient, and Sartre's unrevised prose reads like an uninterrupted free-associating monologue. Flaubert's early fiction is full of symptoms: here, surely, at least a glimmer is coming from the object of the investigation.

If Roquentin is both more convincing and more entertaining than the semifictional Flaubert who emerges from this *roman vrai,* one reason is that in the thirties Sartre, not yet a public figure, was writing for a public. When his friends accused him of overwriting, he worked hard to trim his prose. In the sixties he was living the other half of his life in public but writing for himself. Any intelligent friend could have advised him, if asked, that the book ought to be no longer than six hundred pages, but he was not open to suggestions of this kind, even from De Beauvoir or Robert Gallimard. He also lacked what Keats called "negative capability" when he praised Shakespeare as a man "capable of being in uncertainties, mysteries, doubts, without any irritable reaching after fact and reason."[16]

Determined "to leave nothing in the dark,"[17] Sartre probes persistently into corners that other writers on Flaubert had been obliged to leave obscure. At the beginning of the fifties Sartre had shown in *Saint Genet* that he was capable of writing a Freudian biography without having made a serious study of Freud; now, after the reading done while preparing for the screenplay, he produces what could be called the most Freudian biography ever written.

It was Freud who pushed biography decisively away from fact toward speculation. Deeply interested in the art, and contemptuous of the insights achieved by nineteenth-century biographers, who knew little and said less about the sexuality of their subjects, Freud wrote several biographical essays, but his theories about Moses, Leonardo, and Dostoevsky have exerted less influence on subsequent biographers than his discoveries about the unconscious and his explorations of his patients' sexual past. In any evolutionary account of biography as an art, space should be given to the way Freud's case histories have prized certainty out of the biographer's grasp. "Dora" never succeeds in making Freud accept her version of what happened; he never succeeds in making her accept his. During the traumatic lakeside experience she underwent at the age of fourteen, when "Herr K." forcibly kissed her, did she feel his erect penis pressing against her? The analyst-narrator is easily able to upstage the subject-patient, whose narrative may distort memories that may themselves distort what actually happened. In effect, Freud has redefined the object of biographical inquiry. The goal is now situated at the far end of a swampy field, and there can no longer be any rules for what constitutes foul play. But no one has been more intrepid than Sartre in playing on the swamp.

Perhaps he never had any dreams or fantasies in which he was an analyst, with Flaubert's putrefying corpse on his couch, but he makes no secret of wanting to write a case history. "For this difficult test case I think it permissible to select a compliant subject who yields himself easily and unconsciously." The analyzable material is plentiful, but is a highly intelligent, highly articulate, highly sophisticated writer such a good subject for what Freud calls "pathography" as an inhibited, undeveloped girl? It is true that writers—to adapt Kafka's remark about the Jews—"have always experienced their joys and sorrows at more or less the same time as their Rashi commentary on them," but while the psychoanalyst is intent on bringing to the surface something that has previously sheltered in the timeless silence of the unconscious or the coded language of dreams and physical symptoms, a biography of Flaubert (or of Sartre) will be mainly concerned with translating the written word into the written word. Is the hidden content of Flaubert's fictions really so different from their apparent content? Undeniably there is more difference in the juvenilia than in the mature work, and this is why Sartre postpones his confrontation with *Madame Bovary* for one of the two final volumes he will never write. Analysis of the juvenilia is less interesting to the general reader, but this is not a book for the general reader.

Flaubert once said that his fiction was "the response to a deep and always hidden wound." Sartre joyfully takes up the challenge. What had always been hidden must be uncovered, especially if Flaubert wanted to hide it. But can it be uncovered? The importance of Sartre's gigantic, unbalanced, unfinished, almost unreadable book may turn out to reside in the sheer quantity of the energy it throws into a raid on the unknowable. If Sartre had previously seemed peremptory in contradicting Genet's assertion that he was homosexual before he started stealing, the new biography is still more uncompromising in its refusal to be confined either by ignorance of the facts or by knowledge of facts that contradict the hypotheses. Sartre holds back from speculating about the prenatal life of the fetus in Caroline Flaubert's womb, but he constructs an elaborate fiction to fill the gap that previous biographers had been obliged to leave for the first six years of Gustave's life. If the family is at fault—as all families are, according to Sartre—this is the time to show it. What Sartre hated most about himself was what he hated most about Flaubert—the bourgeois conditioning, the inclination to passivity, the habit of confusing words with things, the cognate tendency to prefer the imaginary to the real. With himself Sartre fights ferociously against these proclivities; with Flaubert he fights by trying to prove that the child was pathologically propelled toward art by damage the family inflicted. The main theme of *L'Idiot de la famille* is close to the main theme of *Les Mots*. Sartre's theory is that the passivity Flaubert acquired between the ages of five and nine had foundations laid for it during the second year of his life as he absorbed his mother's rhythms. In the oral phase of sexuality, filial love is determined by the mother's handling of the baby, and without denying that all he can offer us is guesswork, Sartre tells us in detail about Caroline Flaubert's behavior and baby Gustave's thumb-sucking.

The more a biographer speculates, the more he is liable to slip into disguised autobiography—Achille-Cléophas Flaubert is unmistakably modeled on Charles Schweitzer—and speculations about the subject's infancy can serve as a pretext for smuggling in the biographer's suspicions about his own. Had Sartre ever admitted to himself the possibility that his mother would have preferred a girl? Having claimed that the early death of his father was liberating, he puts the opposite interpretation on the early death of Caroline Flaubert's mother. The baby girl, he insists, must have felt rejected, guilty. Ten years later her father died. His terminal illness was induced, according to Sartre, by an irresistible urge to take revenge on little Caroline for killing her mother in childbirth. When it was her turn to have babies, she gave birth to three boys, two of whom died. After this how could she possibly have wanted another boy? No, if Gustave had been a girl, Caroline could have used her to compensate for memories of her own unhappy childhood. She could have lived vicariously through the child. Yes, disappointed that Gustave was a boy, she must have been dutiful but unloving in bringing him up. Once again Sartre is intent on forging a myth. In reality, there are more grounds for supposing that Anne-Marie Sartre would have preferred a daughter. At the beginning of 1905, when she said that her baby would be either "a little Annie" or "a little Paul,"[18] it was the girl she mentioned first. She went on to let Poulou's hair grow long and to dress him in smocks. And whereas Caroline Flaubert gave birth to a daughter less than a year after Gustave was born—she would then have no reason to go on treating the boy as a girl—Anne-Marie gave birth to no other child.

But in *L'Idiot de la famille* Caroline Flaubert is severely reprimanded for the damage inflicted on the infant who imaginatively tried to be the daughter she wanted. "Putting her imprint on him, she has condemned him forever to have only an *imaginary* sexual life. An unreal woman in men's hands, he will be an unreal man in his relations with women." It would have been interesting to have this thesis tested in an objective analysis of the evidence about Flaubert's relationship with Louise Colet, but Sartre has little to say about this.

The title *L'Idiot de la famille* points to his central assumption that Flaubert's development was retarded. According to his niece Caroline Commanville, who was reminiscing in old age, her uncle once told her that he could not read when he was nine. This is patently untrue. He was born on December 12, 1821, and in a letter written before the end of December 1830 to his school friend Ernest Chevalier, he refers with alarmingly precocious sophistication to his comedies and his "political and constitutional liberal speeches." Undaunted, Sartre decides that the old lady's memory must have been unreliable and that what Flaubert actually said was that he could not read when he was seven. Perhaps someone then told him that he was "the idiot of the family."

THE rising of May 1968 has sometimes been called a Sartrian rebellion, and Lévi-Strauss interpreted it as a triumph of Marxian existentialism over structuralism. "In France, you know," he said at the end of 1969, "structuralism is no longer a fashion. Since May 1968 all objectivity has been repudiated. The position of the youth corresponds to that of Sartre."[19] This is misleadingly simplistic. Though Sartre had done a great deal toward making students more politically aware, he was cooperating with a trend that owed more to the Vietnam War; and from 1966 to 1968, while Louis Althusser and Henri Lefebvre were lecturing at the ENS and at Nanterre, Sartre had little contact with students. He was leading the cosmopolitan life that had become normal for him. In 1966 he spent five weeks in the Soviet Union during the late spring, traveled to Greece in the summer, and in the autumn spent a month in Japan, followed by another week in the Soviet Union, later going to London for a meeting of the Russell tribunal. During February and

March 1967 he would be in Egypt and Israel, then in Stockholm during May, and in Denmark for two weeks of the autumn.

Ideology played a major role both in the 1968 rebellion itself and in the preliminary buildup of pressure, but underlying the appeal of the various radical ideologies was a huge undertow of resentment. If French students could identify better than any other section of the population with the Vietnamese, it was partly through empathic generosity but partly also because the remote, persecuted Asians seemed to reflect their own fate as victims of the Establishment's indifference. Nobody cared about them. Overcrowded, undersubsidized, condescendingly treated, and inefficiently organized while they were at the university, they would probably be unemployed when they graduated. At the same time as Sartre's *tiers-mondisme* was helping to consolidate all these heterogeneous feelings of resentment, the aggressive foreign policy of the United States was helping to recruit support for French Maoism. Not only university students but *lycéens* were joining the action committees formed as branches of the Comité Vietnam National (CVN), but the PCF was as myopically hostile to the committee as it had been to the *italiens,* and as halfhearted about the Vietnamese as it had been about the Algerians. The students cared; the party pretended to care. Whereas the CVN's slogan was "The FLN [Front de Libération Nationale] will win," the PCF's slogan was "Peace in Vietnam."

The pro-Chinese journal *Révolution* had been founded in 1963, with funding from Peking, and since then Maoism had gathered momentum in France. In Paris its principal ideological stronghold was the ENS, where Althusser led a faction strongly critical of the PCF. Since 1960 he had been austerely opposed to rapprochement with the non-Communist left. Roger Garaudy, now one of the party's chief theorists, had been moving toward Sartrian existentialism, a tendency Althusser denounced most outspokenly in his 1964 essay on Marxism and humanism. Referring frequently to Mao, Althusser insisted on the need to retain all the revolutionary purity of Marxist theory; the masses must be indoctrinated with Marxist-Leninist ideas. Ideological purity obviously mattered more to Maoist China than it did in Brezhnev's Soviet Union, and, thanks partly to Althusser, this helped to split the French student left. His disciples demanded that the Union des Etudiants Communistes (UEC) should affiliate with the Mouvement Communiste Français (Marxiste-Léniniste)—the MCF (ML)—France's new pro-Chinese organization, funded by Peking. Intending to counter the danger of disruption, the UEC leaders then expelled about six hundred students in October and November 1966. In December many of these joined to form the Union des Jeunesses Communistes (Marxistes-Léninistes), the UJC (ML).

This accelerated the fragmentation that was already under way. The Jeunesse Communiste Révolutionnaire (JCR) had been founded on April 2, 1966, when about a hundred and twenty young people met in a Paris hall. Trotskyist in ideology but Leninist in organization, the group consisted of "circles": each new recruit would be kept under observation by other members of his circle for three trial months. One of the leaders was Alain Krivine, a tall, dark, eloquent student of history at the Sorbonne, the son of a Jewish dentist. The JCR played a prominent part in creating the CVN and encouraging demonstrations against the Vietnam War.

Of the student "groupuscules" the most obviously Sartrian were the Situationists, whose manifestos bristled with his jargon and derived from his ideas. Positive action and theory, they held, must ensue on the negative liberty acquired during the act of revolt. As in the manifestos of other groups, the borrowings from the *Critique* sometimes look like disguised pieces of plagiarism in student essays, but, unlike Althusser and Lefebvre, Sartre was not trying to keep *au courant* with radical student writing. In 1966 he was more ambivalent than they were about wanting a revolution.

WHEN he and De Beauvoir went back to the USSR at the beginning of May 1966, they found Ehrenburg and their other friends depressed and anxious about the outlook for the intellectuals. Tried in February, Daniel and Sinyavsky had been sentenced to reeducation in a labor camp for five and seven years respectively. Sixty-two writers had put themselves at risk by signing a petition for their release and offering themselves as surety, but at the twenty-third party congress Sholokhov deplored the leniency of the sentence.

After publishing three of Solzhenitsyn's stories in *Les Temps Modernes*, Sartre and De Beauvoir would have liked to meet him, but after parleying with Solzhenitsyn on their behalf for an hour, Lena Zonina came back with a refusal. According to her, he had said he would suffer too much if he met a writer who was free to publish his work. But in *The Oak and the Calf* Solzhenitsyn explains his reason for refusing: Sartre had insulted Russian literature by saying that a Nobel Prize ought to be awarded to the "hangman" Sholokhov.

Sartre and De Beauvoir stayed in the Soviet Union over a month, visiting Yalta, Odessa, Lvov, and Kishinev. After returning to Paris on

June 6, Sartre left again in July for a vacation in Greece before going on to Rome. In the middle of September he and De Beauvoir went to Japan, accepting an invitation from his publisher there, Watanabe, and the University of Kyoto. They flew over the North Pole, and when they landed in Tokyo, about two hundred photographers and journalists and over a thousand students were waiting for them. But the first meal of raw fish made Sartre violently sick; afterward he could swallow nothing for two days.[20] Mr. Watanabe arranged for them to see a private performance of a Noh play and a *kyōgen.* But after the performance the meal was cut short: a typhoon was expected. They were awakened in the night by the wind. Their rooms were full of dust, and uprooted trees lay in the street.[21] From Tokyo they went on to visit Kyoto and Nagasaki. They lectured, they appeared on television, and, on their last day in Japan, they both addressed a big rally in Tokyo against the Vietnam War. After a month in Japan (September 18 to October 16) they went on to Moscow, staying there from October 17 to 22.

In November they left Paris again, this time to visit London for a meeting convened by the ninety-two-year-old Bertrand Russell, who during the summer had formed the International Tribunal Against War Crimes in Vietnam, the idea being to use the Nuremberg trials as a model for judging the American tactics in Vietnam. In July, Sartre had been approached by a chief secretary of the Russell Foundation and had agreed to be involved. At the two-day meeting in mid-November, Sartre was elected executive president of the tribunal. On November 23, when an antiwar meeting was held at the Mutualité, the huge audience of young people gave Sartre's speech an enormous ovation.[22] After the writer Alejo Carpentier had headed a commission to visit Vietnam for the tribunal, he reported that planes were bombing schools, hospitals, leper colonies, and churches, which were all better targets than straw huts. In January 1967 Sartre and De Beauvoir went back for a meeting in London to formulate questions for the tribunal to investigate, and at a Paris press conference on February 2 Sartre and the mathematician Laurent Schwartz, one of the "121," who had been dismissed from his chair at the Ecole Polytechnique, presented a report on the commission's findings. The tribunal was planning to hold most of its meetings in Paris, but a key member, the Yugoslav historian Vladimir Dedijer, who had fought with Tito in the Resistance, was refused a visa to attend the meeting convened for February.

Sartre and De Beauvoir did not go to Vietnam, but they had been planning for more than a year to visit Egypt and Israel in the hope of

arting a dialogue between left-wingers in the two countries. Writing
n anti-Semitism in 1945, Sartre had said that so long as there was a
ngle Jew who could not feel safe in the world, Christians would also be
n danger; but since the Algerian war had brought him close to so many
rabs, friendships and loyalties had been pulling him in opposite direc-
ons. In December 1965 he had announced that after visiting both
gypt and Israel he would bring out an issue of *Les Temps Modernes* pre-
nting both viewpoints.[23] He had planned to make the journey with
e Beauvoir in December 1966, but they postponed it to February
967.

Before leaving for Cairo they were asked to approach Nasser on be-
alf of eighteen young men who had been imprisoned without a trial
or attempting to reconstitute a Communist party. Together with
anzmann and an Egyptian journalist, Ali el-Saman, who had both re-
orted in *Les Temps Modernes* on the situation in the two countries,
artre and De Beauvoir flew to Cairo on February 25 for three weeks in
gypt. They saw the City of the Dead, visited temples, floated down the
ile on a boat, cruised over it in a plane.[24] When Nasser received them
t Heliopolis, Sartre asked whether the eighteen young men could be
ut on trial soon. If they were, said Nasser, they might get a ten-year
entence. It would be better to keep them a little longer and release
hem quietly.

Visiting the Palestinian refugees in a crowded Gaza camp, Sartre had
he impression that the display of misery had been carefully staged, and
t a banquet, not far from the starving refugees, given by the Egyptian
overnor of the Gaza zone, the Palestinian leaders tried to convince him
hat the Jews should be expelled from Israel.[25] Back in Cairo, it was
ood to learn that the eighteen young Communists had been released.

Lanzmann could stay for only the first three days of the seventeen in
srael, but Arlette Elkaim came out to join Sartre and De Beauvoir.
hough they had been invited by a group that included political and
ntellectual figures, the visit was less official than the one to Egypt.
hey traveled all over the country, visiting kibbutzim, where the divi-
on of labor between men and women struck De Beauvoir as unfair.
artre spoke at a meeting called against the Vietnam War. They met a
umber of Arabs, not one of whom felt satisfied with his rights or with
he life he had in Israel, and they met Israeli Jews who were campaign-
ng to give the Arabs a better deal. In one kibbutz they met survivors of
he Warsaw ghetto uprisings. On their last day they were received by
he prime minister, Levi Eshkol, and Sartre held a press conference. He
as now convinced that Israel's right to national existence was incom-

patible with the right of a million Palestinian refugees to live in th
country from which they had been expelled.

After two days in Athens[26] the three of them arrived back in Pari
only a few days before war broke out between Israel and Syria. At th
end of May, Sartre was one of the French signatories to an appeal fo
Israel to be guaranteed its sovereignty, its independence, and its right t
use international waterways. For many Arabs this was enough to mean
that Sartre had sided against them.[27]

On April 13 he dispatched a letter—handwritten on square
paper—to De Gaulle asking whether the refusal to give Vladimir De
dijer a visa meant that the government intended to stop the Russell tri
bunal from meeting in Paris. De Gaulle's reply, which began "Mon
cher Maître," confirmed this ban. "You will not be the one," wrote D
Gaulle, "to teach me that all justice, in principle as well as practice, be
longs to the state." Sartre then gave an interview to say that the govern
ment must be afraid of the tribunal.[28] It met on May 2 at Stockholm
The judges, who had been recruited by Russell's secretary, Ralph
Schoenman, from all over the world, included the historian Isaac
Deutscher and the American pacifist David Dellinger, editor of *Libera
tion;* the playwright Peter Weiss, secretary-general of the Swedish com
mittee, was co-opted as a judge. The languages used were English
French, and Spanish. Dedijer presided, assisted by Laurent Schwartz
Altogether there were about two hundred people in the hall.[29]

In his opening speech Sartre made the point that the tribunal could
enforce its verdict only through public opinion. Unlike the Nuremberg
tribunal, it was not backed by a victorious government, but impotence
was a guarantee of independence.[30] Two American international law
yers argued that America had disregarded the Geneva Convention and
artificially established a South Vietnamese state; a French physicis
demonstrated that the antipersonnel bombs—which could not be used
against targets protected by sandbags—were designed to kill civilians
Photographs and films showed burned and mutilated corpses, children
who had lost limbs, others who had been disfigured by napalm burns
The mutilated Vietnamese civilians who appeared before the tribuna
included a twelve-year-old boy who took off his clothes to reveal hid
eous burns.[31] The evidence was examined in hearings that continued
until May 10, when the tribunal concluded unanimously that the
Americans were guilty of aggression against the Vietnamese and of ter
roristic bombing to undermine the people's morale. "What has been
important for me," said Sartre, "is the progress from this vague, already
intolerable idea: 'Children, women and elderly people are being killed

n Vietnam' to this precise and odious idea: 'It is being done deliberately.' "[32] At a press conference in the Mutualité on May 19 he presented the tribunal's verdict.

SINCE 1962 Sartre and De Beauvoir had traveled eight times to the Soviet Union, but in May 1967, to protest against the treatment of Sinyavsky and Daniel, they refused an invitation to the tenth congress of
the Union of Soviet Writers. Their only regret, retrospectively, was at
having missed their last chance to meet Ilya Ehrenburg, who died on
August 31. "We liked his intelligence, his courage, the charm of his old,
tired face."[33]

In May, Sartre was also involved in writing the preface for a special
issue of *Les Temps Modernes* dealing with the Arab-Israeli conflict. Over
the opening of the Gulf of Aqaba he supported Israel, offending Frantz
Fanon's widow, who refused to allow *Les Damnés de la terre* to go on
being reprinted with his preface.

ANOTHER session of the Russell tribunal was to be held during November in Denmark. In September, Sartre and De Beauvoir went to Brussels for a preliminary discussion. Dellinger, who was going to lead a big
pacifist march in America on October 21, asked that the session start
late in November. He hoped to bring some American servicemen to
testify. The pacifist march culminated in the siege of the Pentagon, at
which Norman Mailer was arrested.

On November 19 Sartre and De Beauvoir flew to Copenhagen. The
sessions were to be held in a trade union building, FjordVilla, at Ros-
kilde, twenty miles from the capital. The hall was used as a ballroom on
Saturday evenings, and the judges sat behind a long table on a stage,
with the dance floor closed off by railings.[34] One question was whether
the Americans were attempting genocide. A Japanese delegate revealed
that rice, sugar cane, and vegetables were being sprayed with poison; it
was not only guerrillas who were harmed. A twenty-three-year-old
American, a former member of the Special Forces, testified that he
taught Vietnamese government troops how to torture and had seen
American officers pushing pieces of bamboo under prisoners' nails. Senior American officers knew that torture was being used, and a lieuten-
ant or captain was invariably present.[35] Another American described
how the wounded were finished off and how tanks and machine guns
would fire for what was called a "crazy moment" at everyone and

everything in a village. Another described the "strategic hamlets" into
which Vietnamese civilians were herded and kept without beds, water
latrines, or adequate food. His evidence was substantiated by a French
journalist's film. A Vietnamese woman told the tribunal how she had
been hung up by her wrists and had been tied half naked to a tree
swarming with ants that could bite. She also described how soldiers had
poured over a woman's head a bowl full of pus, the sputum of con
sumptives, vomit, and water in which lepers had washed.[36] A West
German surgeon gave evidence about peasants machine-gunned from
the air and about depopulated tracts of country—four million Viet
namese had been relocated in the south. There was film, most of it shot
by American servicemen, to confirm the stories of gratuitous killing and
torture. When Bost arrived to report on the hearing for *Le Nouvel Obser
vateur,* he was against using the word "genocide"; three days later he
agreed it was unavoidable.

The sessions lasted from November 20 to December 1. To prepare for
the statement he was to make as executive president at the final session
Sartre had to work at night after the long, exhausting days, but he pro
duced a cogent indictment of the Americans. When Dean Rusk, the
American secretary of state, had said "It is ourselves we are defending,'
he had meant that the first aim was military—to encircle Communist
China. But since 1965 there had been increased evidence of racism—
anti-Negro, anti-Asian, anti-Mexican—among American soldiers, and
as there was no possibility of inflicting a military defeat on thirty-one
million Vietnamese, systematic bombing of such crowded cities as
Hanoi and Haiphong was insidiously calculated to prepare world opin
ion for the idea of genocide. To denounce what the Americans were
doing in Vietnam was the only alternative to being their accomplice.[37]
What Sartre could not resolve was the fundamental ambiguity in his
own position as executive president. His Marxist condemnation of the
violence as indispensable to neocolonialism had to be reconciled with
his condemnation of it for violating international law—a bourgeois
concept. In any event his speech was effective: afterward the tribunal
unanimously upheld the charge of genocide. But the press systemati
cally ignored the proceedings, and the world remained ignorant of what
was going on until March, when the My Lai massacre was exposed.

Sartre returned to Paris at the beginning of December, intending to
leave again in January 1968 for a cultural congress in Havana, but he
succumbed to an inflammation of the arteries. On the telephone to a
Cuban journalist he expressed his admiration for the example Cuba
was setting: "I believe that for a European today it is in Vietnam, in
Cuba and in Latin America that his fate is sealed."[38] But it was ru-

mored in Cuba that Sartre's illness was a fiction, that he was absenting himself from the congress to avoid confrontations with Arab journalists.[39]

IN his address to the nation at the beginning of 1968 De Gaulle had greeted the new year "with serenity," and during the spring *Le Monde*'s analysis of the political situation was headlined "France Is Bored." In the universities a proliferation of strikes suggested that students were becoming less tractable, while their demonstrations were more violent. Bombs were exploded outside the offices of American organizations.

Henri Lefebvre, who believed in confrontation and resistance to all forms of alienation, allowed classroom discussion to become militant, and one of his most vociferous sociology students, an excitable young German, Daniel Cohn-Bendit, helped a demonstration to form itself into a movement. What happened on March 22 was that news about the arrest of local CVN militants arrived during a meeting in a lecture hall. The group proceeded to invade the administration building, occupying the council room on the top floor. The Mouvement du 22 Mars (M22M) was formed by spontaneous combustion. Later Cohn-Bendit, who called himself not the leader but the spokesman of the movement, would say that some of its members had read Marx, "perhaps Bakunin, and of the moderns, Althusser, Mao, Guevara, Lefebvre. Nearly all the militants of the M22M have read Sartre."[40]

TO prevent a teach-in on the struggle against imperialism, the campus was closed for three days, and the tension was exacerbated by news that in West Berlin an attempt had been made to kill Rudi Dutschke, the student leader, and by rumors that attacks were to be expected from right-wing commando groups. On May 3, when all teaching was suspended at Nanterre, a demonstration was staged at the Sorbonne. The police were called in to evacuate the buildings. The students agreed to leave quietly, but about 500 of them were put into police vans, watched by a crowd of about 2000 people, who jeered and yelled. Soon paving stones were being hurled at the police, who fought back with tear gas and clubs. They were brutal not only with demonstrators but with passive onlookers. Three days later there was twelve hours of vicious fighting between police and students. On May 6, when Cohn-Bendit and other student leaders were due to appear before the Sorbonne's disciplinary council, the Union Nationale des Etudiants de France (UNEF) organized a demonstration, and in the Latin Quarter throughout the day students, using paving stones as weapons, clashed with police using clubs, tear gas, and fire hoses. The ferocity of the police, which amazed onlookers, generated extra sympathy for the students. Barricades were built, cars set on fire, students taken off in police vans and beaten up. The next day a procession of perhaps 35,000 demonstrators marched from the Place Denfert-Rochereau to the Etoile, some waving red or black flags, some singing the "Internationale."[41]

This was the day Sartre appeared in the foreground. He condemned the police and, together with De Beauvoir, Colette Audry, Michel Leiris, and Daniel Guérin, signed a manifesto calling on all workers and intellectuals to give the students moral and material support.[42] More demonstrations followed. The students were demanding that the Sorbonne be reopened, that the arrested students be released, that the police withdraw from the Latin Quarter. On May 9, the day that De Gaulle made the education minister, Alain Peyrefitte, announce that the Sorbonne would remain closed, Sartre, Lefebvre, and Jacques Lacan signed a manifesto: "It's scandalous not to recognize what this movement is aimed at and what is at stake: the wish to escape at any price from an order which is alienated but so strongly structured and integrated that it can turn the simplest dispute to its advantage."[43]

Taking sides against the students, L'Humanité had attacked "the German anarchist Cohn-Bendit." It was obvious that the unions were not going to let the students lead the workers into a revolution, but on May 8 the two largest unions, the Confédération Générale du Travail (CGT) and the Confédération Française Démocratique du Travail (CFDT), began talks with UNEF and the university lecturers' union, Syndicat National de l'Enseignement Supérieur (SNESup), and the teachers' Fédération de l'Education Nationale (FEN). The two students' unions, UNEF and Union des Etudiants Communistes (UEC), called for a twenty-four-hour general strike, starting on the thirteenth, and a demonstration against repression. In the evening the Latin Quarter was again a battlefield, with barricades in the Rue Gay-Lussac and vicious fighting between riot police and students. The Cs gas and the tear gas had their effects, but the students were throwing Molotov cocktails as well as paving stones.

Interviewed for Radio Luxembourg on Sunday, May 12, Sartre reiterated what he had written in his preface to Aden-Arabie: "These youngsters don't want the future of their fathers—our future—a future which proved we were cowardly, worn out, weary, stupefied by total obedience. . . . Violence is the one thing that remains, whatever the régime, for the students. . . . The only relationship they can have to this university is to smash it."[44] This message, which was printed in a leaflet and distributed in the Latin Quarter, was in line with the revolutionary slogans that had appeared in the corridors of the Sorbonne and on the walls outside, predicting a violent death for consumer society. Bureaucracy, alienation, capitalism, industrialism, boredom were all anathematized.[45] Every day new slogans and messages appeared.

On May 11 De Gaulle promised to meet the students' demands, but the concession came too late to stave off the twenty-four-hour general strike. Relations between students and workers did not improve when Cohn-Bendit described Communist leaders as Stalinist filth, but there was massive support for the demonstrations, both in Paris and in the provinces. Leaders of left-wing parties marched with students and workers, chanting slogans, and though the CGT, using loudspeaker trucks in the Place Denfert-Rochereau, tried to make the workers disperse, some of them joined with the students to rally in the Champ-de-Mars.

In the Sorbonne red flags flew over the chapel and the statues; the look of the place gave De Beauvoir the impression of an enormous party. Bands were playing jazz and dance music. Hot meals, sandwiches, and fruit juice were brought by sympathizers for the students, many of whom were spending the night there in sleeping bags. There was a crèche in the attic. Press offices were set up in lecture rooms, debate raged endlessly, much of it about the Israeli-Arab conflict. The "left-wing Zionists" had a stall next to the Palestinians, and a huge variety of leaflets was being distributed.[46]

On May 15 the students swarmed into the Place de l'Odéon and occupied the theater. Soon their black flag was flying from its roof. Passersby were friendly, and the atmosphere must have been similar to that of Berlin during November 1918 after the abdication of Kaiser Wilhelm. Power appeared to be in the hands of the people. In Paris, though De Gaulle had not abdicated, people had the impression at least momentarily that they were no longer to be excluded from decision making. Strangers entered into long conversations about education or public transport or taxation as if consensus between private citizens could from now on make itself felt. When cafés were raided by the police, it seemed to confirm that the government was apprehensive about free discussion. The rebels may have got only halfway to revolution, but they had shown that revolution was feasible.

Two days later students carried the Sorbonne's red flag to the huge Renault factory at Billancourt with a placard declaration: "The working class takes the battle flag from the students' frail hands." The next day strikes began to paralyze France. In Paris public transport stopped and banks closed. Gasoline and cigarettes were in short supply. Ambulance drivers had to appeal for fuel; garbage cans overflowed onto the sidewalks.[47] Factories were occupied by workers. Soon it was the biggest strike in the history of France, but the rebels were not trying to take power. They were fighting for a fair deal.[48] Different factions made different demands. Workers were asking for participation in management, and middle-class rebels supported them. In her dispatch to *The New Yorker* Janet Flanner pointed out that in the past De Gaulle had offered the French people a choice between him and chaos. Now they had both.[49]

By interviewing Cohn-Bendit, Sartre helped him to improve his image. He could not be just a hotheaded radical student if the *Nouvel Observateur* was printing a rational conversation between him and a great thinker in its special supplement. At the end Sartre praised him and the students for "putting the imagination in power." The slogans on the walls of the Sorbonne proved how imaginative they were. "This is what I'll call extending the field of the possible."[50] On the same day that the interview appeared, May 20, Sartre, who had been briefed by the secretary of SNESup, Alain Geismar, in a two-hour session during the small hours of the morning, debated in the great hall of the occupied Sorbonne with the leaders of the rebellion. He praised Cohn-Bendit and derided the CGT for having to follow his lead. From then on, Sartre kept in close touch with the rebels. Many of his young supporters were members of action committees, sold the paper *Action*, distributed leaflets.

On the night of the twenty-third, in protest against the expulsion of Cohn-Bendit from the university, students again built barricades and fought with the riot police. The next day two demonstrations were organized by the CGT to drum up support for the strikers.

At least nine million people were on strike by May 24, when De Gaulle promised on television and radio to hold a referendum, offering to resign if it went against him. Students with transistors, listening en masse outside the Gare de Lyon, booed, and afterward, led by Alain Geismar, marched to the stock exchange, where they started fires.[51] The premier, Georges Pompidou, formerly De Gaulle's private secretary, offered substantial concessions on wages, working hours, and workers' rights, but the strike continued.

On May 27, at a meeting in the Stade Charléty, the two Socialist leaders Mendès-France and Mitterrand were reconciled, and on the twenty-ninth the CGT, which had been absent from the meetings, held a demonstration. The disunity of the left added to the pandemonium. To the middle classes it looked as though France might be on the verge of another revolution. Panic-stricken parents moved with their children from Paris to the country, and on May 29, when De Gaulle vanished, the panic increased. It looked as though he had run away in despair of bringing the situation under control. An evening paper carried the headline "French President Lost for Seven Hours." In fact, he knew that, as in the Algerian troubles, he was safe so long as the army remained loyal, and he had gone to consult General Massu in Baden-Baden. Reappearing on May 30, he cleverly regained control by dissolving the Assembly and announcing that he would hold an election. When a large Gaullist procession marched down the Champs-Elysées the same evening, the unions chose not to counter it with an anti-Gaullist demonstration. From now on the split between workers and students would be increasingly apparent; the students would try in vain to convince voters that they should boycott the elections. The occupation of the Sorbonne and the Odéon lasted only till the middle of June.

Defending student violence in an interview, Sartre called it "counterviolence" provoked by the police. It was not desire for disorder but desire for a different order; the intellectual must be willing to fight for his political and social ideals. Inevitably the rift widened between Sartre and more conservative intellectuals, such as his old friend Raymond Aron. Aron's question, formulated in *Le Figaro*, was "Do you expect a bourgeois state to finance a Cuban university?" To Sartre, reasoning and reasonableness of this kind seemed antiquated. His riposte was that since Aron had never become embattled, he was not fit to teach.[52] Sartre also defended the students against Communist criticism. Whether they were bourgeois or not, they had stood up for a truly socialist democracy.[53] The rebellious students approximated closely to what he had described in the *Critique* as a group-in-fusion. Later he would call the rebellion "the first large-scale social movement which has realized, momentarily, something close to liberty, and which, from then on, has tried to devise liberty in action. And this movement has produced people—me among them—who have decided that it is now necessary to try to describe positively what liberty is when conceived as a political objective."[54] After the election had given the Gaullists 358 of the 485 seats, Sartre categorically blamed the Communists for the failure of the rebellion. "In this crisis I think the Communist party had an attitude which was not at all revolutionary or even reformist."[55] The PCF's official explanation of its inaction was that the conflict could not have been genuinely revolutionary since it had been initiated by neither the revolutionary class nor its accredited organization. Unimpressed by this argument, Sartre still gave no sign of regret at having refused to support Defferre.

Though it is easy to overestimate Sartre's influence on the events of May to June, it would be hard to overestimate their influence on him. He had never been closer to a revolution, and it changed his life. The most apparent change was that he never again wore a suit or a tie: even for formal occasions he would turn up informally dressed. This was superficial but symptomatic.

WHAT had been happening in Czechoslovakia during April 1968 was what had failed to happen in France during May: workers and intellectuals joined forces. For twenty years no one had been able to tell the truth about the alienation, the bureaucracy, the nationwide depression caused by an imported, prefabricated socialism, but suddenly the democratic impulse had robustly reasserted itself. A reformist party leadership was outstripped by popular experiment in electing workers' councils and by solidarity between workers and intellectuals clamoring for the right to unrestricted information. In March, after the resignation of the Stalinist president, Antonin Novotný, parliamentary elections were announced. In June the workers' right to self-management was conceded, and "committees for the freedom of expression" were set up by factory workers. But on July 1 the "Letter of the Five Powers" was signed by the Soviet Union, Hungary, Poland, Bulgaria, and East Germany, calling on Czech Communists to oppose the policies of Alexander Dubček, who had become first secretary of the party in January and had taken bold liberalizing initiatives. Lenin had said of the Soviet masses that the new society could be built only by them and with them, but in 1968 the Soviet system was still intent on keeping tight control over the masses in Eastern Europe, and in August the Russian tanks arrived in Prague.

Sartre, who had gone on to Rome after vacationing in Yugoslavia, found himself at a point on the spiral visibly in line with the point he had reached in 1956 during the Soviet attack on Budapest. He had spoken out then against the "crime" that "had been made possible and perhaps necessary (from the Soviet viewpoint) by twelve years of terror and imbecility." The slaughter of Hungarian workers proved "the complete failure of socialism as merchandise imported from the USSR." The terror and imbecility had continued: the same merchandise was being exported during Sartre's eight years of friendship with the Soviet Union, but he had forgotten the lesson that, as he had said, "the Hungarians are teaching us with their blood." Thanks to the new lesson, taught with Czech blood, his break with the Kremlin would be final. The Soviet aggression, he told the Communist paper *Paese Sera,* was "what is called in international law a war crime. . . . It is because I have profound respect for the history of the Soviet Union and am by no means an anti-Communist that I feel obliged to condemn unreservedly the invasion of Czechoslovakia. . . . Today the Soviet example, smothered as it is with bureaucracy, is no longer valid."[56] Disappointingly, Castro applauded the Soviet action, as did most of the prominent Soviet writers except Tvardovsky; the PCF, which had supported the aggression against Hungary, dissociated itself from the new aggression but expelled Roger Garaudy for criticizing it too vigorously.

In another interview for *Paese Sera,* published four days earlier, on August 17, Sartre spoke to four young Italian film makers about the Venice Film Festival, which was to open in September. The national association of Italian *cinéastes* (ANAC) had demanded that the festival should be radically changed and the industry restructured. Siding with them, Sartre declared himself hostile not only to prizes and competitions but to evaluative film criticism. This is in line with his attitude toward literary criticism. Even in the Communist countries, he said, competitive festivals were "symptomatic of a reformism which is no longer revolutionary," while "the critics' function should be expository, informative. They should not pass judgment on merit, because it is for the mass audience to judge. The juries are only supercritics and therefore represent the opposite of what culture ought to be."[57]

FOR ten years since his narrow escape from a stroke in 1958, Sartre's health had been holding up well, but one day in Rome he had an ominous attack of dizziness. He was with De Beauvoir and her schoolteacher friend Sylvie Le Bon. In the Piazza Santa Maria in Trastevere his legs gave way, and he clutched hold of the two women as if he had been drinking heavily, but he had not.[58]

He soon recovered, and, back in Paris, resumed his normal routine. He did not attend the meeting on October 11 at the Mutualité but sent a message, which was read aloud. Denouncing all forms of oppression, he condemned Soviet surveillance of the Czechs and police repressiveness toward the French working class.[59]

He had begun to suspect, as Bertrand Russell did, that the shifting balance of power might bring Russia and America into alliance against China. Along with Schwartz and Dedijer, Sartre and Russell signed a letter in *Le Monde* provoked by Soviet and Bulgarian threats against Yugoslavia: "The secret diplomacy of the rulers of the USSR and the US is a threat to the liberty and sovereignty of men, wherever they are. It is essential that in order to safeguard truth this identity of interest between American capitalism and Soviet bureaucracy should be clearly understood and fought."[60] Later in the month Sartre and Russell again collaborated as signatories—this time with Herbert Marcuse—in an appeal to have Soviet troops withdrawn immediately from Czechoslovakia, where intellectuals and militant workers were being intimidated and blacklisted.

When Sartre was invited by the Czech Writers' Union to the Prague premiere of *Les Mouches,* he spent three days in the city (November 28 to December 1) without going to see *Les Mains sales,* which was also receiving a Czech premiere. Interviewed on television and by journalists, he was encouraging though cautious. "Those who believe the Czechs are defeated may find they are making a mistake."[61] But after the Soviet aggression and the 1968 rebellion, he no longer felt loyal to international communism. Disunited though they were, the extremist groups had crystallized radical opinion to the left of the party, and they showed that he was in no danger of isolation. Without offering any of them his exclusive allegiance, he could believe what he badly needed to believe—that, unlike most left-wingers of his generation, he was in touch with the young.

SARTRE'S mother was now eighty-six and in poor health, with rheumatism, headaches, high blood pressure, and a weak heart. Since 1962 she had been living at the Hôtel l'Aiglon in the Boulevard Raspail, not far from Sartre and De Beauvoir, who had both been paying her visits. Afraid that she might become dizzy in the street, she stayed in her room nearly all the time. On Christmas Day Sartre and De Beauvoir went to drink champagne with her, but on New Year's Eve and New Year's Day she was unwell, and on January 3, 1969, she had a heart attack. She was taken to the Fernand-Widal Hospital in the Rue Faubourg Saint-Denis, where she stayed for a week, sharing a room with another woman, but after a serious attack of uremia, she was moved to the Lariboisière Hospital, in the Rue Ambroise-Paré, where she had a stroke, with hemiplegia. Sartre found her unconscious in a cubicle, surrounded by medical equipment; she was taken back to the Fernand-Widal, given a room to herself, and again surrounded by apparatus. For two weeks she was comatose, her right side paralyzed, her lower lip twisted. Sartre spent hours at her bedside; twice, recovering consciousness, she put her good hand on his wrist, squeezed it, signaled him to go away. On January 30 he was summoned to the hospital, but half an hour before he and De Beauvoir arrived she died quietly. The body was very white; the lips, slightly parted, had resumed their normal shape.[62]

Believing that Sartre had cut his autobiography short for fear of upsetting her, she had expected him to resume it after her death, but he no longer had any desire to analyze the personal factors that had fomented his hatred of the bourgeoisie. In his biography of Flaubert he was coordinating social and familial pressures, but he did not want to deal directly with the hostility he still felt toward Charles Schweitzer and Joseph Mancy. Nor did he resume work on his "dialectical morality." After writing copious notes during 1964–65 for the Cornell lecture he canceled, and adding to them before delivering his 1966 lecture at the Istituto Gramsci, he had the feeling that a new book on ethics existed inside his head; all he would have to do was to put it down on paper.[63] But for this there was no time. He was not only giving priority to the Flaubert biography but allowing it, like *Saint Genet,* to absorb material that had been prepared or half prepared for more philosophical work.

He was also trying to arrive at a new compromise—necessary after his rapprochement with Freud—over the unconscious. The new term Sartre introduced was *le vécu*—lived experience. He had previously used a distinction, borrowed from Jaspers, between knowing and comprehending. Knowledge is factual and analytic; comprehension involved intuition and empathy. A biography that merely depicts the subject's experience factually cannot be adequate; the biographer must use his imagination if he is to convey an impression of emotional living. No longer so hostile to *la vie intérieure,* Sartre deduces subjectivity from external events. Like his earlier term "bad faith," *le vécu* gives him an alternative to Freud's way of dealing with the kind of consciousness that can always elude the spotlight that consciousness throws on itself. "What I call *le vécu* is the accumulation of the dialectical process of psychic life insofar as this process remains obscure to itself as a constant totalization. It is impossible to be conscious of a totalization which also totalizes consciousness. *Le vécu,* in this sense, is permanently susceptible of comprehension but never of knowledge."[64] The experience of the moment always consists of an attempt to unify whatever is confronting consciousness with the residue of all previous experiences. In family life the hierarchical conventions and values create pressures that are internalized by the child, who subsequently externalizes them. His actions reflect what the family has made of him. Sartre's emphasis is no longer on freedom but on conditioning: the child is only choosing to be what he has been made to be.

The overall purpose of the book is to show that Flaubert was the victim of a double conditioning. He was what he was partly because of the family, partly because of literature and language in the state they had reached by the nineteenth century. The phenomenon of Flaubert's art is only a neurotic reaction to his subjective malaise and to the disturbed state of French literature. To describe the cultural situation, Sartre brings out his old notion of the practico-inert—literature and language as the residue of past *praxis*. This idea is combined with the argument he had developed in dealing with Mallarmé, depicting the French nineteenth-century writers as "knights of nothingness." Flaubert is guilty because he developed ideas that were then taken to their logical extreme by Mallarmé. This use of one writer to denigrate another is characteristic of Sartre's methodology. His quarrel with Flaubert is only part of his quarrel with literature, and having spent so much time with Flaubert after deriding him as a man you would not want to spend much time with, Sartre widens the focus of his attack. Even Kafka comes under fire. He too had a bullying father; for him too remorse and resentment are indistinguishable. "Gustave's intention—we guess at it when we reread *Metamorphosis* . . . Something is going to happen to him, something atrocious—death, old age, the name doesn't matter: the point is that he will be *other*. Different and degraded . . . In horror Gustave sees the time and place approaching for his metamorphosis into vermin."

Sartre was seeing himself as a spokesman. Conducting a literary battle against literature without using literary criteria, he was a spokesman for active involvement in contemporary history. Returning in the spring to activism, he spoke out against the Loi d'Orientation, the law based on a prescription by Edgar Faure, the former radical premier, for a structural reorganization of higher education. Uneasy about the radicals, De Gaulle was supporting him against the more reactionary Gaullists, and Faure was expected to compromise between preserving and democratizing the antiquated educational system. The problem of overcrowding, which had prompted the rioting, concealed the more fundamental problem of objectives. And the rebels had challenged the tendency of French society to use the educational system as a means of teaching the skills and cultivating the attitudes it needed for its own existence to continue undisturbed. The Loi d'Orientation, which had been passed in October 1968, involved students and nonteaching staff in electing councils to govern the new "teaching and research units" that replaced the faculties. But the Ministry of Education kept control over awarding degrees, and while administration remained centralized, the autonomy of the individual universities was more apparent than real. In February, after thirty-four students had been expelled from the University of Paris, Sartre and Foucault both spoke at a protest meeting in the Mutualité. Sartre, who attacked the Loi d'Orientation, was given a huge ovation by the students, and in a March interview for the *Nouvel Observateur* he said that a university should not create an elite but should bring culture to everybody—students and nonstudents alike. If he were still a philosophy teacher, he said, he would let students decide both the topics for discussion and whether or not they wanted him to be present. He would support them in their struggle and above all teach them "that they aren't petty bourgeois nihilists but simply youngsters caught in a trap, refusing an education designed to make them servile."[65] This provoked a heated controversy, and Faure replied in the *Nouvel Observateur.*

DURING the May rebellion one of the slogans painted on the walls of the Sorbonne was "Analyzed of the earth, arise." And in the early spring of 1969 the editorial board of *Les Temps Modernes* was acrimoniously divided over whether to publish the transcript of a quarrel between an analyst and a patient who, after twelve years of analysis, had taken a tape recorder into the consulting room and terrorized the doctor by refusing either to switch it off or to leave. Introducing the "document," entitled "L'Homme au magnétophone," in the April issue of the review, Sartre describes himself as a "critical fellow traveler" of psychoanalysis. Though he does not go back to denying the existence of the unconscious, he supports the patient's insurrection against the doctor, who never looks him in the face. How can he be cured when there is no reciprocity, when he is constantly being judged by a man who sees him without being seen? Only by rebelling can the object turn himself into a subject. Granted, the doctor is being threatened with violence, but the "inversion of *praxis* demonstrates clearly that the psychoanalytical relationship is *intrinsically* violent."[66] This conclusion was unacceptable to both Pontalis and Pingaud, who formulated their reservations in short statements printed after the dialogue. Pontalis recognized the affinity between Sartre's attitude and that of the student revolutionaries. Pingaud concedes that there can be no equality in the relationship until the moment of cure but defends the situation as contrived to decenter the subject in such a way that the process will culminate in the restitution of reciprocity.[67]

By using his editorial authority to get the transcript into print Sartre was resuming his warfare against Freud at a moment when France's greatest representative of authoritarianism was about to topple. After surviving the crisis of 1968, De Gaulle was defeated in the spring of 1969 by a smaller crisis, which was largely of his own making. It is still hard to be sure whether he was trying to consolidate his strength or duck out of his economic problems by committing political suicide. Wanting to rob the Senate of its legislative powers and to ensure that in the future only half of it would be elected, the other half being nominated by interest groups, he decided cavalierly to present the nation with a referendum, making it vote both on this issue and on a plan for a limited degree of decentralization in favor of regional government. To these two disparate questions voters had to respond with a single yes or no, knowing that unless De Gaulle got a majority of affirmatives, he would resign. In the past none of his referenda had been rejected, but this time just over 53 percent of the voters refused to support him, and he resigned on April 24.

In the presidential elections that followed, Sartre, De Beauvoir, Colette Audry, Marguerite Duras, and Michel Leiris were among those who signed a letter in *Le Monde* urging voters to support the Communist League candidate, Alain Krivine. But in the ensuing campaign Sartre gave Krivine no active support, and in June, when the only candidates left in the field were Pompidou and Alain Poher, the president of the Senate, neither Sartre nor De Beauvoir voted. They were not alone in abstaining; only 69 percent of the electorate voted, so Pompidou, who won 58 percent of the votes cast, had only 37½ percent of the voters behind him.

PART VI

BEYOND COMMUNISM

(1968–80)

(25)

With the Maoists

It was obvious that the *gauchistes* who had shown their strength in 1968 would be powerless in the new political situation unless a degree of unity could be achieved, and it was natural that Sartre should want to help by using *Les Temps Modernes* as a forum for the young leaders of radical groups—natural, that is, insofar as it had become second nature for him to ignore the lessons of his own writing. The group, he had written in the *Critique*, can achieve cohesion and dynamism unavailable to the collective. But the group, which starts out with a genuine dedication to its class interests, develops vested interests of its own. The party is a group that takes its power from the class it represents but survives by letting the class fall into passive seriality. Born from the heat of conflict, the group proceeds to snatch defeat from its own victory. This is what the student groupuscules had done, and when, after vacationing in Yugoslavia during the summer of 1969, Sartre went on with De Beauvoir to Rome, where they had meetings with Daniel Cohn-Bendit and his brother, with Marc Kravetz, with François George, and with others, the young extremists were hostile both toward each other and toward *Les Temps Modernes*, which, according to them, had become an institution.

At the beginning of January 1970, five immigrant African workers were asphyxiated in their huts at Aubervilliers when they were trying to use gas as a source of heat. Sartre was present on the tenth when the corpses were carried out of the building. To demonstrate against the deaths, a group of people occupied the offices of the employers' organization, the Conseil National du Patronat Français (CNPF). The group included Roland Castro, an activist belonging to Vive la Révolution (VLR), a libertarian movement trying to preserve the fighting spirit of

May, Maurice Clavel, Genet, and Michel Leiris. The riot police were called in to remove the demonstrators, which they did brutally, pushing Genet and Clavel down a staircase and herding them all into police vans. Castro, who tried to escape when a van stopped at a red light, was beaten up and held when the others were released. He was charged with assaulting a police officer. At the trial Sartre appeared as a witness for the defense.

In May 1968 Castro had been editing *La Cause du Peuple* for the union of young Maoists who called themselves Marxists-Leninists (UJC [ML]). The object of the paper was to help anyone contemplating subversive action. It published information about strikes, sabotage, squatting, and other militant actions that might be emulated, and in interviews and articles it let the workers speak in their own language to other workers about the bosses. Twenty-one issues had come out in May and June 1968, and it reappeared in November, after being taken over by the Gauche Prolétarienne (GP), which had evolved out of the UJC (ML) and Cohn-Bendit's M22M. The GP was Maoist, hierarchical and traditionally Leninist in its methods of organizing activism. To Michel Contat, who knew Sartre well, it seemed odd that he should have sided with the GP in preference to VLR.[1] *La Cause du Peuple* would not serve as an organ of liaison between factories where the GP had a base.

In the first months of 1970 Sartre, who was close to completing the third volume of his Flaubert biography, was giving a lot of time to activism directed against a government that since 1968 had tightened its grip and against the residue of colonial oppression. On January 13 he signed a statement on Biafra: "After the assassination of Biafran hope, the reign of political gangsterism has spread all over the planet."[2] Thanks partly to Russell, he had come to feel strongly, *pace* De Gaulle, that the state had no monopoly of legality, that illegal means must be used to fight legalized gangsterism. Two days later he addressed a meeting at the Mutualité on the situation in Brazil. In February he gave a filmed interview to an international committee formed to support the Mexican people. In March he joined the Israel-Palestine committee formed by the independent revolutionary militants of the *gauchiste* groups. Though his Maoist friends complained about the time he was devoting to a biography that could appeal to only a small minority, he refused to abandon it. He was still a writer, and his quarrel with Flaubert had not been settled.

In the middle of April he had lunch at the Coupole with the two leaders of the GP, Geismar and Benny Lévy, and with other leading *gauchistes.* He had only a rough idea of the GP's policies and had recently come under acid attack in the paper, but the impression he gave Geismar was that he felt honored by the invitation to become involved. *La Cause du Peuple* was in danger of being suppressed. It had not been banned, but two successive editors, Jean-Pierre Le Dantec and Michel Le Bris, had been arrested; as soon as copies of the paper came off the press they were regularly, though illegally, confiscated by the police. When De Gaulle said "You don't arrest Voltaire," Sartre had been irked by his immunity, but now he could use it as a weapon. Within two weeks he had agreed to take over nominal responsibility for the paper and its supplements, together with the Maoist-Communist *La Parole au Peuple* and *Révolution,* a paper published by a dissident group from the Communist League. He was not being asked to edit the papers but to let his name be used. From May onward *La Cause du Peuple* gave him back-page credit as managing director, and, along with De Beauvoir's, his name appeared on every other page. Printed in red and black on cheap beige paper, *La Cause du Peuple* proclaimed itself a Communist, revolutionary, proletarian newspaper. The issue dated May 1 printed Sartre's declaration: "I affirm my solidarity with all the acts which, like those which have been indicted, will translate the violence which *actually* exists today among the masses, to underline its revolutionary character." But the issue of May 8 carried a correction: the word "articles" should have appeared instead of the word "acts."

Once again Sartre's continuing movement leftward was dividing the editorial committee at *Les Temps Modernes.* The April issue contained a demand by André Gorz for the system of higher education to be scrapped—"Détruire l'université." After "L'Homme au magnétophone" Pontalis and Pingaud had been persuaded not to resign, but there was no persuading them now.

For twenty years Sartre had been ambivalent about revolution. The ideal had been present in the name Rassemblement Démocratique Révolutionnaire, but it had not been a revolutionary organization, and it was only after May 1968 that Sartre felt in no doubt: a revolution was what he wanted. In May, after the twenty-second issue of *La Cause du Peuple* had been confiscated, he said: "What this is about is making it possible through prolonged effort, extending over years, for 97 percent of the French people one day to make a revolution."[3] If the interview of May 1968 had helped to confer respectability on Cohn-Bendit, Sartre performed the same service for Alain Geismar, interviewing him about the GP for the *Nouvel Observateur.*[4] The next day, May 25, Sartre took the chair and Geismar was one of the speakers at the Mutualité in a protest

organized by the *gauchiste* groups against the arrests of Le Dantec and
Le Bris. About five thousand people attended. Except during the occupation, said Sartre, it was the first time since 1881 that two editors had
been imprisoned. The only one of the speakers to be arrested was Geismar, who said nothing more inflammatory than the others.[5]

While the two editors were being tried, on May 27, the Palais de Justice was surrounded by police vans, and there were two rows of plainclothes policemen in the court. Appearing as a witness for the defense,
Sartre complained about the police. "Threats, searches and arrests have
been on the increase for months. This land of liberty has the most conspicuous police force in the world." And the principal victims were
young people. "The government is framing laws to protect us against
the younger generation."[6] The public prosecutor asked for *La Cause du
Peuple* to be suspended for a year. The judge refused but sentenced Le
Dantec to a year in prison and Le Bris to eight months. When Sartre,
going up to the bench, expressed surprise at being free, the judge said
there was nothing he could do about it.[7]

On the same day Raymond Marcellin, the minister of the interior,
announced that he was dissolving the GP. He was expecting the militants to put themselves on the wrong side of the law by trying to reorga-
nize it. The same evening there was a demonstration in the Latin
Quarter: the police threw tear-gas grenades, and the demonstrators responded by throwing back the pins. No one was injured, but Geismar,
who was illogically held responsible, was sentenced to eighteen months
in prison.[8]

At the beginning of June, when Sartre proposed to form a new association, the "friends" of *La Cause du Peuple,* the police refused to authorize
it until legal action was brought against them: the new association
could subsequently be dissolved, but they could not stop him from
forming it.[9] With ironical opportunism he was using his fame as a strategic weapon. His thirst for martyrdom, wrote François Mauriac in *Le
Figaro Littéraire,* was "no reason for putting this incurably offensive person in prison."[10]

The creation of the "friends" was followed a week later by the formation of the Secours Rouge. On June 18 Sartre gave a press conference, saying the object was to provide legal, moral, and material
support for victims of oppression and their families. But the organization was soon to extend its political activities, trying to coordinate *gauchiste* groups and organize demonstrations. What Sartre wanted above
all was to encourage solidarity between workers and intellectuals. Useful though he was, the radical leaders thought him politically naïve.[11]

On June 20, together with the film director François Truffaut, he was distributing *La Cause du Peuple* in the marketplace on the Rue Daguerre when a policeman, taking him by the arm, told him to come along to the station. Someone in the crowd shouted: "You're arresting a Nobel Prize [winner]." Immediately the policeman let go and hurried away. Sartre followed him, and people yelled "Stop, thief!" but the policeman got away.[12] Six days later, when Sartre, accompanied by twenty-seven other people, including the film directors Louis Malle and Alexandre Astruc and the actor Sami Frey, was distributing copies in the Grands Boulevards, a summons was issued, but he was released after an hour and a half.

Summer brought its usual reprieve from agitprop activity. In July he traveled in Scandinavia with Arlette and Vladimir Dedijer, going on to join De Beauvoir in Rome. They came back to Paris in September. The vacation had not given him any regrets about his involvement with the *gauchistes;* he was willing to go still further. In his view the role of the intellectuals had changed since May 1968; their duty now was to reeducate themselves by serving the masses directly.[13] In *La Cause du Peuple* Sartre was signing articles he had not written and giving his name to ideas he consciously disagreed with. This was in line with his old antipathy to individual personality, but he was trying harder to make himself plural than he ever had when backing Merleau-Ponty's articles in *Les Temps Modernes*. On the eleventh, when the distributors of *La Cause du Peuple* had to appear in court, he did not attend but sent written testimony: "If they are guilty, I am more guilty than they are; if they are innocent, they are more innocent than I am." He had decided to make himself available for any "politically just task" he was asked to perform. He announced this in an interview with *L'Idiot International,* and after taking over the editorship of the Maoist *Tout,* which had been started by militants of Vive la Révolution, he declared in the first issue: "I am making myself available to any revolutionary newspaper in order to make the middle classes either bring me to a political trial which will be clearly concerned for once with the freedom of the press or—by not bringing charges against me—reveal the deliberate illegality of its repression."[14] The result was that he nominally became editor of at least a dozen extremist papers, but he was not always told when his name was being used. Nor was he even prepared to defend the quality of these papers. He told *L'Idiot International* that the bourgeois papers were more truthful and generally superior.[15]

Despite all this strenuous activism and despite the two packs of Boyards he smoked every day, his health had not let him down since the moment of near collapse in Rome during the summer of 1968. But one Saturday evening in September, after he had drunk a lot of vodka during dinner with De Beauvoir and Sylvie Le Bon at a restaurant, he fell asleep at De Beauvoir's flat and dropped his cigarette. In the morning he seemed well enough, but when the two women arrived to accompany him for lunch at La Coupole, he bumped into the furniture at each step he took, and after the meal he was staggering. After Sartre's doctor, Dr. Zaidmann, had been called in, he went away to get a specialist, Dr. Lebeau, who said that the disequilibrium might be caused by a malfunction of the inner ear or the brain. An encephalogram revealed nothing abnormal. On October 8, when the third volume of the biography was delivered to Gallimard, Sartre had an abscess in his mouth and felt as though flu was beginning. He was halfway through a series of eleven consultations with specialists. The circulation in the left hemisphere of his brain was found to be seriously impaired, and his arteries, congenitally narrow, had been narrowed further. It was important for him to smoke less. A series of injections was prescribed, and on October 15 the doctors made him cancel a trip organized by the Maoists to study the living conditions of the workers in several industrial towns. But he refused to rest. On the sixteenth he helped to move copies of *La Cause du Peuple* from the printer to the bookshop La Joie de Lire, and he distributed the paper in the Rue Saint-Séverin. In the Boulevard Saint-Michel two of the young people distributing the papers were arrested and escorted to a waiting police van by two policemen who ignored the questions of the journalists: "What have they done? Why are you arresting them?"[16]

On the twenty-first, when Geismar was tried, Sartre, instead of appearing in court, went to address the Renault workers at Billancourt. With Georges Michel and two Maoists he waited outside the main entrance, but the trade union had been alerted about his plans and had arranged for the workers to leave by a side entrance. The four men went to the Pont de Bir-Hakeim. With his leg paining him, Sartre climbed on an empty barrel and spoke through a hand microphone to a small crowd including activists, journalists, and plainclothes police. He was not at the trial, he said, because class justice had already decided to punish Geismar. The intellectuals, he said, should be the allies of the people, as they had been in the nineteenth century; this was why he wanted to testify in the street.[17] "Geismar," he went on, "the man on trial, he is the people himself."[18] This was an equation reminiscent of his 1952 equation of the party with the people, and he went on talking to the tiny audience as if something was beginning there that would revive the alliance between workers and intellectuals. Meanwhile Geismar was sentenced to eighteen months in prison.

TOGETHER with Jean-Luc Godard, André Glucksmann (a former student of Althusser's and author of two books, *Le Discours de la guerre,* 1967, and *Stratégie et révolution en France,* 1968), and some other friends, Sartre was setting up another paper, *J'Accuse,* which appeared on November 1. But he was suffering from bouts of drowsiness and, when consulted on November 5, Dr. Lebeau reduced the doses of the medicines prescribed for his dizziness; the somnolence was probably due to these. After another encephalogram had been taken on the twenty-second, Lebeau declared that his patient was cured.[19]

Sartre's next idea was to test whether the premise of the Russell tribunal could be used against injustice inside France. In an accident during February 1970 sixteen miners had been killed by a carbureted hydrogen explosion at Hénin-Liétard. In protest, Molotov cocktails were thrown into the offices of the management, causing a fire, for which four Maoists and two ex-convicts—probably not the men responsible—were arrested, but the trial was not due to be held till December 14. Secours Rouge therefore organized a "people's tribunal" in the town hall at Lens. Since responsibility for the explosion lay with the state, Sartre concluded: "The state-proprietor is guilty of the murder committed on February 4, 1970. . . . They consciously gave output priority over safety; in other words, they valued the production of material objects higher than human life."[20] Two days later the six men were acquitted.

At the beginning of 1971 his health was still standing up to the strain. On January 7, speaking at a Mutualité protest meeting about the situation of the Jews in Russia, he demanded the release of Kuznetsov and ten others who had tried to escape by hijacking a plane and had been severely sentenced in December. Sartre also wrote for the first issue of *J'Accuse,* which appeared on January 15. Analyzing the concept of popular justice as compared with class justice, he told the story of the people's tribunal at Lens.

In February he narrowly escaped violence at the hands of the police when he took part in a Maoist occupation of the Sacré-Coeur. The idea was to publicize the injury done to a boy, Richard Deshayes, who had been disfigured by a tear-gas grenade during a Secours Rouge demonstration. Along with the photographer Liliane Siegel, some other Maoist friends, and about two hundred militants, Sartre asked to see the rector, Monseigneur Charles, who was expected to be sympathetic. But all the doors were shut, trapping the demonstrators inside the church until the riot police arrived, hitting out indiscriminately. Sartre hid in a corner; one man had his thigh pierced by a spike from a railing. On February 15, together with Jean-Luc Godard, Sartre held a press conference about the incident, but three days later, resenting the unfair Maoist domination over Secours Rouge, he resigned from the management committee.

To any casual observer in the Paris streets it was obvious that the police were prepared for outbreaks of violence, and sometimes there were scuffles between leftists and members of the right-wing group L'Ordre Nouveau. When a *lycéen* called Guiot was arrested after being charged with hitting a policeman, thousands of *lycéens* protested by sitting down on pavements in the Latin Quarter. Eventually Guiot was acquitted.[21]

In April, Sartre took a vacation in Saint-Paul-de-Vence with Arlette, De Beauvoir, and Sylvie Le Bon, staying with Arlette in the annex of a hotel while the others slept in a building at the back of a garden. They went for walks and visited Cagnes, going back to the hotel where he had stayed with De Beauvoir in 1949. When, after returning to Paris, he found advance copies of the first two volumes of *L'Idiot de la famille,* he said he was as glad to see it in print as he had been to see the first copies of *La Nausée.*

SINCE Fidel Castro's support for the Soviet invasion of Czechoslovakia, Sartre had not been in touch with Cuba, but in April he was asked to sign an appeal for the release of Heberto Padilla, a poet who had been arrested on Castro's orders. The charge was sodomy. After he was released, he and his wife wrote such violent letters of self-criticism that torture may have been used to extort these. In a letter to Castro, Sartre pleaded with him to "spare Cuba from dogmatic obscurantism, cultural xenophobia and systematic repression such as Stalin imposed on the socialist countries."[22] From now on Castro regarded him as an enemy, but Sartre made no attempt to repudiate the influential articles he had published in *France-Soir,* where he had eulogized Castro as "at the same time the island, the men, the cattle, and the earth. . . . He *is* the whole island because he refuses to take it or keep a single patch of ground for himself. The Cubans must win, or we shall lose everything, even hope."

SARTRE was still spending time with Wanda and Michelle, but his routine was to pass the evening with De Beauvoir, except on the two days each week when he stayed overnight with Arlette.[23] On Monday, May 17, he was feeling unwell when he arrived at her flat, and during the night he had a slight stroke. The next day he was not only walking with difficulty but speaking stammeringly and indistinctly out of a twisted mouth. In the evening, with De Beauvoir, he insisted on drinking whiskey, which made him worse, and on Wednesday morning Liliane Siegel went with him to Dr. Zaidmann, who found that the circulation of the blood in the left side of the brain had deteriorated since October. In the previous two months Sartre had not been taking his medicine, and sometimes, when the elevator was out of order, he had walked up ten flights of stairs. The doctor now ordered him to do a minimum of walking.

In the evening his cigarette kept dropping out of his lips, and when De Beauvoir unthinkingly played a recording of Verdi's *Requiem*, he murmured: "How apt!"[24] When he woke up in the morning his right arm felt heavy and numb. Dr. Lebeau could not come but sent another specialist, Dr. Mahoudeau, who attributed the stammer to the twist in the mouth and the lower blood pressure to the medicines. But Sartre still found it difficult to hold a cigarette, and four days later Dr. Zaidmann told Arlette that he might never be entirely cured. Within two days, though, he seemed to have recovered, and one day, lunching with De Beauvoir at La Coupole, he pointed out a blue-eyed girl with dark hair and a round face: "Do you know whom she reminds me of?" "No." "You at her age."[25]

He did not give himself leave to take things easy. On June 4 he resumed control of the Maoist paper *Révolution,* and in the middle of the month, with Maurice Clavel, he launched the Libération Press Agency (APL), intending to produce a daily news bulletin. The agency was to be "a new platform for journalists who want to tell the whole truth to people who want to hear the whole truth." Calling him "the nation's Red cancer," the right-wing weekly *Minute* said he should be in prison.[26]

By the end of the month he could neither speak nor eat without hurting his tongue. "Oh, it makes no difference," he said. "When you're old it doesn't matter. . . . It can't go on much longer. . . . It's natural to get gradually bogged down." To his friends he seemed detached, unconcerned. But he was cheerful when he spent the evening with De Beauvoir and Sylvie, especially on June 21, when they celebrated his sixty-sixth birthday.[27]

Without expecting to live long, he was intending to carry on the fight for an alternative justice powered by public opinion. The next project was to investigate police activity since the beginning of the year.[28] Two hundred and thirty-seven intellectuals signed an appeal for the police to be given a "people's trial." It was scheduled for the Cité Universitaire but then banned by the police, and on June 19 Sartre was summoned to court and informed that Marcellin and Pleven, ministers of justice and of the interior, were bringing charges against him for libel of the police department and the police system. The evidence against him consisted mainly of two unsigned articles in La Cause du Peuple (June 16 and June 23) and an article on drugs in Tout (February 1, 1971).

The tribunal was replaced by a combination of meetings and press conferences at the Mutualité on June 30. Sartre was not well enough to attend, but he sent a letter and an interview that he had just recorded for Luxembourg radio and television.

Still sectioning his summer vacation, he was planning to spend three weeks with Arlette and two with Wanda before joining De Beauvoir in Rome. But in the middle of July, while in Switzerland with Arlette, he had another minor stroke during his sleep. When he woke up his mouth was even more twisted than before, his speech indistinct, his arm insensitive to heat and cold. When Arlette telephoned Dr. Zaidmann she was told: "If he's having spasms like that, the arteries must be exhausted."[29]

With Wanda in Naples he went for long walks and revisited Pompeii. When he arrived in Rome his face was swollen because of an abscessed tooth, but he was cheerful and full of vitality. He took his medicine obediently, drank no coffee or tea, enjoyed one glass of wine at lunchtime, slept for a couple of hours in the afternoon, drank beer at dinner, followed by two glasses of whiskey on the terrace of the hotel.[30]

No longer needing to sleep in the afternoon when he was back in Paris, he went to bed about midnight and got up at half past eight. His mouth was still partly paralyzed, making it hard for him to chew, but he started on the fourth volume of the biography, which was to deal with Madame Bovary, and he toyed with the notion of writing something for the theater or a new novel. Another possibility was to write a "political testament." Benny Lévy, the GP leader, wanted him to write a popular novel, and what tempted him about the idea was the possibility of writing a political testament as a continuation of his autobiography. "It's time that I finally told the truth. But I could only tell it in a work of fiction."[31] The novel remained unwritten.

On September 24 he had to appear in court before two judges. He was immediately released, but he said: "From now on an article constitutes a problem for the rulers, and there is no more freedom in France."[32] On October 27, in the Goutte-d'Or district, which was inhabited mainly by North Africans, a fifteen-year-old Algerian boy, Djelalli, was shot dead by his concierge, who said that he was making too much noise. In November, Sartre took part in two antiracist demonstrations in the area, making speeches through a megaphone. Genet, Foucault, and the writer Claude Mauriac, François Mauriac's son, were also involved. A Djelalli Committee was set up. Sartre volunteered for some work at the committee's headquarters, but Genet persuaded him that he wasn't well enough, and at the beginning of December he abruptly told De Beauvoir: "I've spent all the health in my account. I shan't get past the age of seventy."[33] He asked to be cremated and not to be buried between his mother and stepfather in the Père Lachaise cemetery. The ceremony should be simple, but he hoped that a lot of Maoists would follow his coffin.[34]

Early in 1971, after Geismar had been involved in a hunger strike at the Santé, demanding better conditions for prisoners, Pleven had made promises but had not honored them, and before the end of the year, at a prison in Nancy, there was an eight-day revolt by the prisoners. At a meeting held on January 5, 1972, to inform the public about the facts of the revolt, Sartre made a statement: "We're law-abiding citizens only because we've given in and given up; they are in prison only because they've rebelled." Sartre, Foucault, and the critic Gilles Deleuze were among those who asked for a committee of the prisoners' information group to investigate the uprising. And on January 17 or 18 Sartre went with Michelle Vian, Foucault, Gilles Deleuze, Claude Mauriac, and other members of the Secours Rouge to hold a press conference about the prison system inside the Ministry of Justice. Quickly evicted, they adjourned to the Libération Press Agency, where Sartre and Foucault spoke.

At the end of February, Sartre went back to Belgium. Lallemant, a lawyer who had helped Algerians cross the frontier and had arranged for Sartre to lecture in Brussels on the Algerian war, had now had him invited to lecture as a guest of the Jeune Barreau de Bruxelles, the Brussels young lawyers' association. Appearing in a black sweater to give his talk, "Justice and the State," he found himself facing a fashionably dressed audience. Undeterred, he explained the difference between bureaucratic justice, which "ties the proletariat to its condition," and wild justice, which he defined as "the profound movement by which the proletariat and the plebs assert their freedom against proletarianization."[35] The audience would have been unconvinced even if it had not been distracted by Alexandre Astruc, who was making a film about Sartre. He caught his trousers against something while crawling along the floor with his camera, and suddenly his bottom was exposed.[36]

On the same day the unrest at the Renault factory in Billancourt culminated in a killing. Since the end of January, Maoist militants had been distributing leaflets at the factory gates. Some militants were fired, and two of them, a Tunisian and a Portuguese, started a hunger strike, sheltering in a Boulogne church. On February 14 Sartre, together with Michelle Vian and some journalists, had been taken inside the factory hidden in a van, only to be thrown out when they started distributing leaflets about the dismissals. In protest against these a demonstration was called for February 25, and when the workers were beginning to come out, Pierre Overney, who had been fired a year earlier and now worked as a truck driver, was shot in a scuffle between Maoists and eight armed security guards.

Back in Paris after the killing, Sartre, with Maurice Clavel, called on all democratic citizens to accompany him to Billancourt on the twenty-eighth to investigate what had happened. The investigation yielded little, but more than 30,000 people took part in a protest march the same day, and six days later, before Overney's funeral, Sartre was one of about 160,000 people who marched in protest, though his legs were too weak for him to go more than part of the way. When Renault's personnel chief, Robert Nogrette, was kidnapped, Sartre and Clavel declared that this reprisal was only a "normal response to the repression rampant at Renault." The inadequacy of the PCF's response to the killing provoked Sartre into the most hostile statement he had yet made about the party. Together with De Beauvoir and Philippe Sollers, a novelist and critic associated with *Tel Quel,* he put his name to the statement: "The real struggle against the capitalist slave system is from this point on inseparable from the struggle against the PCF in its effort to pervert the Communist idea." He also accused the Communists of being "in league with the government against the Maoists."[37]

Privately Sartre had misgivings about the kidnapping,[38] which had been carried out by the Nouvelle Résistance Populaire, a militant section of the GP which had gone underground, but having felt sympathetic toward terrorism since the fifties, he was now closer to involvement in it, and prefacing Michèle Manceaux's book *Les Maos en France,* he wrote: "Revolutionary violence is immediately *moral* because workers become the subject of their history." (This parallels Sartre's argument about the patient who rebels against being an object to the analyst.) According to the Maoists, wrote Sartre, it was desire for freedom that gave a festive mood to the actions of the masses fighting for "a moral society" in which "man, overcoming his alienation, can find himself in his true relationships with the group." Behind this sentence is an understandable nostalgia for the gaiety that had erupted during the violence of May 1968. Sartre's activism during the seventies was part of a desperate attempt to revive the revolution that had stopped. He was still theorizing, but he had shifted from the generalizations of the *Critique* to collaboration with activists who had been influenced by it. He could not have moved further from his earlier view that violence was an immoral interference with other people's freedom.

After another spring visit to Saint-Paul-de-Vence with Arlette, De Beauvoir, and Sylvie, he threw himself energetically back into radical politics, protesting against police treatment of squatters in the unoccupied buildings of Paris—especially in the Goutte-d'Or district. On April 11 he took part with Roland Castro and Claude Mauriac in a Secours Rouge press conference about squatters. He also contributed a preface to a book published in Heidelberg by a group of therapists who were carrying out what he called "the only possible radicalization of anti-psychiatry."[39] The relationship with the patient should be dialectical, he said. But he was becoming more critical of both the Maoists and *La Cause du Peuple–J'Accuse*—as it had been called since the papers had merged. After a murder committed at Bruay-en-Artois at the beginning of April, the paper suggested that Leroy, the lawyer accused of the crime, ought to be lynched. "He must be taken by the balls." "Give him to us and we'll cut him to pieces with a razor." The language of violence upset Sartre, who—perhaps thinking of mob justice at the Liberation of Paris—retorted in the issue dated May 17 that popular justice should assume that a man is innocent until proved guilty. But the same issue contained an article signed "La Cause du Peuple" insisting that it was wrong to stand in the way of the people's natural instinct for justice. In the next issue (June 21) Sartre formulated his misgivings about the didactic and working-class orientation of the paper, which was "less and less democratic." He accused it of ignoring such minorities as the young, women, intellectuals, and homosexuals. In 1970 it had given new voices a chance to be heard, but now it was becoming "as edifying as a bosses' newsletter . . . it's becoming factional and it reflects today's struggles in a very narrow way."[40] But when the paper, which was doing badly, suspended publication, Sartre went every morning to discussions on how to keep it alive.[41]

He did his best to ignore his own disabilities, but the impaired circulation of the blood in his brain was making his memory defective, while his gums were troubling him and he was sleeping badly at night, often dropping off to sleep during the early evening. A single glass of whiskey could reduce him to talking nonsense and lurching when he walked.

One evening when André Puig, who had replaced Claude Faux as his secretary, arrived just before midnight at Arlette's flat, he found Sartre lying on the floor drunk. On the way back to his flat, accompanied by Puig, Sartre fell, bruising his nose and his lips.[42]

Before leaving Paris in July for a vacation with Arlette in Austria he signed nineteen appeals and protests, including a statement in support of a hunger strike by Basque political refugees in Paris and a demand that General Massu should be prosecuted for championing torture in his memoirs of the Algerian war. From Austria, Sartre went on to meet De Beauvoir in Rome on August 12. (Wanda was sometimes and Michelle was always being left out of his summer vacation plans, though his friendship with both continued.) Alone on the train to Rome he drank too much wine in the restaurant car, but the vacation in Rome was free from the fits of absentmindedness that had afflicted him in June.[43] De Beauvoir noticed, though, that after eating ice cream he would hurry to the bathroom, and one afternoon in October, when, with Sylvie, they were passing the Pantheon on the way back to the hotel, he was walking in front of the two women when he stopped. "Some cats have just pissed on me," he said. "I went close to the balustrade and they wetted on me." Sylvie laughed, but De Beauvoir knew he had become incontinent. They did not talk about it at first. Twice in her flat he left a mark on her chair before going to the bathroom. When she finally said he should speak to the doctor, he was surprisingly resigned: "I've told him. It's been going on for a long time. It's those cells I lost." In the morning, asked whether he found it embarrassing he answered: "You have to be modest when you're old."[44]

The trouble with his gums had continued: he was suffering constantly from painful abscesses, and the only cure was to have all his teeth pulled out. What scared him was the prospect of being unable to speak in public, but once accustomed to wearing dentures, he was glad to know abscesses would never trouble him again. As the year ended he was quite cheerful.[45] La Cause du Peuple was resurrected, and in October he contributed to "We Accuse the President of the Republic," which was printed as a poster. In December he was among one hundred and thirty-seven intellectuals who denounced "The New Racism" in an appeal published in both La Cause du Peuple and in the Nouvel Observateur.

The most important of all these projects was the creation of a new newspaper, Libération. When he had admitted to L'Idiot International that revolutionary journalism was inferior to that of the Establishment, he was implicitly recognizing the need for a revolutionary paper of higher quality. As he said in a broadcast, "We believe in direct democracy and we want the people to speak to the people. . . . If a means could be found of using what's arresting in popular speech, this would be a new form of writing. . . . We need to reinvent gestures and intonations . . . if we find this style, which should be the style of all the articles in *Libéra-tion,* I think we'll pass muster."[46] This is Rimbaudian both in its fervor and in its formulation about the need for a new language. After admiring the way *La Cause du Peuple* addressed the workers in their own language, Sartre was envisaging a colloquial journalism liberated from the academic prose used in the conventional papers.[47] This idea excited him so much that he was willing to put the Flaubert biography aside for six months to devote all his energy to bringing *Libération* into existence. To raise money for it, in November 1972 he started on a series of conversations with Benny Lévy and Philippe Gavi, which were to be published under the title *On a raison de se révolter* (*It's Right to Rebel*). It was this book more than any other that displaced his critique of *Madame Bovary.* Lévy, an Egyptian Jew, was using the pseudonym Pierre Victor; he had been at the ENS. A member of Vive la Révolution, Gavi had contributed to *Les Temps Modernes.* It was Gavi who set out the program for the new paper. Sartre excitedly took part in planning it; his original intention was to write a daily editorial.[48]

THE spiral of Sartre's development was bringing him back to a new emphasis on freedom. Between 1958, when he wrote the *Critique,* and the rising of 1968 the word had almost dropped out of his vocabulary, but his involvement with the *gauchistes* renewed his faith in "conceiving a political struggle centered on freedom," though he recognized that he was now concerned less with the freedom of the individual than with "the freedom of the militant."[49] He had always had strong anarchist leanings, but while he had vigorously contested De Gaulle's claim to a state monopoly of justice, he would not have declared in 1967, as he did in 1973, "I believe in illegality."[50]

At the same time his resistance to parliamentary democracy had hardened. As a student he had not troubled to vote, and, much later, he attributed this reluctance to an obscure feeling "that a vote could never represent a man's concrete thought."[51] *Les Temps Modernes* had often advised readers either not to vote or to feel that they were voting against one candidate rather than for another. De Gaulle's cynical and repeated use of the referendum had shown that autocracy could be given a democratic veneer, and in the January 1973 issue of the review Sartre advanced a reasoned attack on the voting system: "When I vote I abdicate my power—that's to say the opportunity each person has of forming with everyone else a sovereign group which has no need of representatives—and I affirm that we, the voters, are always other than ourselves and that none of us can rise out of seriality into the group, except through intermediaries." To vote is above all "to vote for voting, as Kravetz puts it, that is to vote for the political institution which keeps us in a state of serial impotence."[52] As in many similar statements, Sartre was using his own *Critique* as his theoretical model and the May rebellion as practical model.

In February he was doing all he could to prepare for the launching of *Libération*. He disliked television—he had no set in his flat and, not wanting to collaborate with a state-controlled organization, he had consistently refused to appear on television—but he did agree to appear in the series *Radioscopie*. On February 7, 1973, he was to be seen fending off the interviewer's questions about his life and his books to talk about the new paper. He also traveled to Lyons and Lille for meetings about *Libération;* he went with a team of *Libération* journalists to investigate housing complexes at Villeneuve-la-Garenne.[53]

Anxiety about his health caught him in odd ways. Once he said: "They'll end up by cutting my legs off. . . . Oh, my legs! I could manage without them." At the end of February he caught bronchitis, and though he seemed to recover quickly, he overtaxed his strength working on an article for the first issue of *Libération* about the first round of the presidential elections on March 4. At about ten on the evening of the fifth, while he was watching a film on television at Arlette's flat, his face twisted and his cigarette fell from his fingers. His arm was paralyzed. Dr. Zaidmann prescribed a course of injections, which restored the use of his arm, but he had enormous difficulty in remembering who people were or what had just happened. When Dr. Lebeau arranged for him to see a neurologist, her encephalogram was reassuring, but, disobeying her instructions, he went on drinking and smoking. He would mistake one friend for another, and even after a doctor at the Salpêtrière had diagnosed anoxia—asphyxia of the brain—caused partly by smoking, partly by the state of his arteries and arterioles, he obstinately refused to stop drinking or smoking; and when the elevator in his apartment house broke down again, he disobediently climbed the ten flights of stairs to continue an article he had started about the Greek resistance.[54]

He let himself be persuaded to take a vacation with Arlette at Junas in the south of France, where he read detective stories, became confused about why he was there, expected Hercule Poirot to arrive, and mistook André Puig, who came for two days, for Vladimir Dedijer. When Sartre went on to join De Beauvoir in Avignon, he was uncertain which of the two women was which. Later he talked about feeling invisible and about having relations with people only if he caused them to exist. Twice he said: "I'm going to be sixty-eight." Back in Paris, he did not notice that Sylvie had diluted the whiskey by pouring water into the bottle.[55] After examining Sartre again the doctor from the Salpêtrière warned De Beauvoir that another stroke could be fatal. Sartre, who had not overheard the conversation, was aware of the danger: "One will have to end up by ending up. After all, I've done what I could. I've done what I had to do."[56]

(26)

Fading Vision

In April 1973 Sartre seemed better, though not well enough to work much. He wrote a letter to *The New York Review of Books* asking for American deserters from Vietnam to be amnestied.[1] He went back to Junas for a few days with Arlette. After driving down, De Beauvoir and Sylvie took them both on to Saint-Paul-de-Vence, where Sartre, who was listless, complained of senile decay—he could no longer work.

Back in Paris, he alternated between liveliness and lethargy, lucidity and confusion. What looked like a perpetual smile was due to partial paralysis of the muscles in his face.[2] Once, when Arlette said she had seen a private screening of a film by Lanzmann about Israel, he told her: "You aren't the only one. Arlette went too."[3] On May 21 he was well enough to resume the conversations with Gavi and Lévy, but an ophthalmic examination revealed that he had lost 40 percent of the vision in his one good eye. Even with a magnifying glass he found it difficult to read newspaper articles. In July, after another attack of dizziness, he was found to have a thrombosis in a temporal vein and a triple hemorrhage at the back of the eye, but a course of treatment cured two of the three hemorrhages and restored 20 percent of his vision.[4] He went on trying to write, knowing he would not be able to read what he had written, not knowing that no one else would. "I was heartbroken when I looked at this scribble," wrote Georges Michel. "Totally illegible lines. His handwriting was barely recognizable. Overlapping letters heaped together, lines not straight, rising, falling, like the handwriting of some people who are mentally ill."[5]

The launching of *Libération* had been delayed, but the first issue had appeared on May 22, and he participated in a discussion with workers at Villeneuve-la-Garenne; extracts were published in four issues of the paper during the third week of June.[6] He signed an appeal for an Ordre

Nouveau meeting to be banned, and when it went ahead, published an attack on Marcellin's decision to authorize it.[7]

In July he spent another three weeks with Arlette in Junas, doing very little. He would sit on her balcony for hours, gazing at the village. At the end of the month De Beauvoir and Sylvie picked him up for the four-day car ride to Venice, where he was to stay with Wanda. He was lucky to have retained the devotion of women who made themselves available whenever he needed them, though he was mostly unavailable when they needed him. Michelle Vian had been his mistress since 1945.[8] Despite jealousy, rivalry, and quarrels, the relationships survived. Though Arlette, the youngest and newest of the long-term mistresses, was in the most favored position, the tolerance of the others was boundless. Eating lunch at Menton with De Beauvoir and Sylvie, he overturned a plate of fish soup and seemed unconcerned when the two women mopped at his feet. They drove him to a hotel on the Grand Canal, and he went in a motorboat to meet Wanda at the airport.[9]

Wanda was not an early riser, and until De Beauvoir left Venice about two weeks later he would often meet her in the mornings; he went for walks with Wanda in the afternoon and spent a great deal of time listening to music on the transistor radio De Beauvoir and Sylvie had given him. On August 16, when he flew to meet them in Rome, his eyesight had noticeably deteriorated since the beginning of the month. The oculist recommended by the hotel found a hemorrhage in the middle of the eye, together with the beginnings of glaucoma, for which he prescribed Pilocarpine. There was also too much pressure within the eye, though this was soon alleviated by doses of Diamox. In the mornings De Beauvoir read to Sartre—mainly books about Flaubert. After lunch he slept for a couple of hours. She read to him from the newspapers when he woke up, and they usually had dinner with Sylvie. No longer incontinent, Sartre drank only the prescribed rations of alcohol, coffee, and tea, but he did not like De Beauvoir to cut up his food for him. With his impaired vision, his false teeth, and his partially insensitive lips, he could not help eating messily but became irritable when told to wipe away traces of food from around his mouth.[10]

Sitting on the balcony of his hotel room, he could enjoy the sunlight: as he described it later, it was a beautiful white light, very bright, very luminous.[11] He went on hoping that he would be able to resume work, but uncertainty about his eyesight was torture, and, as De Beauvoir noticed, the need to sleep during the day was mainly need for respite from it. He was no longer capable of living on his own, and when they returned to Paris, Arlette and Liliane Siegel found him a flat with two bedrooms in a large, ugly modern apartment house on the Boulevard

Edgar-Quinet. The bedrooms looked out on an inner garden, and the Eiffel Tower was visible from the window of the study. Like his flat on the Boulevard Raspail, the new one was on the tenth floor, but there were two elevators in the house. Before he moved, the elevator in his old house had again stopped running, and again he insisted on climbing ten flights of stairs. After this he stayed at De Beauvoir's flat most nights until the new one was ready. He was having injections twice a day and was still sleeping heavily in the afternoons, still uncertain whether he would ever again read and write. Dr. Zaidmann explained that he had a thrombosis which made hemorrhages inevitable; the oculist advised him that he would never get his sight back entirely and that he would have to go for a long time without reading.[12] Depressively he let the women make all the arrangements for his move into the new flat, showing interest neither in the furniture nor in what they did with his papers.[13]

In October, he was finally brought to trial by the right-wing paper *Minute*. It was nearly two and a half years since it had demanded a prison sentence for him. Attacked by *La Cause du Peuple*, which had called *Minute*'s editorial staff "a bunch of thugs, unpurged at the Liberation, part-time members of the OAS and professionals in the art of inciting murder,"[14] *Minute* sued *La Cause du Peuple* for 800,000 francs as damages for libel and intimidation; Sartre employed Gisèle Halimi as his defense counsel. The line of argument had to be that *Minute* had provoked the denunciation. At the trial Gisèle Halimi spoke for more than an hour about *Minute*'s hard-line support for the OAS and its encouragement of racist murders. The judge in the end fined Sartre 400 francs, ordering him to pay damages of one franc.

After the trial he went with Arlette to the oculist, who told him that his retina was incurably damaged toward the center; with special apparatus he might be able to read for an hour a day, using lateral vision. But the apparatus turned out to be useless: the words went by much too slowly. Another examination at the Salpêtrière revealed that he was now diabetic.[15] De Beauvoir took him to a specialist, who diagnosed mild glycemia, prescribed pills and a sugarless diet without even the fruit juice Sartre had been drinking in the evening. He tried to go on working at the Flaubert biography, but when De Beauvoir read *Madame Bovary* out loud he fell asleep. Irrationally, he went on believing that his sight would improve within three months.[16]

After he moved into the new flat De Beauvoir regularly spent the evening with him, sleeping in one of the bedrooms five nights a week, while Arlette slept there the other two. One morning, when De Beauvoir wiped some saliva off the front of his shirt, he remarked with equanimity that looked like indifference: "Yes, I dribble. I've been dribbling for two weeks." When with friends he was mostly silent and listless. On November 23, when he saw a new doctor at the Bicêtre, Dr. Lapresle, he was strongly advised to give up smoking. At first he intended to disobey but soon made up his mind to cut down by restricting himself to a diminishing daily quota. De Beauvoir and Arlette both spent a great deal of time reading to him until this function was taken over by Benny Lévy, who had given up the GP. A refugee from his native Cairo, Lévy was stateless. Known to the police as a *gauchiste,* he was making his life still more dangerous by going around like a spy in a comic, wearing dark glasses and a false beard. It occurred to Geismar that Lévy's life would be less insecure if Sartre employed him, and when Liliane Siegel broached the question, Sartre agreed immediately. Arlette was apprehensive that Lévy would take unfair advantage of the ailing man, and De Beauvoir was ambivalent, though she would no longer have to give up so much of her working day. Sartre went on sleeping a great deal of the time while Lévy was reading to him.

In December 1973 De Beauvoir took him to see a new ophthalmologist, Dr. Ciolek, who reported that the hemorrhage had left permanent scars on the middle of the retina, which was now dead tissue. On the way back Sartre asked: "So I'll never be able to read again?" but then dropped off to sleep in the taxi. In the next few days he went on talking as if he could still read. He dozed during *Temps Modernes* editorial meetings and often sank into bouts of depression. He disliked the flat, he said. "It's the place where I no longer work." Accustomed to a chaotic proliferation of books, periodicals, typescripts, and files in his study, friends were saddened to see immaculate order. Like a prisoner in privileged solitary confinement, he moved only from his leather armchair to his telephone or his radio and back to his leather armchair.[17] Sometimes he forgot that he was in Paris; often he had the impression that his sight was improving. He said: "Obviously it's unbearable unless one takes it to be temporary." On January 8, 1974, when Lanzmann, saying goodbye, kissed him on the cheek, Sartre remarked: "I don't know whether you're kissing a bit of a tomb or a living man." Later on in the evening he asked De Beauvoir: "I'll never get my eyes back?" She was afraid not, she said, and went on weeping all night.[18]

Though Sartre impressed all his friends by his uncomplaining matter-of-factness, it took him a long time to realize that his eyesight was not going to improve. In another consultation at the end of January 1974, Dr. Ciolek assured him that his sight had not deteriorated. Sartre said: "He doesn't seem to think I'll be able to read and write again" and couldn't help adding, "—for a long time."[19] Two days later, picking up a paperback in his flat, he held it near the lamp to see whether he could read the title. He could, but he often failed to read newspaper headlines. A side effect of the medicines was to make him lose control of his bladder again and of his bowels too.[20] De Beauvoir was tactful and self-effacing in helping him to clean up.

After the final conversations in the series with Gavi and Lévy, he left on March 17 for a few days with Arlette in Junas, going on to meet De Beauvoir and Sylvie in Avignon. They traveled by train to Milan, spending a night at the Hotel di La Scala, where they had stayed in 1946, and went on to Venice, where they had rooms at the Hotel Monaco on the Grand Canal. The previous year's routine was resumed: De Beauvoir read to him in the morning; he slept in the afternoon; the three of them went for a walk in the early evening. At a Donizetti opera, *Maria di Rohan,* Sartre could see almost nothing of the action onstage.

Back in Paris, he went for checkups to Ciolek, to the diabetes specialist, and to Dr. Lapresle, who were all satisfied that his condition was stable. He was becoming more resigned, but there was little that gave him pleasure. "I have the feeling of living through the same day again and again," he told De Beauvoir. "I see you, I see Arlette, medicines, and then it starts all over again."[21] But for urgent persuasion from her he would often have absented himself from editorial meetings of *Les Temps Modernes.*

Over the presidential elections, which ensued on the death of Pompidou (April 2, 1974), the editorial board was divided. Together with De Beauvoir, Bost and Lanzmann wanted to support Mitterrand, while Sartre, like Pouillon and Gorz, favored "revolutionary abstention."[22] If the activist Charles Piaget had been a candidate, Sartre would have voted for him, he told *Libération,* but only because he'd have stood no chance of getting in.[23]

When *On a raison de se révolter* was published, Herbert Marcuse, who was in Paris, took part in a discussion with Sartre, Gavi, and Lévy. This was reported for *Libération* by an attractive young Greek girl Sartre had befriended, Hélène Lassithiotakis. Marcuse, who was meeting Sartre for the first time, admitted privately: "Sartre has always been my superego. He may not want to be the world's conscience, but that's what he is."[24]

Though unable to write by dictating into a tape recorder, he still enjoyed being interviewed, and the indefatigable De Beauvoir suggested that during the summer vacation she should question him about his life, so that he could approximate the autobiography he had never completed. Toward the end of June he went with Arlette to Junas and then traveled to Florence for a vacation with Wanda. When De Beauvoir, who was going to Rome with him on the train, picked him up at the hotel, the reunion was reminiscent of her 1939 visit to the army camp in Brumath. Once again he was almost unrecognizable behind a mossy beard, only this time it was white. He could no longer shave, and he disliked going to the barber. But in Rome, De Beauvoir helped the hotel barber win his confidence, and when Sylvie arrived a few days later, she bought him an electric shaver.[25]

In Rome, De Beauvoir began the long interview that was to continue after their return to Paris. Her motivation, naturally, was mixed. She wanted above all to rally his flagging interest in life, helping him to produce an oral continuation of *Les Mots*. This was how he regarded the interview;[26] he also told another interviewer that he would like it "to constitute *our* biography, that of our relationship" as well as an account of his life, but he says little about De Beauvoir or about their relationship. Even if he had been in better health she would have been an indulgent interviewer, more concerned to reassure than to challenge. In detail, many of his memories are inaccurate. He now thought that in the stalag the Germans had presented him with Heidegger's *Sein und Zeit* after an officer had inquired whether he needed anything,[27] and he claimed that he had not read Kafka until after writing *La Nausée*. In fact, he had read *Der Prozess* (*The Trial*) in 1934 while still working on the novel.

Essentially a writer, Sartre could not feel fully alive when unable to write, and, back in Paris, could not stop himself from making such remarks as "You've come to see the dead man's house?" and "Well, yes, I'm a living corpse."[28] Sometimes the idea of suicide occurred to him.[29] After a routine, stretching over fifty years, of writing for nearly ten hours nearly every day, it was not easy to face a future with no writing in it. In conversation he was slower than before but lucid, though he still had nominal aphasia and he tired easily. The brain was softening because the blood was not circulating sufficiently.[30]

While the salaried job had produced a permit for Lévy to live in France, he was still stateless, though the principal of the Ecole Normale, Robert Flacelière, had made several attempts to obtain French nationality for his gifted pupil. But when Sartre wrote to the new president, Giscard d'Estaing, he received a handwritten reply, and naturalization followed promptly. Sartre sent only a brief letter of thanks, but it led to a correspondence with the president. "Though I'm not on his side," Sartre told an interviewer in 1978, "this doesn't mean I don't sympathize with him." But after adding that he had been having a "dialogue by letters" with Giscard, he stipulated that the interview should not be published until after his death.[31]

Sartre had been waging a lifelong war against himself—not only thinking against himself but persecuting his body, not so much to gratify his mind as to make it more productive. With his tough constitution he had survived without paying the full price for rejecting moderation and ignoring his doctor's advice, but his period of impunity was over. The war, of course, went on, but for the rest of his life he would be paying a young ally to fight with him against himself. Benny Lévy's task was exceedingly tricky. His main battle was against the apathy that had been encroaching on Sartre—it has left its mark on the long interview with De Beauvoir—and the enemy forces were so formidable that Lévy thought seriously of giving up. When he arrived in the morning he would ring the bell—like Cau and the two other secretaries, he was given no key—and Sartre often failed to hear it, especially if the radio was on.[32] For the work Sartre had done Lévy had unbounded admiration, but his task was to maintain a lively rapport with a somnolent old man who in losing his sight had lost what had always mattered to him most—his future as a writer. It was not easy to make Sartre live in the present. In conversation he was obliged to concentrate, but when Lévy read aloud, as he did for much of the time they were together, he could not always be sure whether or not Sartre was half asleep.

Sartre could not afford to be realistic about his condition. "My mind is probably as clear," he claimed in 1975, "as it was ten years ago, and my sensitivity has remained the same. . . . I feel neither sad nor melancholy about what I've lost."[33] His emotional dependence on Lévy would increase proportionately to Lévy's success in making him believe he still had a future, if not as a solo writer at least as a duettist. They could collaborate. Though many of those who disliked Lévy would have agreed with Pierre Goldmann that he was a Talmudist who had strayed into Maoism,[34] he appeared to correspond with Sartre's lifelong fantasy of himself as a man of action. The old man who had always detested privacy and *la vie intérieure* could make a fresh attempt, collaborating with a young ex-leader, to write in the first person plural. Thirty years earlier he had started *Les Temps Modernes* with the ideal of involving readers, coeditors, and himself in thinking that was done collectively. About Merleau-Ponty he had written: "He showed me what my own thoughts were." Now Lévy could not only show him but help him to develop them in the direction of a new socialism. "Of all the people I've known he's the only one who from this point of view gives me complete satisfaction."[35] While still accepting Marx's ideas about the class struggle and surplus value, Sartre no longer trusted Marxism as a philosophy of power: what was needed now was "another way of thinking which takes account of Marxism to go beyond it, to reject it and take it up again, to subsume it."[36]

In some ways Lévy's inconsiderateness was advantageous. Instead of making tiresome allowances for Sartre's frailty, he carried on as if there were nothing wrong with him, sometimes reading in a provocative tone, sometimes posing a demanding question when Sartre appeared to be on the point of succumbing to fatigue.[37] Like an intellectual nurse, Lévy needed to have control over his patient, but the stronger his control became, the more his presence was resented by the women who surrounded Sartre. The only one to be won over was Arlette, who not only typed out transcripts of their conversations but began to study Hebrew with Lévy. What they had in common, apart from Judaism and their North African background, was their youth. They were the last young couple to arouse the jealousy of their seniors, as Olga and Bost once had when Sartre had preferred their company; now the Bosts were among the seniors. Watching a loving interdependence develop between the blind old man and the young Jew, friends and colleagues on *Les Temps Modernes* could not be sure whether Lévy was abusing his position of trust, controlling the direction of the old man's thinking, using him as a mouthpiece for his own ideas, which had been changing rapidly. During the triangular conversations with Gavi, the differences of opinion had been small in comparison with the consensus. But Lévy had been drifting from Maoism toward Judaism. To De Beauvoir, Sartre could say that he did not consider the Torah to be the source of all morality, but his conversations with Lévy had become inseparable from readings in which Lévy did the selecting. One day, when Georges Michel called, he saw an enormous book on Sartre's table—Baron's *Histoire d'Israël*. "It's not uninteresting," said Sartre. "It teaches me things I didn't know." According to Michel, he spoke "like a punished child putting on a good face against misfortune."[38]

To a large extent, though, Sartre was responsible for Lévy's frenetic pursuit of his Jewishness. A Sartrian idea was, ironically, boomeranging. According to *Réflexions sur la question juive*, a Jew cannot be authentic unless he lives out fully his condition as a Jew. The young Sartre who wrote this did not know that the old Sartre would be in the hands of a young man who would rebound from fanatical Maoism into the equally fanatical pursuit of his Jewish identity.

Sartre could no longer make any important decisions independently. When he was approached about appearing on television in a series about his life, his first instinct was to refuse, but conversations with Lévy and Gavi led to the idea of programs about twentieth-century history as he had experienced it. Marcel Jullian, the controller of the channel Antenne Deux, agreed to a series of ten programs. Discussing it in an interview, Sartre said: "We'll see how far we can go."[39]

THE March 1974 issue of *Les Temps Modernes* had contained an article on "torture by sensory deprivation," inflicted in prison on members of the Baader-Meinhof group, and an article by their lawyer, Klaus Croissant, about torture by isolation. After this, Croissant asked Sartre to go and see for himself how members of the group, the Rote Armee Fraktion, were being treated in prison. At the beginning of November 1974 he applied to the German authorities for permission to interview Andreas Baader in prison, and eventually this was granted. In an interview that appeared in *Der Spiegel* on December 2, Sartre explained that though he disapproved of the group's violence, he wanted to show solidarity with an imprisoned revolutionary militant.[40] On December 4, accompanied by Lévy, Croissant, and Cohn-Bendit, who was to be his interpreter, Sartre visited Baader in the Stammheim prison at Stuttgart, where he was in the fourth week of a hunger strike. Afterward Sartre gave a press conference and later, together with Heinrich Böll, appeared on German television to appeal for the creation of an international committee to protect the interests of political prisoners. But, as Sartre realized, his efforts were ineffectual or possibly counterproductive. It was useless to explain that he was not condoning what Baader had done, only protesting against the conditions of his imprisonment. The intervention was treated abusively by the German press.

Sartre gave another press conference in Paris, on December 10, with Croissant and Geismar on the platform. By then he was having three meetings a week with De Beauvoir, Lévy, and Gavi to plan for the ten television programs. Each program was to last for ninety minutes, with the final fifteen minutes devoted to present-day problems. In December, Gavi made a serious tactical mistake, writing in *Libération* that if Sartre had agreed to work for television, it was only in order to make it look ridiculous. But during the first three months of 1975, preparations for the series went ahead. To do the research a team of young historians was recruited, mostly by Lévy and Gavi. After preliminary meetings on January 5 and February 1, they settled down to a routine of monthly meetings. They were divided into groups working separately on the themes Sartre, De Beauvoir, Lévy, and Gavi had planned. Jullian made preliminary payments on January 22 and March 6, but no contract had been signed. The historians did not want to be mere researchers, with no control over how their contributions were used, and Sartre was in no state to dominate meetings. Unable to see other people, he tended to remain silent, while Lévy did most of the talking, authoritatively but not always tactfully.

In March, Sartre left Paris to stay with Arlette at Junas, where they were joined by Michel Contat, who tape-recorded a long interview spanning three days. Contat, who had written a study of *Les Séquestrés d'Altona*, was doing a lot of underpaid bibliographical work on *Les Ecrits de Sartre*, which was to be published by Gallimard, and Sartre agreed to his proposal that they should have equal shares in earnings from the interview, which could be sold all over the world. It yielded each of them about fifty thousand francs.

Nothing had been settled about the television programs when Sartre left Paris again on March 23 for a trip with De Beauvoir to Portugal. What had originally been planned as a vacation turned into a fact-gathering tour; they were joined by Lévy and the editor of *Libération*, Serge July. In April 1974 the fascistic Portuguese government had been overturned by a military coup, and the Armed Forces Movement (MFA) had gained popular support. Sartre and De Beauvoir stayed at a hotel in the center of Lisbon near a noisy open-air market. Generally the mood of the city seemed cheerful. Sartre met members of the MFA, lectured to unresponsive students, visited a democratic factory near Oporto. In a series of five interviews published between April 22 and 26 in *Libération*, Sartre came out on the side of the MFA. As during his visit to Cuba, he was naïvely optimistic about the "creativity of the masses" and even about the prospects that genuine democracy could spread to France. "They have self-management there; groups create entire hospitals by occupying buildings and even palaces and mobilizing the whole district. They are taking action with the support of the population and are forming a people's power. . . . It is such a people's power that we would like to encourage through the television programs."[41]

Discussion about the series was continuing inconclusively. Much time was spent on planning for it, while Sartre made headway in collaborating with Lévy on a book to be called "Pouvoir et liberté" ("Power and Liberty"). The object, as Sartre summarized it in 1976, was to show that there could be no ethics without freedom and no freedom until both the concept and the reality of power had been demolished. "A society without power starts to become an ethical society."[42]

In June a contract for the television programs was drafted, but Jullian procrastinated so long over signing that Sartre had to take his summer vacation in a state of uncertainty. He started the vacation with

Arlette, continued it with Wanda, and finished it with De Beauvoir and Sylvie, this time—since he wanted to be with Hélène—in Greece instead of Rome. The two women, who had driven southward, picked him up at the airport in Athens. Hélène was working at the university there, and Sartre, De Beauvoir, and Sylvie divided their time between Crete, Rhodes, and Athens.

Back in Paris, they had an angry confrontation with Jullian, who had asked them to make a pilot program. Behind this disingenuous proposal was the fact that their synopses for the series had been submitted to the prime minister, Jacques Chirac, who wanted the idea to be dropped. Two days after the meeting with Jullian, Sartre gave a press conference. "I have been made to give up: it's a case of formal indirect censorship." He would never again appear on television either in France or abroad, he promised.[43] He did take part in a program put out by Radio-Télévision Luxembourgeoise to explain what had happened, but he was depressed and exhausted.

At times the corner of his mouth and the tip of his tongue were partially paralyzed, and early in October he collapsed or lost his balance several times. Dr. Zaidmann gave him injections. His blood pressure had risen from 140 to 200, and he could not walk even from his bed to the bathroom without help. De Beauvoir stayed in his flat to nurse him. Two days later his blood pressure was 215. Dr. Zaidmann and Dr. Lapresle visited him together and prescribed medicines that reduced the blood pressure to 160 within a week at the cost of reducing his control over bladder and bowels. Seeming indifferent, he declared his intention of continuing to smoke but relented, either because of De Beauvoir's protest or because of an article Michelle read: with arteritis, smoking could make it necessary for a leg to be amputated.[44]

He was in no state to be interviewed, and when Gavi persuaded him to talk about Spain for *Libération,* he made the mistake of describing Franco, who was on his deathbed, as having "the foul face of a Latin swine."[45]

When Sartre woke in the morning his mouth and his throat were partially paralyzed: it took him half an hour to drink a cup of tea or a glass of juice. He also had difficulty in walking even short distances, and on October 20 Dr. Lapresle told De Beauvoir that physically Sartre had sunk to a level from which he would never again rise.[46] Mentally he was lucid enough to work regularly with Lévy on "Pouvoir et liberté." Arlette rented a television set for him and, sitting close to the screen, he could enjoy watching films.

When a threatening letter arrived from an extreme right-wing group that claimed to have blown up Photo-Libération, the picture library offshoot of the press agency, he seemed unperturbed, but De Beauvoir had an armored door installed in his flat. Before the year ended he had recovered sufficiently to take a short vacation with her and Sylvie in Geneva.

During 1976 he was able, without too much exertion, to support demonstrations and appeals that struck him as important. In January he declared his solidarity with a group of Paris militants who had been imprisoned for occupying an annex of the Soviet Embassy in protest against oppression in the USSR; in February, to help the dissident Dr. Mikhail Stern, who was in prison there, Sartre and De Beauvoir arranged for fifty Nobel prizewinners to join them in signing a *Libération* appeal for his release. In March, after thinking for some time about the murder of Pier-Paolo Pasolini, Sartre took only three hours to produce an article about him. After writing it out illegibly, he dictated it from memory to De Beauvoir, and it was published in the *Corriere della Sera*.[47]

Later in the month he left for Venice with De Beauvoir and Sylvie. Though he could take only short steps, he willingly went on long walks with De Beauvoir. "It doesn't bore you having a little friend who walks so slowly?" But when, suffering from a neuralgic pain in her right arm, she was talking about old age and said: "There's always something wrong somewhere," he retorted with conviction: "Not me. There's nothing wrong with me." She had to laugh, and so, after a moment, did he.[48]

He had not been back in Paris for long when the news broke about the death of Ulrike Meinhof in a German prison. Sartre expressed his "horror at a tragic end."[49] Nor did he stay in Paris long. He left to stay with Arlette in Junas and with Wanda in Venice, dividing a month between them before spending nearly three weeks with De Beauvoir and Sylvie in Capri. After driving to Rome, he stayed there with De Beauvoir for nearly a fortnight before they flew to Athens, where he passed the days with De Beauvoir and the evenings with Hélène.

In the autumn he stayed away from editorial meetings but resumed his routine of working three hours a day with Lévy. When new members were needed for the editorial committee at *Les Temps Modernes*—Bost was becoming too deaf and Lanzmann too busy—Lévy was co-opted, together with François George, Pierre Rigoulot, Pierre Goldmann, and Claire Etcherelli. Because of Lévy, Sartre started coming to the meetings again.[50]

In November he accepted an honorary degree from the University of Jerusalem but not without declaring—in a speech that he learned by heart—his concern about the Palestinian refugees and his willingness to accept a degree from Cairo University, should he be offered one.[51]

By January 1977 he could hardly walk. He had pains in his left leg, and when he went with De Beauvoir to the Brazilian restaurant—a short walk that had been easy in December—he had to stop three times on the way, arriving breathless and in pain. Of the women who were seeing him regularly Michelle had always been the least strict about letting him drink, but De Beauvoir and Arlette saw no danger in letting her sleep in his flat on Saturday nights. On Saturday evenings Wanda was with him until eleven, and it was not easy for De Beauvoir or Arlette to take over from her so late. One Sunday evening at nine he was so ill that De Beauvoir dialed SOS on the telephone to call a doctor. Sartre's blood pressure was 250, but it dropped to 140 after an injection. Told that she could no longer sleep in the flat on Saturday nights, Michelle said she had been trying to let him die cheerfully, believing this to be what he wanted.[52]

In the middle of February he was well enough to fly with Lévy to Athens for a week. Hélène had arranged for him to give a lecture at the university there on the twenty-second. After six days of lunching with Lévy, dining with Hélène, and thinking about the lecture, he gave his talk, "What Is Philosophy?" to an audience of about fifteen hundred.[53]

Just over two weeks later Hélène came to Paris, but on her first evening, after taking her to the Brazilian restaurant, Sartre collapsed on the way back. In the morning his blood pressure was 220, although he had drunk very little, and Dr. Cournot, who came in the evening, discovered there had been a spasm in his leg. The next day he had several falls, and when he was taken to Broussais Hospital it was found that his blood pressure, good on the right side, was poor on the left. After inspecting the results of an extensive X-ray examination Dr. Housset delivered an ultimatum: unless he gave up smoking, it would be necessary to cut off first his toes, then his feet, then his legs. Visibly disconcerted, Sartre promised to think it over. Two days later he sadly handed his cigarettes and lighters to De Beauvoir.[54]

At the next consultation Housset prescribed a series of intravenous injections, warning Sartre that any cramp meant he must immediately stop walking to avert the danger of a stroke or heart attack. Housset was not in favor of a vacation in Junas, and he gave De Beauvoir a bulky envelope for Dr. Cournot. Together with Liliane Siegel she steamed it open, but most of the contents were incomprehensible to them. Liliane took them to a medical friend, who explained that Sartre had only 30 percent circulation in his legs. "If he's careful," she said, "he can live for a few more years."[55]

Dr. Cournot advised Sartre to walk very little during the next few weeks, and, arriving with him in Venice, De Beauvoir persuaded him to ask for a wheelchair. From the hotel, where they were given the same rooms as before, he seldom went farther than the bar on the other side of the street. Most of his time was spent either sleeping or listening to music.[56]

When they arrived back in Paris, Hélène was there, and in her company, he said, he felt thirty-five. He was still suffering a lot of pain in his legs, but he celebrated his seventy-second birthday with an eloquent protest against Soviet oppression. While President Giscard d'Estaing was receiving Brezhnev at the Elysée, Sartre was one of the intellectuals receiving a group of dissidents at the Théâtre Récamier. He sat next to Mikhail Stern, who had been released after the appeal on his behalf. But as Sartre's health went on deteriorating, his need for alcohol was increasing; at the end of each session with Lévy he insisted on whiskey.[57]

At the beginning of July, Sartre drove to Junas with Arlette, Puig, and Puig's girl friend. After going on, as usual, to spend a fortnight with Wanda in Venice, he was picked up by De Beauvoir and Sylvie, who drove him to Rome, stopping en route to spend a night in Florence. He and De Beauvoir stayed for thirty-five days in Rome, where Bost and Olga came to visit them. It was hard for Sartre to walk, but he gave a long interview to a left-wing paper, *Lotta Continua.* His progressive disillusionment with Marxism now culminated in the explicit declaration "I am no longer a Marxist."[58] It was at about this time that Hélène lost her power to rejuvenate him: he decided that he wanted neither to have her visit him in Rome nor to visit her in Athens, but he would go on giving her money to stay in Paris. When she came to see him there after his return, he reduced her to tears by saying that he no longer loved her. He told De Beauvoir that he had never been so surrounded by women.[59]

His feelings about terrorism were ambivalent. In the September interview he had said: "Each time the state police shoot at a young militant, I'm on the young militant's side."[60] And after Baader and his group had, according to official bulletins, shot themselves in prison, Sartre, while reiterating his disapproval of the Baader-Meinhof gang's terrorism, had no doubt that they had been assassinated, and he protested vigorously.

After years of trying to encourage peace between Israel and the Arab countries, he was pleased when the courageous Egyptian President Sadat took the initiative of visiting Israel. Early in December, Sartre published an approving article,[61] and in February 1978, with Lévy and

Arlette, he traveled to Jerusalem so that he could find out what was going on and perhaps even contribute to a détente. After five days of interviewing Palestinians he and Lévy both put their names to a piece written mainly by Lévy about the situation. When it was sent to the *Nouvel Observateur,* Bost telephoned De Beauvoir: "It's horribly bad. At the paper we're all quite appalled. Do persuade Sartre to withdraw this piece." Equally appalled when she read it, De Beauvoir passed on Bost's request. Sartre was quite willing to comply, but Lévy was furious, and at a *Temps Modernes* editorial meeting, he insulted Pouillon and Gorz when they told him what they thought of the article. After pronouncing them all to be corpses, Lévy never again came to an editorial meeting and never again spoke to De Beauvoir, who kept away from Sartre's flat while he was there. Nor did she ever go with Sartre to what Lévy called his "community," a suburban house he and his wife shared with another couple.[62]

Sartre was now under serious financial pressure. Along with Hélène, Wanda and Michelle were receiving a monthly allowance, and he owed money to Gallimard. When De Beauvoir told him to buy himself new shoes, he said he couldn't afford them.[63] But he took an Easter vacation with her and Sylvie at Sirmione, where they had hotel rooms on the shores of Lake Garda. After returning to Paris he went on working with Lévy. They were accumulating an enormous amount of material on tape—the conversations had been going on since 1975—but Sartre was increasingly unrealistic about the outcome, believing that the resultant book would contain the tension of disagreements between him and Lévy, whom he still called Pierre. Some passages would be

> written by both of us: the beginning of the sentence will be Pierre's, I'll add a secondary proposition which will introduce a detail; perhaps I'll finish the sentence, or Pierre. The written sentence in these passages will have the value of registering a deeper research than that of one person, because the other will not enter easily into the sentence, he'll want to change it a bit, so that both make every effort to put the best of themselves into the form which has emerged. It will therefore be *better written* by two people than the same ideas could have been by one.[64]

It is not hard to see why Sartre wanted to believe this. His habit was to take less pride in what he had achieved than in what he was going to achieve. To a man who had been proving his freedom by refusing to accept the limitations his body tried to impose, what Lévy appeared to be offering was irresistible: at the same time as breaking down the barriers of the private self, Sartre could feel that he was still active as a writer, still living when he was half dead. More than anyone else Lévy personified the future. But he was no altruist. When he had been a Maoist leader, Sartre had said explicitly that he had no objection to being used and no illusion that the Maoists had approached him for any other reason than his usefulness. He was still useful to Lévy but in different ways.

One result of the unlikely partnership was an Israeli-Palestinian conference. As an Egyptian Jew, Lévy had an almost congenital interest in reconciliation between Israel and the Arab countries, and since accompanying Sartre to Jerusalem in February 1978, he had kept in touch with Eli Ben Gal, an Israeli journalist Sartre had met during his 1967 visit. Another liberal Israeli journalist, Flapan, had taken the chair in 1978 at an Arab-Israeli conference and had kept a record of the discussion, but he was asking *Les Temps Modernes* an exorbitant price for the rights to publish this. Lévy's counterproposal was to hold a similar conference in Paris. Gallimard agreed to pay the delegates' traveling expenses, and Foucault allowed his large flat to be used for the discussions. On March 14, 1979, Sartre made the opening speech but said little subsequently, and it would have been impossible anyway for the delegates to reach any useful conclusions or to provide *Les Temps Modernes* with the "international scoop" Lévy had promised.[65]

For the Easter vacation De Beauvoir and Sylvie drove Sartre to Provence, but soon after their return to Paris he was attacked and wounded in the hand by a half-mad Belgian poet, Gérard de Clèves. Sartre had often given him a hundred-franc note or two when, between periods of confinement in an asylum, De Clèves came to his door asking for money. Eventually wearying of this, Sartre told him not to come anymore, and when he did come, refused to let him in, opening the door only on the chain. De Clèves then produced a knife, slashed at Sartre's hand, and battered so vigorously at the armored door that it began to give way. Arlette, who was in the flat, telephoned for the police, who took De Clèves away, but Sartre refused to prefer charges. There was a deep gash in his thumb and he had to wear a bandage for weeks.[66]

It was at this time that Françoise Sagan became a friend. After obtaining his permission through an intermediary, she had published in *L'Egoïste* a "Lettre d'amour à Jean-Paul Sartre" eulogizing him as the only contemporary "man of justice, honor and generosity," the only great writer who was equally admirable as a man. "In short, you have loved, written, shared, given all you had to give, which was important, at the same time as you rejected everything offered to you, which was importance."[67] He asked to meet her, and they went out to lunch at the Closerie des Lilas. They had not seen each other for twenty years, and she was stammering with nervousness, but as they walked she held his hand to stop him from falling. After this they ate together at intervals of about ten days. When she picked him up at his flat, he would be waiting in his duffel coat. Though the food traveled unsteadily on his fork, journeying blindly to his mouth, his voice was still bright and brave. She enjoyed listening to music with him, making tea for him, cutting up his meat, especially when he managed to joke about it: "You're beginning to cut my steak into pieces that are too big. Are you losing respect for me?" He had been embarrassed, he said, to ask for her "love letter" to be read to him more than once, so she made a recording, which he played during evenings of depression.[68]

Before leaving Paris for the summer vacation he took part in a press conference to raise money for aid to Vietnamese who were running away from the pressure put on the south by the north. Many refugees had been collected in a boat, the *Ile-de-Lumière*, anchored off Pulo-Bidong, and the organizing committee now wanted to create an airlift. André Glucksmann took Sartre to the press conference at the Hôtel Lutétia,[69] where he shook hands with Aron in front of newspaper photographers. But later, after a visit to the Elysée, he recoiled when Aron tried to embrace him. To his former friend's nostalgic "Bonjour, mon petit camarade!" Sartre replied only "Bonjour."[70]

In the summer he went to Aix with De Beauvoir and Sylvie before flying to Rome with De Beauvoir; in the autumn he resumed the conversations with Lévy. In 1976 he had been confident the book would be published by 1979; he now said they needed another two or three years for readings, followed by two years for writing the book.[71]

At the beginning of February 1980 a checkup at Broussais Hospital confirmed that his condition was unchanged. He was still enjoying life and still finding it easy to make friends with young girls, who were glad to spend time with him. Freedom now meant freedom to forget the restrictions imposed by his deteriorating body. In the same way that he had fought fatigue by swallowing corydrane, he fought back against the doctors' regimen and the surveillance of the loyal De Beauvoir. Michelle had been wrong to think he wanted to die but right about his antipathy to discipline. The caring De Beauvoir seemed like a reactionary enemy, who could be outwitted by subversive friends willing to smuggle in cigarettes, whiskey, vodka, which he hid behind books. One Saturday night early in March he spent the night alone in the flat, and in the morning Arlette found him lying on his bedroom floor with a hangover. When De Beauvoir arrived, the two women searched the flat and confiscated the alcohol they found. After scolding Sartre, who tried to laugh it off, De Beauvoir telephoned the girl friends to warn them of the danger.

AT the beginning of 1980 Lévy started to prepare three installments of excerpts from their dialogue to be published in Le Nouvel Observateur. Sartre had always enjoyed quarreling with his earlier self, but there was no precedent for this attack on the sincerity of his philosophical statements. "I talked about despair, but it's nonsense. I talked about it because it was being talked about; it was fashionable. People were reading Kierkegaard. . . . I've never experienced despair, nor seen it as a quality that could be mine. It was Kierkegaard's influence on me." Angst had been "one of the key notions of philosophy from 1930 to 1940 . . . one of the notions I made use of all the time but which didn't correspond to anything for me." In November 1976 he had said "Anguish and flight from anguish are one and the same for me,"[72] but while the earlier statement prefigures the later, the two remain irreconcilable.

Not content with excerpting statements of self-accusation, Lévy made it appear that Sartre would have tended, had he been more honest, to be less relativistic: "What I did not say in L'Etre et le Néant, at least not in this form, is that each man . . . has an end which I'd call . . . transcendent or absolute, and all these practical ends have no meaning except in relation to it . . . and hope is attached to this absolute end." Lévy presents a Sartre who displays all the contrition of a convert: "I kept the idea that a man's life manifests itself as a failure: what he has attempted he has not achieved. He doesn't even think what he wants to think or feel what he wants to feel. That leads in sum to an absolute pessimism. Which I did not say in L'Etre et le Néant but which I'm forced to affirm now."

Questioned about morality, Sartre answers: "Each consciousness has a dimension I have not studied in my philosophical works . . . the dimension of obligation . . . a sort of requirement which goes beyond the actual and which makes the action I intend conform to an interior constraint." Sartre also blames himself for placing too much emphasis on individual freedom: "Other people are always there and they condition me—I left people too independent in L'Etre et le Néant. Each individual is dependent on every other."[73]

Dutifully optimistic, he now holds out humanistic hopes in solidarity: "What a morality needs is to extend the idea of fraternity until it becomes a unique and evident connection between everybody." Lévy also led him to a remorseful recantation about Jews: "What precisely was lacking was the reality of the Jew. Notice that this kind of reality, which is on the whole metaphysical, did not figure much in my philosophy. . . . I now see men differently." Sartre's final declaration of faith in history borders on the religious: "Revolutionaries want a society which would be humane and satisfying to men but they forget that a society of this kind is . . . a society in which relations between men are moral. . . . Well, this idea of ethics as the ultimate end of revolution—it's by a sort of messianism that you can truly conceive it."

Reading Lévy's excerpts from the conversations before they were published in Le Nouvel Observateur De Beauvoir was aghast, but Sartre brushed her protests aside: he wanted the interview to appear in exactly this form. The first installment was published on March 10, the second a week later. On Wednesday, March 19, before going to bed he asked her whether anyone at Les Temps Modernes had talked about the published conversation. No, she said.

In the morning, when she went in to wake him at nine, he was sitting on the edge of the bed, gasping. For four hours, since the attack had started, he had been too weak to reach the door of the other bedroom. De Beauvoir tried to telephone for help, but the line had been cut off because of an unpaid bill. Using the concierge's telephone, she rang a nearby doctor, who came immediately, and, after seeing Sartre, called from a neighbor's flat for the emergency service. Blood was taken and an injection given, followed by a treatment that lasted almost an hour. With an oxygen mask over his face, Sartre was wheeled on a gurney to an ambulance, which took him to Broussais Hospital, where he was put into intensive care. The newspapers were quick to pick up the news, and, disguised as male nurses, two photographers tried to get into his room. They were ejected, and the photograph in Paris Match showing Sartre asleep in a hospital bed was presumably taken with a telescopic lens from a neighboring rooftop.[74]

He had a pulmonary edema, which had been caused by an arterial blockage that stopped his lungs from being irrigated adequately. He had a high temperature and he was delirious. In the morning, thinking both he and Arlette were dead, he asked her what it had felt like to be cremated. Once his pulmonary circulation had been restored, he recovered his lucidity. The doctors would allow him only one visitor at a time, so Arlette spent the mornings with him, De Beauvoir the afternoons, and Arlette came again in the evenings, sometimes alternating with Lévy. Sartre sat in an armchair to eat his meals and receive De Beauvoir but spent the rest of the time in bed. She had already reserved rooms for a vacation they had planned in Belle-Ile, but it was clear he would not be well enough. He was moved to a bigger, brighter room, but he had begun to develop bedsores and his bladder was functioning badly. When he got out of bed he trailed a small plastic bag of urine. No longer adequately supplied with blood, his kidneys could not eliminate urea, and he was too weak for an operation to save one of them. His circulation was so poor that his bedsores became gangrenous.

When Pouillon came to see him, Sartre, after asking for a glass of water, promised: "Next time we have a drink it'll be whiskey at my place." But the next day he asked De Beauvoir: "How will we pay for the funeral?" The following day, with his eyes closed, he took her by the wrist and told her: "I love you very much, my dear Beaver." When she came on Monday, April 14, he murmured a few words without opening his eyes, and when he pursed his lips to be kissed, she kissed both his mouth and his cheek. By the evening he was in a coma, and he did not recover consciousness, though it was about twenty-four hours before he died. Arlette, who was with him, telephoned De Beauvoir, who called Sylvie, who called Bost, Lanzmann, Pouillon, and Gorz. The seven of them stayed overnight with the body, but when De Beauvoir, asking to be left alone with it, tried to lie down next to him under the sheet, a nurse warned her that the gangrene was dangerous. She lay down on top of the sheet and slept—or thought she slept—for a while. In the middle of the night press photographers tried to enter the room. At five in the morning male nurses covered the body and took it away.

He was to be buried in the afternoon of Saturday, April 19, and disinterred four days later for cremation.

Wanting to see the body again on Friday, De Beauvoir went with Bost to the lecture theater of the hospital, a large, cold room with a tiled floor, and the double coffin was brought in. Inside it Sartre was dressed in the clothes Sylvie had found in De Beauvoir's flat, clothes he had worn for going to an opera—a maroon corduroy suit, a light shirt, a tie with an abstract pattern on it. The spectacles were missing, the hair carefully combed, the well-shaven face made up.[75]

On Saturday morning he was again brought to the lecture theater. The lid of the coffin was placed to reveal the upper half of his body. His hands were clasped; a red rose rested against his neck. De Beauvoir asked Pingaud to take some photographs. Embarrassed, he dropped the camera, which hit the coffin and then the tiled floor. He picked it up, stood on a chair, took about four shots.

De Beauvoir had already dosed herself heavily with Valium, and when she asked for more, Sylvie refused at first, only to give in. De

Beauvoir swallowed two tablets. She could hardly see. When she was unable to hold her tears back she let them flow, trying neither to conceal them nor to wipe them away. From time to time she put her hand on Sartre's cold forehead. Dr. Housset came to bow in front of the body. So did the actor François Périer. The president of the Republic, Giscard d'Estaing, had already come to pay his tribute and had stayed for an hour, alone with the coffin. When people approached De Beauvoir to console her, she said, "He didn't suffer," as if she were consoling them. When four black-clad men approached the coffin, she leaned over to give Sartre a final kiss on the mouth, before the sheet was folded back over his face. The coffin was closed and an official from the police commissariat put seals on the inner coffin, which would go into the furnace at the cremation; the men in black arranged the straps that would be used to lift it from the outer coffin. This too was sealed.

From the hospital, which is in the middle of the fourteenth arrondissement, to the cemetery in Montparnasse the hearse had to travel through narrow streets that were more than usually congested. Outside the hospital a woman in black had been waiting for hours, carrying a red rose in silver paper. Before the hearse emerged about 20,000 people were crowding round her. Inside the hearse De Beauvoir, Arlette, Sylvie, and De Beauvoir's sister sat with the coffin. Traffic was halted as the procession, moving slowly through the streets, doubled in size and went on growing till about 50,000 people were following the coffin. It was like a demonstration, bigger than any he had attended while alive. For days the newspapers had been publishing articles about Sartre, and Parisians who had not turned out into the street were watching the procession on television. Hundreds of people had brought their cameras, and around the hearse friends linked hands to protect De Beauvoir from being photographed.

Filing through Saint-Germain, the cortège passed the cafés, the restaurants, the brasseries he had frequented. Finally it reached Montparnasse. Outside his flat in the Boulevard Edgar-Quinet it had to slow down because the mass of people following the hearse had met the mass waiting at the cemetery. Many were standing on top of tombstones; those who were straddling crosses had the best view. At the approach of the procession applause broke out, and it continued until the hearse stopped. Around it the crowd was so dense that it was impossible to take out the coffin until several appeals had been made for the crowd to move back. Packed tightly together and struggling to catch a glimpse of what was going on, people trampled on the neighboring graves. One man was taken to the hospital after being knocked to the ground, and another, pushed from behind, fell into the grave dug for Sartre. There was no ceremony, no speech. De Beauvoir did not get out of the hearse until the coffin had been lowered into the grave. After asking for a chair, she sat at the edge of the open grave for at least ten minutes surrounded by the vast mass of people. All around her camera shutters never stopped clicking.[76] Sartre could not have pictured anything like this when at the age of twenty he had written the one-act comedy *J'aurai un bel enterrement* (*I'll Have a Nice Funeral*).

Not a Conclusion:
Sartre's Continuing Life

In *Les Séquestrés d'Altona* the action goes on after the principal character has made his final exit: not yet resigned to a future without him, the women listen to the monologue he has tape-recorded for posterity. Apart from the work Sartre left to be published posthumously, including the war diaries and the second part of his *Critique*, he was also the author of a remarkable drama to be improvised after his death. Without knowing what form it would take, he had been mischievously aware that conflict would break out between De Beauvoir and Arlette. By making a will he could have arbitrated, but this would have been to make his intentions clear. He preferred ambiguity. To die intestate was to leave everything, including his literary estate, in the hands of his adopted daughter; but at least it might look as if he had not been deliberate in giving her control—even over the letters he had written to De Beauvoir. The pieces of paper still belonged to her, but she could not publish them legally without Arlette's consent. This was not forthcoming, so she published them illegally.

She had tried not to be proprietorial sexually, but as an autobiographer she had enjoyed writing in the first person plural. The world would go on thinking of him and her as a couple, and in 1983, when she defiantly brought out two volumes of his letters, she was showing the world how ardently he had declared his love to her during the first sixteen years of their relationship. What followed the appearance of the book was an undignified quarrel with Arlette, who took no legal action but reviled her in the press. They were fighting over Sartre as they never could when he was alive. This is only one of the ways in which Sartre survived himself. His influence is still enormous, but it cannot be analyzed because it cannot be isolated. Particles of Sartre are in the blood that flows through our brains; his ideas, his categories, his formulations, his style of thinking are still affecting us. Ripples are still spreading from pebbles he threw into the water.

Even contemporary feminism would not be quite what it is but for the initiative he took in encouraging De Beauvoir to analyze the extent to which her life had been conditioned by an upbringing different from a boy's. *Le Deuxième Sexe* (1949) is very much more than an answer to that question, but it is also an extremely Sartrian book. The first paragraph of the second volume begins: "You are not born a woman: you become one. The figure presented in society by the human female is not determined by biological, psychological or economic fatality; it is civilization as a whole which produces this creature, half way between male and eunuch, which is called female." This is a direct application of Sartre's idea about our freedom to recreate ourselves.

No one has been more directly or deeply influenced than De Beauvoir; his effect on other leading contemporary thinkers is less definable, but to take as an example a man twenty-one years his junior, Michel Foucault would probably not have worked in quite the same way but for having Sartre as a model. Much of Foucault's work turns on a challenge, not unlike Sartre's, to the conventional categorizations of knowledge and on the problem of the subject. As Foucault defines it himself, his objective has been "to create a history of the different modes by which human beings, in our culture, are made subjects." People are reduced to object status by being classified and segregated as criminal or insane, by being studied as objects suitable for scientific classification, or by being subjected to processes of domination by a class or group in a stronger position. Foucault is by no means Sartrian in either his approach or his methodology, but it is doubtful whether, without Sartre as his precursor, he would have taken the same kind of interest in insanity or made the same kind of attempt as he does in *L'Archéologie du savoir* (1969) to subvert the traditions of dealing with history in terms of period, with culture in terms of totality, and with literature in terms of the individual writers's oeuvre.

It is easier to demonstrate the indebtedness of R. D. Laing, who draws openly, gratefully, and fruitfully on Sartre's proposals for an existentialist psychoanalysis and on his ideas about the reduction of people to object status. Sartre, Foucault, and Laing have been among the most influential of those who have taught us to distrust the idea of a boundary between sanity and madness and to listen more sympathetically to the "insane" discourse of those who might formerly have been dismissed as incapable of communicating with us.

A major part of Sartre's achievement rests on his courage and obstinacy in asserting that we are what we make of ourselves. The idea which De

Beauvoir handed, like a flag, to the feminists is essentially the same idea that was later handed by Sartre first to the working class and then to Third World victims of colonialism. *Les Communistes et la paix* tells us that "classes do not exist; they are made." In his preface to Fanon's *Les Damnés de la terre* he explains that the native is free to cure himself of the "colonial neurosis" by using violence against the oppressive intruder. The problem of violence is central in Sartre's work, and to say that he has altered our thinking about violence is to say that he has altered our violence. He was the greatest and most influential of all the thinkers who sanctioned the concept of "counterviolence" as the only effective retaliation against the legalized violence of the state. No great mind has ever been tugged more painfully between the Western moral tradition and the homicidal mania of contemporary terrorism.

Since the American massacres in Vietnam and the Communist invasions of Hungary, Czechoslovakia, Cambodia, and Afghanistan, and after the wars, massacres, and famines in India and Africa, where the apathy of governments with the power to distribute supplies has been matched only by the apathy of richer countries with the power to send more help, it has been impossible to go on believing that the state is the chief custodian of morality. Before the end of the nineteenth century Nietzsche had already shown that the concept of goodness did not originate from neighborly altruism. The evolution of language had been determined by the dominant groups, which used their name-giving prerogatives to glorify themselves and their qualities while denigrating those of weaker rivals. "Good" had been cognate with "noble," "evil" with "plebeian," "fair" with "just," "black" with "evil." But even Sartre, who was familiar with Nietzsche's work, could not simply carry on as a moral philosopher from where Nietzsche had left off. The ideas of good and evil established by the Judeo-Christian tradition are not easily overturned, and we are rightly reluctant to abandon our belief in the rule of law, even when the laws are made by a government we distrust. We also distrust terrorists. Sartre was in the same quandary, and though, like Nietzsche, he failed to find a satisfactory escape route, we cannot ignore the discoveries he made while looking for one.

Situations is the right title for his essays because his ideas changed with changing circumstances and he was constantly propelled into what he called thinking against himself by what Marxists call contradictions in the situation. Despite his precocity he did not come of age as a philosopher until the war, when the quarrel between his instincts and his ideas about violence was precipitated by the situation of France in defeat. As a passionate advocate of individual liberty he was bound to condemn violence as theft of the other person's freedom: by using force we are making him into an object. But what about the freedom fighters who were sabotaging German freight trains? Counterviolence was the only effective way of fighting back against the Nazis, whose power was founded on violence.

Violence is not a crucial issue in most of the fiction Sartre had written or sketched out before the war, but from *L'Engrenage* onward he is preoccupied with the question of whether power can be wielded without violence, and, if not, whether violence can be humane. *Les Mains sales* plunges him deeper into the problem. Like Jean in *L'Engrenage,* Hoederer understands that a leader cannot expect to keep his hands clean. Violence is the only viable route to a future in which freedom may be available to everybody. In spite of the sympathy Sartre felt toward the Communists, the play turned out to be a powerful weapon in the hands of anti-Communists, and by banning performances of his play he was in effect denying himself freedom of expression.

The word "freedom" does not disappear from his vocabulary, but instead of being designated as something that is destroyed when force is used, it reappears as something that can flicker into life only briefly during moments of collective violence. There can be no true freedom for the individual until there is freedom for everyone. The *Critique* looks forward to the initiative taken collectively by the students in 1968; they will seize hold of their own liberty like the crowd that marched on the Bastille in 1789.

It is easy to understand how Sartre, who never said that he was a Maoist and sometimes said that he wasn't, came to join forces with extremist former students after the rebellion failed. When, at the end of the war, he wrote that France had never been so free as during the occupation, he meant that moral decisions had never been so clear-cut. But they had been almost equally clear-cut during the period of tension that preceded the rebellion. Against a government that allowed Algerians to be tortured in Algeria and murdered in France, counterviolence was hardly less attractive than it had been when the Nazis were in control. But in the seventies, when Sartre sided with the militants, he balked at the mindless anarchic violence they would have welcomed in their hatred of the status quo. The hunger for the justice of the lynch mob was as erratic as the clamor for vengeance against collaborators after the liberation of Paris, when mobs prowled savagely through the streets.

From 1968, when he appeared on Czech television trying to encourage movement toward liberalization, to 1979, when he was still trying to promote peace between Israel and the Arab countries and to help the Vietnamese boat people, he was pragmatically siding with the forces of good against evil, though he was still unable to formulate any adequate moral theory. After he helped to launch *Libération* and helped it to weather a major financial crisis, it is still in existence—tangible evidence of his power. But between his writing and his activism the lack of coordination was more debilitating than it had been when he launched *Les Temps Modernes* and tried to rally support for the RDR. In the forties and fifties the public he had addressed in his writing was the same public he was trying to involve in political action: the tone, the style, and the level of his Baudelaire biography are no different from those of *Qu'est-ce que la littérature?*, which made its first appearance in *Les Temps Modernes*. But the Flaubert biography is not written for the same public as *Libération*. It had been dangerous to regard abstraction as a cleansing force, and it had been dangerous to cultivate two styles of writing, one depending on careful revision, the other depending on drugs, haste, and disregard for style.

If the whole of his postwar career was bedeviled by the difficulty of integrating literary and political activity, he not only failed to solve the problem but let the two halves of his life become progressively separated. But his importance rests more on this failure, I believe, than on any of his successes. He could not have clung more tightly to both sides of the dilemma; his main achievement is the trajectory of his life. Undeniably, he ends up in a position of error—a non-Maoist editor of Maoist papers, a blind writer collaborating verbally for five years with an ex-Maoist Talmudist on a book that will never be finished—but there is something heroic in Sartre's indomitable persistence, in his boundless willingness to be wrong.

DURING the nineteenth century, biography tended to emulate the pattern of the *Bildungsroman*: the heroic subject would be observed progressing from the romantic excesses of youth to wisdom and maturity. He would seem to learn from each adventure, each mistake, ending up at dignified peace with a society that appreciates and rewards him. Sartre's life was less a pilgrimage toward the truth than a series of intellectual and political adventures in which he strenuously entangled himself in self-deception and angrily extricated himself. But if he has survived himself, it is because he came so close, while living autobiographically, to giving his experiences the quality of myth. In his UNESCO lecture he quoted Kierkegaard's remark "My own untruth is something I can discover only by myself because it is discovered only when I have discovered it, even if the rest of the world knew it already." Here the word "untruth" points to what is predictable and confounding in the situation from which he starts, trapped within a historical progression. He can liberate himself only by experiencing his subjective truth.

Together with Nietzsche, Kierkegaard inaugurates a phase of philosophy in which truth and experience are tightly intertwined. Sartre quotes from Antoine de Waelhens: "When Kierkegaard, Nietzsche and Bergson arrived on the scene, philosophy ceased to be *detached explanation* and claimed from now on to be *at one* with experience." It was necessary "to give up the ideal of philosophy as a rigorous science." Instead of illuminating human life it "aspired to become this life in its complete consciousness of itself." Sartre was a philosopher of this kind. Judged by the standards of rigorous science or even of academic philosophy, his thinking may fail to pass muster, but, like Kierkegaard and Nietzsche he has succeeded in "designating himself as a transhistorical absolute"—this is the phrase he uses about Kierkegaard. His discovery of his own untruth was so forceful that the resonance is still audible. Like Nietzsche and Kierkegaard, he cannot be reduced to what he wrote. When we try to extrapolate the statements from the situations, the pronouncements about liberty and violence merely contradict each other and eventually cancel each other out. But when we put the texts into their context, we see that each *volte-face*, each failure to fulfill a promise or complete a work is only superficially an interruption of the progress he is making. Without these discontinuities the movement itself is unthinkable. Which is not to say that he should never have attempted it. But it was essential for him to assert his freedom repeatedly in the way Antoine Roquentin had—by abandoning the book he was writing. No less ambitious than Nietzsche in the tasks he set himself—to write a phenomenological ethic, to prove that history has a single meaning, to create a dialectical morality, to reconcile psychoanalysis with Marxism—he cannot possibly fulfill them. But he could not have done what he did if he had been realistic about what he could do.

Sartre's life will continue indefinitely; less forcefully, though, since Simone de Beauvoir's death on April 14, 1986, almost exactly six years after his on April 15, 1980. In many ways their relationship had continued throughout the six years. In April 1980 she had been thrown into a depression from which she never recovered fully. Like him, she believed in the therapeutic value of work, and eventually she settled down to write *La Cérémonie des adieux*, which was ready to be published by the end of 1981. The first 150 pages, a disturbingly honest account of the last ten years in his life, are closely based on the diaries she had kept; the remaining 400 pages comprise an almost unedited transcript of the interviews she had conducted with him in Rome during the summer of

1974. In 1982 she published his letters to her but not hers to him, and she had no wish to make any other use of the material in her diaries. After her moving 1964 book about the death of her mother, *Une Mort très douce* (*A Very Easy Death*), and her 1970 book on old age (*La Vieillesse*), it might have seemed natural to write about her own experience of old age in a sequel to the four volumes of autobiography, but she had lost the one person who could possibly have persuaded her to write another book.

Like Sartre, she adopted a grown-up daughter. Thirty-four years her junior, Sylvie Le Bon had shared her life for more than eight years before his death and went on sharing it until the end. But without him De Beauvoir had only a limited interest in staying alive. At first she took an active part in running *Les Temps Modernes,* and she went on supporting the causes she believed in. In 1972 she had repudiated the statement made at the end of *Le Deuxième Sexe*—that she was not a feminist—and she went on, generously and judiciously, being helpful to the movement. But in 1984, when Claude Chabrol's film of her second novel, *Le Sang des autres,* was shown in Paris, she had no desire to see it, and though her mind was still quick, active, lucid, it had become apparent that no one had paid sufficient attention to the first sentence in her preface to *La Cérémonie des adieux:* "Here is the first of my books—no doubt the only one—that you will not have read before it was printed."

Their partnership had been extraordinary, not only as an experiment in personal relationships but as a literary phenomenon. The voice of Sartre's "little judge" survives in his work, just as his voice survives in her work.

Chronology

1905	6/21	Jean-Paul Sartre born, son of Jean-Baptiste Sartre (b.1874) and Anne-Marie, née Schweitzer (b. 1882).
1906	9/17	Jean-Baptiste Sartre dies.
1907		Sartre and his mother move in with her parents, Charles Schweitzer (b.1844) and Louise, née Guillemin (b.1848), in Meudon.
1908	1/9	Simone de Beauvoir born.
1909		A severe cold causes leucoma in Sartre's right eye, leading to strabismus and partial loss of sight.
1910		
1911		The Schweitzer-Sartre family moves to Paris.
1912		
1913	AUTUMN 10/22	Sartre starts at Lycée Montaigne. Paternal grandfather, Eymard Sartre (b.1837), dies.
1914		Attends communal school at Arcachon and later the Poupon school in Paris.
1915		After a period of private tutoring, is sent, in October, to the Lycée Henri IV.
1916		In the *sixième* Paul Nizan becomes a classmate.
1917	 NOV.	Anne-Marie marries Joseph Mancy and settles with him at La Rochelle. Jean-Paul moves in with them and starts at the lycée there.

6/28	Mutiny on battleship *Potemkin*.
10/20	General strike in Russia; 10/26, workers in St. Petersburg form the first Soviet.
7/12	Rehabilitation of Alfred Dreyfus.
7/25	Japan given protectorate over Korea.
JULY	Clemenceau resigns as French premier. Aristide Briand forms government.
7/25	Blériot flies across the English Channel.
5/6	George V succeeds Edward VII.
8/22	Japan annexes Korea.
5/26	Germany grants partial autonomy to Alsace-Lorraine.
10/26	Chinese republic proclaimed.
1/14	Raymond Poincaré becomes French premier.
FEB.–MARCH	Miners' strike starts in Britain.
7/10	Proportional representation used in French elections.
10/17–10/3/13	First Balkan War.
1/17	Poincaré becomes president; 1/21, Briand forms cabinet.
2/3–4/23	Second Balkan War.
5/19–8/10	Third Balkan War.
6/28	Assassination of Austrian archduke Francis Ferdinand at Sarajevo.
7/30	Socialist leader Jean Jaurès assassinated in Paris.
8/1–23	Declarations of war involving major European powers and Japan.
4/22	Germans use poison gas.
9/29	Briand becomes French premier.
1/29	First Zeppelin raid on Paris.
9/15	British use tanks for first time on the western front.
12/7	Lloyd George becomes prime minister of British coalition government.
4/2	US declares war on Germany.
5/15	Pétain appointed French commander in chief.
9/12	Paul Painlevé forms cabinet.
9/15	Russian republic proclaimed, with Kerensky as premier.
11/7	(10/26 old style) Bolshevik revolution in Russia.

1917
(cont'd.)

1918		Writes a novel about Götz von Berlichingen.
1919	SPRING	Steals money from his mother.
1920	AUTUMN	Returns to Lycée Henri IV in Paris.
1921	JUNE	Passes first part of *baccalauréat*.
1922	JUNE	Passes second part of *baccalauréat*. Writes the story "L'Ange du morbide" and the unfinished novel *Jésus la Chouette*.
	AUTUMN	Moves to the Lycée Louis-le-Grand as a day boarder, living with mother and stepfather in the Place de Clignancourt.
1923		Publishes "L'Ange du morbide" and several chapters of *Jésus la Chouette* in *La Revue Sans Titre*.
	SUMMER	Writes two chapters of *La Semence et le scaphandre*.
1924		Starts at the Ecole Normale Supérieure.
1925	SEPT.	Meets Simone Camille Sans (later known as Simone Jollivet).
1926	SEPT.	Nizan's departure for Aden cements Sartre's friendship with Guille and Maheu.

11/8	Lenin becomes chairman of council of people's commissars.
11/16	Clemenceau succeeds Paul Painlevé and forms cabinet.
12/5	Germans and Russians sign armistice; 12/21, peace negotiations start.

7/16	Execution of Tsar Nicholas II, who had abdicated 3/17.
10/12	Germany and Austria agree to withdraw troops before armistice is signed.
11/9	Republic proclaimed in Bavaria; revolution in Berlin.
11/11	Allies sign armistice with Germany.

1/5–11	Spartacist revolt in Berlin.
6/28	Peace treaty signed at Versailles; Alsace-Lorraine returned to France.

1/10	League of Nations founded.
FEB.	German Workers' party (which had 6 members when Hitler joined in 1919) changes its title to National Socialist party.
12/29	Socialist congress at Tours votes in favor of affiliation with Moscow International. Minority withdraws, splitting party. *L'Humanité* taken over by Communist majority.

3/8	French troops occupy some Ruhr towns because Germany delays reparations.
3/28	British Independent Labour party refuses to affiliate with Moscow.
10/6	Franco-German agreement on reparations in kind.

2/15	Court of International Justice holds first sessions at The Hague.
10/30	Benito Mussolini invited by the king to form fascist government.

1/11	French and Belgian troops occupy the Ruhr because of nonpayment of reparations.
8/10–13	Strikes and riots in Germany.
11/8–9	Hitler attempts a putsch in Munich.

JAN.	Kuomintang congress admits Communists to the party and encourages Russian "advisers."
6/13–15	Gaston Doumergue becomes French president and Edouard Herriot chosen as premier.
11/30	Franco-Belgian evacuation of the Ruhr completed.

1/16	Trotsky dismissed as chairman of Military Council.
4/10	Herriot defeated; Paul Painlevé becomes French premier.
4/25	Hindenburg elected president of Germany.
11/27	Briand forms government.

5/4–12	General strike in Britain.
7/15	Briand's government overturned by financial crisis.
7/23	Poincaré premier again.
8/10	Franc devalued and sinking fund established.
OCT.	Stalin expels Trotsky and Zinoviev from Politburo.

1927	MAY	Nizan returns.
		Sartre writes thesis, "L'Image dans la vie psychologique."
	SUMMER	In Usson-en-Forez. Unofficial engagement to daughter of a grocer.

| 1928 | JULY | Fails *agrégation*. |

1929	JULY	Meets Simone de Beauvoir.
		Comes out first in *agrégation* exam; she is second.
	NOV.	Begins 18 months' military service at Saint-Cyr.

| 1930 | JAN. | Transferred to Saint-Symphorien. |
| | | Inherits money when his grandmother dies. |

1931	2/28	Demobilized.
	APRIL	Teaching job in Le Havre.
	JUNE	"La Légende de la vérité" published in *Bifur*.
	SUMMER	Vacation in Spain with De Beauvoir.
		Starts "Factum sur la contingence" (first version of *La Nausée*).

1932	EASTER	In Britanny with De Beauvoir.
	SUMMER	In Morocco and Spain.
	OCT.	De Beauvoir takes teaching job in Rouen.

1933		Aron talks to Sartre about Husserl and phenomenology.
	EASTER	In London with De Beauvoir.
	SUMMER	With her in Italy.
	SEPT.	Starts a year's study at the French Institute in Berlin.

1934		Completes second version of *La Nausée* and writes *La Transcendance de l'Ego*.
	EASTER	In Paris.
	SUMMER	With De Beauvoir in Germany, Austria, Prague, and Alsace.
	OCT.	Resumes teaching in Le Havre.

1935	FEB.	Injected with mescaline.
	3/21	Charles Schweitzer dies, aged 91.
	SUMMER	Tour with mother and stepfather in Norway followed by hiking with De Beauvoir in France.
	AUTUMN	Triangular friendship with Olga Kosakiewicz and De Beauvoir.
	CHRISTMAS	In Switzerland with De Beauvoir.

5/13	"Black Friday": breakdown of German economy.
5/20–21	Lindbergh's transatlantic flight.
2/27	Trotsky expelled from party.

4/22	Union of left parties wins French elections.

1/31	Trotsky exiled.
7/27	Poincaré resigns; Briand premier again.

0/29	Wall Street crash, followed by European financial crisis.

3/12	Gandhi starts campaign of civil disobedience in India.
6/30	Last Allied troops leave Rhineland.
2/12	Last Allied troops leave the Saar.

1/27	Pierre Laval premier.
FEB.	Oswald Mosley forms his New party.
7/13	All German banks closed.
8/1	Franco–US loan to Britain.
9/21	Britain abandons gold standard. Pound falls from $4.86 to $3.49.

2/21	André Tardieu forms government.
4/10	Hindenburg reelected German president with 19 million votes, against Hitler's 13 million.
5/1	Left parties win French elections.
6/4	Herriot forms government.
7/31	Nazis win majority in German elections.
8/10	Sanjurjo attempts coup in Spain.
2/18	Herriot resigns, and Joseph-Paul Boncour forms cabinet.

1/30	Hitler appointed chancellor.
1/31	Daladier becomes French premier.
2/27	Reichstag fire; civil liberties and freedom of press suspended.
APRIL	Nazi persecution of Jews begins.
11/22	Camille Chautemps forms government.
DEC.	Stavisky scandal. Maurras's Action Française denounces corruption: a Jewish swindler has been protected by highly placed friends. When Stavisky is found dead, Chautemps comes under suspicion.

2/8	After rioting in Paris, encouraged by the reactionary league Croix-de-Feu, Gaston Doumergue forms coalition government.
2/12–13	General strike in France.
8/19	Hitler voted Führer by plebiscite.

3/7	Saar restored to Germany after plebiscite of 1/13.
6/4	Pierre Laval forms government.
7/27	Government granted extraordinary financial powers.

1936		*L'Imagination* published by Alcan.
		Writes story "Erostrate."
	5/3	Does not vote at elections.
	SUMMER	With De Beauvoir in Italy.
		Writes story "Dépaysement."
	JULY	Starts new teaching job in Laon.

1937		*La Transcendance de l'Ego* published in *Recherches Philosophiques*.
		Melancolia accepted by Gallimard.
	JULY	Story "Le Mur" published in *La Nouvelle Revue Française*.
	SUMMER	With De Beauvoir and Bost in Greece.
	OCT.	Starts teaching job in Neuilly.

1938		Writes 400 pages of "Le Psyché."
		Stories "La Chambre," "Intimité," and "Nourritures" (formerly "Dépaysement") published.
	APRIL	*La Nausée* published.
	JULY	Finishes story "L'Enfance d'un chef."
	SUMMER	With De Beauvoir in Morocco.
	AUTUMN	Starts *L'Age de raison*.

1939	FEB.	Publishes *Le Mur*.
	EASTER	With De Beauvoir in Provence.
	MAY	Meets Ilya Ehrenburg at antifascist conference.
	SUMMER	In south of France.
	9/2	Called up.
	DEC.	*Esquisse d'une théorie des émotions* published.

1940	FEB.	On leave in Paris.
	MARCH	*L'Imaginaire* published.
	APRIL	On leave again; awarded the Populiste Prize.
	5/23	Nizan killed in action.
	6/21	Sartre taken prisoner.
	12/24	*Bariona* staged in stalag.

1941	MARCH	Escapes from stalag.
	APRIL	Resumes teaching in Neuilly.
		Founds resistance group Socialisme et Liberté.
	6/21	Article on *Moby Dick* published in *Comoedia*.
		Finishes *L'Age de raison*.
	SUMMER	Cycling trip in Free Zone with De Beauvoir.
	OCT.	Teaching job at Lycée Condorcet.
		Dissolves Socialisme et Liberté.
	DEC.	Works on *L'Etre et le Néant*.

1942		Finishes *Les Mouches;* starts *Le Sursis*.
	SUMMER	Cycling trip in Free Zone with De Beauvoir; they then stay at La Pouèze.
	OCT.	Completes *L'Etre et le Néant*.

1/22	Albert Sarraut succeeds as French premier.
5/3	Popular front wins French elections.
6/4	Léon Blum forms government.
6/12	Forty-hour week introduced.
6/30	Croix-de-Feu suppressed.
7/18	Spanish civil war begins.
10/2	Devaluation of the franc.

JAN.	Show trials start in Moscow. Karl Radek among accused.
2/27	French Ministry of Defense created, Maginot Line extended, and Schneider-Creusot factory nationalized.
6/21	Blum resigns; Chautemps forms Radical Socialist government.

3/2–15	Trial of Bukharin in Moscow.
3/23	Blum forms popular front government.
4/10	Daladier forms government with Blum's support.
5/19–20	France and Britain support Czechoslovakia against Hitler.
8/12	Germany mobilizes.
9/7	French reservists called up.
9/29	Munich conference: Sudetenland given to Hitler; Czech frontiers guaranteed.
10/4	End of popular front in France.

2/27	France and Britain recognize Franco's government.
3/16	German army occupies Czechoslovakia.
3/28	Spanish civil war ends with surrender of Madrid.
8/23	Nonaggression pact between Hitler and Stalin.
9/1	Germany invades Poland.
9/3	France and Britain declare war on Germany.

3/20	Paul Reynaud replaces Daladier as premier.
5/7	Churchill replaces Chamberlain as British prime minister.
5/14	Dutch army surrenders.
5/28	Belgium surrenders.
6/14	Germans enter Paris.
6/16	Marshal Pétain takes over from Reynaud.
6/22	Concludes armistice with Germany.
8/23	German blitz on London begins.

5/14	Vichy government supports Admiral Darlan's commitment to give Hitler naval help.
6/22	Hitler invades Russia.
7/12	Anglo-Russian alliance.
12/7	Japanese bomb Pearl Harbor.
12/8	Britain and US declare war on Japan.
12/11	US declares war on Germany and Italy.

SEPT.	US bombers raid German positions in France.
11/8	Allies land in French North Africa.
12/24	Darlan assassinated.

1943	JAN.	Sartre joins Comité Nationale des Écrivains and contributes to underground papers.
	6/2	*Les Mouches* premiered; meets Camus.
	AUTUMN	Writes *Huis clos* in two weeks.
	NOV.	Finishes *Le Sursis*.
	DEC.	Finishes *Réflexions sur la question juive*.

1944	MAY	Meets Genet.
	5/27	*Huis clos* premiered.
	JULY	Escapes from Paris with De Beauvoir.
	AUG.–SEPT.	Reports for *Combat* on the liberation of Paris.
		Forms editorial committee for *Les Temps Modernes*.

1945		Refuses the Légion d'Honneur.
	1/12	Flies to the US. Meets Dolores Vanetti.
	1/21	Joseph Mancy dies.
	MAY	Returns to France.
	SUMMER	Vacation with his mother in the country and with De Beauvoir at La Pouèze. Writes *Morts sans sépulture*.
	AUTUMN	Existentialism in vogue.
	OCT.	Lectures on existentialism in Brussels and in Paris at the Club Maintenant.
	12/12	Returns to the US.

1946	APRIL	Returns to France; meets Boris and Michelle Vian.
	MAY–JUNE	Lectures in Switzerland on existentialism.
	JUNE–JULY	Publishes "Matérialisme et révolution" in *Les Temps Modernes*.
	SEPT.	Stays in Rome to work on *Huis clos* screenplay.
	OCT.	Moves into flat, 42 Rue Bonaparte, with his mother.
	11/8	*Morts sans sépulture* and *La Putain respectueuse* premiered in double bill.
	NOV.	Trip to Holland.

1947		*Baudelaire* published.
	FEB.–JULY	*Que'est ce que la littérature?* published in *Les Temps Modernes*.
	JULY	Visit to London for double bill of *Morts sans sépulture* and *La Putain respectueuse*.
	AUG.–SEPT.	Trip to Sweden and Lapland with De Beauvoir.
	SEPT.	*Les Jeux sont faits* presented at Cannes Film Festival.
	OCT.	*Situations I* published.
	OCT.–NOV.	Series of radio programs, *La Tribune des Temps Modernes*.
	CHRISTMAS	With De Beauvoir at La Pouèze. Starts *Les Mains sales*.

1948	FEB.	Joins Rassemblement Démocratique Révolutionnaire (RDR).
	4/2	*Les Mains sales* premiered.
	MAY	*Situations II* published.

1/30–31	German army defeated at Stalingrad.
5/12	German army in Tunisia surrenders.
6/4	French Committee of National Liberation formed.
7/26	Mussolini loses control of Italy.

6/6	D-Day: landings in Normandy.
8/15	Allied forces land on the Riviera.
8/25	Allied troops enter Paris.
10/23	Allies recognize De Gaulle as head of French provisional government.

2/4–11	Yalta conference: Churchill, Stalin, and Roosevelt agree on spheres of influence.
4/12	Roosevelt dies; succeeded by Truman.
4/30	Hitler dies in bunker.
5/8	VE Day.
6/5	Germany divided by Allies into four zones.
7/26	Conservatives defeated in Britain: Attlee replaces Churchill.
8/6–9	Atomic bombs dropped on Hiroshima and Nagasaki.
8/14	Japan surrenders.
10/9	Laval sentenced to death for collaborating.
10/21	Left triumphant in French elections.
11/13	De Gaulle elected president of provisional government.
11/20	Trials of Nazi war criminals begin at Nuremberg.

1/20–22	De Gaulle resigns as president. Félix Gouin succeeds him.
3/6	France recognizes Vietnam as a free state.
5/5	Referendum rejects French draft constitution.
JUNE	MRP wins majority in French elections.
6/19	Georges Bidault elected president.
10/13	Revised constitution adopted.
11/10	In elections Communists win 186 seats, MRP 166, Socialists 103.
12/16	Blum forms Socialist government.

1/16	Vincent Auriol elected president.
1/21	Blum resigns, Ramadier forms coalition government
3/29	Revolt against France in Madagascar.
4/14	De Gaulle heads anti-Communist Rassemblement du Peuple Français (RPF).
MAY	Series of strikes in France.
6/5	George Marshall, US secretary of state, announces program of economic aid for Europe.
10/19–26	RPF triumphs in municipal elections.
11/14	UN recognizes Korean independence.
11/19–23	Ramadier resigns; Robert Schuman forms government with support of MRP and Socialists.

2/25	Communist coup d'état in Czechoslovakia.
3/31	US Congress passes law for aid under the Marshall Plan.

1948	SUMMER	With De Beauvoir in Algeria.
(cont'd)	10/30	Sartre's books put on Index by Vatican.
	DEC.–JUNE	
	1949	*La Mort dans l'âme* published in *Les Temps Modernes*.

1949	MARCH	Stays at Cagnes working on ethical notes and novel.
	JUNE	*Situations III* published.
		Convenes and subsidizes meeting of RDR.
	SUMMER	South American vacation with Dolores Vanetti.
		Meets Hemingway in Cuba.
	10/6	Resigns from RDR.
	NOV.–DEC.	Excerpts from *Drôle d'amitié* published in *Les Temps Modernes*.

1950	JAN.	Sartre and Merleau-Ponty denounce Soviet labor camps.
	SPRING	With De Beauvoir to Sahara and black Africa.
	JUNE	Breach with Dolores.
	JULY	Starts publishing series of six articles on Genet in *Les Temps Modernes*.

1951	JAN.	Works on *Le Diable et le Bon Dieu*.
	6/7	Premiere of play.
	SUMMER	With De Beauvoir in Norway, Iceland, Scotland.

1952	JAN.	Agrees to work with Communists in protest over Henri Martin affair.
	JUNE	Reads *Le Coup du 2 décembre* by Guillemin.
	JULY	*Saint Genet* published; works on novel.
	JULY AND	Publishes *Les Communistes et la paix*, Parts 1 and 2, in *Les Temps Modernes*.
	OCT.–NOV.	
	AUG.	Publishes reply to Camus in *Les Temps Modernes*.
	SUMMER	In Italy.

6/24	Russians blockade West Berlin; airlift starts.
6/28	Yugoslavia expelled from Cominform.
7/29	Tito defies charges and wins support of party in Yugoslavia.
8/15	Republic of Korea proclaimed under Syngman Rhee.
9/9	North Koreans proclaim republic and claim whole country.
9/10	Henri Queuille, radical, forms government.
11/7	RPF succeeds in French elections.

JAN.	Kravchenko trial.
3/8	France recognizes non-Communist Vietnam as independent state.
4/4	North Atlantic Treaty signed.
5/5	Council of Europe established.
5/12	End of Berlin blockade.
5/23	German Federal Republic established.
9/15	Heuss and Adenauer elected as president and chancellor.
10/1	People's Republic of China proclaimed.
7/10	German Democratic Republic established under Pieck (president) and Grotewohl (minister-president).
10/28	Henri Queuille resigns, and Bidault forms coalition.
12/30	France gives Vietnam sovereignty.

3/8	Soviet Union reveals it has atomic weapons.
3/21	Adenauer proposes Franco-German economic union.
6/24	Bidault resigns.
6/25	North Koreans invade south.
7/11	René Pleven forms government after Queuille has tried (7/2) unsuccessfully.
9/15–10/1	UN forces land in South Korea and advance to beyond 38th parallel.

2/28	Pleven's coalition defeated.
3/10	Queuille forms government.
4/18	Treaty for single coal and steel authority in Western Europe.
6/17	French elections: Gaullists win 117 seats, socialists 104, Communists 101.
8/11	Pleven forms centrist coalition.
9/10	NATO foreign ministers consider use of German troops.
12/13	National Assembly ratifies treaty for single coal and steel authority.

1/7–22	Pleven's ministry falls; Edgar Fauré forms coalition.
2/29	After collapse of Fauré's government, Antoine Pinay assumes power.
3/30	Anti-French rioting in Tangier.
4/28	General Ridgway replaces Eisenhower as Supreme Allied Commander in Europe.
5/27–31	Paris signing of treaty for European Defense Community (EDC).
5/28	Communist demonstrations in Paris; Dubois arrested.
7/25	European coal and steel community established.
10/5	First postwar party congress in USSR.
11/27	Slansky (former party secretary) tried in Czechoslovakia.
12/12	Communist peace congress in Vienna.

1953	APRIL	Publishes "Réponse à Claude Lefort" in *Les Temps Modernes*
	MAY	Merleau-Ponty withdraws from *Les Temps Modernes*.
	JUNE	Sartre stays in Venice; condemns execution of Rosenbergs.
	NOV.	*Kean* opens.

1954	JAN.–FEB.	Makes speeches in protest against European Defense Community.
	FEB.	Meets Brecht at international writers' conference.
	APRIL	*Les Communistes et la paix*, Part 3, published in *Les Temps Modernes*.
	5/24–25	Attends Berlin meeting of World Peace Conference.
	5/26–6/23	First visit to USSR.
	SUMMER	In Italy. Meets Togliatti. Travels with De Beauvoir in Germany, Austria, Czechoslovakia. Returns to Italy.
	DEC.	Becomes vice-president of Franco-Soviet Association.

1955	JAN.	*Les Temps Modernes* supports rebels in Algeria.
	SPRING	Sartre starts working on biography of Flaubert.
	6/8	*Nekrassov* premiered.
	6/26	Attends peace conference at Helsinki; meets Lukács.
	JUNE	Merleau-Ponty's *Les Aventures de la dialectique* published, with a chapter attacking Sartre for "ultra-bolshevism."
		Revival of *Huis clos*. Sartre meets Evelyne Rey, who plays Estelle.
	SEPT.–NOV.	To China with De Beauvoir.
	NOV.	Starts working on a screenplay of Arthur Miller's *The Crucible*.

1956	FEB.	Controversy with Pierre Hervé and Pierre Naville about Communist party.
	MARCH	Meets Arlette El Kaïm.
	3/26–31	Takes part in Communist-organized cultural congress in Venice.

1/12	Tito elected president of Yugoslavia.
1/14–2/10	Constitution drafted for European political community.
2/24	Conference of foreign ministers on European Defense Community.
3/5	Stalin dies.
6/17	Rising in East Berlin.
6/19	Rosenbergs executed as atomic spies in US.
6/26	Joseph Laniel forms government.
8/6	New series of strikes starts in France.
9/12	Khrushchev becomes first secretary of Central Committee.
10/20	Adenauer forms new government.
12/23	René Coty elected president of France.
	L. P. Beria (former Soviet minister of internal affairs) shot as traitor.

1/25–2/18	Soviet and Western foreign ministers meet in Berlin. USSR vetoes idea of free elections in Germany.
3/9	Center and right victorious in French elections.
4/18	Colonel Nasser becomes Egypt's premier.
5/7	French defenders of Dien Bien Phu in North Vietnam defeated by Communist Viet-Minh.
6/18	Pierre Mendès-France becomes premier.
7/2	French retreat in Indochina.
7/20–23	Settlement in Indochina: Cambodia, Laos, and Vietnam given independence.
8/22	French intransigence sabotages Brussels negotiations on EDC treaty.
10/3	West Germany invited to enter NATO.
10/8	Communists occupy Hanoi, capital of Vietnam.
10/23	Four-power agreement to end occupation of Germany; nine-power agreement on Western European union.
10/26	Economic and cultural agreement between France and West Germany.
11/3	Terrorist activity in Algeria.
DEC.	Twenty thousand French troops sent to Algeria.

1/25	Jacques Soustelle appointed governor-general of Algeria.
2/5–23	Mendès-France resigns; Edgar Fauré forms government.
3/11–27	Treaty for European union ratified.
4/5–6	Churchill resigns; Anthony Eden succeeds him.
5/5	Occupation of Germany ends.
6/15	Anglo-American atomic energy agreement.
10/2	France withdraws from UN, angered at Algerian interference.
10/23–26	Referendum in South Vietnam: emperor deposed, republic proclaimed.

JAN.	East German army formed.
FEB.	Guy Mollet forms government.
2/14	Twentieth party congress in USSR; Khrushchev denounces Stalin.
3/12	Communists in Assembly vote to give government special powers in Algeria.

| 1956
(cont'd) | SUMMER | With Michelle Vian, Simone de Beauvoir, and Claude Lanzmann in Italy, Yugoslavia, and Greece; then long stay in Italy till November. |
| | NOV. | Condemns Soviet intervention in Hungary and Anglo-French intervention in Suez. |

1957	JAN.	To Poland for Polish premiere of *Les Mouches*.
	SUMMER	To Rome and Capri with Michelle Vian. Writes introduction to Gorz's *Le Traître*.
	SEPT.	Claude Faux, a party member, succeeds Jean Cau as Sartre's secretary.
	SEPT.–OCT.	*Questions de méthode* published in *Les Temps Modernes*.
	12/10	Appears as witness in trial of Ben Saddok.

1958	MARCH	Reviews Alleg's *Le Question* in *L'Express*. Paper seized by police.
	SPRING	Works on *Critique de la raison dialectique*.
	MAY	Accepts commission to write a screenplay for John Huston's film about Freud.
	5/22	Publishes anti-Gaullist article in *L'Express*.
	5/30	Participates in press conference about violation of human rights in Algeria.
	6/16–9/15	In Italy; works on *Les Séquestrés d'Altona*.
	SEPT.	Campaigns in *L'Express* for a "No" vote in the referendum.
	OCT.	Cardiac illness.

1959		Completes *Critique*, Part 1, and works on Freud screenplay.
	MAY	Interviewed by Jeanson for *Vérités pour. . . .*
	SUMMER	In Rome and Venice.
	AUG.	Completes *Les Séquestrés d'Altona*.
	9/24	*Les Séquestrés d'Altona* premiered in Paris.
	SEPT.	Stays with John Huston in Ireland.

1960	1/7	Article on Camus in *France-Observateur*.
	2/22–3/20	In Cuba with De Beauvoir. Writes preface to new edition of Nizan's *Aden-Arabie*.
	MAY	Visits Yugoslavia.
	AUG.	Is one of 121 signatories of manifesto favoring civil disobedience.
	AUG.–NOV.	Visits Brazil with De Beauvoir.
	12/1	Press conference advocating "No" vote in referendum.

1961	FEB.	Péju "secretary-general" of new editorial committee of *Les Temps Modernes* including Bost, Gorz, Lanzmann, Pingaud, Pontalis, and Pouillon.
	MAY	Merleau-Ponty dies.
	JUNE	Sartre installs Mme. Mancy in a hotel and moves into a flat with De Beauvoir.

JUNE	Rioting brutally crushed in Poznań.
7/26	Nasser seizes Suez Canal.
10/22-24	Demonstrations in Hungary; Soviet intervention.
10/31	Anglo-French bombing of Egyptian airfields.
11/4	Soviet attack on Budapest.
11/5	Soviet threat to use rockets unless Britain and France accept Middle East cease-fire.
12/8	General strike in Hungary; martial law proclaimed.

3/25	Rome treaties signed for Common Market and Euratom.
5/21	Mollet resigns.
6/12	Maurice Bourgès-Maunoury, radical, forms government.
10/30	Félix Gaillard, radical socialist, forms government.
12/8	Union de la Gauche Socialiste formed.

4/5	In Cuba, Fidel Castro opens battle against Fulgencio Batista's government.
4/16	Gaillard resigns.
5/14	Pierre Pflimlin (MRP) forms government.
5/29	De Gaulle forms government of national safety.
9/28	Referendum on constitution for Fifth Republic.
10/5	"Yes" vote strengthens De Gaulle.
11/30	Gaullist victory in elections.
12/12	Salan made inspector general of national defense in Algeria.
12/21	De Gaulle elected president.

1/1-2	Batista flees Cuba, and Manuel Urrutia is appointed provisional governor, but Castro postpones elections.
1/8	De Gaulle becomes president, with Michel Debré as prime minister.
2/16	Fidel Castro made Cuban premier.
9/16	De Gaulle broadcasts on Algeria's future.

1/24-2/1	Rioting in Algiers.
MARCH-JUNE	Ten-power disarmament committee meets in Geneva.
5/16-19	Khrushchev, De Gaulle, Eisenhower, and Macmillan meet in Paris.
6/14	FLN agrees to negotiate cease-fire but rejects De Gaulle's terms.
6/30	Lumumba becomes premier of newly independent Congolese republic.
AUG.-SEPT.	Belgian troops evacuate Congo.
9/5	Lumumba dismissed by President Kasavubu.
11/8	Kennedy elected US president.
12/13	Lumumba arrested.

1/6-8	Massive support for De Gaulle's referendum on Algeria.
1/17	Execution of Lumumba; danger of civil war in Congo.
4/17	Castro defeats Bay of Pigs invasion.
4/21-6	Army revolt in Algeria.

1961	7/19	Bomb attack on Sartre's flat, 42 Rue Bonaparte.
(cont'd)	JULY–OCT.	Stays in Rome. Writes essay on Merleau-Ponty and meets Frantz Fanon.
	NOV.	Takes part in pro-Algerian demonstrations.
	DEC.	Gives lecture "Subjectivity and Marxism" at Istituto Gramsci, Rome.
	DEC.	Resumes work on Flaubert biography.
1962	1/7	Second bomb attack on flat in Rue Bonaparte; Sartre moves to flat in Quai Blériot and later to 222 Boulevard Raspail.
	3/14	Elected vice-president of Congrès de la Communanté Européenne des Ecrivains (COMES).
	JUNE	Péju fired and replaced by Jeanson.
	6/1–24	To Russia with De Beauvoir.
	7/9–14	Returns to Moscow for peace conference; makes speech. Stays in Rome; works on adaptation of Euripides' *Alcestis*.
	12/28–1/13	Returns to Moscow.
1963	JULY	Essay on Lumumba published in *Présence Africaine*.
	AUG.–SEPT.	COMES conference in Leningrad; received by Khrushchev in Georgia.
	SEPT.	André Puig replaces Claude Faux as Sartre's secretary.
	OCT.–NOV.	Publishes *Les Mots* in *Les Temps Modernes*.
	11/12–14	Visits Czechoslovakia with De Beauvoir.
1964	4/21	Lectures for UNESCO on Kierkegaard.
	5/23	Lectures on morality and society at Istituto Gramsci.
	6/1–7/10	Visit to Russia.
	JULY–SEPT.	Stays in Rome; works on *Les Troyennes*.
	10/16–22	Refuses Nobel Prize.
	11/19	Gives interview for first issue of *Le Nouvel Observateur*.
1965	1/25	Applies to adopt Arlette Elkaim as his daughter.
	3/10	*Les Troyennes* premiered.
	MARCH	Cancels lecture at Cornell University.
	JUNE	Campaigns against Gaston Defferre's proposals for amalgamation of SFIO and MRP.
	JULY	To USSR and Helsinki.
	10/6	Speaks at a COMES meeting and is elected vice-president.
	DEC.	Gives qualified support to Mitterrand in elections.
1966	FEB.	Writes preface for *La Promenade du dimanche*, by Georges Michel, who becomes a friend.
	5/2–6/6	In USSR.
	JULY	Joins Bertrand Russell's tribunal to investigate American war crimes in Vietnam.
	JULY–AUG.	To Greece.
	9/18–10/16	Visits Japan with De Beauvoir.
	10/17–22	Stays in Moscow.
	11/13–15	Russell tribunal meets in London.

8/17–18	Berlin Wall built.
8/27	Provisional government formed in Algeria under Ben Kheddha.
11/8	Negotiations begin for Britain to enter Common Market.

FEB.	Riots in Paris against the OAS.
3/14	France boycotts Geneva disarmament conference attended by 17 foreign ministers.
3/18	Cease-fire in Algeria; provisional FLN government established.
4/14–15	Debré resigns and Georges Pompidou forms ministry.
7/3	After referendum France gives Algeria independence.
8/16	Algeria admitted to Arab League.
OCT.–NOV.	Crisis over installation of Russian missile base in Cuba.
11/2–3	Base dismantled and missiles removed.

1/22	Franco-German treaty of cooperation.
1/29	De Gaulle vetoes British entry to Common Market.
10/15	Adenauer succeeded by Erhard as German chancellor.
11/22	President Kennedy assassinated.

1/27	France enters into diplomatic relations with China.
7/7	France starts selective military service.
8/2	Fighting begins in North Vietnam.
10/15	Khrushchev is replaced by Brezhnev and Kosygin.
10/16	China explodes atom bomb.

2/7	US air raids on North Vietnam begin.
3/21	US spacecraft lands on moon.
6/19	President Ben Bella of Algeria deposed by Houari Boumedienne, who forms new government.
6/25	Hungarian president Kádár resigns. Succeeded by Gyula Kallai.
7/10	World Peace Congress in Helsinki.
11/11	Ian Smith's unilateral declaration of Rhodesian independence.
12/5	De Gaulle gets only 44 percent of votes but is reelected president, defeating Mitterrand.

1/10–14	Sinyavsky and Daniel tried and sentenced to 7 and 5 years respectively in labor camps.
2/21	De Gaulle calls for NATO to be dismantled and (3/10) threatens to withdraw French troops.
6/20	De Gaulle pays 12-day official visit to Moscow.
7/29	US government "dissociates" itself from bombing populated areas in North Vietnam.
8/25	De Gaulle visits French nuclear testing center in Pacific.
11/13–25	Israel attacks Jordan and is censured by UN Security Council.
12/1	Kiesinger succeeds Erhard as chancellor.
12/13	US bombs Hanoi suburbs.

1967	2/2	Participates in Russell tribunal press conference.
	3/2	To Egypt and Israel with De Beauvoir.
	4/13	Writes to De Gaulle about Russell tribunal.
	5/2–10	Presides over tribunal's meeting in Stockholm.
	5/30	Meeting about Regis Debray at Mutualité.
	11/20–12/1	Second session of tribunal outside Copenhagen.
	12/12	Simone Jollivet ("Toulouse") dies.

1968	JAN.	Ill with arteritis.
	MARCH–APRIL	Visit to Yugoslavia.
	APRIL	Appears on Czech television: hopeful about "Prague Spring."
	5/6	Supports student rebellion.
	5/11	Interviewed on Radio Luxembourg.
	5/20	Interview with Cohn-Bendit published.
		Speaks at Sorbonne.
	JULY	In *Spiegel* interview accuses PCF of betraying student revolution.
	SUMMER	In Italy.
	8/24	Condemns Soviet intervention in Czechoslovakia.
	11/14	Successful revival of *Le Diable et le Bon Dieu* at the TNP.
	11/28–12/1	To Czechoslovakia.

1969	1/30	Sartre's mother dies.
	2/10	Speaks at meeting to protest against expulsion of 34 dissident students.
	APRIL	Controversial psychoanalytical dialogue published in *Les Temps Modernes*.
	MAY	Gives limited support to Communist candidate in presidential elections.
	JUNE	Abstains from voting in second round.
	SUMMER	To Yugoslavia and Italy; meets student leaders in Rome.
	12/11	Appears on French television to denounce My Lai massacre.
	12/19	Chairs press conference on massacre.

1970	2/23	Appears as witness at trial of Roland Castro.
	APRIL	Becomes nominal editor of *La Cause du Peuple*.
	MAY	Pontalis and Pingaud resign from *Les Temps Modernes*.
	5/27	Gives evidence at trial of two previous editors of *La Cause du Peuple*.

2/24	Former Nazis sentenced in Munich for murder of over 80,000 Dutch Jews.
3/5	In elections for National Assembly, Gaullist majority reduced to one.
4/20	Bolivian police arrest Regis Debray for guerrilla involvement. US bombs Haiphong.
5/2–10	Bertrand Russell's international war crimes tribunal meets in Stockholm.
5/16	De Gaulle obstructs Britain's entry into EEC.
6/5–10	War between Israel and UAR.
10/9	Che Guevara killed in guerrilla clash with Bolivian army.
11/15	Fédération de la Gauche Démocratique formed.
1/5	Dubček replaces Novotný as first secretary of Czech Communist party.
1/30–3/11	Clashes between students and police in Poland.
3/5	Czech government announces relaxation of censorship.
3/22–30	Novotný resigns and is succeeded by Svoboda.
4/8	New Czech government formed under Oldrich Černik.
4/11	German students riot after assassination attempt on Rudi Dutschke.
5/3	Clashes begin between students and police in Paris.
5/13	Vietnam peace talks begin in Paris.
6/23–7/9	Landslide victory for De Gaulle in elections.
7/9	Couve de Murville succeeds Pompidou as premier.
8/20	Warsaw Pact troops enter Czechoslovakia.
9/24	France explodes hydrogen bomb.
10/31	President Johnson announces end of Vietnam bombing.
11/5	Nixon elected US president.
12/14	Education minister Edgar Faure announces sanctions for students sabotaging reforms.
3/28	Anti-Soviet demonstrations in Prague.
4/17	Dubček resigns as leader of party; succeeded by Gustav Husák.
4/27	De Gaulle announces resignation when his referendum is defeated.
6/10	International Red Cross suspends operations in Nigeria-Biafra War.
6/15–20	Pompidou becomes president and Jacques Chaban-Delmas premier.
7/17	General Franco names Prince Juan Carlos as his eventual successor.
10/21	Willy Brandt becomes chancellor as SDP and FDP form coalition.
11/12	Solzhenitsyn expelled from Union of Soviet Writers.
11/19	My Lai massacre exposed.
1/15	Unconditional surrender of Biafra to Nigeria.
2/14	Tvardovsky removed from editorship of *Novy Mir*.
5/23–28	Portuguese troops destroy guerrilla center in Angola.
5/27	Gauche Prolétarienne (GP) banned by French government.

1970 6/11   Secours Rouge founded.
(cont'd) 6/20 and 26   Distributes *La Cause du Peuple* in the street.
          JULY   Visits Norway.
          SEPT.   Assumes nominal editorship of other extremist papers.
          10/21   Makes speech to Renault workers outside factory.
          12/12   Takes part in a people's trial charging state with responsibility for industrial accidents.

1971 1/15   Starts contributing regularly to new paper *J'Accuse.*
          2/13   Takes part in attempt to occupy Sacré-Coeur.
          2/18   Secours Rouge dissolved.
          APRIL   Breaks with Fidel Castro.
          5/14   *L'Idiot de la famille,* Vols. 1 and 2 published.
          JUNE   Takes over *Révolution* and helps to found Libération Press Agency.
          SUMMER   In Rome.
          11/7 AND 27   Joins in demonstrations against racism in Goutte-d'Or district.

1972 FEB.–MARCH   Gives long filmed interview.
          2/14   Ejected from Renault factory with group of militants.
          3/4   Attends funeral of Pierre Overney, Renault worker killed by guard.
          SUMMER   In Italy.
          NOV.   Starts conversations with Benny Lévy and Philippe Gavi.
          WINTER   Involved in preparations for launching daily paper, *Libération.*

1973 JAN.   Publishes "Elections, piège à cons" in *Les Temps Modernes.*
          FEB.   *Spiegel* interview condemning imprisonment of Baader-Meinhof gang.
          5/22   *Libération* begins publication.
          JUNE   Sartre's eyesight deteriorates.
          SUMMER   In Italy.
          AUTUMN   Benny Lévy becomes his secretary.
          OCT.   Moves from Boulevard Raspail to larger flat in Boulevard Edgar-Quinet.
          10/8   Sued by the weekly *Minute,* he appears in court and is fined one franc.
          DEC.   Campaigns to rescue *Libération* from financial problems.

1974 APR.   Recommends "revolutionary abstention" in elections.
          MAY   Publication of *On a raison de se révolter.*
          5/21   Withdraws from some of the extremist papers to which he had lent his name.
          SUMMER   Vacation in the south of France and Italy; records long interview with De Beauvoir.

6/12	Twelve Russians (including several Jews) try to hijack an airplane at Leningrad airport.
6/28	US troops begin withdrawal from Cambodia.
9/28–29	Nasser dies, succeeded by Anwar Sadat.
11/9	De Gaulle dies.
12/20	Gomulka replaced by Edward Gierek as first secretary.

2/5	US manned spacecraft *Apollo 2* lands on moon.
4/25	Two hundred thousand protesters march on Capitol in Washington, DC, against Vietnam War.
5/3	In East Germany, Ulbricht succeeded by Honecker as first secretary.
6/8	Sinyavsky released.
11/12	Nixon announces withdrawal of 45,000 soldiers from Vietnam and end of US offensive role.
12/3–17	Indo-Pakistan War.

2/25–27	Israel bombs southern Lebanon in reprisal for guerrilla raids.
5/1–15	Ulrike Meinhof and six other urban guerrillas arrested in West Germany.
5/22	Nixon visits Moscow—first US president to do so.
6/27	PCF and Socialists agree on joint policy.
7/5	Chaban-Delmas succeeded by Pierre Messmer as premier.
7/17–8/11	Trial of political dissenters in Prague: 46 of them jailed.
9/5	Terrorists kill Israeli Olympic athletes at Munich airport.
9/8	Israeli planes attack guerrilla bases in Syria and Lebanon.
11/7	Nixon reelected.
12/18–30	US resumes heavy bombing of North Vietnam.

6/30	Nixon makes television statement on Watergate and accepts responsibility for bugging.
8/6–8	Accidental US bombing of friendly villages in Cambodia.
10/6	Arab states attack Israel on Yom Kippur.
11/11	Israel and Egypt sign cease-fire agreement.

2/13	Solzhenitsyn deported and deprived of Soviet citizenship.
2/28	Heath succeeded by Wilson as minority Labour government takes office.
4/2	Pompidou dies.
4/25	Military coup overthrows Dr. Caetano's régime in Portugal.
5/8	Willy Brandt resigns after spying incident involving aide.
5/15	Civilian government installed in Portugal.
5/16	Helmut Schmidt becomes chancellor.
5/19	Giscard d'Estaing defeats Mitterrand in presidential elections.

| 1974 | NOV. | Plans for television series. |
| (cont'd) | 12/4 | Meeting with Andreas Baader in Stammheim prison. |

1975	4/6–13	In Portugal with De Beauvoir.
	MAY	*L'Arc* publishes joint interview with Sartre and De Beauvoir on feminism.
	6/21	Sartre's seventieth birthday: *Le Nouvel Observateur* publishes long interview with Michel Contat.
	9/21	Press conference on cancellation of television series.

1976	MARCH	Fifty Nobel prizewinners participate in Sartre's campaign to secure release of Mikhail Stern, political prisoner in USSR.
	3/14	Article on Pasolini published in *Corriere della Sera*.
	10/27	Film *Sartre par lui-meme* released in Paris.
	11/7	Accepts doctorate from Jerusalem University.

1977	6/21	Attends reception given at the Théâtre Récamier for Russian dissidents.
	SEPT.	Interview in *Lotta Continua.* Declares he is no longer a Marxist.
	OCT.–NOV.	Protests against "assassination" of Baader and his comrades.
	4/12	Publishes an appeal in *Le Monde:* Israel should respond to Sadat's peace initiative.

| 1978 | 2/2–7 | Visit to Israel with Arlette and Benny Lévy. |

5/27	Jacques Chirac becomes premier.
8/8	Nixon announces resignation; 9/8, Gerald Ford sworn in as president.

1/14	US–Soviet trade agreement falls through because USSR refuses to let Jews emigrate.
2/11	Thatcher becomes Conservative party leader.
3/12	In Portugal armed forces movement sets up supreme revolutionary council.
4/10	Giscard pays first state visit to independent Algiers.
4/17	Cambodia falls to Communist Khmer Rouge.
4/30	Unconditional surrender of South Vietnam to Vietcong.
5/21	Trial opens in West Germany of Baader and Meinhof.
6/5	Sadat reopens Suez Canal, closed since Six-Day War (1967).
11/20	Franco dies; 11/22, King Juan Carlos I sworn in.

4/15	In Spain general union of workers holds first congress in 44 years.
4/25	In Portugal first elections in 40 years; Socialist party victorious under Mario Soares.
5/9	Ulrike Meinhof found hanged in prison; leftist demonstrators riot.
6/16	In Soweto, South African police fire on protesting students.
8/25	Chirac resigns, replaced by Raymond Barre.
10/10	First elections in Cuba since Castro took power.
11/19	Algerians vote for new constitution with National Assembly and elected president.

1/20	Jimmy Carter becomes US president.
5/17	Israeli Labour party defeated after 29 years in office; Begin becomes prime minister.
5/24	In France 24-hour general strike against government's austerity program.
7/31	Twenty thousand demonstrators fight police at Creys-Malville nuclear reactor site.
10/18	Baader and two other terrorists found dead in Stammheim jail.
11/19–21	Sadat visits Israel.
12/2	Other Arab states unite against peace initiative.

3/12	In first round of French elections left wins absolute majority for first time.
3/19	In second ballot ruling, Gaullist coalition retains majority.
4/19	France explodes neutron device in Pacific.
5/15–18	Yuri Orlov, leader of group monitoring Soviet violations of human rights, tried and sentenced to seven years in labor camp.
9/5–17	Carter, Sadat, and Begin meet at Camp David.
9/20–29	Vorster resigns as South African premier; Botha succeeds him.
11/12	Anti-Shah riots in Iran.
12/15	Carter announces opening of diplomatic relations with China.
12/25	Vietnamese invade Cambodia to support rebels against Pol Pot.

1979	3/5	Speaks at colloquium organized by Benny Lévy and *Les Temps Modernes* for Israelis and Palestinians to discuss peace.
	JUNE	Françoise Sagan's open "love letter to Sartre" published in *Le Matin*.
	6/20	Takes part in press conference to help Vietnamese boat people.
	6/26	Received by Giscard d'Estaing with other delegates from committee helping boat people.

1980	3/10, 17, and 24	Conversations with Lévy published in *Nouvel Observateur*.
	3/20	Taken to Broussais Hospital.
	4/13	Sinks into coma.
	4/15	Dies at 9:00 P.M.
	4/19	Buried in the Montparnasse cemetery.
	4/23	Cremated at Père Lachaise; ashes buried again at Montparnasse.

1/16	Shah and family leave Iran.
2/1	Ayatollah Khomeini returns after 15 years of exile and takes power.
5/4	Thatcher becomes prime minister with majority of 44 seats in the House of Commons.
5/28	British government offers homes to 982 Vietnamese boat people.
6/7	Voting for first directly elected European parliament.
10/12	Castro addresses UN General Assembly.
10/23	Six Czech dissidents, including Václav Havel, sentenced.
12/25	USSR invades Afghanistan.

1/11	Castro and his brother Raul assume greater powers.
1/22	Dissident physicist Andrei Sakharov exiled from Moscow.
3/6	The first woman is elected to the French Academy—Marguerite Yourcenar.
5/6	After relaxation of emigration, 10,000 Cubans seek political asylum at Peruvian Embassy.

Abbreviations

ANAC	National association of Italian *cinéastes*
APL	Libération Press Agency
ASR	Action Socialiste Révolutionnaire
CFDT	Confédération Française Démocratique du Travail (second largest union, originally Christian)
CGT	Confédération Générale du Travail (largest union, dominated by the PCF)
CNE	Comité National des Ecrivains
COIC	Comité d'Organisation de l'Industrie Cinématographique
COMES	Congrès de la Communauté Européenne des Ecrivains
CP	Communist Party
CVN	Comité Vietnam National
EDC	European Defense Community
ENS	Ecole Normale Supérieure
FAC	Front pour l'Action et Coordination (antifascist organization)
FEN	Fédération de l'Education Nationale (main federation of teachers' unions)
FFI	Forces Françaises de l'Intérieur
FLN	Front de Libération Nationale
GP	Gauche Prolétarienne (Maoist amalgamation of UJC [ML] and M22M)
JCR	Jeunesses Communistes Révolutionnaires (Trotskyist)
JEC	Jeunesse Etudiante Chrétienne
MCF (ML)	Mouvement Communiste Français (Marxiste-Léniniste) (Maoist)
MFA	Armed Forces Movement (Portuguese)
MRP	Movement Républicain Populaire
M22M	Mouvement du 22 Mars (Maoist)
NRF	*Nouvelle Revue Française*
OAS	Organisation de l'Armée Secrète
PCF	Parti Communiste Français
RDA	Révolution Démocratique Africaine
RDR	Rassemblement Démocratique Révolutionnaire
RNP	Rassemblement Nationale Populaire
RPF	Rassemblement du Peuple Français (Gaullist)
SFIO	Section Française de l'Internationale Ouvrière

SNESUP	Syndicate National de l'Enseignement Supérieur (university teachers' union, controlled by left)
TNP	Théâtre National Populaire
UEC	Union des Etudiants Communistes
UJC (ML)	Union des Jeunes Communistes (Marxistes-Léninistes) (Maoist)
UJRF	Union de la Jeunesse Républicaine de la France
UNEF	Union Nationale des Etudiants de France
UNR	Union for the New Republic
VLR	Vive la Révolution (libertarian)

Notes

FREQUENTLY CITED WORKS

Carnets	Sartre, *Les Carnets de la drôle de guerre*
Cérémonie	De Beauvoir, *La Cérémonie des adieux*
Critique 1	Sartre, *Critique de la raison dialectique,* Part 1 (1960)
Critique 2	Sartre, *Critique de la raison dialectique,* Part 2 (1986)
Ecrits	Contat and Rybalka, *Les Ecrits de Sartre*
Force de l'âge	De Beauvoir, *La Force de l'âge*
Force des choses	De Beauvoir, *La Force des choses*
Idiot	Sartre, *L'Idiot de la famille*
Jeune fille rangée	De Beauvoir, *Mémoires d'une jeune fille rangée*
LC	Sartre, *Lettres au Castor et à quelques autres*
Astruc	*Sartre par lui-même* (film interview)
LTM	*Les Tempe Modernes*
Mots	Sartre, *Les Mots*
OR	Sartre, *Oeuvres romanesques*
Situations	Sartre, *Situations,* I-X
TCF	De Beauvoir, *Tout compte fait*

In the notes, an author's name followed by a page number refers the reader to an entry in the bibliography, pp. 535–540.

A page or chapter number standing alone refers to the work last cited above.

LIFE BEGINS TOMORROW

1. Michel Contat and Michel Rybalka, in *Le Monde,* April 17, 1980.
2. *Qu'est-ce que la littérature?*
3. *Questions de méthode.*
4. Scriven, p. 6.
5. Cau, p. 234.
6. Interview, *New Left Review,* Nov.–Dec. 1969.
7. Roland Barthes, *Le Degré zéro de l'écriture* (Paris, 1953), p. 43.
8. Cau, pp. 233–234.
9. Michelle Vian, interviewed by the author, July 2, 1985.
10. Cau, pp. 233–237.
11. Nietzsche, *Fenseits von Gut and Böse,* Sec. 6.
12. *Cérémonie,* p. 368.
13. *Critique,* p. 332.
14. *Carnets,* p. 175.
15. Jean Cau, interviewed by the author, July 6, 1985.
16. *Idiot,* Vol. 2, p. 1488.
17. Marcel Péju, interviewed by the au-

thor, June 28, 1985.

CHAPTER 1
POULOU

1. *Mots*, p. 11.
2. Cohen-Solal, *Sartre*, pp. 17–33.
3. Pp. 45–46.
4. P. 73.
5. *Mots*, p. 14.
6. De Beauvoir, *La Vieillesse*. Charles Schweitzer's identity is concealed under the name Durand.
7. *Mots*, pp. 17–18.
8. *Carnets*, p. 93.
9. *Mots*, p. 73.
10. P. 85.
11. Cohen-Solal, *Sartre*, p. 40.
12. P. 45.
13. *Carnets*, p. 100.
14. Cohen-Solal, *Sartre*, p. 56.
15. *Mots*, p. 60.
16. P. 109.
17. P. 174.
18. P. 182.
19. P. 186.
20. *Ecrits*, p. 22.
21. *Mots*, p. 189.
22. P. 190.
23. Cohen-Solal, *Sartre*, p. 26.
24. *Ecrits*, p. 22.
25. *Mots*, p. 191.

CHAPTER 2
NITRE AND SARZAN

1. *Baudelaire*, p. 21.
2. Interview with Jean Gérassi, *OR*, p. xxxviii.
3. Astruc, p. 16.
4. Interview, "Autoportrait à 70 ans," *Situations X*.
5. Astruc, p. 18.
6. *Cérémonie*, p. 197.
7. P. 192.
8. P. 403; interview, rptd. in Chapsal.
9. Astruc, p. 18.

10. Michel Guillet, "Jean-Paul Sartre au lycée," *Sud-Ouest Dimanche*, Oct. 25, 1964.
11. *Cérémonie*, p. 416.
12. Jeanson, *Sartre dans sa vie*, p. 291.
13. Ibid.
14. *Cérémonie*, p. 193.
15. Jeanson, *Sartre dans sa vie*, p. 292.
16. *Ecrits*, p. 511.
17. Astruc, p. 27.
18. P. 24.
19. *Cérémonie*, p. 374.
20. Astruc, pp. 19–20.
21. *Saint Genet*, p. 21.
22. *Cérémonie*, p. 186.
23. Astruc, p. 20.
24. *Cérémonie*, p. 167.
25. P. 374.
26. Cohen-Solal/H. Nizan, p. 33.
27. Astruc, p. 30.
28. *Cérémonie*, p. 167.
29. P. 166.
30. Preface to *Aden-Arabie*, rptd. in *Situations IV*.
31. Ibid.
32. Cohen-Solal/H. Nizan, p. 34.
33. *Ecrits*, p. 22.
34. Interview, in Schilpp.
35. *Ecrits*, p. 22.
36. *Jésus la Chouette*, rptd. in *Ecrits*, pp. 506–516.
37. Jeanson, *Sartre dans sa vie*, p. 285.
38. Nizan, *La Conspiration*, p. 46.
39. Georges Canguilhem, untitled article in collection of brief memoirs about Sartre's schooldays, in *Arts*, Jan. 11–17, 1961.
40. Preface to *Aden-Arabie*.
41. First chap. of *La Semence et le scaphandre*, in *Magazine Littéraire*, No. 59 (Dec. 1971).

42. Ibid.
43. *Jeune fille rangée*, pp. 440–444.
44. First chap. of *La Semence et le scaphandre*.
45. *Obliques*, No. 18–19.
46. Ibid.
47. Astruc, p. 24.
48. *Cérémonie*, pp. 178–179.
49. Ibid.
50. Cohen-Solal/H. Nizan, pp. 34–35.
51. *Libération*, édition spéciale Sarte (supplement to No. 1932), p. 18.
52. Astruc, p. 40.
53. Canguilhem, in *Arts*.
54. *Cérémonie*, p. 375.
55. Aron, *Mémoires*, p. 35.
56. *Cérémonie*, p. 181.
57. Preface to *Aden-Arabie*.

CHAPTER 3
SCHOOL FOR
SUPERIORS

1. Jeanson, *Sartre dans sa vie*, p. 289.
2. *Situations IV*, p. 149.
3. Cohen-Solal, *Sartre*, p. 95.
4. Georges Canguilhem, untitled article in collection of brief memoirs about Sartre's schooldays, in *Arts*, Jan. 11–17, 1961; "Paul Nizan," in *Situations IV*.
5. *Cérémonie*, p. 329.
6. P. 315.
7. Jean Fabre, interview, *Revue d'Histoire Littéraire de la France*, No. 6 (Nov.–Dec. 1975).
8. Canguilhem, in *Arts*.
9. Daniel Lagache, untitled article in

collection of brief memoirs about Sartre's schooldays, in *Arts*, Jan. 11–17, 1961.
10. *Cérémonie*, p. 409.
11. Library register of loans at the Ecole Normale.
12. "L'Enfance d'un chef," in *Le Mur*.
13. Ibid.
14. Library register of loans at the Ecole Normale.
15. "Paul Nizan," in *Situations IV*.
16. Cited by Jacqueline Leiner in *Le Destin littéraire de Paul Nizan* (Paris, 1970), p. 40.
17. Advertisement in *Europe* (Jan. 1925), cited by N. Racine, *Les Ecrivains communistes en France, 1920–36*, p. 213.
18. Letter from Louis Aragon and André Breton to Jacques Doucet, Feb. 1922, cited by Roger Garaudy, *L'Itinéraire d'Aragon* (Paris, 1961), p. 132.
19. Henri Lefebvre, *La Somme et le reste*, p. 389.
20. *Cérémonie*, pp. 234–235.
21. André Breton, *Les Pas perdus* (Paris, 1924), p. 206.
22. Lefebvre, p. 373.
23. Notebook in Henriette Nizan's archives; Leiner, p. 49.
24. *L'Oeuvre*, March 22, 1926, cited in Cohen-Solal, *Sartre*, p. 97.
25. *Cérémonie*.
26. *LC*, Vol. 1, pp. 28–29.

27. Ibid.
28. P. 30.
29. Ibid.
30. Cohen-Solal/H. Nizan, p. 48.
31. *Jeune fille rangée*, p. 321.
32. *Force de l'âge*, pp. 72–73.
33. Sartre, interview, *OR*, p. 1791.
34. Ibid.
35. *LC*, Vol. 1., pp. 15–16.
36. P. 10.
37. Pp. 10–11.
38. P. 12.
39. Pp. 12–13.
40. P. 13.
41. *Nietzsche: Sa vie et sa pensée* (Paris, 1920–31).
42. *LC*, pp. 12–14.
43. Ibid.
44. P. 15.
45. Pp. 16–17.
46. Ibid.
47. Ibid.
48. Ibid.
49. Ibid.
50. P. 18.
51. P. 20.
52. P. 22
53. Ibid.
54. Pp. 23–24.
55. P. 24.
56. P. 25.
57. P. 26.
58. Aron, *Mémoires*, p. 32.
59. "Paul Nizan," in *Situations IV*.
60. Ibid.
61. *Force de l'âge*, pp. 47–48. (Guille is called Pagniez.)
62. Pp. 39–40.
63. *LC*, Vol. 1, pp. 33–35.
64. *Force de l'âge*, p. 40.
65. *LC*, Vol. 1, p. 27.
66. Astruc, p. 38.
67. Alain, *Système des beaux arts* (Paris, 1920), p. 16.
68. Georges Dumas, *Nouveau traité de la*

psychologie, Vol. 2, p. 594.
69. Alfred Binet, *L'Ame et le corps* (Paris, 1908).
70. *LC*, Vol. 1, p. 27.
71. P. 886.
72. P. 888.
73. H. Nizan, interview, in *Arts*, Jan. 11–17, 1961.
74. *Force de l'âge*, pp. 73–74.
75. *LC*, Vol. 1, p. 32.
76. *Carnets*, p. 342.
77. "Paul Nizan," in *Situations IV*.
78. *LC*, Vol. 1, p. 34.
79. *Situations IV*, p. 147.
80. Canguilhem, in *Arts*.
81. Lagache, in *Arts*.
82. *Critique 1*, p. 22.
83. *Force de l'âge*, p. 47.
84. "Sartre et les femmes," interview in Muchnik.
85. *Ecrits*, p. 24.
86. Ibid.
87. *Force de l'âge*, p. 41.
88. Raymond Aron; interview with Jean Gérassi, *OR*, p. xliv.
89. Aron, *Mémoires*, p. 37.
90. *Les Nouvelles Littéraires*, Feb. 2, 1929.
91. Ibid.
92. *Force de l'âge*, p. 47.
93. Pp. 74–78.
94. Ibid.

CHAPTER 4
THE BEAVER

1. *Jeune fille rangée*, p. 330.
2. P. 335.
3. Pp. 440–445.
4. P. 454.
5. *Vogue* (July 1965), p. 72.
6. *Jeune fille rangée*, pp. 458–459.
7. P. 471.

8. Pp. 475–476.
9. P. 476.
10. P. 477.
11. P. 477–478.
12. P. 478.
13. P. 480.
14. P. 482.
15. Maurice de Gandiller, quoted in Cohen-Solal, *Sartre*, p. 116.
16. *Jeune fille rangée*, p. 482.
17. *Cérémonie*, p. 206.
18. *Jeune fille rangée*, p. 484.
19. P. 485.
20. Pp. 488–489.
21. Ibid.
22. *Force de l'âge*, p. 17.
23. P. 18.
24. Ibid.
25. Ibid.
26. P. 19
27. Ibid.
28. Ibid.
29. Pp. 19–20.
30. P. 21
31. P. 22.
32. P. 24.
33. Pp. 26–27.
34. P. 27.
35. P. 54.
36. *Jeune fille rangée*, p. 403.
37. *Force de l'âge*, p. 35.
38. Ibid.
39. P. 36.
40. P. 38.
41. P. 43.
42. *Carnets*, p. 96.
43. P. 98.
44. *Force de l'âge*, p. 33.
45. *LC*, Vol. 1, pp. 42–43.
46. *Cérémonie*, p. 408.
47. De Beauvoir, *La Vieillesse*, p. 347.
48. *Force de l'âge*, pp. 44–45.
49. *Carnets*, p. 109.
50. *Force de l'âge*, p. 46.
51. Pp. 46–47.
52. P. 49.
53. Ibid.

54. *Ecrits*, p. 53.
55. *Cérémonie*, p. 330.
56. P. 551.
57. *Force de l'âge*, p. 50.
58. Certificate found among the papers of Mme. Mancy, in *Ecrits*, p. xlviii.
59. *Force de l'âge*, pp. 80–81.
60. P. 82.

CHAPTER 5
PROVINCIAL SCHOOL-
MASTER

1. Aron, *Mémoires*, p. 82; Astruc, p. 49.
2. Jean Giustiniani, quoted in Cohen-Solal, *Sartre*, p. 126; Robert Marchandeau, *Bulletin des anciens élèves du lycée François I*, No. 75, in Cohen-Solal, *Sartre*, p. 126.
3. A. Dupuis, untitled article, *OR*, pp. 1678–80.
4. Cohen-Solal, *Sartre*, pp. 127–128.
5. Albert Palle, in *Arts*, Jan. 11–17, 1961.
6. Palle, interview with the author, June 21, 1985.
7. Ibid.
8. *Cérémonie*, pp. 403 and 410.
9. Pp. 330–332.
10. Pp. 252–254.
11. *Force de l'âge*, p. 83.
12. *Ecrits*, pp. 549–550.
13. *Force de l'âge*, p. 86; *Cérémonie*, p. 294.
14. Letter to De Beauvoir, *OR*, pp. 1687–88.
15. Ibid.
16. *Mots*, p. 135.
17. *OR*, p. 1687.
18. P. 6.
19. Pp. 1680–81.
20. P. 1681.
21. *Cérémonie*, p. 394.
22. *OR*, p. 22.

23. Alain Robbe-Grillet, *Le Monde*, Jan. 22, 1982.
24. *OR*, p. 1682.
25. Ibid.
26. P. 1683.
27. P. 1684.
28. Ibid.
29. *Force de l'âge*, p. 111.
30. P. 110.
31. *OR*, p. 1686.
32. P. 5.
33. *Force de l'âge*, p. 115.
34. *Cérémonie*, p. 254.
35. *Force de l'âge*, p. 113.
36. P. 114.
37. Ibid.
38. P. 372.
39. P. 119.
40. P. 121.
41. P. 122.
42. Ibid.
43. P. 128.
44. *Cérémonie*, pp. 406–407.
45. *Force de l'âge*, pp. 136–138.
46. P. 140.
47. Ibid.
48. *Critique 1*, p. 23.
49. Ibid.

CHAPTER 6
A GERMAN CREDO

1. *Force de l'âge*, p. 141.
2. Ibid.
3. P. 142.
4. Ibid.
5. *Situations I*, p. 25.
6. P. 17.
7. Pp. 18–22.
8. *Force de l'âge*, p. 143.
9. P. 145.
10. P. 146.
11. P. 333.
12. P. 149.
13. P. 151.
14. P. 153.
15. P. 154.
16. Jacques-Laurent Bost, in Astruc, p. 50.

17. *Force de l'âge*, p. 161.
18. *Carnets*, p. 100.
19. *Situations I*, p. 31.
20. P. 33.
21. Ibid.
22. "L'Ecrivain et sa langue," *Revue Esthétique* (July–Dec. 1965).
23. Edmund Husserl, *Cartesian Meditations*, trans. David Cairns (The Hague, 1960), pp. 24–25.
24. *La Transcendance de l'Ego*.
25. *LC*, Vol. 1, p. 361.
26. *OR*, pp. 25–26.
27. *La Nausée*, p. 141.
28. P. 232.
29. Heidegger, quoted by Sartre in *Esquisse d'une théorie des émotions*.
30. *La Nausée*, p. 180.
31. *Situations I*, p. 34.
32. *La Nausée*, p. 182.
33. P. 180.
34. Pp. 182–183.
35. P. 185.
36. P. 87.
37. P. 137.
38. P. 31.
39. P. 59.
40. *Carnets*, pp. 225–226.
41. Ibid.
42. *La Nausée*, p. 84.
43. P. 189.
44. Pp. 121–122.
45. *Force de l'âge*, p. 186.
46. P. 188.
47. Pp. 190–191.
48. *Force de l'âge*, p. 203.
49. *OR*, p. 1831.
50. *Carnets*, p. 320
51. *Cérémonie*, p. 396.
52. Ibid.
53. "Strictly Personal," *Harper's Bazaar* (1945), p. 1460.
54. De Beauvoir, *La Vieillesse*, p. 348.

CHAPTER 7
BACK TO BOUVILLE

1. Astruc, p. 51.
2. *Carnets*, pp. 100–101.
3. *Cérémonie*, pp. 419–420.
4. *Force de l'âge*, pp. 209–211.
5. Astruc, p. 42.
6. Ibid.
7. Daniel Lagache, untitled article in collection of brief memoirs about Sartre's schooldays, in *Arts*, Jan. 11–17, 1961.
8. *Force de l'âge*, pp. 216–217.
9. Ibid.
10. Pp. 217–218.
11. Astruc, pp. 53–54.
12. *Force de l'âge*, p. 218.
13. Ibid.
14. *Carnets*, p. 102.
15. P. 156.
16. Ibid.
17. *Force de l'âge*, p. 219.
18. P. 224.
19. *LC*, Vol. 1, pp. 60–61.
20. *Force de l'âge*, p. 255.
21. Interview with Michel Contat, *OR*, p. 1803.
22. Letter to De Beauvoir, July 1935, *LC*, Vol. 1, pp. 58–59.
23. *Force de l'âge*, pp. 226–228.
24. *Carnets*, p. 102.
25. Ibid.
26. *OR*, pp. 446–447.
27. *Force de l'âge*, p. 240.
28. Pp. 240–242.
29. Pp. 248–251.
30. P. 253.
31. Pp. 253–255.
32. P. 258.
33. *OR*, p. 270.
34. Pp. 258–262.

35. Pp. 264–265.
36. Pp. 266–267.
37. Chap. 11.
38. *Force de l'âge*, pp. 269–270.

CHAPTER 8
INTIMACY

1. *LC*, Vol. 1, p. 132.
2. *Cérémonie*, p. 410.
3. *Force de l'âge*, pp. 273–274.
4. *LC*, Vol. 1, p. 70.
5. *Ecrits*, pp. 555–556.
6. *Carnets*, pp. 182–183.
7. *Force de l'âge*, pp. 279–280; *Cérémonie*, pp. 232–233.
8. *LC*, Vol. 1, p. 90.
9. *Force de l'âge*, p. 294.
10. Pp. 287–289.
11. *OR*, p. li.
12. *Cérémonie*, p. 208.
13. *Force de l'âge*, p. 298.
14. De Beauvoir, interviewed by the author, May 1983.
15. *Carnets*, pp. 14–15.
16. *Force de l'âge*, p. 301.
17. *LC*, Vol. 1, p. 96.
18. P. 103.
19. Pp. 117–118.
20. P. 129.
21. Pp. 117–118.
22. P. 136.
23. P. 145.
24. P. 147.
25. *Carnets*, p. 234.
26. *Force de l'âge*, pp. 311–317.
27. *LC*, Vol. 1, p. 149.
28. P. 159.
29. P. 157.
30. *Force de l'âge*, p. 323.

CHAPTER 9
BREAKTHROUGH

1. *Carnets*, p. 102.
2. P. 305.
3. Pp. 300–302.
4. P. 302.

5. P. 303.
6. *Esquisse d'une théorie des émotions.*
7. *Force de l'âge,* p. 329.
8. Pp. 329–331.
9. *OR,* p. liii.
10. Pp. 1849–50.
11. *Situations II,* pp. 212–213, in *Ecrits,* p. 70.
12. *Force de l'âge,* p. 335.
13. *Ecrits,* p. 60.
14. *Vendredi,* May 6, 1938; *OR,* p. 1701.
15. *Ce Soir,* May 16, 1938; *OR,* p. 1701.
16. *Journal-Echo de Paris,* May 30, 1938; *OR,* p. 1703.
17. *Nouvelles Littéraires,* June 18, 1938; *OR,* p. 1703.
18. *Alger Républicain,* Oct. 20, 1938; *OR,* p. 1709.
19. *Force de l'âge,* p. 336.
20. *Situations I,* p. 29.
21. P. 8.
22. *Force de l'âge,* p. 337.
23. *LC,* Vol. 1, p. 180.
24. P. 184.
25. Ibid.
26. P. 185.
27. P. 187.
28. Pp. 188–189.
29. Pp. 190–195.
30. P. 194.
31. P. 199
32. P. 204.
33. P. 207.
34. P. 213.
35. *Force de l'âge,* p. 338.
36. P. 339.
37. *Carnets,* p. 234.
38. *Force de l'âge,* pp. 339–343.
39. Pp. 344–345.
40. Interview in *Marianne,* Dec. 7, 1938, in *Ecrits,* p. 65.
41. *Situations II,* p. 36.
42. Pp. 37–51.

43. *OR,* p. 1860.
44. Ibid.
45. Interview in *Marianne; OR,* p. 1698.
46. Interview in Roger Troisfontaines, *La Choix de Jean-Paul Sartre* (Paris, 1946), in *Ecrits,* p. 145.
47. *Force de l'âge,* pp. 356–362.
48. *LC,* Vol. 1, p. 218.
49. Sartre's blurb for *Le Mur* (1967), in *Ecrits,* pp. 69–70.
50. *Les Livres Littéraires* (June–July 1939); *OR,* p. 1817. *Le Figaro,* March 4, 1939; *OR,* p. 1812. *Le Temps,* March 30, 1939; *OR,* p. 1815.
51. *Alger Républicain,* March 12, 1939; *OR,* p. 1814.
52. *Force de l'âge,* p. 363.
53. *LC,* Vol. 1, pp. 177–178.
54. *OR,* p. 402.
55. De Beauvoir, interviewed by the author, May 1983.
56. *OR,* p. 436.
57. P. 437.
58. P. 438.
59. P. 442.
60. P. 466.
61. *Force de l'âge,* p. 367.
62. P. 370.
63. P. 371.
64. *LC,* Vol. 1, p. 228.
65. P. 229.
66. Pp. 229–230.
67. P. 232.
68. P. 234.
69. P. 235.
70. P. 240.
71. P. 241.
72. P. 239.
73. P. 242, and author's interview with De Beauvoir, May 1983.

74. *LC,* Vol. 1, pp. 242–243.
75. *Cérémonie,* pp. 385 and 400.
76. Pp. 395 and 400.
77. P. 393.
78. Ibid.
79. Pp. 398–399.
80. *Force de l'âge,* pp. 383–385, and *LC,* pp. 246–247.
81. *LC,* Vol. 1, p. 249, and *Force de l'âge,* pp. 383–384.
82. *Cérémonie,* p. 397.
83. *Force de l'âge,* p. 386.
84. *LC,* Vol. 1, p. 270.
85. P. 271.
86. De Beauvoir's diary, Sept. 1, 1939; *Force de l'âge,* pp. 390–392.
87. De Beauvoir's diary, Sept. 2, 1939; *Force de l'âge,* p. 392.
88. *LC,* Vol. 1, p. 274.
89. Ibid.

CHAPTER 10
THE WAR PROFITEER

1. *Cahiers,* p. 14.
2. Jules Romains, *Prélude à Verdun.*
3. *LC,* Vol. 1, p. 275.
4. P. 277.
5. Pp. 279–283.
6. P. 283.
7. Pp. 285–291.
8. Pp. 288–292.
9. Pp. 291–294.
10. Pp. 293–300.
11. P. 377.
12. Pp. 302–319.
13. *L'Etre et le Néant,* pp. 536–537.
14. *LC,* Vol. 1, p. 380.
15. Jean Pierre, "Réponse à Sartre" (unpubl.).
16. Diary entry, Sept. 14, 1939, quoted in *Force de l'âge,* p. 12.

17. *LC*, Vol. 1, pp. 301–321.
18. P. 389.
19. Pierre, "Réponse à Sartre."
20. *LC*, Vol. 1, p. 336.
21. P. 258.
22. P. 263.
23. P. 347, letter to Simone Jollivet.
24. P. 366.
25. P. 358.
26. P. 359.
27. P. 373.
28. Ibid.
29. *OR*, p. 446.
30. P. 523.
31. Interview with Christian Grisoli, *Paru*, No. 13 (Dec. 1943).
32. *OR*, pp. 507–508.
33. *LC*, Vol. 1, p. 304.
34. P. 389.
35. *Carnets*, p. 51.
36. P. 156.
37. *LC*, Vol. 1, p. 337.
38. Pp. 345–346.
39. P. 373.
40. P. 382.
41. Letter to De Beauvoir, Oct. 26, 1939, in *LC*, Vol. 1, pp. 377–380.
42. *Carnets*, p. 175.
43. *OR*, p. 625.
44. *Carnets*, p. 175.
45. P. 172.
46. *LC*, Vol. 1, p. 341.
47. P. 353.
48. P. 365.
49. P. 375.
50. P. 376.
51. P. 386.
52. P. 376.
53. P. 380.
54. Diary, Nov. 1, 1939, *Force de l'âge.*
55. *LC*, Vol. 1, p. 391.
56. P. 390.
57. P. 395.
58. P. 396.

59. P. 401.
60. P. 407.
61. P. 440.
62. Letter to De Beauvoir, Dec. 4, 1939, in *LC*, Vol. 1, pp. 457–459.
63. Letter to De Beauvoir, Dec. 12, 1939.
64. Ibid.
65. *Carnets*, p. 122.
66. Sartre gives the name as Mistler; according to Jean Pierre, the clerk's name was Selzer.
67. *Carnets*, pp. 120–121.
68. *LC*, Vol. 1, p. 407.
69. P. 414.
70. P. 425.
71. P. 427.
72. P. 441.
73. P. 446.
74. P. 447.
75. P. 443.
76. Pp. 465–466.
77. P. 467.
78. P. 465.
79. Jean Pierre, letter to Bernard Poirot-Delpeche (undated, un-publ.).
80. *LC*, Vol. 1, p. 469.
81. P. 492.
82. P. 496.
83. P. 497.
84. P. 490.
85. P. 500.
86. P. 518.
87. P. 506.
88. P. 518.
89. P. 549.
90. P. 548.
91. P. 533.
92. P. 538.
93. P. 548.
94. P. 478.
95. P. 552.
96. Pierre, letter to Bernard Poirot-Delpeche.
97. *LC*, Vol. 1, p. 537.
98. P. 555.

99. P. 556–557.
100. P. 567.
101. P. 543.
102. Pierre, letter to Bernard Poirot-Delpeche.
103. *LC*, Vol. 1, p. 563.
104. *Carnets*, p. 240.
105. Ibid.
106. P. 241.
107. P. 242.
108. P. 267.
109. P. 247.
110. *Force de l'âge, FA*, pp. 443–445.
111. *Carnets*, pp. 308–309.
112. Pp. 338–340.
113. *LC*, Vol. 1, p. 588.
114. P. 586.
115. P. 593.
116. *LC*, Vol. 2, pp. 90–91.
117. P. 89.
118. P. 94.
119. Ibid.
120. P. 98.
121. P. 110.
122. P. 107.
123. P. 111.
124. Ibid.
125. *Carnets*, p. 413.
126. P. 414.
127. *LC*, Vol. 2, p. 145.
128. P. 147.
129. P. 146.
130. P. 147.
131. P. 191.
132. P. 162.
133. P. 201.
134. P. 159.
135. P. 180.
136. Ibid.
137. Pp. 181 and 197; p. 195.
138. Pierre, "Réponse à Sartre."
139. *LC*, Vol. 2, p. 199.
140. Pp. 204–205.
141. Pp. 220–221.
142. P. 235.
143. P. 221.
144. Pierre, "Réponse à Sartre."

145. *LC*, Vol. 2, pp. 226 and 230.
146. P. 222.
147. P. 268.
148. P. 229.
149. Ibid.
150. P. 231.
151. P. 232.
152. P. 236.
153. P. 240.
154. P. 251.
155. Ibid.
156. P. 252.
157. P. 262.
158. P. 268.
159. P. 269.
160. Pp. 275 and 280.
161. Ibid.
162. P. 281.
163. Ibid.
164. P. 287; "La Mort dans l'âme," June 10–11, 1940, in *Ecrits*, pp. 638–649.
165. Pierre, letter to Bernard Poirot-Delpeche.
166. *Cérémonie*, pp. 489–490.
167. *LC*, Vol. 2, pp. 286–287.
168. "Journal de Mathieu," *LTM* (Sept. 1982).
169. *LC*, Vol. 2, p. 285.
170. P. 290.
171. Ibid.
172. P. 289.
173. P. 294.
174. P. 295.

CHAPTER 11
STALAG

1. *Ecrits*, p. 642.
2. *Situations III*, p. 34.
3. *LC*, Vol. 2, pp. 295–296 and 299.
4. Ibid.
5. P. 299.
6. Perrin, pp. 39–66.
7. P. 91.
8. Ibid.
9. *Ecrits*, pp. 565–633.
10. Perrin, p. 97.

11. Interview with Jean Gérassi, *OR*, p. lvi.
12. Perrin, p. 111.
13. P. 112.
14. P. 113.
15. *OR*, p. lxvi.
16. Perrin, pp. 115–120.
17. Pp. 127–128.
18. *LTM* (Sept. 1982).
19. Perrin, p. 127.
20. P. 146.

CHAPTER 12
IN OCCUPIED PARIS

1. *Situations IV*, p. 348.
2. Ibid.
3. Pryce-Jones, pp. 37–42.
4. P. 164.
5. *Force de l'âge*, pp. 492–494.
6. P. 494.
7. Astruc, p. 68.
8. J. B. Pontalis, interviewed by the author, July 3, 1985.
9. "Merleau-Ponty vivant," *Situations IV*.
10. Cohen-Solal, *Sartre*, p. 232.
11. Pryce-Jones, pp. 118, 228–229.
12. *Force de l'âge*, pp. 495–496.
13. Testimony of Simone Debout and Jean-Touissaint Desanti; Cohen-Solal, *Sartre*, pp. 234–235.
14. *Force de l'âge*, pp. 496–497.
15. Pp. 497–498.
16. Pp. 504–505.
17. Pp. 505–506.
18. Interview in *Avant-Scène*, May 1–15, 1968.
19. *Cérémonie*, p. 363.
20. *Force de l'âge*, pp. 506–509.

21. Pp. 509–511.
22. Pp. 511–516.
23. *Situations III*, p. 18.
24. P. 22.
25. Pp. 25–26.
26. Ibid.
27. Pp. 31–32.
28. *Force de l'âge*, pp. 515–520.
29. *Carrefour*, Sept. 9, 1944.
30. Henri Pétain, *La France nouvelle* (Paris, 1943), p. 167.
31. *Force de l'âge*, p. 521.
32. P. 511.
33. P. 509.
34. P. 511.
35. Marcel Péju, interviewed by the author, June 28, 1985.
36. Posthumously published interview, *Libération*, June 8–9 and June 10, 1985.
37. Testimony of Mme. Pierre Kaan and Pierre Piganiol; Cohen-Solal, *Sartre*, pp. 266–267.
38. *Force de l'âge*, pp. 530–531.
39. Pp. 533–534.
40. Pp. 533–535.
41. Pp. 535–537.
42. *L'Etre et le Néant*, pp. 561–562.
43. P. 563.
44. P. 639.
45. Pp. 640–641.
46. *OR*, p. 1033.
47. *Situations IV*, pp. 34–35.
48. *L'Etre et le Néant*, p. 134.
49. *OR*, pp. 1057–58.
50. Henri Bergson, "Essai sur les données immédiates de la conscience" (Paris, 1889), p. 99.

51. *L'Etre et le Néant*, p. 300.
52. Book review, in *New Statesman*, May 25, 1957, pp. 675–676.
53. George Steiner, *Heidegger* (London, 1978).
54. *L'Etre et le Néant*, p. 296.
55. P. 430.
56. P. 451.
57. P. 457.
58. P. 664.
59. P. 660.
60. P. 688.
61. P. 682.
62. P. 684.
63. P. 689.
64. P. 708.
65. Martin Heidegger, "Brief über den Humanismus" (Bern, 1947).
66. Ibid.
67. Ibid.
68. *L'Etre et le Néant*, p. 85.
69. *OR*, p. 1094.
70. "Un Nouveau Mystique," Oct.–Dec. 1943, rptd. in *Situations I*.
71. *L'Etre et le Néant*, p. 89.
72. *Situations I*, p. 23.
73. Heidegger, Section 40, *Sein und Zeit*, 12th ed. (Tübingen, 1972).
74. Ibid., Section 53.
75. *L'Etre et le Néant*, pp. 690–691.
76. *Sein und Zeit*, Section 60.
77. *L'Etre et le Néant*, p. 695.
78. Pp. 697–698.
79. *OR*, p. 1123.
80. Albert Camus, *Oeuvres complètes* (Paris, 1965), Vol. 2, p. 108.
81. *Situations I*, 113.
82. P. 115.
83. P. 121.

CHAPTER 13
THE FUTURE REAPPEARS

1. *Force de l'âge*, pp. 540–542.
2. Pp. 546–549.
3. *Cahiers Charles Dullin*, Vol. 2 (Paris, March 1966).
4. Ibid.
5. *Force de l'âge*, pp. 552–553.
6. P. 553.
7. *Paris Soir*, June 15, 1943.
8. Armory, in *Les Nouveaux Temps*, June 13, 1943.
9. "Oreste et la cité," *Les Lettres Françaises*, No. 12; rptd. in Michel Leiris, *Brisées* (Paris, 1966).
10. Charles Dullin, *Ce sont les dieux qu'il nous faut* (Paris, 1969).
11. *Force de l'âge*, p. 566.
12. Ibid.
13. P. 568.
14. *Ecrits, p. 101*.
15. *L'Etre et la Néant*, p. 276.
16. Pp. 444–445.
17. *Force de l'âge*, p. 576.
18. "Aminadab," in *Cahiers du Sud* (April 1943), rptd., in *Situations I*, p. 127.
19. *Force de l'âge*, pp. 569–570.
20. Maria Casarès, *Résidente privilégiée* (Paris, 1980), p. 232.
21. *Force de l'âge*, p. 584.
22. P. 587.
23. P. 590.
24. Ibid.
25. Pp. 591–593.
26. *Situations X*, p. 196.
27. Lottman, *Albert Camus*, p. 340.

28. *Saint Genet*.
29. *Force de l'âge*, p. 595.
30. Ibid.
31. *Critique 1*, p. 100.
32. *Situations X*, p. 106.
33. *Baudelaire*, p. 245.
34. P. 130.
35. *Carnets*, p. 381.
36. Pp. 308–309.
37. P. 381.
38. P. 391.
39. *Force de l'âge*, p. 597.
40. Spoken preface to Deutsche Grammophon recording of *Huis clos*, rptd. in *Un Théâtre de situations*.
41. *Force de l'âge*, p. 598.
42. P. 599.
43. Pp. 599–600.
44. Sartre, "Colère d'une ville," *Combat*, Aug. 30, 1944, in *Ecrits*, pp. 103–104.
45. Sartre, "L'Insurrection," *Combat*, Aug. 28, 1944, in *Ecrits*, p. 104.
46. *Force de l'âge*, p. 608.
47. "Toute la ville tire," *Combat*, Aug. 31, 1944, in *Ecrits*, p. 104.
48. Sartre, "La Délivrance est à nos portes," *Combat*, Sept. 2, 1944, in *Ecrits*, p. 105.
49. "La République du silence," *Situations III*, p. 12.
50. Ibid., pp. 12–13.
51. *Les Mandarins*, p. 15.
52. *Force des choses*, p. 18.
53. *Réflexions sur la question juive*.
54. *Nouvel Observateur*, March 10, 1980.
55. Werner Cohn, "The 'Aryans' of

Jean-Paul Sartre," *Encounter* (Dec. 1981).
56. *LC*, Vol. 2, p. 25.
57. Sartre's blurb for *L'Age de raison*, in *Ecrits*, p. 113.

CHAPTER 14
MAKING A NEW START

1. Caute, pp. 36–37.
2. Pp. 44–45.
3. *OR*, p. 1921.
4. Pp. 1918–21.
5. "Volcano on Ice," a critical portrait of Raymond Aron. Presented by Richard Mayne and produced by Judith Bumpus, BBC, Radio 3, Jan. 14, 1985.
6. *Force des choses*, p. 27.
7. Ibid.
8. *Les Mandarins*, pp. 25–26.
9. Lottman, *Albert Camus*, pp. 184–185 and 346–347.
10. *Cérémonie*, p. 303.
11. *Situations III*, p. 113.
12. P. 114.
13. Pp. 122–123.
14. P. 93.
15. P. 118.
16. *Force des choses*, p. 45.
17. *Ecrits*, pp. 117–118.
18. *Force des choses*, p. 45.
19. *Situations III*, p. 75.
20. Testimony of Dolores Vanetti; Cohen-Solal, *Sartre*, p. 314.
21. *Le Figaro*, March 11–12, 1945, in *Ecrits*, p. 119.
22. *Situations III*, p. 108.
23. P. 81.
24. P. 85.
25. *Situations II*, pp. 246–247.

CHAPTER 15
CHIEF EXISTENTIALIST

1. *Force des choses*, p. 50.
2. *Les Mandarins*, pp. 204–205.
3. "Présentation des Temps Modernes," *Situations II*, p. 13.
4. P. 14.
5. Pp. 15–16.
6. "La Fin de la guerre," *Situations III*, pp. 63–71.
7. *Ecrits*, p. 131.
8. Pp. 129–30.
9. Pp. 128–129.
10. Interview with Sartre, in *Paru* (Dec. 1945); *OR*, p. 1912.
11. P. 1916.
12. Jean Pouillon, interviewed by the author, June 22, 1985.
13. *Situations II*, pp. 9–15.
14. Pp. 22–23.
15. Lévi-Strauss, inaugural lecture at the Collège de France, published as *Leçon inaugurale* (Paris, 1960).
16. Davies, "*Les Temps Modernes* and Anthropology 1945–81," p. 75.
17. *LTM* (Jan. 1946).
18. "Merleau-Ponty vivant," *Situations IV*.
19. *Cahiers*, p. 120.
20. Sartre, article in *Vogue; OR*, p. 1919.
21. "Merleau-Ponty vivant," *Situations IV*.
22. *LC*, Vol. 2, p. 332.
23. Pp. 850–851.
24. Cohen-Solal, *Sartre*, p. 365.
25. *Force des choses*, p. 82.
26. P. 87.
27. André Gorz, *Le Traître* (Paris, 1958).
28. Ibid.
29. *Cérémonie*, pp. 346–347 and 361.
30. Cau, p. 176.
31. "Matérialisme et révolution," *Situations III*.
32. *LC*, Vol. 2, p. 337.
33. Flanner, *Paris Journal 1944–65*, p. 73.
34. *TCF*, p. 105.
35. Olivier Todd, interviewed by the author, July 1, 1985.
36. Cau, pp. 234–237.
37. Jean Pouillon, interviewed by the author, June 22, 1985.
38. De Beauvoir, interviewed by the author, July 4, 1985.
39. *Force des choses*, p. 123.
40. Arthur and Cynthia Koestler, *Stranger on the Square* (London, 1984), pp. 68–70.
41. *Force des choses*, pp. 123–125.
42. *Ecrits*, p. 157.
43. *Force des choses*, p. 128.
44. Pp. 128–129.
45. *LC*, Vol. 2, p. 338.
46. *Force des choses*, p. 129.
47. P. 132.
48. Jean Cau, interviewed by the author, July 6, 1985.
49. Cau, p. 133.
50. *Force des choses*, pp. 125–126.
51. *LC*, Vol. 2, p. 336.
52. *Situations II*, p. 196.
53. *Force des choses*, pp. 140–142.
54. *Qu'est ce que la littérature?*, *Situations II*.
55. *Situations II*, p. 290.
56. P. 280.
57. P. 285

58. P. 305.
59. P. 308.
60. *Cahiers*, p. 120.
61. Interview in *Mondes Nouveaux*, Dec. 21, 1944.
62. *Cahiers*, p. 90.
63. Pp. 90–97.
64. P. 61.
65. P. 101.
66. P. 86.
67. P. 155.
68. P. 39.
69. P. 169.
70. P. 191.
71. P. 212.
72. *Cérémonie*, p. 512.
73. *Force des choses*, pp. 147–148.
74. Pp. 149–150.

CHAPTER 16
DEMOCRATIC
REVOLUTIONIST

1. Aron, *Mémoires*, p. 317.
2. Interview with Sartre, *Combat*, Oct. 18, 1947, in *Ecrits*, pp. 169–170.
3. *Ecrits*, p. 170.
4. P. 171.
5. P. 172.
6. Aron, *Mémoires*, p. 318.
7. *Ecrits*, pp. 195–197.
8. *Force des choses*, pp. 124–125.
9. Pp. 155–157, and Arthur and Cynthia Koestler, *Stranger on the Square*, pp. 70–71.
10. "Pour un théâtre de situations," *La Rue* (Nov. 1947), rptd. in *Un Théâtre de situations*.
11. Nathalie Sarraute, *International Herald Tribune*, March 17, 1984.
12. *Force des choses*, p. 158.
13. Greco, *Jujube*.
14. *Force des choses*, p. 159.

15. P. 161.
16. *Ecrits*, p. 205.
17. "Appel," in *Ecrits*, p. 198.
18. P. 200.
19. Flanner, *Paris Journal 1944–65*, p. 84.
20. *La Gauche*, May 15–30, 1948.
21. Interview, New York *Herald Tribune*, Paris ed., June 2, 1948.
22. *La Gauche* (July 1948).
23. Burnier, p. 55.
24. *Les Lettres Françaises*, Feb. 10, 1949.
25. *Le Monde*, April 17, 1980.
26. Interview, *OR*, p. 1915.
27. P. 1323.
28. P. 1337.
29. P. 1425.
30. *Cahiers*, pp. 211–215.
31. P. 265.
32. P. 268.
33. *OR*, p. 1426.
34. P. 1284.
35. Geneviève Idt, in *Obliques*, No. 18–19, p. 90.
36. *OR*, p. 1160.
37. *LC*, Vol. 2, p. 340.
38. *Force des choses*, p. 179.
39. *LC*, Vol. 2, pp. 340–344.
40. *Force des choses*, pp. 180–181.
41. David Rousset, interviewed by the author, July 5, 1985.
42. *Ecrits*, p. 209.
43. Ibid.
44. *OR*, p. 2147.
45. P. 1596.
46. P. 1498.
47. P. 1520.
48. P. 1522.
49. *Cahiers*, pp. 332–334.
50. Pp. 309–320.
51. Pp. 338–344.

52. P. 352.
53. P. 390.
54. Ibid.
55. P. 403.
56. P. 409.
57. P. 280.
58. P. 169.
59. Pp. 183–188.
60. P. 189.
61. P. 188.
62. *The Nation*, April 9, 1949, cited by Burnier.
63. "Défense de la culture française par la culture européenne," *Politique Etrangers* (June 1949), in *Ecrits*, pp. 212–215.
64. Note by Sartre, quoted in De Beauvoir, *Force des choses*, p. 194.

CHAPTER 17
COMMUNIST VALUES

1. Mary Welsh Hemingway, *How It Was* (New York, 1951), pp. 280–281.
2. Interview, *Franc-Tireur*, Oct. 24, 1949, in *Ecrits*, p. 219.
3. Interview, *Franc-Tireur*, Oct. 21, 1949, in *Ecrits*, p. 218.
4. Cohen-Solal, *Sartre*, pp. 437–438.
5. Letter to Simone Jollivet, in *LC*, Vol. 2, p. 346.
6. *Cahiers*, p. 501.
7. Aron, *Mémoires*, p. 198.
8. Interview in Chapsal.
9. "L'Engagement de Mallarmé," *Obliques*, No. 18–19, p. 192.
10. P. 177.
11. P. 190.
12. P. 182.

13. P. 190.
14. P. 188.
15. P. 186.
16. "Merleau-Ponty vivant," *Situations IV.*
17. Ibid.
18. *Le Monde,* Oct. 27, 1949, cited by Burnier, p. 64.
19. Arthur and Cynthia Koestler, *Stranger on the Square* (London, 1984), p. 71.
20. Letter to Simone Jollivet, in *LC,* Vol. 2, pp. 348–349.
21. *Force des choses,* p. 230.
22. Pp. 230–231.
23. P. 233.
24. Todd, p. 106.
25. *Force des choses,* p. 250.
26. "Merleau-Ponty vivant," *Situations IV.*
27. Ibid.
28. *Situations IV,* p. 240.
29. *Lebensbeschreibung Herrn Götzens von Berlichingen* (Nuremberg, 1731).
30. Jouhandeau, quoted by Sartre, *Saint Genet,* p. 213.
31. Interview in *L'Avant-Scène,* May 1–15, 1968.
32. Ibid.
33. Interview in *New Left Review,* No. 58 (1969).
34. Interview, *Samedi-Soir,* June 2–8, 1951, in *Ecrits,* p. 237.
35. "Merleau-Ponty vivant," *Situations IV.*
36. Note by Sartre, quoted in *Force des choses,* p. 262.
37. Cau, p. 251.

38. *Force des choses,* p. 256.
39. Ibid.
40. P. 258.
41. Cau, p. 239.
42. The passage from Odo of Cluny is quoted in *Un Théâtre de situations* but is omitted from the standard translation of Huizinga's *The Waning of the Middle Ages.*
43. *Force des choses,* p. 260.
44. Jeanson, *Le Problème moral,* p. 159.
45. "Merleau-Ponty vivant," *Situations IV.*
46. *Force des choses,* p. 268.
47. Todd, p. 58.
48. Marcel Péju, interviewed by the author, June 28, 1985.
49. Lottman, *Albert Camus,* p. 496.
50. P. 500.
51. *Saint Genet,* p. 265.
52. P. 341
53. P. 512.
54. *Situations I,* p. 31.
55. *Saint Genet,* p. 363.
56. Pp. 364–365.
57. P. 512.
58. P. 421.
59. Ibid.
60. P. 500.
61. P. 289.
62. Pp. 304–305.
63. P. 81.
64. Angelo Hesnard, *L'Univers morbide* (Paris, 1948), p. 180, quoted by Collins, p. 95.
65. *Le Mur,* p. 165. The relevance of this was spotted by Pacaly, p. 246.
66. *Saint Genet,* p. 487.
67. P. 491.
68. P. 487.
69. P. 486.
70. P. 488.

71. P. 516.
72. P. 550.
73. Ibid.
74. Cocteau, pp. 314–318.
75. *Force des choses,* p. 275.
76. P. 273.
77. Cau, p. 234.
78. Pp. 229–257.

CHAPTER 18
UNDER OATH TO HATE

1. *Ecrits,* p. 261.
2. *L'Affaire Henri Martin* (1952).
3. Lottman, *Albert Camus,* p. 498.
4. *Force des choses,* p. 279.
5. Lottman, *Albert Camus,* p. 500.
6. *Force des choses,* p. 279, and *Ecrits,* p. 250.
7. Ibid.
8. *LTM* (May 1952).
9. Casarès, cited by Lottman, *Albert Camus,* p. 502.
10. *Force des choses,* p. 278.
11. Michelle Vian, interviewed by the author, July 2, 1985.
12. "Merleau-Ponty vivant," *Situations IV.*
13. Jeanson, *Sartre par lui-même,* p. 91.
14. *Cérémonie,* p. 217.
15. *Situations IV,* p. 249.
16. *Force des choses,* p. 281.
17. *Situations VI,* p. 85.
18. P. 96.
19. Mark Poster, cited by Aronson, p. 219.
20. Burnier, p. 76.
21. *LTM* (Aug. 1952), rptd. in Albert Camus, *Actuelles 2* (Paris, 1953) and

in *Oeuvres complètes*, Vol. 2.
22. Jeanson's testimony, cited by Lottman, *Albert Camus*, p. 503.
23. "Réponse à Albert Camus," *LTM* (Aug. 1952), rptd. in *Situations IV*, p. 90.
24. *Situations IV*, pp. 91–92.
25. Pp. 108 and 100, fns.
26. Pp. 95–96.
27. P. 107.
28. P. 106.
29. P. 111.
30. Pp. 122–125.
31. P. 125.
32. Albert Camus, Diary, rptd. in *Oeuvres complètes*, Vol. 2.
33. *Ecrits*, pp. 251–252.
34. *Situations VI*, pp. 208–210.
35. P. 247.
36. Leon Trotsky, *Terrorism and Communism: A Reply to Karl Kautsky* (Ann Arbor, MI, 1961), p. 60.
37. *Situations IV*, p. 251.
38. Pp. 253–254.
39. Davies, "*Les Temps Modernes* and Anthropology 1945–81."
40. *Ecrits*, pp. 251–252.
41. Marcel Péju, interviewed by the author, June 28, 1985.
42. *Ecrits*, p. 257.
43. *Force des choses*, p. 310.
44. *Ecrits*, p. 255.
45. *Force des choses*, p. 311.
46. Cau, pp. 253–254.
47. *Situations IV*, pp. 257–259.

48. *LTM* (April 1953), pp. 1541–1629.
49. *Situations VI*, pp. 259–260.
50. Marcel Péju, interviewed by the author, June 28, 1985.
51. "Les Animaux malades de la rage," *Libération*, June 22, 1953, rptd. in *Ecrits*, pp. 704–708.
52. Aron, *Mémoires*, p. 308.
53. Jeanson, *Sartre par lui-même*, p. 78.
54. Program note, rptd. in *Ecrits*, p. 268.
55. Interview, *Les Lettres Françaises*, Nov. 12–19, 1953, rptd. in *Un Théâtre de situations*.
56. Ibid.
57. Interview rptd. in *Un Théâtre de situations*.
58. *Force des choses*, p. 319.
59. Ibid.
60. *Combat*, Oct. 31–Nov. 1, 1953, in *Ecrits*, p. 266.
61. Astruc, pp. 110–111.
62. *Cérémonie*, p. 275.
63. Marcel Proust, *Jean Santeuil* (Paris, 1952), p. 198.
64. Interview, *Le Monde*, June 1, 1955, in *Ecrits*, p. 386.
65. Interview, *The Listener*, June 6, 1957.
66. *Cérémonie*, p. 275.
67. P. 274.
68. Interview, *Le Monde*, June 1, 1955, in *Ecrits*, p. 386.
69. *Cérémonie*, p. 274.
70. Interview, *Le Monde*, April 18, 1964, in *Ecrits*, p. 387.

71. *Situations VI*, pp. 279–280.
72. P. 283.
73. Pp. 372–373, fn.
74. P. 350.
75. P. 382.
76. P. 334.
77. P. 353.
78. P. 351.
79. P. 352.
80. Merleau-Ponty, p. 138.
81. *Force des choses*, p. 327.
82. "A nos lecteurs," *LTM* (May 1954), in *Ecrits*, p. 277.
83. *Libération*, May 17, 1954, in *Ecrits*, p. 277.
84. Julius Fucik, *Ecrit sous la potence* (Paris, 1954).
85. *Force des choses*, p. 327.
86. Pp. 328–329.
87. *Libération*, July 5–19, 1954, in *Ecrits*, p. 279.
88. *Ecrits*, p. 280.
89. *Cérémonie*, p. 462, and Cau interview.
90. *Force des choses*, p. 331.
91. P. 333.
92. *Ecrits*, pp. 288–289.
93. *Situations VII*, p. 112.
94. *Ecrits*, p. 303.
95. Shusha Guppy, conversation with the author, 1985.
96. *Force des choses*, p. 347.
97. P. 348.
98. *Ecrits*, pp. 287–288.
99. *Force des choses*, p. 354.
100. "La Chine que j'ai vue," *France-Observateur*, Dec. 18, 1955, in *Ecrits*, pp. 292–293.

101. Ibid.
102. *Force des choses,* pp. 355–356.
103. Pp. 356–357.
104. Pp. 357–358.
105. Marcel Péju, interviewed by the author, June 25, 1985.
106. "Colonialisme et guerre d'Algérie," *LTM* (March–April 1956), in *Situations V* and *Ecrits,* p. 297.
107. Todd, p. 143.
108. *Situations VII,* p. 109.
109. P. 113.
110. P. 111.
111. Ibid.
112. P. 113.
113. Pp. 110–111.
114. P. 117.
115. *The Observer,* March 25, 1956, cited in Caute, p. 224.
116. Roger Garaudy, "A propos d'un article de Jean-Paul Sartre sur Pierre Hervé," *La Nouvelle Critique* (May 1956), cited in Caute, p. 255.
117. *LC,* Vol. 2, p. 327.
118. *Situations IV,* p. 280.
119. Ibid.
120. *Ecrits,* p. 301.
121. Ibid.
122. P. 304.
123. P. 303.
124. *Force des choses,* p. 373.
125. András Hegedüs, *Memoirs.*
126. *LTM,* No. 129–131 (1956–57), p. 678.
127. *Force des choses,* p. 382.
128. *L'Express,* Nov. 9, 1956, in *Ecrits,* pp. 305–306.

129. *Force des choses,* p. 384.
130. *Situations VII,* p. 158.
131. P. 219.
132. P. 217.
133. P. 191.
134. P. 188.
135. P. 193.
136. P. 257.
137. Pp. 162–163.
138. P. 271.
139. "Le Fântome de Staline," *Situations VII.*
140. Caute, p. 227.
141. Burnier, p. 105.
142. *Situations VII,* p. 290.
143. P. 307.
144. *L'Humanité,* Nov. 5, 1956; Caute, p. 230.

CHAPTER 19
BACK TO PHILOSOPHY

1. Preface to *Critique 1.*
2. *LTM* (Feb.–March, 1957).
3. *LTM* (May 1957), rptd. in *Situations V.*
4. *Force des choses,* p. 392.
5. *Le Monde,* May 14, 1971.
6. See p. 157.
7. Olivier Todd, interviewed by the author, June 16, 1985.
8. "Le Séquestré de Venise," *Situations IV.*
9. Ibid.
10. "Des Rats et des hommes," *Situations IV.*
11. Ibid.
12. *Critique 1,* p. 48.
13. P. 47.
14. *LTM* (Sept.–Oct. 1957), rptd. as "Questions de Méthode" in *Critique 1.*

15. *Word: Journal of the Linguistic Circle of New York* (Aug. 1945).
16. *Situations X,* pp. 149–150.
17. *Critique 1,* p. 28.
18. P. 40.
19. Ibid.
20. P. 17.
21. Ibid.
22. P. 18.
23. P. 28.
24. Pp. 41–42, fn.
25. Henri Lefebvre, "Perspectives de sociologie rurale," *Cahiers de Sociologie* (1953).
26. *L'Etre et le Néant,* p. 537.
27. P. 536.
28. Claude Lévi-Strauss, "Histoire et ethnologie," *Revue de Métaphysique et de morale,* Nos. 3–4 (1949), rptd. as introduction to *Anthropologie structurelle* (Paris, 1958).
29. Marx, *Das Kapital,* Vol. III.
30. *Critique 1,* p. 32.
31. Burnier, p. 120.
32. P. 114.
33. *Situations V,* p. 52.
34. P. 55.
35. Ibid.
36. *Force des choses,* p. 403.
37. P. 404.
38. *Situations V,* p. 70.
39. P. 86.
40. *Force des choses,* p. 407.
41. *Cérémonie,* pp. 404–406.
42. Interview, rptd. in Chapsal.
43. *Critique 1,* p. 142.
44. P. 125, fn.
45. P. 369.
46. Pp. 453–454.
47. P. 144.
48. P. 442.
49. P. 431.

50. P. 454.
51. *Critique 1*, p. 74, including fn.
52. Lévi-Strauss, Chap. 9.
53. Davies, "*Les Temps Modernes* and Anthropology 1945–81," p. 261.
54. Lévi-Strauss, Chap. 4.
55. Ibid.
56. Davies, "*Les Temps Modernes* and Anthropology 1945–81," p. 266.
57. P. 308.
58. P. 290.
59. *Cérémonie*, p. 418.
60. "Le Prétendant," *Situations V*.
61. De Beauvoir diary, May, 27 (1958); *Force des choses*, p. 414.
62. "Le Théâtre peut-il aborder l'actualité politique?" *France-Observateur*, Feb. 13, 1958, rptd. in Arthur Adamov, *Ici et maintenant* (Paris, 1964).

CHAPTER 20
FREUDIAN INTERLUDE

1. De Beauvoir diary, June 3 (1958); *Force des choses*, p. 428.
2. De Beauvoir diary, June 16 (1958); *Force des choses*, p. 437.
3. *Situations X*, p. 150.
4. "Le Théâtre peut-il aborder l'actualité politique?" *France-Observateur*, Feb. 13, 1958, rptd. in Arthur Adamov, *Ici et maintenant* (Paris, 1964).
5. *Force des choses*, p. 475.

6. De Beauvoir diary, Aug. 17 (1958); *Force des choses*, p. 455.
7. *Le Scénario Freud*, p. 531.
8. De Beauvoir diary, Sept. 23 (1958); *Force des choses*, pp. 466–467.
9. De Beauvoir diary, Sept. 29 (1958); *Force des choses*, p. 470.
10. *Force des choses*, pp. 473–475.
11. P. 476.
12. *Le Scénario Freud*, p. 535.
13. Interviews, "L'Ecrivain et sa langue," *Revue d'Esthétique*, Dec. 7, 1965; interview, rptd. in Chapsal.
14. Interview, rptd. in Chapsal.
15. *Ecrits*, p. 728.
16. H. Hamon and P. Rotman, *Les Porteurs de valise* (Paris, 1981), p. 158.
17. *Force des choses*, p. 491.
18. Cohen-Solal, *Sartre*, p. 495.
19. *Interview with Bernard Dort, rptd. in Un Théâtre de situations.*
20. Interview with A. Koehler, ibid.
21. *LC*, Vol. 2, p. 360.
22. Ibid.
23. P. 563.
24. P. 361 and *Force des choses*, p. 498.
25. John Huston, *An Open Book* (New York, 1980), pp. 289–296.

CHAPTER 21
UNOFFICIAL AMBASSADOR

1. Jeannine Gallimard's testimony.

Lottman, *Albert Camus*, pp. 661–664.
2. "Albert Camus," rptd. in *Situations IV*.
3. *Sartre on Cuba*, p. 7.
4. Pp. 8–10.
5. *France-Soir*, July 12, 1960, in *Ecrits*, p. 349.
6. *France-Soir*, July 9, 1960, in *Ecrits*, p. 348.
7. *Sartre on Cuba*, p. 94.
8. P. 98.
9. *France-Soir*, July 14, 1960, in *Ecrits*, pp. 349–350.
10. *Sartre on Cuba*, pp. 137–139.
11. *Cérémonie*, p. 503.
12. Interview, in *Nouvel Observateur*, Nov. 19, 1964, in *Ecrits*, p. 407.
13. *Force des choses*, p. 514.
14. P. 515.
15. Merleau-Ponty, Introduction, *Signes*.
16. *Le Semeur*, Feb. 7–8, 1960, in *Ecrits*, pp. 352–353.
17. *Les Cahiers libres de la jeunesse*, Feb. 15, 1960.
18. "Paul Nizan," *Situations IV*.
19. Ibid.
20. Ibid.
21. Merleau-Ponty, Introduction, *Signes*.
22. Ibid.
23. *Force des choses*, p. 516.
24. P. 522.
25. J. G. Weightman, *Encounter* (June 1961); *Force des choses*, p. 523.
26. *Critique 2*, typescript, p. 20.
27. *Critique 1*, p. 131.
28. *Critique 2*, typescript, p. 20.
29. P. 59.

30. Pp. 78, 102, and 41.
31. P. 291.
32. P. 212.
33. P. 317.
34. P. 379.
35. Pp. 393–394.
36. P. 409.
37. Pp. 415 and 450.
38. P. 460.
39. P. 435.
40. P. 466.
41. Pp. 471 and 488.
42. P. 490.
43. P. 505.
44. P. 526.
45. P. 500.
46. Ibid.
47. Ibid.
48. Michel, pp. 52–53.
49. P. 24.
50. Interview, *Obliques*, No. 18–19, p. 14.
51. Interview, *New Left Review*, No. 58.
52. *Ecrits*, p. 359.
53. *Force des choses*, p. 526.
54. P. 534.
55. Interview, *Verité-Liberté* (July–Aug. 1960), in *Ecrits*, p. 356.
56. *Force des choses*, p. 536.
57. P. 540.
58. P. 541.
59. P. 543.
60. Pp. 541–546.
61. P. 554.
62. P. 559.
63. P. 563.
64. Pp. 563–564.
65. H. Hamon and P. Rotman, *Les Porteurs de valise* (Paris, 1981), pp. 300–306.
66. *Le Figaro*, Sept. 21, 1960.
67. *Force des choses*, p. 574.
68. Ibid.
69. P. 577.
70. P. 579.
71. P. 594.
72. P. 597.
73. Interview with Laszlo Robert, *The New Hungarian Quarterly*, Dec. 10, 1982.

CHAPTER 22
"KILL SARTRE"

1. Michel, p. 64.
2. *Force des choses*, p. 603.
3. Ibid.
4. *LTM.*
5. Interview, *L'Express*, Jan. 4, 1961, rptd. in *Situations V*.
6. *L'Arc*, No. 30, 1966.
7. *Interview, France-Observateur*, May 8, 1961, in *Ecrits*, p. 366.
8. *Force des choses*, p. 617.
9. P. 618.
10. P. 620.
11. P. 622.
12. P. 624.
13. *Cahiers*, p. 191.
14. Preface to *Les Damnés de la terre*, rptd. in *Situations V*, p. 174.
15. Regis Debray, cited by Cohen-Solal, *Sartre*, p. 576.
16. Flanner, *Paris Journal 1944–65*, p. 512.
17. *Force des choses*, pp. 626–627.
18. "Merleau-Ponty" (first version), trans. William S. Hamrick, in *The Review of Metaphysics* (Washington, DC, March 1984).
19. *Force des choses*, p. 631.
20. P. 633.
21. P. 636.
22. P. 639.
23. P. 647.
24. "Albert Schweitzer 1875–1975," catalogue of exhibition at National and University Library of Strasbourg, *OR*, p. lxxxii.
25. *Force des choses*, p. 640.
26. P. 641.
27. Pp. 646–647.
28. P. 650.
29. Interview, in *La Voie Communiste* (June–July 1962), in *Ecrits*, pp. 378–379.
30. *Situations V*, pp. 176–185.
31. *Situations X*, p. 221.
32. *Force des choses*, pp. 654–657.
33. P. 662.
34. P. 665.
35. Pp. 665–666.
36. "La Démilitarisation de la culture," *Situations VII*, pp. 326–327.
37. *Le Figaro*, Nov. 20, 1962, in *Ecrits*, p. 367.
38. *TCF*, p. 320.
39. Jean Pouillon, interviewed by the author, June 22, 1985.

CHAPTER 23
WRITING IS NEUROSIS

1. *Cérémonie*, p. 275.
2. Interview, *Le Monde*, April 18, 1964, in *Ecrits*, pp. 387 and 398.
3. *Mots*, p. 57.
4. P. 23.
5. P. 22.
6. This point has been made by Howard Davies in Jameson, *Sartre after Sartre*.
7. *Mots*, p. 21
8. *Novy Mir*, Oct 10, 1964, in *Ecrits*, p. 388.
9. *Mots*, p. 11.
10. P. 137.
11. P. 111.
12. P. 161.

13. Pp. 127–128.
14. Pp. 131–132.
15. *La Nausée*, pp. 60–61.
16. *Mots*, p. 84.
17. P. 136.
18. P. 113.
19. P. 125.
20. *Cérémonie*, p. 276; *Mots*, p. 275; *Novy Mir*, Oct. 10, 1964.
21. "La Pensée politique de Patrice Lumumba," *Présence Africaine* (July–Aug. 1963); *Situations V*.
22. *TCF*, pp. 321–322.
23. Pp. 322–326.
24. Interview, *La Nouvelle Critique* (June–July 1964), in *Ecrits*, pp. 399–400.
25. "Kafka 10 ans après," *LTM* (July 1973), cited in *OR*, p. lxxxiv.
26. *Ecrits*, p. 399.
27. *Situations V*, p. 172.
28. P. 189.
29. Flanner, *Paris Journal 1944–65*, pp. 589–590.
30. Speech, rptd. in *Kierkegaard vivant* (Paris: UNESCO, 1966).
31. Ibid.
32. Ibid.
33. *Ecrits*, p. 425.
34. "Détermination et liberté," *Ecrits*, pp. 735–745.
35. *TCF*, pp. 338–339.
36. *Un Théâtre de situations*.
37. *L'Humanité*, July 16, 1964, in *Ecrits*, p. 400.
38. *LTM* (Oct. 1964).
39. *Le Monde*, Oct. 24, 1964, in *Ecrits*, p. 403.
40. *Nouvelles Littéraires*, Oct. 29, 1964, in *Ecrits*, p. 405.
41. *La Brèche* (Dec. 1964), in *Ecrits*, p. 405.
42. *TCF*, p. 138.
43. Interview, in *Nouvel Observateur*, Oct. 24, 1964, in *Ecrits*, pp. 405–406.
44. Cohen-Solal, *Sartre*, p. 585.
45. *TCF*, p. 216.
46. "Pourquoi je refuse d'aller aux Etats-Unis," *Nouvel Observateur*, April 1, 1965, in *Ecrits*, pp. 412–413.
47. "Up All Night," *The Nation*, May 31, 1965, in *Ecrits*, p. 416.

CHAPTER 24
HALFWAY TO REVOLUTION

1. *Nouvel Observateur*, June 17, 1965, in *Ecrits*, p. 417.
2. *Nouvel Observateur*, June 24, 1965, in *Ecrits*, p. 417.
3. Davies, "*Les Temps Modernes* and Anthropology 1945–81," p. 283.
4. Hirsh, pp. 143–145 and 155.
5. *TCF*, pp. 351–353.
6. P. 351.
7. P. 356.
8. "Avant-garde? De quoi et de qui?" *Nouvel Observateur*, Sept. 20–Oct 6, 1965, in *Ecrits*, pp. 421–422.
9. Interviews in various Greek daily papers, Nov. 9, 1965, and in *Le Monde*, Nov. 10, 1965, in *Ecrits*, p. 422.
10. *Le Monde*, Dec. 4, 1965, in *Ecrits*, pp. 422–423.
11. *Situations IX*, pp. 48–49.
12. *Cahiers de Philosophie* (Feb. 1966), in *Ecrits*, pp. 429–430.
13. *L'Arc* (Oct. 1966), in *Ecrits*, pp. 433–434.
14. Henry James, *The Art of Fiction* (New York, 1948), pp. 126 and 131.
15. *La Nausée*, p. 26.
16. Letter to George and Thomas Keats, Dec. 22, 1817, *The Letters of John Keats*, ed. Maurice Buxton Forman, 4th ed. (London, 1952), p. 71.
17. *Idiot*, p. 657.
18. Cohen-Solal, *Sartre*, p. 42.
19. *The New York Times*, Dec. 31, 1961, cited by Poster, p. 386.
20. *TCF*, pp. 279–284.
21. Pp. 285–296.
22. P. 377.
23. Interview, in *Al Ahram* (Cairo), Dec. 25, 1965, in *Ecrits*, pp. 440–441.
24. *TCF*, pp. 403–415.
25. Pp. 415–423.
26. Pp. 423–442.
27. *Le Monde*, June 1, 1967, in *Ecrits*, p. 444.
28. *Nouvel Observateur*, April 26–May 3, 1966, in *Ecrits*, p. 447.
29. *TCF*, pp. 383–384.
30. *Tribunal Russell: Le jugement de Stockholm* (Paris, 1967), in *Ecrits*, pp. 447–448.
31. *TCF*, pp. 385–389.
32. Interview, in *Nouvel Observateur*, May 24–30, 1967, in *Ecrits*, p. 448.
33. *L'Unità*, Sept. 3, 1967, in *Ecrits*, p. 451.

34. *TCF*, pp. 391–392.
35. P. 393.
36. P. 395.
37. "Le Genocide,"
    LTM (Dec. 1967).
38. *Granma* (Havana,
    Jan. 1968), in
    Ecrits, pp. 459–466.
39. *Ecrits*, p. 460.
40. Daniel Cohn-Ben-
    dit, *The French Stu-
    dent Revolt*, trans. B.
    Brewster (New
    York, 1968), p. 58.
41. *TCF*, pp. 469–470.
42. *Le Monde*, May 8,
    1968, in *Ecrits*, pp.
    462–463.
43. *Le Monde*, May 10,
    1968, in *Ecrits*, p.
    463.
44. *Ecrits*, pp. 463–464.
45. J. Besançon, *Les
    Murs ont la parole*
    (Paris, 1948), cited
    by Hirsh, p. 140.
46. *TCF*, pp. 469–470.
47. P. 470.
48. *Situations X*, p. 184.
49. Flanner, *Paris Jour-
    nal 2, 1965–71*, p.
    255.
50. *Nouvel Observateur*,
    special supple-
    ment, May 20,
    1968, in *Ecrits*, p.
    464.
51. *TCF*, p. 474.
52. *Le Figaro*, June 14,
    1968; *Nouvel Obser-
    vateur*, June 19–25,
    1968; both in
    Ecrits, pp. 467–468.
53. *Nouvel Observateur*,
    June 26–July 2,
    1968, in *Ecrits*, pp.
    466–467.
54. *Situations X*, p. 184.
55. *Der Spiegel*, July 15,
    1968, in *Ecrits*, pp.
    467–468.
56. *Paese Sera*, Aug. 25,
    1968, in *Ecrits*, p.
    470.
57. *Paese Sera*, Aug. 21,
    1968, in *Ecrits*, p.
    469.
58. *Cérémonie*, p. 8.

59. *Nouvel Observateur*,
    Nov. 4–10, 1968, in
    Ecrits, pp. 471–472.
60. *Le Monde*, Oct. 17,
    1968, in *Ecrits*, p.
    471.
61. *Le Monde*, Dec. 3,
    1968, in *Ecrits*, pp.
    472–473.
62. *TCF*, pp. 108–111.
63. *Ecrits*, p. 426.
64. *Idiot*, Vol. III, p.
    1753.
65. *Nouvel Observateur*,
    March 17–23,
    1969, in *Ecrits*, p.
    477.
66. "L'Homme au
    magnétophone,"
    Situations X.
67. Ibid.

CHAPTER 25
WITH THE MAOISTS

1. *Situations X*, pp.
   184–185.
2. *Le Monde*, Jan. 13,
   1970, *OR*, p. xcii.
3. *Le Monde*, May
   17–18, 1970.
4. *Nouvel Observateur*,
   May 24, 1970.
5. Lecture, "Justice et
   l'Etat," Feb. 25,
   1972, to Jeune
   Barreau, Brussels;
   Situations X, p. 67.
6. *Situations VIII*.
7. Lecture, "Justice et
   l'Etat," Feb. 25,
   1972, *Situations X*.
8. Ibid.
9. Ibid.
10. *Le Figaro Littéraire*,
    June 15–21, 1970.
11. Roland Castro, in-
    terviewed by the
    author, July 1,
    1985.
12. *TCF*, p. 481.
13. *L'Idiot Internationale*
    (Sept. 1970), rptd.
    in *Situations VIII*.
14. *Tout*, Sept. 23,
    1970.
15. *L'Idiot Internationale*
    (Sept. 1970).

16. Michel, p. 84.
17. Pp. 86–87.
18. *L'Idiot Internationale*
    (Nov. 1970).
19. *Cérémonie*, p. 11.
20. P. 12.
21. P. 14.
22. *Le Monde*, May 22,
    1971.
23. *Cérémonie*, p. 7.
24. P. 32
25. P. 34.
26. *Minute*, June 16,
    1971, cited in Con-
    tat and Rybalka,
    *The Writings of
    Sartre*.
27. *Cérémonie*, p. 34.
28. *Le Monde*, June 24,
    1971.
29. *Cérémonie*, p. 35.
30. P. 36.
31. *OR*, p. xcv.
32. *Le Monde*, Sept.
    26–27, 1971.
33. *Cérémonie*, pp.
    37–38.
34. P. 38.
35. *Situations X*, p. 52.
36. *Cérémonie*, p. 26.
37. P. 28.
38. Ibid.
39. P. 48.
40. *La Cause du Peu-
    ple/ J'Accuse*, No.
    25.
41. *Cérémonie*, p. 49.
42. Ibid.
43. Pp. 50–51.
44. Pp. 51–52.
45. Pp. 52–53.
46. Broadcast of Feb.
    7, 1973, cited in
    Contat and Ry-
    balka, *The Writings
    of Sartre*.
47. Serge July, inter-
    viewed by the au-
    thor, July 5, 1985.
48. Ibid.
49. *On a raison de se
    révolter*, pp. 17–18.
50. Interview, *Actuel*
    (Feb. 1973);
    Obliques, No.
    18–19, p. 336.
51. *On a raison de se
    révolter*, pp. 23–24.

52. *Situations X,* p. 81.
53. *Cérémonie,* pp. 38–39.
54. Pp. 39–42.
55. Pp. 42–46.
56. Pp. 67–68.

CHAPTER 26
FADING VISION

1. *The New York Review of Books,* April 19, 1973; *Obliques,* No. 18–19, p. 336.
2. *Cérémonie,* p. 49.
3. P. 69.
4. Pp. 48–51.
5. Michel, p. 102.
6. *Libération,* June 15, 18, 19, and 20, 1973; *Obliques,* No. 18–19.
7. *Libération,* June 29, 1973.
8. Michelle Vian, interviewed by the author, June 17 and 19, 1985.
9. *Cérémonie,* pp. 51–53.
10. Pp. 53–54.
11. Michel, p. 103.
12. *Cérémonie,* pp. 77–78.
13. Cohen-Solal, *Sartre,* p. 621.
14. *Cérémonie,* p. 77.
15. Pp. 79–81.
16. Pp. 82–83.
17. Michel, pp. 104–105.
18. Remark to Contat, *Cérémonie,* pp. 85–87.
19. P. 89.
20. Ibid.
21. P. 94.
22. *Situations X,* p. 214.
23. Interview, *Libéra-*

tion, April 13–14, 1974.
24. Remark to Contat, *OR,* p. xlviii.
25. *Cérémonie,* pp. 96–97.
26. *Situations X,* p. 152.
27. Charlesworth, p. 143.
28. *Cérémonie,* p. 97.
29. Sagan, p. 134.
30. Michel, p. 107.
31. *Le Monde,* April 17, 1980.
32. Cohen-Solal, *Sartre,* p. 631.
33. Interview, *Nouvel Observateur,* June 23 and 30 and July 7, 1975; *Situations X.*
34. Pierre Goldmann, *Souvenirs d'un juif polonais né en France* (Paris, 1975).
35. *Situations X,* p. 193.
36. Ibid.
37. Cohen-Solal, *Sartre,* p. 636.
38. Michel, p. 188.
39. *Cérémonie,* p. 99.
40. *Der Spiegel,* Dec. 2, 1974; *Obliques,* No. 18–19, p. 338.
41. Schilpp, p. 26.
42. Interview, Silverman and Elliston, p. 233.
43. *Cérémonie,* p. 114; *Obliques,* No. 18–19, p. 340.
44. *Cérémonie,* pp. 116–117.
45. *Libération,* Oct. 28, 1975; *Obliques,* No. 18–19, p. 350.
46. *Cérémonie,* p. 118.
47. *Corriere della Sera,* March 14, 1976; *Cérémonie,* p. 120.

48. *Cérémonie,* p. 121.
49. *Le Monde,* May 12, 1976; *Obliques,* No. 18–19, p. 342.
50. *Cérémonie,* pp. 125–126.
51. Pp. 124–125.
52. Pp. 127–128.
53. Pp. 128–129.
54. Pp. 129–130.
55. Pp. 130–131.
56. Pp. 131–132.
57. P. 133.
58. *Lotta Continua,* Sept. 15, 1977; *OR,* p. cii.
59. *Cérémonie,* p. 136.
60. *Lotta Continua,* July 15, 1977; *Obliques,* No. 18–19, p. 343.
61. *Le Monde,* Dec. 4–5, 1977.
62. *Cérémonie,* p. 140.
63. P. 139.
64. Interview, in *Obliques,* No. 18–19, p. 16.
65. *Cérémonie,* pp. 143–145.
66. Ibid., pp. 145–146, and Michel, pp. 121–122.
67. Sagan, p. 129.
68. Pp. 131–134.
69. *Cérémonie,* p. 115.
70. Todd, pp. 267–268.
71. Michel, p. 27.
72. Interview, in Silverman and Elliston, p. 239.
73. *Nouvel Observateur,* March 10, 1980.
74. *Cérémonie,* p. 157.
75. Michel, p. 30.
76. Ibid., pp. 30–38; *Cérémonie,* pp. 157–159.

Bibliography

SARTRE'S WORKS IN FRENCH

The publisher is Gallimard except where another name is given.

1936 *L'Imagination.* Presses Universitaires de France
1937 *La Transcendance de l'Ego.* Vrin
1938 *La Nausée*
1939 *Le Mur.* (In addition to the title story this contains "L'Enfance d'un chef,"
        "Intimité," "La Chambre," and "Erostrate."
        Esquisse d'une théorie des émotions. Hermann
1940 *L'Imaginaire*
1943 *L'Etre et le Néant*
        Les Mouches
1944 *Huis clos*
1945 *L'Age de raison*
        Le Sursis
1946 *L'Existentialisme est un humanisme.* Nagel
        Morts sans sépulture
        La Putain respectueuse
        Réflexions sur la question juive
        Baudelaire
1947 *Situations I*
        Les Jeux son faits. Nagel
1948 *Les Mains sales*
        L'Engrenage. Nagel
        Situations II
1949 *La Mort dans l'âme*
        Situations III
        Entretiens sur la politique (with David Rousset and Gérard Rosenthal)
1951 *Le Diable et le Bon Dieu*
1952 *Saint Genet, comédien et martyr*
1953 *L'Affaire Henri Martin*
1954 *Kean*
1955 *Nekrassov*
1959 *Les Séquestrés d'Altona*
1960 *Critique de la raison dialectique,* prefaced by *Questions de méthode*
1963 *Les Mots*

1964   *Situations IV*
       Situations V
       Situations VI
1965   *Les Troyennes*
       Situations VII
1970   *Ecrits de Sartre.* Ed. Michel Contat and Michel Rybalka. (In addition to
       the bibliography this contains the play *Bariona* and several previously un-
       collected pieces.)
1971   *L'Idiot de la famille.* Vols. I and II
1972   *Situations VIII*
       Situations IX
1973   *Un Théâtre de situations*
1974   *On a raison de se révolter* (with Philippe Gavi and Pierre Victor)
1976   *Situations X*
1977   *Sartre par lui-même* (transcript of sound track from an interview film
       directed by Alexandre Astruc and Michel Contat)
1981   *Oeuvres romanesques.* Ed. Michel Contat and Michel Rybalka, with Gene-
       viève Idt and George H. Bauer.
1983   *Les Carnets de la drôle de guerre*
       Cahiers pour une morale
       Lettres au Castor et à quelques autres. 2 vols.
1984   *Le Scénario Freud.* Ed. J. B. Pontalis.
1986   *Critique de la raison dialectique.* Vol. 2.

SARTRE'S WORKS IN ENGLISH TRANSLATION

FICTION

The Age of Reason. Trans. Eric Sutton. New York and London, 1947.
The Reprieve. Trans. Eric Sutton. New York and London, 1947.
Intimacy (Le Mur). Trans. Lloyd Alexander. New York and London, 1949.
Nausea. Trans. Lloyd Alexander. New York and London, 1949. Publ. in London
as *The Diary of Antoine Roquentin.*
Iron in the Soul (La Mort dans l'âme). Trans. Gerard Hopkins. London, 1950; New
York, 1951. Publ. in New York as *Troubled Sleep.*

PHILOSOPHICAL AND PSYCHOLOGICAL WORKS

Existentialism. Trans. Bernard Frechtman. New York, 1947.
Existentialism and Humanism. Trans. Philip Mairet. London, 1948.
Outline of a Theory of the Emotions. Trans. Bernard Frechtman. New York, 1948.
Psychology of the Imagination. Trans. Bernard Frechtman. New York, 1948; London,
1949.
Being and Nothingness. Trans. Hazel Barnes. New York, 1956; London, 1957.
The Transcendance of the Ego. Trans. Forrest Williams and Robert Kirkpatrick.
New York, 1957.
Sketch for a Theory of the Emotions. Trans. Philip Mairet. London, 1962.
Search for a Method. Trans. Hazel Barnes. New York, 1963.
The Problem of Method. Trans. Hazel Barnes. London, 1964.
Critique of Dialectical Reason, Vol 1: *Theory of Practical Ensembles.* Trans. Alan Sheri-
dan Smith. London, 1976.

BIOGRAPHICAL AND AUTOBIOGRAPHICAL WORKS

Baudelaire. Trans. Martin Turnell. New York, 1950.
Saint Genet: Actor and Martyr. Trans. Bernard Frechtman. New York, 1963.

The Words. Trans. Bernard Frechtman. New York, 1964:
Words. Trans. Irene Clephane. London, 1964.
The Idiot of the Family. Trans. Hazel Barnes. New York and London, 1982.
War Diaries. Trans. Quintin Hoare. London, 1984.

PLAYS
The Flies and *In Camera* (*Huis clos*). Trans. Stuart Gilbert. London, 1946.
The Flies. Trans. Stuart Gilbert. New York, 1947.
No Exit (*Huis clos*). Trans. Stuart Gilbert. New York, 1947.
The Respectful Prostitute. Trans. Kitty Black. London, 1947.
————. Trans. Lionel Abel. New York, 1949.
Dirty Hands. Trans. Lionel Abel. New York, 1949.
————. Trans. Kitty Black. London, 1949.
Men Without Shadows. Trans. Kitty Black. London, 1949.
The Victors. Trans. Lionel Abel. New York, 1949.
Lucifer and the Lord. Trans. Kitty Black. London, 1953.
Kean, or Disorder and Genius. Trans. Kitty Black. London, 1954; New York, 1960.
Nekrassov. Trans. Sylvia and George Leeson. Toronto, 1957; London, 1958; New York, 1960.
The Devil and the Good Lord. Trans. Kitty Black. New York, 1960.
Loser Wins. Trans. Sylvia and George Leeson. London, 1960.
The Condemned of Altona. Trans. Sylvia and George Leeson. New York, 1961.
The Trojan Women. Trans. Ronald Duncan. New York and London, 1967.

SCREENPLAYS
The Chips Are Down. Trans. Louise Varèse. New York, 1948; London, 1951.
In the Mesh (*L'Engrenage*). Trans. Mervyn Savill. London, 1954.
The Freud Scenario. Trans. Quintin Hoare. London, 1985.

ESSAYS AND INTERVIEWS
Anti-Semite and Jew. Trans. George J. Becker. New York, 1948.
Portrait of the Anti-Semite. Trans. Eric de Mauny. London, 1948.
What Is Literature? Trans. Bernard Frechtman. New York, 1949.
Literary and Philosophical Essays. Trans. Annette Michelson. New York and London, 1955.
Literary Essays. Trans. Annette Michelson. New York, 1957.
Sartre on Cuba. New York, 1961.
Essays in Aesthetics. Trans. Wade Baskin. New York, 1963.
Situations. Trans. Benita Eisler. New York, 1965.
The Communists and Peace. Trans. Martha H. Fletcher, with John R. Kleinschmidt. New York, 1968.
The Spectre of Stalin. Trans. Irene Clephane. London, 1969.
Politics and Literature. Trans. J. A. Underwood and John Calder. London, 1973.
Between Existentialism and Marxism. Trans. John Mathews. London and New York, 1974.
Sartre on Theater. Trans. Frank Jellinek. New York and London, 1976.
Life Situations: Essays Written and Spoken. Trans. Paul Auster and Lynda Davis, New York, 1977.
Sartre by Himself. Trans. Richard Seaver. New York, 1978.
Simone de Beauvoir, *Adieux.* Trans. Patrick O'Brian. New York, 1984.

BIBLIOGRAPHIES IN FRENCH AND ENGLISH
Contat, Michel, and Michel Rybalka, eds. *Les Ecrits de Sartre.* Paris, 1970.

Contat, Michel, and Michel Rybalka, eds. *The Writings of Sartre*. 2 vols. Trans. Richard McCleary. Evanston, IL, 1974.

Lapointe, François, and Claire Lapointe. *Jean-Paul Sartre and His Critics: An International Bibliography (1938–75)*. Bowling Green, OH, 1975.

Wilcocks, Robert. *Jean-Paul Sartre: A Bibliography of International Criticism*. Edmonton, Alberta, 1975.

SELECT BIBLIOGRAPHY OF WORKS ON SARTRE AND HIS BACKGROUND

Alleg, Henri. *La Question*. Paris, 1961.

Aron, Raymond. *L'Opium des intellectuels*. Paris, 1955.

———. *Les Marxismes imaginaires*. Paris, 1970.

———. *Histoire et dialectique de la violence*. Paris, 1973.

———. *Mémoires*. Paris, 1983.

Aronson, Ronald. *Sartre: Philosophy in the World*. London, 1980.

Barnes, Hazel. *Sartre*. New York, 1973.

———. *Sartre and Flaubert*. New York, 1982.

de Beauvoir, Simone. *L'Invitée*. Paris, 1943.

———. *Les Mandarins*. Paris, 1954.

———. *La Longue Marche*. Paris, 1957.

———. *Mémoires d'une jeune fille rangée*. Paris, 1958.

———. *La Force de l'âge*. 2 vols. Paris, 1960.

———. *La Force des choses*. 2 vols. Paris, 1963.

———. *La Vieillesse*. Paris, 1970.

———. *Tout compte fait*. Paris, 1972.

———. *La Cérémonie des adieux*. Paris, 1981.

Boschetti, Anna. *Sartre et Les Temps Modernes*. Paris, 1985.

Brée, Germaine. *Camus and Sartre*. New York, 1972.

Burnier, Michel Antoine. *Les Existentialistes et la politique*. Paris, 1966.

Camus, Albert. *Oeuvres complètes*, ed. Roger Quilliot. 2 vols. Paris, 1965.

Casarès, Maria. *Résidente privilégiée*. Paris, 1980.

Cau, Jean. *Croquis de mémoire*. Paris, 1985.

Caute, David. *Communism and the Intellectuals*. London, 1964.

Caws, Peter. *Sartre*. London, 1979.

Cazalis, Anne-Marie. *Les Mémoires d'une Anne*. Paris, 1976.

Chapsal, Jacques. *La Vie politique sous la Ve république*. Paris, 1981.

Chapsal, Madeleine. *Les Ecrivains en personne*. Paris, 1960.

Charlesworth, Max. *The Existentialists and Jean-Paul Sartre*. Brisbane, 1975.

Charme, Stuart L. *Meanings in the Studies of Lives: Sartre as Biographer*. Cambridge, MA, 1984.

Chiodi, Pietro. *Sartre and Marxism*. Trans. Kate Soper. Hassocks, Sussex, Eng., 1976.

Cocteau, Jean. *Journal: Le Passé défini*. Paris, 1984.

Cohen-Solal, Annie. *Sartre (1905–80)*. Paris, 1985.

———, with Henriette Nizan. *Paul Nizan: Communiste impossible*. Paris, 1980.

Collins, Douglas. *Sartre as Biographer*. Cambridge, MA, and London, 1980.

Colombel, Jeannette. *Sartre ou le parti de vivre*. Paris, 1981.

Cranston, Maurice. *Sartre*. Edinburgh, 1962.

Davies, Howard. *"Les Temps Modernes* and Anthropology 1945–81: A Contribution to the Analysis of the Sartrian Notion of 'Anthropologie Synthétique' " (unpubl. diss., Univ. of London, 1982).

Flanner, Janet. *Paris Journal 1944–65*. London, 1966.

———. *Paris Journal 2, 1965–71*. Ed. William Shawn. New York, 1971.

———. *Uncollected Writings*. New York, 1979.

Frears, J. R. *France in the Giscard Presidency.* London, 1981.
George, François. *Sartre.* Paris, 1976.
Goldmann, Pierre. *Souvenirs d'un juif polonais né en France.* Paris, 1975.
Goldthorpe, Rhiannon. *Sartre: Literature and Theory.* Cambridge, MA, 1984.
Gorz, André. *Le Traître.* Paris, 1958.
———. *Adieux au prolétariat.* Paris, 1980.
Greco, Juliette. *Jujube.* Paris, 1983.
Grisoni, Dominique, ed. *Politiques de la philosophie.* Paris, 1976.
Halpern, Joseph. *Critical Fictions: The Literary Criticism of Jean-Paul Sartre.* New Haven and London, 1976.
Hanley, D. L., A. O. Kerr, and N. H. Waites. *Contemporary France: Politics and Society Since 1945.* London, 1979.
Heller, Gerhard. *Un Allemand à Paris.* Paris, 1981.
Hirsh, Arthur. *The French Left: A History and Overview.* Quebec, 1982.
Hollier, Denis. *Politique de la prose: Jean-Paul Sartre et l'an quarante.* Paris, 1982.
Idt, Geneviève, ed. *Études Sartriennes I.* Paris, 1984.
Jameson, Frederick. *Sartre: The Origins of a Style.* New Haven, 1961.
———. *Marxism and Form.* Princeton, NJ, 1971.
———, ed. *Sartre after Sartre.* Yale French Studies No. 68. Binghamton, NY, 1985.
Jeanson, Francis. *Le Problème moral et la pensée de Sartre.* Paris, 1947.
———. *Sartre par lui-même.* Paris, 1955.
———. *Sartre dans sa vie.* Paris, 1974.
Johnson, Richard. *The French Communist Party Versus the Students: Revolutionary Politics in May–June 1968.* New Haven and London, 1972.
Lecarme, Jacques. *Les Critiques de notre temps et Sartre.* Paris, 1973.
Lejeune, Philippe. *Le Pacte autobiographique.* Paris, 1975.
Lévi-Strauss, Claude. *La Pensée sauvage.* Paris, 1962.
Lévy, Benny. *Le Nom de l'homme: Dialogue avec Sartre.* Paris, 1984.
Lottman, Herbert. *Albert Camus: A Biography.* London, 1979.
———. *Left Bank.* London, 1982.
McCarthy, Patrick. *Camus: A Critical Study of His Life and Work.* London, 1982.
McMahon, Joseph H. *Humans Being: The World of Jean-Paul Sartre.* Chicago and London, 1971.
Marcuse, Herbert. *Studies in Critical Philosophy.* Boston, 1973.
Merleau-Ponty, Maurice. *Les Aventures de la dialectique.* Paris, 1955.
———. *Signes.* Paris, 1961.
Michel, Georges. *Mes Années Sartre.* Paris, 1981.
Muchnik, Nicole, ed. *De Sartre à Foucault: Vingt ans de grands entretiens dans Le Nouvel Observateur.* Paris, 1984.
Murdoch, Iris. *Sartre.* Cambridge, Eng., 1953.
Nizan, Paul. *Le Cheval de Troie.* Paris, 1935.
———. *La Conspiration.* Paris, 1938.
Pacaly, Josette. *Sartre au miroir.* Paris, 1980.
Perrin, Marius. *Avec Sartre au Stalag XIID.* Paris, 1980.
Poster, Mark. *Existential Marxism in Post-War France: From Sartre to Althusser.* Princeton, NJ, 1975.
Pryce-Jones, David. *Paris in the Third Reich.* London, 1981.
Sagan, Françoise. *Avec mon meilleur souvenir.* Paris, 1984.
Schilpp, Paul-Arthur, ed. *The Philosophy of Jean-Paul Sartre.* La Salle, IL, 1982.
Schwarzer, Alice. *Simone de Beauvoir Today.* London, 1984.
Scriven, Michael. *Sartre's Existential Biographies.* London, 1984.
Seale, Patrick, and Maureen McConville. *French Revolution 1968.* London, 1968.

Sendick-Siegel, Liliane. *Sartre: Images d'une vie.* Paris, 1978.

Sicard, Michel, ed. "Sartre" and "Sartre et les arts." Two special issues of the review *Obliques,* No. 18–19 and No. 24–25, both undated.

Silverman, Hugh J., and Frederick J. Elliston, ed. *Jean-Paul Sartre: Contemporary Approaches to His Philosophy.* Brighton, Eng., 1980.

Singer, Daniel. *Prelude to Revolution: France in May 1968.* London, 1970.

Steiner, George. *Heidegger.* London, 1978.

Suhl, Benjamin. *Jean-Paul Sartre: The Philosopher as Literary Critic.* New York, 1970.

Thody, Philip. *Jean-Paul Sartre: A Literary and Political Study.* London, 1960.

Thompson, Kenneth, and Margaret Thompson. *Sartre: Life and Works.* New York and Bicester, Oxfordshire, Eng., 1984.

Tint, Herbert. *France Since 1918.* London, 1970.

Todd, Olivier. *Un fils rebelle.* Paris, 1981.

Touraine, Alain. *The May Movement: Revolt and Reform.* Trans. Leonard F. X. Mayhew. New York, 1979.

Vèrdes-Leroux, Jeannine. *Les Intellectuals au service du parti.* Paris, 1983.

Verstraeten, Pierre. *Violence et éthique.* Paris, 1972.

Vian, Boris. *L'Ecume des jours.* Paris, 1963.

Warnock, Mary. *The Philosophy of Jean-Paul Sartre.* London, 1965.

———, ed. *Sartre: A Collection of Critical Essays.* New York, 1971.

Webster, Paul, and Nicholas Powell. *Saint-Germain-des-Prés: French Post-War Culture from Sartre to Bardot.* London, 1984.

Photo Credits

PAGE 289:   top, Documentation Obliques; bottom, Bibliothèque de l'Ecole Normale Supérieure.

PAGE 290:   top, author's collection; bottom, Yves Colin.

PAGE 291:   top, Documentation Obliques; bottom, Gisele/John Hillelson.

PAGE 292:   Elliot Erwitt/Magnum from John Hillelson.

PAGE 293:   top, George Henri; bottom, Yves Manciet.

PAGE 294:   top, Documentation Obliques; bottom, Jacques de Poitier/Paris Match.

PAGE 295:   top, Brinon-Gamma; bottom, Agence France-Presse.

PAGE 296:   top, Lipnitski-Viollet; bottom, Keystone.

PAGE 297:   top, Agence France-Presse; bottom, D. Berretty/Magnum, from John Hillelson.

PAGE 298:   top, Henri Bureau/Sygma, from John Hillelson; bottom, Bruno Barbey/Magnum, from John Hillelson.

PAGE 299:   top, Alain Nogues/Sygma, from John Hillelson; bottom, Agence France-Presse.

PAGE 300:   both photos, Agence France-Presse.

Index

Abetz, Otto, 179–80, 217
absurdity notion, 105, 202, 236
18. Brumaire des Louis-Napoleon, Der (Marx), 353
Action, 220, 232, 260, 426
Action Socialiste Révolutionnaire (ASR), 259
Adamov, Arthur, 349
Aden-Arabie (Nizan), 371–72, 373, 378, 383, 424
Advicovitch, Stépha (later Stépha Gérassi), 78, 89, 229
Aeschylus, 182, 186
aesthetics, Sartre's theory of, 75, 116, 247–49, 250–51
Africa, Sartre's trip to, 274–75
Afrique fantôme, L' (Leiris), 237
Age de raison, L' (*The Age of Reason*) (Sartre), 120, 140, 177, 198, 199, 200, 201, 220, 260
  characterization of Marcelle in, 158–59
  characterization of Mathieu in, 154, 156, 166
  De Beauvoir's editorial assistance on, 157, 158, 166, 168
  Mathieu and Marcelle's relationship in, 140–41, 155
  model for Boris in, 118–19
  model for Ivich in, 117
  prologue to, 166
  publication of, 232, 302
  writing of, 150, 151, 153, 154, 161, 163–64, 165–66, 168, 169, 171
Akhmatova, Anna, 238

Alain (Emile Auguste Chartier), 55, 64, 67, 70, 73, 99
A la recherche du temps perdu (Proust), 45
Alban (author), 64
Alcan, 111, 118
Alcestis (Euripides), 391, 402
Algerian war, 320–21, 331, 332, 339–41, 348–49, 352, 361–62, 377–90, 405, 419
  Algerian terrorism in, 384, 385
  ceasefire in, 389
  generals' uprising in, 382–83
  "Manifesto of the 121" in, 378, 380, 381, 383, 418
  OAS terrorism in, 382, 386–90
  referendums on, 382, 389
  Les Temps Modernes and, 320, 332, 339, 340, 341, 381–82, 387
  torture in, 332, 339, 341, 382, 450
  violence against Sartre in, 383, 387–89
Alger Républicain, 133, 139, 341
Algren, Nelson, 250, 254, 263, 270, 404
alienation notion, 197, 202, 271, 346
Alleg, Henri, 341
Allégret, Yves, 220
Allgemeine Psychopathologie (Jaspers), 63, 70
Alphen, Henriette, *see* Nizan, Henriette Alphen
Althusser, Louis, 11, 386, 410, 415, 416, 417, 423
Altman, Georges, 258, 269, 304

Amado, Jorge, 378, 380
Amphitryon 38 (Giraudoux), 187
analytical reason, Sartre's attack on, 342, 346–47
Andler, Charles, 64
"Ange du morbide, L' " ("The Angel of Morbidity") (Sartre), 47, 58, 358
angst, 471
"Anna O." (Bertha Pappenheim), 357
Anthropologie structurale, L' (Lévi-Strauss), 335
anthropology, 248, 250, 307
  Mallarmé biography and, 272
  structuralism and, 335, 338, 347–48, 410
  Les Temps Modernes and, 236–37, 347–48
  terminology of, 237, 307, 347
anti-Americanism, 11, 17, 230, 309–10, 410
anticommunism, 268–69, 308, 318, 328
antifascist conference (1939), 142
Antigone (Sophocles), 175
anti-Semitism, 17, 220–21, 233, 419
Antoine Bloyé (Nizan), 66
anxiety:
  in Heidegger's philosophy, 201
  Sartre's depiction of, 201–2
APL (Libération Press Agency), 445, 446
appeasement, 136, 141–42
"A propos de l'existentialisme: Mise au point" (Sartre), 232
Arab-Israeli conflict, 418–20, 421, 425, 467–68, 469
Aragon, Louis, 58, 99, 308, 326, 327
Arbalète, L', 207, 208, 212
"Arbre, L' " ("The Tree") (Sartre), 81
Ardennes offensive (1944–45), 227–28
Ariel (Maurois), 64
Aristotle, 74
Arland, Marcel, 211
Armed Forces Movement (MFA), 463
Arnaud, Georges, 377–78
Aron, Dominique, 226, 247
Aron, Raymond, 51, 68, 75, 76, 78–79, 80, 97, 108, 111, 171, 271, 310, 470
  at ENS, 55, 57, 62, 71
  Sartre's philosophical discussions with, 78, 81, 83, 101

Sartre's rupture with, 254–55
student rebellion and, 427
Les Temps Modernes and, 226, 227, 241, 242
ASR (Action Socialiste Révolutionnaire), 259
Art d'être grandpère, L' (Hugo), 396
Association of Revolutionary Writers, 99
Astruc, Alexandre, 441, 447
Atlantic Pact, 264, 268–69, 303, 310, 376
atomic bomb, 230, 235, 313
Aubervilliers, Africans' deaths at (1970), 437–38
Audiberti, Jacques, 201
Audry, Colette, 95, 113–14, 142, 183, 424, 434
Audry, Jacqueline, 95
Auriol, Vincent, 288
authenticity notion, 156, 165, 221
Autres, Les (Sartre), *see Huis clos*
Aventures de la dialectique, Les (Merleau-Ponty), 336
Axelos, Kostas, 403
Aymé, Marcel, 323

Baader, Andreas, 462
Baader-Meinhof group, 462, 465, 467
Baal (Brecht), 64
Babinski, Joseph, 70
Badel, Anet, 215
Bakunin, Mikhail, 423
Balachova, Tania, 215
Balzac, Honoré de, 107
Barbezat, Marc, 207, 212
Barbusse, Henri, 99
Bariona, ou Le Fils du tonnerre (*Bariona, or the Thunder's Son*) (Sartre), 174–76, 186
Barrault, Jean-Louis, 138, 179, 182, 190, 211, 215, 277, 280
Barrault (teacher), 36
Barthes, Roland, 19–20, 307, 386, 410
Basque refugees, 450
Bataille, Georges, 199, 211
Battle of San Pietro, The, 366
Baudelaire, Charles, 15, 47, 199–200, 251, 286
Baudelaire (Sartre), 40, 213–14, 285, 334, 351, 361, 481
BBC (British Broadcasting Corporation), 188, 205, 207, 218, 220

Beauvoir, Georges de (father), 76
Beauvoir, Hélène de (Poupette) (sister), 74, 81, 94, 125, 126, 127, 165, 184, 474
Beauvoir, Simone de, 16, 19, 20, 25, 56, 59, 67, 80–81, 87, 88, 94, 97–102, 108–10, 112–14, 115, 118, 124, 131, 133, 138, 139, 144–45, 146, 163, 200, 208, 209, 228, 230, 241, 247, 254–58, 263, 265, 268, 280, 282, 302, 309, 311, 316–17, 318, 324, 327, 340, 341, 342, 348, 349, 366, 369, 381, 382, 387, 389, 392, 402, 403, 430, 434, 439, 441, 444–45, 446, 448, 449, 454, 461, 462, 463, 465, 468, 469, 472
  in Africa, 274–75
  L'Age de raison and, 157, 158, 166, 168
  Algerian war and, 361–62, 388
  books written by, 120, 140, 219, 227, 233–34, 250, 348, 477, 482–83
  in Brazil, 378–80
  Castor (beaver) as nickname of, 75
  childbearing unimportant to, 83, 140–41
  in China, 319–20
  in Cuba, 370–72, 380
  in Czechoslovakia, 399
  death of, 482
  feminism of, 478, 479, 483
  in Great Britain, 252–53
  in Greece, 127–28
  illnesses of, 125, 126, 132, 380
  infidelities of, 250, 270, 311
  in Italy, 121–23, 243, 301, 305, 352, 355, 383–84, 386
  in Japan, 418
  in Middle East, 418–19
  in Morocco, 135–36, 220
  La Nausée and, 91, 92–93, 126
  in occupied France, 180, 182–85, 186, 188–89, 191–92, 204–5, 207, 210, 211, 212, 215, 216, 217, 218, 219
  Olga and, 114, 116–18, 119–20, 128, 140, 163, 234
  physical appearance of, 186
  political views of, 141–42
  religious upbringing of, 75, 83
    Sartre interviewed by, 458, 459, 460, 482–83
    Sartre's death and, 447, 472–75, 477, 483
    as Sartre's editorial adviser, 91, 92–93, 126, 157, 158, 166, 168, 362–63, 365, 412
    Sartre's first meeting with, 73–74
    Sartre's illnesses and, 356, 429, 442, 445, 450, 452–53, 455, 456–58, 464, 466, 470–71, 472–73
    Sartre's influence on, 478
    Sartre's letters to, 150, 151, 152, 153, 155, 157–58, 160, 161, 162, 167, 168, 171, 176, 229, 477, 483
    Sartre's mistresses and, 109, 127, 134, 135, 140, 143–44, 152, 153, 158, 161, 164–65, 167–68, 229, 240, 243, 249–50, 263, 275, 404–5, 477
    Sartre's relationship with, 73–78, 82–84, 109–10, 120, 125, 126–27, 128, 139–41, 152, 153, 154–55, 157, 179, 227, 229, 234, 275–76, 404–5, 482
    Les Séquestrés d'Altona and, 362–63, 365
    in Soviet Union, 320, 390, 391, 398–99, 402, 408–9, 417, 418, 421
    in Spain, 89–90, 95
    student rebellion and, 424, 425
    teaching career of, 77, 82, 94, 123, 127, 210
    Les Temps Modernes and, 225–26
    Vietnam War and, 418, 421
Beckett, Samuel, 15
Being, 166
  in L'Etre et le Néant, 194, 195–96, 197, 198
  For-itself vs. In-itself and, 194, 197
  Heidegger's idea of, 104, 105, 195, 197, 308, 336
  in La Nausée, 104–5, 195
Being and Nothingness (Sartre), see Etre et le Néant, L'
being-for-others notion, 194, 208
Belgium, Nazi invasion of (1940), 168
Belleville, Pierre, 408
Bénard (lycéen), 38–39
Bénard, Marc, 173–74, 175, 188, 204
Ben Bella, Ahmed, 332
Ben Gal, Eli, 469
Bénouville, Guillain de, 254

Ben Saddok, 340
Bergson, Henri, 51, 67–68, 91, 102, 103, 111, 193–94, 213, 482
Beria, Lavrenty P., 322
Berland, Jacques, 206
Berlin, Sartre's studies in, 97, 100–101, 102
Bernal, J. D., 323
Bernes (teacher), 49, 56
Berriau, Simone, 280, 318, 349, 352, 356
Bestiaires, Les (Alban), 64
"Bewilderment" (Sartre), *see* "Dépaysment"
Biafra, 438
Bidault, Georges, 315
Bienenfeld, Bianca, 142–43, 144, 162
Biffures (Leiris), 248
Bifur, 89
Billancourt, Renault factory in, 425, 442, 448
Billoux, François, 205
Binet, Alfred, 67
Blanchot, Maurice, 210, 284
Blin, Roger, 160
Bloch, Marc, 307
Blum, Léon, 115, 121, 124
Boisselot, Père, 173
Böll, Heinrich, 462
Bompiani (publisher), 242
Bonnafé, Alphonse, 88–89, 254
Bonnes, Les (Genet), 96
Borderie, Bernard, 323
boredom, metaphysical reality of, 92
Bost, Jacques-Laurent, 113, 119, 123, 127, 128, 131, 168, 171, 228, 249, 280, 287, 301, 369, 381, 382, 392, 422, 458, 465, 467, 473
    in occupied France, 180, 181, 182, 184, 186, 191, 210, 215, 216
    Sartre influenced by, 112, 118, 124
    Sartre's relationship with, 118, 125, 126, 212, 461, 468
Bost, Mme., 211
Bost, Pierre, 111, 118, 124, 125, 126
Boston University, 405
Boulez, Pierre, 378
Bourdin, Captain, 172–73
bourgeoisie, 96, 249, 272, 314, 342, 345
    Sartre's hatred for, 302, 311, 331, 333, 394–95, 411, 414, 431
Bourgès-Maunoury, Maurice, 340

Bourguiba, Habib, 341
Bourla, Jean-Pierre, 212
Boutillier (*lycéen*), 43–44
Boyer, Charles, 264
Braco (poacher), 177–78
Brandys, Kazimierz, 390
Braque, Georges, 211
Brasseur, Pierre, 280–81, 310, 311
Brazil, 385, 438
    Sartre's trip to, 378–80
Brecht, Bertolt, 17, 64, 210, 220, 250, 277, 313, 333, 345, 390
Bréhier (professor), 55
Brentano, Franz, 100
Breton, André, 58, 60, 97, 229, 255, 264, 403, 409
Brezhnev, Leonid, 408, 467
"Brief über den Humanismus" (Heidegger), 195, 197, 308
British Broadcasting Corporation (BBC), 188, 205, 207, 218, 220
Brodsky, Joseph, 409
Brontë, Emily, 72
Brook, Peter, 252
Brunschvicg, Léon, 57, 70, 71, 73, 358
Buddenbrooks (Mann), 137
Bulganin, Nikolay A., 324
Burgos, cathedral at, 90, 102–3
Butor, Michel, 349

Cacoyannis, Michael, 405
Cahiers de Philosophie, 410
Cahiers libres de la jeunesse, 372
Calder, Alexander, 229
Camus, Albert, 10, 105, 139, 215, 216, 218, 227, 228, 249, 250, 255, 259, 262, 264, 276, 281, 331
    absurdity notion of, 202, 236
    Algerian war and, 321, 340
    books written by, 202–3, 215, 226, 228, 262, 282–83, 288–301, 304, 305
    death of, 369–70
    dissociation of, from existentialism, 236
    La Nausée reviewed by, 133
    Nobel Prize won by, 340, 402
    political views of, 244, 246, 247
    as proletarian culture hero, 211, 212
    prose style of, 203
    Sartre's first meeting with, 206

Sartre's relationship with, 212, 281,
   282–83, 304–5, 306
 Les Temps Modernes and, 226,
   282–83, 288–301, 304–5, 369–70
 as theater director, 208–9, 211, 215
Camus, Francine, 212, 228, 247, 276
Canguilhem, Georges, 51, 55
capitalism, 59, 77, 96, 259, 265, 374,
   401
Carnets de la drôle de guerre (War
   Diaries) (Sartre), 27, 106, 150,
   151–52, 153, 154, 156–57, 161,
   162, 163, 168, 192, 251, 344, 392,
   477
Carpentier, Alejo, 418
Cartel des Gauches, 58–59, 94
Cartier-Bresson, Henri, 315, 319
Casarès, Maria, 211, 212, 215, 280,
   281
Castro, Fidel, 370–71, 372, 380, 382,
   406, 429, 444
Castro, Roland, 437–38, 449
Catholic Church, 407
Cau, Jean, 19, 21, 242, 244, 279, 280,
   287, 316, 460
 daily schedule of, 245–46
Cause du Peuple, La, 438, 439–40, 441,
   442, 446, 450, 451, 456
 "friends" of, 440
Cause du Peuple—J'Accuse, La, 449
Cavaillès, Jean, 181, 183
Caves du Vatican, Les (Gide), 137
Cazalis, Anne-Marie, 258
Céline, Louis-Ferdinand, 97–98, 179,
   409
Central Intelligence Agency (CIA),
   268
Cérémonie des adieux, La (De Beauvoir),
   482–83
Cervantes, Miguel de, 277, 278
Ce Soir, 132–33, 307
CFDT (Confédération Française
   Démocratique du Travail), 424
CGT (Confédération Générale du
   Travail), 307, 424, 425, 426
Chabrier (teacher), 46–47
Chabrol, Claude, 483
Chaintron, Jean, 288
Chamberlain, Neville, 136
"Chambre, La" ("The Room")
   (Sartre), 102, 126, 138, 363
Chambure, Guy de, 282
Chaplin, Charlie, 65, 118, 226

Chateaubriant, Alphonse de, 219
Chauffard, R.-J., 208, 215, 254, 318
Chaumis (prisoner of war), 173
Chemins de la liberté, Les (*The Roads to
   Freedom*) (Sartre), 18, 27, 78, 133,
   198, 221, 373
 as continuation of *La Nausée*,
   137–38
 fragmentary fourth volume of, 18,
   249, 265–66, 311, 314, 360
 see also *Age de raison, L'*; *Mort dans
   l'âme, La*; *Sursis, Le*
Cheval de Troie (Nizan), 115
Chevalier, Ernest, 415
China, 264, 276, 416, 422, 429
 Sartre's trip to, 319–20
 Soviet split with, 408, 409
Chips Are Down, The (Sartre), see *Jeux
   sont faits, Les*
Chirac, Jacques, 464
Christian Socialists, 240
Churchill, Winston, 230
CIA (Central Intelligence Agency),
   268
cinema:
 and Sartre's home movies, 79
 Sartre's interest in, 35, 52, 79, 89,
   98, 109
 Sartre's screenplays for, 206–7,
   209–10, 220, 239, 256, 257, 323,
   351–61, 362, 364–68
Ciolek, Dr., 457, 458
class system, 251, 344, 374
 see also bourgeoisie; working class
Claudel, Paul, 19, 173, 254
Clavel, Maurice, 438, 445, 448
Clement VII, Pope, 281
Cleopatra, 386
Clephane, Irene, 394
Clift, Montgomery, 368
CNE (Comité National des Ecri-
   vains), 205, 209, 210, 225, 307,
   315, 326, 327
CNPF (Conseil National du Patronat
   Français), 437
Cocteau, Jean, 62, 175, 179, 206, 212,
   215, 260, 287
cogito, Cartesian, 105, 197, 198
Cohn-Bendit, Daniel, 423, 424, 425,
   426, 437, 438, 439, 462
COIC (Comité d'Organisation de
   L'Industrie Cinématographique),
   206

Cold War, 11, 263–64, 279, 302, 313, 319, 390
  Atlantic Pact and, 264, 268–69, 303, 310, 376
  Korean War and, 276, 279, 281, 306
  peace movement and, 307–8, 315, 319, 326, 328, 331
  Sartre's radio broadcasts and, 254–55
  thaw in, 318, 322, 323–234
Colet, Louise, 415
Collins, Douglas, 285
colonialism, 77, 320
  Sartre's opposition to, 264, 307, 331, 382, 385, 402, 406, 422, 438, 479
  violence as necessary response to, 384–85, 422, 479
  see also Algerian war
Colonna d'Istria (teacher), 51, 71
Columbia University, 240
Combat, 10, 190, 212, 216, 217, 218, 227, 228, 241
COMES (Community of European Writers), 398–99
Cominform, 263, 274, 324
Comintern, 181, 317
Comité d'Organisation de l'Industrie Cinématographique (COIC), 206
Comité National des Ecrivains (CNE), 205, 209, 210, 225, 307, 315, 326, 327
Comité National du Théâtre, 210–11, 219
Comité Parisien de la Liberation, 218
Comité Vietnam National (CVN), 416, 417, 423
Commanville, Caroline, 415
Commune, 99
communism, 59, 60, 232, 235, 236, 251, 332, 372, 430
  anticommunism and, 268–69, 308, 318, 328
  freedom antithetical to, 243
  Gide's views on, 273–74
  polycentrism and, 316
Communisme yougoslave depuis la rupture avec Moscou, Le (Dalmas), 274
Communistes et la paix, Les (The Communists and Peace) (Sartre), 12, 18, 326, 331, 344, 479
  first part of, 302, 304, 305,
    second part of, 305–6, 309
    third part of, 313–15
Communist party, working class and, 301–2, 303–4, 305–6, 309, 314–15
Communist party of France, see Parti Communiste Français
Communist party of Germany, 99
Communist party of Italy, 316, 402
Community of European Writers (COMES), 398–99
Comoedia, 182
concentration camps, 141, 184, 239, 273
Condemned of Altona, The (Sartre), see Séquestrés d'Altona, Les
Confédération Française Démocratique du Travail (CFDT), 424
Confédération Générale du Travail (CGT), 307, 424, 425, 426
Conrad, Joseph, 117
conscience, as depicted in Les Mouches, 186–87
consciousness, 159, 249, 284, 345, 353
  dialectical materialism and, 243
  in L'Etre et le Néant, 193–94, 195, 196–97, 198, 356–57, 361
  Freud's theory of, 22, 57, 356–57, 361
  history and, 336, 343
  Husserl's theory of, 100, 101
  in La Nausée, 102–3, 104
  sexuality and, 201–2
  in Le Sursis, 198
  unconscious and, 199, 237, 356–57, 361, 376, 413, 431, 433
"Consciousness of Duration" (Sartre), 51
Conseil National de la Résistance, 190
Conseil National du Patronat Français (CNPF), 437
Conspiration, La (Nizan), 133
"Constitution du mépris, La" ("The Constitution of Contempt") (Sartre), 355
constitutions, French, 181, 240, 244, 302, 355
Contat, Michel, 132, 438, 463
contingency notion, 52, 71, 76, 81, 89, 91–93, 98, 104, 236
Copeau, Jacques, 205
Corbin (translator), 139
Cornell University, 405, 431

Corriere della Sera, 465
corydrane, 341–42
Coty, René, 348
Coup du 2 Décembre, Le (Guillemin), 302
Courcel, Nicole, 323
Cournot, Dr., 466–67
Cournot, Patrice, 371–72
Courtade (author), 322
"creature of distances" notion, 139, 175
Crime and Punishment (Dostoevsky), 248
Critique de la raison dialectique (Critique of Dialectical Reason) (Sartre), 331, 335, 336, 341–48, 349, 359, 384, 385, 393, 398, 400, 401, 412, 417, 427, 437, 451, 452, 480
  anti-individualism in, 343, 344–46, 353, 362
  critics of, 347–48
  dialectical reversals in, 23–24, 344
  dialectical vs. analytical reason in, 342, 346–47
  drug-taking during writing of, 23, 341–42, 346
  as muddled and jargon-ridden, 342–43, 359–60, 375, 376
  practico-inert notion in, 376
  public response to, 373
  Sartre's goals in, 20, 342, 343
  second part of, 20, 343, 373–77, 477
  as unfinished text, 17–18, 343, 376–77
Croissant, Klaus, 462
Crucible, The (Miller), 323
Cuba, 374, 378, 379, 382, 385, 405, 422–23, 444
  Sartre's trips to, 370–72, 380
Cuzin, Jean, 180
CVN (Comité Vietnam National), 416, 417, 423
Cynara, 98–99
Czechoslovakia:
  Nazi invasion of (1939), 136, 142, 198, 201, 172
  Prague Spring in (1968), 17, 428
  Sartre's trips to, 399–400
  Soviet invasion of (1968), 12, 428–29, 430, 444
Czech Writers' Union, 430

Daladier, Edouard, 115, 136, 142, 355
Dalmas, Louis, 274

Damnés de la terre, Les (Fanon), 384–85, 421, 479
Daniel, Yuli (Arzhak), 409, 417, 421
Darbon, François, 365
Darlan, Jean, 190
Dasein, 105, 195, 197, 201
Davies, Howard, 348
Davis, Gary, 264
Déat, Marcel, 180, 184
de Beauvoir, Simone, *see* Beauvoir, Simone de
Debray, Regis, 386
Debré, Michel, 355, 382
de Clèves, Gérard, 469
de Courcy (playwright), 310
Dedijer, Vladimir, 418, 420, 429, 441, 452
"Défaite, Une" (later "Empédocle") (Sartre), 64, 65, 68, 71
Defferre, Gaston, 406, 408, 410, 427
de Gaulle, Charles, 10, 228, 240, 244, 250, 254, 266, 378, 379, 406, 407, 409, 420, 432, 438, 439, 451
  Algerian war and, 382–83, 384, 386–87
  and dropping of charges against Sartre, 381
  power assumed by, 348–50, 352, 355, 356
  resignation of, 433–34
  in Resistance, 170, 176, 189, 216, 219
  student rebellion and, 423–27
Delacroix, Henri, 111
Delange, René, 182
Delannoy, Jean, 206–7, 209
Deleuze, Gilles, 447
Dellinger, David, 420, 421
"Demilitarization of Culture, The" (Sartre), 390
democracy, 259
  parliamentary, Sartre's disdain for, 451–52
Demongeot, Mylène, 323
Denmark, Sartre's trip to, 253
"Dépaysement" ("Bewilderment") (Sartre), 122, 124, 138
Depression, Great, 77, 94, 96, 111
Dernier des métiers, Le (Bost), 212
Dernière Chance, La (Sartre), 18, 265–66, 311, 314, 360
Derrida, Jacques, 386
Desanti, Dominique, 180

Desanti, Jean, 180
Descartes, René, 56, 62, 66, 74, 111, 192, 337
Deshayes, Richard, 443
Désir attrapé par la queue, Le (Picasso), 211
Deutscher, Isaac, 420
Deuxième Sexe, Le (De Beauvoir), 83, 348, 478, 483
Diable et le Bon Dieu, Le (The Devil and the Good Lord) (Sartre), 110, 276–81, 282, 283, 310, 318, 339, 351, 385
  autobiographical aspects of, 278–79
  dramatic shortcomings of, 277–78
  first production of, 280–81
Dialectical and Historical Materialism (Stalin), 243
dialectical materialism, 20, 243, 252, 335–36, 373
dialectical reason, Sartre's attraction to, 271, 342, 346–47, 359
Dirty Hands (play) (Sartre), *see Mains sales, Les*
"Dirty Hands" (screenplay) (Sartre), *see* Mains sales, Les
Djamila Boupacha (De Beauvoir and Halimi), 389
Djelalli (Algerian boy), 446–47
Dollfuss, Engelbert, 109
"Dora" (Freud's patient), 413
Dorosh (writer), 390
Dort, Bernard, 282
Dos Passos, John, 97, 98, 106, 199, 200, 227
Dostoevsky, Fyodor, 50, 126, 248, 390, 412
Drôle d'amitié (Sartre), 304
Dubček, Alexander, 428
Duclos, Jacques, 301, 308, 313, 322
Duhamel, Georges, 66
Dulles, John Foster, 260
Dullin, Charles, 72, 94, 95, 109, 124, 125, 138, 210, 215, 287
  Les Mouches and, 190–91, 205–6
  Sartre influenced by, 174, 205–6, 208, 277
Dumas, Alexandre, *père,* 310
Dumas, Georges, 55, 67
Duras, Marguerite, 260, 378, 434
Dürer, Albrecht, 72
Dutschke, Rudi, 423

Ecole Normale Supérieure (ENS), 47–48, 237, 285, 318, 323, 386, 415, 451
  Maoism at, 416
  Sartre at, 54–62, 64, 66–70, 71–75, 87, 100, 350, 351
  Sartre's failure to rebel at, 371, 372
Ecrits de Sartre, Les (bibliography), 463
Editions de l'Europe, 82
Editions du Cerf, 232
Education sentimentale, L' (Flaubert), 161
education system, 407, 432–33, 439
Egoïste, L' (Sagan), 469–70
Egypt, Sartre's trip to, 418–19
Ehrenburg, Ilya, 123, 142, 260, 316, 319, 391, 399, 408, 409, 417, 421
Einstein, Albert, 60
Eisenhower, Dwight D., 204, 207, 218, 301
elections:
  of 1945, 240–41
  of 1946, 244–45
  of 1956, 320–21
  of 1965, 406, 410
  of 1968, 427
  of 1969, 434
  of 1973, 452
  of 1974, 458
Electre (Giraudoux), 186, 187
Elizabeth II, Queen of England, 263
Elkaim (El Kaïm), Arlette, 364, 365, 366, 419, 441, 449, 450, 458, 463, 465, 467, 468, 469, 474, 477
  adopted by Sartre, 403–5
  Sartre's illnesses and, 445, 446, 452, 454–57, 461, 464, 466, 460, 472, 473
  Sartre's relationship with, 323, 358, 444
Eluard, Paul, 58, 205, 210
Emmanuel, Pierre, 236
emotion, 81
  as means of perceiving, 104–5
  Sartre's hostility toward, 130–31
Emotions, Outline of a Theory (Sartre), *see Esquisse d'une théorie des émotions*
"Empédocle" (formerly "Une Défaite") (Sartre), 64, 65, 68, 71
end, as justification of means, 267, 273, 282
"End of the War, The" (Sartre), *see* "Fin de la guerre, La"

Enfance des hommes illustres, L', 37

"Enfance d'un chef, L' " (Sartre), 33, 52, 57, 58, 131–32, 138, 213, 285–86, 398

Engels, Friedrich, 96, 243, 283, 333, 334, 343

Engrenage, L' (In the Mesh) (Sartre), 239, 245, 251, 256, 257, 480

Enrico (Mouloudji), 211

ENS, *see* Ecole Normale Supérieure

"Enterprise de démoralisation, Une" (Sartre), 332

Entretiens sur la politique (Sartre), 321

"Epoche" method, 102

Er l'Arménien (Sartre), 71, 76, 81

"Erostrate" (Sartre), 112, 119, 127, 138, 261

Eshkol, Levi, 419

Espoir, L' (Malraux), 166, 262

Esprit, L', 59

Esquisse d'une théorie des émotions (Sketch for a Theory of the Emotions) (Sartre), 129–31, 237

Essai sur le don (Mauss), 237, 248, 347, 394

"Essai sur les données immédiates de la conscience" (Bergson), 51

Etchegoyen, Abbé, 173

Etcherelli, Claire, 465

ethics and moral theories, 18, 165, 251, 265, 312, 431, 481

   in *Le Diable et le Bon Dieu*, 276–80, 283

   in Lévy-Sartre dialogues, 471–72

   "moral health" as defined in, 61, 68

   "morality of complaisance" and, 159–60

   reconciliation of politics and, 245, 252, 261–62, 268, 270–71, 339, 463, 479

   Saint Genet and, 270–71

ethnography, anthropology vs., 237, 307, 347

Etiemble, René, 235, 242, 304

Etranger, L' (Camus), 202–3, 228, 305

Etre et le Néant, L' (Being and Nothingness) (Sartre), 12, 28, 151, 171, 192–97, 206, 208, 243, 251, 266, 267, 286, 306, 308, 315, 323, 338, 339, 346

   acquisitive impulse as explained in, 196

   consciousness notion in, 193–94, 195, 196–97, 198, 356–57, 361

   critique of, 200–201

   freedom as envisioned in, 192–94, 197

   Heidegger criticized in, 196–97

   key terms in, 194–95

   Sartre's later criticisms of, 471

   sexuality as viewed in, 195

   theology and, 196, 197

   as unfinished text, 17–18

Etude expérimentelle de l'intelligence (Binet), 67

Eugénie (housekeeper), 245

Euripides, 391, 402

European Defense Community, 331

existentialism, 9, 11, 162, 336, 415, 416

   clothing fashions and, 258

   Communists' denunciations of, 220, 232, 252

   critics of, 236, 265

   evolution of, 155–56, 157

   Heidegger's critique of, 195, 308

   of Kierkegaard, 400–401

   label of, repudiated by Sartre, 232

   Marxism and, 16–17, 232, 236, 331–32, 335, 337, 339

   popularity of, 193, 232–34, 236, 257–58, 302, 339

   Sartre's critique of, 337

   Sartre's lectures on, 235–36, 240, 241

"Existentialisme est un humanisme, L' " ("Existentialism is a Humanism) (Sartre), 235–36

Existentialisme n'est pas un humanisme, L' (Kanapa), 252

Existentialisme ou marxisme? (Lukács), 265

Expérience intérieure, L' (Bataille), 199

Express, L', 325–26, 341, 349, 355, 382

Fables choisies (La Fontaine), 35

Fabre, Jean, 55

FAC (Front for Action and Coordination . . .), 389

"Factum sur la contingence" (later *La Nausée*) (Sartre), 91

family, Sartre's disdain for, 317–18, 394–95, 404, 414, 431

Fanon, Frantz, 384–85, 386, 400, 406, 421, 479

"Fantôme de Staline, Le" (Sartre), 326, 332, 333
fascism, 274
  ascribed to United States, 310
  in Italy, 99–100
  opposition to, 142, 387, 388, 389
Faulkner, William, 133
Faure, Edgar, 432, 433
Faux, Claude, 387, 388, 450
Fédération de l'Education Nationale (FEN), 424
Feller, Paul, 173, 174
feminism, 478, 479, 483
Ferron, Louise, 126
Fejtö, François, 326
FFI (Forces Françaises de l'Intérieur), 216, 217, 218, 219, 283
"fiestas," 211, 212, 214–15
Fifth Republic, founding of, 348–50, 352, 355, 356
Figaro, Le, 139, 227, 228, 380, 391, 427
Figaro Littéraire, Le, 273, 283, 403, 440
"Fin de la guerre, La" ("The End of the War") (Sartre), 235
Flacelière, Robert, 459
Flanner, Janet, 244, 426
Flapan (Israeli journalist), 469
Flaubert, Achille-Cléophas, 414
Flaubert, Caroline, 414–15
Flaubert, Gustave, 17, 27, 33, 90–91, 107, 110, 161, 213, 214, 234, 249, 251, 303, 410, 455
  Sartre's biography of, see Idiot de la famille, L'
Flies, The (Sartre), see Mouches, Les
Fliess, Wilhelm, 357–58
FLN (Front de Libération Nationale) (Algeria), 320, 378, 380, 382, 387, 389, 402
Forces Françaises de l'Intérieur (FFI), 216, 217, 218, 219, 283
Foreign Legion, 382
For-itself, 192, 193, 194, 195, 197, 315
Foucault, Michel, 386, 410, 432, 447, 469, 478
Fouchet, Christian, 407
Fourth Republic, 340–41
  end of, 348–50, 352, 355
Francastel, Pierre, 307
France Libre, La, 226
France-Observateur, 322, 340, 369–70, 383

France-Soir, 316, 379, 444
Franco, Francisco, 95, 124, 131, 142, 464
Franco-Soviet Association, 317, 326
Franc-Tireur, 258–59, 264, 269
Franqui, Carlos, 370
freedom notion, 9–10, 11, 52, 80, 83, 92, 99, 144, 162, 177, 198, 199, 206, 208, 256, 267, 271, 344, 346, 451, 479–80
  in L'Etre et le Néant, 192–94, 197
  in Les Mouches, 186–88
  revolution and, 243, 252, 259, 339, 448–49
  violence as interference with, 252, 448–49
Free French movement, 170
French Institute (Berlin), Sartre's studies at, 97, 100–101, 102
French League for a Free Palestine, 249
French League for Human Rights (French League for the Rights of Man), 246, 288
French Revolution, 280, 313–14, 344, 345–46, 360, 374, 375–76
Freud, Jakob, 354
Freud, Sigmund, 53, 57, 60, 70, 199, 272, 317, 338, 376, 393, 400, 431, 433
  biographical methods and, 412–13
  consciousness as viewed by, 22, 57, 356–57, 361
  Sartre's change of heart, 352–53
  Sartre's identification with, 353–54, 358–59
  Sartre's screenplay about, 351–61, 362, 364–68
  see also psychoanalysis
Frey, Sami, 441
Friedmann, Georges, 59
"Frogs Who Want a King, The" (Sartre), see "Grenouilles qui demandent un roi, Les"
Front de Libération Nationale (FLN) (Algeria), 320, 378, 380, 382, 387, 389, 402
Front de Libération Nationale (FLN) (Vietnam), 416
Front for Action and Coordination . . . (FAC), 389
Front Républicain, 321
Fucik, Julius, 315

Gaillard, Félix, 340–41, 348
Galindo, Pierre, 228
Gallimard, 210, 212, 221, 270, 393, 403, 442, 463, 468, 469
  La Nausée published by, 123–24, 125–26, 206
Gallimard, Anne, 369
Gallimard, Gaston, 124, 126
Gallimard, Janine, 369
Gallimard, Michel, 369
Gallimard, Robert, 412
Gandhi, Mohandas K., 77
Garaudy, Roger, 225, 317, 322, 331, 337, 416, 429
Gau, Abbé, 332
Gauche, La, 259
Gauche Prolétarienne (GP), 438–39, 440, 448, 457
Gaulle, Charles de, see de Gaulle, Charles
Gaullism, 226, 254–55, 266
Gavi, Philippe, 451, 454, 458, 461, 462, 464
Geismar, Alain, 426, 438–40, 442–43, 447, 457, 462
General Introduction to Psychoanalysis (Freud), 356
Genet, Jean, 96, 119, 211, 215, 219, 312, 334, 397, 438, 447
  homosexuality of, 285–86, 414
  language of, 283, 284
  reacts to Sartre's biography, 287
  Sartre influenced by, 267–68
  Sartre's biography of, see Saint Genet
  Sartre's first meeting with, 212
  Sartre's identification with, 286–87
Geneva conference (1955), 318
Geneva Convention, 420
Gensac, Claude, 311
George, François, 437, 465
Georgin (teacher), 45, 46
Gérassi, Fernando, 78, 89–90, 114, 124, 131, 145, 229
Gérassi, Stépha Advicovitch, 78, 89, 229
German Institute, 179
Germany, 111
  appeasement of, 136, 141–42
  France invaded by (1940), 168–70
  Holland and Belgium invaded by (1940), 167, 168
  rise of Nazism in, 77, 99, 100, 109
  Sartre's studies in, 97, 100–101, 102

  see also Nazis; occupation; Paris, occupied; World War II
Gestalt psychology, 81
Giacometti, Alberto, 123, 241–42, 315
Giacometti, Annette, 241
Gide, André, 19, 45, 137, 153, 183, 187, 228, 236, 312, 396
  disillusionment of, with Soviet Union, 273–74, 316, 339
Gide, Catherine, 183
Girard, Marie, 101, 109
Giraudoux, Jean, 45, 175, 186, 187
Giscard d'Estaing, Valéry, 459–60, 467, 474
Glucksmann, André, 443, 470
God, 196, 197, 198, 252, 336
Godard, Jean-Luc, 443, 444
Goethe, Johann von, 276
Goldmann, Pierre, 460, 465
Gombrowicz, Witold, 15
Gomulka, Wladyslaw, 324–25
Gorz, André (Michel Bosquet), 21, 241, 333–34, 408, 439, 458, 468, 473
Götz, von Berlichingen, 43, 276–81, 283
Götz von Berlichingen mit der eisernen Hand (Goethe), 276
Goût du définitif, Le (Nizan), 59
GP (Gauche Prolétarienne), 438–39, 440, 448, 457
Gramsci, Antonio, 316
Grass, Günter, 108
Great Britain, 249, 264, 325
  Sartre's plays staged in, 252–53
  Sartre's trip to, 98–99
  in World War II, 142, 169, 170, 181, 317
Greco, Juliette, 258
Greece, Sartre's trip to, 127–28
"Grenouilles qui demandent un roi, Les" ("The Frogs Who Want a King") (Sartre), 355
Griaule, Marcel, 237
Groupe d'Information Internationale, 59
group-in-fusion notion, 344
Guéhenno, Jean, 205
Guérin, Daniel, 424
Guevara, Ernesto (Che), 370, 371, 423
Guille, Pierre, 80, 81, 115, 121, 152, 171
  at ENS, 54, 55, 63, 66–67, 71

Guille, Pierre (*cont.*)
  Sartre influenced by, 79
  Sartre's vacations with, 94–95, 116,
    122
Guillemin, Henri, 302, 307
Guillemin, Jacques, as Sartre's pseu-
    donym, 58
Guillemin, Louise (later Louise
    Schweitzer) (grandmother), 31,
    32–33, 35, 76, 80
Guiot (*lycéen*), 444
Gute Mensche von Sezuan, Der (Brecht),
    390
Guterman, Norbert, 59

Halimi, Gisèle, 389, 456
Hegedüs, Lorant, 325
Hegel, Georg Wilhelm Friedrich, 23,
    60, 70, 154, 194, 208, 266, 267,
    282, 337, 346, 373, 376
Heidegger, Martin, 15, 22, 162, 173,
    174, 176, 186–87, 336, 337, 401,
    459
  "creature of distances" notion of,
    139, 175
  L'Etre et le Néant and, 193, 194–95,
    196–97, 201
  La Nausée influenced by, 103–4,
    105, 106–7
  Sartre compared with, 197
  Sartrean existentialism attacked by,
    195, 308
  Sartre's meeting with, 308
Heller, Gerhard, 180
Helsinki conference (1955), 319
Helsinki peace congress (1964), 408,
    409
Hemingway, Ernest:
  Camus influenced by, 203
  Sartre influenced by, 97, 98, 139
  Sartre's consciousness notion and,
    100, 106
  Sartre's meetings with, 227, 270
Hénin-Liétard, miners killed at
    (1970), 443
Hernani (Hugo), 310
Herriot, Edouard, 59, 94
Hervé, Pierre, 321, 331
Hesnard, Angelo, 285
"Histoires pour l'oncle Jules"
    (Sartre), 153, 161
history, 359, 362, 374, 401
  individual in relation to, 412

responsibility and, 199
Sartre's philosophical concern with,
    20, 336, 342, 343, 375–76
History and Class Consciousness (Lukács),
    336
Hitler, Adolf, 99, 109, 115, 123, 124,
    131, 146, 181–82, 184, 186, 190,
    217, 254
  appeasement of, 136, 141–42
Hoffmeister, Adolf, 399
Holland:
  Nazi invasion of (1940), 167, 168
  Sartre's trip to, 247–48
Homme révolté, L' (Camus), 282–83,
    288–301, 304
Hommes de bonne volonté, Les (Romains),
    159
homosexuality, 45, 285–86, 414
Honegger, Arthur, 182
Housset, Dr., 466, 474
Hugo, Victor, 303, 310, 396
Huis clos (formerly *Les Autres*) (*In
    Camera; No Exit*) (Sartre), 207–9,
    215, 220, 241, 258, 267, 319, 363,
    377
  being-for-others notion in, 208
  Broadway production of, 240, 351
Humanité, L', 59, 260, 322, 326, 328,
    424
Hume, David, 111
Hungary, uprising in (1956), 12, 18,
    324, 325–28, 331, 361, 428
Huracán sobre el azucar (*Hurricane on the
    Sugar*) (Sartre), 379
Husserl, Edmund, 20, 107, 159, 162,
    180, 196, 197, 284, 337
  phenomenology of, 97, 100–101,
    102–5, 193
  Sartre's image theories and, 111–12
Huston, John, 351, 352, 353, 357, 361,
    365, 366–68, 386
Hyppolite, Jean, 54

I Chose Freedom (Kravchenko), 265
idealism, 67, 73
  realism vs., 97, 100, 105, 162
Idiot de la famille, L' (The Idiot of the
    Family) (Sartre), 12, 15, 16, 20,
    27, 108, 213, 271–72, 285, 398,
    401, 411–15, 431–32, 444, 456,
    481
  bourgeois family condemned in,
    317–18, 414, 431

Critique de la raison dialectique and, 18, 343, 377, 412
  as disguised autobiography, 414–15
  as Freudian biography, 412–13
  Marxian and Freudian insights combined in, 25, 317–18, 334
  speculation about Flaubert's childhood in, 413–15
  title of, 415
  writing of, 317, 331, 388, 438, 446, 451
Idiot International, L', 441, 450
Idt, Geneviève, 262
I'll Have a Nice Funeral (Sartre), *see J'aurai un bel enterrement*
"Image, L' " (Sartre), 111–12, 118
"Image dans la vie psychologique: Rôle et nature, L' " (Sartre), 67–68, 70
image theories, 67–68, 93, 111–12, 130
Imaginaire, L' (*The Psychology of Imagination*) (Sartre), 118
imagination, 70, 111–12
  emotion and, 130
Imagination, L' (*Imagination*) (Sartre), 70, 118
Immaculée Conception, L' (Eluard), 58
In Camera (Sartre), *see Huis clos*
indicative vs. intuitive acts, 102–3
individualism, 273
  Sartre's disdain for, 333–34, 343, 344–46, 353, 362, 441
Indochina War, First, 288, 315, 332
Indochina War, Second, *see* Vietnam War
In-itself, 193, 194, 196, 197, 201, 315
intentionality notion, 100
International Day of Resistance to Dictatorship and War (1948), 268
International Tribunal Against War Crimes in Vietnam (Russell tribunal), 415, 418, 420–22, 443
In the Mesh (Sartre), *see Engrenage, L'*
"Intimité" ("Intimacy") (Sartre), 124–25, 132, 138
intuitive vs. indicative acts, 102–3
Invitée, L' (De Beauvoir), 120, 140, 234
Ionesco, Eugène, 15

Iron in the Soul (Sartre), *see Mort dans l'âme, La*
Isherwood, Christopher, 100
Isoré (teacher), 88, 89
Israel, 16
  Arab-Israeli conflict and, 418–20, 421, 425, 467–68, 469
  Sartre's trips to, 418–20, 467–68
  Zionism and, 249, 258, 263
Istituto Gramsci, 401, 431
italiens, 408, 416
Italy, 131, 169
  Communists in, 242, 316, 402
  Sartre's trips to, 99–100, 242–43, 301, 305, 316, 324, 352, 355, 383–86, 391, 446, 450, 455, 458, 459, 465, 467
  in World War II, 207, 211–12
It's Right to Rebel (Gavi, Lévy, and Sartre), *see On a raison de se révolter*
Ivan's childhood, 390

J'Accuse, 443, 449
Jaloux, Edmond, 133
James, Henry, 411
Jankélévitch, Vladimir, 189, 404
Japan, 288
  Sartre's trips to, 415, 418
  teaching post sought by Sartre in, 78, 82, 87
  in World War II, 184, 230
Jaspers, Karl, 63, 70, 337, 401, 431
J'aurai un bel enterrement (*I'll Have a Nice Funeral*)(Sartre), 61, 457
Jaurès, Jean-Léon, 59, 345
jazz, 9, 46, 61, 74, 227, 258
JCR (Jeunesse Communiste Révolutionnaire), 417
"Jean-sans-terre" (Sartre), *see Mots, Les*
Jean Santeuil (Proust), 312
Jeanson, Francis, 281, 283, 301, 304, 305, 310, 332, 361, 377, 379–80
JEC (Jeunesse Etudiante Chrétienne), 407
Jésus la Chouette (Jesus the Owl) (Sartre), 43, 47, 58
Jeune Barreau de Bruxelles, 447
Jeunesse Communiste Révolutionnaire (JCR), 417
Jeunesse Etudiante Chrétienne (JEC), 407

Jeux sont faits, Les (*The Chips Are Down*) (Sartre), 209–10
Jews:
  anti-Semitism and, 17, 220–21, 233, 419
  Lévy-Sartre dialogue on, 471–72
  Nazi persecution of, 141, 182, 189, 204, 206, 212, 220, 233
  Sartre's essay on, 220–21, 419, 461
  Les Séquestrés d'Altona and, 404
  in Soviet Union, 310, 443
  Zionism and, 249, 258, 263
Jollivet, Simone, *see* Sans, Simone-Camille
Jollivet (teacher), 121
Jones, Ernest, 351, 353, 355
Jouhandeau, Marcel, 277
Journal du voleur (Genet), 267
Journal-Echo de Paris, 133
Jouvet, Louis, 280, 281
Joyce, James, 93, 108, 399, 409
Judaism, 461
  see also Jews
Jullian, Marcel, 462, 463, 464
July, Serge, 463

Kaan, Pierre, 190
Kádár, János, 327, 328
Kafka, Felice, 127
Kafka, Franz, 21, 100, 107, 126, 127, 132, 146, 202, 279, 390, 399, 409, 413, 432, 459
Kanapa, Jean, 235, 252, 304
Kant, Immanuel, 77, 337
Kapital, Das (Marx), 96, 339
Kean (Sartre), 246, 310–11, 351, 352
Kean ou Désordre et génie (*Kean, or Chaos and Genius*) (Dumas, *pere*), 310–11
Keats, John, 412
Khrushchev, Nikita, 313, 322, 372, 390, 391, 399, 408
Khrushchev, Nina, 372–73
Kierkegaard, Sören, 161, 201, 337, 400–401, 471, 481–82
Koestler, Arthur, 159, 244, 246–47, 249, 255–56, 274
Koestler, Mamaine, 247, 255, 274
Korean War, 276, 279, 281, 306
Korène, Véra, 365
Kosakiewicz, Olga (Olga Dominique), 115, 136, 138, 143, 164, 168, 211, 215, 240, 257, 287, 358, 381, 461, 467
  as actress, 138, 182, 205, 206
  De Beauvoir's relationship with, 114, 116–18, 119–20, 128, 140, 163, 234
  in occupied France, 182, 184, 186
  Sartre's relationship with, 114, 116, 117–18, 119–20, 123, 124, 125, 126, 128, 133, 140, 157, 208, 229, 234
Kosakiewicz, Wanda (Marie-Olivier), 125, 126, 211, 221, 257, 351, 444, 446, 450, 455, 459, 464, 465, 466, 467, 468
  as actress, 207, 208, 230, 278, 311, 318, 360, 363
  in occupied France, 184, 186
  Sartre's marriage proposal to, 167–68, 229, 404
  Sartre's relationship with, 123, 129, 134, 135, 142, 143–44, 152, 153, 158, 160, 161, 162, 163, 164–65, 240, 244, 275, 319
Kosma, Joseph, 258
Kosygin, Andrey, 408
Kott, Jan, 390
Kravchenko, Victor, 264–65
Kravetz, Marc, 437, 452
Krivine, Alain, 417, 434
Kubitschek, Juscelino, 380
Kundera, Milan, 399
Kuznetsov, Eduard, 443

labor camps, Soviet, 265, 273, 304, 390
Lacan, Jacques, 194, 211, 386, 387, 410, 424
Lachelier, Jules, 70
Lacoste, Robert, 332
Lagache, Daniel, 55, 60, 68, 113
Laing, R. D., 478
Lallemant (lawyer), 447
language, reality dissolved by, 283–84
Lannier, Jean, 205, 206
Lanson, Gustave, 54, 60, 69, 318, 350
Lanzmann, Claude, 318, 319, 324, 340, 369, 384, 419, 454, 457, 458, 473
  Algerian war and, 362, 378, 379, 380, 381, 382

De Beauvoir's relationship with, 309, 311, 404
Rosenberg executions and, 309–10
Les Temps Modernes and, 282, 382, 465
Lapresle, Dr., 457, 458, 464
Lassithiotakis, Hélène, 458, 464, 465, 466, 467, 468
Laval, Pierre, 111, 170, 184, 190, 205
Lawrence, D. H., 17, 200
Lawrence, T. E., 235–36
Lazareff, Hélène, 316
Lazareff, Pierre, 316
League for Anti-Fascist Movements, 387, 389
League of Nations, 131
Lebeau, Dr., 442, 443, 445, 452
Le Bon, Sylvie, 429, 442, 444, 445, 449, 453, 454, 455, 458, 459, 464, 465, 467, 468, 469, 470, 473, 474, 483
Le Bris, Michel, 439, 440
Leclerc, Jacques, 218
Le Dantec, Jean-Pierre, 439, 440
Ledoux, Fernand, 365
Lefebvre, Georges, 307
Lefebvre, Henri, 11, 59, 232, 236, 331–32, 338, 415, 417, 423, 424
Lefort, Claude, 309, 331
Légende de la vérité, La (*Legend of Truth*) (Sartre), 81–82, 89, 90, 98
Léger, Fernand, 229, 245
Le Havre:
    Allied bombing of, 188
    chestnut tree observed in, 90–91, 103–5
    Sartre as teacher in, 82, 87–89, 90, 111, 112
Leibniz, Gottfried Wilhelm von, 74, 111
Leibowitz, René, 211
Leiris, Michel, 209, 211, 215, 219, 226, 237, 242, 248, 274, 307, 362, 396, 424, 434, 438
Leiris, Zette, 209, 215, 219
Le Léap, Alain, 307
Lemaître, Frédérick, 310
Lemarchand, Jacques, 211
Lenin, V. I., 60, 252, 274, 303–4, 306, 308, 325, 336, 428
Lens, people's tribunal at, 443
Leonardo da Vinci, 20, 412

Leroy, Henri, 173, 174
Leroy (lawyer), 449
Let There Be Light, 351, 366, 367
Lettre à Sartre (Hervé), 322
Lettres Françaises, Les, 190, 206, 219, 226, 260, 265
Levi, Carlo, 243, 264, 313
Levi, Silone, 243
Lévinas, Emmanuel, 97
Lévi-Strauss, Claude, 229, 237, 306–7, 335, 345, 347, 348, 386, 387, 410, 415
Lévy, Benny (Pierre Victor), 18, 221, 438–39, 446, 451, 454, 457, 458, 459, 460–62, 463, 464, 465, 466, 467–69
    Jewishness of, 461, 471–72
    Sartre's dialogue with, 468–69, 470, 471–72
Liberation (1944–45), 216–19, 225
Libération, 307, 309, 315, 316, 450–51, 452, 454, 458, 462, 463, 464, 465, 481
Libération Press Agency (APL), 445, 446
Liehm, Antonin, 399–400
Lindbergh, Charles, Jr., 69, 318
linguistics, 237, 307
Lisowski, Jerzy, 331–32
littérature engagée, la, 234–35, 238
"Living Kierkegaard" colloquium (1964), 400–401
Locke, John, 99, 337
Loi d'Orientation (1968), 432–33
Loosdregt (teacher), 43, 47
Loser Wins (Sartre), see *Séquestrés d'Altona, Les*
Lotta Continua, 467
Lottman, Herbert, 228
"Lucifer" (Sartre), 133
Luguet, André, 260
Lukács, Georg, 265, 319, 336, 343
Lumumba, Patrice, 398
Luther, Martin, 277
Luxemburg, Rosa, 308
Lycée Condorcet, 180, 184, 185, 190, 210
Lycée Henri IV, 38, 45–48, 55
Lycée Louis-le-Grand, 48–53, 56
Lycée Montaigne, 36
Lycée Pasteur, 127, 128, 180
Lyric Theatre (London, W14), 252–53

Maar, Dora, 211
Mabille, Zaza, 81
Madame Bovary (Flaubert), 110, 411,
    412, 413, 446, 451, 456
Magre, Judith, 319
Maheu, René, 49, 51, 54, 55, 62,
    66–67, 69, 71, 78, 171, 400
  De Beauvoir's relationship with, 73,
    74–75
Mahoudeau, Dr., 445
Mailer, Norman, 421
Mains sales, Les (Dirty Hands) (play)
    (Sartre), 256–57, 258, 260, 262,
    264, 266, 282, 358, 430, 480
  Vienna production of, 307–8, 317
"Mains sales, Les" ("Dirty Hands")
    (screenplay) (Sartre), 239
Maîtres et esclaves (Freyre), 379
Malentendu, Le (Camus), 215
Mallarmé, Stéphane, 18, 107, 108,
    263, 271–72, 284, 301, 432
Malle, Louis, 441
Mallet, Serge, 308
Malraux, André, 10, 124, 166, 173,
    183, 220, 226, 246, 262, 378, 379
Manceaux, Michèle, 448
Mancy, Anne-Marie (mother) (for-
    merly Anne-Marie Schweitzer
    Sartre), 31–37, 38, 42, 44–45, 49,
    51, 57, 65, 70, 80, 83, 94, 110,
    115, 120, 128, 143, 146, 152, 157,
    162, 167, 176, 188, 230, 263, 282,
    351, 359, 383, 388, 447
  daughter wanted by, 414–15
  death of, 430–31
  De Beauvoir's relationship with,
    116
  family background of, 31
  first marriage of, 32
  home shared by Sartre and, 21,
    245
  as mother, 33, 34, 37
  Les Mots and, 394, 395, 396, 398,
    431
  second marriage of, 24, 40–41, 78,
    245
  stealing incident and, 44, 45
Mancy, Joseph (stepfather), 57, 70,
    94, 110, 116, 146, 152, 167, 447
  death of, 230
  marriage of, 40–41
  Norwegian vacation of, 115, 282
  Sartre's relationship with, 44, 45,
    47, 49, 52, 120, 128, 132, 139,
    143, 171, 188, 431
Mandarins, Les (De Beauvoir), 219,
    227, 233–34, 250
Mandelstam, Osip, 238
"Manifesto Against the Cold War,"
    307
"Manifesto of the 121," 378, 380, 381,
    383, 418
Mann, Thomas, 47, 137
Mansfield, Katherine, 122
Maoists, 12, 416, 469, 480, 481
  Sartre's agitprop activities with,
    437–44, 445–51
  Sartre's criticisms of, 449
Maos en France, Les (Manceaux),
    448–49
Mao Tse-tung, 264, 319, 423
Marcel, Gabriel, 62, 139, 232, 236,
    337, 403
Marcellin, Raymond, 440, 446, 455
"Marchand de bananes, Le" (Sartre),
    35
Marcuse, Herbert, 430, 458
Marshall, George, 250
Marshall Plan, 250, 252, 268
Martin, Henri, 288, 311–12, 331
Marx, Karl, 23, 57, 60, 70, 96, 181,
    194, 197, 243, 271, 272, 282, 283,
    303, 308, 333, 336, 337, 343, 344,
    345, 346, 353, 374, 375, 376, 423
Marxism, 11, 17, 20, 66, 96, 197, 232,
    238, 250, 308, 317, 321, 322, 360,
    386, 416, 460–61
  existentialism and, 16–17, 232, 236,
    331–32, 335, 337, 339
  history as viewed in, 336
  psychoanalysis and, 12, 25, 321,
    323–24, 331, 335, 351–52, 364
  Sartre's disillusionment with, 467
  Sartre's philosophical analysis of,
    342–48, 385–89
  of students, 11, 17
"Marxism and Existentialism"
    (Sartre), 332
Massnahme, Die (Brecht), 345
Masson, André, 229, 378
Massu, Jacques, 427, 450
master-slave relationship, Hegel's,
    194, 243, 266–67, 268
"Matérialisme et révolution" (Sartre),
    243
Matignon Agreement (1936), 121

Maulnier, Thierry, 380
Maupassant, Guy de, 90–91
Mauriac, Claude, 447, 449
Mauriac, François, 137, 205, 284, 310, 440
Maurois, André, 64
Mauss, Marcel, 237, 248, 272, 347, 394
MCF (ML) (Mouvement Communiste Français (Marxiste-Léniniste)), 416
means, end as justification for, 267, 273, 282
Meinhof, Ulrike, 465
Melville, Herman, 182
Memmi, Albert, 340
Mendès-France, Pierre, 426
Men Without Shadows (Sartre), see Morts sans sépulture
Merleau-Ponty, Maurice, 81, 134, 180, 184, 254, 259, 269, 336, 343, 372, 383, 460
    anthropology and, 237
    disillusionment of, with Communists, 276, 281
    pro-Soviet apologias by, 244, 249, 273, 274
    Sartre's conflicts with, 301, 306, 308, 309, 323–24, 331
    Sartre's political analysis criticized by, 314–15
    as Sartre's political mentor, 237, 243, 250, 276
    structuralism and, 307
    Les Temps Modernes and, 226, 242, 251, 273, 276, 282, 306, 308, 309, 347–48, 387, 441
Messages, 169
Meteorological Corps, 75
    Sartre's service in, 79–80, 81, 82, 83, 97, 145, 146, 149–78, 182, 183
Mexico, 438
Meyer, Jean, 318
Meyerson, L., 67
MFA (Armed Forces Movement), 463
Michel, Georges, 442, 454, 461
"Midnight Sun" ("Soleil de Minuit") (Sartre), 115, 116, 119, 122, 282
Mikoyan, Anastas, 409
Miller, Arthur, 323
Minute, 445, 456
Mirande, Yves, 280
Misrahi, Robert, 258

Miterrand, François, 408, 410, 426, 458
Moby Dick (Melville), 182
Moch, Jules, 260
Modern Times, 118
Molière (Jean Baptiste Poquelin), 391
Mollet, Guy, 321, 332, 339–40, 349, 356
Mondadori, Arnoldo, 242–43
Monde, Le, 99, 273, 283, 332, 402, 429, 434
Monnier, Adrienne, 80
Monroe, Marilyn, 367
Montand, Yves, 323
Montherlant, Henry Millon de, 64, 219
morality, see ethics and moral theories
Morand, Paul, 45
Moravia, Albert, 97
Moreau (professor), 356
Morel, Albert, 63, 67
Morel, Dr., 192
Morel, Mme., 67, 71, 79, 94–95, 115, 129, 134–35, 140, 142, 145, 167, 183, 188, 189, 192, 207, 256, 270, 382, 388
Morgan, Claude, 205, 215, 327
Morhange, Pierre, 59
Morocco, Sartre's trip to, 135–36, 220
Mort dans l'âme, La (Iron in the Soul) (novel) (Sartre), 18, 155, 260–63, 302
    "duty" derided in, 261–62
    final scene in, 260–61
"Mort dans l' âme, La" (essay) (Sartre), 169
Morts sans sépulture (Men Without Shadows) (Sartre), 244, 256, 319
    London production of, 252–53
    synopsis of, 230–31
    torture sequences in, 230–31, 247, 363
    violence and lateral reciprocity of love in, 344–45
Moscow trials, 124, 244, 246, 249
Moses, 412
Mots, Les (The Words) (Sartre), 24, 26, 34, 90, 154, 163, 272, 286, 312–13, 316, 333, 393–98, 414, 431
    as anti-literature, 396–97
    bourgeois family disdained in, 394–95

Mots, Les (*The Words*) (Sartre) (*cont.*)
  factuality of, 391–92, 397
  "Jean-sans-terre" as original title
    of, 312, 394, 398
  motives for writing of, 393
  narrative voice in, 394
  oral continuation of, 458, 459, 460
  prose style of, 398
  public response to, 400, 402
Mouches, Les (*The Flies*) (Sartre), 127,
  183, 190, 233, 258, 262, 332, 358,
  402, 430
  analysis of, 186–88
  first production of, 190–91, 205–6,
    207
  reviews of, 206
Moulin, Jean, 189–90
Mouloudji, Marcel, 164, 211
Mounier, Emanuel, 264
Mouvement Communiste Français
  (Marxiste-Léniniste) (MCF
  (ML)), 416
Mouvement du 22 Mars (M22M),
  423, 438
Mouvement Républicain Populaire
  (MRP), 240, 244
Müller (soldier), 149–51, 152–53, 155
Mur, Le (*The Wall*) (book) (Sartre),
  131, 138–39
"Mur, Le" ("The Wall") (short story)
  (Sartre), 124, 126, 127, 133, 138,
  142, 145
Murdoch, Iris, 194
Musil, Robert, 100
Mussolini, Benito, 99, 124, 131, 136,
  207
Mutter Courage (Brecht), 277
M22M (Mouvement du 22 Mars),
  423, 438
mysticism, of surrealists, 59
Mythe de Sisyphe, Le (Camus), 202

Nagel, Louis, 264
Nagy, Imre, 324, 325, 327
Nasser, Gamal Abdel, 419
NATO (North Atlantic Treaty Organization), 313, 328, 331
Nausée, La (*Nausea*) (Sartre), 10, 15,
  17, 27, 81, 89, 90–93, 102–8, 111,
  112, 114, 138, 139, 169, 200, 248,
  308, 312, 396–97, 400, 444, 459
  absurdity notion in, 105
  L'Age de raison as continuation of,
    137–38

Anny's emotionality in, 130–31
Anny's resistance to pain in, 95
antihumanistic viewpoint of, 119
Being as issue in, 104, 105
chestnut tree episode in, 90–91,
  103–5, 107, 108, 110, 131, 346
emotion as means of perceiving in,
  104–5
"Epoche" method in, 102
L'Étranger and, 202
familiarity vs. strangeness of world
  in, 91–92
fragments of café conversations in,
  124–25
gallery episode in, 108
Heidegger's influence on, 103–4,
  105, 106–7
L'Idiot de la famille vs., 411, 412
language in, 107
literary influences on, 97–98
model for Anny in, 72
narrative form of, 92–93
nature of consciousness in, 102–3,
  104
past vs. present in, 106
phenomenology and, 97, 100–101,
  102–5
Proust parodied in, 103
publisher sought for, 123–24,
  125–26, 206
reviews of, 132–33
Roquentin's abandoned book in,
  18, 19, 213, 482
Roquentin's nausea in, 106, 131,
  201, 202
Roquentin's reversals in, 24–25
superfluity vs. contingency in,
  104–5
title of, 126
writing of, 100, 102, 108
Naville, Pierre, 309, 322
Nazis (National Socialists), 9, 94, 100,
  109, 141–42, 177, 225, 233, 254,
  258, 480
  rise to power of, 77, 99, 100, 109
Nekrassov (Sartre), 318–19, 331, 349
New Yorker, 244, 426
New York Review of Books, 454
New York Times, 228
Niemeyer, Oscar, 380
Nietzsche, Friedrich, 22, 23, 64, 65,
  68, 72, 81–82, 143, 159, 166, 261,
  271, 351, 401, 479, 482

Nizan (father), 46, 51
Nizan, Henriette Alphen (Rirette), 62, 68, 71, 74, 75, 77, 78, 79, 125, 145, 229, 404
Nizan, Paul-Yves, 67, 68, 69, 70, 73, 74, 75, 76, 77, 79, 83, 87, 145, 152, 154, 171, 229, 251, 387, 393
  books written by, 115, 133, 371-72, 373, 378, 383, 424
  death of, 176
  depressions and morbidity of, 50, 58
  at ENS, 54, 55, 57, 58, 60, 62
  as lycéen, 39, 45-46, 47-51, 52
  La Nausée reviewed by, 132-33
  PCF left by, 265, 266
  political views of, 58-59, 60, 66, 70, 94, 124, 372
  in publishing of Sartre's works, 82, 89, 123
  romance and marriage of, 62, 70-71
  Sartre's estrangements from, 48-49, 54, 58, 63, 78
Nobel Prize, 16, 340, 402-3, 417
Nodier, Pierre, 73
Noël (teacher), 39
No Exit (Sartre), see Huis clos
Nogrette, Robert, 448
North Atlantic Treaty Organization (NATO), 313, 328, 331
nothingness, 161, 168, 194-95, 196, 198, 201, 249
Notre-Dame des fleurs (Genet), 212, 267, 284
Nouveau traité de la psychologie (Dumas), 67
Nouvelle Classe Ouvrière, La (Mallet), 408
Nouvelle Classe Ouvriére, Une (Belleville), 408
Nouvelle Encyclopédie Philosophique, 111
Nouvelle Résistance Populaire, 448
Nouvelle Revue Française, 62, 125-26, 127, 133, 226
Nouvelles Littéraires, Les, 72, 133
Nouvel Observateur, Le, 406, 408, 422, 426, 433, 439, 450, 468, 471-72
Novotný, Antonin, 428
Novy Mir, 391, 395, 409
Nuremberg tribunal, 418, 420

OAS, (Organisation de l'Armée Secrète), 382, 386-90, 456
"Oath, The" (Sartre), see "Serment, Le"
Oberammergau, Passion play at, 109
objectification, 346, 353
objectivity, 101, 248
objects:
  Sartre's hatred of, 346
  see also possessions
occupation, German of France, 9, 10, 170-219, 238, 283, 302, 345, 480
  Camus's vs. Sartre's response to, 283
  collaborators in, 179-80, 232-33
  deterioration of French-German relations in, 184
  L'Etre et le Néant and, 192-93, 197
  fall of France and, 168-70
  food shortages in, 184-85, 191-92, 207
  of Free Zone, 204
  French cinema in, 206-7
  Liberation and, 216-19, 225
  Les Mouches and, 186-88, 192, 206
  Nazis' final acts of vengeance in, 216
  psychological effects of, 232-33
  Sartre and De Beauvoir's crossings into Free Zone in, 182-84, 191-92
  Sartre as prisoner of war in, 170-78, 184
  Vichy government in, 170, 181, 190, 204, 262, 349
  see also Paris, occupied; Resistance; World War II
Odo of Cluny, Bishop, 281
Oedipus Rex (Sophocles), 175
Oeuvre, L', 60
Office of War Information, U.S., 227, 228, 229
Ollivier (teacher), 38
Ollivier, Albert, 226, 241, 242
Ombre, L' (Sans), 94
On a raison de se révolter (It's Right to Rebel) (Gavi, Lévy, and Sartre), 451, 458
oppression:
  Sartre's analyses of, 266-67, 340
  see also colonialism
Ordre Nouveau, L', 444, 454-55

Oresteia (Aeschylus), 186
Organisation de l'Armée Secrète
    (OAS), 382, 386–90, 456
  demonstrations against, 388, 389
  Sartre as target of, 387–89
Orgueilleux, Les (*The Proud Ones*)
    (Sartre), 220
Origins of Psychoanalysis, The (Freud),
    357–58
Overney, Pierre, 448
ownership, Sartre's analysis of,
    196

Paci, Enzo, 402
Padilla, Heberto, 444
Paese Sera, 428–29
Palestinian refugees, 419–20, 465
Palle, Albert, 89
Paolo Pauli (Adamov), 349
Pappenheim, Bertha ("Anna O."),
    357
Papin sisters, 96
Parain, Brice, 126
Paris, occupied, 179–219, 230
  air-raid sirens in, 185–86, 188
  bombing of, 211, 219
  city life in, 186
  complicity of French writers and
    artists in, 179–80
  liberation of (1944), 216–19
  theatrical activity in, 182, 190–91,
    205–6, 208–9
  see also occupation; Resistance
Paris Match, 472
Paris-Soir, 206, 209
Parodi, Alexandre, 94
Parole au Peuple, La, 439
Parti Communiste Français (PCF),
    11, 12, 16, 17, 18, 26, 58–59, 60,
    66, 70, 75, 96, 111, 115, 229, 243,
    244, 246, 247, 249, 250, 251, 252,
    255, 257, 259, 260, 268, 273, 274,
    275, 281, 282, 309, 349, 372, 376,
    385, 399, 402, 406, 407, 408, 429,
    480
  Algerian war and, 320, 389
  in elections of 1945, 240, 241
  Hervé expelled by, 321–22
  Hungarian uprising and, 324, 325
  Maoists and, 448
  mystification ascribed to, 251
  Nizan's departure from, 265, 266
  Sartre denounced by, 178, 219–20

  Sartre's alignment with, 301–4,
    305–6, 307, 321–22, 331
  Sartre's break from, 325–28
  Sartre's disenchantment with,
    261–62
  in Sartre's fiction, 154, 177, 261,
    278
  student rebellion and, 427
  Vietnam War and, 288
  in World War II, 205, 216, 225
Paru, 236
Pascal, Blaise, 345
Pasolini, Pier-Paolo, 465
Pasternak, Boris, 402, 403, 409
Pathé, 207, 209
Paulhan, Jean, 125–26, 138, 153, 205,
    210, 226
PCF, *see* Parti Communiste Français
peace movement (1950s), 307–8, 315,
    319, 326, 328, 331
Péju, Marcel, 282, 309, 320, 362,
    379–80, 381
Pelletier (*lycéen*), 43–44
Pensée sauvage, La (Lévi-Strauss), 347,
    387
Pentagon, 181
perception, 79, 162, 284
  emotionality and, 130–31
  emotions as means of, 104–5
  imagining vs., 112
  nausea and, 131
Périer, François, 260, 474
Péron, Alfred, 70
Perret, Olga, 207, 208, 209, 215
Perrin, Marius, 173, 174, 176, 177
Peste, La (Camus), 226, 262
Pétain, Marshal Henri Philippe, 170,
    186, 187, 228, 223, 266
Petitjean, A. M., 132
Petit Parisien, Le, 69
Peyrefitte, Alain, 424
Pflimlin, Pierre, 348–49
phenomenological psychology, 112,
    129–31
Phénoménologie de la perception, La (Mer-
    leau-Ponty), 180
phenomenology, 67, 97, 100–101,
    102–5, 119, 162, 173, 193, 195
Phenomenology of Mind, The (Hegel),
    194
Philosophies, 59, 73
Piaget, Charles, 70, 458
Picasso, Pablo, 205, 211, 268

Pierre, Jean, 149–51, 152–53, 155, 160, 161, 162, 163, 167, 168, 170, 172

Pieterkowski (Pieter) (soldier), 149–51, 152–53, 155, 157, 160, 169, 170, 171, 172, 198, 221, 262

Pingaud, Bernard, 410, 433, 439, 473

Plato, 71, 104

Plekhanov, Georgy V., 375

Pleven, René, 446, 447

poetry:
by Sartre, 81
Sartre's disdain for, 214

Poher, Alain, 434

Poil de Carotte (Renard), 68

Poland, 142, 331–32
Sartre's trips to, 390
uprising in (1956), 324–25, 327

police department, investigation of, 445–46

Politecnico Il, 242

Politzer, Georges, 59, 75, 76, 181, 189, 321

polycentrism, 316

Pompes funèbres (Genet), 286

Pompidou, Georges, 426, 434, 458

Ponge, Francis, 208, 236

Pontalis J.-B. (psychoanalyst), 254, 306, 393–94, 433, 439

Portrait du colonisateur (Memmi), 340

Portrait du colonisé (Memmi), 340

Portugal, 463

possessions:
Sartre's analysis of desire for, 196
Sartre's disdain for, 20–21, 61, 77, 84, 129, 312

Potomak (Cocteau), 62

Pouillon, Jean, 180, 181, 235, 306, 335, 347, 348, 381, 410, 458, 468, 473

Poupon school, 36–37, 38

Pour la Victoire, 228

"Pour un papillon" (Sartre), 35

Pouvoir et liberté (Power and Liberty) (Lévy and Sartre), 18, 463, 464

practico-inert notion, 346, 348, 376, 410, 432

Pravda, 252, 322, 391

praxis, 334, 343, 344, 345–46, 347, 348, 374, 375, 376, 410, 432, 433

"Présentation" (Sartre), 234–35, 236–37, 242, 281–82

Presle, Micheline, 209

"Prétendant, Le" (Sartre), 349

Prévert, Jacques, 205, 206

Prix de la Pléiade, 210–11

Prix Interallié, 133

Problème moral et la pensée de Sartre, Le (Jeanson), 283

Prodromides, John, 405

proletariat, see working class

"Prométhée" (Sartre), 161

Propos (Alain), 99

Proudhon, Pierre-Joseph, 181

Proud Ones, The (Sartre), see Orgueilleux, Les

Proust, Marcel, 15, 60, 71, 117, 141, 399
Sartre influenced by, 45
Sartre's disdain for, 106, 107, 235, 312
subjectivity of, 98, 103, 157, 193

Prozess, Der (The Trial) (Kafka), 146, 459

Pryce-Jones, Alan, 323

Psyché, La (Sartre), 18, 129–31, 136

psychoanalysis, 199, 338, 354, 357, 478
biography and, 334, 412, 413
considered by Sartre, 393–94
doctor-patient relationship in, 433
Marxism and, 12, 25, 321, 323–24, 331, 335, 351–52, 364
see also Freud, Sigmund

psychology:
of consciousness, 196–97
phenomenological, 112, 129–31
Sartre's early studies of, 55, 57, 81, 351

Psychology of Imagination, The (Sartre), see Imaginaire, L'

Puig, André, 450, 452, 467

Pushkin, Aleksandr, 409

Putain respectueuse, La (The Respectful Prostitute) (Sartre), 244, 247, 252–53, 319

400 Coups, Les, 390

Queneau, Jeanine, 209, 215

Queneau, Raymond, 209, 210, 211, 215

Querelle de Brest (Genet), 267

Qu'est-ce que la littérature? (What Is Literature?) (Sartre), 231, 242, 247–51, 284, 302, 303, 481
motivation for writing of, 247–48

Question, La (Alleg), 341
Questions de méthode (Search for a Method) (Sartre), 308, 335–39, 344, 346–47

racism, 220, 229, 244, 247, 249, 387, 388, 422, 447, 450
Radioscopie, 452
Radio-Télévision Luxembourgeoise, 464
Rákosi, Matyas, 324, 325
Ramadier, Paul, 250, 254, 255
Rasquin (teacher), 88, 89
Rassemblement Démocratique Révolutionnaire (RDR), 259, 260, 264, 268–69, 273, 279, 304, 321, 387, 406, 439, 481
Rassemblement du Peuple Français (RPF), 250, 254, 255
realism, idealism vs., 97, 100, 105, 162
reality, language and, 283–84
reason, analytical vs. dialectical, 271, 342, 346–47, 359
reciprocity notion, 343–44
    writer-reader relationship and, 250–51
Red Gloves, 264
"Réflexions sur la mort" (Sartre), 153
Réflexions sur la question Juive (Sartre), 220–21, 419, 461
"Réformisme et les fétiches, Le" (Sartre), 307
Reggiani, Serge, 365, 366
regressive-progressive method, 338, 343
Reinhardt, Wolfgang, 365, 367–68
Relations Culturelles Françaises, 239
Renard, Jules, 68
Renault, Billancourt factory of, 425, 442, 448
Reprieve, The (Sartre), *see Sursis, Le*
Republic, The (Plato), 71
Resistance, 10, 19, 183, 204, 209, 226, 232–33, 234, 251, 305, 340, 345, 372, 379
    formation of, 189–90
    intellectual, 205, 208
    in liberation of Paris, 216–19
    PCF and, 181, 184, 205, 225
    reprisals against, 184, 190, 210
    sabotage by, 184, 190
    Sartre criticized for lack of participation in, 189

Sartre's group in, 180–81, 182, 184, 189
Respectful Prostitute, The (*La Putain Respectueuse*) (Sartre), 244, 247, 252–53, 319
responsibility notion, 159–60, 165, 186–88, 193, 198, 199, 234, 235
Retour de l'URSS (Gide), 274
"Révolte, La" (Sartre), 133
Revolución, 370
revolution, 325, 376, 385, 408, 439–40
    end as justification of means in, 252, 282
    freedom and, 243, 252, 259, 339, 448–49
    proletariat's role in, 303–4
    violence and, 252, 267, 282, 400, 448–49
Révolution, 416, 439, 445
Révolution et les fétiches, La (Hervé), 321
Revue sans titre, La, 58
Rey, Evelyne, 319, 323, 360, 361, 363
Reynaud, Paul, 355
Ricardou, Jean, 386
Ridgway, Matthew, 301
Rieder (publisher), 89, 90
Rigoulot, Pierre, 465
Rilke, Rainer Maria, 173
Rimbaud, Arthur, 333, 342
Roads to Freedom, The (Sartre), *see Chemins de la liberté, Les*
Robbe-Grillet, Alain, 92, 409
Robespierre, Maximilien, 334, 375
Rochet, Waldeck, 407, 408
Rolland, J. F., 327, 328
Romains, Jules, 149, 159
"Room, The" (Sartre), *see* "Chambre, La"
Roosevelt, Franklin D., 205, 229–30
Rosenberg, Ethel, 309–10
Rosenberg, Julius, 309–10
Rote Armee Fraktion, 462
Roubaud (teacher), 49
Rouleau, Raymond, 25, 323
Rous, Jean, 258
Rousseau, Jean-Jacques, 56, 74
Rousseaux, André, 139
Rousset, David, 255, 258, 259, 264, 268, 269, 273, 406
Roy, Claude, 288, 304, 306, 319, 327, 328, 378

RPF (Rassemblement du Peuple Français), 250, 254, 255
Rusk, Dean, 422
Russell, Bertrand, 418, 429–30, 438
Russell tribunal, 415, 418, 420–22, 443
Russian Revolution, 60, 374
Rybalka, Michel, 132

Sacré-Coeur, Maoist occupation of (1971), 443–44
Sadat, Anwar, 467
Sagan, Françoise, 469–70
Saint-Exupéry, Antoine de, 159
Saint Genet (Sartre), 12, 15, 18, 44, 108, 272, 283–87, 317, 334, 339, 351, 361, 385, 412, 431
    canonization of Genet in, 277
    as discourse on nature of good and evil, 270–71
    facts distorted in, 285
    Genet's reaction to, 287
Saint George and the Dragon (Tintoretto), 383
Salacrou, Armand, 211
Salan, Raoul, 349, 382
Saman, Ali el-, 419
Samedi-Soir, 282
Sang des autres, Le (De Beauvoir), 234, 483
Sanjurjo, José, 95
Sans, Simone-Camille (Toulouse) (Simone Jollivet), 67, 95, 114, 120, 129, 214–15, 287, 391, 397
    as actress, 72, 94
    Sartre's relationship with, 62–66, 68–69, 70, 72, 144, 240
Santé, prisoners' uprising at (1971), 447
Sartoris (Faulkner), 133
Sartre, Anne-Marie Schweitzer (mother), *see* Mancy, Anne-Marie
Sartre, Eymard (grandfather), 31, 40
Sartre, Hélène (aunt), 62, 65
Sartre, Jean-Baptiste (father), 31, 32, 354, 395, 398, 414
Sartre, Jean-Paul:
    abstraction in writings of, 107–8
    absurdity notion of, 105, 202, 236
    adventure stories and thrillers enjoyed by, 35–36, 89
    aesthetic theory of, 75, 116, 247–49, 250–51
    analytical reason attacked by, 342, 346–47
    anthropological thinking of, 236, 237, 248, 250, 272, 335, 338, 347–48
    anti-Americanism of, 11, 17, 230, 309–10, 410
    antihumanism in works by, 119, 138
    assessment of, 9–13, 15–28, 477–83
    authenticity notion of, 156, 165, 221
    aversion of, to viscosity, 201–2
    biographical method of, 213–14, 272, 317, 334–35, 431–32
    biography as interest of, 24, 92, 213
    birth of, 32
    body distasteful to, 131, 144
    boldy maltreated by, 21–22, 23, 342, 460
    books read by, 57, 64, 67, 131, 139, 146
    bourgeoisie hated by, 302, 311, 331, 333, 394–95, 411, 414, 431
    boxing enjoyed by, 56, 88–89
    brothel first visited by, 99, 111
    chess played by, 166–67, 169
    childbearing disdained by, 140–41
    childhood of, 32–47, 312–13, 391, 394–98
    cinema as interest of, 35, 52, 79, 89, 98, 109
    collective life enjoyed by, 176
    colonialism opposed by, 264, 307, 331, 382, 385, 402, 406, 422, 438, 479
    competitiveness of, 103
    consciousness as viewed by, 102–3, 104, 159, 193–99, 201–2, 243, 249, 284, 336, 343, 345, 353, 356–57, 361, 376, 413, 431, 433
    contingency notion of, 52, 71, 76, 81, 89, 91–93, 98, 104, 236
    country abhorred by, 110
    crimes fascinating to, 96
    critical essays and reviews by, 133, 137, 202, 203
    death of, 472–73
    defective vision of, 33, 454, 455, 456, 457–58
    depressions of, 113, 378, 457

Sartre, Jean-Paul (*cont.*)
  detective fiction enjoyed by, 89,
    92–93
  dialectical reason attractive to, 271,
    342, 346–47, 359
  dialectical reversals of, 23–26, 278,
    304, 344, 352–53, 400, 471, 482
  dramaturgical principles of, 205–6,
    256
  dreams of, 112
  drugs used by, 21, 23, 26, 112,
    113–14, 126, 248–49, 286,
    341–42, 346, 348, 352, 367, 383,
    411
  early fiction by, 35, 43, 47, 48–49,
    58, 64, 65, 68, 71, 81–82, 89
  early intellectual development of,
    34, 36–37, 38–39
  early philosophical studies of,
    46–47, 49, 50, 51, 56, 57, 64, 66,
    67–68, 70, 72, 100
  early romances of, 62–66, 68–69,
    70, 72
  at Ecole Normale Supérieure,
    54–62, 64, 66–70, 71–75, 87, 100,
    350, 351, 371, 372
  ethics and moral theories of, 18, 61,
    68, 159–60, 165, 245, 251, 252,
    261, 265, 268, 270–71, 276–80,
    312, 339, 431, 463, 471–72, 479,
    481
  evaluative film or literary criticism
    opposed by, 429
  fame of, 10, 11, 12, 15, 16, 24, 132,
    232–34, 236, 257–58, 287, 302,
    373, 403, 410–11
  family as viewed by, 317–18,
    394–95, 404, 414, 431
  family background of, 31–32
  fearful of being influenced, 106–7,
    359
  financial affairs of, 80, 281, 351,
    393, 468
  first play by, 174–76
  first sexual experience of, 49
  freedom notion of, 9–10, 11, 52, 80,
    83, 92, 99, 144, 162, 177, 186–88,
    192–94, 197, 198, 199, 206, 208,
    243, 252, 256, 259, 267, 271, 339,
    344, 346, 448–49, 451, 479–80
  friendships of, 142, 209, 212, 333,
    358
  funeral of, 15, 447, 473–75

  gentle side of, 55
  group-in-fusion notion of, 344
  hallucinogen taken by, 113–14,
    126
  hearing problem of, 342, 383
  home movies of, 79
  illnesses of, 315, 316, 355–56, 360,
    378, 379, 429, 441–42, 443, 445,
    446, 449–50, 452–53, 454, 455,
    456–58, 459, 460, 464–65, 466,
    470–71, 472–73
  image theories of, 67–68, 93,
    111–12, 130
  immortality sought by, 360
  impossible tasks attempted by,
    376–77, 482
  indifference of, to present and past,
    20, 233
  individualism disdained by,
    333–34, 343, 344–46, 353, 362,
    441
  infidelities of, 48, 84, 99, 101, 109,
    126–27, 133–35, 140, 142–44,
    152, 153, 158, 160, 161, 162, 163,
    164–65, 167–68, 229, 239–40,
    243–44, 249–50, 263, 270, 275,
    301, 319, 323, 359, 390, 455, 467
  influence of, 477–78
  isolation of, 279, 287, 410
  Jacques Guillemin as pseudonym
    of, 58
  jazz enjoyed by, 9, 46, 61, 74, 227,
    258
  language-reality relationship as
    viewed by, 283–84
  letter-writing style of, 127, 128
  literary executor of, 404, 477
  "literary neurosis" of, 393, 395–96
  literary vs. philosophical or politi-
    cal writings of, 26–27, 136–37,
    248–49, 342, 481
  "living autobiographically"
    ascribed to, 156, 481
  long summer vacations taken by,
    252
  lycée education of, 36–37, 38–39,
    41–53
  mild homosexual inclinations of, 45
  military service of, 79–80, 81, 82,
    83, 97, 145, 146, 149–78, 182, 183
  mistress adopted by, 403–5
  "moral health" as defined by, 61,
    68

Nobel Prize rejected by, 402–3
notebooks of, 50, 91, 93, 265, 266–67
objects hated by, 346
oppression analyzed by, 266–67, 340
pain resisted by, 95–96
parliamentary democracy disdained by, 451–52
as performer, 36, 51, 60–61
philosophizing and theorizing of, 27–28, 81, 99, 156–57
physical appearance of, 25, 33, 34, 41, 43, 51, 61–62, 91–92, 132, 144, 241–42, 428
piano played by, 41, 61
poetry written by, 81
poetry disdained by, 214
polished prose devalued by, 248, 333, 360
political action vs. literary creation, 302–3
as political activist, 273, 387, 437–44, 445–51, 454–55, 456, 458, 462, 463, 465
possessions disdained by, 20–21, 61, 77, 84, 129, 312
"Poulou" as nickname of, 33, 245
in practical politics, 258–59, 264, 269, 307–8, 331, 332
practico-inert notion of, 346, 348, 376, 410, 432
as prisoner of war, 170–78, 184, 459
privacy unimportant to, 152, 194, 234, 266, 460
psychoanalysis considered by, 393–94
psychology studied by, 55, 57, 81, 351
radicalization of, 301–4, 306
radio broadcasts of, 254–55
religious training of, 33
in Resistance, 180–81, 182, 183, 184, 189, 190, 205
responsibility notion of, 159–60, 165, 186–88, 193, 198, 199, 234, 235
salvation sought by, 393
as screenwriter, 206–7, 209–10, 220, 239, 256, 257, 323, 351–61, 362, 364–68
self-destructiveness of, 359

self-generation complex of, 107
self-hatred of, 231, 333, 345, 400
sexual preferences of, 45, 144
shellfish phobia of, 116, 123, 201, 363
as social and economic historian, 313–15
sociological perspective assumed by, 333–39
speaking voice and verbal virtuosity of, 51, 56
stabbing of, 469
stealing incident and, 44, 45
students' relationship with, 11–12, 17, 373, 378, 386, 406–8, 415, 417, 423–28, 430, 432–33, 437
teaching career of, 78, 82, 87–89, 90, 99, 111, 112, 120, 121, 180, 184, 185, 190, 210, 220
television appearances of, 452, 461–64
theology and, 196, 197–98, 252, 336
tiers-mondisme of, 12, 385, 386, 406, 416
tiredness as experienced by, 109, 151
totalization notion of, 213, 334–36, 337, 346, 347, 359, 373, 374, 375, 376, 413
trial of, 456
uncompleted projects of, 17–18, 23–24, 333, 343, 376–77, 398, 482
violence as viewed by, 247, 252, 267, 271, 280, 282, 344–45, 384–85, 400, 422, 448–49, 479–80
war diaries of, 27, 106, 150, 151–52, 153, 154, 156–57, 161, 162, 163, 168, 192, 251, 344, 392, 477
weight gained by, 114–15
will of, 477
work habits of, 56, 102, 263
working class and, 96, 173, 211, 219, 301–2, 303–4, 305–6, 309, 313–15, 344, 442–43
working in cafés preferred by, 129, 138
writing enjoyed by, 19, 21, 333
see also specific topics and works
Sartre, Joseph (uncle), 40, 65
Saussure, Ferdinand de, 137, 237
Savonarola, Girolamo, 281
Schoenman, Ralph, 420
Schubert, Franz, 263

Schuman, Robert, 255, 257, 264
Schwartz, Laurent, 387, 418, 420, 429
Schweitzer, Albert, 31, 388
Schweitzer, Anne-Marie (mother) *see*
    Mancy, Anne-Marie
Schweitzer, Georges, 32
Schweitzer, Karl (Charles) (grandfa-
    ther), 31, 32–35, 37, 40, 44, 45,
    76, 80, 87, 90–91, 110, 115, 354,
    414, 431
  infidelities of, 32–33
  Les Mots and, 395, 396, 398
  in Sartre's early intellectual devel-
    opment, 34–35, 36, 38
Schweitzer, Louis, 31
Schweitzer, Louise Guillemin (grand-
    mother), 31, 32–33, 35, 76, 80
Scottsboro case, 244
Secours Rouge, 440, 443, 444, 447,
    449
Section Française de l'Internationale
    Ouvrière (SFIO), 58–59, 78, 94,
    111, 115, 240, 244, 250, 259, 349,
    350, 406, 408
Seed and Safeguard (Sartre), *see Semence
    et le scaphandre, La*
Seghers, Anna, 313
Sein und Zeit (Heidegger), 107, 173,
    194, 201, 308, 459
self, disunity of, 385–86
Selzer (clerk), 159–60
Semence et le scaphandre, La (*Seed and
    Safeguard*) (Sartre), 48–49, 58, 261
Semeur, Le, 372
"Séquestré de Venise, Le" (Sartre),
    363
Séquestrés d'Altona, Les (*The Condemned
    of Altona; Loser Wins*) (Sartre),
    110, 360, 362–66, 377, 393, 404,
    463, 477
  De Beauvoir's editorial assistance
    on, 362–63, 365
  first production of, 366
  Marxian and Freudian insights
    combined in, 364
  synopsis of, 362–63
  title of, 363
"Serment, Le" ("The Oath") (Sartre),
    133
Servan-Schreiber, Jean-Jacques, 355
sexuality, 195
  desire and, 267
  viscosity and, 201–2

SFIO, *see* Section Française de l'Inter-
    nationel Ouvrière
Shakespeare, William, 130, 277, 412
Shelley, Percy Bysshe, 64
Shevchenko, Taras Grigorievich, 401
Sholokhov, Makhail, 403, 417
Siegel, Liliane, 443, 445, 455, 457,
    462, 466
Signes (Merleau-Ponty), 383
Signoret, Simone, 323, 378
Si le grain ne meurt (Gide), 396
Silone, Ignazio, 97
Simmonot, Emile, 31, 34
Simonov, Konstantin, 315, 320
"singular universal" notion, 401
Sinyavsky, Andrei (Avram Tertz),
    409, 417, 421
"Situation de l'écrivain en 1947, La"
    (Sartre), 250
Situationists, 417
Situations (Sartre), 28, 479
Sketch for a Theory of the Emotions
    (Sartre), *see Esquisse d'une théorie
    des émotions*
Skira (publisher), 241
Slansky (Rudolf Salzmann), 309
smoking, Sartre's philosophical analy-
    sis of, 196
SNESup (Syndicat National de l'En-
    seignment Supérieure), 424, 426
socialism, 83, 152, 180, 259, 327, 460
Socialisme et Liberté, 180–81, 182,
    184, 190, 226
Socialist party, *see* Section Française
    de l'Internationale Ouvrière
Société Européenne de Culture, 323
Socrates, 62, 104
"Soleil de minuit" ("Midnight Sun")
    (Sartre), 115, 116, 119, 122, 282
Sollers, Philippe, 448
Solzhenitsyn, Aleksandr, 391, 409,
    417
Sophocles, 175
Sorbonne, 55, 97, 247, 373, 379, 407,
    433
  student rebellion at, 423–28
  see also Ecole Normale Supérieure
Sorcières de Salem, Les (Miller, trans-
    lated by Aymé), 323
Sorokine, Nathalie, 182, 184, 186,
    188, 204, 212, 227
Soulier de satin, Le (Claudel), 173
Soustelle, Jacques, 227, 340

Soviet Union, 17, 142, 145, 238, 304, 416, 429–30, 465
  analyzed in *Critique de la raison dialectique*, 374–76
  censorship in, 409
  Chinese split with, 408, 409
  Cold War and, 11, 254, 255, 263–64, 268–69, 276, 279, 281, 302, 307, 313, 318, 319, 322, 323–24, 390
  Czechoslovakia invaded by (1968), 12, 428–29, 430, 444
  Gide's disillusionment with, 273–74, 316, 339
  Jews in, 310, 443
  labor camps in, 265, 273, 304, 390
  Moscow trials in, 124, 244, 246, 249
  1956 uprisings and, 12, 324–28, 331, 361, 428
  Sartre's allegiance to, 304
  Sartre's disillusionment with, 325–28
  Sartre's trips to, 11, 315–16, 320, 339, 390–91, 398–99, 401–2, 408–9, 415, 417, 418. 421
  in World War II, 181–82, 184, 205, 207, 210, 317
Spain:
  civil war in, 121–22, 123, 124, 131, 142
  coup d'état attempted in (1932), 95
  Sartre's trips to, 89–90, 95
Spanish Testament (Koestler), 159
Spender, Stephen, 323
Sperber, Manès, 246, 255
Spiegel, Der, 462
Spinoza, Baruch, 25, 56, 111, 159
squatters, Sartre's support for, 449
Stalag XII-D:
  Sartre as prisoner of war at, 172–76, 459
  Sartre's escape from, 176–78, 184
Stalin, Joseph, 181, 184, 230, 243, 246, 255, 276, 313, 324, 327, 343, 374, 375
  Khrushchev's condemnation of, 322
Stalinism, 239, 256, 259, 309, 316, 326, 327, 332, 374, 399
state, Sartre's views on, 344
State Department, U.S., 228
Steiner, George, 194
Stendhal (Marie-Henri Beyle), 25, 57, 76, 117, 130, 411

Stéphane, Roger, 307
Stern, Mikhail, 465, 467
Stern Gang, 258
Stibbe, Pierre, 340
Stratégie ouvrière et néo-capitalisme (Gorz), 408
structuralism, 106, 213, 307, 335, 338, 347–48, 386, 410–11, 415
student rebellion (1968), 12, 17, 423–28, 437, 480
  Aden-Arabie preface and, 371–72
  education system and, 407, 432–33
  events leading to, 406–8, 415–17
  Sartre influenced by, 428
  Vietnam War and, 415, 416, 417
  workers and, 424, 425–26, 427
subjectivity, 98, 101, 103, 104, 105, 157, 193, 194, 195, 248, 249, 431
Sudermann, Hermann, 352, 363
Suez Canal incident (1956), 325
Suppliant Women, The (Aeschylus), 182
surrealists, 57–58, 59–60, 137, 249, 251, 284, 342
Sursis, Le (*The Reprieve*) (Sartre), 192, 193, 197–200, 207, 208, 220, 221, 261
  contrast between Mathieu and Daniel in, 198–99
  narrative technique in, 199–200
  publication of, 232, 302
  rape of Ivich in, 201–2
  theology and, 197–98
  totalization notion in, 334–35
Switzerland, Sartre's trips to, 240, 241
Sylvia, Gaby, 215, 319
Syndicat National de l'Enseignment Supérieur (SNESup), 424, 426
Syria, 420

Tabou Club, 258
Taine, Hippolyte, 111
Tanguy, Yves, 229
Tarkovsky, Andrei, 390
television:
  Sartre's appearances on, 452, 461–64
  Sartre's hatred of, 452
Tel Quel, 386, 410–11
Temps, Le, 139
Temps Modernes, Les, 10, 12, 27, 118, 209, 225–27, 236–39, 241, 243, 248, 249, 251, 252, 263, 283, 306–7, 308–9, 313, 315, 322, 326,

Temps Modernes, Les (cont.)
  331, 335, 361, 386, 399, 402, 410,
  417, 433, 439, 441, 451–52, 457,
  458, 460, 461, 462, 468, 469, 472,
  481, 483
  Algerian war and, 320, 332, 339,
    340, 341, 381–82, 387
  anthropology and, 236–37, 347–48
  Arab-Israeli conflict and, 419, 421
  Camus and, 226, 282–83, 288–301,
    304–5, 369–70
  editorial committee of, 226, 236,
    242, 306, 465
  first issue of, 226–27, 234–35,
    236–37
  Italian Communists and, 316
  literary policy of, 235, 242
  political alignment of, 235, 238,
    276, 281–82, 304, 306, 307, 308–9
  pro-Soviet apologias in, 273
  Sartre's editorial function at,
    347–48
  student radicals and, 408, 437
  title of, 226
Terre des hommes (Saint-Exupéry), 159,
  236
terrorism, 448, 467, 479
  in Algerian war, 340, 382, 384, 385,
    386–90
  see also violence
Théâtre Antoine, 244, 247, 260, 280
Théâtre de la Cité, 190
Théâtre de l'Atelier, 72
Theodorakis, Mikis, 410
theology, 196, 197–98, 252, 336
Thérive, André, 139
Third World, 12, 385, 386, 406, 479
Thorez, Maurice, 115, 316, 399, 402,
  407
tiers-mondisme, 12, 385, 386, 406, 416,
  479
Tillon, Charles, 181
Tintoretto (Jacopo Robusti), 18, 333,
  363, 383
Tito, Marshal (Josip Broz), 274, 324,
  377
Todd, Olivier, 282, 402
Togliatti, Palmiro, 316, 402, 408
Töpffer, Rodolphe, 132
Torrès, Henri, 254
torture, 307, 349, 462, 480
  in Algerian war, 332, 339, 341, 382,
    450

in *Morts sans sépulture*, 230–31, 247,
  363
  torturer-victim relationship in, 231,
    341
  in Vietnam War, 421
  see also violence
totalization notion, 213, 334–36, 337,
  346, 347, 359, 373, 374, 375, 376,
  431
Toulouse, *see* Sans, Simone-Camille
Tout, 441, 446
*Tragédie hongroise ou Une Révolution so-
  cialiste antisoviétique, La* (Fejtö),
  326
Traître, Le (Gorz), 21, 333–34
Transcendance de l'Ego, La (Sartre), 101,
  115, 159, 194
"Tree, The" (Sartre), *see* "Arbre, L'"
Tribune des Temps Modernes, La, 254–55
Triolet, Elsa, 313
Trojan Women, The (Euripides), 402
Trotsky, Leon, 257, 267, 306, 374
Troyennes, Les (Sartre), 402, 405
Truffaut, François, 390, 441
Truman, Harry S., 230
Tual, Roland, 210
Tunisia, 341, 384
Tvardovsky, Aleksandr, 399, 409,
  429
Twórczość, 331–32, 335
Typhus (Sartre), 220

UEC (Union des Etudiants Commu-
  nistes), 407, 408, 416–17, 424
UFC (ML) (Union des Jeunesses
  Communistes (Marxistes-Lénin-
  istes)), 417, 438
Unamuno, Miguel de, 69
unconscious, 199, 237, 356–57, 361,
  376, 413, 431, 433
UNEF (Union Nationale des Etu-
  diants Français), 407, 408
UNESCO, 400–401
Ungaretti, Giuseppe, 399
Union de la Jeunesse Républicaine de
  la France, 225
Union des Etudiants Communistes
  (UEC), 407, 408, 416–17, 424
Union des Jeunesses Communistes
  (Marxistes-Léninistes) (UJC
  (ML)), 417, 438
Union for the New Republic (UNR),
  356

Union Nationale des Etudiants Français (UNEF), 407, 408
Union of Soviet Writers, 390, 398–99, 421
United Nations, 264
United States, 10, 16, 325, 326, 429–30
    Cold War and, 11, 254, 255, 263–64, 268–69, 276, 279, 281, 302, 307, 313, 318, 319, 322, 323–24, 390
    racism in, 220, 229, 244, 247, 249
    Sartre's anti-Americanism and, 11, 17, 230, 309–10, 410
    Sartre's trips to, 227, 228–30, 239–40, 372
    in Vietnam War, 405, 409, 416, 418, 420–22
    in World War II, 169, 184, 317
University of Jerusalem, 465
Univers morbide, L' (Hesnard), 285
UNR (Union for the New Republic), 356

Vailland, Roger, 327
"Vainqueurs, Les" ("The Victors") (Sartre), 230
Valdé, Pierre, 260
Valéry, Paul, 19, 60
Vanetti, Dolores, 229, 234, 239–40, 243, 244, 249–50, 263, 270, 274, 275, 370, 404
Van Gogh, Vincent, 248
Vautour de la Sierra, Le, 79
vécu, le, 431
Vendredi, 132
Venice conference (1956), 323–24, 331
Venice Film Festival, 129
Vercors (Jean Bruller), 327
Verdun (Romains), 159
Vérités pour . . . (Jeanson), 332
Vers le concret (Wahl), 67
Verstraeten, Pierre, 410
Vian, Boris, 249, 258
Vian, Michelle, 19, 21, 249, 309, 310, 316, 324, 355, 366, 447, 448
    Sartre's illnesses and, 464, 466, 470
    Sartre's relationship with, 243–44, 275, 301, 351, 358, 444, 450, 455, 468
Vichy government, 170, 181, 190, 204, 262, 349
Victor, Pierre, see Lévy, Benny

"Victors, The" ("Les Vainqueurs") (Sartre), 230
Vie et les oeuvres de Hans Sachs, La (Schweitzer), 396
Vieillesse, La (De Beauvoir), 348
vie intérieure, la, 58, 74, 98, 110, 431, 460
Vienna congress (1952), 307–8
Vietnamese boat people, 470
Vietnam War, 16, 405, 408, 409, 419, 454
    First Indochina War and, 288, 315, 332
    Russell tribunal and, 415, 418, 420–22, 443
    student rebellion and, 415, 416, 417
Vigier, Jean-Pierre, 387
Vilar, Jean, 215, 280
violence, 247, 280, 448–49, 479–80
    freedom and, 252, 271
    and lateral reciprocity of love, 344–45
    as response to colonial oppression, 384–85, 422, 479
    revolution and, 252, 267, 282, 400, 448–49
    of students, 424–25, 427
    see also terrorism; torture
Vitold, Michel, 318, 319
Vitold, Roger, 215
Vittorini, Elio, 242–43
Vive la Révolution (VLR), 437–38, 441, 451
Voie Communiste, La, 389
Voltaire (François-Marie Arouet), 381
Voznesensky, Andrey, 390, 391

Waelhens, Antoine de, 482
Wagner, Cosima, 64, 65, 68
Wagner, Richard, 64, 65
Wahl, Jean, 67, 189
Wall, The (book) (Sartre), see Mur, Le
"Wall, The" (short story) (Sartre), see "Mur, Le"
Was Ist Metaphysik? (Heidegger), 139
Watanabe (publisher), 418
Weil, Simone, 73, 95, 124
Weiss, Peter, 420
Wilde, Oscar, 278
will, in Sartre's moral theory, 159
Wittgenstein, Ludwig, 15
Woolf, Virginia, 199
Words, The (Sartre), see Mots, Les

working class, 173, 211, 219, 327, 344, 385, 389, 401, 408, 438, 439, 342-43, 451, 479
    in Marx's view of history, 336
    party's relationship with, 301-2, 303-4, 305-6, 309, 314-15
    Sartre's lack of contact with, 96
    strike of June 1952 and, 301-2, 313
    student rebellion and, 424, 425-26, 427
World Congress for Peace (1952), 308
World War I, 37, 60
World War II, 149-219
    armistice talks after, 301
    bombing of France in, 184-85, 188, 210, 211, 219
    bombing of Germany in, 205, 210, 211
    end of, 230
    events leading to, 115, 131, 136, 141-42, 145, 146, 198
    fall of France in, 168-70
    final days of, 215-19, 230
    North African and Italian fronts in, 181, 204, 207
    persecution of Jews in, 141, 182, 189, 204
    Sartre as prisoner of war in, 170-78, 184
    Sartre's military service in, 145, 146, 149-78, 182, 183
    and Sartre's views on violence, 479-80
    Soviet front in, 181-82, 184, 205, 210, 317
    see also occupation; Paris, occupied; Resistance
Wright, Richard, 220, 264, 269

Yeats, W. B., 22
Yevtushenko, Yevgeny, 391
Yogi and the Commissar, The (Koestler), 244
Yogi et le prolétarien, Le (Merleau-Ponty), 244-45, 249
York, Susannah, 368
Yugoslavia, 263, 274, 429-30
    Sartre's trip to, 377

Zadkine, Ossip, 123
Zaidmann, Dr., 442, 445, 446, 452, 456, 464
Zhdanov, Andrey, 310
Zionism, 249, 258, 263
Zola, Emile, 206
Zonina, Lena, 390, 399, 417

FINE WORKS OF NON-FICTION AVAILABLE IN QUALITY PAPERBACK EDITIONS FROM CARROLL & GRAF

☐ Anderson, Nancy/WORK WITH PASSION $8.95
☐ Arlett, Robert/THE PIZZA GOURMET $10.95
☐ Asprey, Robert/THE PANTHER'S FEAST $9.95
☐ Athill, Diana/INSTEAD OF A LETTER $7.95
☐ Bedford, Sybille/ALDOUS HUXLEY $14.95
☐ Berton, Pierre/KLONDIKE FEVER $10.95
☐ Blake, Robert/DISRAELI $14.50
☐ Blanch, Lesley/PIERRE LOTI $10.95
☐ Blanch, Lesley/THE SABRES OF PARADISE $9.95
☐ Bowers, John/IN THE LAND OF NYX $7.95
☐ Buchan, John/PILGRIM'S WAY $10.95
☐ Carr, John Dickson/THE LIFE OF SIR ARTHUR
    CONAN DOYLE $8.95
☐ Carr, Virginia Spencer/THE LONELY HUNTER: A
    BIOGRAPHY OF CARSON McCULLERS $12.95
☐ Cherry-Garrard/THE WORST JOURNEY IN THE
    WORLD $13.95
☐ Conot, Robert/JUSTICE AT NUREMBURG $11.95
☐ Cooper, Lady Diana/AUTOBIOGRAPHY $13.95
☐ De Jonge, Alex/THE LIFE AND TIMES OF GRIGORII
    RASPUTIN $10.95
☐ Edwards, Anne/SONYA: THE LIFE OF COUNTESS
    TOLSTOY $8.95
☐ Elkington, John/THE GENE FACTORY $8.95
☐ Farson, Negley/THE WAY OF A TRANSGRESSOR $9.95
☐ Freudenberger, Dr. Herbert/SITUATIONAL
    ANXIETY $9.95
☐ Garbus, Martin/TRAITORS AND HEROES $10.95
☐ Gill, Brendan/HERE AT THE NEW YORKER $12.95
☐ Golenbock, Peter/HOW TO WIN AT ROTISSERIE
    BASEBALL $8.95
☐ Green, Julian/DIARIES 1928-1957 $9.95
☐ Harris, A./SEXUAL EXERCISES FOR WOMEN $8.95
☐ Haycraft, Howard (ed.)/MURDER FOR
    PLEASURE $10.95
☐ Hook, Sidney/OUT OF STEP $14.95
☐ Lansing, Alfred/ENDURANCE: SHACKLETON'S
    INCREDIBLE VOYAGE $8.95
☐ Lifton, David S./BEST EVIDENCE $11.95
☐ Macmillan, Harold/THE BLAST OF WAR $12.95

☐ Madden, David and Bach, Peggy/REDISCOVERIES II $9.95
☐ Martin, Jay/NATHANAEL WEST: THE ART OF HIS
    LIFE $8.95
☐ Maurois, Andre/OLYMPIO: THE LIVE OF VICTOR
    HUGO $12.95
☐ Maurois, Andre/PROMETHEUS: THE LIFE OF
    BALZAC $11.95
☐ Maurois, Andre/PROUST: PORTRAIT OF
    GENIUS $10.95
☐ McCarthy, Barry and Emily/FEMALE SEXUAL
    AWARENESS $9.95
☐ McCarthy, Barry/MALE SEXUAL AWARENESS $9.95
☐ McCarthy, Barry & Emily/SEXUAL AWARENESS $9.95
☐ Mizener, Arthur/THE SADDEST STORY: A
    BIOGRAPHY OF FORD MADOX FORD $12.95
☐ Montyn, Jan & Kooiman, Dirk Ayelt/A LAMB TO
    SLAUGHTER $8.95
☐ Moorehead, Alan/THE RUSSIAN REVOLUTION $10.95
☐ Morris, Charles/IRON DESTINIES, LOST
    OPPORTUNITIES: THE POST-WAR ARMS
    RACE $13.95
☐ O'Casey, Sean/AUTOBIOGRAPHIES I $10.95
☐ O'Casey, Sean/AUTOBIOGRAPHIES II $10.95
☐ Poncins, Gontran de/KABLOONA $9.95
☐ Pringle, David/SCIENCE FICTION: THE 100 BEST
    NOVELS $7.95
☐ Proust, Marcel/ON ART AND LITERATURE $8.95
☐ Richelson, Hildy & Stan/INCOME WITHOUT
    TAXES $9.95
☐ Roy, Jules/THE BATTLE OF DIENBIENPHU $8.95
☐ Russell, Franklin/THE HUNTING ANIMAL $7.95
☐ Salisbury, Harrison/A JOURNEY FOR OUR
    TIMES $10.95
☐ Schul, Bill D./ANIMAL IMMORTALITY $9.95
☐ Scott, Evelyn/ESCAPADE $9.95
☐ Sloan, Allan/THREE PLUS ONE EQUALS
    BILLIONS $8.95
☐ Stanway, Andrew/THE ART OF SENSUAL
    LOVING $15.95
☐ Stanway, Dr. Andrew/SECRET SEX $15.95
☐ Trench, Charles/THE ROAD TO KHARTOUM $10.95
☐ Werth, Alexander/RUSSIA AT WAR: 1941-1945 $15.95
☐ White, Jon Manchip/CORTES $10.95
☐ Wilmot, Chester/STRUGGLE FOR EUROPE $14.95
☐ Wilson, Colin/BEYOND THE OCCULT $10.95

☐ Wilson, Colin/A CRIMINAL HISTORY OF
  MANKIND $13.95
☐ Wilson, Colin/THE MAMMOTH BOOK OF TRUE
  CRIME $8.95
☐ Zuckmayer, Carl/A PART OF MYSELF $9.95

Available from fine bookstores everywhere or use this coupon for ordering.

FINE WORKS OF FICTION
AVAILABLE IN QUALITY
PAPERBACK EDITIONS FROM
CARROLL & GRAF